NEUE
HORIZONTE

NEUE HORIZONTE

A FIRST COURSE IN GERMAN LANGUAGE AND CULTURE

Third Edition

David B. Dollenmayer

Worcester Polytechnic Institute

Thomas S. Hansen

Wellesley College

D. C. HEATH AND COMPANY

Lexington, Massachusetts   Toronto

Address editorial correspondence to:

D. C. Heath
125 Spring Street
Lexington, MA 02173

About the Authors

David B. Dollenmayer is an Associate Professor of German at the Worcester Polytechnic Institute (Worcester, Massachusetts). He received his B.A. and Ph.D. from Princeton University and was a Fulbright Fellow at the University of Munich. He has written articles on Alfred Döblin, Joseph Roth, Christa Wolf, and Ingeborg Bachmann. He is the author of *The Berlin Novels of Alfred Döblin* (University of California Press, 1988).

Thomas S. Hansen is Professor of German at Wellesley College (Wellesley, Massachusetts). He studied at Tufts University and the University of Tübingen before receiving his Ph.D. from Harvard University. He has published articles on German Exile Literature (1933–1945). His current research focuses on the twentieth-century writer Arno Schmidt and on German-American literary relations, with emphasis on Edgar Allan Poe.

Preface

Neue Horizonte, Third Edition, is a complete first-year German program for college and university students. In it you will learn the basic structures and vocabulary of German and practice the four skills of speaking, listening, reading, and writing. In addition, you will learn about the culture of contemporary Germany, Austria, and Switzerland.

The goal of the program is to help you achieve a basic level of linguistic proficiency in German. To achieve this goal, the text emphasizes communicative competency, that is to say, speaking the language to communicate your thoughts, ideas, and feelings to others. After completing *Neue Horizonte*, you will be prepared to go directly to a German-speaking country and, after a brief period of acclimatization, be able to communicate in most everyday situations and to continue to build on what you have already learned.

In addition, the text aims to excite your curiosity and help you view your own culture through the prism of another, thereby expanding your intellectual horizons in the spirit of the Austrian philosopher Ludwig Wittgenstein's maxim, "Die Grenzen meiner Sprache sind die Grenzen meiner Welt" (The boundaries of my language are the boundaries of my world).

The Text

Neue Horizonte consists of a short introduction and sixteen chapters. After every four chapters is a summary and review section with self-correcting tests.

The *Einführung* (introductory chapter) permits you to begin talking in German with your fellow students on the very first day. In this chapter you will learn greetings and farewells, basic vocabulary such as the names of classroom objects and people, and the days of the week. You will also learn how to spell, count to twenty, tell time, talk about the weather, describe how you feel, and say where you are from.

Each subsequent chapter contains the following sections:

Dialoge und Variationen *(Dialogues and Variations)*

The dialogues introduce new grammatical structures and vocabulary through idiomatic conversations reflecting everyday situations. There are two or three dialogues per chapter, all short enough to be memorized, with English translations printed on the following page. The *Variationen* that follow contain activities that encourage you to use the dialogue material creatively to express your own thoughts, ideas, and experiences.

Lyrik zum Vorlesen *(Poetry for Reading Aloud)*

The poem in each chapter is related to the chapter's cultural theme. It may be used for both pronunciation and intonation practice and can serve as a basis for simple interpretive class discussion. Unfamiliar vocabulary is glossed in the margins so that you can readily understand the poem without resorting to a dictionary.

Grammatik   *(Grammar)*

The grammar explanations in *Neue Horizonte* are brief, but complete, and do not presuppose familiarity with grammatical terminology. Following each major concept, a variety of activities practice what you have learned. So that class time can be devoted to communication, you should do the recorded exercises—indicated in your text by a cassette icon (⌷☐⌷)—immediately after you study grammar explanations. The sequence of in-class exercises moves from theory to practice. The *Übungen* (Exercises) are directed by the instructor and reinforce grammatical competence. The activities called *Gruppenarbeit* and *Partnerarbeit* (Group Work and Work with Partners) allow you to use the new structures with more freedom and creativity, promoting self-expression and communicative competence.

Wortschatz 1 und Wortschatz 2   *(Vocabulary 1 and Vocabulary 2)*

Each chapter contains two lists of important words and phrases you need in order to communicate in German. *Wortschatz 1* follows the dialogues; *Wortschatz 2* immediately precedes the reading selection. The words and expressions are arranged alphabetically by parts of speech; nouns are arranged by gender to facilitate learning. Each *Wortschatz* includes a list of antonyms (*Gegensätze*–Opposites) for newly introduced adjectives, adverbs, and verbs, as well as a special section called *Mit anderen Worten* (In Other Words). Here you learn some of the more colorful idiomatic language that characterizes the casual, everyday speech of native German speakers. Intensified forms of adjectives such as **steinalt** (*old as the hills*), or colloquialisms such as **prima** (*great*) and **Kram** (*stuff*) are defined in German. By the end of *Neue Horizonte* you will have acquired an active vocabulary of about 1600 words and phrases.

Tips zum Lesen und Lernen   *(Tips for Reading and Learning)*

This pre-reading section includes tips for learning and expanding your German vocabulary, presents easily recognized cognates such as **Universität**, and teaches some basic strategies for approaching a reading selection in German.

Lesestück   *(Reading)*

The *Lesestück* is the core of the cultural presentation of each chapter. In Chapters 1–8 the readings provide basic information on daily life in the German-speaking countries. Topics include the family, geography, secondary schools, work and professions, travel, and university and urban life. The readings in Chapters 9–16 address important topics regarding twentieth-century German history and culture; for example, the Weimar era and the legacy of World War II, foreign workers, and women in modern society. New readings on the environment (Chapter 9) and German reunification (Chapter 11) raise issues of contemporary global concern. The readings in Chapters 13 and 14 are devoted to Switzerland and Austria, respectively. Chapters 12 and 15 present authentic, unedited nonfiction texts by the modern writers Anna Seghers and

Max von der Grün. After each reading, the *Fragen zum Lesestück* (Questions on the Text) check your understanding of the reading and sometimes ask for interpretive responses.

Situationen aus dem Alltag *(Situations from Everyday Life)*

This section contains activities and optional vocabulary that emphasize "survival skills" in everyday situations such as using public transportation, eating in a restaurant, introducing oneself in various social situations, and expressing feelings.

Zum Schluß *(And finally)*

The oral and written exercises in this section integrate and combine the grammatical and cultural material covered in the chapter. They emphasize free oral and written expression of your own ideas. The last written exercise, *Wie sagt man das auf deutsch?* (How do you say that in German?) is an English-to-German translation activity that combines the major grammar points in the chapter.

Almanach *(Almanac)*

The final section of each chapter provides either more detailed information in English on the cultural topic of the chapter or presents authentic material related to the chapter's theme, for example, help-wanted ads in Chapter 5 or excerpts from an environmental brochure in Chapter 9.

Appendices, Vocabularies, and Index

Neue Horizonte includes two appendices to facilitate your study of German:

1. an answer key to the "Test Your Progress" quiz following each of the four review sections
2. a table of the principal parts of strong and irregular verbs

Note that maps of Germany and the German-speaking countries and of Europe, as well as a table of equivalent weights and measures, appear on the inside text covers.

Both the German-English and the English-German vocabularies include all the active vocabulary in the *Wortschatz* lists and the optional vocabulary introduced in the *Situationen aus dem Alltag*. For quick reference, the book ends with a comprehensive index to grammatical and cultural topics included in the text.

The Workbook/Laboratory Manual and Cassette Program

The Workbook/Laboratory Manual and the cassette program for *Neue Horizonte* are fully integrated with the student text. A cassette icon ([▢]) next to an exercise lets you know that it is recorded. A similar icon ([▣]) indicates that you can find different but related oral exercises on the tape. The workbook supplies further writing practice of the vocabulary and grammar structures for each textbook chapter.

The Video Program

D. C. Heath and Company offers a video program that can be used in conjunction with *Neue Horizonte*. Next to selected dialogues and several *Situationen aus dem Alltag* sections you will see a video icon (⬛). This signals that related material appears in the designated video module, allowing you to view situations similar to those in your text that have been filmed in an authentic setting enacted by native speakers of German.

As you begin your study of German, we wish you **viel Spaß und viel Erfolg!**

Acknowledgments

We wish to express our appreciation to Fabian Becker for his painstaking reading of the entire manuscript and his many valuable suggestions for improvements, as well as to Joan Schoellner and Janice Molloy at D. C. Heath and Company for their unfailing patience, flexibility, and attention to detail. We would also like to thank our colleagues and students at Wellesley College, Worcester Polytechnic Institute, and Massachusetts Institute of Technology, whose valuable criticism has helped us make *Neue Horizonte* an effective tool for the teaching of German.

We wish to thank especially the following colleagues for their help and advice:

Prof. John Austin, Georgia State University
Ms. Ellen Crocker, Massachusetts Institute of Technology
Dr. Karl-Heinz Finken, Wellesley College
Dr. Diethild Harrington, Worcester Polytechnic Institute
Prof. Wighart von Koenigswald, Universität Bonn, and the Hessisches
  Landesmuseum (Darmstadt, Germany)
Prof. Jens Kruse, Wellesley College
Prof. Michael Resler, Boston College
Prof. Margaret Ward, Wellesley College
Prof. Christiane Zehl-Romero, Tufts University

In addition, we would like to thank the following colleagues who reviewed the manuscript at various stages of its development:

Mary Bassett, University of Arizona
Barbara Bopp, formerly of University of California at Los Angeles
Alfred Cobbs, Wayne State University
Eugene Dobson, University of Alabama
Ronald Gougher, West Chester University
Charles James, University of Wisconsin at Madison
Dieter Jedan, Murray State University

William Keel, University of Kansas
Harvey Kendall, California State University at Long Beach
John Lalande, University of Illinois at Urbana
Hans Mussler, Utah State University
Gertraud Rosenbladt, Foothill College
Maria Stoffers, Queensborough Community College
David Weible, University of Illinois at Chicago

David B. Dollenmayer
Thomas S. Hansen

Contents

KAPITEL 4   Land und Leute   94

KAPITEL 5   Arbeit und Freizeit   130

KAPITEL 6 An der Universität **158**

KAPITEL 7   Auf Reisen   **188**

KAPITEL 8   Das Leben in der Stadt   **214**

KAPITEL 11   Deutschland nach der Mauer   **310**

KAPITEL 12   Erinnerungen   **340**

KAPITEL 13   Die Schweiz   **386**

KAPITEL 14 Österreich   **412**

KAPITEL 15 Gastarbeiter in Deutschland   **440**

KAPITEL 16   Die Frau: neue Wege und Rollen   **466**

NEUE
HORIZONTE

Einführung
Introduction

Communicative Goals
- Greeting people and asking their names
- Identifying classroom objects
- Saying good-bye
- Naming the days of the week
- Spelling in German and asking how words are spelled
- Describing how you feel
- Talking about the weather
- Counting up to 20
- Telling time
- Telling where you are from and in what month you have your birthday

Stufe 1

Step 1

Guten Tag! *Hello!*

German speakers greet each other in various ways. What greeting you use depends on the time of day:

Guten Morgen!   *Good morning!* (until about 10:00 A.M.)
Guten Tag!   *Hello!* (after 10:00 A.M.)
Guten Abend!   *Good evening!* (after 5:00 P.M.)

where you live:

Grüß Gott!   *Hello!* (in Southern Germany and Austria)

and how well you know each other and what the social situation is:

Hallo!
Tag!   *Hi!* (informal greetings)

1 **Gruppenarbeit:** Guten Tag!
Group Work

When German speakers meet friends and acquaintances, they not only greet each other, but they also shake hands. Greet the students next to you in German. Don't forget to shake hands!

2 **Partnerarbeit:** Was sagen diese Leute?
Work with Partners: What are these people saying?

With a partner, complete the following dialogues by saying them aloud.

> **Herr** = *Mr.*
> **Frau** = *Mrs. or Ms.*
> **Fräulein** = *Miss*

1. _____, Herr Lehmann!

   _____, Frau Schmidt!

2. _____, Brigitte!

   _____, Heinz!

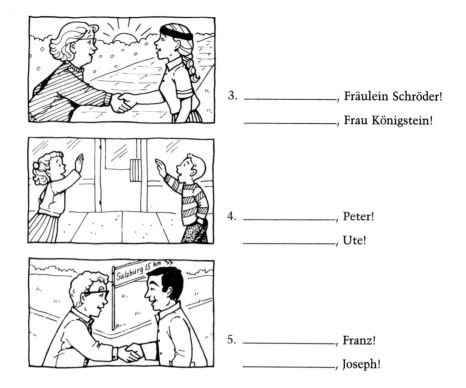

3. _____, Fräulein Schröder!

   _____, Frau Königstein!

4. _____, Peter!

   _____, Ute!

5. _____, Franz!

   _____, Joseph!

Wie heißen Sie? *What's Your Name?*

> **you   *du* or *Sie***
>
> German has two forms of the pronoun "you." If you're talking to a relative or good friend, use the familiar form **du**. University students call each other **du** even when they're meeting for the first time. If you're talking to an adult whom you don't know well, use the formal **Sie**.

When you meet people for the first time, you want to learn their names. Listen to your instructor, then repeat the following dialogue.

—Hallo, ich heiße Anna. Wie heißt du?   *Hello, my name is Anna. What's your name?*

—Hallo Anna. Ich heiße Thomas.   *Hello Anna. My name's Thomas.*

—Freut mich, Thomas!   *Pleased to meet you, Thomas.*

If you're meeting an adult who is not a fellow student, the dialogue would go like this:

—Ich heiße Schönhuber, und wie heißen Sie?

—Guten Tag, Herr Schönhuber. Ich heiße Meyer.

—Freut mich, Herr Meyer.

---

heißen X's name is

German verbs have endings that must agree with the subject of the sentence:

ich heiße	my name is (literally: *I am called*)
du heißt ⎫	
Sie heißen ⎭	your name is
er heißt	his name is
sie heißt	her name is
Wie heißt du? ⎫	What's your name? (literally: *How*
Wie heißen Sie? ⎭	*are you called?*)

---

3 **Partnerarbeit:** Wie heißt du?

Say the first dialogue at the bottom of page 4 several times with a partner, substituting your own names for Anna and Thomas.

4 **Partnerarbeit:** Und wie heißt du?

Now find a new partner and complete the following dialogue together.

A: Hallo!

B: _____!

A: Ich heiße _____. Wie heißt du?

B: Freut mich! Ich heiße _____.

5 **Gruppenarbeit:** Ich heiße . . .

Walk around the classroom and greet other students. Tell them your name and ask theirs. Use **du** and don't forget to shake hands.

Wie heißt du?

Wie heißt er?

Wie heißt sie?

6 Gruppenarbeit: Wie heißt . . . ?

Your instructor will ask you the names of other students. If you can't remember someone's name, just ask that person, „Wie heißt du?"

Wie geht's?   *How Are You?*

---

dir or Ihnen

Wie geht's dir? ⎫
Wie geht es Ihnen? ⎭   (literally) *How goes it for you?*

After you've said hello, you want to find out how someone is. With a relative or fellow student, the conversation goes like this:

—Wie geht's dir heute, Franz?   *How are you today, Franz?*
—Sehr gut, danke. Und dir?   *Very well, thanks. And you?*
—Prima, danke.   *Great, thanks.*

With an adult you know less well, the exchange goes like this:

—Wie geht es Ihnen, Frau   *How are you, Mrs. Müller?*
 Müller?
—Leider nicht so gut.   *Unfortunately, not so well.*
—Oh, das tut mir leid.   *Oh, I'm sorry.*

7 Partnerarbeit: Wie geht's?

With a partner, practice the two preceding dialogues several times until you can say them with books closed.

8 Partnerarbeit: Wie geht's dir?

Complete this dialogue with a new partner. You're both students or good friends and so say **du** or **dir** to each other.

A: Hallo! Wie geht's dir heute, _____?

B: _____, danke. Und _____?

A: _____, danke.

9 Partnerarbeit: Wie geht es Ihnen?

Now you have a more formal relationship. Use **Sie** and **Ihnen**.

A: Guten Tag, Frau/Herr _____. Wie geht es Ihnen heute?

B: Leider _____.

A: Oh, _____.

Was ist das? *What Is That?*

1. der Professor (der Lehrer)	6. der Tisch	11. die Tür
2. die Professorin (die Lehrerin)	7. die Uhr	12. die Landkarte
3. der Student (der Schüler)	8. die Wand	13. das Poster
4. die Studentin (die Schülerin)	9. das Fenster	14. die Kreide
5. die Tafel	10. der Stuhl	15. der Wischer

1. das Buch
2. das Heft
3. das Papier
4. der Bleistift
5. der Kugelschreiber
6. der Radiergummi

—Was ist das?
—Das ist der Tisch.
     das Buch.
     die Tafel.

What is that?
That's the table.
    the book.
    the blackboard.

the der, das or die

Every German noun belongs to one of three classes, traditionally called *masculine*, *neuter*, and *feminine*. The form of the definite article (**der**, **das**, **die** = *the*) shows which class each noun belongs to. This article *must* be learned with each noun.

masculine	**der** Mann	*the man*
	der Stuhl	*the chair*
neuter	**das** Kind	*the child*
	das Buch	*the book*
feminine	**die** Frau	*the woman*
	die Tafel	*the blackboard*

—Wer ist das?	*Who is that?*
—Das ist Thomas.	*That's Thomas.*
die Professorin.	*the (female) professor.*
der Professor.	*the (male) professor.*
die Studentin.	*the (female) student.*
der Student.	*the (male) student.*

The **-in** suffix denotes a female.

10 Partnerarbeit: Was ist das?

Work together and see how many people and things in the room you can identify.

A: Was ist das?

B: Das ist der/das/die _____.

A: Wer ist das?

B: Das ist _____.

Question Words

wie?	*how?*
was?	*what?*
wer?	*who?*

Auf Wiedersehen! *Good-bye!*

There are several expressions you can use when leaving.

Auf Wiedersehen!	*Good-bye!*
Tschüs!	*So long! (informal, among friends)*
Schönes Wochenende!	*(Have a) nice weekend!*
Danke, gleichfalls!	*Thanks, same to you! (You too!)*
Bis morgen!	*Until tomorrow!*
Bis Montag!	*Until Monday!*

Die Wochentage *Days of the Week*

Montag	*Monday*
Dienstag	*Tuesday*
Mittwoch	*Wednesday*
Donnerstag	*Thursday*
Freitag	*Friday*
Samstag (in southern Germany)	*Saturday*
Sonnabend (in northern Germany)	
Sonntag	*Sunday*

11 Gruppenarbeit: Auf Wiedersehen!

At the end of class, turn to your neighbors and say good-bye until next time. Tell your instructor good-bye too.

Stufe 2

Das Alphabet

The name of almost every letter in German contains the sound ordinarily represented by that letter. You should memorize the German alphabet. Listen to the alphabet on the tapes and to your instructor.

a	ah	**j**	jot	**s**	ess
b	beh	**k**	kah	**t**	teh
c	tseh	**l**	ell	**u**	uh
d	deh	**m**	emm	**v**	fau
e	eh	**n**	enn	**w**	weh
f	eff	**o**	oh	**x**	iks
g	geh	**p**	peh	**y**	üppsilon
h	hah	**q**	kuh	**z**	tsett
i	ih	**r**	err	**ß**	ess-tsett

Notes on capitalization:

- All nouns are capitalized, wherever they occur in the sentence.

- Adjectives denoting nationality are *not* capitalized.

deutsch	*German*
amerikanisch	*American*
kanadisch	*Canadian*

12 Partnerarbeit: Wie schreibt man das? *How do you write that?*

A. Ask each other how you spell your names. Write the last name as your partner spells it, then check to see whether you've written it correctly.

—Wie heißt du?
—Ich heiße Jay Schneider.
—Wie schreibt man Schneider? *How do you write "Schneider"?*
—Man schreibt das S-C-H-N-E-I-D-E-R. *You write it . . .*

B. Now turn to the classroom objects pictured on p. 7. One partner spells four or five of the objects pictured; the other partner says each word as it is spelled. Then switch roles.

13 Gruppenarbeit: Wie sagt man das? *How do you say that?*

Here are some abbreviations used in both English and German. Take turns saying them in German:

VW	BMW	ISBN	BASF
IBM	MP	EKG	TNT
USA	PVC	UdSSR	

14 Gruppenarbeit: Wie spricht man das aus? *How do you pronounce that?*

A. Let's move from individual letters to pronouncing entire words in German. Here are some well-known German surnames. Take turns saying them aloud.

Fahrenheit	Kissinger	Nietzsche	Bach
Jung	Freud	Luther	Schönberg
Diesel	Ohm	Zeppelin	Schwarzenegger
Beethoven	Röntgen	Bunsen	Goethe
Hesse	Mozart		

B. Now here are some words that English has borrowed from German. Caution: in English, their pronunciation has been anglicized. Be sure to pronounce them in German, and see if you know what they mean.

Angst	Kindergarten	Strudel
Ersatz	Kitsch	Wanderlust
Gestalt	Poltergeist	Weltanschauung
Gesundheit	Rucksack	Zeitgeist
Hinterland	Spiel	Zwieback
Flak	Leitmotiv	Schmalz

Wie geht's?

Now let's get beyond the basics of "How are you?" "I'm fine" and find out more detail about how you're feeling.

—Wie geht's heute? Bist du guter Laune? *How are you today? Are you in a good mood?*
—Nein, ich bin nicht guter Laune. Ich bin schlechter Laune. *No, I'm not in a good mood. I'm in a bad mood.*

sein   to be

The most frequently occurring verb in German is **sein**. It is very irregular in the present tense.

ich bin	*I am*
du bist ⎫	*you are*
Sie sind ⎭	
er ist	*he is*
sie ist	*she is*

Negation

Nicht (*not*) is placed in front of the adjective it negates:

—Bist du müde?	*Are you tired?*
—Nein, ich bin **nicht** müde.	*No, I'm not tired.*

Practice saying how you feel. Use the following phrases:

Es geht mir gut. (*I'm fine.*)

Ich bin . . .
guter Laune (*in a good mood*).
munter (*lively, cheerful*).
fit (*in good shape*).

Es geht mir nicht so gut. (*I'm not
   so well.*)

Ich bin . . .
schlechter Laune (*in a bad mood*).
müde (*tired*).
krank (*sick*).
sauer (*ticked off, sore*).

Reaktionen (*Reactions*)
Das freut mich! (*I'm glad!*)

Das tut mir leid. (*I'm sorry.*)

15 Gruppenarbeit

Take turns describing these six people in German.

Er/sie ist _____.

16 Partnerarbeit

With a partner, complete the following dialogues.

GERTRUD: Grüß Gott Melanie! Wie geht's _____ heute?

MELANIE: Hallo, Gertrud. Leider geht's mir _____ gut. Ich bin heute _____.

GERTRUD: Oh, _____.

FRAU PABST: Guten Tag, Herr Hauser! Wie geht es _____?

HERR HAUSER: Guten Tag, Frau Pabst! Sehr gut, danke. Ich bin heute _____!

FRAU PABST: Oh, _____!

17 Gruppenarbeit: Bist du . . . ?

Form groups of three or four for this guessing game. Each person in turn acts out one of the adjectives listed on page 11. The others ask questions until they guess what the mood is.

—Bist du müde?

—Ja, ich bin müde.   ODER   Nein, ich bin nicht müde.

Das Wetter   *The Weather*

The weather is a frequent topic of conversation everywhere.

—Wie ist das Wetter heute?
—Es ist **herrlich** (*great, terrific*).   ODER   Es ist **furchtbar** (*terrible*).

Es ist kühl.   Es ist warm.   Es ist kalt.   Es ist heiß.

Scheint die Sonne heute?   *Is the sun shining today?*

Ja, die Sonne scheint.   *Yes, the sun is shining.*   Nein, es regnet.   *No, it's raining.*

18 **Partnerarbeit:** Wie ist das Wetter heute?

Chat briefly with a partner about today's weather. Use the words and phrases above. Here are more weather words. Listen and repeat them after your instructor.

Es ist heute . . . wolkig.   *Today it's . . . cloudy.*
                   neblig.   *foggy.*
                   sonnig.   *sunny.*
                   windig.   *windy.*
Es schneit.   *It's snowing.*

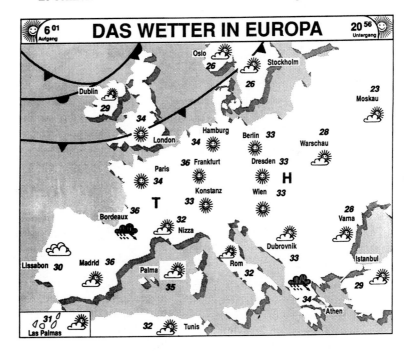

DAS WETTER IN EUROPA

19 **Gruppenarbeit:** In London ist es . . .

Describe the weather in the following places.

Wie ist das Wetter in . . .

Oslo?

Cannes?

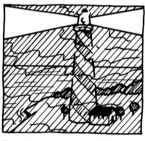

Boston?

Berlin?

Hamburg?

Stufe 3

Wie viele? *How Many?*

0	null	11	elf
1	eins	12	zwölf
2	zwei	13	dreizehn
3	drei	14	vierzehn
4	vier	15	fünfzehn
5	fünf	16	sechzehn
6	sechs	17	siebzehn
7	sieben	18	achtzehn
8	acht	19	neunzehn
9	neun	20	zwanzig
10	zehn		

20 **Gruppenarbeit:** Wie ist die Telefonnummer? *What is the telephone number?*

Read these business telephone numbers aloud.

NATURKOST · NATURKOSMETIK
belladonna 694 3731
BERGMANNSTR. 101

mitfahr zentrale **Berlin 15**
030-8827606

SCHALLPLATTEN + CD's
ANKAUF · VERKAUF · TAUSCH
LP's ab 4 DM · Sl ab 1 DM
Ständiger Barankauf von LP's + CD's (Sammlungen)
Mo–Fr 12.00–18.30
Sa 10.00–14.00
Bergmannstraße 10
Telefon: 6 93 19 98

Dortmund
0231/82 34 45
82 20 67

EIGENER ABSCHLEPPDIENST
K. Walter
vorm. ZINNEKER
1230 WIEN, BREITENFURTERSTR. 213
804 21 42
KAROSSERIE-FACHWERKSTÄTTE
Einbrenn- und Sonderlackierung
Autokosmetik

21 **Kettenreaktion:** Wie ist deine Telefonnummer? *Chain Reaction: What's your telephone number?*

Follow the model. One student asks the next.

BEISPIEL: STUDENT A: Wie ist deine Telefonnummer?

STUDENT B: Meine Telefonnummer ist _____. Wie ist *deine* Telefonnummer?

STUDENT C: _____.

Wie spät ist es, bitte? *What Time Is It, Please?*

Es ist drei Uhr.

Es ist Viertel nach sieben.

Es ist Viertel vor zehn.

Es ist ein Uhr. *or* Es ist eins.

Es ist elf (Minuten) nach zehn.

Es ist vierzehn vor acht.

The half hour is counted in German in relation to the following full hour, not the preceding hour as in English.

Es ist halb acht.
(literally) *It is halfway to eight.*

„Wie spät ist es?" (Turmuhr
[*tower clock*] und Sonnenuhr
in Würzburg)

22 Gruppenarbeit: Wie spät ist es, bitte?

Persönliche Fragen   *Personal Questions*

Question Words	
woher?	*from where?* (origin)
wo?	*where?* (location)

When you meet people, you usually want to find out some basic facts about them, such as where they come from. Listen to the following dialogue and repeat it after your instructor.

—Woher kommst du?   *Where do you come from?*
—Ich komme aus Minnesota.   *I come from Minnesota.*
—Wo wohnst du jetzt?   *Where do you live now?*
—Ich wohne jetzt in Kalifornien. *I'm living in California now.*

kommen *to come*		**wohnen** *to live*	
ich komme	*I come*	ich wohne	*I live*
du kommst	*you come*	du wohnst	*you live*
Sie kommen		Sie wohnen	
er kommt	*he comes*	er wohnt	*he lives*
sie kommt	*she comes*	sie wohnt	*she lives*

23 Gruppenarbeit

Walk around the classroom and find out what cities, states, or foreign countries your classmates are from. Your instructor can help you with the German names of other countries. Then find out where your classmates live, on campus or otherwise.

—Woher kommst du?

—Ich komme aus ———.

—Wo wohnst du jetzt?

—Ich wohne in Davis Hall.

Listen to the dialogue and repeat it after your instructor.

—Wann hast du Geburtstag?   *When is your birthday? (literally: When do you have birthday?)*

—Ich habe im Januar Geburtstag.   *My birthday is in January.*

haben *to have*	
ich **habe**	*I have*
du **hast**	*you have*
Sie **haben**	
er **hat**	*he has*
sie **hat**	*she has*

Die Monate (*The Months*)

im Januar	im Juli
im Februar	im August
im März	im September
im April	im Oktober
im Mai	im November
im Juni	im Dezember

24   **Kettenreaktion**

Find out in what months your classmates were born.

BEISPIEL: STUDENT A: Wann hast du Geburtstag?

STUDENT B: Ich habe im _____ Geburtstag. Wann hast *du* Geburtstag?

STUDENT C: _____.

Useful Classroom Expressions

Wie sagt man „the book" auf deutsch?	*How do you say "the book" in German?*
Man sagt „das Buch".	*You say "das Buch."*
Übersetzen Sie bitte.	*Please translate.*
Wiederholen Sie bitte.	*Please repeat.*
Üben wir!	*Let's practice!*
Machen sie Nummer drei, bitte.	*Please do number three.*
Alle zusammen, bitte.	*All together, please.*
Sie sprechen zu leise.	*You're speaking too softly.*
Sprechen Sie bitte lauter.	*Please speak more loudly.*
Sie sprechen zu schnell.	*You're speaking too fast.*
Sprechen Sie bitte langsamer.	*Please speak more slowly.*
Wie bitte?	*I beg your pardon? What did you say?*
Antworten Sie bitte auf deutsch!	*Please answer in German.*
Das ist richtig.	*That's correct.*
Das ist falsch.	*That's incorrect.*
Verstehen Sie das?	*Do you understand that?*

Profile of the Federal Republic of Germany

Area: 357,050 square kilometers; 135,679 square miles
Population: 79 million, or 222 people per sq. kilometer (582 per sq. mile)
Currency: Deutsche Mark; 1 DM = 100 Pfennige
Major Cities: Berlin (largest city, official capital, pop. 3.9 million); Bonn (seat of government, pop. 300,000); Munich (pop. 1.3 million); Frankfurt am Main (pop. 594,000); Hamburg (pop. 1.6 million); Cologne (pop. 914,000); Düsseldorf (pop. 561,000); Leipzig (pop. 554,000); Stuttgart (pop. 563,000); Dresden (pop. 519,000).
Religions: Protestant: 50%; Catholic: 37%; other: 13% (est.)

After Germany's defeat in the Second World War, the allied powers supported the creation of two German states in 1949: the Federal Republic of Germany (FRG or "West Germany") and the German Democratic Republic (GDR or "East Germany"). These two states existed side by side for forty-one years. The reunification of 1990 merged one of the most affluent capitalist countries with one of the most prosperous countries in the Eastern bloc. The fifteen administrative districts of the GDR were restructured into five new states (*Länder*) of the Federal Republic.

Today, the unified nation has roughly the same area as Minnesota and Wisconsin combined. Unification increased the gross national product by 24% and the total population by 27%, making Germany the most populous country in the European Community (EC).

But the revolutionary changes in Germany are still difficult to assess. Many of the statistics sound very promising: Germany produces 30% of all exports from the EC (35% of all cars, 29% of electricity, and 26% of steel).

However, forty years of state ownership and lack of competition left East Germany's industry obsolete and unable to compete in the western marketplace. The infrastructure of the former GDR must now be modernized, a process that has caused inflation in the entire country and high rates of unemployment in the former East German workforce. Unification has thus come at a high price to German taxpayers. In the long run, Germany will emerge richer and stronger, but in the short run, Germans will have to make economic sacrifices to resolve differences, overcome disparities, and achieve genuine national unity.

In Deutschland leben 79 Millionen Menschen.

Wie geht es Ihnen?

Communicative Goals
- Making statements
- Asking simple questions answered by yes or no
- Asking for information: when, why, who, where, what, etc.

Cultural Goal
- Using the correct forms of address ("you") in social situations

Lyrik zum Vorlesen   *Kinderreime, Zungenbrecher*

Grammatik   Personal Pronouns   •   Verbs: Infinitive and Present Tense   •   Noun Gender and Pronoun Agreement   •   Noun Plurals   •   Nominative Case   •   The Sentence: German Word Order   •   The Flavoring Particle *ja*

Lesestück   Wie sagt man „you" auf deutsch?

Situationen aus dem Alltag   „Sie" oder „du"?

Almanach   Where Is German Spoken?

In Eile

HERR LEHMANN: Guten Morgen, Frau Hauser!

FRAU HAUSER: Morgen, Herr Lehmann. Entschuldigung, aber ich bin in Eile. Ich fliege um elf nach Wien.

HERR LEHMANN: Wann kommen Sie wieder zurück?

FRAU HAUSER: Am Mittwoch . . . also dann, auf Wiedersehen!

HERR LEHMANN: Auf Wiedersehen! Gute Reise!

Die Mensa

KARIN: Tag, Michael! Wie ist die Suppe heute?

MICHAEL: Tag, Karin! Sie ist ganz gut. . . . Übrigens, arbeitest du viel im Moment?

KARIN: Nein, nicht sehr viel. Warum fragst du?

MICHAEL: Ich gehe heute abend zu Horst. Du auch?

KARIN: Ja, natürlich.

MICHAEL: Prima! Also tschüs, bis dann.

Typisch für September

FRAU BACHMANN: Guten Tag, Frau Kuhn! Wie geht's?

FRAU KUHN: Tag, Frau Bachmann! Sehr gut, danke, und Ihnen?

FRAU BACHMANN: Danke, auch gut. Was machen die Kinder heute?

FRAU KUHN: Sie spielen draußen, das Wetter ist ja so schön.

FRAU BACHMANN: Ja, endlich scheint die Sonne. Aber vielleicht regnet es morgen wieder.

FRAU KUHN: Das ist typisch für September.

„Wie ist die Suppe heute?"

Wortschatz 1
Vocabulary 1

wohnen — to live

fly

In a Hurry

MR. LEHMANN: Good morning, Ms. Hauser.

MS. HAUSER: Morning, Mr. Lehmann. Forgive me, but I'm in a hurry. I'm flying to Vienna at eleven.

MR. LEHMANN: When are you coming back again?

MS. HAUSER: On Wednesday. . . . Well then, good-bye.

MR. LEHMANN: Good-bye. Have a good trip!

The University Cafeteria

KARIN: Hi, Michael! How's the soup today?

MICHAEL: Hi, Karin! It's pretty good. . . . By the way, are you working a lot at the moment?

KARIN: No, not very much. Why do you ask?

MICHAEL: I'm going to Horst's tonight. You too?

KARIN: Yes, of course.

MICHAEL: Great! Well, so long until then.

Typical for September

MRS BACHMANN: Hello, Mrs. Kuhn. How are you?

MRS. KUHN: Hi, Mrs. Bachmann. Very well, thanks, and you?

MRS. BACHMANN: Thanks, I'm fine too. What are the kids doing today?

MRS KUHN: They're playing outside—the weather is so nice.

MRS. BACHMANN: Yes, the sun is finally shining. But maybe it will rain again tomorrow.

MRS. KUHN: That is typical for September.

Verben *Verbs*

arbeiten to work
fliegen to fly
fragen to ask
gehen to go; walk
kommen to come
machen to make; do
regnen to rain
scheinen to shine; seem
sein to be
spielen to play

Substantive *Nouns*

der **Herr, -en** gentleman
  Herr Lehmann Mr. Lehmann
der **Morgen, -** morning
der **September** September
der **Tag, -e** day

das **Büro, -s** office
das **Kind, -er** child
das **Wetter** weather
(das) **Wien** Vienna

die **Frau, -en** woman
  Frau Kuhn Mrs./Ms. Kuhn
die **Mensa** university cafeteria
die **Sonne** sun
die **Straße, -n** street; road
die **Suppe, -n** soup

Adjektive and Adverbien[2] *Adjectives and Adverbs*

auch also, too
da there
dann then
draußen outside
endlich finally
gut good; well
  ganz gut pretty good; pretty well
heute abend this evening, tonight
hier here
morgen tomorrow
natürlich natural(ly); of course
schön beautiful(ly)
sehr very
typisch typical(ly)
vielleicht maybe, perhaps
wieder again

Andere Vokabeln *Other Words*

aber but
also well, *therefore*
bis until; by
  bis dann until then; by then
danke thanks
für for
in in
ja yes; *untranslatable "flavoring particle," see p. 35.*
nach to (*with cities and countries*)

---

1. The definite article is seldom used with the names of cities. It occurs in phrases such as **das alte Wien** = *old Vienna*. All city and most country names are neuter in German.

2. There is no German equivalent to the English adverb ending -ly (*natural–naturally*). For example, the German word **natürlich** can mean both *natural* and *naturally*, depending on the context. Similary, **gut** means both *good* and *well*.

nein no
nicht not
übrigens by the way
um at (*with expressions of time*)
und and
usw. (= **und so weiter**) etc. (= and so forth)
viel much, a lot
warum? why?
wie how; like, as
zu to (*with people*); too (*as in "too much"*)
zurück back

Nützliche Ausdrücke
Useful Expressions

am Mittwoch (Donnerstag usw.) on Wednesday (Thursday, etc.)

Auf Wiedersehen! Good-bye!
Entschuldigung! Pardon me! Excuse me!
Guten Morgen! Good morning!
 Morgen! Morning!
Guten Tag! Hello! (*literally* "Good day")
 Tag! Hi! (*short for* Guten Tag)
Gute Reise! (Have a) good trip!
im Moment at the moment
in Eile in a hurry
Prima! Terrific! Great!
Tschüs! So long! (*informal, among friends*)
Wie geht's? How are you? (*informal*)

Gegensätze *Opposites*
gut ≠ schlecht good ≠ bad
hier ≠ da here ≠ there
schön ≠ häßlich beautiful ≠ ugly
der Tag ≠ die Nacht day ≠ night
viel ≠ wenig much, a lot ≠ not much, little

Mit anderen Worten
In Other Words
wunderschön = sehr schön
prima = sehr gut

Variationen *Variations*

A **Persönliche Fragen** *Personal Questions*

1. Wo wohnen Sie?
2. Wie geht es Ihnen heute?
3. Arbeiten Sie viel im Moment?
4. Was machen Sie heute abend?

B **Partnerarbeit** *Work with a Partner*
Now ask each other the same questions as in A. Use the **du**-form.

C **Partnerarbeit:** Wann fliegst du?

The clock faces show departure times from the Frankfurt airport. Ask each other when you're flying to various places.

> BEISPIEL (*Example*): Wann fliegst du nach _____?
> Ich fliege um _____.

1. nach Prag

2. nach Moskau

3. nach Kopenhagen

4. nach Madrid

5. nach Toronto

6. nach Singapur

D **Übung** *Exercise*

Respond to these greetings and farewells.

1. Guten Morgen!
2. Wie geht es Ihnen?
3. Guten Tag!
4. Auf Wiedersehen!
5. Gute Reise!

6. Tschüs, bis dann.
7. Tag!
8. Hallo!
9. Schönes Wochenende!

E **Übung:** Und Sie?

Respond to your instructor, saying you also feel the same way.

> BEISPIEL: Richard ist heute guter Laune. Und Sie?
> Ja, *er* ist guter Laune, und *ich* bin es auch.

1. Maria ist fit. Und Sie?
2. Herr Schrödinger ist krank. Und Sie?
3. Frau Bachmann ist munter. Und Sie?
4. Christian ist guter Laune. Und Sie?
5. Wir sind schlechter Laune. Und Sie?
6. Ich bin heute sauer. Und Sie?

Lyrik zum Vorlesen

Poetry for Reading Aloud

In each chapter this section presents some short selections of original German poetry (**Lyrik**), rhymes, or song texts for your enjoyment. Read them aloud. Don't worry about understanding everything. The emphasis here is on the *sound* of German.

Kinderreime   *Children's Rhymes*

A Traditional Counting-out Rhyme

Eins zwei drei,
du bist frei.°   *free*
Vier fünf sechs,
du bist weg.°   *out*
Sieben acht neun,
du mußt's sein.°   *you are it*

Children's Alphabet Rhyme

A b c d e f und g,
h i j k l m n o p,
q r s t u v w,
x y z und o weh°,   **o weh** = *oh my*
jetzt kann ich das ABC°.   *now I know the ABC*

Ich heiße Peter, du heißt Paul.
Ich bin fleißig,° du bist faul.°   *hard-working/lazy*

Zungenbrecher°   *Tongue twisters*

In Ulm,[3] um Ulm°   *In Ulm, around Ulm,*
und um Ulm herum.°   *and round about Ulm.*

Fischers Fritz fischt frische Fische,°   *Fischer's (boy) Fritz fishes fresh*
frische Fische fischt Fischers Fritz.°   *fish,*
                                                        Fresh fish is what Fischer's
                                                        Fritz fishes.

3. Southern German city on the Danube River.

Grammatik *Grammar*

Personal Pronouns

Personal pronouns as the subject of a sentence:

		Singular		Plural
1st person	ich	*I*	**wir**	*we*
2nd person	du	*you* (familiar)	**ihr**	*you* (familiar)
	Sie	*you* (formal)	**Sie**	*you* (formal)
3rd person	er	*he, it*		
	es	*it*	**sie**	*they*
	sie	*she, it*		

The Three "you's" of German

German has three words for the personal pronoun "you": **du, ihr,** and **Sie.**

The familiar pronouns **du** (*singular*) and **ihr** (*plural*) are used when addressing children, family members, close friends, animals, and the deity. Members of certain groups (students, blue-collar workers, soldiers, athletes) converse among themselves almost exclusively with **du** and **ihr.**

Sie is used when addressing one or more adults who are not close friends of the speaker. In writing, **Sie** meaning *you* is distinguished from **sie** meaning *they* by always beginning with a capital letter.

The pronoun **ich** is not capitalized except when it is the first word in a sentence.

„Tag, Frau Breitenkamp! Wie geht es Ihnen?"

Verbs: Infinitive and Present Tense

The Infinitive

German verbs are found in a dictionary in the infinitive form. In English, the infinitive is usually preceded by *to*.

> *to play*   *to hike*

In German, the infinitive consists of the verb stem plus the ending **-en** or **-n**.

spiel-	**spielen**	*to play*
wander-	**wandern**	*to hike*

Present Tense Endings

German verbs have various endings in the present tense. The ending used depends on the subject of the verb.

Das Kind spiel**t** draußen.	*The child plays outside.*
Die Kinder spiel**en** draußen.	*The children play outside.*

In order to form the present tense of a German verb, find the stem by dropping the infinitive ending **-en** or **-n**:

> komm- ~~en~~

Then add the personal endings:

	stem + ending		Present Tense	
ich	komm- **e**	ich	komme	*I come*
du	komm- **st**	du	kommst	*you come*
Sie	komm- **en**[4]	Sie	kommen[4]	
er, es, sie	komm- **t**	er, es, sie	kommt	*he, it, she comes*
wir	komm- **en**	wir	kommen	*we come*
ihr	komm- **t**	ihr	kommt	*you come*
Sie	komm- **en**[4]	Sie	kommen[4]	
sie	komm- **en**	sie	kommen	*they come*

1 Übung: Wer kommt morgen?

Use the pronoun provided by your instructor to say who is coming tomorrow.

BEISPIEL: ich
Ich komme morgen.

1. er
2. Sie, Frau Bachmann
3. wir
4. sie (*they*)
5. sie (*she*)
6. du, Michael
7. ich
8. ihr

4. The third person plural **sie kommen** (*they come*) is also the polite form of address: **Sie kommen** (*you come*—singular and plural). These forms are always identical except for capitalization. From now on, the **Sie**-form will be given with the third person plural in verb paradigms: **sie, Sie kommen**.

2 **Kettenreaktion:** Wo wohnst du?

Say where you live and then ask the next student.

> BEISPIEL: Ich wohne in Atlanta. Wo wohnst du?
> Ich wohne in _____.

Regular Variations in Personal Endings

Verbs with stems ending in **-d**, **-t**, or a consonant cluster such as **-gn** require an **-e-** before the **du**, **er**, and **ihr** endings to make them pronounceable.

arbeiten		stem: **arbeit-**		**regnen**	stem: **regn-**
ich arbeite		wir arbeiten			
du arbeitest		ihr arbeitet		es regnet	
er, es, sie arbeitet		sie, Sie arbeiten			

3 **Übung:** Wer arbeitet heute?

Use the pronoun or name provided by your instructor to say who is working today.

> BEISPIEL: wir
> Wir arbeiten heute.

1. ich
2. Herr Lehmann
3. sie (*they*)
4. du

5. ihr
6. Frau Kuhn
7. wir
8. Michael

to make

4 **Gruppenarbeit:** Was machst du heute?   *4 Studenten*

Read the following conversation together. Supply the missing verbs to say what you're doing today.

STUDENT 1: Was machst du heute?

STUDENT 2: Ich _____. Was machst *du* heute?

STUDENT 3: Ich _____. Was machst du heute?
usw. (*etc.*)

English and German Present Tense Compared

German present tense is equivalent to three English forms:

ich gehe $\begin{cases} I\ go \\ I\ am\ going \\ I\ do\ go \end{cases}$

Present Tense with Future Meaning

In German the present tense often expresses future meaning, especially when another element in the sentence makes the future meaning clear.

Ich fliege um elf nach Wien.	*I'm flying to Vienna at eleven.*
Heute abend gehe ich zu Horst.	*I'm going to Horst's tonight.*
Mittwoch bin ich wieder zurück.	*I'll be back Wednesday.*

Note that English often uses the present progressive (*I'm flying, I'm going*) for the same purpose.

The Verb *sein*

Like *to be* in English, the verb **sein** is irregular; its forms must be memorized.

ich	**bin**	*I am*	wir	**sind**	*we are*
du	**bist**	*you are*	ihr	**seid**	*you are*
er, es, sie	**ist**	*he, it, she is*	sie, Sie	**sind**	*they, you are*

Noun Gender and Pronoun Agreement

You have learned that German has three genders for nouns, shown by the definite article (**der, das, die**). When a pronoun is substituted for a noun (*the chair = it*), it must have the same gender.

Wo ist **der** Stuhl?	**Er** ist hier.	*It's here.*
Wo ist **das** Buch?	**Es** ist hier.	*It's here.*
Wo ist **die** Tafel?	**Sie** ist hier.	*It's here.*

Note that **er, es,** and **sie** can all mean "it."

It's helpful to remember the similarities between the definite article and its corresponding pronoun.

der Stuhl → **er**
das Buch → **es**
die Tafel → **sie**

Gender distinctions disappear in the plural. The definite article **die** is used with all plural nouns, and the pronoun **sie** replaces all plural nouns.

Wo sind **die** Stühle?		
Wo sind **die** Bücher?	**Sie** sind hier.	*They are here.*
Wo sind **die** Tafeln?		

  5 Übung

Answer your instructor's questions affirmatively. Use a pronoun.

BEISPIEL: Ist Rolf heute guter Laune?
Ja, *er* ist heute guter Laune.

1. Ist das Buch gut?
2. Ist Frau Schmidt sehr müde?
3. Spielen die Kinder draußen?
4. Ist das Wetter typisch für September?

Wie geht es Ihnen? **29**

5. Scheint die Sonne endlich? *sie*

sie 7. Ist die Suppe gut?

sie 6. Sind Karin und Michael Studenten?

er 8. Ist der Tag schön?

6 **Partnerarbeit:** Hier oder da?

Partner A asks where the things in the left-hand column are. Partner B answers with the correct pronoun, pointing to the object. Reverse roles for the right-hand column.

BEISPIEL: PARTNER A: Wo ist die Tafel?
PARTNER B: Sie ist da.

das Buch
das Heft
die Tür
der Bleistift
die Wand
die Landkarte

der Radiergummi
das Fenster
der Professor/die Professorin
der Tisch
der Stuhl
das Poster

Noun Plurals

The most common plural ending for English nouns is *-s* or *-es*: chair, chairs; dish, dishes. Some nouns have irregular plurals: man, *men*; mouse, *mice*; child, *children*; sheep, sheep.

German has a much greater variety of plural forms. There is no one basic rule, nor is any one form the most common. The following list gives examples of all the plural forms.

	Singular	Plural
No change	der Lehrer	die Lehrer
Umlaut added to stem vowel	die Mutter	die Mütter
Add ending **-e**	der Tisch	die Tische
Umlaut + ending **-e**	der Stuhl	die Stühle
Add ending **-er**	das Kind	die Kinder
Umlaut + ending **-er**	das Buch	die Bücher
Add ending **-en**	die Frau	die Frauen
Add ending **-n**	die Straße	die Straßen
Add ending **-s**	das Büro	die Büros

It is customary in dictionaries and vocabulary lists to indicate the plural by an abbreviation. An umlaut above the hyphen indicates that the stem (stressed) vowel is umlauted in the plural.

Dictionary Entry	*You Must Learn*
der **Lehrer,** -	der **Lehrer,** die **Lehrer**
die **Mutter,** ¨	die **Mutter,** die **Mütter**
der **Tag,** -e	der **Tag,** die **Tage**
der **Stuhl,** ¨e	der **Stuhl,** die **Stühle**

7 Übung

Look at the following vocabulary and say aloud both the singular and plural forms with their articles.

1. das Kind, -er
2. das Büro, -s
3. der Tisch, -e
4. die Mutter, ¨

5. die Tafel, -n
6. die Straße, -n
7. der Stuhl, ¨e
8. die Frau, -en

 8 Übung

Now substitute the plural for the singular and change the verbs accordingly.

BEISPIEL: *Der Herr kommt um elf.*
Die Herren kommen um elf.

1. Das Büro ist sehr schön.
2. Die Frau fliegt nach Wien.
3. Das Kind kommt heute abend.

4. Die Straße ist sehr schön.
5. Das Buch ist gut.
6. Der Lehrer arbeitet morgen im Büro.

Nominative Case

The case of a noun or a pronoun is a signal of its function in the sentence. German has four cases: nominative, accusative, dative, and genitive. The article used with the noun shows its case.

Der Schüler fragt den Lehrer.	*The pupil asks the teacher.*
Der Lehrer fragt **den** Schüler.	*The teacher asks the pupil.*

nominative case   *accusative case*

der Schüler		**den** Schüler
subject	vs.	direct object
person asking		person being asked

In this chapter we are using only the nominative case, which is used for the subject of a sentence and for a predicate nominative (see page 32).

Definite Article in the Nominative Case

You have already learned the definite articles (*the*) in the nominative:

	singular	*plural*
masculine	**der** Mann	**die** Männer
neuter	**das** Kind	**die** Kinder
feminine	**die** Frau	**die** Frauen

Here are the indefinite articles (*a, an*) in the nominative:

	singular	*plural*
masculine	**ein** Mann	Männer
neuter	**ein** Kind	Kinder
feminine	**eine** Frau	Frauen

Note: Masculine and neuter singular indefinite articles are identical in the nominative: **ein** Mann, **ein** Kind. The indefinite article has no plural:

ein Kind → Kinder

The personal pronouns you have learned in this chapter (**ich, du,** etc.) are all in the nominative case.

9 **Übung:** Was ist das?

Say what your instructor is pointing to. Use the indefinite article.

BEISPIEL: PROFESSORIN: Was ist das?
STUDENTIN: Das ist **ein** Fenster.

Use of the Nominative Case

The subject of the sentence is always in the nominative case. Notice that the subject does not have to come at the beginning of the sentence.

Der Herr ist in Eile.	*The gentleman is in a hurry.*
Endlich kommt **die Suppe.**	*The soup is finally coming.*
Morgen fliegt **sie** zurück.	*She's flying back tomorrow.*

A predicate nominative is a noun that refers to the same person or thing as the subject of the sentence. It follows the subject and the linking verb **sein.**[5]

Das ist **Frau Schmidt.**	*That is Mrs. Schmidt.*
Paul ist **ein Kind.**	*Paul is a child.*

10 **Gruppenarbeit:** Was ist das? Wer ist das?

One student leads the game. The rest are divided into two teams. The leader points to an object or a person in the room and asks:

Wer / Was ist das?
Das ist ein(e) / der / das / die _____.

Teams answer alternately. The team with the most correct answers wins.

---

5. Other linking verbs (**bleiben,** *to remain;* **heißen,** *to be called;* **werden,** *to become*) also take the predicate nominative. You will learn them later.

The Sentence: German Word Order

Statements: Verb-Second Word Order

In declarative sentences (statements) in English, the subject comes immediately before the verb phrase, with very few exceptions.

> *subject* *verb*
> **We** **are going** to Richard's tonight.

Other elements may precede the subject-verb combination:

> Tonight **we are going** to Richard's.

In German statements, only the verb has a fixed position. *It is always the second element.*

> 1   2   3   4
> Wir **gehen** heute abend zu Richard.

This is an ironclad rule and must be learned well. If an element other than the subject begins the sentence, the verb *remains* in second position and the subject then *follows* the verb. Note the difference from English, where the subject always precedes the verb.

> 1   2   3   4
> Heute abend **gehen** wir zu Richard.
> Zu Richard   **gehen** wir heute abend.

A time phrase (**heute abend**) or a prepositional phrase (**zu Richard**) may consist of two or more words, but counts as *one* grammatical element.

> Initial **ja, nein, und,** and **aber** do *not* count as the first element.

> 0   1   2   3
> Ja,   wir gehen   zu Richard.
> Aber wir gehen   zu Richard.

First position is usually used to restate what's being talked about. A new element with information value—the answer to a question, for instance—is usually placed at the end of the statement.

> Was machen wir?   Wir gehen **zu Claudia.**
> Was machen wir heute abend?   Heute abend **gehen wir zu Claudia.**
> Wann gehen wir zu Claudia?   Zu Claudia gehen wir **heute abend.**

11 Übung

Restate the sentences, beginning with the word or phrase in italics.

> BEISPIEL: Ich arbeite *übrigens* viel.
>   *Übrigens* arbeite ich viel.

1. Die Lehrerin geht *morgen* zu Frau Bachmann.

2. Die Sonne scheint *endlich* wieder.

3. Es regnet *heute*.

4. Wir fliegen *um elf* nach Wien.

5. Das ist *vielleicht* die Straße.

6. Ich arbeite viel *im Moment*.

7. Die Suppe ist *heute* ganz gut.

8. Es regnet *natürlich* viel.

Questions

There are two main types of questions in German:

- Yes/no questions are answered by **ja** or **nein**. In a yes/no question, the verb is always the first element.

Ist Andrea hier?	*Is Andrea here?*
Arbeitet sie in Berlin?	*Does she work in Berlin?*
Kommst du wieder zurück?	*Are you coming back again?*

- Questions asking for information start with a question word (*what, how, when,* etc.) and have the same verb-second word order as statements.

Was	macht	er?	*What is he doing?*
Wie	geht	es Ihnen?	*How are you?*
Wann	kommen	Sie wieder zurück?	*When are you coming back again?*

Here are some question words:

wann	*when*	**Wann** kommt sie zurück?
warum	*why*	**Warum** fragst du?
was	*what*	**Was** macht er?
wer	*who*	**Wer** ist das?
wie	*how*	**Wie** geht es dir?
wo	*where*	**Wo** wohnen Sie?
woher	*from where*	**Woher** kommt ihr?

Do not confuse **wer** (*who*) and **wo** (*where*)!

12 Übung

Change these statements to yes/no questions.

BEISPIEL: Stefan arbeitet in Stuttgart.
Arbeitet Stefan in Stuttgart?

1. Das ist typisch für September.
2. Ihr geht wieder zu Karin.
3. Es regnet.
4. Herr Hauser fliegt nach Berlin.
5. Frau Kuhn kommt auch.
6. Im Moment arbeitest du viel.
7. Er ist sehr in Eile.
8. Der Herr kommt am Mittwoch zurück.

13 Übung

Ask the questions for which the following statements are answers.

BEISPIEL: Das ist der Professor.
Wer ist das?

1. Er fliegt um elf.
2. Sie sind im Büro.
3. Das ist Frau Bachmann.
4. Das ist die Mensa.
5. Die Suppe ist gut, danke.
6. Sie kommt aus Deutschland.

Time before Place

In German, adverbs like **heute** and adverbial phrases like **nach Wien** *must* come in the sequence *time before place*. The usual sequence in English is exactly the reverse: place before time.

	time	*place*		*place*	*time*
Sie fliegt	morgen	nach Wien.	She's flying to Vienna tomorrow.		
Wir gehen	heute abend	zu Horst.	We're going to Horst's tonight.		

14 **Übung:** Heute oder morgen?

Answer your instructor with a complete sentence, using either **heute** or **morgen**.

> BEISPIEL: Wann gehen Sie zu Stefanie?
> Ich gehe heute zu Stefanie.

1. Wann fliegt Stefan nach Wien?

2. Wann geht Frau Bachmann zu Frau Kuhn?

3. Wann spielen die Kinder draußen?

4. Wann kommt Herr Lehmann zurück?

The Flavoring Particle *ja*

German adds various kinds of emphasis to sentences by using intensifying words known as "flavoring particles." These can seldom be directly translated into English, but it is important to become familiar with them and understand what intensity or emotional "flavor" they add to a sentence.

One flavoring particle frequently used in declarative sentences (i.e., statements) is **ja**. As a flavoring particle, **ja** does not mean *yes*, but rather adds the sense of *after all, really*.

In the third dialogue at the beginning of this chapter, Frau Kuhn says about her children:

Sie spielen draußen, das Wetter ist **ja** so schön.	They're playing outside—the weather (as is obvious) really is so beautiful.

The flavoring particle **ja** is usually placed immediately after the verb and personal pronouns. Here is how **ja** might be added to some other sentences from the dialogues:

Ich bin **ja** in Eile.	I'm in a hurry, after all.
Ich gehe **ja** heute abend zu Horst.	I'm going to Horst's tonight, you know.

Lesestück

Wie sagt man „you" auf deutsch?

Tips zum Lesen and Lernen *Tips for Reading and Studying*

Tips zum Vokabelnlernen *Tips for Learning Vocabulary*

The feminine suffix -*in* You will have noticed that German often has two different nouns to distinguish between a male and a female.

Professor/Professorin	Lehrer/Lehrerin
Schüler/Schülerin	Partner/Partnerin
Student/Studentin	

The suffix **-in** always denotes the female, and its plural is always **-innen**.

-in	**-innen**
die Studentin	die Studentinnen

Partnerarbeit: Wie heißt der Mann, wie heißt die Frau?

With a partner, fill in the blanks.

	Mann	*Frau!*	*zwei!*
1.	Amerikaner	*Amerikanerin*	*Amerikanerinnen*
2.	Tourist	_____	_____
3.	Nachbar (*neighbor*)	_____	_____
4.	Lehrer	_____	_____
5.	Professor	_____	_____
6.	Schüler	_____	_____
7.	Student	_____	_____
8.	Partner	_____	_____

German has many words that look so much like their English equivalents that you can easily guess their meanings. Both languages have borrowed many of these words from Latin or French. When such words occur in the readings, we will preview them in this special section called *Leicht zu merken*. If the German word is stressed on a different syllable than the English, this will be indicated to the right. You should have no trouble guessing the meanings of these cognates:

formell	for*mell*
die Solidarität	Solidari*tät*
der Tourist	Tour*ist*

Einstieg in den Text   *Getting into the Text*

Here are some tips to help you get the most out of the reading (*Lesestück*) in each chapter.

- Read the title. How does it anticipate the text? The title "Wie sagt man 'you' auf deutsch?", for example, lets you know that the text is about the various forms of second-person address. You have already used these.

- Read out loud the new active vocabulary for the reading (*Wortschatz 2*). Try to identify similarities between English and German forms that will help you remember the words; for example, **grüßen** (*greet*), **Haus** (*house*), **Gruppe** (*group*); **freundlich** (*friendly*), **oft** (*often*).

- Read the text once through aloud without referring back to the vocabulary. Do not try to translate as you read. Your purpose is to get a rough idea of content from the key words you recognize in each paragraph. For example, in the first paragraph of the following reading, you will recognize the words **Touristen, Deutschland,** and **Amerikaner.** A good working assumption is that the paragraph deals with tourists in Germany—perhaps American tourists.

- Once you have a general idea of the content of each paragraph, read the text at least one more time, again without trying to translate. Your object this time is to begin to understand the text on the sentence level. The marginal glosses (marked by the sign°) will help you to understand words and phrases not for active use.

- Read and try to answer the content questions (*Fragen zum Lesestück*). Refer back to the text only if necessary.

Wortschatz 2

Verben

bedeuten to mean, signify
  Was bedeutet das? What does that mean?
grüßen to greet, say hello to
meinen to be of the opinion, think
sagen to say; tell
(stimmen) das stimmt that's right, that's true
studieren to attend a university; study (*a subject*); major in

Substantive

der **Amerikaner, -** American (*m.*)[6]
der **Deutsche, -n** German (*m.*)
der **Schüler, -** secondary school pupil (*m.*)
der **Student, -en** university student (*m.*)
der **Tourist, -en** tourist (*m.*)

(das) **Deutschland** Germany
das **Haus, -̈er** house

die **Amerikanerin, -nen** American (*f.*)
die **Deutsche, -n** German (*f.*)
die **Gruppe, -n** group
die **Klasse, -n** class; grade
die **Schülerin, -nen** secondary school pupil (*f.*)
die **Studentin, -nen** university student (*f.*)
die **Touristin, -nen** tourist (*f.*)

Adjektive and Adverbien

freundlich friendly
höflich polite(ly)

immer always
oft often
so so; like this
viele many
wahrscheinlich probably
ziemlich fairly, quite

Andere Vokabeln

man one (*indefinite pronoun*)[7]
oder or

Nützliche Ausdrücke

zum Beispiel for example
auf deutsch in German

Gegensätze

immer ≠ nie
  always ≠ never
oft ≠ selten often ≠ seldom

Vor der Uni in Bonn.

6. See list of abbreviations in the Appendix, p. 509.
7. This pronoun is often best translated with "we," "you," or "they": **Das sagt man oft.** = *They (people) often say that.* See p. 83 for a complete explanation.

Wie sagt man „you" auf deutsch?

Touristen in Deutschland sagen oft, die Deutschen sind sehr
freundlich und höflich. Das stimmt, aber wahrscheinlich
meinen viele Amerikaner auch, die Deutschen sind ziemlich formell.

5   Frau Bachmann und Frau Kuhn sind zum Beispiel Nach-
barinnen.° Sie wohnen im selben° Haus und sind auch
befreundet,° aber Frau Bachmann fragt nicht: „Wie geht es
dir, Gisela?" Nein, sie sagt: „Wie geht es Ihnen, Frau Kuhn?"
Sie grüßen einander° formell.

10 Die Lehrer duzen° die Schüler von Klasse eins bis Klasse
zehn. Aber ab° Klasse elf sagen sie „Sie." Die Schüler siezen°
die Lehrer natürlich immer.

    Heute ist das „du" auch ein Ausdruck der° Solidarität.
Für die Studenten bedeutet es: wir sind eine Gruppe. Karin
15 und Michael, zum Beispiel, studieren.[8] Sie sagen von Anfang
an° „du" zueinander.°

neighbors / **im selben** = *in the same*
on friendly terms

each other
address with **du**
beginning in / *address with* **Sie**

Ausdruck der = *expression of*

von . . . an = *from the beginning* / *to each other*

Fragen zum Lesestück   *Questions on the Reading*

1. Wer meint, die Deutschen sind ziemlich formell?
2. Was sagt Frau Bachmann zu Frau Kuhn?
3. Sagen Lehrer und Schüler „du"?
4. Was sind Karin und Michael?
5. Sagen Karin und Michael „Sie"?
6. Was bedeutet das „du" für die Studenten?

„Diese Studenten sagen 'du' zueinander." (Heidelberg)

8. Note that **studieren** means to attend college or university and is not used
to describe the student's daily activity of studying. Thus, "I'm studying
tonight" (i.e., doing homework) is translated as "Ich **arbeite** heute abend,"
or "Ich **lerne** heute abend."

Situationen aus dem Alltag   *Situations from Everyday Life*

Partnerarbeit: „Sie" oder „du"?

Frau Professor Ullman   *Herr Kuhn*   *Karoline und Dieter*   *Niklas Schuhmacher*

1. Take turns asking the people pictured
   a. what their names are.
   b. whether they're working at the moment.
   c. whether they're tired today.
   d. where they live.
   e. where they work.

2. Partner A plays one of the people pictured above and responds to Partner B's questions. Then Partner B plays another of these people and answers Partner A's questions.

   BEISPIEL: Wo wohnen Sie, Herr Kuhn?
   　　　　　　 Ich wohne in Wien.

3. Now ask each other personal questions using the **du**-form.

Zum Schluß   *And finally . . .*

Sprechen wir miteinander!   *Let's Talk Together!*

A **Partnerarbeit:** Ist es wahrscheinlich?

Partner A uses the cues to ask questions. Partner B responds, beginning with one of the three adverbs in the right-hand column.

   BEISPIEL: fliegen / Berlin?
   　　　　　 PARTNER A: Fliegst du nach Berlin?
   　　　　　 PARTNER B: Vielleicht fliege ich nach Berlin.

Partner A	*Partner B*
gehen / zu Marion?	Natürlich . . .
studieren / in Konstanz?	Wahrscheinlich . . .
arbeiten / im Moment?	Vielleicht . . .
kommen / zurück?	
wohnen / hier?	
fliegen / nach Leipzig?	

B **Partnerarbeit:** An welchem Tag?   *On which day?*

Review the days of the week together as a class. Then use the cues below to ask each other questions. Your partner answers with any day of the week, beginning the sentence with **Am** . . .

BEISPIEL: Wann / kommen / zurück?
PARTNER A: Wann kommst du zurück?
PARTNER B: Am Dienstag komme ich zurück.

1. Wann / arbeiten?
2. Wann / haben / Deutsch?
3. Wann / gehen / zu Gisela?

4. Wann / fliegen / nach Hamburg?
5. Wann / kommen / zurück?
6. Wann / spielen /Tennis?

C **Partnerarbeit:** Seid ihr auch so?

With your partner, look at the following adjectives you can use to describe your personality. You shouldn't have trouble understanding them, because they all have English cognates. Ask each other questions to find out which of these characteristics you have in common. Make a list of three or four characteristics you share.

BEISPIEL: Ich bin sehr emotional. Bist du auch emotional?
Ja, ich bin auch (oft / ziemlich / sehr) emotional.

emotional	modern	kreativ	konservativ
sentimental	aktiv	dynamisch	objektiv
subjektiv	kompetent	progressiv	optimistisch
pessimistisch	naiv	athletisch	originell
intelligent	clever		

D **Gruppenarbeit**

Now go with your partner to another pair of students and ask questions to find out how they describe themselves. Use the words listed in exercise C.

BEISPIEL: GRUPPE A: Seid ihr auch emotional?
GRUPPE B: Nein, wir sind nicht emotional, wir sind . . . Und ihr?

E **Übung:** Wie ist das Wetter?

Your instructor will ask your opinion about various things. Be sure to use the correct pronoun in your answer. The list of adjectives below will give you some ideas.

BEISPIEL: Wie ist die Suppe heute?
Sie ist ganz gut.

gut	freundlich	höflich	munter
schön	typisch	heiß	sauer
kalt	herrlich	guter Laune	windig

Schreiben Sie zu Hause   *Write at Home*

F **Zwei Studenten im Gespräch** (*Two Students in Conversation*)   Write a dialogue using the following cues. You will need to provide verb endings, correct word order, etc.

ULLI: Tag / Dieter! du / arbeiten / morgen?
DIETER: Nein. warum / du / fragen?
ULLI: morgen / wir / gehen / zu Hans. du / kommen / auch?
DIETER: natürlich / ich / kommen

G „**Was machst du?**"   Answer each question according to the cue in English. Answer appropriately for the way you're addressed (**Was machst du? Ich mache . . . Was macht ihr? Wir machen . . .**)

BEISPIEL: Was machst du morgen? (*flying to Vienna*)
Ich fliege morgen nach Wien.

1. Was macht ihr heute? (*going to Stefan's*)

2. Was machst du im Moment, Richard? (*working a lot*)

3. Was machen Sie, Frau Gruber? (*finally studying*)

4. Was machst du, Regina? (*playing outside*)

5. Was macht ihr am Mittwoch, Rolf und Helene? (*flying to Hamburg*)

6. Was machen Sie, Frau Bachmann? (*greeting Mrs. Kuhn*)

H **Antworten Sie bitte auf deutsch!** (*Please answer in German!*)   Answer the yes/no questions affirmatively and with complete sentences.

1. Was machst du heute abend?

2. Bist du in Eile?

3. Fliegt der Professor nach New York?

4. Wer wohnt hier?

5. Regnet es wieder?

6. Was machen wir im Moment?

7. Arbeitest du vielleicht morgen?

8. Ist das typisch?

I Wie sagt man das auf deutsch?

1. When are you coming back, Jürgen and Katrin?

2. We are coming back tomorrow.

3. Excuse me, are you in a hurry?

4. Yes, I'm going to Helene's.

5. She says the Germans are friendly.

6. Yes, that's right.

7. How are you, Herr Beck?

8. Fine thanks, and you?

9. The sun is shining again.

10. Good! We'll work outside.

Where Is German Spoken?

German is the language of the Federal Republic of Germany (**die Bundesrepublik Deutschland**), Austria (**Österreich**), Liechtenstein, and parts of Switzerland (**die Schweiz**) and Luxembourg (**Luxemburg**). Scattered linguistic enclaves of German speakers in the U.S. (notably in Pennsylvania), Canada, Brazil, Africa (especially in Namibia, where it is one of the official languages), Australia, and the South Tirol (in northern Italy) bring the number of native German speakers to around 118 million, with another 100 million for whom German is a second language. Here are some comparative statistics on the world's major languages, showing numbers of native and non-native speakers in 1989. Notice that the names of almost all languages in German end with **-sch**.

Chinesisch	1 Milliarde 44 Million[9]
Englisch	437 Million
Spanisch	331 Million
Russisch	291 Million
Arabisch	192 Million
Portugiesisch	171 Million
Japanisch	124 Million
Französisch	119 Million
Deutsch	118 Million
Italienisch	63 Million

9. **Eine Milliarde** = (American) *billion*; **Eine Billion** = (American) *trillion*. Source: *World Almanac Book of Facts* (1990) and *Cambridge Encyclopedia of Language* (1987).

KAPITEL 2

Familie und Freunde

Communicative Goals
- Talking about families
- Asking people what they are looking for
- Saying what belongs to whom
- Counting above 20

Cultural Goal
- Learning some differences and similarities between German and American family life

Lyrik zum Vorlesen „Du bist mein"

Grammatik The Accusative Case •
More on Verbs in the Present Tense •
Possessive Adjectives • Cardinal Numbers
above 20

Lesestück Die Familie heute

Situationen aus dem Alltag Die Familie

Almanach Die ganze Familie

Dialoge

Wer liest die Zeitung?

VATER: Kurt, ich suche meine Zeitung. Weißt du, wo sie ist?

SOHN: Deine Zeitung? Ich lese sie im Moment.

VATER: Was liest du denn?

SOHN: Ich lese einen Artikel über unsere Schule.

Ich hab' eine Frage

ANNETTE: Katrin, ich hab' eine Frage. Kennst du den Mann da drüben?

KATRIN: Wen meinst du denn?

ANNETTE: Er spricht mit Stefan. Ich sehe, er kennt dich.

KATRIN: Natürlich kenn' ich ihn—das ist mein Bruder Max!

ANNETTE: Ach, du hast auch einen Bruder! Ich kenne nur deine Schwester.

Georg sucht ein Zimmer

GEORG: Kennst du viele Leute in München?

STEFAN: Ja, meine Familie wohnt da. Warum?

GEORG: Ich studiere nächstes Semester dort und brauche ein Zimmer.

STEFAN: Unser Haus ist ziemlich groß. Sicher haben meine Eltern ein Zimmer frei.

GEORG: Phantastisch! Vielen Dank!

STEFAN: Bitte, bitte. Nichts zu danken.

Notes on Usage

Dropping Unstressed *e* In informal conversation, Germans often drop the unstressed ending **-e** in the first person singular.

Katrin, ich **hab'** eine Frage.
Natürlich **kenn'** ich ihn.

The Flavoring Particle *denn* Probably the most frequently used flavoring particle is **denn**. It adds an element of personal interest to a question. **Denn** is never stressed and usually comes immediately after the verb and personal pronouns.

Was liest du denn?
Wen meinst du denn?
Wer ist denn das?

Wortschatz 1

Who's Reading the Newspaper?

FATHER: Kurt, I'm looking for my newspaper. Do you know where it is?

SON: Your newspaper? I'm reading it at the moment.

FATHER: What are you reading?

SON: I'm reading an article about our school.

I Have a Question

ANNETTE: Katrin, I have a question. Do you know that man over there?

KATRIN: Whom do you mean?

ANNETTE: He's talking with Stefan. I see he knows you.

KATRIN: Of course I know him—that's my brother Max!

ANNETTE: Oh, you have a brother too! I only know your sister.

Georg Is Looking for a Room

GEORG: Do you know many people in Munich?

STEFAN: Yes, my family lives there. Why?

GEORG: I'm studying there next semester and need a room.

STEFAN: Our house is pretty big. My parents surely have a room free.

GEORG: Fantastic! Thanks a lot!

STEFAN: You're welcome. Don't mention it.

Verben

brauchen to need
essen (ißt) to eat
haben to have
heißen to be called
  Er heißt Max. His name is Max.
kennen to know, to be acquainted with
lesen (liest) to read
  lesen über (+ *acc.*) to read about
meinen to mean
nehmen (nimmt) to take
sehen (sieht) to see
sprechen (spricht) to speak, talk
  sprechen über (+ *acc.*) to talk about
suchen to look for, seek
wissen (weiß) to know (*a fact*)

Substantive

der **Artikel, -** article
der **Bruder, ⁻** brother
der **Freund, -e** friend
der **Joghurt** yoghurt
der **Mann, ⁻er** man; husband
der **Sohn, ⁻e** son
der **Vater, ⁻** father

das **Fleisch** meat
das **Gemüse** vegetables
das **Obst** fruit
das **Semester, -** semester
das **Zimmer, -** room

die **Familie, -n** family
die **Frage, -n** question
die **Schule, -n** school
die **Schwester, -n** sister
die **Zeitung, -en** newspaper

die **Leute** (*pl.*) people
die **Eltern** (*pl.*) parents

Adjektive und Adverbien

(da) drüben over there
dein (*fam. sing.*) your
dort there
frei free; unoccupied
groß big
mein my
nur only
sicher certain, sure
unser our

Andere Vokabeln

ach oh, ah
bitte you're welcome
denn *flavoring particle, see p. 45*
mit with
über (+ *acc.*) about
wen? whom?
wie viele? how many?

Nützliche Ausdrücke

Phantastisch! Fantastic!
vielen Dank many thanks, thanks a lot
nächstes Semester next semester
Nichts zu danken! Don't mention it!

Gegensätze

danke ≠ bitte thank you ≠ you're welcome
groß ≠ klein big ≠ little

Variationen

A Persönliche Fragen

1. Wie viele Studenten kennen Sie hier? Wie heißen sie?

2. Georg studiert nächstes Semester in München. Wo studieren Sie nächstes Semester?

3. Stefan kommt aus München. Woher kommen Sie?

4. Kurt liest die Zeitung im Moment. Lesen Sie auch eine Zeitung? Oft, oder nur manchmal? Wie heißt sie?

B Partnerarbeit: Wie heißt . . . ?

Help each other recall the names of other students in the class.

STUDENT A: Wie heißt die Studentin/der Student da drüben?

STUDENT B: Sie/er heißt . . . .

C Gruppenarbeit: Wen kennen Sie hier?

Say whom you know and how well.

INSTRUCTOR: Wen kennen Sie hier?

STUDENT: Ich kenne . . .

INSTRUCTOR: Kennen Sie ihn/sie gut?

STUDENT: Ja, sehr gut. *oder*: Nein, nicht sehr gut.

Vielleicht sprechen die Frauen über das Wetter. Was sagen sie zueinander?

D Partnerarbeit: Was suchst du?

Tell what you're looking for. Try to remember the correct gender of these nouns, then put them into the corresponding column.

Buch	Stuhl	Professor
Bleistift	Kugelschreiber	Professorin
Heft	Landkarte	Zeitung
Uhr		

Ich suche:

meinen (masculine)	**mein** (neuter)	**meine** (feminine)
_____	_____	_____
_____	_____	_____
_____	_____	_____
_____	_____	_____
_____	_____	_____

Conduct the following dialogue, using each object above.

STUDENT A: Was suchst du?

STUDENT B: Ich suche meinen/mein/meine _____.

STUDENT A: Er/es/sie ist nicht hier.

E Gruppenarbeit: Was brauchen wir?   *4 Studenten*

You and three friends are going to Munich to study. Decide together on some things you'll need.

Wir brauchen:

einen (masculine)	**ein** (neuter)	**eine** (feminine)
_____	_____	_____
_____	_____	_____
_____	_____	_____
_____	_____	_____

Lyrik zum Vorlesen

This is one of the earliest surviving love poems in German. It was found in the Latin text of a letter written ca. 1160 A.D. by a lady to her lover. The original medieval German has been translated into modern German.

Du bist mein, ich bin dein,
Des sollst du gewiß sein.°
Du bist verschlossen°
In meinem Herzen,°
Verloren° ist das Schlüsselein:°
Du mußt immer drinnen° sein.

Des . . . sein = *of that you can*
  be certain / locked up
heart
lost / little key
inside (cf. **draußen**)

Grammatik

The Accusative Case

In *Kapitel 1* you learned the forms and functions of the nominative case. In this chapter you will learn the accusative case. The direct object of a verb is in the accusative.

The Direct Object

The direct object is the thing or person acted upon, known, or possessed by the subject.

Subject *(nominative)*			Direct Object *(accusative)*	
Sie	lesen	→	das Buch.	*They're reading the book.*
Anna	kennt	→	meine Eltern.	*Anna knows my parents.*
Karl	hat	→	einen Bruder.	*Karl has a brother.*

With the exception of the masculine singular articles, the accusative is identical in form to the nominative:

	Nominative	Accusative
masc:	Hier ist **der** / **ein** Bleistift.	Ich habe **den** / **einen** Bleistift.
neut:	Hier ist **das** / **ein** Zimmer.	Ich habe **das** / **ein** Zimmer.
fem:	Hier ist **die** / **eine** Zeitung.	Ich habe **die** / **eine** Zeitung.
plur:	Hier sind **die** / **meine**[1] Bücher.	Ich habe **die** / **meine** Bücher.

---

1. The indefinite article **ein** has no plural form. We therefore use the possessive adjective **mein-** (*my*) to show the plural endings.

1 **Übung:** Wer hat ein Deutschbuch?

Your instructor asks who has various things. Say that you have them.

> BEISPIEL: Wer hat ein Deutschbuch?
> Ich habe ein Deutschbuch.

neu — ein
f. eine
m. einen
p meine

 2 **Übung:** Was suchen Sie?

Your instructor asks what you are looking for. Say you are looking for one of the things in the picture (they are all masculine).

> BEISPIEL: Was suchen Sie?
> Ich suche einen _____.

 3 **Kettenreaktion:** Was brauchst du?

Now ask each other what things in the picture you need.

> BEISPIEL: Was brauchst du?
> Ich brauche den _____. Und was brauchst du?

Fragewort

The accusative form of the question word **wer** is **wen**:

Wen kennst du in München?   *Whom do you know in Munich?*

Accusative of the Personal Pronouns

	Singular			*Plural*	
nom.	*acc.*		*nom.*	*acc.*	
ich	**mich**	*me*	wir	**uns**	*us*
du	**dich**	} *you*	ihr	**euch**	} *you*
Sie	**Sie**		Sie	**Sie**	
er	**ihn**	*him, it*			
es	**es**	*it*	sie	**sie**	*them*
sie	**sie**	*her, it*			

4 **Übung:** Brauchen Sie etwas?

Your instructor asks whether you need something. Say that you do need it.

    BEISPIEL: Brauchen Sie den Stuhl?
      – Ja, ich brauche ihn.

5 **Partnerarbeit:** Wen kennst du hier?

Conduct the following dialogue with your partner, naming as many students in your class as possible.

PARTNER A: Wen kennst du hier?

PARTNER B: Ich kenne Barbara / Robert.

PARTNER A: Ich kenne sie / ihn auch.

PARTNER B: Wen kennst *du* hier?

6 **Übung**

Answer your instructor's question affirmatively.

    BEISPIEL: Suchst du mich?
      Ja, ich suche dich.

1. Kennst du mich?
2. Brauchst du uns?
3. Seht ihr uns?
4. Kenne ich dich?
5. Kenne ich euch?
6. Fragst du mich?
7. Brauche ich dich?
8. Brauche ich euch?
9. Kennen Sie mich?
10. Kenne ich Sie?

More on Verbs in the Present Tense

Contraction of *du*-form: *heißen*

Verbs with stems ending in **-s, -ß,** or **-z** contract the **du**-form ending **-st** to **-t.** In these verbs, the **du**-form and the **er**-form are identical. You used some of the forms of **heißen** in the *Einführung*. Here is the complete conjugation in the present tense.

heißen *to be called*	stem: **heiß-**
ich heiße	wir heißen
du **heißt**	ihr heißt
er, es, sie heißt	sie, Sie heißen

Verbs with Stem-Vowel Change *e* to *i(e)*

Some German verbs change their stem vowel in the **du**- and **er**-forms of the present tense.

e → i **sprechen** *to speak*	
ich spreche	wir sprechen
du **sprichst**	ihr sprecht
er, es, sie **spricht**	sie, Sie sprechen

e → ie **sehen** *to see*	
ich sehe	wir sehen
du **siehst**	ihr seht
er, es, sie **sieht**	sie, Sie sehen

e → ie **lesen** *to read*	
ich lese	wir lesen
du **liest**	ihr lest
er, es, sie **liest**	sie, Sie lesen

Stem-vowel change will be indicated in the *Wortschatz* sections by inclusion of the **er**-form: **sehen (sieht)** *to see.* Two other verbs in this group are **essen,** *to eat;* and **nehmen,** *to take.* They change not only their stem vowel, but also some consonants.

essen to eat	**nehmen** to take
ich esse	ich nehme
du **ißt**[2]	du **nimmst**
er, es, sie **ißt**	er, es, sie **nimmt**

7 **Gruppenarbeit**

1. Say what you eat, then ask the next person.

   BEISPIEL: Ich esse Fleisch, was ißt du?

Fleisch · Suppe · Gemüse · Obst · Brot · Wurst · Joghurt

2. Say what you read, then ask the next person.

   BEISPIEL: Ich lese den *Spiegel*, was liest du?

Die Zeit · einen Artikel · DER SPIEGEL · den Spiegel · die Zeitung · ein Buch · einen Brief

3. Say what languages you speak and then ask the next person.

   BEISPIEL: Ich spreche _____, was sprichst du?

Chinesisch	Polnisch	Deutsch	Englisch	Spanisch
Italienisch	Schwedisch	Französisch	Japanisch	Russisch

2. Diagraph-s (**ß**) is called „ess-zett" in German. It regularly replaces **ss** 1. at the end of a word (**groß**); 2. before personal endings beginning with **t** (**du ißt, ihr eßt**); and 3. between vowels when the first vowel is long or a diphthong (**heißen**). **Füße** (*feet*) has a long **ü**, but **Flüsse** (*rivers*) has a short **ü**. You will gradually get used to the ess-zett as you write more German.

4. Say what you see. The next student repeats what you see, then adds what he/she sees.

> BEISPIEL: A: Ich sehe ein Fenster.
> B: Sie sieht ein Fenster, und ich sehe eine Tafel.

The Verb *wissen*

The verb **wissen** (*to know*) is irregular in the singular present. Its forms must be memorized.

ich	**weiß**	wir	wissen
du	**weiß**t	ihr	wißt
er, es, sie	**weiß**	sie, Sie	wissen

Both the first person singular and the third person singular lack endings: **ich weiß, er weiß.**

wissen vs. kennen Both **wissen** and **kennen** may be translated as "to know," but **wissen** means "to know a fact" and **kennen** means "to be familiar, acquainted with" and is used when the direct object is a person or place.

> **Weißt** du, wer das ist? Ja, ich *Do you know who that is? Yes, I*
> **kenne** ihn sehr gut. *know him very well.*
> **Kennen** Sie Berlin, Herr Brandt? *Do you know Berlin, Mr. Brandt?*
> Nein, nicht sehr gut. *No, not very well.*

8 **Übung:** *Wissen oder kennen?*

> BEISPIEL: ich / Georg   Ich kenne Georg.

1. er / Michael
2. wir / Berlin
3. Katrin / wo ich wohne
4. ihr / was sie macht
5. ich / Stefan und Annette
6. du / München
7. ich / wer das ist
8. die Schüler / was der Lehrer meint

The Verb *haben*

The verb **haben** (*to have*) is irregular in the present singular.

ich	habe	wir	haben
du	**hast**	ihr	habt
er, es, sie	**hat**	sie, Sie	haben

 9 **Übung:** Wer hat die Zeitung?

Your professor asks you who has the newspaper, while pointing to somebody. Say that that person has the newspaper.

> BEISPIEL: Wer hat die Zeitung? (*points to Sean*)
> Sean hat sie.

Possessive Adjectives

	Singular			Plural	
personal pronoun	possessive adjective		personal pronoun	possessive adjective	
ich	mein	my	wir	unser	our
du	dein	} your	ihr	euer	} your
Sie	Ihr		Sie	Ihr	
er	sein	his; its			
es	sein	its	sie	ihr	their
sie	ihr	her; its			

Note that formal **Ihr** (*your*), like formal **Sie** (*you*), is always capitalized.

Possessive adjectives must agree with the nouns they modify in case, number, and gender. This agreement is shown by endings. As the following table shows, the endings of the possessive adjectives are the same as the endings of **ein**. Possessive adjectives are therefore called **ein**-words.

Endings of **ein**-words

	masc.	neut.	fem.	plur.
nom.	ein	ein	eine	(no plural)
	mein	mein	meine	meine
	ihr	ihr	ihre	ihre
	unser	unser	unsre	unsre
	euer	euer	eure	eure
acc.	einen	ein	eine	(no plural)
	meinen	mein	meine	meine
	ihren	ihr	ihre	ihre
	unsren	unser	unsre	unsre
	euren	euer	eure	eure

Note: The **-er** on **unser** and **euer** is *not* an ending, but part of the stem. When **euer** and **unser** take endings, the second **-e-** of the stem is dropped.[3]

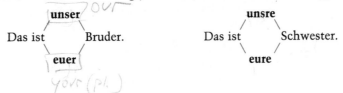

3. The **e** *must* be dropped from **euer** (→ **euren**) and *may* be dropped from **unser**.

Note: The endings for nominative and accusative are identical *except in the masculine.*

masculine nominative	masculine accusative
Das ist mein Bruder.	Ich sehe mein**en** Bruder.
Das ist ihr Bruder.	Sie sieht ihr**en** Bruder.
Das ist unser Bruder.	Wir sehen unsr**en** Bruder.
Das ist euer Bruder.	Ihr seht eu**ren** Bruder.

Fragewörter

wer?	*who?*
wen?	*whom?*
wessen?	*whose?*

---

10 **Übung:** Wessen Buch ist das?

Tell your instructor whose book is being pointed to.

> BEISPIEL: Wessen Buch ist das?
> Das ist *mein* Buch.

11 **Übung:** Wessen Freund kennen Sie?

Tell your instructor whose friend you know.

> BEISPIEL: *Wessen* Freund kennen Sie?
> Ich kenne *seinen* Freund.

Cardinal Numbers above 20

The English nursery rhyme "Sing a Song of Sixpence" contains the phrase "four-and-twenty blackbirds." German forms the cardinal numbers above twenty in the same way: 24 = **vierundzwanzig.**

20	zwanzig	30	dreißig
21	einundzwanzig	31	einunddreißig (usw.)
22	zweiundzwanzig	40	vierzig
23	dreiundzwanzig	50	fünfzig
24	vierundzwanzig	60	sechzig
25	fünfundzwanzig	70	siebzig
26	sechsundzwanzig	80	achtzig
27	siebenundzwanzig	90	neunzig
28	achtundzwanzig	100	hundert
29	neunundzwanzig	1 000	tausend

4 982 viertausendneunhundertzweiundachtzig

German numbers above twelve (**zwölf**) are seldom written as words, except on checks. When they *are* written out, each number is one continuous word. German uses a period *or* a space where English uses a comma to divide thousands from hundreds, etc.

German	English
4.982 oder 4 982	4,982

German uses a comma where English uses a decimal point. The comma is read as **Komma**.

0,5	0.5
(null Komma fünf)	(zero point five)

Bankleitzahl
641 500 20

Kreissparkasse Tübingen

Zahlen Sie gegen diesen Scheck aus meinem/unserem Guthaben

ein hundert siebenundzwanzig

Deutsche Mark in Buchstaben

DM
127,50

wie nebenstehend
Pf

an *Buchhandlung Gaste*

oder Überbringer

Tübingen, den 28.8.91

Ausstellungsort, Datum

Jens Kruse

Unterschrift des Ausstellers

Verwendungszweck *Bücher*

(Mitteilung für den Zahlungsempfänger)

Der vorgedruckte Schecktext darf nicht geändert oder gestrichen werden. Die Angabe einer Zahlungsfrist auf dem Scheck gilt als nicht geschrieben.

Scheck-Nr.	Konto-Nr.	Betrag	Bankleitzahl	Text

0000026126112⌡   849 883⊓   64150020⌡ 01⊓

Bitte dieses Feld nicht beschriften und nicht bestempeln

12 Übung

Read these numbers aloud in German.

26	1 066	3 001
69	533	0,22
153	985	3,45
4 772,08	48	71
1992	1971	1800

Wie weit ist es nach Garmisch-Partenkirchen?

Lesestück Die Familie heute

Tips zum Lesen und Lernen

Tips zum Vokabelnlernen

Compound Nouns A characteristic feature of German is its formation of compound nouns from two or more nouns. You should get used to analyzing these words and should learn to identify their component parts. You will frequently see similarities to English compound nouns:

Hausfrau	*housewife*
Hausarbeit	*housework*

Often a connecting -(e)s- or -(e)n- is inserted between the components.

das **Eigentum** + die **Wohnung** = die **Eigentumswohnung**
  (*property*)   (*apartment*)   (*condominium*)

der **Bund** (*federation*) + die **Republik** = die **Bundesrepublik**

die **Familie** + die **Diskussion** = die **Familiendiskussion**

The gender of the *last* component noun is *always* the gender of the entire compound.

das **Haus** + die **Frau** = die **Hausfrau**

das **Wort** + der **Schatz** = der **Wortschatz**
  (*word*)   (*treasure*)   (*vocabulary*)

Leicht zu merken

die **Alternative, -n**	Alternative
der **Konflikt, -e**	Konflikt
(das) **Nordamerika**	
relativ	
sozial	sozial
traditionell	traditionell

Einstieg in den Text

- Review the tips for reading on page 37 in *Kapitel 1*.
- The following text is entitled „Die Familie heute." This gives you a good idea of what sort of information to expect.
- Before reading, recall the vocabulary you already know that relates to the topic of family, e.g., **Bruder**, **Schwester**, etc.

- **Guessing from context**   The first sentence of a paragraph (sometimes called the "topic sentence") often announces the primary topic of what follows. An example is page 60, line 11 of „Die Familie heute." It announces that **die typische Familie** is the topic of this paragraph. Later in the paragraph comes this sentence:

  Fast alle Familien besitzen ein Auto und einen Fernseher.

  The words that are probably immediately comprehensible to you are **alle Familien** and **Auto.** Knowing the topic, you can make an educated guess at the meaning of **fast** and **besitzen.** Such educated guessing, or finding context clues, is very important when reading texts with many unfamiliar words.

Wortschatz 2

Verben

besitzen   to own
bleiben   to stay, remain
finden   to find
geben (gibt)   to give
kochen   to cook
leben   to live, be alive

Substantive

der **Beruf, -e**   profession, vocation
der **Fernseher, -**   TV set
der **Großvater, ⁝**   grandfather
der **Onkel, -**   uncle

das **Auto, -s**   car
das **Essen**   food; meal
das **Geld**   money
das **Klischee, -s**   cliché
das **Problem, -e**   problem

die **Arbeit**   work
die **Bundesrepublik (Deutschland)**   the Federal Republic (of Germany)
die **BRD**   the FRG
die **Diskussion, -en**   discussion
die **Großmutter, ⁝**   grandmother

die **Hausfrau, -en**   housewife
die **Mutter, ⁝**   mother
die **Rolle, -n**   role
die **Stelle, -n**   job, position
die **Tante, -n**   aunt
die **Tochter, ⁝**   daughter

die **Großeltern** (*pl.*)   grandparents

Adjektive und Adverbien

anders   different
berufstätig   employed
deutsch   German
fast   almost
jung   young
manchmal   sometimes
mehr   more
  nicht mehr   no longer, not any more
noch   still
  noch ein   another, an additional
normal   normal
sogar   even, in fact
überall   everywhere
wenigstens   at least
wichtig   important

Andere Vokabeln

alle (*pl.*)   all; everybody
niemand   nobody, no one
zwischen   between

Nützliche Ausdrücke

es gibt (+ *acc.*)   there is, there are
das sind (*pl. of* **das ist**)   those are
zu Hause   at home
eine Rolle spielen   to play a role

Gegensätze

jung ≠ alt   young ≠ old
niemand ≠ jemand   no one ≠ someone
wichtig ≠ unwichtig   important ≠ unimportant

Mit anderen Worten

Kinder sagen:
  Vati = Vater
  Mutti = Mutter
  Oma = Großmutter
  Opa = Großvater

Die Familie heute

„Der Vater hat einen Beruf und verdient das Geld, die Mutter ist Hausfrau. Sie bleibt zu Hause, kocht das Essen und ver- sorgt° die Kinder." Die Klischees kennen wir schon. Heute stimmen sie aber nicht mehr, wenigstens nicht für junge[4] Familien in Deutschland. Dort ist die Rollenverteilung° oft anders. Viele Frauen sind berufstätig oder suchen eine Stelle. Tagsüber° ist manchmal niemand zu Hause. Oft machen der Mann und die Frau die Hausarbeit gemeinsam,° und in Familiendiskussionen haben die Kinder heute auch eine Stimme.°

Die typische Familie ist relativ klein: ein oder zwei Kinder, das ist normal. Manchmal wohnen auch die Groß- eltern mit ihnen zusammen.° Viele Familien in der Bun- desrepublik haben ein Haus oder eine Eigentumswohnung.° Fast alle Familien besitzen ein Auto und einen Fern- seher. Der Lebensstandard° ist heute sogar höher als° in Nordamerika.

Aber gibt es denn keine° Konflikte? Natürlich! Man fin- det in Deutschland, wie überall, Probleme zwischen Eltern und Kindern. Viele junge Leute suchen Alternativen. Sie wohnen manchmal in Wohngemeinschaften° oder Land- kommunen.° Aber für die Mehrheit° bleibt die traditionelle Familie—Mutter, Vater und Kinder—noch die wichtigste° soziale Gruppe.

takes care of

assignment of roles

during the day
jointly

voice

mit . . . zusammen = *with them*
condominium

standard of living / **höher als** = *higher than*
no

communal living groups / rural communes / majority
most important

Fragen zum Lesestück

1. Was sind die Klischees über die traditionelle Familie?
2. Was suchen heute viele Frauen?
3. Haben Familien in Deutschland viele Kinder?
4. Wie heißt Deutschland offiziell?
5. Besitzen alle Familien in Deutschland ein Haus?
6. Ist die Familie auch heute noch wichtig?

Junge Familie aus Eibelstadt. Wie alt sind die Kinder?

4. When German adjectives are used attributively (before nouns), they receive endings, most often **-e** or **-en.** You will learn how to use these endings actively in *Kapitel 9.*

Situationen aus dem Alltag

Die Familie

Here is some useful vocabulary for talking about your family. You already know some of these words.

die **Großeltern**	
die **Großmutter, ⸚**	
die **Oma, -s**	*grandma*
der **Großvater, ⸚**	
der **Opa, -s**	*grandpa*
die **Eltern**	
die **Mutter, ⸚**	
die **Mutti, -s**	*mama, mom*
der **Vater, ⸚**	
der **Vati, -s**	*papa, dad*
der **Sohn, ⸚e**	
die **Tochter, ⸚**	
die **Geschwister** (*pl.*)	*siblings, brothers and sisters*
der **Bruder, ⸚**	
die **Schwester, -n**	
der **Onkel, -**	
die **Tante, -n**	
die **Kusine, -n**	*cousin* (f.)
der **Vetter, -n**	*cousin* (m.)

Partnerarbeit: Fragebogen   *Questionnaire*

You are a German sociologist studying the American family. Use the questionnaire below to interview your partner. Be ready to report the information that you collect to the class.

1. **Großeltern:** Leben sie noch?   ja / nein

2. **Mutter:** wie alt? _____   berufstätig?   ja / nein   Beruf? _____

3. **Vater:** wie alt? _____   berufstätig?   ja / nein   Beruf? _____

4. **Geschwister:** wie viele Brüder? _____   wie alt? _____
   wie viele Schwestern? _____   wie alt? _____

5. **Autos:** wie viele? _____

6. **Fernseher:** wie viele? _____

7. **Heimcomputer?**   ja / nein

8. Wer kocht das Essen? _____

9. Wer macht die Hausarbeit? _____

10. Besitzt Ihre Familie ein Haus?   ja / nein

Bring to class photographs or your own drawing of some of your family members. Tell the others in the group about the people in the picture.

Zum Schluß

Sprechen wir miteinander!

A **Übung:** Wer ist in der Familie?

Answer your instructor's questions about Sylvie, Felix, and their families.

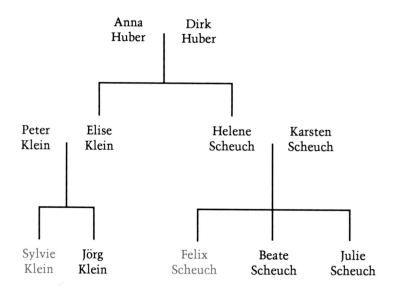

1. Das ist Sylvie Klein. Sie hat eine Mutter und . . .
   Wer ist Herr Klein? . . . Er ist ihr Vater.
   Wer ist Frau Klein?
   Wer ist Jörg?
   Wer sind Herr und Frau Huber?

2. Das ist Felix Scheuch. Er hat einen Vater und . . .
   Wer sind Beate und Julie? Herr Scheuch? Frau Scheuch? Elise Klein?

B **Gruppenarbeit:** Was gibt es hier?

Say what's in your classroom.

BEISPIEL: Hier gibt es _____.

C **Partnerarbeit**

Take turns saying what is in the pictures below.

BEISPIEL: Es gibt einen Wagen.

der Fernseher   das Essen   das Gold   die Familie

das Auto

einen (den) Artikel   die Tür   das Fenster

fem
eine

D **Gruppenarbeit**   *3 oder 4 Personen*

How many answers can you give to the following questions?

1. *Was liest du denn?*

   Ich lese _____.
   _____.
   _____.
   _____.

2. *Was kochst du?*

   Ich koche _____.
   _____.
   _____.
   _____.

3. *Wen kennst du?*

   Ich kenne _____.
   _____.
   _____.
   _____.

4. *Was suchst du?*

   Ich suche _____.
   _____.
   _____.
   _____.

5. *Was brauchst du denn?*

   Ich brauche _____.
   _____.
   _____.
   _____.

6. *Was siehst du denn?*

   Ich sehe _____.
   _____.
   _____.
   _____.

E Übung

You're an interpreter for your instructor, who doesn't know German. Ask your classmates the questions in German and have them answer in German.

BEISPIEL: I: Where does she live?
S1: Wo wohnst du denn?
S2: Ich wohne in Toronto.

1. Where are his/her books?
2. When is he/she going to Germany?
3. What is his/her mother's name?
4. Who is his/her teacher?
5. Does it rain here often?
6. Is he/she employed?
7. Whom does he/she know here?
8. Does he/she have a brother?

Schreiben Sie zu Hause

F Write sentences using the cues provided. Add verbs, articles, and endings to verbs and possessive adjectives where necessary.

BEISPIEL: ich / suchen / mein / Geschwister
Ich suche meine Geschwister.

1. kennen / du / mein / Bruder?
2. Frau Huber / lesen / Artikel
3. unser / Mutter / haben / Beruf
4. dein / Eltern / auch / berufstätig?
5. mein / Familie / besitzen / Fernseher
6. Karin / suchen / ihr / Bruder
7. sehen / du / unser / Professor?
8. kennen / ihr / Mann / da drüben?

G Construct dialogues from the following cues (a double slash indicates a comma).

1. Sie / kennen / Berlin?
ja // mein / Familie / wohnen / dort. warum / Sie / fragen?
ich / studieren / im Oktober / da / und / suchen / Zimmer
2. wie / du / heißen?
ich / heißen / Klaus
wen / du / suchen / denn?
mein / Bruder. du / wissen // wo / er / sein?

H **Wissen** oder **kennen?** Choose the correct equivalent of the verb "to know."

A: _Kennst_ du den Mann da drüben?

B: Natürlich _kenne_ ich ihn.

A: _weißt_ du, wie er heißt?

B: Ja, er heißt Wolf Breisacher.

A: Ich _weiß kenne_ München gut.

B: Das _kenne weiß_ ich. Du kommst ja aus München!

A: _Kennst_ du Julian Wegener? Er studiert dort.

B: Wirklich? Ich _kenne_ ihn nicht gut, aber ich _weiß_, er wohnt in München.

I Wie sagt man das auf deutsch?

1. Her family is quite typical.

2. Their name is Schölz and they live in Munich.

3. Does her brother work, or is he looking for a job?

4. He's studying in Heidelberg.

5. I'm looking for my newspaper.

6. Fritz has it.

7. He's reading an article.

8. Where are your children now, Mr. Asch?

9. They're living at home.

10. When are you eating, children?

11. Probably at six.

Die ganze Familie *The Whole Family*

Der Vater, der heißt Daniel,
der kleine Sohn heißt Michael,
die Mutter heißt Regine,
die Tochter heißt Rosine.

Der Bruder, der heißt Kristian,
der Onkel heißt Sebastian,
die Schwester heißt Johanna,
die Tante heißt Susanna.

Der Vetter, der heißt Benjamin,
die Kusine, die heißt Katharin,
die Oma heißt Ottilie—
nun kennst du die Familie!

Some first names currently popular in Germany:

Namen für Mädchen

Christine	Katharina
Sabrina	Anna
Kathrin	Julia
Stefanie	Nadine
Melanie	Nicole

Namen für Jungen

Christian	Michael
Stefan	Andreas
Matthias	Daniel
Markus	Sebastian
Thomas	Alexander

Increasingly popular among Germans are English names such as Jessica, Jennifer, Oliver, and Patrick.

Die Familie ist zusammen. Sie trinken Kaffee und sprechen miteinander.

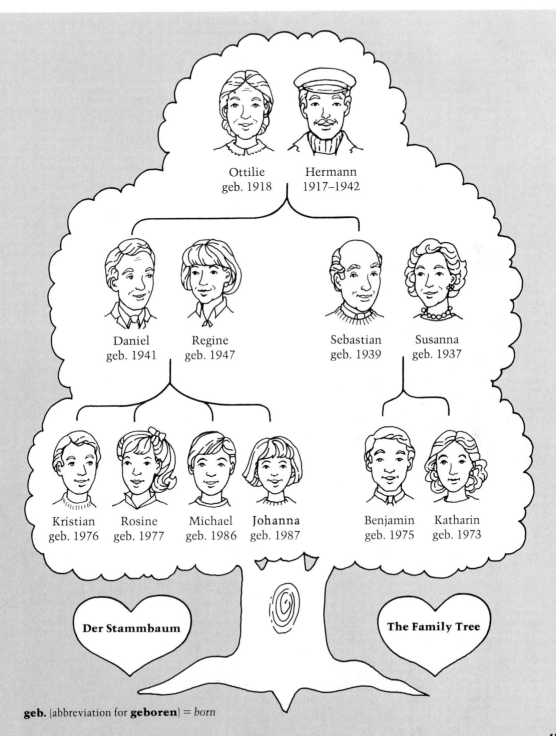

Ottilie
geb. 1918

Hermann
1917–1942

Daniel
geb. 1941

Regine
geb. 1947

Sebastian
geb. 1939

Susanna
geb. 1937

Kristian
geb. 1976

Rosine
geb. 1977

Michael
geb. 1986

Johanna
geb. 1987

Benjamin
geb. 1975

Katharin
geb. 1973

Der Stammbaum

The Family Tree

geb. (abbreviation for **geboren**) = *born*

Jugend und Schule

Communicative Goals
- Negating statements and questions
- Contradicting
- Requesting confirmation
- Expressing opinions
- Asking where and how long
- Talking about clothing

Cultural Goal
- Comparing schools in America and Germany

Lyrik zum Vorlesen   „Das Lied vom Jockel"

Grammatik   Verbs with Stem Vowel Change *a* to *ä*, *au* to *äu* • The Predicate • Modal Verbs • Negation with *nicht* (not) • Negation with *kein* • Expecting an Affirmative Answer: *nicht wahr?* • Contradicting a Negative Statement or Question: *doch* • The Indefinite Pronoun *man*

Lesestück   Eine Klassendiskussion

Situationen aus dem Alltag   Kleidung und Farben

Almanach   A Note about Schools in German-Speaking Countries

Dialoge

Du hast es gut!

MONIKA: In Frankfurt[1] hast du es gut, Renate! Hier in Hinterwalden ist es stinklangweilig.

RENATE: Dann mußt du mich bald besuchen. Oder hast du keine Lust?

MONIKA: Doch, ich möchte schon nach Frankfurt, aber ich habe leider kein Geld.

RENATE: Das verstehe ich nicht. Verdienst du nicht genug?

Eine Pause

Kurt und Stefan fahren nach Innsbruck

KURT: Wir müssen noch eine Stunde nach Innsbruck fahren.

STEFAN: Können wir nicht eine Pause machen? Ich möchte ein bißchen laufen.

KURT: Ich auch. Da drüben kann man halten, nicht wahr?

STEFAN: Ja . . . Mensch! Der Berg ist wahnsinnig steil!

KURT: Was ist denn los? Bist du nicht fit?

STEFAN: Doch! Das schaff' ich leicht.

Ich habe leider keinen Wagen

CAROLA: Klaus, wie spät ist es denn?

KLAUS: Um Gottes Willen! Es ist schon halb zwölf.

CAROLA: Mußt du jetzt nach Hause?

KLAUS: Ja, und ich muß zu Fuß gehen. Ich habe leider keinen Wagen.

CAROLA: Warum denn nicht?

KLAUS: Mein Mitbewohner hat ihn heute abend. Er hat viel zu tun.

Note on Usage: The Flavoring Particle *schon*

As a flavoring particle, **schon** is often used to strengthen, confirm, or reinforce a statement. It adds the sense of "really," "indeed." In the first dialogue, Monika protests:

Ich möchte **schon** nach Frankfurt, aber ich habe leider kein Geld.	*I really would like to go to Frankfurt (indeed I would), but unfortunately I don't have any money.*

Here are some other examples.

Du weißt schon warum.	*You know perfectly well why.*
Ich komm' schon!	*Coming!*

---

1. Two cities in Germany are named Frankfurt. They are distinguished by the rivers on which they are situated: Frankfurt am Main (also written Frankfurt a. M. or Frankfurt/Main) in the state of Hessen; and Frankfurt an der Oder (Frankfurt a. d. O. or Frankfurt/Oder) in the state of Brandenburg.

Wortschatz 1

You've Got It Made

MONIKA: You've got it made in Frankfurt, Renate. It's really boring here in Hinterwalden.

RENATE: Then you have to visit me soon. Or don't you want to?

MONIKA: Sure I do. I really would like to go to Frankfurt, but unfortunately I don't have any money.

RENATE: I don't understand that. Don't you earn enough?

A Break

Kurt and Stefan are driving to Innsbruck.

KURT: We still have an hour to drive to Innsbruck.

STEFAN: Can't we take a break? I'd like to walk a bit.

KURT: Me too. We can stop over there, can't we?

STEFAN: Yes . . . Man, the mountain is really steep!

KURT: What's the matter? Aren't you in shape?

STEFAN: Sure! I can handle that easily.

Unfortunately, I Don't Have a Car

CAROLA: Klaus, what time is it?

KLAUS: For heaven's sake. It's already 11:30.

CAROLA: Do you have to go home now?

KLAUS: Yes, and I have to walk. Unfortunately I don't have a car.

CAROLA: Why not?

KLAUS: My roommate has it tonight. He has a lot to do.

Verben

besuchen   to visit
fahren (fährt)   to drive, go (*by vehicle*)
halten (hält)   to stop (*intrans.*); hold
können (kann)   can, to be able to
laufen (läuft)   to run; to go on foot, walk (*colloq.*)
ich möchte   I would like to[2]
müssen (muß)   must, to have to
schaffen (*colloq.*) to handle, manage, get done
schlafen (schläft)   to sleep
sollen (soll)   should, to be supposed to
tragen (trägt)   to carry; wear
tun   to do
verstehen   to understand
wollen (will)   to want to

Substantive

der **Berg, -e**   mountain
der **Wagen, -**   car
der **Mitbewohner, -**   roommate (*m.*)

die **Freundin, -nen**   friend (*f.*)
die **Minute, -n**   minute
die **Pause, -n**   break; intermission
  eine Pause machen   to take a break
die **Stunde, -n**   hour; class hour
  die **Deutschstunde**   German class
die **Mitbewohnerin, -nen**   roommate (*f.*)

Adjektive und Adverbien

bald   soon
fit   in shape
jetzt   now
langweilig   boring
leicht   easy; light (*in weight*)
leider   unfortunately
schon   already
spät   late
steil   steep
wahnsinnig   1. (*adj. & adv.*) insane(ly), crazy 2. (*colloq. adv.*) extremely, incredibly, awfully
wahr   true

Andere Vokabeln

doch   yes I *do*, yes I *am*, etc. (*contradictory*, see p. 82)
genug   enough
kein[3]   not a, not any, no
nichts   nothing

Nützliche Ausdrücke

ein bißchen   a little; a little bit; a little while
Ich habe keine Lust.   I don't want to.
Mensch!   Man! Wow!
nicht (wahr)?   isn't it?, can't you?, doesn't he?, etc. (see p. 81)
nach Hause   home (*as destination of motion*)
  Ich fahre nach Hause.   I'm driving home.

2. For an explanation of **möchte**, see pp. 76 and 420.
3. For the endings of **kein**, see p. 80.

Um Gottes Willen! For heaven's sake!

Was ist los? What's the matter?; What's going on?

zu Fuß gehen to go on foot, walk

Gegensätze

spät ≠ früh late ≠ early

langweilig ≠ interessant boring ≠ interesting

nichts ≠ etwas nothing ≠ something

leicht ≠ schwer light (*in weight*); easy ≠ heavy; difficult, hard

stinklangweilig = sehr, sehr langweilig

wahnsinnig (*colloq.*) = sehr, sehr

Variationen

A Persönliche Fragen

1. Wo sind Sie zu Hause?

2. Gibt es da viel zu tun, oder ist es langweilig?

3. Brauchen Sie heute einen Wagen, oder laufen Sie nach Hause?

4. Besitzen Sie einen Wagen?

5. Sind Sie fit oder nicht?

6. Haben Sie genug Geld?

7. Wen besuchen Sie bald?

So üben Sie mit Sicherheit richtig!

Das sind nur einige Beispiele aus FIT UND GESUND

Falsch   Richtig

B Übung

1. Kurt möchte ein bißchen laufen. Ich möchte zu Hause bleiben.
   Was möchten Sie denn machen?
   Ich möchte _____.

2. Kurt und Stefan wollen da drüben halten. Ich will nach Hause laufen.
   Was wollen Sie denn machen?
   Ich will _____.

3. Klaus muß morgen arbeiten. Ich muß kochen.
   Was müssen Sie denn morgen machen?
   Ich muß _____.

C Übung: Doch!

Use **doch** to contradict what your instructor says.

BEISPIEL: Sie besuchen mich nicht!
Doch, ich besuche Sie!

1. Sie sind nicht fit!

2. Der Tourist kommt nicht aus Amerika!

3. Sie verstehen mich nicht!

4. Wir arbeiten heute nicht!

5. Die Studenten gehen nicht nach Hause!

6. Robert ist nicht Ihr Freund!

7. Der Berg ist nicht steil!

8. Es ist nicht spät!

This traditional humorous rhyme is about the long chain of events that must occur before the servant Jockel finally carries out his master's order to cut the oats. Each verse adds an object and activity to bring him home. English parallels are rhymes like "The House That Jack Built" and "There Was an Old Lady Who Swallowed a Fly." The later verses have not been printed out in their entirety. Supply the chain of events in place of "usw."

Das Lied vom Jockel° ⟶ *The Song About Jockel*

Der Herr, der schickt den Jockel aus,°
er soll den Hafer° schneiden.°
Der Jockel schneidet den Hafer nicht
und kommt auch nicht nach Haus.

Der . . . aus = *The master (he)
sends out Jockel / oats / cut*

Da° schickt der Herr den Pudel° aus,
er soll den Jockel beißen.°
Der Pudel beißt den Jockel nicht,
der Jockel schneidet den Hafer nicht
und kommt auch nicht nach Haus.

then / poodle
bite

Da schickt der Herr den Prügel° aus,
er soll den Pudel schlagen.° (usw.)

cudgel
beat

Da schickt der Herr das Feuer° aus,
es soll den Prügel brennen.° (usw.)

fire
burn

Da schickt der Herr das Wasser° aus,
es soll das Feuer löschen.° (usw.)

water
quench

Da schickt der Herr den Ochsen° aus,
er soll das Wasser saufen.° (usw.)

ox
drink

Da schickt der Herr den Schlächter° aus,
er soll den Ochsen schlachten.° (usw.)

butcher
slaughter

Da schickt der Herr den Henker° aus,
er soll den Schlächter hängen.° (usw.)

hangman
hang

Da schickt der Herr den Teufel° aus,
er soll den Henker holen.° (usw.)

devil
fetch

Da geht der Herr nun selbst hinaus°
und macht gar bald ein End daraus.°
Der Teufel holt den Henker nun,
der Henker hängt den Schlächter nun,
der Schlächter schlacht den Ochsen nun,
der Ochse säuft das Wasser nun,
das Wasser löscht das Feuer nun,
das Feuer brennt den Prügel nun,
der Prügel schlägt den Pudel nun,
der Jockel schneidet den Hafer nun
und kommt auch gleich° nach Haus.

Da . . . hinaus = *So now the
master goes out himself / **und
. . . daraus** = and soon puts an
end to this*

right away

Grammatik

Verbs with Stem-Vowel Change *a* to *ä, au* to *äu*

a → ä	fahren	*to drive; go by vehicle*	
ich	fahre	wir	fahren
du	**fährst**	ihr	fahrt
er, es, sie	**fährt**	sie, Sie	fahren

Other verbs in this group are: **halten (hält),**[4] *to stop or hold;* **schlafen (schläft),** *to sleep;* **tragen (trägt),** *to carry or wear.*

au → äu	laufen	*to run*	
ich	laufe	wir	laufen
du	**läufst**	ihr	lauft
er, es, sie	**läuft**	sie, Sie	laufen

Fragewort

wie lange?   *how long?*

---

 1 Kettenreaktion

Say how you get home, then ask your classmates how they get home.

> BEISPIEL: S1: Ich fahre nach Hause. Fährst du auch nach Hause?
> S2: Nein, ich laufe nach Hause. Läufst du auch nach Hause?

2 Kettenreaktion

Wie lange schläfst du?

> BEISPIEL: Ich schlafe acht Stunden. Wie lange schläfst du?

---

4. Stem-changing verbs whose stem ends in **-t** do *not* insert **-e-** between stem and personal ending: **du hältst, er hält** (in the latter form, the ending **-t** merges with the **-t** of the stem).

3 **Gruppenarbeit:** Mit offenen Büchern   *With open books*

Tell one thing that you're wearing, then one thing the person next to you is wearing.

BEISPIEL: Ich trage _____ und er/sie trägt heute _____.

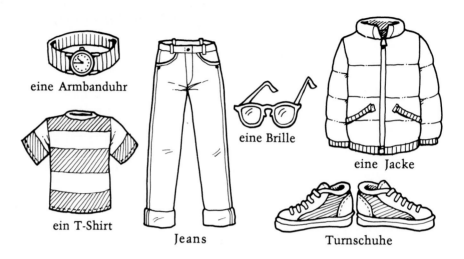

eine Armbanduhr

eine Brille

eine Jacke

ein T-Shirt

Jeans

Turnschuhe

The Predicate

At this point, it is important to say a few more words about the structure of sentences. In both German and English, all statements and questions contain a subject (S) and an inflected verb (V):

S *V*	*S* *V*
Ich arbeite viel.	*I work a lot.*

V *S*	*V* *S*
Schläfst du?	*Are you sleeping?*

The verb by itself, however, is not always adequate to express the entire action or condition in which the subject is involved. For example, consider the simple English statement

John is young.

"John" is the subject and "is" is the verb. When taken by themselves, however, the words

John is

are not a meaningful utterance in English.[5] The verb "is" must be completed by a complement, in this case, the adjective "young." The verb and its complement together make up the entire verbal idea, or predicate. In the example

---

5. Except as an abbreviated answer to a question, with repetitious elements omitted but understood: "Who is playing the harmonica?" "John is (playing it)."

sentence, "young" is called a predicate adjective because it is used together with the verb "is" to form the entire predicate.

Similarly, in the sentence

Herr Beck ist unser Lehrer.   *Mr. Beck is our teacher.*

unser Lehrer—a noun phrase in the nominative case—is the complement of the verb **sein**; it is therefore called a predicate nominative.[6]

In both German and English, various kinds of words and phrases can complement the verb to form the complete predicate. In the sentence

She can ski.

the verb "can" is complemented by a second verb "ski" to form the predicate "can ski." You will learn about verbs like "can" in the following section.

Modal Verbs

There is a group of six verbs in German called *the modal verbs.* They do not express an action or condition by themselves, but rather the subject's *attitude* or *relation* to the action expressed by another verb.

Wir **müssen** noch eine Stunde **fahren.**   *We still **have to drive** for an hour.*

The modal verb **müssen** (*have to*) indicates that it is *necessary* for the subject (**wir**) to perform the action of driving (**fahren**). **Müssen** is the first part of the predicate, and the infinitive **fahren** is the second part of the predicate. The German modals are:

		expresses
dürfen	*to be allowed to, may*	permission
können	*to be able to, can*	ability
müssen	*to have to, must*	necessity
sollen	*to be supposed to, should*	obligation
wollen	*to want to; intend to*	desire; intention
(ich) **möchte**[7]	*(I) would like to*	inclination, desire

Lehrer und Schüler

6. See p. 32.
7. **Möchte** (*would like to*) is a subjunctive form of the modal verb **mögen**. See pp. 108 and 420.

The modal auxiliaries take no endings in the **ich-** and **er**-forms, and most have a changed stem vowel in the singular.

---

dürfen   *to be allowed to*

permission (handwritten)

ich	darf
du	darfst
er, es, sie	darf
wir	dürfen
ihr	dürft
sie, Sie	dürfen

Darf ich draußen **spielen?**
May I play outside?

---

können   *to be able to*

ability (handwritten)

ich	kann
du	kannst
er, es, sie	kann
wir	können
ihr	könnt
sie, Sie	können

Wir **können** da drüben **halten.**
We can stop over there.

---

müssen   *to have to*

necessity (handwritten)

ich	muß
du	mußt
er, es, sie	muß
wir	müssen
ihr	müßt
sie, Sie	müssen

Heute **muß** ich zu Fuß **gehen.**
Today I have to go on foot.

---

sollen   *to be supposed to*[8]

obligation (handwritten)

ich	soll
du	sollst
er, es, sie	soll
wir	sollen
ihr	sollt
sie, Sie	sollen

Sollen wir eine Pause **machen?**
Should we take a break?

---

wollen   *to want to*

desire (handwritten)
intension (handwritten)

ich	will
du	willst
er, es, sie	will
wir	wollen
ihr	wollt
sie, Sie	wollen

Willst du jetzt **essen?**
Do you want to eat now?

---

ich möchte[9]   *I would like to*
(infinitive: **mögen**)

desire (handwritten)
inclination (handwritten)

ich	möchte
du	möchtest
er, es, sie	möchte
wir	möchten
ihr	möchtet
sie, Sie	möchten

Ich **möchte** dich **besuchen.**
I would like to visit you.

---

8. Notice that only **sollen** does not have a stem-vowel change in the singular.
9. **Möchte** has endings different from the other modals.

When a modal verb is present, it is *always* the inflected verb. The complementary infinitive (which is the second part of the predicate) comes at the end of the sentence. Note the difference from English, in which the dependent infinitive immediately *follows* the modal verb.

Wir **können** da drüben **halten.**   We *can stop* over there.
Das **muß** ich für morgen **lesen.**   I *have to read* that for tomorrow.
Marie **soll** ihre Eltern **besuchen.**   Marie *is supposed to visit* her
                                      parents.

It is important that you get used to this two-part predicate, since it is a central structural feature of German sentences.

4 Übung: Was möchten Sie heute tun?

Here are some things people in the dialogues are doing.

Monika besuchen   Geld verdienen
nach Frankfurt fahren   eine Pause machen
ein bißchen laufen   da drüben halten
nach Hause fahren   zu Fuß gehen

Choose from these activities to answer your instructor's questions.

     BEISPIEL: Was möchten Sie heute tun?
               Ich möchte Monika besuchen.

1. Was können Sie heute tun?
2. Was müssen Sie heute tun?

5 Gruppenarbeit: Was willst du machen?   *4 Studenten*

Ask each other about what you intend to do or be some day. This list will provide some ideas. What others can you find?

     BEISPIEL: Was willst du denn machen?
               Ich will in Deutschland studieren, und du?

eine Familie haben   Freunde in Europa besuchen
viel Geld verdienen   fit sein
berufstätig sein   nie krank werden
ein Haus besitzen   in Deutschland studieren

Omission of the Infinitive

Certain infinitives may be omitted from sentences with modal verbs when they are clearly implied.

■ **haben**

     Möchten Sie ein Zimmer   *Would you like a room?*
     [**haben**]?

- **machen, tun**

Das kann ich leider nicht [**machen/tun**].	*Unfortunately I can't do that.*

- verbs of motion (**gehen, fahren, fliegen, laufen**) when destination is expressed

Mußt du jetzt nach Hause [**gehen, fahren**]?	*Do you have to go home now?*

- **Sprechen** is usually omitted in the following expression.

Kannst du Deutsch?	*Can you speak German?*
Ja, ich kann Deutsch.	*Yes, I can speak German.*

6 **Übung:** Wie sagt man das auf englisch?

1. Wollen Sie jetzt nach Hause?
2. Er kann das noch nicht.
3. Willst du meinen Bleistift?
4. Mein Vater will das nicht.

5. Sie können schon gut Deutsch.
6. Möchten Sie das Geld?
7. Darf man denn das?
8. Wann wollen Sie nach Amerika?

Fragewort

wohin?[10]   *where to?*

---

7 **Partnerarbeit:** Wohin wollen wir im Februar?

By the time the semester break comes in mid-February, many German students want to travel where it is warm. Use the map of Europe on the back inside cover to plan such a trip with your partner.

> BEISPIEL: STUDENT A: Wohin willst du im Februar?
> STUDENT B: Ich will nach . . . . Wohin willst du?

Negation with *nicht* (not)

Nicht is used to negate a sentence.

Karin ist meine Schwester.	*Karin is my sister.*
Karin ist **nicht** meine Schwester.	*Karin is not my sister.*

In the example above, the position of **nicht** is exactly parallel to the position of *not* in English. In most German sentences, however, this will not be the case. Here are some preliminary guidelines for the position of **nicht**.

10. Recall the analogous question word **woher?**—*from where?* The particle **her** indicates motion *toward* the speaker, **hin** indicates motion *away from* the speaker (see pp. 454–56).

- **Nicht** usually *follows* the subject, verb, and direct object.

Ich kenne deinen Freund **nicht**.	*I don't know your friend.*
Er sagt das **nicht**.	*He doesn't say that.*
Wir besitzen das Auto **nicht**.	*We don't own the car.*

- **Nicht** also usually follows expressions of definite time.

Sie können heute abend **nicht** kommen.	*They can't come tonight.*
Hans arbeitet jetzt **nicht**.	*Hans isn't working now.*

8 Übung

Negate these sentences by adding **nicht**.

1. Kurt besucht seinen Bruder.
2. Ich kenne eure Mutter.
3. Frau Schmidt besucht uns morgen.
4. Monika macht das heute abend.
5. Ich verstehe ihn.
6. Am Donnerstag kochst du.
7. Er liest sein Buch.
8. Mein Großvater schläft.

- **Nicht** *precedes* complements that constitute the second part of the predicate.[11] These include:

Predicate adjectives

Der Berg ist **steil**.	*The mountain is steep.*
Der Berg ist **nicht** steil.	*The mountain is not steep.*

Predicate nominatives[12]

Das ist **Herr Böhm**.	*That is Mr. Böhm.*
Das ist **nicht** Herr Böhm.	*That is not Mr. Böhm.*

Adverbs modifying the verb

Margit geht **zu Fuß**.	*Margit is going on foot.*
Margit geht **nicht** zu Fuß.	*Margit isn't going on foot.*

Prepositional phrases that show destination (**nach Wien, nach Hause**) or location (**in Berlin, zu Hause**)

Sie geht **nach Hause**.	*She's going home.*
Sie geht **nicht** nach Hause.	*She's not going home.*
Er arbeitet **in Berlin**.	*He works in Berlin.*
Er arbeitet **nicht** in Berlin.	*He doesn't work in Berlin.*

Infinitives complementing modal verbs

Er kann mich **sehen**.	*He can see me.*
Er kann mich **nicht** sehen.	*He can't see me.*

11. See page 74.
12. See page 75.

9 Übung

Negate these sentences by adding **nicht.**

1. Das Wetter ist schön.
2. Ich kann dich besuchen.
3. Unsere Freunde kommen morgen.
4. Ich möchte Berlin sehen.
5. Der Berg ist steil.
6. Wir wollen halten.
7. Frau Mackensen ist unsere Lehrerin.
8. Ich muß nach Hause gehen.
9. Margit läuft gut.
10. Er kann mich sehen.

10 Übung

Answer your instructor's questions negatively.

BEISPIEL: Kennen Sie Berlin?
Nein, ich kenne Berlin nicht.

1. Müssen Sie nach Hause?
2. Wollen wir halten?
3. Kennt er deinen Freund?
4. Ist das der Berg?
5. Schaffen Sie das?
6. Darf sie nach München fahren?
7. Kommt Carola heute abend?
8. Ist Ihre Mitbewohnerin freundlich?
9. Ist es heute schön?
10. Fahren wir heute abend?
11. Ist es langweilig in Frankfurt?
12. Studiert Stefan in München?

Negation with *kein*

Kein (*not a, not any, no*) is the negative of **ein.** It negates nouns preceded by **ein** or nouns not preceded by any article.

Morgen will ich ein Buch lesen.	*I want to read a book tomorrow.*
Morgen will ich **kein** Buch lesen.	*I don't want to read a book tomorrow.*
Hier wohnen Studenten.	*Students live here.*
Hier wohnen **keine** Studenten.	*No students live here.*

Kein is an **ein**-word and takes the same endings as **ein** and the possessive adjectives.

Das ist $\begin{cases} \textbf{ein} \text{ Fernseher.} \\ \textbf{kein} \text{ Fernseher.} \\ \textbf{unser} \text{ Fernseher.} \end{cases}$ Er hat $\begin{cases} \textbf{einen} \text{ Wagen.} \\ \textbf{keinen} \text{ Wagen.} \\ \textbf{meinen} \text{ Wagen.} \end{cases}$

Nicht and **kein** are mutually exclusive. In any given situation, only one will be correct. If a noun is preceded by the definite article or by a possessive adjective, use **nicht** rather than **kein** to negate it.

Ist das die Professorin?	*Is that the professor?*
Nein, das ist **nicht** die Professorin.	*No, that's not the professor.*
Ist das eure Professorin?	*Is that your professor?*
Nein, das ist **nicht** unsere Professorin.	*No, that's not our professor.*
Ist das eine Professorin?	*Is that a professor?*
Nein, das ist **keine** Professorin.	*No, that's not a professor.*

11 **Übung**

Negate the sentence, using **kein.**

1. Meine Familie besitzt einen Wagen.

2. Maria hat heute Geld.

3. Es gibt hier ein Problem.

4. Hier wohnen Studenten.

5. Morgen gibt es eine Diskussion.

6. Herr Meyer hat Kinder.

12 **Übung**

Respond negatively to your instructor's questions, using **kein** or **nicht.**

BEISPIEL: Hat Barbara einen Freund? Nein, sie hat keinen Freund.
Ist das ihr Freund? Nein, das ist nicht ihr Freund.

1. Haben Sie einen Freund in Amerika?

2. Haben Sie Freunde in Washington?

3. Ist das der Lehrer?

4. Verdient er Geld?

5. Sehen Sie das Haus?

6. Ist das seine Freundin?

7. Suchen Sie das Buch?

8. Suchen Sie ein Buch?

13 **Partnerarbeit:** Meine Familie

Ask each other about your families. (Names for family members are on p. 61.)

BEISPIEL: S1: Hast du einen Sohn?
S2: Nein, ich habe keinen Sohn.

Expecting an Affirmative Answer: *nicht wahr?*

Nicht wahr? (literally, "not true?"), when added to a positive statement, anticipates confirmation (English: *doesn't she? wasn't he? wasn't it? didn't you?* etc.) In spoken German, you may shorten it to **nicht?**

Heute ist es schön, **nicht wahr?**	*It's beautiful today, isn't it?*
Sie studieren in Freiburg, **nicht?**	*You're studying in Freiburg, aren't you?*
Gisela kennst du, **nicht wahr?**	*You know Gisela, don't you?*

14 **Übung:** Das ist ein Tisch, nicht wahr?

Contradict your instructor if necessary.

> BEISPIEL: Das ist ein Tisch, nicht wahr?
> Nein, das ist kein Tisch, das ist ein(e) _____.

15 **Übung:** Wie sagt man das auf deutsch?

1. You have a car, don't you?
2. You're learning German, aren't you?
3. You'll visit me soon, won't you?
4. He's in good shape, isn't he?
5. We can work today, can't we?
6. You can understand that, can't you?

Contradicting a Negative Statement or Question: *doch*

To contradict a negative statement or question, use **doch** instead of **ja**.

Ich spreche nicht gut Deutsch.	*I don't speak German well.*
Doch, Sie sprechen sehr gut Deutsch!	*Yes you do, you speak German very well.*
Kennst du Ursula nicht?	*Don't you know Ursula?*
Doch, ich kenne sie sehr gut!	*Sure, I know her very well.*

16 **Übung:** Doch!

Contradict your instructor's negative statements and questions, beginning your response with a stressed **doch.**

> BEISPIEL: Schaffst du das nicht?
> *Doch*, ich schaffe das!

1. Wir wollen nicht hier halten.
2. Wir haben nicht genug Geld.
3. Hast du keinen Bruder?
4. Es ist nicht sehr spät.
5. Kannst du kein Deutsch?

17 **Übung**

Contradict your instructor if necessary.

> BEISPIEL: Das ist kein Tisch.
> *Doch!* Natürlich ist das ein Tisch!

The Indefinite Pronoun *man*

The indefinite pronoun **man** refers to people in general rather than to any specific person. Although the English indefinite pronoun "one" may sound formal in everyday speech, **man** does not sound this way in German. It is used in both colloquial and formal language. It is often best translated into English as "people," "they," "you," or even "we."

You can use **man** only as the subject of a sentence, and only with a verb in the third person singular.

In Deutschland sagt **man** das oft.	*They often say that in Germany.*
Das muß **man** lernen.	*You've got to learn that.*
Das weiß **man** nie.	*One never knows.*

Do not confuse **man** with **der Mann** (*the man*).

Der Mann spricht Deutsch.   Hier spricht man Deutsch.

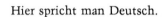

18 **Übung**

Change the subject to **man.**

1. In Hinterwalden können die Leute genug verdienen.

2. Um elf Uhr machen wir eine Pause.

3. Hoffentlich können wir drüben halten.

4. Hier können Sie gut essen.

5. Dürfen wir hier schlafen?

19 **Übung:** Wie sagt man das auf deutsch?

Use **man** as the subject.

1. In America we don't say that.

2. You've got to stop here.

3. One has to do that.

4. People say there are problems here.

5. Can we go on foot?

Tips zum Lesen und Lernen

Tip zum Vokabelnlernen

Masculine nouns ending in **-er** almost never change in the plural.

singular	*plural*
der Lehrer	die Lehrer
der Amerikaner	die Amerikaner
der Schüler	die Schüler
der Europäer	die Europäer
der Pullover	die Pullover

Resist the temptation to add an **-s** as in the English plural (*two pullovers*). Remember that *very few* German nouns take **-s** in the plural.

Übung   Answer your instructor's questions with the plural form.

1. Wie viele Lehrer haben Sie?

2. Wie viele Amerikaner gibt es hier im Zimmer?

3. Wie viele Schüler kennen Sie?

4. Wie viele Europäer studieren hier?

5. Wie viele Pullover besitzen Sie?

Leicht zu merken

international	intern**a**tion**a**l
die **Jeans** (*pl.*)	
optimistisch	optim**i**stisch
pessimistisch	pessim**i**stisch
das **System, -e**	Syst**e**m
das **Schulsystem**	**Schul**system

Einstieg in den Text

Remember that word order in German is in some ways freer than in English. It is true that the verb must be in second position in statements. In place of the subject, however, an object, an adverb, or some other element can be in first position. You will often find sentences beginning with the direct object:

Das finde ich auch.	*I think so too.* (literally: *I find that too.*)
Angst habe ich auch.	*I'm afraid too.* (literally: *I have fear too.*)

The clue to understanding such sentences is the personal ending of the verb. Words like **habe** and **finde** are obviously first-person and go with the subject pronoun **ich**.

Wortschatz 2

Verben

besprechen (bespricht) to discuss
entscheiden to decide
hassen to hate
hören to hear
lachen to laugh
  lachen über (+ *acc.*) to laugh about
lernen to learn
schreiben to write
  schreiben über (+ *acc.*) to write about
singen to sing

Substantive

der **Europäer, -** European (*m.*)
der **Mantel, ⁻** coat
der **Pullover, -** pullover, jersey, sweater
  also: der **Pulli, -s**
der **Schuh, -e** shoe
  der **Turnschuh** sneaker, gym shoe

(das) **Amerika** America
(das) **Deutsch** German (*language*)
(das) **Englisch** English (*language*)
(das) **Europa** Europe
  Mitteleuropa Central Europe
das **Gymnasium,** die **Gymnasien** secondary school (*prepares pupils for university*)

das **Hemd, -en** shirt
das **Kleid, -er** dress; *pl.* = dresses *or* clothes

die **Angst, ⁻e** fear
  Angst haben to be afraid
  Ich habe Angst. I am afraid.
die **Bluse, -n** blouse
die **Europäerin, -nen** European (*f.*)
die **Hausaufgabe, -n** homework assignment
die **Hose, -n** trousers, pants
die **Jacke, -n** jacket
die **Musik** music
die **Reise, -n** trip
  eine Reise machen to take a trip
die **Sprache, -n** language
  die **Fremdsprache** foreign language
die **Umwelt** environment
die **Welt, -en** world
die **Zeit, -en** time

die **Pommes frites** (*pl.,* pronounced *"Pomm fritt"*) French fries

Adjektive und Adverbien

ähnlich similar
also thus, for that reason
amerikanisch American
darum therefore, for that reason
ehrlich honest
eigentlich actually, in fact

fremd strange; foreign
heutzutage nowadays
neu new
schnell fast
toll (*colloq.*) great, terrific

Nützliche Ausdrücke

bitte please
Das finde ich auch. I think so too.
gar nicht not at all
Stimmt schon. That's right.

Gegensätze

hassen ≠ **lieben** to hate ≠ to love
lachen ≠ **weinen** to laugh ≠ to cry
neu ≠ **alt** new ≠ old
schnell ≠ **langsam** fast ≠ slow
Stimmt schon. ≠ **Stimmt nicht.** That's right. ≠ That's wrong.

Mit anderen Worten

steinalt = **sehr, sehr alt**
blitzschnell = **sehr, sehr schnell**

Eine Klassendiskussion

Last spring class 10a from the Kepler Gymnasium in Hannover visited a high school in California. Now they are discussing their impressions of the States with their teacher, Herr Beck; they also plan to write an article for their school newspaper.

HERR BECK: Können wir jetzt unsere Amerikareise ein bißchen besprechen? Rolf, möchtest du etwas sagen? . . . Ach, er schläft ja wieder. (*Alle lachen.*)

5 ROLF: Meinen Sie mich? Entschuldigung! Unsere Reise? Sie war° doch toll.   *was*

KIRSTEN: Das finde ich auch. Die Amerikaner sind wahnsinnig freundlich, und jetzt weiß ich, die Schüler in Amerika sind eigentlich gar nicht so anders. Dort trägt man ja auch Jeans und Turnschuhe, hört Rockmusik, singt dieselben° Schlager und ißt Pommes frites.   **dieselben Schlager** = *the same hits*

10

HERR BECK: Stimmt schon, aber haben die amerikanischen Schüler auch ähnliche Probleme wie ihr?

Der Schüler hat eine Frage. (Hannover)

15	ANDREAS:	Ach, wissen Sie, alle Schüler hassen Hausaufgaben! (*Alle lachen*) Nein, aber im Ernst,° wir sind alle manchmal pessimistisch. Man meint, man kann später° keine Arbeit finden, und auch die Umweltprobleme sind heute international.	*seriously* *later*
20		Heutzutage haben die Schüler überall ein bißchen Angst.	
	HERR BECK:	Angst habe ich auch, muß ich ehrlich sagen. Aber gibt es denn keine Unterschiede° zwischen hier und dort?	*differences*
25	KIRSTEN:	Doch, natürlich! Dort besuchen° alle Schüler die high school, bis sie 18 sind. Mit zehn Jahren müssen wir aber entscheiden: Gymnasium, Realschule oder Hauptschule.¹³ Die zwei Schulsysteme sind also ganz anders.	*here = attend*
30	CHRISTA:	Ich finde, wir müssen hier mehr und schneller° lernen. Deutschland ist in Mitteleuropa und hat viele Nachbarländer.° Darum müssen wir ja Fremdsprachen lernen. Viele Europäer können z.B. gut Englisch, aber relativ wenige Amerikaner lernen Fremdsprachen.	*faster* *neighboring countries*
35			
	HERR BECK:	Jetzt haben wir leider keine Zeit mehr. Aber morgen können wir unseren Artikel über die Reise für die Schülerzeitung schreiben. Auf Wiedersehen bis dann.	

Fragen zum Lesestück

1. Wer bespricht die Amerikareise?

2. Wie war die Reise?

3. Sind die Schüler in Amerika sehr anders, oder sind sie ähnlich?

4. Was trägt man auch in Amerika?

5. Was ißt man auch dort?

6. Was hassen alle Schüler?

7. Warum sind Schüler heutzutage manchmal pessimistisch?

8. Warum müssen die Deutschen Fremdsprachen lernen?

9. Was müssen die deutschen Schüler mit 10 Jahren machen?

10. Was schreibt die Klasse für ihre Schülerzeitung?

13. See *Almanach*, p. 93.

Situationen aus dem Alltag

Was soll ich heute tragen?

You already know some of this vocabulary.

die **Kleidung**	*clothing*
1. der **Anzug, ̈e**	*suit*
2. die **Bluse, -n**	
3. die **Brille** (*sing.*)	*glasses*
4. der **Handschuh, -e**	*glove*
5. das **Hemd, -en**	
6. die **Hose, -n**	
7. der **Hut, ̈e**	*hat*
8. die **Jacke, -n**	
9. das **Kleid, -er**	
10. die **Krawatte, -n**	*tie*
11. der **Mantel, ̈**	
12. der **Pulli, -s**	
13. der **Rock, ̈e**	*skirt*
14. der **Schuh, -e**	
15. die **Tasche, -n**	*pocket; handbag, shoulder-bag*
16. das **T-shirt, -s**	*T-shirt*
17. der **Turnschuh, -e**	
18. der **Regenschirm, -e**	*umbrella*
19. die **Mütze, -n**	*cap*

Gruppenarbeit: Was tragen Sie heute?

> BEISPIELE: PROFESSOR: Was tragen Sie heute, Mary?
> STUDENTIN: Ich trage _____ und _____.

Partnerarbeit: Was trägst du heute?

> BEISPIELE: STUDENT A: Was trägst du heute?
> STUDENT B: Ich trage _____ und _____. Was trägst du?

Gruppenarbeit: Was tragen Sie in diesen Situationen?

> BEISPIELE: Es regnet.
> Dann trage ich . . .

1. Es regnet (Es schneit. Es ist windig.)
2. Die Sonne scheint, und es ist sehr warm.
3. Sie suchen eine Stelle und haben heute ein Interview.
4. Sie und Ihre Mitbewohner machen heute abend eine Party.

Welche Farbe hat das?

die **Farbe, -n**	color
bunt	colorful, multi-colored
blau	blue
braun	brown
gelb	yellow
grau	gray
grün	green
rot	red
schwarz	black
weiß	white
dunkel	dark
hell	light
dunkelblau	dark blue
hellgrün	light green

Partnerarbeit

Ask each other about the colors of various things in the classroom and of clothing people are wearing.

> BEISPIELE: Welche Farben hat die Landkarte?
> Sie ist _____.
>
> Welche Farbe hat Peters Hemd?
> Sein Hemd ist _____.

Zum Schluß

Sprechen wir miteinander!

A Übung

Answer each of your instructor's questions in the negative, making sure to use **nicht** or **kein** correctly.

1. Wollen Sie Ihre Hausaufgaben heute abend machen?
2. Besitzen Sie ein Motorrad?
3. Können wir jetzt arbeiten?
4. Sind Ihre Freunde fit?
5. Machen Sie im Dezember eine Reise?
6. Wollen Sie das?
7. Hören Sie mich?
8. Lachen die Kinder laut?
9. Haben Sie Angst?
10. Tragen Sie eine Mütze?
11. Ist ihre Bluse grün?
12. Ist Frau Wenger oft im Büro?

B Gruppenarbeit: Mit offenen Büchern   *3 oder 4 Studenten*

Take turns changing each sentence by substituting the new elements provided.

BEISPIELE: Ich möchte morgen nach Berlin. (wollen)
STUDENT A: Ich will morgen nach Berlin. (Wien)
STUDENT B: Ich will morgen nach Wien.

1. Ich möchte morgen nach Berlin.
   wollen
   München
   müssen
   wir
   Kopenhagen
   nächstes Semester

2. Im Juni kannst du viel Geld verdienen.
   müssen
   September
   ich
   haben
   wollen

3. Wir können da drüben halten.
   sollen
   eine Pause machen
   ich
   möchte
   arbeiten
   zu Hause

4. Er geht jetzt nach Hause.
   fahren
   morgen
   Max
   bald
   ihr

C Gruppenarbeit: Was meinen Sie? *4 Personen*

Here are some topics of conversation and some adjectives. Using the verbs **meinen** and **finden,** take turns expressing opinions about these topics. Others in the group agree or disagree.

BEISPIEL: STUDENT A: Ich finde (meine), die Umwelt ist wichtig.
STUDENT B: Das finde (meine) ich auch. *oder*
Das finde (meine) ich nicht.

Schulen in Amerika	schön / häßlich
Schulen in Deutschland	wichtig / unwichtig
Rockmusik	interessant / langweilig
klassische Musik	toll
Umwelt	prima
Fremdsprachen	stinklangweilig
Hausaufgaben	wahnsinnig gut

D Gruppenarbeit: Stimmt nicht! *3 Personen*

Play this game with two other partners. One says something obviously false. The others contradict that statement and give the correct information. Then the next player takes a turn.

BEISPIELE: —Kirsten trägt heute einen Pulli.
—Stimmt nicht! Sie trägt keinen Pulli! Sie trägt eine Bluse.

E Partnerarbeit: Interview—*heute* und *morgen*

Interview each other. Give as many answers as possible to the following questions.

1. Was möchtest du heute abend machen? Ich möchte _____.

2. Was mußt du morgen machen? Morgen muß ich _____.

3. Was willst du in 10 Jahren (*in 10 years*) machen? In 10 Jahren will ich

_____.

Schreiben Sie zu Hause

F Udo is throwing a party, but nobody can come. Finish writing him the following note explaining why. There are some cues to help you.

Lieber Udo (*Dear Udo*),

Leider kann niemand zur Party kommen. Monika muß zu Hause bleiben. Klaus
. . .

Klaus / müssen / für morgen / machen / seine Hausaufgaben

Ruth / möchten / fahren / nach Berlin

Peter und Ute / wollen / besuchen / ihre Tante / in Wien

Herr Beck / können / leider / finden / seinen Anzug / nicht

Andreas / dürfen / nicht so spät / kommen / nach Hause

ich / wollen / gar nicht / kommen

G Finish the following dialogue by completing the sentences.

ANNA: Hallo Klaus!
KLAUS: _____, wie geht's?
ANNA: _____. Was machst du denn heute?
KLAUS: Heute muß ich _____.
    Und du?
ANNA: Heute soll ich _____, aber ich will _____. Also tschüs!
KLAUS: Tschüs Anna!

H Wie sagt man das auf deutsch?

1. Wouldn't you like to stay a bit?

2. Unfortunately, I have to work this evening.

3. How long do you have to work?

4. Only one hour.

5. Don't you have any friends in Hinterwalden?

6. Yes, I do. Unfortunately they're quite boring.

7. Then you have to visit us soon.

8. You want to come to Berlin, don't you?

9. Yes. I can't stay in Hinterwalden.

10. Why not? Aren't there any jobs there?

11. Yes, but not enough. I have to look for a job in Berlin.

A Note about Schools in German-Speaking Countries

The public school systems in Germany, Austria, and Switzerland all differ from American public schools in the degree to which they track pupils. Relatively early in their schooling, children are steered toward apprenticeships, commercial training, or preparation for university study. In the Federal Republic of Germany, each **Land** (province) has authority over its own school system. In all **Länder,** children attend four years of elementary school **(Grundschule)** together. At the end of the fourth, fifth, or sixth grade (depending on the **Land**), they are then tracked into separate schools. The decision is made on the basis of grades and conferences between teachers and parents.

There are three possibilities: the **Hauptschule,** the **Realschule,** or the **Gymnasium.** The first two are oriented respectively toward trades and business and prepare the pupils for various forms of apprenticeship and job training. The **Gymnasium** is the traditional preparation for university study. After passing their final examination, called the **Abitur** in Germany and the **Matura** in Austria and Switzerland, pupils may apply to a university.

Since 1971, there has been some experimentation in the Federal Republic with **Gesamtschulen** (unified schools) comprising all three types of secondary schools. These are schools designed on the American model, where pupils need not make their important decision at the age of ten, but can wait until they are sixteen. **Gesamtschulen,** however, comprise only a small percentage of the total number of secondary schools.

Schüler in einer Grundschule.

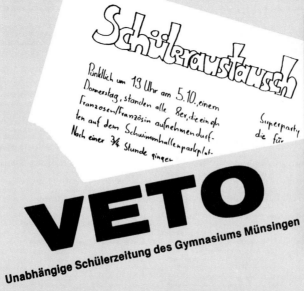

Schüleraustausch

Pünktlich um 19 Uhr am 5.10., einem Donnerstag, standen alle 8er, die einen Franzosen/Französin aufnehmen durften auf dem Schwimmhallenparkplatz. Nach einer ¾ Stunde ginger

Superparty die für

VETO
Unabhängige Schülerzeitung des Gymnasiums Münsingen

Land und Leute

Am See

FRAU MÜLLER: Wollen Sie noch einmal schwimmen gehen, Frau Brinkmann?

FRAU BRINKMANN: Nein, lieber nicht. Ich bin ein bißchen müde. Und das Wasser ist so wahnsinnig kalt. Gehen Sie doch ohne mich.

FRAU MÜLLER: Möchten Sie vielleicht lieber Karten spielen?

FRAU BRINKMANN: Ja, gerne!

Winterurlaub

RICHARD: Möchtest du im Winter nach Österreich?

EVA: Super! Fahren wir doch im Januar nach Innsbruck!

RICHARD: Hoffentlich können wir noch ein Hotelzimmer bekommen.

EVA: Ich glaube, es ist noch nicht zu spät.

Morgens um halb zehn

ANITA: Also tschüs! Ich muß jetzt weg.

BEATE: Warte mal! Ohne Frühstück geht's nicht! Iß doch wenigstens ein Brötchen.

ANITA: Leider habe ich keine Zeit mehr. Mein Seminar beginnt um zehn, und unterwegs muß ich noch ein Heft kaufen.

BEATE: Nimm doch das Brötchen mit. Später wirst du sicher hungrig.

ANITA: Du hast recht . . . Also, bis nachher!

Beim Bäcker kauft man frische Brötchen.

Wortschatz 1

At the Lake

MRS. MÜLLER: Do you want to go swimming again, Mrs. Brinkmann?

MRS. BRINKMANN: No, I'd rather not. I'm a little tired. And the water is so awfully cold. You go without me.

MRS. MÜLLER: Maybe you'd rather play cards?

MRS. BRINKMANN: Yes, gladly!

Winter Vacation

RICHARD: Would you like to go to Austria this winter?

EVA: Great! Let's go to Innsbruck in January!

RICHARD: I hope we can still get a hotel room.

EVA: I don't think it's too late yet.

9:30 in the Morning

ANITA: So long then. I've got to go now.

BEATE: Wait a second! Not without breakfast! Eat a roll at least.

ANITA: Unfortunately I have no more time. My seminar begins at ten, and on the way I still have to buy a notebook.

BEATE: Take the roll along. Later you're sure to get hungry.

ANITA: You're right . . . Well, see you later!

Verben

beginnen to begin
bekommen to receive
frühstücken to eat breakfast
glauben to believe; think
kaufen to buy
mögen (mag) to like
schwimmen to swim
warten to wait
werden (wird) to become, get (*in the sense of* "become")

Substantive

der **See, -n** lake
  am See at the lake
der **Urlaub, -e** vacation (*from a job*)
der **Winter, -** winter
  im Winter in the winter

das **Brötchen, -** roll[1]
das **Frühstück** breakfast
  zum Frühstück for breakfast
das **Hotel, -s** hotel
(das) **Österreich** Austria
das **Seminar, -e** (*university*) seminar
das **Wasser** water

die **Karte, -n** card; ticket; map

Adjektive und Adverbien

einmal once
  noch einmal once again, once more

gern gladly, with pleasure
gern (+ *verb*) like to
  Ich spiele gern Karten. I like to play cards.
etwas oder jemand gern haben to like something or someone
  Ich habe dich gern. I like you.
hoffentlich I hope . . .
hungrig hungry
kalt cold
lang(e) long; for a long time
lieber (+ *verb*) prefer to, would rather
  Ich spiele lieber Karten. I'd rather play cards.
morgens (*adv.*) in the morning(s)
müde tired, weary
nachher later on, after that
noch nicht not yet
später later
super (*colloq.*) super, great
unterwegs on the way; en route; on the go
weg away, gone

Andere Vokabeln

doch (*flavoring particle with commands, see p. 99*)
durch through
mal (*flavoring particle with commands, see p. 99*)
mit along (with me, us, etc.)
ohne without
zusammen together

---

1. **Brötchen** (or, in Southern Germany, **Semmeln**) are crusty rolls baked fresh daily and are the most common breakfast food.

Nützliche Ausdrücke

Bis nachher! See you later!
Das (es) geht. That's (it's) all right. It's possible. It can be done.
Das (es) geht nicht. That's (it's) out. Nothing doing. You can't do that.
Lieber nicht. I'd rather not. No thanks. Let's not.

recht haben to be right
  Du hast recht. You're right.
Warte mal! Wait a second! Hang on!

Gegensätze

kalt ≠ heiß cold ≠ hot
kaufen ≠ verkaufen to buy ≠ to sell

lang ≠ kurz long; for a long time ≠ short; for a short time
zusammen ≠ allein together ≠ alone

Mit anderen Worten

todmüde = sehr müde
super = phantastisch = prima = sehr gut

Variationen

A Persönliche Fragen

1. Frau Brinkmann und Frau Müller spielen gern Karten. Was machen Sie gern?
2. Spielen Sie lieber Karten, oder gehen Sie lieber schwimmen?
3. Frau Brinkmann sagt, sie ist ein bißchen müde. Sind Sie heute müde?
4. Wohin wollen Sie im Winter?
5. Was möchten Sie dort machen?
6. Essen Sie immer Frühstück, oder haben Sie manchmal keine Zeit?
7. Essen Sie gern Brötchen?
8. Wann beginnt die Deutschstunde?
9. Müssen Sie heute etwas kaufen? Was denn?

B Gruppenarbeit: Gegensätze *Mit offenen Büchern*

Contradict each other. You may refer to your books.

    BEISPIEL: STUDENT A: Fremdsprachen sind unwichtig.
            STUDENT B: Nein, sie sind wichtig.

1. 8:15 Uhr ist zu früh.
2. Dieses Buch ist langweilig.
3. Dieses Zimmer ist schön.
4. Wir kennen hier niemand.
5. Bernd haßt Rockmusik.
6. Du trägst oft Turnschuhe.
7. Sie sind immer müde.

For each sentence in the left column choose an appropriate response or responses from the right column.

1. Gehen wir noch einmal schwimmen!	Super!
	Du hast recht.
2. Das Wasser ist zu kalt!	Stimmt schon.
3. Ohne Frühstück geht's nicht.	Stimmt nicht.
4. Es gibt keine Hotelzimmer mehr.	Das finde ich auch.
5. Spielen wir zusammen Karten.	Gar nicht!
6. Das schaffst du leicht.	Es tut mir leid.
7. Bist du hungrig?	Was ist denn los?
8. Ein Hotelzimmer mit Frühstück kostet DM 250!	Um Gottes Willen!
	Nichts zu danken.
9. Du kommst wieder zu spät.	Mensch!
10. Mensch, bin ich müde.	Phantastisch!
	Doch!
	Prima!
	Gerne!

Now choose one of the exchanges above and expand it into a mini-dialogue. Prepare to say it for the whole class.

> BEISPIEL: A: Es gibt keine Hotelzimmer mehr.
> B: Um Gottes Willen! Was machen wir denn?
> A: Ich weiß nicht. Hoffentlich . . .

Lyrik zum Vorlesen

Viele deutsche Kinder lernen dieses traditionelle Gedicht (*poem*) über die Jahreszeiten.

Die Jahreszeiten°

Es war° eine Mutter,	*there was*
Die hatte° vier Kinder:	*who had*
Den Frühling, den Sommer,	
Den Herbst und den Winter.	
Der Frühling bringt Blumen,°	*flowers*
Der Sommer bringt Klee,°	*clover*
Der Herbst, der° bringt Trauben,°	*it / grapes*
Der Winter bringt Schnee.	

seasons (°Die Jahreszeiten)

Grammatik

Commands: The Imperative

The imperative form of German verbs is used either to make suggestions ("Let's go swimming") or to give commands ("Wait!").

"Let's do something": The *wir*-Imperative

Fahren wir nach Innsbruck.	**Let's go** to Innsbruck.
Spielen wir Karten.	**Let's play** cards.

The **wir**-imperative has the same word order as a yes/no question, but at the end of the sentence, the voice drops instead of rising. Compare the following intonation curves:

Gehen wir nach Hause?   Gehen wir nach Hause!

"Do something!": The *Sie*-Imperative

Fahren Sie nach Innsbruck!	*Go to Innsbruck!*
Bitte **besuchen Sie** mich im Mai!	*Please visit me in May!*

Use the **Sie**-imperative to tell someone you address as **Sie** what to do.

Flavoring Particles *doch* and *mal* with Commands

doch   why don't you . . .   You can soften a command to a suggestion by adding the unstressed flavoring particle **doch.**

Gehen Sie nach Hause!	*Go home!*
Gehen Sie **doch** nach Hause.	*Why don't you go home.*

mal   You can make a command more peremptory by adding the unstressed flavoring particle **mal.**

Warte!	*Wait!*
Warte **mal!**	*Wait a second!*
Hören Sie **mal!**	*Just listen here!*

1 **Übung:** Machen Sie das doch!

Encourage your instructor to do what he or she would like to do.

BEISPIEL: Ich möchte eine Reise machen.
　　　　　Machen Sie doch eine Reise!

1. Ich möchte morgen schwimmen.
2. Ich möchte meinen Wagen verkaufen.
3. Ich möchte nach Hause gehen.
4. Ich möchte Karten spielen.
5. Ich möchte Frau Klein besuchen.
6. Ich möchte eine Pause machen.

2 **Übung:** Nein, machen Sie das nicht!

Now tell your instructor *not* to do the things listed in *Übung 1*.

> BEISPIEL: Ich möchte nach Hause gehen.
> Nein, gehen Sie nicht nach Hause!

3 **Gruppenarbeit:** Ja, machen wir das!

Here are some activities you could do today. Take turns suggesting them to each other.

> BEISPIEL: schwimmen gehen
> STUDENT A: Gehen wir heute schwimmen!
> STUDENT B: Ja, machen wir das! *oder*
> Nein, lieber nicht.

jetzt frühstücken	eine Reise machen
Karten spielen	eine Pause machen
eine Zeitung kaufen	nach Hause laufen
zu Hause arbeiten	den Wagen verkaufen

Now suggest other things to do today.

Imperative Forms for *du* and *ihr*

To give commands or make suggestions to people whom you address with **du**, you need to learn the forms of the **du**- and **ihr**-imperatives.

The *du*-imperative The **du**-imperative of most verbs is simply the verb stem without ending.

Geh ohne mich.	*Go without me.*
Frag mich nicht.	*Don't ask me.*
Fahr schnell nach Hause!	*Drive home quickly!*
Sei nicht so langweilig.	*Don't be so boring.*

Note: The pronoun **du** is *not* used with the **du**-imperative!

If the verb changes its stem vowel from **e** to **i(e)**, the *changed* stem is used:

verb	*statement*	*du-imperative*
lesen	Du **liest** das für morgen.	**Lies** das für morgen.
geben	Du **gibst** Peter das Buch.	**Gib** Peter das Buch.
essen	Du **ißt** ein Brötchen.	**Iß** ein Brötchen.

Note that the stem-vowel change **a(u)** to **ä(u)** does *not* appear in the **du**-imperative:

fahren	Du **fährst** nach Hause.	**Fahr** nach Hause.
laufen	Du **läufst** zu schnell.	**Lauf** nicht so schnell!

Verb stems ending in **-d** or **-t** add an **-e** to the stem:

Arbeite nicht so viel.	*Don't work so hard.*
Warte doch!	*Wait!*

4 Übung: Ja, tu das doch!

Your instructor plays the part of your friend Beate. Tell her to go ahead and do the things she asks about.

BEISPIEL: Soll ich da drüben halten?
Ja, halte doch da drüben.

1. Soll ich das tun?
2. Soll ich mit Hans sprechen?
3. Soll ich Peter das Buch geben?
4. Soll ich schnell laufen?
5. Soll ich hier warten?

6. Soll ich Pommes frites essen?
7. Soll ich etwas singen?
8. Soll ich zu Fuß gehen?
9. Soll ich eine Zeitung lesen?
10. Soll ich eine Jacke tragen?

5 Übung: Nein, lieber nicht.

Now tell Beate *not* to do the things listed in *Übung 4.*

BEISPIEL: Soll ich drüben parken?
Nein, park nicht drüben.

Wie bitte? Was sollen wir essen?

The *ihr*-imperative The **ihr**-imperative is identical to the present-tense **ihr**-form, but without the pronoun.

Present tense:	Ihr **bleibt** hier.	*You're staying here.*
	Ihr **singt** zu laut.	*You sing too loudly.*
	Ihr **seid** freundlich.	*You are friendly.*

Imperative:	**Bleibt** hier.	*Stay here.*
	Singt nicht so laut.	*Don't sing so loudly.*
	Seid freundlich.	*Be friendly.*

6 Übung: Dürfen wir das machen?

A. Your instructor plays one of a group of children and asks you if they're allowed to do certain things.

BEISPIEL: Sollen wir bald nach Hause kommen?
Ja, kommt bald nach Hause.

1. Dürfen wir Karten spielen?
2. Dürfen wir das Buch lesen?

3. Sollen wir nach Hause laufen?
4. Sollen wir die Brötchen essen?

B. Now tell them what not to do.

BEISPIEL: Sollen wir nach Hause kommen?
Nein, kommt nicht nach Hause.

1. Sollen wir Jeans tragen?
2. Sollen wir heute kommen?

3. Sollen wir hier bleiben?
4. Sollen wir das sagen?

Imperative of *sein*

The verb **sein** is irregular in the **Sie**- and **wir**-imperatives (the **du**- and **ihr**-forms are regular):

Seien Sie bitte freundlich, Herr Kaiser.	*Please be friendly, Mr. Kaiser.*
Seien wir freundlich.	*Let's be friendly.*
Seid freundlich, Kinder.	*Be friendly, children.*
Sei freundlich, Rolf.	*Be friendly, Rolf.*

 7 Übung: Sei doch . . . !

A. Tell the following people to be honest.

BEISPIEL: Richard
Sei doch ehrlich, Richard!

1. Kinder
2. Herr Bachmann

3. wir
4. Barbara

B. Now tell them not to be so boring.

BEISPIEL: Herr Stolze
Seien Sie doch nicht so langweilig, Herr Stolze!

1. Ute
2. Frau Klein

3. Thomas und Beate
4. wir

The Verb *werden*

The verb **werden** *to become* is irregular in present tense **du**- and **er**-forms.

ich	werde	wir	werden
du	**wirst**	ihr	werdet
er, es, sie	**wird**	sie, Sie	werden

Werden is a frequently used verb. Its basic English equivalent is "to become, get." It can be translated in various ways, depending upon context.

Es **wird** kalt.	*It's getting cold.*
Ihre Kinder **werden** groß.	*Your children are getting big.*
Meine Schwester will Professorin **werden.**	*My sister wants to become a professor.*
Am Montag **werde** ich endlich 21.	*I'm finally turning 21 on Monday.*

8 Übung: Wer wird müde?

Say who is getting tired.

BEISPIEL: Barbara
Barbara wird müde.

1. wir
2. die Kinder
3. meine Mutter
4. ihr
5. du
6. ich

9 Übung: Wie sagt man das auf englisch?

1. Morgen wird es heiß.
2. Wann wirst du denn zwanzig?
3. Draußen wird es warm.
4. Das Buch wird endlich interessant.
5. Meine zwei Freunde wollen Lehrer werden.

Negating *müssen*

Ich brauche nicht zu . . .   *I don't need to . . .*

This is the most common way to say that you don't have to do something:

Mußt du heute arbeiten?   *Do you have to work today?*
Nein, heute brauche ich nicht zu   *No, today I don't have to work.*
arbeiten.

If you want to say that you don't *have* to do something, but you *choose* to or *want* to, then negate **müssen** in the following way.

Mußt du denn heute arbeiten?   *Do you **have** to work today?*
Nein, ich **muß** nicht arbeiten,   *No, I don't **have** to work, but I*
aber ich will.   *want to.*

10 Übung: Müssen Sie das machen?

Your instructor asks if you must do certain things, and you reply that you don't have to.

BEISPIEL: Müssen Sie bleiben?
Nein, ich brauche nicht zu bleiben.

1. Müssen Sie Deutsch lernen?
2. Müssen Sie nach Österreich fahren?
3. Müssen Sie Ihre Professorin fragen?
4. Müssen Sie eine Reise machen?
5. Müssen Sie zu Fuß gehen?
6. Müssen Sie ein Heft kaufen?
7. Müssen Sie lange warten?
8. Müssen Sie Ihren Mantel verkaufen?

11 Übung: Ich muß nicht, aber ich will.

Say you don't have to do the following, but you want to.

> BEISPIEL: *Müssen* Sie denn so ehrlich sein?
> Nein, ich *muß* nicht so ehrlich sein, aber ich *will* ehrlich sein.

1. Müssen Sie denn Karten spielen?
2. Müssen Sie denn nach Hause?
3. Müssen Sie denn im Winter schwimmen?
4. Müssen Sie denn so schnell sprechen?
5. Müssen Sie denn Suppe kochen?
6. Müssen Sie denn bis sieben arbeiten?

Negating *schon* and *noch*

There are two ways to negate **schon:**

positive	*negative*
schon	{ noch nicht { noch kein

Bist du **schon** hungrig? Nein, **noch nicht.**	*Are you hungry yet?* *No, not yet.*
Wollen Sie **schon** gehen? Nein, ich will **noch nicht** gehen.	*Do you want to leave already?* *No, I don't want to leave yet.*
Habt ihr **schon** Karten? Nein, wir haben **noch keine** Karten.	*Do you have tickets yet?* *No, we don't have any tickets yet.*

 12 Übung: Nein, noch nicht.

Answer the questions negatively, saying that things haven't happened yet.

1. Ist Rolf schon da?
2. Studiert sie schon in Berlin?
3. Ist es schon zu spät?
4. Soll ich schon entscheiden?
5. Verdienst du schon genug?
6. Kannst du schon beginnen?

 13 Übung

Say you don't have any of these things yet.

1. Haben Sie schon Kinder?
2. Haben Sie schon eine Karte?
3. Haben Sie schon ein Hotelzimmer?
4. Besitzen Sie schon einen Wagen?
5. Haben Sie schon Angst?
6. Besitzen Sie schon einen Computer?

Noch also has two different negations:

positive   *negative*

noch   { nicht mehr
              { kein- . . . mehr

Regnet es **noch?**   *Is it still raining?*
Nein, **nicht mehr.**   *No, not any more.*

Ich glaube, Rita studiert **noch.**   *I think Rita's still in college.*
Nein, sie studiert **nicht mehr.**   *No, she's no longer in college.*

Hast du **noch** Geld?   *Do you have any more money?*
Nein, ich habe **kein** Geld **mehr.**   *No, I have no more money.*

Können wir **noch** Karten   *Can we still get tickets?*
  bekommen?
Leider habe ich **keine** Karten   *Unfortunately I don't have any*
  mehr.   *more tickets.*

 14 Übung

Answer your instructor's questions negatively.

1. Ist Ihr Wagen noch neu?   4. Wohnen Sie noch zu Hause?

2. Geht Ihre Uhr noch?   5. Können Sie noch warten?

3. Können Sie uns noch besuchen?   6. Ist es draußen noch kalt?

  15 Übung

Answer your instructor's questions negatively.

1. Hat er noch Arbeit?   4. Ist er noch ein Kind?

2. Haben Sie noch Zeit?   5. Gibt es noch Probleme?

3. Hat Ihre Großmutter noch einen   6. Hören Sie noch Rockmusik?
   Wagen?

Prepositions with the Accusative Case

Prepositions are a class of words that show relationships of space (*through* the mountains), time (*until* Tuesday), or other relationships (*for* my friend, *without* any money). A preposition with the noun or pronoun that follows it is called a prepositional phrase. German prepositions are used with nouns in specific grammatical cases. Here is the list of prepositions that are always followed by the accusative case. Learn this list by heart.

bis	*until, by*	Wir warten **bis Dienstag.**
		Ich muß es **bis morgen** lesen.
durch	*through*	Er fährt **durch die Berge.**
für	*for*	Sie arbeitet **für ihren Vater.**
gegen	*against*	Was hast du **gegen mich?**
	around, about (with times)	Karl kommt **gegen drei.**

ohne	*without*	Wir gehen **ohne dich.**
um	*around* (the outside of)	Das Auto fährt **um das Hotel.**
	at (with times)	Karl kommt **um drei.**

16 **Übung:** Für wen?

Sie kaufen ein Buch. Für wen kaufen sie es?

Ich kaufe es für meine_____.

Sie machen heute das Frühstück. Für wen machen Sie es?

Ich mache es für mein-_____.

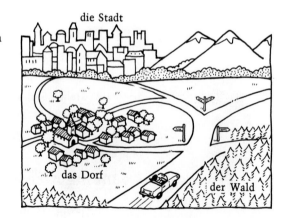

17 **Übung:** Ich mache das allein.

Your instructor asks if you do things with other people in your class. Say that you do everything without them. Use pronouns in your answer.

1. Spielen Sie mit Richard Karten? Nein, ohne _____.

2. Arbeiten Sie morgen mit Ingrid zusammen? Nein, leider ohne _____.

3. Gehen Sie mit Robert und Susan schwimmen?

4. Frühstücken Sie am Mittwoch mit mir?

18 **Übung:** Wohin fährt Monika?

Monika is going to drive through various locations. Tell where she's driving.

Sie fährt durch _____.

Dann fährt sie durch _____.

die Stadt

das Dorf

der Wald

19 **Übung:** *gegen* oder *um?*

BEISPIEL: Wann frühstücken wir denn? (6:57)
Wir essen gegen sieben.

1. Wann gehen wir denn schwimmen? (3:00)

2. Wann frühstücken Sie? (7:55)

3. Wann sehen wir unseren Professor? (1:00)

4. Wann besucht uns Tante Amalie? (8:00)

5. Wann machen wir denn eine Pause? (4:54)

Equivalents of English "like"

verb + *gern(e)*

Gern(e) plus a verb corresponds to English "to like to (do something)."

Ich **schwimme gern.**	*I like to swim.*
Sie **geht gern** zu Fuß.	*She likes to walk.*
Hören Sie **gerne** Musik?	*Do you like to listen to music?*

Gern(e) generally comes immediately after the subject and verb. The negation of **gern** is **nicht gern.**

Ich schwimme **nicht gern.**	*I don't like to swim.*

20 **Partnerarbeit:** Ich höre gern Musik.

Take turns saying what you like to eat (**essen**), read (**lesen**), play (**spielen**), and listen to (**hören**). Here are some suggestions.

BEISPIEL: Ich höre gern Rockmusik. Und du?

Jazz	Fußball	Frühstück
Pizza	Brötchen	Volksmusik
Mozart	Zeitungen	Bücher
Tennis	Tischtennis	Lyrik (*poetry*)

21 **Kettenreaktion:** Was machen Sie gern? Was machen Sie lieber?

STUDENTIN 1: Ich spiele gern Tennis.

STUDENT 2: Sie spielt gern Tennis, aber ich lese lieber Bücher.

STUDENT 3: Er liest gern Bücher, aber ich _____ lieber _____.
usw.

etwas mögen or *etwas gern haben*

There are two ways to say you like someone or something: **etwas mögen** or **etwas gern haben.**

Ich **habe** dich sehr **gern.** ⎱	*I like you very much.*
Ich **mag** dich sehr. ⎰	

Negation: Ich habe dich **nicht gern.**
Ich mag dich **nicht.**

Mögen is a modal verb. Its present-tense forms are

mögen *to like (something)*			
ich	**mag**	wir	mögen
du	**magst**	ihr	mögt
er, es, sie	**mag**	sie, Sie	mögen

Unlike the other modals, it is usually used without an infinitive.

Ich **mag** Maria.	*I like Maria.*
Mögen Sie die Suppe nicht?	*Don't you like the soup?*

Remember that the form **möchte** means "would like to (do something)" and *is* used with an infinitive.

Ich **möchte** Maria besuchen.   *I would like to visit Maria.*

 22 Übung

Tell who likes Frau Brandt. Use the appropriate form of **mögen**.

BEISPIEL: die Schüler
Die Schüler mögen Frau Brandt.

1. du
2. wir
3. Franz

4. meine Eltern
5. ich
6. ihr

23 Übung: Was haben Sie gern?

Say which things and people you like or dislike. Here are some ideas. Add some of your own. Use **gern haben** or **mögen**.

meine Mitbewohner

das Essen hier

den Winter

Hausaufgaben

die Uni

meine Arbeit

meine Geschwister

Fremdsprachen

Three German Equivalents for "like"

Distinguish carefully among the three German equivalents for English "like":

- **Möchte** means "would like to" do something and is used with a complementary infinitive (which may sometimes be omitted, see pp. 77–78):

    Ich **möchte** Innsbruck besuchen.
    Ich **möchte** nach Innsbruck (fahren).

- A verb + **gern** means "to like to" do something.

    Ich spiele **gern** Karten.

Möchte expresses a wish for something, while a verb + **gern** makes a general statement about your likes or dislikes:

Ich **möchte** Karten spielen.	*I would like to play cards.*
Ich spiele **gern** Karten.	*I like to play cards.*

- **Mögen** or **gern haben** means "to like" people or things and is used with a noun or pronoun:

    Ich **mag** Professor Jäger.
    Ich **habe** ihn **gern**.

24 **Übung:** Wie sagt man das auf deutsch?

1. I like the soup.
2. I like to eat soup.
3. I would like the soup.
4. They would like to study in Germany.
5. Karl doesn't like to wait.

6. Do you like Professor Lange?
7. Our children like to play outside.
8. We would like to drive home.
9. I don't like that.
10. I like her.

Sentence Adverbs

Sentence adverbs modify entire sentences and express the speaker's attitude toward the content of the whole:

Natürlich bin ich morgens müde.   *Of course I'm tired in the morning.*

Du hast **sicher** genug Geld.   *You surely have enough money.*
Leider habe ich keine Zeit mehr.   *Unfortunately I have no more time.*

Learn these important German sentence adverbs:

Gott sei Dank	*thank goodness*
hoffentlich	*"I (or) Let's hope that . . ."*
leider	*unfortunately*
natürlich	*naturally, of course*
selbstverständlich	*"It goes without saying that . . . ," of course*
sicher	*certainly, surely*
übrigens	*by the way, incidentally*

Note on punctuation: When sentence adverbs come at the beginning of a sentence, they are not followed by a comma, as they are in English:

Übrigens studiert sie noch.   *Incidentally, she's still a student.*

 25 **Übung:** Selbstverständlich!

Your instructor will ask you a question. Show that your answer is obvious by beginning it with **Selbstverständlich** . . . or **Natürlich** . . .

BEISPIEL: Lernen Sie Deutsch?
     Selbstverständlich lerne ich Deutsch!

1. Frühstücken Sie?
2. Sind Sie hungrig?
3. Haben Sie Zeit für mich?
4. Möchten Sie nach Österreich?
5. Schwimmen Sie gern?
6. Spielen Sie gern Karten?

26 Übung: Leider!

Your instructor will ask you a question. Show that you regret having to answer "yes" by beginning your answer with **Ja, leider . . .**

> BEISPIEL: Regnet es noch?
> Ja, leider regnet es noch.

1. Schneit es noch?
2. Haben Sie ein Problem?
3. Sind Sie sehr müde?

4. Ist der Berg sehr steil?
5. Gehen Sie ohne mich?
6. Ist das Wasser zu kalt?

27 Übung: Gott sei Dank!

Now indicate your relief at being able to answer the same questions negatively by beginning your answer with **Nein, Gott sei Dank . . .**

> BEISPIEL: Regnet es noch?
> Nein, Gott sei Dank regnet es nicht mehr.

gehen + infinitive

The verb **gehen** is often used with an infinitive as its complement.

> Sie **geht** oft **schwimmen.**   *She often goes swimming.*
> Ich **gehe** jetzt **schlafen.**   *I'm going to bed now.*

The complementary infinitive (**schwimmen** and **schlafen** in the examples) is the second part of the predicate and comes at the end of the sentence.

> **Gehen** wir noch einmal   *Let's go swimming again!*
>   **schwimmen!**
> Ich **gehe** mit Dieter **schwimmen.**   *I'm going swimming with Dieter.*

Note what happens when the entire verbal idea **schwimmen gehen** (to go swimming) is used as the complement of a modal verb:

> Wir wollen heute **schwimmen**   *We want to go swimming today.*
>   **gehen.**

28 Partnerarbeit: Dann geh doch . . . !

Partner 1 reads the sentences on the left. Partner 2 then tells partner 1 what to do, choosing an appropriate activity from the right-hand column.

> BEISPIEL: Ich bin müde.
> Dann geh doch schlafen!

1. Ich muß Geld verdienen.

2. Ich bin hungrig.

3. Ich möchte gern fit bleiben.

4. Ich bin müde!

arbeiten gehen

schlafen gehen

essen gehen

Tennis spielen gehen

Tips zum Lesen und Lernen

Tips zum Vokabelnlernen

■ Note that the four compass points are all masculine:

der Norden	der Osten
der Süden	der Westen

Remember that the days, seasons, and the months are also masculine:

der Montag	der Januar
der Dienstag	der Februar
der Mittwoch	der März
der Donnerstag	der April
der Freitag	der Mai
der Samstag (oder Sonnabend)	der Juni
der Sonntag	der Juli
	der August
der Frühling	der September
der Sommer	der Oktober
der Herbst	der November
der Winter	der Dezember

■ The prefix **Haupt-** is attached to nouns and adds the meaning *main, chief, primary, principal, most important.*

die **Haupt**regionen	*the principal regions*
die **Haupt**frage	*the main question*
die **Haupt**stadt	*the capital city*
die **Haupt**rolle	*the leading role*
die **Haupt**straße	*the main street*

Leicht zu merken

die **Alpen**	
barbarisch	
die **Geographie**	*Geographie*
geographisch	
die **Kolonie, -n**	*Kolonie*
der **Kontrast, -e**	*Kontrast*
die **Kultur, -en**	*Kultur*
mild	
die **Region**	*Region*
der **Rhein**	
wild	
zirka	

Einstieg in den Text

The reading in this chapter builds on familiar vocabulary about the weather (**das Wetter**) and discusses climate and geography (**Klima und Geographie**).

Study this map and try to guess the meanings of the new words.

Wortschatz 2

Verben

beschreiben to describe
fließen to flow
liegen to lie; be situated
trinken to drink
wandern to hike; wander

Substantive

der **Baum, ⸚e** tree
der **Fluß, Flüsse** river
der **Frühling** spring
der **Herbst** fall, autumn
der **Hügel, -** hill
der **Norden** the North
der **Osten** the East
der **Schnee** snow
der **Sommer** summer
der **Süden** the South
der **Wald, ⸚er** forest
der **Wein, -e** wine
der **Westen** the West

das **Bier, -e** beer
(das) **Italien** Italy
das **Klima** climate
das **Land, ⸚er** country
das **Leben** life
das **Lied, -er** song
   das **Volkslied, -er** folk
   song
das **Märchen, -** fairy tale
das **Meer, -e** sea
das **Tal, ⸚er** valley

die **Landschaft, -en**
   landscape
die **Schweiz** Switzerland
die **Stadt, ⸚e** city

Adjektive und Adverbien

flach flat
hoch high
immer noch / noch immer
   still (*intensification of*
   noch)

modern modern
naß wet, damp
schrecklich terrible
sonnig sunny
trocken dry

Andere Vokabeln

von from

Nützliche Ausdrücke

im Süden (im Norden, usw.)
   in the South (in the North,
   etc.)
im Winter (im Sommer, usw.)
   in the winter (in the
   summer, etc.)
Gott sei Dank! Thank
   goodness!

Gegensätze

naß ≠ trocken wet ≠ dry
modern ≠ altmodisch
   modern ≠ old-fashioned

Deutschland: Geographie und Klima

Für die alten Römer° war° das Leben in der Kolonie Germania nicht sehr schön. Der Historiker° Tacitus (zirka 55 bis 115 n.Chr.°) beschreibt das Land als° kalt und neblig.° Über die Germanen° schreibt er: „Sie sind ohne Kultur, haben keine Städte und leben im Wald. Sie sind wild und barbarisch, wie ihr Land."

Das moderne Deutschland liegt in Mitteleuropa, und die „wilden Germanen" wohnen heute zum größten Teil° in der Stadt. Es gibt keinen Urwald° mehr, aber der Wald ist immer noch typisch und wichtig für die Landschaft in Deutschland, Österreich und der Schweiz. Am Sonntag wandert man gern durch die Wälder, und die Kinder hören auch heute noch gern Märchen wie „Hänsel und Gretel" oder „Schneewittchen." In solchen° Märchen und auch in deutschen Volksliedern spielt der Wald eine große Rolle.

Auch das Klima in Deutschland ist Gott sei Dank nicht so schrecklich, wie° Tacitus meint. Selbstverständlich ist es nicht so warm und sonnig wie in Italien, aber das deutsche Klima ist eigentlich ziemlich mild. In den Flußtälern wird

Romans / was
historian
nach Christus = *A.D.* / *as*
foggy / *Germanic peoples*

zum . . . Teil = *for the most part*
primeval forest

such

so . . . wie = *as . . . as*

Familienwanderung im Regen.

es zum Beispiel im Winter nicht sehr kalt. Die großen
20 Flüsse—der Rhein, die Weser, die Elbe und die Oder—fließen durch das Land von Süden nach Norden. Nur die Donau[2]
fließt von Westen nach Osten. Am° Rhein und an der° Donau   **am** *and* **an der** = *on the*
trinkt man gern Wein; die Römer brachten° den Weinbau°   brought / viniculture
25 nach Deutschland. Die Deutschen trinken also nicht nur
Bier.

Es gibt in Deutschland drei geographische Hauptregionen. Im Norden ist das Land flach und fruchtbar und
ohne viele Bäume. Hier beeinflußt° das Meer—die Nordsee   *influences*
30 und die Ostsee—Landschaft und Klima. Diese° Region   *this*
nennt man das Tiefland.° In der Mitte des Landes aber gibt   *lowland*
es viele Hügel und kleine Berge. Man nennt diese Region
das Mittelgebirge.° Im Süden liegt das Hochgebirge°—die   *central mountains / high mountains*
Alpen. Hier gibt es natürlich viel Schnee im Winter, denn°   *because*
35 die Berge sind sehr hoch. Deutschlands höchster° Berg ist   *highest*
die Zugspitze (2 963 m). Man sieht also, in Deutschland gibt
es viele Kontraste: Wald und Feld,° Stadt und Land, Berge   *field*
und Meer.

**Burgruine [*castle ruin*] Ehrenfels am
Rhein.**

Fragen zum Lesestück

1. Wie beschreibt Tacitus die Kolonie Germania?
2. Was ist noch immer typisch für die Landschaft in
   Deutschland?
3. Was macht man gern am Sonntag?
4. Was spielt eine große Rolle in „Hänsel und Gretel"?
   Kennen Sie andere Märchen?
5. Wie ist das Klima in Deutschland?
6. Ist es so warm und sonnig wie in Italien?
7. Wo trinkt man viel Wein?
8. Wie ist das Land im Norden?
9. Wo gibt es viel Schnee im Winter?
10. Wie heißen die drei geographischen Hauptregionen?

2. See the map on the inside of the front cover.

Situationen aus dem Alltag

Klima, Wetter und Landschaft

You already know some of these words from the introductory chapter (see pp. 12–14).

Klima und Wetter

die **Luft** *air*
der **Regen** *rain*
  regnerisch *rainy*
  Es regnet.
der **Schnee**
  Es schneit.
der **Wind** *wind*
  Es ist windig.
wolkig
neblig
sonnig *sunny*
windig *windy*
kalt ≠ **heiß**
warm ≠ **kühl**
naß ≠ **trocken**
mild

Landschaft

der **Baum, ⸚e**
der **Berg, -e**
  bergig *mountainous*
der **Wald, ⸚er**
das **Meer, -e**

der **Hügel, -**
hügelig *hilly*
das **Tal, ⸚er**

Gruppenarbeit: Sprechen wir über Klima und Landschaft

Beschreiben wir die Landschaft in diesen Fotos.

1.

2.

3.

Partnerarbeit: Landschaft und Klima, wo ich wohne.

Find out where your partner comes from and ask about the climate and geography there.

BEISPIEL: Woher kommst du denn?
         Wie ist das Klima dort im Sommer?
         Kannst du die Landschaft beschreiben?

Zum Schluß

Sprechen wir miteinander!

A Partnerarbeit: Sei doch (nicht) . . . !

Suggest some self-improvement to your partner. Take turns telling each other how you should be (or not be).

> BEISPIEL: Sei doch ehrlich!
> Sei doch nicht sauer!

guter Laune	sauer	höflich
schlechter Laune	munter	fit
glücklich	freundlich	ehrlich

B Partnerarbeit: Nein, das darfst du nicht!

Ask your partner for permission to do something. Your partner tells you to do something else. The list will help you get started. Then try inventing some of your own exchanges.

> BEISPIEL: zu Hause bleiben?   draußen spielen
> STUDENT A: Darf ich zu Hause bleiben?
> STUDENT B: Nein, spiel doch draußen!

nach Hause fahren?	zu Fuß gehen
jetzt Pizza essen?	bis heute abend warten
Tennis spielen?	deine Hausaufgaben machen

C Partnerarbeit: Macht das bitte für uns!

Machen Sie zusammen eine Liste: Was können andere Studenten für Sie machen? Seien Sie kreativ!

> BEISPIEL: Sie können für uns . . .
> die Bücher tragen
> die Hausaufgaben schreiben   usw.

Sie und Ihr Partner sagen jetzt zwei anderen Studenten, sie sollen etwas für Sie machen. Die anderen antworten „ja" oder „nein".

> BEISPIEL: Jennifer und Brian, tragt bitte die Bücher für uns.
> Ja, O.K., das machen wir gern für euch. *oder*
> Nein, das brauchen wir nicht zu machen.

D Gruppenarbeit

Say what you like and don't like about university life. Also say what you like and don't like to do. Your instructor will write your responses on the board.

> BEISPIEL: Ich mag meine Mitbewohnerin sehr.
> Ich habe das Essen nicht sehr gern.

E Gruppenarbeit: Was wollen wir denn machen?

Planen wir einen Urlaub. Lesen wir zusammen diese Anzeigen für Ferienorte. Hier gibt es sehr viel zu tun! Was machen Sie gerne? Was machen Sie lieber? Wollen wir schwimmen oder wandern gehen?

Die
Landschaft
für Aktivurlaub
und
echte Erholung

Wandern, Tennis, Reiten, Wintersport, heilklimatischer Jahreskurort, Luftkurort, Kur- und Höhenbäder, beheiztes Freibad, Schwarzwälder Gastlichkeit, sonnige Höhenlage.

Natur erleben
Kanu + Wandern
Ausgerüstete Touren in
Skandinavien u. Grönland
Auch für Unerfahrene.
Informationen bei
SUN-TEAM, 2 HH 76
Lachnerstr. 1/1
Tel. 040/279 88 88

Schreiben Sie zu Hause

F Phantasiefrage   You are the Roman historian Tacitus. You have returned to contemporary Germany to update your impressions. Write in German about the country. What do people still (**noch**) do or no longer (**nicht mehr**) do? What plays a role in modern life? How are things nowadays, such as the cities, the wine, etc.?

G Write sentences using the elements below. You may have to add words.

1. wer / wollen / wandern / durch / Berge?

2. er / möchten / fahren / ohne / sein / Freund

3. leider / wir / haben / kein / mehr / Brötchen (*pl.*)

4. du / können / vier Uhr / gehen / schwimmen

5. wir / gehen / zusammen / zu Fuß / durch / Tal

6. im Winter / ich / haben / gern / Berge

H Wie sagt man das auf deutsch?

1. The sun is shining and the water is warm. Let's go swimming.

2. I don't want to go swimming yet. Go without me.

3. But I don't like to swim alone.

4. Do you like the winter, Rolf?

5. No, I don't like it any more.

6. I don't like to walk through the snow.

7. Wait here, Eva and Andrea.

8. We don't need to wait.

9. I hope that you still have money.

10. Unfortunately, I don't have any more money.

11. Can you do something for me?

12. Unfortunately, I have to go home now.

The Common Origin of German and English

Although Tacitus thought the Germanic tribes had "always been there," they in fact originated in the Baltic region around the second millenium B.C. As the Roman Empire began to collapse in the fourth century A.D., the Germanic peoples migrated south, a movement that continued for nearly two hundred years. The **Germani** (as they were called by the Romans) displaced the Celts from the heart of the European continent, pushing them as far west as Ireland. The Romans temporarily halted Germanic expansion southwards by establishing their own northern frontier, a series of fortifications called the **limes,** literally the "limits" or boundaries of their empire. Remains of the **limes** can be seen in Germany today. Contemporary dialects and regional differences within the German-speaking countries have their origins in the various Germanic tribes of the early Middle Ages.

Thanks to the migration of the Germanic Angles and Saxons to the British Isles in the fifth century A.D., the Germanic language that was to evolve into modern English was introduced there. German and English thus share common origins. Some other languages included in the Germanic family are Yiddish, Dutch, Flemish, Norwegian, Swedish, Danish, and Icelandic. You will easily recognize cognates (words that have the same etymological root) in English and German, although different meanings may have developed. These words can be readily identified by some regularly occurring consonant shifts. Try guessing the English equivalents for the following words:

German	English	Related Words
z	t	zehn = ten
		Herz =
ss	t	Wasser =
		groß =
pf	p	Pflanze =
		Pflug = plough
ff	p or pp	Schiff =
		Pfeffer und Salz =
ch	k	machen =
		Milch =
t	d	Tag =
		Tür =
d	th	du =
		drei =

Zusammenfassung und Wiederholung

Summary and Review (Kapitel 1–4)

This section is always set off by blue page edges and follows every fourth chapter of *Neue Horizonte*. In it you will find a review of the structures and functions of the preceding chapters. These are not detailed grammar explanations, but rather tables and summaries of structures you have already learned. In the page margins are cross references to the more complete explanations in the *Grammatik* sections of the preceding chapters. Although this section emphasizes form and structure rather than spoken communication, each *Zusammenfassung und Wiederholung* also reviews the useful colloquial expressions and slang words and phrases from the four preceding chapters.

This section can be used both for current review and for future reference. To use the following *Zusammenfassung und Wiederholung* most effectively for review of Chapters 1–4, first look at pp. 119–27 to recall and summarize what you have learned. Then test your understanding with the "Test Your Progress" quiz. Answers are provided in Appendix 1 at the back of the book. If you need to review a specific grammar topic, refer to the page number noted in the margin.

FORMS

1. Verbs

A. Infinitive: ends in **-en** or **-n**

komm**en**	*to come*
tu**n**	*to do*
arbeit**en**	*to work*
heiß**en**	*to be called*

B. Stem: infinitive minus **-en** or **-n**

p. 27

komm-
tu-
arbeit-
heiß-

C. Present tense: *stem + personal endings*

1. Basic paradigms

p. 27

ich	komme	wir	kommen
du	kommst	ihr	kommt
er, es, sie	kommt	sie, Sie	kommen

ich	tue	wir	tun
du	tust	ihr	tut
er, es, sie	tut	sie, Sie	tun

Stems Ending in **-t** or **-d**

p. 28

ich	arbeite	wir	arbeiten
du	arbeit**est**	ihr	arbeit**et**
er, es, sie	arbeit**et**	sie, Sie	arbeiten

Stems Ending in **-s**, **-ß**, or **-z**

p. 52

ich	heiße	wir	heißen
du	heiß**t**	ihr	heißt
er, es, sie	heißt	sie, Sie	heißen

2. Stem-vowel change: only in **du**- and **er**-forms

pp. 52, 73

	sehen e → ie	**sprechen** e → i	**tragen** a → ä	**laufen** au → äu
ich	sehe	spreche	trage	laufe
du	**siehst**	**sprichst**	**trägst**	**läufst**
er, es, sie	**sieht**	**spricht**	**trägt**	**läuft**

similarly:

lesen (**liest**) besprechen (**bespricht**) fahren (**fährt**)
essen (**ißt**) halten (**hält**)
geben (**gibt**) schlafen (**schläft**)
nehmen (**nimmt**)

p. 73

3. Verbs with irregular present tense

sein *to be*

p. 29

ich	**bin**	wir	**sind**
du	**bist**	ihr	**seid**
er, es, sie	**ist**	sie, Sie	**sind**

	haben *to have*		p. 54

ich	**habe**	wir	**haben**
du	**hast**	ihr	**habt**
er, es, sie	**hat**	sie, Sie	**haben**

	werden *to become*		p. 102

ich	**werde**	wir	**werden**
du	**wirst**	ihr	**werdet**
er, es, sie	**wird**	sie, Sie	**werden**

	wissen *to know (facts)*		p. 54

ich	**weiß**	wir	**wissen**
du	**weißt**	ihr	**wißt**
er, es, sie	**weiß**	sie, Sie	**wissen**

4. Modal verbs

(a) Conjugation: changed stem in singular, no ending for **ich**- and **er**-forms

	dürfen *to be allowed to, may*		p. 75

ich	**darf**	wir	**dürfen**
du	**darfst**	ihr	**dürft**
er, es, sie	**darf**	sie, Sie	**dürfen**

similarly:

können (ich **kann**)	*to be able to, can*	p. 76
mögen (ich **mag**)	*to like*	
müssen (ich **muß**)	*to have to, must*	
sollen (ich **soll**)	*to be supposed to, should*	
wollen (ich **will**)	*to want to*	

Mögen occurs most often in the following form:

	ich möchte *I would like to*		p. 76

ich	**möchte**	wir	**möchten**
du	**möchtest**	ihr	**möchtet**
er, es, sie	**möchte**	sie, Sie	**möchten**

(b) modal verb + infinitive   pp. 75, 77

The complementary infinitive comes at the end of the sentence or clause.

Modal	**Infinitive**
Ich **darf** heute abend nicht	**mitkommen.**
Willst du denn gar nichts	**trinken?**
Robert **möchte** Lehrer	**werden.**

(c) Infinitive omitted (implicit **fahren, gehen, haben, machen, tun**)   pp. 77–78

Modal	
Ich **muß**	in die Schule.
Dürfen	wir denn das?
Hannah **möchte**	ein Bier.

The infinitive is also omitted in the idiom

Ich **kann** Deutsch.

2. Noun Phrases: article or possessive adjective + noun

A. *Definite article* (**der, das, die**) + *noun*   pp. 31, 37, 49

		Singular		**Plural**
masculine	*nom.*	**der** Mann		
	acc.	**den** Mann		
neuter	*nom.*	**das** Kind	*nom.*	**die** Männer, Kinder, Frauen
	acc.		*acc.*	
feminine	*nom.*	**die** Frau		
	acc.			

B. **Ein**-words (Indefinite Article and Possessive Adjectives)   pp. 32, 49, 55

	ein	*a, an* (unstressed); *one* (stressed)
	kein	*not a, no*
	mein	*my*
	dein	*your*
	sein	*his* (*its*)
possessive	**sein**	*its*
adjectives	**ihr**	*her* (*its*)
	unser	*our*
	euer	*your*
	ihr (Ihr)	*their* (*your*)

C. **Ein**-word + *noun*

		Singular		Plural
masculine	nom. acc.	**kein** Mann **keinen** Mann		
neuter	nom. acc.	**kein** Kind	nom. acc.	**keine** Männer, Kinder, Frauen
feminine	nom. acc.	**keine** Frau		

3. Pronouns

A. Personal pronouns: replace nouns

pp. 26, 51

	Singular		Plural	
	nom.	*acc.*	*nom.*	*acc.*
1st person	ich	mich	wir	uns
2nd person familiar	du	dich	ihr	euch
2nd person formal	Sie	Sie	Sie	Sie
3rd person *masculine*	er	ihn		
neuter	es	es	sie	sie
feminine	sie	sie		

B. Indefinite pronoun **man**: refers to people in general

p. 83

man = *one, they, people, we*

The indefinite pronoun **man** can only be the *subject* of a sentence and is always used with a verb in the 3rd person singular.

In Deutschland wandert man   *In Germany they (people) like to go hiking*
gern am Sonntag.   *on Sunday.*

4. Prepositions with accusative case

pp. 105–6

bis	*until, by*
durch	*through*
für	*for*
gegen	*against; around, about* (with times)
ohne	*without*
um	*around* (the outside of); *at* (with time)

FUNCTIONS

1. Making statements

Declarative sentences: verb in second position   p. 33

Heute abend	**kommt**	Richard.
Seit April	**wohnt**	sie bei ihrer Tante.
Die Studenten	**haben**	keine Zeit.
Ich	**kann**	meine Schuhe nicht finden.

2. Asking questions

A. Yes/no questions: verb first   p. 34

Kommt	er?
Wohnen	Sie in Berlin?
Müßt	ihr gehen?

B. Information questions: question word first

Was	trinkst du gern?
Warum	sagen Sie das?
Für wen	arbeiten Sie denn?
Woher	kommst du?
Wohin	fährst du im Sommer?
Wessen	Pulli ist das?

Other question words: **wann, wie, wo, wer, wen, wie lange**

3. Giving commands and suggestions

A. **wir**-Imperative: suggestion—"Let's do something"   p. 99

Sprechen wir über unsere Probleme.
Gehen wir nach Hause.

B. **Sie**-Imperative   p. 99

Warten Sie noch ein bißchen.
Lesen Sie das Buch.

C. **ihr**-Imperative   p. 101

Wartet noch ein bißchen.
Lest das Buch.

D. **du**-Imperative   p. 100

1. Basic form: verb stem

   Komm doch um neun.
   Frag mich nicht.
   Lauf schnell, Konrad!

2. Verbs with stem-vowel change **e → i(e)**

   Lies das Buch. (**lesen**)
   Sprich bitte nicht so schnell. (**sprechen**)

3. Verbs with stems ending in **-t** or **-d**: stem + **e**

   Arbeite nicht so viel.
   Warte noch ein bißchen.

E. Imperative of **sein**   p. 102

   Seien wir doch freundlich!
   Seien Sie doch freundlich, Herr Schmidt!
   Seid doch freundlich, Kinder!
   Sei doch freundlich, Anna!

4. Negating   pp. 80–81

A. **kein**

   1. **kein** negates **ein** + noun

      Hast du **einen Bruder?**
      Nein, ich habe **keinen Bruder.**

   2. **kein** negates nouns without articles

      Braucht sie **Geld?**
      Nein, sie braucht **kein Geld.**

B. **nicht**   pp. 78–79

   1. **nicht** follows:

      a. the subject and the inflected verb

         Ich esse.
         Ich esse **nicht.**

      b. the direct object

         Sie liest das Buch.
         Sie liest das Buch **nicht.**

      c. expressions of definite time

         Sie kommen morgen.
         Sie kommen morgen **nicht.**

   2. **nicht** precedes verbal complements (the second part of the predicate)   p. 79

      a. adverbs

         Der Lehrer spricht schnell.
         Der Lehrer spricht **nicht** schnell.

      b. predicate adjectives

         Der Wald ist dunkel.
         Der Wald ist **nicht** dunkel.

      c. predicate nominatives

         Er ist der Chef.
         Er ist **nicht** der Chef.

d. prepositional phrases showing destination or location

Sie fliegt nach Wien.
Sie fliegt **nicht** nach Wien.

e. infinitives complementing verbs

Du sollst es kaufen.
Du sollst es **nicht** kaufen.

C. Negating **schon** and **noch** pp. 104–5

1. **schon** ≠ $\begin{cases} \textbf{noch nicht} \\ \textbf{noch kein-} \end{cases}$

Ist Peter **schon** hier? Nein, er ist **noch nicht** hier.
Habt ihr **schon** Kinder? Nein, wir haben **noch keine** Kinder.

2. **noch** ≠ $\begin{cases} \textbf{nicht mehr} \\ \textbf{kein- . . . mehr} \end{cases}$

Wohnt Ute **noch** hier? Nein, Ute wohnt **nicht mehr** hier.
Hast du **noch** Angst? Nein, ich habe **keine** Angst **mehr.**

5. Specifying time and place

Word order of adverbs: TIME before PLACE (*reverse of English*) p. 35

Dr. Bachmann fliegt morgen nach Europa.   *Dr. Bachmann is flying to Europe tomorrow.*

Bleiben wir am Mittwoch zu Hause.   *Let's stay home on Wednesday.*

6. Translating English "like"

A. *to like something or someone:* **mögen** or **gern haben** pp. 107–8

Ich **mag** dich sehr.
Ich **hab'** dich sehr **gern.** } *I like you a lot.*

Die Farbe **mag** ich nicht.
Die Farbe **habe** ich nicht **gern.** } *I don't like the color.*

B. *to like to do something:* verb + **gern(e)**

Ich **schwimme gern.**   *I like to swim.*
Machen Sie das **gerne?**   *Do you like to do that?*

C. *would like to:* **möchte** + infinitive

Ich **möchte** etwas **sagen.**   *I would like to say something.*
Möchten Sie eine Zeitung **kaufen?**   *Would you like to buy a newspaper?*

USEFUL IDIOMS AND EXPRESSIONS

1. **Personal questions, feelings, and emotions**

Bist du heute müde / guter Laune / schlechter Laune / munter / sauer / glücklich?
Woher kommst du?
Wo wohnst du denn?

Wann hast du Geburtstag?
Wie alt bist du?
Was ist los?

2. **Greeting and parting**

Guten Morgen!	Wie geht's?	Tschüs!
Guten Tag!	Gute Reise!	Auf Wiedersehen!
Guten Abend!	Wie geht es Ihnen (dir)?	Bis dann. Bis nachher. Bis Montag.
Hallo!	Schönes Wochenende!	

3. **Polite expressions**

Danke!   Entschuldigung!   Nichts zu danken!
Vielen Dank!   Bitte!

4. **Reactions and opinions**

Gott sei Dank!   Das mache ich gern.
Phantastisch! / Toll! / Super!   Das spielt keine Rolle.
Hoffentlich!   Das freut mich.
Um Gottes Willen!   Das tut mir leid.
Mensch!   Lieber nicht.
Das geht. ≠ Das geht nicht.
Du hast recht. / Stimmt schon. / Das finde ich auch.

5. **Time and place**

Bist du heute (morgen) zu Hause?   Im Norden ist es im Sommer kühl.
Fährst du bald nach Hause?   Wie spät ist es? Es ist halb neun.

6. **Colloquialisms**

wunderschön   phantastisch   steinalt
prima   stinklangweilig   blitzschnell
super   todmüde

TEST YOUR PROGRESS

You will find an answer key on page 503.

A. Provide the verb form to agree with the German subject. Then give the English infinitive.

1. scheinen: es _____   to _____

2. spielen: die Kinder _____   to _____

3. gehen: ihr _____   to _____

4. bedeuten: es _____   to _____

5. meinen: ich _____   to _____

6. laufen: er _____   to _____

7. stimmen: es _____   to _____

8. schlafen: du _____   to _____

9. fahren: wir _____ to _____

10. besuchen: ihr _____ to _____

11. wollen: sie (*sing.*) _____ to _____

12. dürfen: ich _____ to _____

13. werden: du _____ to _____

14. schneien: es _____ to _____

15. bekommen: Sie _____ to _____

16. lesen: du _____ to _____

17. tragen: ihr _____ to _____

18. können: er _____ to _____

19. warten: ich _____ to _____

20. sollen: er _____ to _____

B. Rewrite each sentence with the new subject provided.

1. Ich möchte schon nach Berlin. (Barbara)

2. Ich will noch ein bißchen bleiben. (die Studenten)

3. Was tragen die Kinder am Freitag? (du)

4. Nehmen Sie ein Brötchen? (Karin)

5. Lesen alle Menschen die Zeitung? (du)

6. Schlaft ihr bis neun? (er)

7. Wißt ihr, wie er heißt? (Gisela)

8. Warten wir bis zehn? (er)

9. Essen wir Pommes frites? (Oliver)

10. Wir laufen durch den Wald. (Horst)

C. Give the definite article and plural forms of the following nouns.

BEISPIEL: _____ Buch / die _____
das Buch / die Bücher

1. _____ Schule / die _____

2. _____ Hemd / die _____

3. _____ Mutter / die _____

4. _____ Schuh / die _____

5. _____ Sprache / die _____

6. _____ Freund / die _____

7. _____ Freundin / die _____

8. _____ Bruder / die _____

9. _____ Schwester / die _____

10. _____ Klischee / die _____

11. _____ Sohn / die _____

12. _____ Tochter / die _____

13. _____ Haus / die _____

14. _____ Zeitung / die _____

15. _____ Beruf / die _____

16. _____ Land / die _____

17. _____ Stuhl / die _____

18. _____ Frau / die _____

19. _____ Lehrer / die _____

20. _____ Lehrerin / die _____

D. Answer the following questions negatively.

1. Bist du schon müde?
2. Wohnt ihr noch zu Hause?
3. Ist sie noch Studentin?
4. Kennst du schon meine Schwester?
5. Habt ihr schon Kinder?
6. Schreibst du noch Briefe?
7. Muß ich immer noch hier bleiben?
8. Haben Sie noch Angst?

E. Fill in the blank with the correct article or correct ending. Some blanks may need to be left empty.

1. Mein _____ Freunde haben morgen kein _____ Zeit.
2. Für _____ Fernseher habe ich im Moment kein _____ Geld.
3. Ihr _____ Sohn habe ich sehr gern.
4. Hoffentlich hast du nichts gegen mein _____ Bruder.
5. Kaufst du etwas für unser _____ Essen morgen?
6. Leider muß ich ohne mein _____ Freunde gehen.
7. _____ Studenten müssen zu Fuß gehen.
8. Ich kenne Ihr _____ Familie nicht.
9. Mein _____ Vater und mein _____ Mutter sind jetzt zu Hause.
10. _____ Klima ist oft sehr kalt, aber das spielt kein _____ Rolle.

F. Fill in the blanks with the correct pronouns or possessive adjectives.

1. Das ist nicht _____ Buch. (her)
2. Kennst du _____ gut? (her)
3. Geht _____ jetzt nach Hause? (you)
4. Ich möchte _____ Freunde besuchen. (his)
5. Das kann nicht _____ Vater sein. (her)
6. _____ Vater kenne ich leider noch nicht. (her)
7. Kinder, ich kann _____ sehen. (you)
8. Sind das _____ Kinder, Frau Overholzer? (your)
9. Ist _____ Freund Amerikaner, Frau König? (your)
10. Ich will _____ morgen sehen. (them)

G. Wie sagt man das auf deutsch?

1. I like you a lot.
2. Don't you like my friends?
3. I'd like to be alone.
4. I like to be alone.
5. Would you like to go swimming?
6. I like to hike.
7. I do not like the climate.

Arbeit und Freizeit

Communicative Goals
- Talking about work and professions
- Learning how to show, give, and tell things to people
- Asking about prices in shops
- Saying when and for how long things happen

Cultural Goal
- Understanding some differences and similarities between the world of work in Germany and America

Lyrik zum Vorlesen   Richard Dehmel, „Der Arbeitsmann"

Grammatik   Verbs with Separable Prefixes • Verbs with Inseparable Prefixes • Dative Case • Dative Personal Pronouns • Word Order of Noun and Pronoun Objects • Prepositions with Dative Case • Time Phrases in Accusative Case • Omission of Indefinite Article with Professions and Nationalities

Lesestück   Drei Deutsche bei der Arbeit

Situationen aus dem Alltag   Berufe

Almanach   Stellenangebote (*Help Wanted Ads*)

Dialoge

Der neue Bäckerlehrling kommt an

Morgens um 6.00. Georg macht die Bäckerei auf.

MARTIN: Morgen. Ich heiße Martin Niedermayer. Ich fange heute bei euch an.

GEORG: Morgen, Martin. Mein Name ist Georg. Den Chef lernst du gleich kennen.

MARTIN: Ist gut. Seit wann arbeitest du denn hier?

GEORG: Erst seit einem Jahr. Komm jetzt mit, und ich zeige dir den Laden.

Beim Bäcker

VERKÄUFERIN: Was darf's sein, bitte?

KUNDE: Geben Sie mir bitte sechs Brötchen und ein Bauernbrot.

VERKÄUFERIN: (*Sie gibt ihm das Brot.*) So, bitte sehr. Sonst noch etwas?

KUNDE: Sind diese Brezeln frisch?

VERKÄUFERIN: Ja, von heute morgen.

KUNDE: Dann geben Sie mir doch sechs Stück. Wieviel kostet das bitte?

VERKÄUFERIN: Das macht zusammen DM 6,80, bitte sehr.

KUNDE: Danke. Auf Wiedersehen.

VERKÄUFERIN: Wiedersehen.

Schule oder Beruf?

VATER: Warum willst du denn jetzt die Schule verlassen? Deine Noten sind ja ganz gut, und du hast nur noch ein Jahr.

KURT: Aber das Abitur brauch' ich nicht. Ich will ja Automechaniker werden.

VATER: Sei nicht so dumm! Als Lehrling verdienst du schlecht.

KURT: Aber ich hab' die Nase einfach voll. Ich möchte lieber mit den Händen arbeiten.

VATER: Quatsch! Du schaffst das Abitur, und ich schenke dir ein Motorrad. Einverstanden?

KURT: Hmmm.

Wortschatz 1

The New Baker's Apprentice Arrives

Six A.M. Georg is opening the bakery.

MARTIN: Morning. My name is Martin Niedermayer. I'm starting here today.

GEORG: Morning, Martin. My name is Georg. You'll meet the boss soon.

MARTIN: O.K. How long have you been working here?

GEORG: Only for a year. Now come with me and I'll show you the shop.

At the Baker's

SALESWOMAN: May I help you?

CUSTOMER: Give me six rolls and one loaf of dark bread, please.

SALESWOMAN: (*She gives him the bread.*) There you are. Anything else?

CUSTOMER: Are these pretzels fresh?

SALESWOMAN: Yes, from this morning.

CUSTOMER: Then give me six. How much is that, please?

SALESWOMAN: Together that comes to six marks eighty.

CUSTOMER: Thank you. Good–bye.

SALESWOMAN: Bye.

School or Profession?

FATHER: Why do you want to leave school now? Your grades are pretty good and you've only got one more year.

KURT: But I don't need the **Abitur.** I want to be a car mechanic.

FATHER: Don't be so dumb. You won't earn much as an apprentice.

KURT: But I'm fed up. I'd rather work with my hands.

FATHER: Nonsense! You pass your **Abitur** and I'll give you a motorcycle. Is it a deal?

KURT: Hmmm.

Verben

an·fangen (fängt an)[1]   to begin, start

an·kommen   to arrive

an·rufen   to call up

auf·hören (mit etwas)   to cease, stop (*doing something*)

auf·machen   to open

auf·stehen   to stand up; get out of bed

kennen·lernen   to get to know; meet

kosten   to cost

mit·kommen   to come along

schenken   to give (*as a gift*)

stehen   to stand

verlassen (verläßt) (*trans.*)   to leave (*a person or place*)

zeigen   to show

Substantive

der **Automechaniker, -**   auto mechanic

der **Bäcker, -**   baker

der **Bauer, -n**   farmer

der **Chef, -s**   boss

der **Kunde, -n**   customer (*m.*)

der **Laden, ∸**   shop, store

der **Lehrling, -e**   apprentice

der **Name, -n**   name

das **Abitur**   final secondary school examination

das **Brot**   bread
  das **Bauernbrot**   dark bread

das **Jahr, -e**   year

das **Motorrad, ∸er**   motorcycle

das **Stück, -e**   piece
  sechs Stück   six (*of the same item*)

die **Bäckerei, -en**   bakery

die **Brezel, -n**   soft pretzel

die **Chefin, -nen**   boss (*f.*)

die **Deutsche Mark (DM)**   the German mark   DM 6,80 (*spoken:* „**sechs Mark achtzig**")

die **Hand, ∸e**   hand

die **Kundin, -nen**   customer (*f.*)

die **Nase, -n**   nose

die **Note, -n**   grade

Adjektive und Adverbien

dieser, dieses, diese; (*plur.*) **diese**[2]   this; these

dumm   dumb

einfach   simple, easy

erst   not until; only

fertig (mit)   done, finished (with); ready

Mit den Hausaufgaben bin ich bald fertig.   I'll be done with my homework soon.

Das Essen ist fertig.   The meal is ready.

frisch   fresh

gleich   right away, immediately

---

1. See p. 136 for an explanation of the raised dot.

2. Note that the endings of **dieser** are almost exactly like the endings of the definite article **der:**

	masc.	neut.	fem.	plur.
nom.	dieser	dieses	diese	diese
acc.	diesen			

Both **der** and **dieser** are called "**der**-words." See p. 201.

heute morgen this morning
voll full

Andere Vokabeln

als as a
als Lehrling/Kind as an
apprentice/as a child
bei at, near
bei euch with you, at
your place (*i.e., where you
work or live*)
dir (*dat. form of* **du**) (to *or*
for) you
euch (*dat. form of* **ihr**) (to *or*
for) you (*pl.*)
seit since
seit 5 Jahren for (the past)
5 years
**Ich arbeite seit 5 Jahren
hier.** I've been working
here for five years.
wieviel? how much?

Nützliche Ausdrücke

Bitte sehr. Here it is. There
you are.
Einverstanden. Agreed. It's a
deal. O.K.
Ich habe die Nase voll. I'm
fed up. I've had it up to
here.
Was darf es sein? What'll it
be? May I help you?
Sonst noch etwas? Will
there be anything else?
Das macht zusammen . . .
All together that comes to
. . .
Ist gut. (*colloq.*) O.K. Fine
by me.
Quatsch! Rubbish! Baloney!
Nonsense!
Wieviel kostet das bitte?
How much does that cost,
please?

Gegensätze

an·fangen ≠ auf·hören
to start ≠ to stop
dumm ≠ klug
dumb ≠ smart, bright
einfach ≠ schwierig
simple ≠ difficult
voll ≠ leer full ≠ empty

Mit anderen Worten

das Abitur = das Abi
(*Schülerslang*)
dumm = blöd

Variationen

A Persönliche Fragen

1. Der Vater schenkt Kurt ein Motorrad. Was schenkt Ihnen Ihr Vater?
Er schenkt mir _____.

2. Georg zeigt Martin den Laden. Was möchten Sie *mir* zeigen?
Ich möchte Ihnen _____ zeigen.

3. Kurt sagt, das Abitur braucht er nicht. Was brauchen *Sie* nicht?

4. Kurt hat nur noch ein Jahr, und dann ist er mit der Schule fertig. Wie viele
Jahre haben Sie noch an der Uni?

5. Kurt arbeitet gern mit den Händen. Und Sie?

6. Martin lernt den Chef gleich kennen. Wen möchten *Sie* kennenlernen?

B Partnerarbeit: Was darf's denn sein?

Partner A spielt den Verkäufer oder die Verkäuferin, Partner B spielt eine Kundin oder einen Kunden. Für das Semester müssen Sie viel kaufen. Spielen Sie diesen Dialog zusammen. Hier sehen Sie, was man kaufen kann.

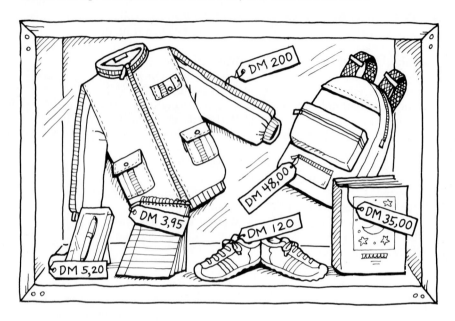

VERKÄUFERIN: Guten Tag. Was darf's denn sein, bitte?

KUNDE: Zeigen Sie mir bitte _____.

VERKÄUFERIN: Bitte sehr.

KUNDE: Was kostet denn _____?

VERKÄUFERIN: Das kostet _____.

KUNDE: Ich möchte gern _____, _____ und _____ kaufen.

VERKÄUFERIN: Das macht zusammen DM _____, bitte sehr.

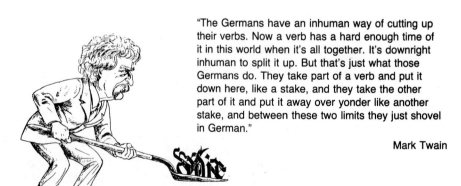

"The Germans have an inhuman way of cutting up their verbs. Now a verb has a hard enough time of it in this world when it's all together. It's downright inhuman to split it up. But that's just what those Germans do. They take part of a verb and put it down here, like a stake, and they take the other part of it and put it away over yonder like another stake, and between these two limits they just shovel in German."

Mark Twain

Richard Dehmel (1863–1920) worked as a journalist in Berlin and was active in progressive literary circles. The language of his revolutionary lyric poetry was influenced by Nietzsche. In this poem, an **Arbeitsmann** (*day laborer*) reflects on a life of toil and deprivation. The swallows he observes on a Sunday walk with his child provide a counter-image of freedom, beauty, and fearlessness.

Der Arbeitsmann

Wir haben ein Bett,° wir haben ein Kind,   *bed*
Mein Weib!°   **mein Weib** = *meine Frau*
Wir haben auch Arbeit, und gar zu zweit,°   **und . . . zweit** = *and even*
Und haben die Sonne und Regen und Wind.   *together*
Und uns fehlt nur eine Kleinigkeit,°   **uns . . . Kleinigkeit** = *we lack*
Um so frei zu sein,° wie die Vögel° sind: *only a small thing* / **um . . .**
Nur Zeit.   **zu** = *in order to* / *birds*

Wenn wir sonntags° durch die Felder° gehn,   *on Sundays / fields*
    Mein Kind,
Und über den Ähren weit und breit°   **über . . . breit** = *above the*
Das blaue Schwalbenvolk blitzen sehn,°   *grain far and wide* / **Das . . .**
Oh, dann fehlt uns nicht das bißchen   **sehn** = *see flocks of blue*
Kleid,   *swallows flashing*
Um so schön zu sein, wie die Vögel sind:
Nur Zeit.

Nur Zeit! wir wittern° Gewitterwind,°   *smell / stormwind*
Wir Volk.°   *common folk*
Nur eine kleine Ewigkeit;°   *eternity*
Uns fehlt ja nichts, mein Weib, mein Kind,
Als all das, was durch uns gedeiht,°   **als . . . gedeiht** = *except for all*
Um so kühn° zu sein, wie die Vögel sind.   *that prospers through us /*
Nur Zeit!   *daring*

Richard Dehmel (1863–1920)

Grammatik

Verbs with Separable Prefixes

The meanings of many English verbs can be changed or modified by the addition of another word.

> to find → to find out
> to look → to look up
> to burn → to burn down
> to hang → to hang around

Likewise, the meanings of many German verbs are modified—or even changed completely—by a similar process, the addition of a prefix to the root verb.

> stehen *to stand* → **auf**stehen *to stand up; get out of bed*
> kommen *to come* → **mit**kommen *to come along*
> hören *to hear* → **auf**hören *to cease, stop*
> fangen *to catch* → **an**fangen *to begin*

Similarly:

ankommen	*to arrive*
anrufen	*to call up*
aufmachen	*to open*
kennenlernen	*to get to know, meet*
zurückkommen	*to come back*

Such verbs are called *separable prefix verbs.* Separable prefix verbs have the primary stress on the prefix (**an**kommen, **auf**hören).

In the present tense and the imperative, the prefix is *separated* from the verb and placed at the end of the sentence or clause. It is the second part of the predicate.

Ich **stehe** morgen sehr früh **auf.**	*I'm getting up very early tomorrow.*
Wann **stehst** du **auf?**	*When are you getting up?*
Stehen Sie bitte **auf!**	*Please get up!*
Steht ihr denn bald **auf?**	*Are you getting up soon?*

When a verb with a separable prefix complements a modal verb, the separable prefix is again attached to the root verb infinitive at the end of the sentence or clause.

without a modal	*with a modal*
Er **fängt** morgen **an.**	Er soll morgen **anfangen.**
Ich **lerne** sie **kennen.**	Ich möchte sie **kennenlernen.**

Note: Separable prefixes will be indicated in the *Wortschatz* sections by a raised period between prefix and root verb: **an·fangen.** This symbol is used only in this textbook, *not* in conventional German spelling.

1 Übung

Ihre Professorin sagt, Sie sollen etwas machen. Antworten Sie, Sie können es nicht machen.

> BEISPIEL: Fangen Sie doch heute an.
> Ich kann heute nicht anfangen.

1. Hören Sie doch auf.
2. Kommen Sie doch mit.
3. Machen Sie den Laden auf.

4. Rufen Sie doch Ihre Mutter an.
5. Stehen Sie bitte auf.
6. Kommen Sie bitte heute an.

2 Übung

Ihr Professor sagt, Sie müssen etwas machen. Sie antworten, Sie sind einverstanden.

> BEISPIEL: Sie müssen um sieben aufstehen.
> Einverstanden, ich stehe um sieben auf.

1. Sie müssen jetzt anfangen.
2. Sie müssen früh aufstehen.
3. Sie müssen um acht aufmachen.
4. Sie müssen Helena anrufen.
5. Sie müssen aufhören.
6. Sie müssen gleich mitkommen.

3 Partnerarbeit: Mach das bitte für mich.

1. **aufmachen** Partner A asks partner B to open various things, and B agrees.

> BEISPIEL: A: Mach doch _____ auf.
> B: Gut, ich mache _____ auf.

Buch	Laden	Rucksack	Zeitung
Fenster	Tür	Tasche	

2. **anrufen** Partner B tells A to call up various relatives and friends. A says he/she doesn't want to.

> BEISPIEL: A: Ruf doch dein-_____ an.
> B: Aber ich will mein-_____ nicht anrufen.

Onkel	Tante	Freund/-in	Lehrer
Bruder	Schwester	Großeltern	Professorin
Mutter	Vater	Geschwister	

3. **Um 7.00 Uhr** Your partner wants to know when you're going to do various things. Answer with the time.

> BEISPIEL: Wann kommst du denn zurück?
> Um 7.00 komme ich zurück.

ankommen	mit deiner Arbeit aufhören
zurückkommen	morgens aufstehen
anfangen (fängst an)	den Chef kennenlernen

Verbs with Inseparable Prefixes

There are also German verbs with *inseparable* prefixes. These prefixes *never* separate from the root verb. You can tell them from separable prefixes in these ways:

- They are *never* stressed.

- They have no independent meaning of their own, while separable prefixes resemble other parts of speech such as prepositions (**mit**kommen) and adverbs (**zurück**kommen).

The inseparable prefixes are: **be-, ent-, er-, ge-, ver-,** and **zer-.** Here are the verbs with inseparable prefixes that you have already learned: **bedeuten, beginnen, bekommen, beschreiben, besitzen, besprechen, besuchen, entscheiden, verdienen, verlassen, verstehen.**

4 Übung

Say these verb pairs aloud to practice the difference between stressed separable prefixes and unstressed inseparable prefixes. Then complete the following sentences with the appropriate verb.

inseparable	*separable*
verstehen	**auf**stehen
beschreiben	**auf**schreiben (*to write down*)
gehören (*to belong to*)	**auf**hören
bekommen	**mit**kommen
erfahren (*to find out*)	**ab**fahren (*to depart*)

1. Ich _____ dich nicht. (*understand*)
   Ich _____ um 7 Uhr _____. (*get up*)

2. _____ Sie es bitte! (*describe*)
   _____ Sie es bitte _____! (*write down*)

3. Harald _____ heute ein Motorrad. (*is getting*)
   Bernd _____ heute _____. (*is coming along*)

Dative Case

The dative case is used in German for the indirect object of a verb, that is, the person or thing *for* whom an action is performed or *to* whom it is directed.[3]

Sie gibt **ihm** das Brot.   *She gives him the bread.* or
                               She gives the bread to him.

English shows the indirect object by means of word order and in some cases also uses a preposition (*to him, for the teacher*).

---

3. Other uses of the dative case will be covered later in this chapter and in subsequent chapters.

Identify the direct object and the indirect object in the following English sentences.

1. We owe him a debt of gratitude.
2. I'm buying my father a necktie.
3. Tell me what you think.
4. We're cooking spaghetti for the kids.
5. Peel me a grape.
6. To whom did you say that?

German versus English Indirect Object

In German, the dative case is shown by the form of the personal pronoun (e.g., **dir** = *to/for you*) or of the article or possessive adjective used with a noun (**dem** Lehrer = *to/for the teacher*, **ihrer** Tochter = *to/for her daughter*).

German does *not* use a preposition to show the indirect object. It is signalled by case alone.

$$\overset{i.o.}{\hphantom{}} \quad \overset{d.o.}{\hphantom{}}$$
Ich kaufe **dir das Motorrad.** { *I'll buy you the motorcycle.*
I'll buy the motorcycle for you.

Sag **dem Lehrer guten Morgen.** { *Tell the teacher good morning.*
Say good morning to the teacher.

Sie gibt **ihrer Tochter das Geld.** { *She's giving her daughter the money.*
She's giving the money to her daughter.

The German case system allows more flexibility in word order than English. The following sentences all say basically the same thing, with some minor shifts in emphasis.

Sie gibt **ihrer Tochter das Geld.**
Sie gibt **das Geld ihrer Tochter.**
Das Geld gibt sie **ihrer Tochter.**
Ihrer Tochter gibt sie **das Geld.**

By mastering the case endings, you can always find your way through such sentences.

Forms of the Dative Case

The definite article, indefinite article, and possessive adjectives all share the same set of dative endings (nominative and accusative, the cases you have already learned, are included in the following table for comparison and review).

	masc.	*neut.*	*fem.*	*plural*
nom.	der Vater	das Kind	die Frau	die Leute
acc.	den Vater			
dat.	-em	-em	-er	-en -n
	dem Vater	**dem** Kind	**der** Frau	**den** Leuten
	ein**em** Vater	ein**em** Kind	ein**er** Frau	kein**en** Leuten
	unser**em** Vater	dein**em** Kind	sein**er** Frau	mein**en** Leuten

Note: *All nouns* in the dative plural add an **-n** to the noun itself (**den** Leuten, **den** Händen), except those nouns already ending in **-n** (den Frauen) and those ending in **-s** (den Hotels).

Fragewörter

wer?	*who?*
wen?	*whom?* (direct object)
wessen?	*whose?*
wem?	*to/for whom?*

Wem geben Sie das Geld?   ***To whom*** *are you giving the money?*

---

 6 Übung: Wem soll sie es geben?

Beate kann ihr Brötchen nicht essen. Wem soll sie es geben?

BEISPIEL: die Lehrerin
           Sie soll es der Lehrerin geben.

feminine

1. ihre Freundin
2. ihre Schwester
3. die Professorin
4. die Chefin

neuter and masculine

5. ein Kind
6. ihr Freund
7. der Lehrer
8. mein Vater
9. dieser Automechaniker

plural

10. die Kinder
11. diese Leute
12. die Studenten
13. ihre Freunde

7 Kettenreaktion: Wem schenkst du den Pulli?

Sie kaufen einen schönen Pulli für jemand in Ihrer Familie. Wem schenken Sie ihn?

BEISPIEL: STUDENT A: Wem schenkst *du* den Pulli?
           STUDENT B: Meiner Schwester. Wem schenkst *du* den Pulli?
           STUDENT C: Mein-_____. Wem . . . ?

8 Übung: Wie sagt man das auf deutsch?

Benutzen Sie (*Use*) den Du-Imperativ.

BEISPIEL: *Read the child a book.*   Lies dem Kind ein Buch.

1. Buy your sister a book.

2. Give my parents the money.

3. Describe the problem to the mechanic.

4. Write your mother a card.

5. Cook the food for your friends.

6. Show my friend the city.

Dative Personal Pronouns[4]

In the following table, the nominative and accusative forms of the personal pronouns are included for review and comparison.

	singular			plural	
nom.	acc.	dat.	nom.	acc.	dat.
ich	mich	**mir**	wir	uns	**uns**
du	dich	**dir**	ihr	euch	**euch**
Sie	Sie	**Ihnen**	Sie	Sie	**Ihnen**
er	ihn	**ihm**			
es	es	**ihm**	sie	sie	**ihnen**
sie	sie	**ihr**			

Note the similarities between the third-person dative pronouns and the dative endings of the articles and possessive adjectives.

ihm → **dem** Mann, **meinem** Kind
ihr → **der** Frau, **seiner** Schwester
ihnen → **den** Freunden, **unseren** Kindern

9 Übung

You're buying bread. Your instructor will ask whom you're buying it for and will give you a visual cue.

BEISPIEL: Wem kaufen Sie das Brot? (*points to another student*)
Ich kaufe es *ihm/ihr.*

10 Partnerarbeit: Kaufst du mir etwas?

Taking turns and using the cues below, ask your partner what he or she will do for you.

BEISPIEL: Kaufst du mir eine Brezel?
Ja, ich kaufe dir eine Brezel. *oder*
Nein, ich kaufe dir keine Brezel.

dein Motorrad verkaufen

deine Fotos zeigen

deine Reise beschreiben

Geld schenken

eine Karte kaufen

ein Brötchen geben (gibst)

---

4. Note that English pronouns do not have different forms for the direct object and the indirect object, whereas German pronouns (except **uns** and **euch**) do.

I see **him**. Ich sehe **ihn.**
I'm giving **him** the book. Ich gebe **ihm** das Buch.

Word Order of Noun and Pronoun Objects

Verbs such as **geben, schenken, kaufen, beschreiben,** and **zeigen** often have two objects. One is usually the person (in the dative case) *to whom* something is given, shown, etc., or *for whom* something is done. The second object is usually the thing (in the accusative case) that is being given, shown, bought, etc.

Note that the order of pronoun objects in German is the same as in English.

Ich schenke **meiner Freundin eine Uhr.**	*I'm giving **my girlfriend a watch.***
Ich schenke **ihr eine Uhr.**	*I'm giving **her a watch.***
Ich schenke **sie meiner Freundin.**	*I'm giving **it to my girlfriend.***
Ich schenke **sie ihr.**	*I'm giving **it to her.***

Any personal pronouns that are not in the first position are placed *immediately after the inflected verb.*

Ich gebe **ihm** mein Buch.	*I'm giving **him** my book.*
Ich gebe **es** meinem Bruder.	*I'm giving **it** to my brother.*

If more than one personal pronoun follows the verb, they come in the order *nominative, accusative, dative.* Again, this is just like English word order: *subject pronoun, direct object pronoun, indirect object pronoun.*

Ich gebe **es Ihnen** heute.	*I'm giving **it to you** today.*
Heute gebe **ich es Ihnen.**	*Today **I'm giving it to you.***

 11 Übung: Wem schenken Sie die Uhr?

You've bought a watch as a present. Your instructor will ask whom you're giving it to. Answer the questions affirmatively, using pronouns.

BEISPIEL: Wem schenken Sie die Uhr? Schenken Sie sie Ihrer Mutter?
Ja, ich schenke sie ihr.

1. Schenken Sie sie Ihrem Vater?
2. den Kindern?
3. Ihrem Freund?
4. Ihrer Mitbewohnerin?
5. mir?
6. uns?

 12 Übung: Wem zeigen Sie heute das Haus?

You're a realtor showing people a new house. Tell your instructor whom you're showing it to today.

BEISPIEL: Wem zeigen heute das Haus? Zeigen Sie es dem Professor?
Ja, heute zeige ich es ihm.

1. Zeigen Sie es heute der Professorin?
2. dieser Frau?
3. mir?
4. uns?
5. den drei Studenten?
6. meinem Freund?

Prepositions with Dative Case

Another use of the dative case is as the object of certain prepositions. (See pp. 105–6 for prepositions with the accusative case.) The following prepositions *always* have an object in the dative case. Memorize the list.

aus	*out of*	Sie sieht **aus** dem Fenster.	*She's looking out of the window.*
	from (native country, city or region)	Ich komme **aus** Amerika.	*I'm from America.*
außer	*except for*	**Außer** ihm sind wir alle hier.	*We're all here except for him.*
	besides, in addition to	**Außer** ihm wohnt auch sein Bruder hier.	*Besides him, his brother lives here too.*
bei	*in the home of*	Ich wohne **bei** meiner Tante.	*I live at my aunt's.*
	near	Das Kind spielt **beim** Fenster.	*The child is playing near the window.*
	at	Er ist **bei** der Arbeit.	*He's at work.*
mit	*with*	Ich arbeite **mit** den Händen.	*I work with my hands.*
nach	*after*	**Nach** der Arbeit bin ich manchmal müde.	*After work I'm sometimes tired.*
	to (with country and city names)	Wir fahren **nach** England.	*We're going to England.*
seit	*since* (referring to times)	**Seit** dem Tag mag ich ihn nicht mehr.	*Since that day I haven't liked him.*
	for (when scanning the past)[5]	Ich arbeite **seit** einem Jahr hier.	*I've been working here for a year.*
von	*from*	Das Buch habe ich **von** meiner Mutter.	*I got that book from my mother.*
	of	Er ist ein Freund **von** mir.	*He's a friend of mine.*
	by	Das ist ein Buch **von** Hermann Hesse.	*That's a book by Hermann Hesse.*
zu	*to* (people and some locations)	Ich gehe **zur** Schule und dann **zu** meinen Freunden.	*I'm going to school and then to my friends' house.*

5. For an action or situation beginning in the past and continuing in the present, English uses *perfect* tense + *for* (*I've been working for a year*), while German uses *present* tense + **seit** (**Ich arbeite seit einem Jahr**). This will be covered in more detail in *Kapitel 10*.

Contractions

The following contractions of prepositions with the dative of the definitive article are standard.

bei dem → **beim**	Das Kind spielt **beim** Fenster.
von dem → **vom**	Ich komme gerade **vom** Chef.
zu dem → **zum**	Ich muß schnell **zum** Professor.
zu der → **zur**	Ich gehe jetzt **zur** Schule.

---

einander **each other**

Several accusative and dative prepositions can combine with the adverb **einander** (*each other*) to show reciprocity. Here are some examples:

Wir kaufen oft **füreinander** ein.	*We often shop for each other.*
Georg und Martin arbeiten **miteinander.**	*Georg and Martin work with one another.*

---

 13 Übung: Bei wem wohnen Sie?

Sie sind alle Studenten in Tübingen. Sie wohnen nicht im Studentenwohnheim (*dormitory*). Sagen Sie Ihrem Professor oder Ihrer Professorin, bei wem Sie wohnen.

BEISPIEL: Bei wem wohnen Sie?
Bei meinem Freund.

Tante	Freundin	Bruder	Großeltern
Familie	Vater	Freund	Frau König

14 Kettenreaktion: Zu wem gehst *du*?

Each student says whom he or she is going to see, then asks the next student.

Automechaniker	Bäckerin	Lehrling
Professorin	Automechanikerin	Amerikaner
Professor	Eltern	Familie
Chef	Amerikanerin	Bäcker

BEISPIEL: LEHRER: Zu wem gehen Sie?
STUDENT A: Ich gehe zu meiner Familie. Zu wem gehst *du*?
STUDENT B: Ich gehe zum Bäcker. Zu wem . . .

15 Übung: Mit wem gehen Sie schwimmen?

Sie gehen mit Freunden aus der Deutschstunde schwimmen. Sagen Sie, mit wem Sie schwimmen gehen.

BEISPIEL: PROFESSOR/IN: Mit wem gehen Sie schwimmen?
STUDENT/IN: (*points to one or more other students in the class*)
Mit ihr/ihm/ihnen.

Time Phrases in Accusative Case

Here are some time phrases telling *when* or *how often* something occurs or *how long* it goes on. The nouns in these phrases are in the *accusative case.*[6]

Wann?

diesen Freitag	dieses Semester	diese Woche
diesen Herbst	dieses Jahr	
diesen März		

Ich studiere **dieses Semester** in Konstanz.   *I'm studying in Konstanz this semester.*

Diese Woche ist Thomas krank.   *Thomas is sick this week.*

Wann/Wie oft?

jeden Morgen	jedes Semester	jede Minute
jeden Abend	jedes Jahr	jede Stunde
jeden Tag		jede Woche
jeden Montag		
jeden September		
jeden Sommer		

Wir gehen **jeden Tag** zum Bäcker.   *We go to the baker's every day.*

Er fährt **jedes Jahr** nach Amerika.   *He goes to America every year.*

Note: Remember that expressions of time (**jeden Tag**) precede expressions of place or destination (**zum Bäcker**).

Wie lange?

einen Tag	eine Minute	drei Tage
ein Jahr	eine Stunde	zwei Semester

Wir bleiben **einen Tag** in London.   *We're staying in London for a day.*

Ich studiere **ein Semester** in Köln.   *I'm studying in Cologne for a semester.*

Note that the German equivalent of *"for a day"* is simply **einen Tag** without a preposition.

16 **Übung:** Mit offenen Büchern

Supply the missing time phrases cued in English.

1. Wie oft stehen Sie um 7.00 Uhr auf?
   Ich stehe _____ um 7.00 Uhr auf. (*every day*)

2. Wann rufen Sie Ihre Eltern an?
   Ich rufe sie _____ an. (*this Wednesday*)

3. Wie lange bleiben Sie in Tübingen?
   Ich bleibe _____ dort. (*a year*)

---

6. Remember that when a time phrase uses a preposition, that preposition will govern the case of the noun: **seit dem Tag** *since that day;* **nach einer Stunde** *after an hour.*

4. Wann arbeitest du denn mit Karl zusammen?
   Wahrscheinlich arbeite ich _____ mit ihm zusammen. (*this week*)

5. Wie lange wartet ihr noch?
   Wir warten noch _____ vor der Bäckerei. (*for an hour*)

6. Hoffentlich kannst du lange bei uns bleiben.
   Nein, leider kann ich nur _____ bei euch sein. (*one day*)

7. Wann ist das Klima bei euch besonders schön?
   Das Wetter ist _____ mild und kühl. (*every October*)

8. Wann kann ich Sie besuchen, Herr Wahrig?
   _____ um 9.00 Uhr bin ich frei. (*every Tuesday*)

Omission of Indefinite Article with Professions and Nationalities

When stating someone's profession or nationality, German does not use an indefinite article before the noun, as does English.

Mein Sohn möchte Automechani-ker werden.	*My son wants to become **an** auto mechanic.*
Frau Gerhard ist Lehrerin.	*Mrs. Gerhard is **a** teacher.*
Scott ist Amerikaner.	*Scott's **an** American.*

To say you are *not* a teacher, mechanic, American, etc., you may use either **nicht** or **kein.**

Rolf, bist du Student?	Nein, ich bin **kein** Student. *or* Nein, ich bin **nicht** Student.

 17 Gruppenarbeit: Bist du Amerikaner/in?

Your instructor will give everyone a card with a profession or nationality (**Bäcker, Studentin, Amerikaner,** etc.). Don't show your card to anyone else. Speak to as many of your classmates as possible and guess what they are until you find the right answer.

BEISPIEL: Bist du Bäckerin?
Nein, ich bin nicht/keine Bäckerin.
Bist du _____?

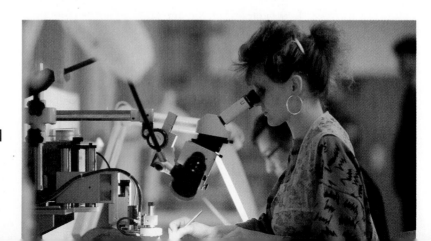

Facharbeiterin [*technician*] in der Optikindustrie.

Tips zum Lesen und Lernen

Tips zum Vokabelnlernen

Agent Nouns Both English and German add the suffix **-er** to a verb stem to form a noun that denotes a person who performs the action (agent). In German, the additional ending **-in** indicates that the agent is female.

arbeiten → **Arbeiter/in**	*to work → worker*
lesen → **Leser/in**	*to read → reader*

Sometimes an umlaut is added in the agent noun:

anfangen → **Anfänger**	*to begin → beginner*
tragen → **Briefträger/in**	*to carry → letter carrier*
backen → **Bäcker/in**	*to bake → baker*
handeln → **Buchhändler/in**	*to trade, deal → bookseller*

Übung

Was machen diese Leute?

1. Herr Kropf ist Kaffeetrinker.

2. Frau Baumann ist Zeitungsleserin.

3. Wir sind alle Anfänger.

4. Albert ist Frühaufsteher.

5. Herr Hanselmann ist Buchhändler.

Adverbs of Time By adding an **-s** to the names of the days or parts of the day, German forms adverbs showing regular or habitual occurrence.

morgens	*in the mornings, every morning*
nachmittags	*in the afternoons, every afternoon*
abends	*in the evenings, every evening*
nachts	*at night, every night*
montags	*Mondays, every Monday*
dienstags	*Tuesdays, every Tuesday*
usw.	*etc.*

Note: These words are *adverbs*, not nouns, and are therefore not capitalized.

MERCEDES-BENZ
Ihr guter Stern auf allen Straßen.

Wann machen Sie das?

> BEISPIEL: Wann essen Sie Brötchen?
> Morgens esse ich Brötchen.

1. Wann haben Sie Deutsch?

2. Wann trinken Sie Kaffee?

3. Wann machen Sie Ihre Hausaufgaben?

4. Wann gehen Sie zum Bäcker?

5. Wann rufen Sie Ihre Familie an?

Leicht zu merken

campen	(pronounced **kämpen**)
die **Industrie, -n**	Indus*trie*
(das) **Kanada**	
der **Korrespondent, -en**	Korrespon*dent*
kritisch	
der **Partner, -**	
der **Sport**	
die **Universität, -en**	Universi*tät*
die **USA** (*pl.*)	

Einstieg in den Text

The title „Drei Deutsche bei der Arbeit" lets you know that the reading will focus on three individuals and their work. What sorts of things would you expect to learn about people's personal and professional lives from such a reading? You can apply to this text the familiar question words that you have been using to ask about each other's lives.

Before reading the whole text, skim the third portrait and see if you can quickly find answers to the following questions:

Wie heißt dieser Mann?
Wie alt ist er?
Was macht er?
Wo wohnt er?
Wer sind die anderen (*other*) Menschen in seiner Familie?

Let these questions guide your reading for information as you work through the entire text.

Wortschatz 2

Verben

ab·holen to pick up, fetch, get

aus·sehen (sieht aus) to appear, look (happy, tired, fit, etc.)
Du siehst schrecklich aus. You look terrible.

bedienen to serve

berichten to report

ein·kaufen to shop for; go shopping

fern·sehen (sieht fern) to watch TV

reisen to travel

schließen to close

spazieren·gehen to go for a walk

sterben (stirbt) to die

vergessen (vergißt) to forget

vorbei·kommen to come by, drop by

zu·machen to close

Substantive

der **Arbeiter, -** worker
der **Fußball** soccer
der **Journalist, -en** journalist
der **Reiseführer, -** (travel) guide book
der **Roman, -e** novel
der **Streß** (*no plural*) stress
der **Verein, -e** club

das **Bild, -er** picture; image
das **Dorf, ̈er** village

(das) **Frankreich** France
das **Geschäft, -e** business; store
(das) **Jugoslawien** Yugoslavia
das **Mittagessen** midday meal, lunch
das **Schaufenster, -** store window
das **Wochenende, -n** weekend
  am Wochenende on the weekend
das **Wort** word (*2 plural forms:* **die Worte:** words in a context; **die Wörter:** unconnected words, as in a dictionary)
das **Wörterbuch, ̈er** dictionary

die **Buchhandlung, -en** bookstore
die **Fabrik, -en** factory
die **Freizeit** free time
die **Mannschaft, -en** team
die **Muttersprache, -n** native language
die **Postkarte, -n** postcard
die **Stimme, -n** voice
die **Wanderung, -en** hike
die **Woche, -n** week
die **Zeitschrift, -en** magazine

die **Lebensmittel** (*pl.*) groceries

Adjektive und Adverbien

abends (in the) evenings
aktuell topical, relevant, current
besonders especially
bunt colorful
fleißig industrious, hard-working
französisch French
jeder, -es, -e[7] each, every
meistens mostly, usually
sauer sour; acidic
  der saure Regen acid rain

Gegensätze

fleißig ≠ faul
  industrious ≠ lazy
aufmachen ≠ zumachen / schließen to open ≠ to close

Mit anderen Worten

stressig (*colloq.*) = **mit viel Streß**

Am Schreibtisch arbeiten

---

7. **Jeder** has the same endings as **dieser**. Both are **der**-words (see p. 201).

Drei Deutsche bei der Arbeit

Man sagt über die Deutschen, sie leben für ihre Arbeit. Stimmt das heute noch? Unsere Beispiele zeigen ein anderes° Bild.

different

Christine Sauermann, Buchhändlerin

Christine Sauermann ist 35 Jahre alt, geschieden,° und hat einen jungen Sohn Oliver (10 Jahre alt). Sie ist seit zehn Jahren berufstätig und besitzt seit fünf Jahren eine Buchhandlung in der Altstadt°[8] von Tübingen.[9] Zwei Angestellte° arbeiten für sie im Laden.

divorced

old city / employees

Das Geschäft geht gut, denn° viele Touristen gehen durch die Altstadt spazieren, und Studenten kommen auch jeden Tag vorbei. Mit den neuesten Romanen sieht ihr Schaufenster immer bunt aus. Den Studenten verkauft sie Wörterbücher und Nachschlagewerke,° aber die Touristen kaufen meistens Reiseführer und Postkarten von der Stadt.

because

reference works

Sie macht um 9 Uhr auf und um 6 Uhr abends zu. Von 1 Uhr bis 3 Uhr macht sie Mittagspause.° Sie schließt den Laden, holt Oliver von der Schule ab, und geht mit ihm nach Hause. Dort kocht sie das Mittagessen[11] und kauft später dann noch Lebensmittel ein.

midday break[10]

Außer sonntags arbeitet Christine Sauermann jeden Tag sehr fleißig in ihrem Laden. In ihrer Freizeit möchte sie also Erholung° vom Streß. Darum macht sie gern Wanderungen mit ihrem Sohn zusammen. Diesen Sommer zum Beispiel gehen sie zusammen in Schottland° campen.

relaxation

Scotland

Jörg Krolow (22 Jahre alt), Fabrikarbeiter

Jörg Krolow arbeitet seit einem Jahr als Mechaniker in einer Autofabrik in Dortmund.[12] Die Arbeit ist schwer, aber gut bezahlt.° Nach der Arbeit trinkt er oft ein Bier mit Freunden zusammen oder sieht fern. Am Wochenende spielt er im Sportverein Fußball.

paid

8. Most German cities and towns have an **Altstadt** ("old city") in their centers. This is the original core of the city, which may date from the Middle Ages. Many of these old city centers have been renovated and closed to motor vehicles.

9. A university town on the Neckar River in Baden-Würtemberg about twenty miles south of Stuttgart. The university was founded in 1477.

10. Many small shops and businesses close from one to two-thirty or three P.M., though this practice is less common nowadays in large cities.

11. The noon meal is traditionally the main meal of the day.

12. An industrial city in North Rhine-Westphalia.

Es ist schon spät, aber die Buchhandlung ist noch offen. (München)

35	Wie alle deutschen Arbeiter in der Schwerindustrie ist Krolow in einer Gewerkschaft.° Sie sichert° jedem Mitglied° einen guten Lohn° und gibt den Arbeitern eine Stimme im Aufsichtsrat.°	union / assures / member wage board of directors[13]
40	Krolow hat wie die meisten Deutschen° fünf Wochen Urlaub im Jahr. Dieses Jahr will er im Sommer mit seiner Freundin nach Jugoslawien. Im Oktober fährt seine Fußballmannschaft nach Amiens,[14] der Partnerstadt von Dortmund, und spielt dort gegen einen französischen Fußballklub.	**wie . . . Deutschen** = *like most Germans*

Klaus Ostendorff (53 Jahre alt), Journalist

45	Klaus Ostendorff ist Korrespondent bei der Deutschen Presseagentur° in Nordamerika. Seit fünzehn Jahren berichtet er über die USA und Kanada für Zeitungen und Zeitschriften in Deutschland. Seine Artikel geben den Lesern ein kritisches Bild von beiden° Ländern.	wire service both
50	Im Moment schreibt Ostendorff einen Artikel über das Waldsterben° in Nordamerika. Dieses Problem ist in Deutschland besonders aktuell: Der saure Regen bedroht° auch die Wälder in Europa.	death of the forests threatens
55	Ostendorff lebt mir seiner Frau Martina und ihren drei Kindern in Washington. Die Kinder sollen ihre Muttersprache nicht vergessen, und darum spricht die Familie zu Hause meistens Deutsch miteinander. Die Kinder besuchen das deutsche Gymnasium in Washington und reisen im Sommer nach Deutschland. Dort macht die ganze° Familie Urlaub bei den Großeltern. Sie wohnen in einem Dorf in den Bayerischen° Alpen.	whole Bavarian

13. German workers in large companies elect up to 50% of the board of directors. This has meant a high degree of cooperation between management and labor and has resulted in fewer strikes than in other industrial nations.
14. Northern French city on the Somme River.

Fragen zum Lesestück

1. Wo arbeitet Christine Sauermann?
2. Wie lange ist sie schon berufstätig?
3. Wer sind ihre Kunden, und was suchen sie bei ihr?
4. Wie sieht ein typischer Tag für Christine aus?
5. Was macht sie gern in ihrer Freizeit?
6. Was macht Jörg Krolow in seiner Freizeit?
7. Wohin fährt er im Urlaub?
8. Über was schreibt Klaus Ostendorff im Moment?
9. Wie ist seine Familie anders als die Familie von Christine oder Jörg?
10. Warum sprechen Ostendorff und seine Frau zu Hause meistens Deutsch?

Situationen aus dem Alltag

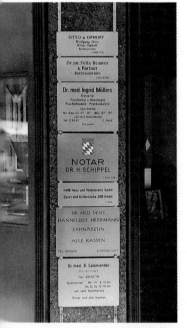

Berufe

Was sind Sie von Beruf?   *What is your profession?*

der **Arzt,** ⁼e	die **Ärztin, -nen**	*physician*
der **Elektrotechniker, -**	die **Elektrotechnikerin**	*electrician* or *electrical engineer*
der **Geschäftsmann** (*pl.*) **Geschäftsleute**	die **Geschäftsfrau**	*businessman/businesswoman*
der **Ingenieur, -e**	die **Ingenieurin, -nen**	*engineer*
der **Kellner, -**	die **Kellnerin, -nen**	*waiter/waitress*
der **Krankenpfleger, -**	die **Krankenschwester, -n**	*nurse*
der **Künstler, -**	die **Künstlerin, -nen**	*artist*
der **Landwirt, -e**	die **Landwirtin, -nen**	*farmer*
der **Politiker, -**	die **Politikerin, -nen**	*politician*
der **Rechtsanwalt,** ⁼e	die **Rechtsanwältin, -nen**	*lawyer*
der **Schriftsteller, -**	die **Schriftstellerin, -nen**	*writer*
der **Verkäufer, -**	die **Verkäuferin, -nen**	*salesperson*

Diese Berufe wissen Sie schon auf deutsch:

der **Bäcker, -**	die **Bäckerin, -nen**
der **Fabrikarbeiter, -**	die **Fabrikarbeiterin, -nen**
	die **Hausfrau, -en**
der **Journalist, -en**	die **Journalistin, -nen**
der **Lehrer, -**	die **Lehrerin, -nen**
der **Mechaniker, -**	die **Mechanikerin, -nen**
der **Professor, -en**	die **Professorin, -nen**

Wer arbeitet in diesem Gebäude? Lesen Sie mal die Schilder [*signs*].

Fragen: Was wissen Sie über diese Berufe?

1. Wer braucht das Abitur?
2. Wer muß für seinen Beruf studieren?
3. Wer macht eine Lehre (*apprenticeship*)?
4. Wer verdient gut? Wer verdient relativ schlecht?
5. Wer hat viel Freizeit? Wer hat nicht viel Freizeit?
6. Wer hat flexible Arbeitszeiten?
7. Wer arbeitet oft nachts / morgens / abends?
8. Wer arbeitet draußen?
9. Wer braucht vielleicht einen Computer bei der Arbeit?
10. Wer arbeitet meistens allein, wer mit anderen Menschen zusammen?

Mit Menschen zu tun haben   **Handwerklich arbeiten**   **Im Labor arbeiten**

Partnerarbeit: Suchen wir eine Stelle.

Sie und Ihr Partner brauchen Geld und suchen Stellen für den Sommer. Im Almanach (S. 157) sind einige Stellenangebote (*job offers, help wanted ads*) aus deutschen Zeitungen. Besprechen Sie sie zusammen. Was möchten Sie gern machen? Was möchten Sie lieber nicht machen?

Gruppendiskussion: Was willst du werden, und warum?   *4 Studenten*

First tell each other what you want to do after college. Then ask questions about each other's career plans.

BEISPIEL: Ich möchte Lehrer werden.
Verdient ein Lehrer genug?
Sind deine Eltern Lehrer?
Wo möchtest du denn arbeiten?
usw.

Zum Schluß

Sprechen wir miteinander!

A **Gruppenarbeit:** Was zeigst du mir? *4 oder 5 Studenten*

One student uses a verb from the list below to ask other students what they are going to do for him or her. Other students use a noun from the list to answer. After asking each person in the group, a new questioner starts over with a different verb.

BEISPIEL: Was kaufst du mir, Joanne?
Ich kaufe dir einen Fernseher.
Vielen Dank! Was _____ du mir, Steve?

Verbs	*Nouns*	
kaufen	Mantel	Hemd
beschreiben	Wagen	Mittagessen
kochen	Artikel	Buch
geben	Stadtplan	Stadt
schenken	Fernseher	Bluse
zeigen	Brot	Tasche
verkaufen	Auto	Zeitung
	Brötchen	Suppe
	Wasser	Uhr

B **Contradicting:** Nein, das stimmt nicht!

Contradict what your instructor says.

BEISPIEL: Dieser Wagen ist *neu!*
Nein, das stimmt nicht. Dieser Wagen ist *alt!*

1. Wir holen die Kinder *früh* ab.
2. Hamburg liegt in *Süddeutschland.*
3. Jetzt *fängt* die Stunde *an.*
4. Der Lehrling *schließt* den Laden.
5. Der Chef möchte *etwas* sagen.
6. Wir essen *viel.*
7. Ich glaube, *jemand* wohnt da drüben.
8. Meine Nase ist *häßlich.*
9. Diese Jacke ist *altmodisch.*
10. Diese Übung ist *schwer.*

C Gruppenarbeit: Mit anderen Worten

With books closed, the class forms two teams. The instructor says a sentence, and the first team to think of a more colorful or colloquial way to say the same thing gets a point.

BEISPIEL: Heute ist es *sehr sehr* kalt.
Heute ist es *wahnsinnig* kalt.

1. Der Film war *sehr langweilig*.
2. Ich schenke meiner *Großmutter* ein Foto von mir.
3. Heute ist das Wasser *sehr kalt*.
4. Die Autos fahren *sehr schnell* durch die Stadt.
5. Gestern abend war ich *sehr sehr müde*.
6. Die Berge in Österreich sind *sehr schön*.

only the
person addressed
All Pronoun
Capitalized!

D Partnerarbeit: Sprechen Sie miteinander!

Take turns asking each other the following questions. Choose your answers from the list of words below. Then ask some questions of your own.

(der) Tag, Morgen, Nachmittag, Abend
Montag, Dienstag, usw.
Januar, Februar, März, usw.
Winter, Frühling, Sommer, Herbst

(das) Semester, Jahr, Wochenende

(die) Stunde, Woche

1. Wie oft gehst du schwimmen?
Ich gehe jed-_____ schwimmen.

2. Wie oft ißt du Brezeln?
Brezeln esse ich _____.

3. Wann fährst du nach Europa?
Ich fahre dies-_____ nach Europa.

4. Wann studierst du in Konstanz?
Ich studiere _____ in Konstanz.

5. Wie lange bleibst du in München?
Ich bleibe ein-_____ da.

6. Wie lange schläfst du morgen?
Morgen schlafe ich _____.

Eure,

Schreiben Sie zu Hause

E Der Arbeitstag Sie haben eine neue Stelle. Schreiben Sie Ihren Eltern und beschreiben Sie ihnen einen typischen Arbeitstag. (*Use the cues to help you*).

Liebe Mutti, lieber Vati!

aufstehen / morgens / 7.00 Uhr

Arbeit / anfangen / 8.30 Uhr

ich / arbeiten / mit / mein Freund Kurt / zusammen

Laden / zumachen / 5.00 Uhr

nach / Arbeit / ich / gehen / Bier / trinken

nach / Essen / fernsehen / oft / ein bißchen

abends / ich / sein / todmüde

Euer Gerd

F **Berufsberatung** (*Career Counseling*) Frau Friedrichsen, a career counselor (**Berufsberaterin**), is advising her client, Herr Liebig. Fill in Herr Liebig's answers to her questions.

FRAU F: Also Herr Liebig, sagen Sie mir bitte, arbeiten Sie lieber mit Menschen oder allein?

HERR L: ______________________________

FRAU F: Sagen Sie mir etwas über Ihre Familie. Wie viele Kinder haben Sie?

HERR L: ______________________________

FRAU F: Ist Ihre Frau auch berufstätig?

HERR L: Ja.

FRAU F: Und was ist sie von Beruf?

HERR L: ______________________________

FRAU F: Was machen Sie besonders gern in Ihrer Freizeit?

HERR L: ______________________________

FRAU F: Wieviel wollen Sie verdienen?

HERR L: ______________________________

FRAU F: Also, Herr Liebig, vielleicht wollen Sie gern ________ werden?

G **Aufsatzthema** (*Essay Topic*): Beschreiben Sie Ihre Arbeit! You have read about the lives of three working Germans. Write a page about your own job or your parents' jobs. How is working in this country different from what you have read about working in Germany?

H Wie sagt man das auf deutsch?

1. When are you getting up tomorrow?
2. At six. I have to leave the house early.
3. Why? What are you doing?
4. I'm driving with my girlfriend to Munich.

5. What are you doing on the weekend?
6. I don't know yet. Why do you ask?
7. Can you come by? A student from Germany is visiting me.
8. Gladly. I'd like to meet him.
9. I want to show him the city.
10. Of course. We can show it to him after the seminar.
11. So long, until then.

Almanach

Stellenangebote (*Help Wanted Ads*)

Here is a selection of help wanted ads from the German press. They range from unskilled labor (**Zeitungsträger/in**) to highly specialized professionals (**Statistiker/in**). Note the amount of English business and computer jargon in the technical fields.

An der Universität

Communicative Goals
- Talking about events in the past
- Talking about German and American university life
- Writing a letter in German

Cultural Goal
- Learning about German student life and the university system

Lyrik zum Vorlesen   Johann Wolfgang von Goethe, „Wanderers Nachtlied II"

Grammatik   Simple Past Tense of *sein*   •   Perfect Tense   •   Two-way Prepositions   •   Masculine N-nouns

Lesestück   Ein Brief aus Freiburg

Situationen aus dem Alltag   Das Studium; Das Studentenzimmer

Almanach   Ein *Vorlesungsverzeichnis*

Karin sucht ein Zimmer

STEFAN: Hast du endlich ein Zimmer gefunden?

KARIN: Nee, ich suche noch. Leider habe ich keinen Platz im Studenten-wohnheim bekommen.

STEFAN: Du! Gestern ist bei uns in der WG[1] die Helga[2] ausgezogen. Also, jetzt ist ein Zimmer frei. Willst du zu uns?

KARIN: Super! Meinst du, das ist möglich?

STEFAN: Selbstverständlich!

Am Semesteranfang

CLARA: Wo warst du denn?

EVA: In der Buchhandlung. Warum?

CLARA: Hast du mir ein Vorlesungsverzeichnis mitgebracht?

EVA: Ja, ich hab's auf den Schreibtisch gelegt.

CLARA: Ach ja, da liegt es unter der Zeitung. Wieviel hat's denn gekostet?[3]

EVA: Vier Mark fünfzig, aber ich schenk's dir.

CLARA: Das ist wirklich nett von dir! Vielen Dank!

An der Uni in Tübingen

PETRA: Hast du den Austauschstudenten aus Kanada schon kennengelernt?

KLAUS: Meinst du den Peter?

PETRA: Ja. Er kann phantastisch Deutsch, nicht?

KLAUS: Ich glaube, er hat schon zwei Semester[4] in Konstanz[5] studiert.

PETRA: Ach, darum!

Note on Usage

In informal, colloquial speech, Germans often use the definite article with proper names. The dialogues contain two examples of this:

Gestern ist bei uns in der WG **die** Helga ausgezogen.	*Yesterday Helga moved out of her apartment.*
Meinst du **den** Peter?	*Do you mean Peter?*

---

1. Because dormitory space is scarce in Germany, many students share houses or apartments in communal living arrangements called **Wohngemeinschaften** (abbreviated **WG, -s**).

2. For an explanation of the use of the definite article with proper names, see Note on Usage.

3. German students buy their course catalogues at the start of each semester in local bookstores.

4. German students calculate their university time in semesters rather than years. Average length of studies is currently twelve semesters.

5. A German city on Lake Constance (in German **Bodensee**), population circa 71,000, with a new university founded in 1966. Konstanz is on the German-Swiss border.

Wortschatz 1

Karin Looks for a Room

STEFAN: Have you finally found a room?

KARIN: Nope, I'm still looking. Unfortunately I didn't get a place in the dorm.

STEFAN: Hey! Yesterday Helga moved out of our apartment. So now there's a room free. Do you want to move in with us?

KARIN: Terrific! Do you think it's possible?

STEFAN: Of course.

At the Beginning of the Semester

CLARA: Where were you?

EVA: In the bookstore. Why?

CLARA: Did you bring me a course catalogue?

EVA: Yes, I put it on the desk.

CLARA: Oh yeah, it's lying under the newspaper. How much did it cost?

EVA: Four marks fifty, but I'll give it to you for free.

CLARA: That's really nice of you! Thanks a lot.

At the University in Tübingen

PETRA: Have you met the exchange student from Canada yet?

KLAUS: Do you mean Peter?

PETRA: Yes. He speaks fantastic German, doesn't he?

KLAUS: I think he's already studied two semesters in Konstanz.

PETRA: So that's why!

Verben

aus·ziehen, ist ausgezogen[6] to move out

bringen, hat gebracht to bring

glauben to believe; think

legen to lay, put down

mit·bringen, hat mitgebracht to bring along, take along

ziehen, hat gezogen to pull

Substantive

der **Anfang, -̈e** beginning
  am Anfang at the beginning

der **Austauschstudent, -en, -en**[7] exchange student

der **Mensch, -en, -en** person, human being

der **Platz -̈e** place; space; city square

der **Schreibtisch, -e** desk

das **Bett, -en** bed

(das) **Kanada** Canada

das **Studentenwohnheim, -e** student dormitory

das **Vorlesungsverzeichnis, -se** university catalogue listing lectures and courses

die **Universität, -en** university
  an der Universität at the university

die **Vorlesung, -en** university lecture; lecture course

die **Wohngemeinschaft, -en** communal living group, co-op apartment

Adjektive und Adverbien

gestern yesterday
möglich possible
nett nice
wirklich real; really

Andere Vokabeln

unter under, beneath

Gegensätze

am Anfang ≠ am Ende at the beginning ≠ at the end

ausziehen ≠ einziehen to move out ≠ to move in

möglich ≠ unmöglich possible ≠ impossible

Mit anderen Worten

die **Uni, -s** (*student slang*) = **Universität**

die **WG, -s** (*student slang*) = **Wohngemeinschaft**

nee (*colloq.*) = **nein**

---

6. For an explanation of the form **ist ausgezogen**, see *Grammatik*, pp. 163–65.
7. For an explanation of the second ending, see *Grammatik*, p. 175.

Variationen

A Persönliche Fragen

1. Karin findet keinen Platz im Studentenwohnheim. Gibt es bei Ihnen genug Zimmer für alle?

2. Wo wohnen Sie: im Studentenwohnheim, bei einer Familie, in einer WG oder zu Hause bei Ihren Eltern?

3. Stefan wohnt in einer WG. Kennen Sie Studenten in WGs? Was ist dort anders als im Studentenwohnheim?

4. Eva kauft ein Vorlesungsverzeichnis. Was müssen Sie am Semesteranfang kaufen?

5. Eva schenkt Clara das Vorlesungsverzeichnis. Was schenken Sie Ihrem Mitbewohner oder Ihrer Mitbewohnerin?

6. An der Uni in Tübingen gibt es viele Austauschstudenten. Gibt es auch an Ihrer Uni Austauschstudenten? Woher kommen sie?

B Übung: Das möchte ich auch.

Your instructor tells you something she or he has done. Respond that you would like to do that too.

BEISPIEL: Ich habe in Berlin gewohnt.
Ich möchte auch in Berlin wohnen.

1. Ich habe einen Sportwagen gekauft.

2. Ich habe um acht Uhr gefrühstückt.

3. Ich habe Karten gespielt.

4. Ich habe Russisch gelernt.

5. Ich habe viel gemacht.

C Übung: Was meinen Sie?

Antworten Sie mit dem Gegensatz.

BEISPIEL: Finden Sie den Film *gut*?
Nein, ich finde ihn *schlecht*.

1. Soll man *spät* aufstehen?

2. Ist dieses Klassenzimmer zu *groß*?

3. Sind Fremdsprachen *unwichtig*?

4. Ist Deutsch *schwer*?

5. Soll man *immer* in Eile sein?

6. Spricht der Professor zu *langsam*?

7. Soll man *allein* arbeiten?

8. Sind die Studenten hier meistens *faul*?

Studenten auf einer Bank im Park. (Kiel)

Lyrik zum Vorlesen

This brief poem, which Goethe first wrote on the wall of a forest hut where he was spending the night, is certainly the most famous poem in the German language. The simplicity of its three main images (mountains, trees, and birds) and the evocative language of stillness make this a profound statement of a relationship with nature.

Wanderers Nachtlied (1780)

Über allen Gipfeln°	*mountain peaks*
Ist Ruh,°	*peace*
In allen Wipfeln°	*tree tops*
Spürest° du	*feel*
kaum° einen Hauch;°	*hardly / breath*
Die Vögelein° schweigen° im Walde.	*little birds / are silent*
Warte nur, balde°	**balde = bald**
Ruhest° du auch.	*rest*

Johann Wolfgang von Goethe (1749–1832)

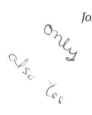

Grammatik

Simple Past Tense of *sein*

To talk about events in the past, German has two tenses. One is called the *perfect tense* and the other, the *simple past tense*. In spoken German, the perfect tense is usually used to talk about the past. You will learn how to use it in this chapter. With the frequently occurring verb **sein,** however, simple past is used more often than perfect. It is therefore very useful for you to learn the following conjugation.[8]

ich **war**	*I was*	wir **waren**	*we were*
du **warst** ⎫ Sie **waren** ⎭	*you were*	ihr **wart** ⎫ Sie **waren** ⎭	*you were*
er/es/sie **war**	*he/it/she was*	sie **waren**	*they were*

1 Übung: Wo waren sie?

Ihr Professor fragt, wo diese Menschen waren. Sagen Sie ihm, sie waren alle in der Buchhandlung.

> BEISPIEL: Wo war Eva?
> Sie war in der Buchhandlung.

1. Wo war Clara?
2. Wo war Franz?
3. Wo warst du?
4. Wo waren die Studenten?

5. Wo war ich?
6. Wo wart ihr?
7. Wo waren wir?
8. Wo waren Sie?

Perfect Tense

In spoken German, one uses the perfect tense with most verbs to talk about events in the past. The perfect tense is a compound tense; that is, it consists of a conjugated *auxiliary* or *helping* verb and a form of the main verb called *past participle*. The participle is the second part of the predicate and is in final position at the end of a sentence or clause.

> *auxiliary   participle*
> Sie **hat** das Buch **gekauft.**   *She bought the book.* or
> *She has bought the book.*

---

8. You will learn how to form the simple past tense of other verbs in *Kapitel 10.*

Conjugation with *haben*

Most German verbs use **haben** as their auxiliary verb. Here is a sample conjugation:

aux. *part.*	
Ich **habe** es **gekauft.**	*I bought it.*
Du **hast** es **gekauft.**	*You bought it.*
Sie **hat** es **gekauft.**	*She bought it.*
Wir **haben** es **gekauft.**	*We bought it.*
Ihr **habt** es **gekauft.**	*You bought it.*
Sie **haben** es **gekauft.**	*They bought it.*

Past Participles of Weak Verbs

There are two basic classes of verbs in German: the *weak* verbs and the *strong* verbs. They are distinguished by the way they form their past participle.

The weak verbs form their past participle by adding the unstressed prefix **ge-** and the ending **-t** or **-et** to the verb stem.[9] Here are some examples of weak verbs you have already learned:

infinitive	*stem*	*auxiliary + past participle*
arbeiten	arbeit-	hat **gearbeitet**
kaufen	kauf-	hat **gekauft**
kosten	kost-	hat **gekostet**
legen	leg-	hat **gelegt**
meinen	mein-	hat **gemeint**

Verbs ending in **-ieren** are *always* weak verbs. They do *not* add the prefix **ge-** in the past participle.

studieren → studier- → hat **studiert**

Er hat in Freiburg **studiert.**   *He studied in Freiburg.*

2 Übung: Was haben Sie gekauft, und was hat das gekostet?

You went on a shopping spree yesterday. Tell your instructor which of the things listed below you bought and what they cost.

1. eine Schreibmaschine (DM 949)
2. einen Taschenrechner (DM 39)
3. ein Regal (DM 98)
4. eine Espressomaschine (DM 129)

Solar-Digital
Taschenrechner
nur 39.–

BEISPIEL: A: Was haben Sie gestern gekauft?
           B: Ich habe ein-_____ gekauft.
           A: Was hat das denn gekostet?
           B: Das hat DM _____ gekostet.

---

9. Stems ending in **-d** or **-t** add **-et: arbeit-** (*stem*), **gearbeitet** (*past participle*)

3 Partnerarbeit: Austauschstudenten

Say where the exchange students come from and where they studied.

> BEISPIEL: Nicole kommt aus Frankreich, und sie hat in Heidelberg
> studiert.

Name	*Heimat (homeland)*	*Universitätsstadt*
Nicole	Frankreich	Heidelberg
Yukiko	Japan	Tübingen
Pedro	Spanien	Saarbrücken
Cathleen	Irland	Wien
Matthew	Kanada	Berlin
Beth	USA	Konstanz

Past Participles of Strong Verbs

The strong verbs form their past participle by adding the prefix **ge-** and the suffix **-n** or **-en** to the verb stem. In addition, many strong verbs change their stem vowel and occasionally also some consonants in the stem. For this reason, *the past participle of each strong verb must be memorized.*[10] Here are some examples of strong verbs you have already learned:

infinitive	*auxiliary + past participle*
geben	hat **gegeben**
stehen	hat **gestanden**
trinken	hat **getrunken**
tun	hat **getan**

4 Übung: Was haben Sie gesehen?

Was haben Sie gestern gesehen? Sagen Sie es der Gruppe.

> BEISPIEL: PROFESSOR: Sagen Sie uns, was Sie gestern gesehen haben.
> STUDENT: Ich habe _____, _____ und _____ gesehen.

5 Kettenreaktion: Was hast du getrunken?

You were all thirsty yesterday. Each person says what he or she drank, then asks the next person.

> BEISPIEL: A: Gestern habe ich _____ getrunken. Was hast du getrunken?
> B: Ich habe _____ getrunken.

Kaffee   Milch

10. Beginning in *Wortschatz 1* of this chapter, the past participle of each new strong verb is given following the infinitive (and present-tense stem-vowel change, when applicable).

Conjugation with *sein*

Some German verbs use **sein** rather than **haben** as their auxiliary verb in the perfect tense.

Gestern **ist** die Helga ausgezogen.   *Helga moved out yesterday.*

To take **sein,** a verb must fulfill two conditions:

1. It must be *intransitive* (i.e., it does *not* take a direct object).

2. It must indicate *change of location or condition.*

Two frequently used verbs are exceptions to this second rule: **sein** itself and **bleiben.** In the perfect tense, these verbs use **sein** as their auxiliary even though they don't show change of location or condition.

Here are some examples of verbs with **sein** as their auxiliary:

infinitive	*aux. + participle*	*shows*
fliegen	**ist geflogen**	
gehen	**ist gegangen**	*change of location*
wandern	**ist gewandert**	
reisen	**ist gereist**	
sterben	**ist gestorben**	*change of condition*
werden	**ist geworden**	
bleiben	**ist geblieben**	*(exceptions)*
sein	**ist gewesen**	

As you can see, verbs with **sein** may be either weak (**gereist**) or strong (**geflogen**).

6 **Kettenreaktion:** Wohin bist du gereist?

Sie haben alle Reisen gemacht. Sagen Sie der Gruppe wohin.

BEISPIEL: STUDENT A: Ich bin nach Mexiko gereist. Wohin bist du gereist?

STUDENT B: Ich bin _____ gereist.
(usw.)

7 **Übung:** Was ist sie geworden?

You've all lost touch with your old school friend Karoline. Tell your instructor what you think she became.

BEISPIEL: Was glauben *Sie?*
Ich glaube, sie ist Ärztin geworden.

Table of Strong Verbs

The following table contains all the strong verbs that you have learned so far.[11] Review your knowledge of the infinitives and stem-vowel changes in the present tense. Note that the verbs that change their stem vowels in the present-tense **du-** and **er-**forms are *always* strong verbs. *Memorize the past participles.*

infinitive	stem-vowel change	aux. + participle	English
ausziehen		*ist* **ausgezogen**	*to move out*
anfangen	fängt an	**hat angefangen**	*to begin*
anrufen		**hat angerufen**	*to call up*
beginnen		**hat begonnen**	*to begin*
besitzen		**hat besessen**	*to possess*
bleiben		*ist* **geblieben**	*to stay*
entscheiden		**hat entschieden**	*to decide*
essen	ißt	**hat gegessen**	*to eat*
fahren	fährt	*ist* **gefahren**	*to drive*
finden		**hat gefunden**	*to find*
fliegen		*ist* **geflogen**	*to fly*
fließen		*ist* **geflossen**	*to flow*
geben	gibt	**hat gegeben**	*to give*
gehen		*ist* **gegangen**	*to go*
halten	hält	**hat gehalten**	*to hold; stop*
heißen		**hat geheißen**	*to be called*
kommen		*ist* **gekommen**	*to come*
laufen	läuft	*ist* **gelaufen**	*to run*
lesen	liest	**hat gelesen**	*to read*
liegen		**hat gelegen**	*to lie*
nehmen	nimmt	**hat genommen**	*to take*
scheinen		**hat geschienen**	*to shine; seem*
schlafen	schläft	**hat geschlafen**	*to sleep*
schließen		**hat geschlossen**	*to close*
schreiben		**hat geschrieben**	*to write*
schwimmen		*ist* **geschwommen**	*to swim*
sehen	sieht	**hat gesehen**	*to see*
sein	ist	*ist* **gewesen**	*to be*
singen		**hat gesungen**	*to sing*
sprechen	spricht	**hat gesprochen**	*to speak*
stehen		**hat gestanden**	*to stand*
sterben	stirbt	*ist* **gestorben**	*to die*
tragen	trägt	**hat getragen**	*to carry; wear*
trinken		**hat getrunken**	*to drink*
tun		**hat getan**	*to do*
vergessen	vergißt	**hat vergessen**	*to forget*
verlassen	verläßt	**hat verlassen**	*to leave*
werden	wird	*ist* **geworden**	*to become*

11. Except for **ausziehen, anfangen, anrufen, besitzen, entscheiden, vergessen,** and **verlassen,** this list includes only the basic verb (e.g., **stehen** but not **aufstehen** or **verstehen**). See pp. 168–69 for the formation of past participles of verbs with separable and inseparable prefixes.

Stop

8 Übung: Heute und gestern.

Ihr Professor sagt etwas über heute. Sie sagen, auch gestern ist es so gewesen.

BEISPIEL: Heute scheint die Sonne.
Auch gestern hat die Sonne geschienen.

1. Heute trägt Thomas einen Pulli.
2. Heute liegt die Zeitung da.
3. Heute finden wir die Vorlesung gut.
4. Heute singt er zu laut.
5. Heute nimmt Vater den Wagen.
6. Heute schließe ich den Laden.
7. Heute steht Markus draußen.
8. Heute liest du einen Artikel.
9. Heute essen wir um sieben.
10. Heute abend wird es kalt.
11. Heute tun wir das.
12. Heute schlafen wir bis acht.
13. Heute läuft Christian durch den Wald.
14. Heute kommt ihr um neun Uhr.
15. Heute geben wir dem Kind ein Brötchen.
16. Heute hält das Auto hier.

Past Participles of Separable-prefix Verbs

Verbs with separable (stressed) prefixes form their past participles by inserting **-ge-** *between* the prefix and the verb stem.

anfangen → hat **angefangen**
aufmachen → hat **aufgemacht**

Das Konzert hat um acht Uhr **angefangen.** — *The concert began at eight o'clock.*
Wann bist du denn **aufgestanden?** — *When did you get up?*
Wer hat den Laden **aufgemacht?** — *Who opened the store?*

9 Übung: Ich habe das schon gemacht!

Ihr Professor sagt Ihnen, Sie sollen etwas tun. Sie sagen, Sie haben es schon getan.

BEISPIEL: Machen Sie doch die Tür auf.
Ich habe sie schon aufgemacht.

1. Fangen Sie doch an.
2. Hören Sie doch auf.
3. Stehen Sie doch auf.
4. Kaufen Sie doch ein.
5. Machen Sie doch die Tür zu.
6. Rufen Sie doch Robert an.

Past Participles of Inseparable-prefix Verbs

Verbs with inseparable (unstressed) prefixes[12] do *not* add the prefix **ge-** in the past participle.

> berichten → hat **berichtet**
> verstehen → hat **verstanden**

> Sie hat uns über Amerika **berichtet.**   *She reported to us about America.*
> Das habe ich nicht **verstanden.**   *I didn't understand that.*

10 **Übung:** Ich habe das schon getan!

Ihr Professor sagt Ihnen, Sie sollen etwas tun. Sie sagen, Sie haben es schon getan.

> BEISPIEL: Beginnen Sie bitte mit Ihrer Arbeit.
> Ich habe mit meiner Arbeit schon begonnen.

1. Beschreiben Sie bitte die Landschaft.
2. Vergessen Sie das.
3. Besuchen Sie Ihre Großeltern.
4. Berichten Sie über Ihre Reise.
5. Besprechen Sie das Problem.
6. Verlassen Sie das Zimmer.

Perfect Tense of Mixed Verbs

There is a handful of German verbs that have the weak participle form **ge—t** but also change their stem. They are called "mixed verbs." The ones you have learned so far are

bringen	hat **gebracht**
mitbringen	hat **mitgebracht**
kennen	hat **gekannt**
wissen	hat **gewußt**

11 **Übung:** Das habe ich schon gewußt!

Your instructor will tell you something obvious. Respond that you already knew that.

> BEISPIEL: Heute ist Donnerstag.
> Ja, das habe ich schon gewußt! *oder*
> Wirklich? Das habe ich nicht gewußt!

12 **Kettenreaktion:** Was hast du heute mitgebracht?

Say what you've brought with you to class today, then ask the next student.

> BEISPIEL: Ich habe heute einen Bleistift mitgebracht. Was hast du mitgebracht?
> Ich habe ein-_____ mitgebracht.

---

12. See p. 138.

The Use of the Perfect Tense

The perfect tense is used much more frequently in German than it is in English. In spoken German, the perfect is the usual tense for talking about events in the past. It is therefore often referred to as the "conversational past." English uses the simple past tense (one-word form) for the same purpose.

Sie **sind** gestern nach Berlin **geflogen.**	They *flew* to Berlin yesterday.
Ich **habe** die Zeitung um sieben **gelesen.**	I *read* the newspaper at seven.

There are no German equivalents for English progressive and emphatic forms in the past.

$$\text{Ich habe } \textbf{gesprochen.} \begin{cases} \textit{I spoke.} \\ \textit{I have spoken.} \\ \textit{I was speaking.} \\ \textit{I did speak.} \end{cases}$$

Two-way Prepositions

You have learned that some prepositions in German are always followed by a prepositional object in the accusative case, while others are always followed by an object in the dative case (review pp. 105–6 and 143–44).

A third group, called the "two-way prepositions," are followed by the *accusative* case when they signal *destination*, and by the *dative* when they signal *location*. Here are some examples:

		Destination (*accusative*)	Location (*dative*)
Preposition		**Answers Wohin?**	**Answers Wo?**
in		Wo gehen die Studenten hin? Sie gehen **in die Mensa.** *They're going (in)to the cafeteria.*	Wo sind die Studenten? Sie sind **in der Mensa.** *They're in the cafeteria.*
auf		Wohin legt Inge das Buch? Sie legt es **auf den Tisch.** *She's putting it on the table.*	Wo liegt das Buch? Es liegt **auf dem Tisch.** *It's lying on the table.*

Fragewörter

The question words **wohin** and **woher** can also be separated in the following way:

Wohin gehst du?	*oder*	**Wo** gehst du **hin**?
Woher kommen Sie?	*oder*	**Wo** kommen Sie **her**?

13 **Übung:** *Wo oder wohin?*

Ihre Professorin fragt Sie, **wo** einige *(some)* Leute sind, oder **wohin** sie gehen. Antworten Sie mit „In der Mensa" oder „In die Mensa."

1. Wo ist Karin?

2. Wo geht ihr jetzt hin?

3. Wo ißt du heute abend?

4. Wo sind Horst und Petra?

5. Wo sollen wir Wolf treffen?

6. Wohin läuft Peter so schnell?

14 **Übung:** *Wo oder wohin?*

Your instructor will ask you some questions about where things are lying or where they are being placed. Answer with „Auf dem Tisch" or „Auf den Tisch" as appropriate.

1. Wo liegt meine Zeitung?

2. Wohin soll ich das Geld legen?

3. Wo liegen die Karten für heute abend?

4. Wohin hast du das Buch gelegt?

Here is a list of two-way prepositions. You should memorize them and their meanings.

preposition	with accusative	with dative
an	to, toward	at, alongside of
auf	onto	on, upon, on top of
hinter	behind	behind
in	into, to	in
neben	beside, next to	beside, next to
über	over, above; across	over, above
unter	under	under, beneath[13]
vor	in front of	in front of
zwischen	between	between

Note: The prepositions **an** and **in** are regularly contracted with the articles **das** and **dem** in the following way:

an das → **ans**
an dem → **am**
in das → **ins**
in dem → **im**

13. **Unter** also has the meaning "among": **Sie hat unter den Studenten gestanden.** *She was standing among the students.*

Here are more examples illustrating how the two-way prepositions are used to show either destination or location. Notice how the verb determines location or destination. For example, verbs like **stehen** and **sein** show location (*dative*); verbs like **fahren** and **gehen** show destination (*accusative*).

	Destination (*accusative*)	Location (*dative*)
Preposition	**Answers Wohin?**	**Answers Wo?**
an	Hans geht **ans Fenster.** *Hans is walking toward the window.*	Hans steht **am Fenster.** *Hans is standing at the window.*
hinter	Das Kind läuft **hinter das Haus.** *The child is running behind the house.*	Das Kind steht **hinter dem Haus.** *The child is standing behind the house.*
neben	Leg dein Buch **neben die Zeitung.** *Put your book next to the newspaper.*	Dein Buch liegt **neben der Zeitung.** *Your book is next to the newspaper.*
über	Wir fliegen **über das Meer.** *We're flying across the ocean.*	Die Sonne scheint **über dem Meer.** *The sun is shining over the ocean.*
unter	Die Katze läuft **unter das Bett.** *The cat runs under the bed.*	Die Katze schläft **unter dem Bett.** *The cat sleeps under the bed.*
vor	Der Bus fährt **vor das Hotel.** *The bus is driving up in front of the hotel.*	Der Bus hält **vor dem Hotel.** *The bus is stopping in front of the hotel.*
zwischen	Er läuft **zwischen die Bäume.** *He's running between the trees.*	Er steht **zwischen den Bäumen.** *He's standing between the trees.*

Note: In their basic meanings, all the two-way prepositions show spatial relations. Many of them can also show non-spatial relationships, e.g., **über** = "about" with verbs like **sprechen, lachen, schreiben,** etc. In this non-spatial meaning, **über** is always followed by accusative case:

Wir haben über **unsere** Amerikareise gesprochen.
Sie schreibt mir über **ihren** Bruder.

15 **Übung:** Wo war Martina heute?

Martina war heute viel unterwegs. Sagen Sie, wo sie war.

BEISPIEL: Sie war in der Stadt.

16 **Gruppenarbeit** *Mit offenen Büchern*

Take turns replacing the verbs in the sentences below with new verbs from
the list. Change the case of the prepositional object according to whether the
verb you use shows destination or location. Choose three or four new verbs
for each sentence.

gehen	liegen	warten
arbeiten	fahren	lesen
laufen	wohnen	halten

1. Wir fahren in die Stadt.

2. Jutta steht hinter dem Haus.

3. Das Kind läuft unter den Tisch.

4. Hans steht am Fenster.

5. Wir sind im Zimmer.

Note on the Prepositions *an* and *auf*

The prepositions **an** and **auf** do not correspond exactly to any English
prepositions.

- **an** generally signals motion *toward* or location *at* a border, edge, or vertical
  surface.

Sie steht **am Tisch.**	*She's standing at the table.*
Gehen Sie bitte **an die Tafel.**	*Please go to the blackboard.*
Wir fahren **ans Meer.**	*We're driving to the ocean.*

- **auf** generally signals motion *onto* or location *upon* a horizontal surface.

Das Buch liegt **auf dem Tisch.**	*The book is (lying) on the table.*
Leg das Buch **auf den Tisch.**	*Put (or lay) the book on the table.*

17 Übung: Wo ist Hans? Wohin geht er?

Sagen Sie, wohin Hans geht oder wo er ist.

18 Übung: *an* oder *auf*?

Complete each sentence with **an** or **auf** and the article.

Wohin? Antworten Sie mit Präposition + *Akkusativ*!

1. Karl geht _____ Tafel.

2. Legen Sie Ihren Mantel _____ Stuhl.

3. Marga fährt im Sommer _____ Meer.

4. Ich habe die Zeitung _____ Schreibtisch gelegt.

Wo? Antworten Sie mit Präposition + *Dativ*!

5. Das Kind steht _____ Stuhl.

6. Karl wartet _____ Tür.

7. Unser Ferienhaus liegt _____ Meer.

8. Das Essen ist schon _____ Tisch.

Masculine N-nouns

A few masculine nouns take the ending **-en** or **-n** in all cases except the nominative singular. They are called "N-nouns."

	singular	*plural*
nom.	der Student	die Studenten
acc.	den Studenten	die Studenten
dat.	dem Studenten	den Studenten

Dieser Student kennt München sehr gut.
Kennst du diesen Student**en**?
Ich habe diesem Student**en** ein Wörterbuch verkauft.

A good rule-of-thumb is that a noun that is masculine, refers to a person or animal, and has the plural ending **-en** or **-n** is an N-noun. Here are the N-nouns you have already learned. Notice the endings; they will be shown in this way in all subsequent *Wortschatz* sections.

der **Bauer, -n, -n**	*farmer*
der **Herr, -n, -en**	*gentleman; Mr.*[14]
der **Journalist, -en, -en**	*journalist*
der **Korrespondent, -en, -en**	*correspondent*
der **Kunde, -n, -n**	*customer*
der **Mensch, -en, -en**	*person, human being*
der **Student, -en, -en**	*student*
der **Tourist, -en, -en**	*tourist*

 19 **Partnerarbeit:** Wer ist das? Ich kenne ihn nicht.

Partner A asks who one of these men is; partner B answers. Partner A says he doesn't know this person. Switch roles for the next man.

BEISPIEL: A: Wer ist das?
           B: Das ist ein Bauer.
           A: Ich kenne diesen _____ nicht.
           B: Wer ist das? (usw.)

14. When **Herr** is used as a title (*Mr.*), it also must have the N-noun singular endings: Das ist Herr Weiß; *but* Kennen Sie Herrn Weiß?

Lesestück — Ein Brief aus Freiburg

Tips zum Lesen und Lernen

Wie schreibt man eine Postkarte oder einen Brief auf deutsch?

Salutation: -e with a female name, -er with a male name

Place and date: day / month / year

Jena, den 20. 5. 91

Liebe Sabine, lieber Markus!

Hallo! Wie geht's Euch denn? Gestern sind wir hier angekommen und haben schon Eure Kusine Gertrud besucht. Sie und ihre Freunde sind wahnsinnig nett und haben uns sehr viel von Jena gezeigt. Morgen fahren wir nach Berlin und sind am Freitag wieder zu Hause. Bis dann.

Viele herzliche Grüße von

Tanja und Fabian

All second person forms capitalized: Euch, Euer, Du, Dein, etc.)

Standard closing = many cordial greetings

Leicht zu merken

automatisch	
finanzieren	finanzieren
der **Film**, -e	
das **Foto**, -s	
das **Konzert**, -e	Konzert
die **Party**, -s	
die **Philosophie**	Philosophie
praktisch	
privat	privat
das **Programm**, -e	Programm
die **Sowjetunion**	Sowjetunion
das **Theater**, -	Theater

Einstieg in den Text

Einen Brief lesen   The following text is a letter written by a German student named Claudia in response to a letter from her American friend Michael, who is coming to Germany as an exchange student. Such informal letters between friends are more loosely structured and associative than formal prose. They tend to be halfway between spoken and written style. As a result, you'll find here conversational phrases and slang (e.g. „Ich kann Dir eine Menge erzählen" or „Da staunst Du wohl, oder?").

Claudia writes first about what she's studying, then tells a bit about student life in Freiburg and compares it to America. Then she describes the difficulty of finding a place to live and talks about the rich cultural life in Freiburg. It is clear that her letter is a response to what Michael has written her. She refers to his letter with the following phrases:

„Dein Brief ist gestern angekommen, . . ." (line 2)

„Du schreibst, . . ." (line 3)

What do you think Michael wrote in his original letter? Claudia also asks some questions of him:

„Wie ist es denn bei Dir? Bekommst Du . . ." (line 43)

How might Michael respond in his next letter to her?

In einer Vorlesung (Darmstadt)

Wortschatz 2

Verben

antworten (+ *dat.*) to answer (*a person*)
Ich kann dir nicht antworten. I can't answer you.

aus·geben, hat ausgegeben to spend (*money*)

beantworten to answer (*a question, letter, etc.*)
Ich kann die Frage nicht beantworten. I can't answer the question.

belegen to register for, to take (*a university course*)

bezahlen to pay for

erzählen to tell, recount

enttäuschen to disappoint

feiern to celebrate, have a party

schicken to send

sitzen, hat gesessen to sit

staunen to be amazed, surprised

Substantive

der Ausweis, -e I.D. card
Studentenausweis student I.D.

der Brief, -e letter

der Bürger, - citizen

der Krieg, -e war

der Stadtplan, ¨e city map

der Termin, -e appointment

das Ende, -n end

das Glück happiness; luck
Glück haben to be lucky

das Haar, -e hair

das Hauptfach, ¨er major field (*of study*)

das Kino, -s movie theater
ins Kino gehen go to the movies

das Nebenfach, ¨er minor field (*of study*)

(das) Polen Poland

das Referat, -e oral report; written term paper

(das) Rumänien Romania

das Stipendium, Stipendien scholarship, stipend

das Studium (university) studies

das Tempo pace, speed, tempo

die Antwort, -en answer

die Geschichte, -n story; history

die Klausur, -en written test

die Kneipe, -n tavern, bar

die Wohnung, -en apartment

die Ferien (*pl.*) (school or university) vacation
die Semesterferien semester break

Adjektive und Adverbien

billig inexpensive, cheap

gerade just, at this moment

je ever

kostenlos free of charge

lieb dear, nice, sweet
Das ist lieb von dir! That's sweet of you!

niedrig low

schlimm bad

selber by oneself (myself, yourself, ourselves, etc.)

sofort immediately, right away

sonst otherwise, apart from that

verantwortlich (für) responsible (for)

wohl probably

Andere Vokabeln

alles (*sing.*) everything

einige some

ein paar a couple (of); a few

Nützliche Ausdrücke

das heißt that means, in other words
d.h. i.e. (= that is)

herzlich willkommen heartily welcome

Gegensätze

billig ≠ teuer cheap ≠ expensive

je ≠ nie ever ≠ never

Glück haben ≠ Pech haben to be lucky ≠ to be unlucky

der Krieg ≠ der Frieden war ≠ peace

Mit anderen Worten

die Bude, -n (*Studentenslang*) = **das Studentenzimmer**

eine Katastrophe = eine schlimme Situation

eine Menge (*colloq.*) = **viel**

Ein Brief aus Freiburg[15]

Claudia Martens hat gerade einen Brief von ihrem amerikanischen Freund Michael Hayward bekommen. Claudia war ein Jahr in Amerika als Austauschschülerin an Mikes high school in Atlanta. Sie schickt ihm sofort eine Antwort.

Freiburg, den 20.2.92

Lieber Michael,

Dein Brief ist gestern angekommen, und ich möchte ihn sofort beantworten. Du schreibst, Du willst zwei Semester an der Uni in Freiburg Geschichte studieren. Das finde ich super! Ich studiere auch Geschichte, aber nur im Nebenfach.
5 Mein Hauptfach ist eigentlich Philosophie. Letztes° Semester habe ich ein sehr interessantes Seminar über den Ersten Weltkrieg belegt. Vielleicht können wir im Herbst zusammen in die Vorlesung über Bismarck und die Gründerjahre[16]
10 gehen.

    Habe ich Dir je über unser Universitätssystem und das Studentenleben bei uns berichtet? Die Semesterferien[17] haben gerade begonnen, also habe ich endlich ein bißchen Freizeit und kann Dir eine Menge erzählen. Im allgemeinen°
15 ist das Tempo bei uns etwas langsamer, und das Studium weniger° stressig als bei Euch. Wir schreiben nicht so viele Klausuren und Referate, und man ist als Student mehr für sich selbst° verantwortlich. Das heißt zum Beispiel, Du kannst abends zu Hause sitzen und Bücher wälzen,° oder
20 mit Freunden in die Kneipe gehen. Erst am Semesterende mußt Du für das Seminar ein Referat schreiben; dann bekommst Du einen Schein.° Bei einer Vorlesung gibt es weder Referate noch° Klausuren! Da staunst Du wohl, oder?°

    Wie Du vielleicht schon weißt, sind unsere Unis staat-
25 lich;° das bedeutet, sie sind für uns Studenten fast kostenlos. Die Studiengebühren° sind sehr niedrig. Ansonsten° muß man praktisch nur für Wohnung, Essen, Bücher und Kleidung Geld ausgeben. Außerdem° bekommen viele Studenten auch das sogenannte° BAföG.[18] Wie finanzierst Du

last

in general

weniger = nicht so

für ... selbst = *for oneself*
Bücher wälzen = *hit the books*

certificate of course credit
weder ... noch = *neither ... nor* /
= *nicht wahr?*
state-run
tuition fees / otherwise

in addition
so-called

---

15. City in Baden-Württemberg near the Black Forest. The Albert-Ludwigs-Universität was founded in 1457.
16. Otto von Bismarck (1815–1898): German statesman and Prussian Chancellor, under whose leadership the German states were united to found the German Empire in 1871. **Gründerjahre:** the "Founders' Years" refers to the period 1870–1900, when many German businesses were founded.
17. The German academic year has a **Wintersemester** that begins in mid-October and ends in mid-February. The **Sommersemester** begins in late April and ends in mid-July. The **Semesterferien** come between semesters.
18. Inexpensive government loans for university students in Germany are mandated by the Federal Education Support Law, or Bundes-Ausbildungsförderungsgesetz (BAföG). This acronym has entered the university vocabulary.

30 eigentlich Dein Jahr in Deutschland? Mit einem Stipendium, oder mußt Du alles selber bezahlen?

Jedenfalls° ist das Essen in der Mensa immer billig und relativ gut, aber mit dem Wohnen ist es manchmal eine Katastrophe: Es gibt nicht genug Studentenwohnheime für alle
35 Studenten, und private Buden sind wahnsinnig teuer geworden. Seit Herbst 1989 ist die Wohnungsnot° besonders schlimm: Wir sind überflutet von° Deutschen aus der ehemaligen° DDR und von den „Aussiedlern" aus Polen, Rumänien und der Sowjetunion.[19] Übrigens habe ich letztes
40 Semester einigen Schulkindern aus zwei Aussiedlerfamilien Nachhilfestunden° in Deutsch gegeben, denn° diese neuen Bürger aus Osteuropa können oft nur wenig Deutsch.

Wie ist es denn bei Dir? Bekommst Du durch das Austauschprogramm automatisch einen Platz im Studenten-
45 wohnheim? Wenn nicht,° dann hast Du Glück: Du kannst zu uns in die WG! Wir haben nämlich° nächstes Semester ein Zimmer frei, und Du bist herzlich willkommen. Michael, Du bist immer so gern ins Kino und Konzert gegangen. Ich bin sicher, die Filme und Konzerte hier werden Dich
50 nicht enttäuschen.° Mit Deinem Studentenausweis bekommst Du im Theater, Kino und Museum immer eine Ermäßigung.°

Jetzt habe ich aber einen Termin beim Arzt und muß nachher für eine Party einkaufen. Wir feiern nämlich heute
55 abend das Semesterende. Also, genug für heute, aber ich schreibe Dir bald wieder. Viele herzliche Grüße an Dich und Deine Familie.

Deine *Claudia*

P.S. Ich hab' Dir einen Stadtplan und ein paar Postkarten von der Altstadt beigelegt,° und dazu° ein neues Foto von mir. Kennst Du mich noch mit kurzen Haaren?

in any case

housing shortage
inundated by
former

tutoring / because

wenn nicht = *if not*
you see

werden . . . enttäuschen = *will . . .*
  disappoint
discount

enclosed / in addition

19. Both citizens of the former German Democratic Republic and the **Aussiedler** ("emigrants," ethnic Germans from other Eastern European countries) have a constitutional right to West German citizenship. Many of them flooded the West German housing and employment markets once *glasnost* permitted mass emigration to the West in the late 1980s.

Fragen zum Lesestück

1. Wo hat Claudia Michael kennengelernt?
2. Was möchte Michael in Freiburg studieren?
3. Wie ist das Tempo im Studentenleben in Freiburg?
4. Warum kostet das Studium in Deutschland nicht sehr viel?
5. Wie finanziert man das Studium?
6. Wo können Studenten billig essen?
7. Warum sind Studentenzimmer manchmal wahnsinnig teuer?
8. Wo kann man sonst leben?
9. Was hat Claudia letztes Semester in ihrer Freizeit gemacht?
10. Wo kann Michael in Freiburg wohnen?
11. Was hat Claudia ihm außer einem Brief geschickt?
12. Was ist für Michael neu auf dem Foto von Claudia?

Situationen aus dem Alltag

Das Studium

Einige von diesen Wörtern kennen Sie schon.

studieren an (+ *dat.*)	*to study at*
Ich studiere an der Uni Freiburg.	
die **Vorlesung, -en**	
das **Seminar, -e**	
das **Fach, ⁻er**	*area of study; subject*
Hauptfach	
Nebenfach	
das **Wintersemester**	*fall term (usually October-February)*
Sommersemester	*spring term (usually April-July)*
die **Bibliothek, -en**	*library*
das **Labor, -s**	*lab*
die **Klausur, -en**	
das **Referat, -e**	
ein Referat halten	*to give a report*
ein Referat schreiben	*to write a paper*
die **Wissenschaft, -en**	*science; scholarship; field of knowledge*

Einige Studienfächer

Note that most academic disciplines are feminine.

die **Anglistik**	Anglisik	*English studies*
die **Betriebswirtschaft**		*management, business*
die **Biologie**	Biologie	*biology*
die **Chemie**	Chemie	*chemistry*
die **Elektrotechnik**		*electrical engineering*
die **Germanistik**	Germanistik	*German studies*
die **Geschichte**		*history*
die **Informatik**	Informatik	*computer science*
Jura (used without article)		*law*
die **Kunstgeschichte**		*art history*
die **Landwirtschaft**		*agriculture*
die **Linguistik**	Linguistik	*linguistics*
die **Mathematik**	Mathematik	*mathematics*
die **Medizin**	Medizin	*medicine*
die **Musikwissenschaft**		*musicology*
die **Pädagogik**	Pädagogik	*education*
die **Philosophie**	Philosophie	*philosophy*
die **Physik**	Physik	*physics*
die **Politikwissenschaft**		*political science*
die **Psychologie**	Psychologie	*psychology*
die **Soziologie**	Soziologie	*sociology*
die **Wirtschaftswissenschaft**		*economics*

Sprechen wir über das Studium

Gruppenarbeit: Was studierst du denn?

Was ist Ihr Hauptfach und was belegen Sie dieses Semester?

> BEISPIEL: Mein Hauptfach ist _____. Dieses Semester belege ich
> _____, _____ und _____. Was studierst denn du?

Partnerarbeit: Interview

Interview each other in more detail about your studies. Take notes if necessary, and be prepared to report to the whole class. Ask each other questions such as the following:

1. Was tust du lieber: Referate schreiben oder Referate halten? Wie oft mußt du das tun?

2. Hast du deine Referate je auf einem Computer geschrieben?

3. Arbeitest du oft in der Bibliothek, oder mehr im Labor?

4. Was willst du nach dem Studium machen?

5. Brauchst du Deutsch für dein Studium oder für deinen Beruf?

6. Wie finanzierst du das Studium? Bekommst du ein Stipendium?

7. Wohnst du im Studentenwohnheim oder privat?

Das Studentenzimmer

Die Möbel (*pl.*)   *furniture*

Dieses Zimmer ist **möbliert** (*furnished*).

1. das Telefon, -e
2. das Bett, -en
3. die Lampe, -n
4. der Teppich, -e
5. die Schreibmaschine, -n
6. die Stereoanlage, -n
7. die Schallplatte, -n
8. das Radio, -s
9. das Bücherregal, -e
10. das Poster, -
11. der Spiegel, -
12. der Wecker, -
13. der Kleiderschrank, ⸚e
14. der Schlüssel, -
15. die Decke, -n
16. der Boden, ⸚

Gruppenarbeit: Beschreiben wir dieses Zimmer.

Wie finden Sie dieses Zimmer? Ist es typisch für die Studentenzimmer bei Ihnen? Kann man hier gut wohnen? Wie sieht *Ihr* Zimmer aus? Was gibt es zum Beispiel *nicht* bei Ihnen?

Zum Schluß

Sprechen wir miteinander!

A **Gruppenarbeit:** Was hat Maria letzte Woche gemacht?

Maria studiert Philosophie an der Uni in Tübingen. Sie ist sehr gut organisiert. Das sieht man an ihrem Terminkalender für letzte Woche. Was hat sie letzte Woche getan?

> BEISPIEL: Am Montag hat sie mit Thomas Kaffee getrunken.

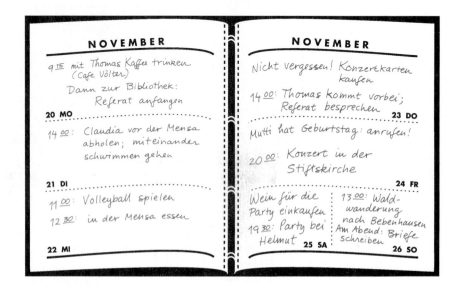

NOVEMBER

9 15 mit Thomas Kaffee trinken
(Café Völter)
Dann zur Bibliothek:
Referat anfangen

20 MO

14 00: Claudia vor der Mensa
abholen; miteinander
schwimmen gehen

21 DI

11 00: Volleyball spielen
12 30: in der Mensa essen

22 MI

NOVEMBER

Nicht vergessen! Konzertkarten
kaufen
14 00: Thomas kommt vorbei;
Referat besprechen

23 DO

Mutti hat Geburtstag: anrufen!

20 00: Konzert in der
Stiftskirche

24 FR

Wein für die
Party einkaufen
19 30: Party bei
Helmut **25 SA**

13 00: Wald-
wanderung
nach Bebenhausen
Am Abend: Briefe
schreiben **26 SO**

B **Gruppenarbeit:** Was haben Sie letzte Woche gemacht?

Jetzt machen Sie *Ihren* Terminkalender auf. Was haben *Sie* letzte Woche getan?

C **Gruppenarbeit:** Wo im Klassenzimmer?

Here is a classroom. Answer the questions about where the people and things are located. Then describe the locations of other people and objects.

> BEISPIEL: Wo sitzt Herr Schröder?
> Er sitzt auf dem Tisch (vor Marie, usw.).

1. Wo sitzt Marie?
2. Wo steht Jutta?
3. Wo steht Karl?
4. Wo steht Gertrud?

5. Wo sitzt der Lehrer?
6. Wo steht Emil?
7. Wo liegt die Zeitung?
8. Wo sind diese Leute?

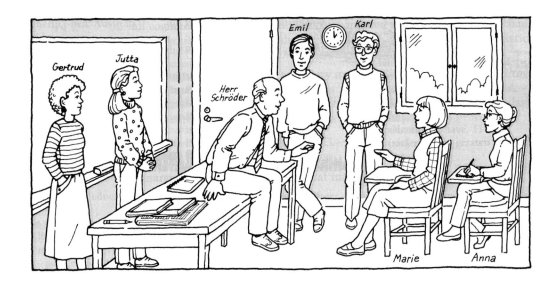

D Gruppenarbeit

Jetzt beschreiben Sie *Ihr* Klassenzimmer. Wo stehen oder sitzen die Menschen?

E Übung

Here is another picture of the same classroom, but now everyone is moving around and doing things. Tell where they are going and what they are doing. Describe any other actions you can.

1. Wohin legt Gertrud ihr Buch?

2. Wo geht Karl hin?

3. Wohin legt der Lehrer das Buch?

4. Wo geht Emil hin?

5. Wo geht Anna hin?

Zwei Studenten sind schon Mitbewohner in einer WG, und zwei andere Studenten wollen in diese WG. Die Mitbewohner interviewen die neuen Studenten über ihr Studium und ihre Interessen (*interests*).

Was studiert ihr?

Habt ihr je in einer WG gewohnt?

Warum wollt ihr bei uns wohnen? usw.

Die neuen Studenten haben auch einige Fragen:

Wie sehen die Zimmer aus?

Gibt es schon einen Schreibtisch im Zimmer? usw.

Schreiben Sie zu Hause

G **Was habe ich letzte Woche gemacht?** In exercise A above you used Maria's appointment calendar to help you describe what she did last week, then in exercise B you described your own activities. Now prepare a more extensive written paragraph in German describing what you did last week.

H „Liebe Claudia, . ." Claudias Brief an Michael Hayward haben Sie schon gelesen. In diesem Brief hat sie ihm das Studentenleben in Freiburg beschrieben. Jetzt spielen Sie die Rolle von Michael Hayward und schreiben Sie eine Antwort an Claudia. Beantworten Sie ihre Fragen und schreiben Sie über das Studentenleben bei Ihnen. Haben Sie andere Fragen an Claudia über Freiburg und das Studium dort? (Review „Wie schreibt man eine Postkarte oder einen Brief" on p. 176).

I Wie sagt man das auf deutsch?

1. I've brought you a course catalogue.

2. Did it cost much?

3. No, it was cheap. Shall I put it on your desk?

4. The lecture began at ten o'clock.

5. Unfortunately, I arrived too late.

6. I stood behind my friends and didn't hear anything.

7. What did you study in Dresden?

8. History was my major but I also studied German.

9. Tonight we're going to the movies together.

10. I hope you haven't forgotten your student I.D.

11. No, it's in my pocket.

12. Good, let's go! We have to be there before 8:00 o'clock.

Almanach

Ein Vorlesungsverzeichnis

Oberseminare:

14169 Aufgaben der Erforschung mittelalterlicher und frühneuzeitlicher Litera- *Harms*
tur, 1stündig, Mo. 16.30—18 (14täglich)

14170 Probleme deutscher Literatur im Mittelalter, 2stündig, Mo. 17—18.30 *Hellgardt*

14171 Probleme der Mediävistik, 1stündig, Mo. 17—19 (14täglich) *Peil*

14172 Probleme von deutscher Sprache und Literatur, 1stündig, Fr. 11—13 *H. F. Rosenfeld*
(14täglich)

14173 Philologisches Seminar: Neuentdeckte Überlieferungen von Minnesang *Worstbrock*
und Sangspruchdichtung, 2stündig, Do. 15—17

14174 Übungen zur spätmittelalterlichen Literatur, 2stündig, Do. 17—19 *Williams*

3.4. Neuere deutsche Literaturgeschichte
Münchner Vorlesung zur Gegenwartsliteratur:

14175 Sten Nadolny: Das Erzählen und die guten Absichten, Mo., 2.7., Di. 3.7.,
Di. 10.7., Mo. 16.7., Di. 17.7., jeweils 19—20 Uhr, Große Aula

Vorlesungen:

14176 Einführung in die Textanalyse, 2stündig, Di. 11—13, HS 201, Hauptgebäu- *Hoffmann*
de

14177 Theorien literarischer Evolution: Vom Formalismus zur Systemtheorie, *Jäger*
2stündig, Fr. 12—14, HS E 02, Schellingstr. 3, VG

14178 Literatur und Lust — Zur Kritik literaturwissenschaftlicher Vernunft, *Anz*
2stündig, Di. 15—17, HS 224, Hauptgebäude

14179 Das Essen und die Literatur, 2stündig, Do. 11—13, HS 133, Hauptgebäu- *Neumann*
de

14180 Literatur im Zeitalter des Absolutismus I (Barock), 2stündig, Fr. 11—13, *Eibl*
HS E 03, Schellingstr. 3, VG

14181 Die deutsche Literatur der Aufklärung, 2stündig, Mi. 15—17, HS E 01, *Schmitz*
Schellingstr. 3, VG

14182 Österreichische Literatur im Exil 1938—1945, 2stündig, Mo. 17—19, HS *Fischer*
217, Hauptgebäude

14183 Friedrich Schiller, der Historiker, Dichter und Theoretiker, 2stündig, Di. *Bauer B.*
9—11, HS 109, Hauptgebäude

14184 Geschichte der deutschen Lyrik von der Romantik bis zum Naturalis- *Häntzschel*
mus, 3stündig, Do. 8.30—11, HS 331, Hauptgebäude

Seminare Stufe I:
Einführung in die Neuere deutsche Literatur

14185 Kurs A: 4stündig, Do. 11—15 *Deubel*

14186 Kurs B: 4stündig, Do. 15—19 *Deubel*

14187 Kurs C: 4stündig, Mo., Do. 11—13 *Dittmann*

14188 Kurs D: 4stündig, Mi. 15—19 *Haefs*

14189 Kurs E: 4stündig, Mi., Do. 9—11 *Henckmann*

14190 Kurs F: 4stündig, Mi., Do. 11—13 *Henckmann*

14191 Kurs G: 4stündig, Di., Do. 17—19 *Hoffmann*

14192 Kurs H: 4stündig, Mi., Fr. 9—11 *Schröder*

14193 Kurs I: 4stündig, Mi., Fr. 11—13 *Schröder*

Deutsch im Rahmen einer Fächergruppendidaktik:

14194 Kurs K: 3stündig, Do. 8.30—11 *Dittmann*

14195 Kurs L: 3stündig, Mo. 12—15 *Hay*

Seminare Stufe II:

14196 Computerphilologie, 2stündig, Mi. 17—19 *Deubel*

14197 Semiotische Grundlagentexte I, 2stündig, Di. 11—13 *Jäger*

14198 Einführung in die Editionskunde, 2stündig, Do. 15—17 *Zehm*

(Einführung in) Feministische Theorie und Literaturwissenschaft

14199 Kurs A: 2stündig, Fr. 9—11 *Henckmann*

Auf Reisen

Communicative Goals
- Expressing intentions, opinions, preferences and polite requests
- Making travel plans and talking about traveling
- Conversing on the telephone

Cultural Goal
- Learning about traveling in Germany and Europe

Lyrik zum Vorlesen   Wilhelm Müller, „Wanderschaft"

Grammatik   Coordinating Conjunctions   •   Verbs with Dative Objects   •   Personal Dative   •   Using *würden* + infinitive   •   More on Two-way Prepositions   •   *Der*-words versus *ein*-words   •   Perfect Tense of Modal Verbs

Lesestück   Unterwegs per Autostop oder mit der Bahn

Situationen aus dem Alltag   Reisen und Verkehr

Almanach   Jugendherbergen (*Youth Hostels*)

Dialoge

Am Bahnhof

GEPÄCKTRÄGER: Darf ich Ihnen helfen?

TOURISTIN: Ja, bitte! Würden Sie mir den Koffer tragen?

GEPÄCKTRÄGER: Gerne. Wohin müssen Sie denn?

TOURISTIN: Gleis drei. Mein Zug fährt gleich ab.

Vor der Urlaubsreise

MARION: Suchst du die Thermosflasche?

THORSTEN: Nein, nicht die Thermosflasche, sondern den Straßenatlas. Ich glaube, ich habe ihn auf den Tisch gelegt.

MARION: Ja, hier liegt er, unter meiner Jacke.

THORSTEN: Häng die Jacke doch auf, dann haben wir mehr Platz. Ich möchte unsere Reise nach Venedig planen.

Am Telefon

Es klingelt lange. Herr Krogmann kommt endlich ans Telefon.

HERR KROGMANN: Krogmann.

MARION: Hallo Papa! Hier ist Marion. Warum hast du nicht gleich geantwortet?

KROGMANN: Ach, Marion, seid ihr wieder zurück? Ich habe auf dem Sofa gelegen und bin eingeschlafen.

MARION: Oh, das tut mir leid.

KROGMANN: Das macht nichts. Ich habe sowieso aufstehen wollen. Wie war denn eure Reise?

MARION: Alles war wunderbar.

Hauptbahnhof in Hamburg.

Wortschatz 1

At the Train Station

PORTER: May I help you?
TOURIST: Yes, please. Would you carry my suitcase?
PORTER: Gladly. Where do you have to go?
TOURIST: Track three. My train is leaving right away.

Before the Trip

MARION: Are you looking for the thermos bottle?
THORSTEN: No, not the thermos bottle, but the road atlas. I think I put it on the table.
MARION: Yes, here it is, under my jacket.
THORSTEN: Hang up the jacket, then we'll have more room. I'd like to plan our trip to Venice.

On the Telephone

The phone rings a long time. Mr. Krogmann finally comes to the telephone.

HERR KROGMANN: Krogmann.
MARION: Hello, Dad. This is Marion. Why didn't you answer right away?
KROGMANN: Oh, Marion, are you back? I was lying on the sofa and fell asleep.
MARION: Oh, I'm sorry.
KROGMANN: That doesn't matter. I wanted to get up anyway. How was your trip?
MARION: Everything was wonderful.

Verben

ab·fahren (fährt ab), ist abgefahren to depart, leave (*by vehicle*)
danken (+ *dat.*) to thank
ein·schlafen (schläft ein), ist eingeschlafen to fall asleep
gefallen (gefällt), hat gefallen (+ *dat.*) to please
  Das Buch gefällt mir. I like the book.
gehören (+ *dat.*) to belong to (*a person*)
hängen, hat gehängt (*trans.*) to hang
  auf·hängen to hang up
hängen, hat gehangen (*intrans.*) to be hanging
helfen (hilft), hat geholfen (+ *dat.*) to help
klingeln to ring
setzen to set (down), put
stellen to put, place
würden (+ *infinitive*) would (do something)[1]

Substantive

der **Bahnhof, -̈e** train station
der **Gepäckträger, -** porter, redcap
der **Koffer, -** suitcase
der **Straßenatlas** road atlas
der **Zug, -̈e** train

das **Gepäck** luggage
das **Gleis, -e** track

das **Telefon, -e** telephone
(das) **Venedig** Venice

die **Flasche, -n** bottle
die **Thermosflasche** thermos bottle

Adjektive und Adverbien

sowieso anyway
wunderbar wonderful

Andere Vokabeln

sondern but rather, but . . . instead

Nützliche Ausdrücke

Das (es) tut mir leid. I'm sorry (about that).
Das (es) macht nichts. That (it) doesn't matter.
Das ist (mir) egal. It doesn't matter (to me). I don't care.

Gegensätze

abfahren ≠ ankommen to depart ≠ to arrive
aufstehen ≠ ins Bett gehen to get up ≠ to go to bed
einschlafen ≠ aufwachen to fall asleep ≠ to wake up

Mit anderen Worten

Das ist mir Wurscht. (*colloq.*) = **Das ist mir egal.**

---

1. **Würden** is a subjunctive form of **werden**. For its use, see p. 198.

Variationen

A Persönliche Fragen

1. Sind Sie je mit dem Zug gefahren? Wohin?

2. Fahren Sie gern mit dem Zug? Haben Sie das schon oft gemacht?

3. Die Touristin muß zu ihrem Zug. Wohin müssen Sie heute?

4. Thorsten und Marion brauchen einen Straßenatlas für ihre Reise. Was brauchen Sie für eine Reise?

5. Thorsten plant eine Reise nach Venedig. Planen Sie eine Reise in den Ferien? Wohin?

6. Herr Krogmann schläft auf dem Sofa. Wo schlafen Sie lieber am Nachmittag, auf dem Sofa oder im Bett?

7. Schlafen Sie auch gern nachmittags?

B Reaktionen

Respond to the statements and questions on the left with an appropriate phrase from the right.

1. Ich kann den Koffer nicht tragen.	Einverstanden!
2. Würden Sie mir bitte helfen?	Doch!
3. Hast du das nicht gewußt?	Oh, das tut mir leid!
4. Wo fährt denn Ihr Zug ab?	Das macht nichts!
5. Waren die Hausaufgaben besonders schwer?	Gerne!
	Auf dem Tisch.
6. Wie war die Reise?	Gar nichts.
7. Wohin hast du den Atlas gelegt?	Auf das Sofa.
8. Wo liegt denn der Stadtplan?	Das finde ich auch.
9. Gehen wir zusammen einkaufen?	Bitte sehr.
10. Was ist denn los?	Auf Gleis zehn.
	Nee, gar nicht.
	Wunderbar!

C Übung: Das würde ich gerne tun.

Ihre Professorin fragt Sie, ob Sie etwas machen wollen. Antworten Sie, Sie würden das gerne tun.

BEISPIEL: Wollen Sie etwas essen?
    Ja, ich würde gerne etwas essen.

1. Wollen Sie etwas lesen?

2. Wollen Sie etwas sehen?

3. Wollen Sie etwas trinken?

4. Wollen Sie in die Bibliothek?

5. Wollen Sie jetzt aufhören?

The literature of the Romantic period in Germany produced poems famous for their expression of themes such as moonlit nights, the language of nature, love, longing, and wandering. In the early 19th century **das Wandern** described the life of an itinerant journeyman. These were artisans who journeyed from town to town, gaining experience with different master craftsmen.

Wilhelm Müller's poem cycle „Die schöne Müllerin" (1820) is unified by the theme of the love of the journeyman for the miller's daughter.[2] In this poem the youth is moved to **Wanderlust** by the mill itself with its rushing water and turning wheels. He ends by asking the miller and his wife for permission to depart.

Wanderschaft°

journeying

Das Wandern ist des Müllers Lust,°
Das Wandern!
Das muß ein schlechter Müller sein,
Dem niemals fiel das Wandern ein,°
Das Wandern.

des . . . Lust = *the miller's desire*

dem . . . ein = *who has never thought of wandering*

Vom Wasser haben wir's gelernt,
Vom Wasser!
Das hat nicht Rast° bei Tag und Nacht,
Ist stets° auf Wanderschaft bedacht,°
Das Wasser.

rest
stets = immer/*intent*

Das sehn wir auch den Rädern ab,°
Den Rädern!
Die gar nicht gerne stille stehn
Und sich mein Tag nicht müde drehn,°
Die Räder.

sehn . . . ab: *see it from the wheels*

Und . . . drehn = *never tire of turning*

Die Steine selbst,° so schwer sie sind,
Die Steine!
Sie tanzen mit den muntern Reihn°
Und wollen gar noch schneller sein,
Die Steine!

Steine selbst = *even the stones*

cheerful dance

O Wandern, Wandern, meine Lust,
O Wandern!
Herr Meister und Frau Meisterin,
Laßt mich in Frieden weiterziehn°
Und wandern!

Laßt . . . ziehn = *let me go in peace*

Wilhelm Müller (1794–1827)

---

2. Set to music by Franz Schubert, this poem is the first song in his cycle „Die schöne Müllerin," op. 5, no. 1 (D 795).

Grammatik

Coordinating Conjunctions

Coordinating conjunctions are words that join clauses that could each stand alone as a simple sentence. The coordinating conjunction joins them into a compound sentence.

Christa ist achtzehn.   Ihr Bruder ist sechzehn.
Christa ist achtzehn, **und** ihr Bruder ist sechzehn.

Kannst du das Fenster aufmachen?   Soll ich es machen?
Kannst du das Fenster aufmachen, **oder** soll ich es machen?

The most common coordinating conjunctions in German are

und	*and*
oder	*or*
aber	*but, however*
sondern	*but rather, instead*
denn	*for, because*

Remember the iron-clad rule that in German statements, the verb is always in second position. A coordinating conjunction is *not* counted as being in first position in its clause. This means that the word order of the second clause is *not* affected by the coordinating conjunction.

$$0 \quad 1 \quad 2$$
Klaus muß bis drei arbeiten, **aber** dann kann er nach Hause.

$$0 \quad 1 \quad 2$$
Ute kommt nicht zu Fuß, **sondern** sie fährt mit dem Auto.

$$0 \quad 1 \quad 2$$
Helmut ißt erst um sieben, **denn** er arbeitet bis sechs.

The coordinating conjunctions are also used to join units smaller than a clause.

Ich habe einen Bruder **und** eine Schwester.
Möchtest du Wein **oder** Bier?
Dieser Laden ist gut, **aber** sehr teuer.
Barbara ist nicht hier, **sondern** in Italien.

Note on punctuation: There is *always* a comma before **aber, sondern,** and **denn.** Before **und** and **oder,** there is only a comma if a complete clause (with subject) follows.

Jens geht in die Stadt **und** kauft Lebensmittel ein.
Jens geht in die Stadt, **und** Maria kauft Lebensmittel ein.

1 **Partnerarbeit**

Use **und, aber, oder,** or **denn** to join each sentence from column A to one from column B. Try to find the most logical pairings. Compare results with other students.

<table>
<tr><td align="center">A</td><td align="center">B</td></tr>
<tr><td>Meine Eltern kommen morgen.</td><td>Ich möchte sie dort besuchen.</td></tr>
<tr><td>Bist du heute krank?</td><td>Willst du in einer WG wohnen?</td></tr>
<tr><td>Gisela studiert in Freiburg.</td><td>Ich zeige ihnen meine Wohnung.</td></tr>
<tr><td>Ich bringe das Buch mit.</td><td>Mein Bruder wohnt auf dem Land.</td></tr>
<tr><td>Ich wohne in der Stadt.</td><td>Du sollst es lesen.</td></tr>
<tr><td>Ich bin jetzt in Eile.</td><td>Sie hat mir nicht geantwortet.</td></tr>
<tr><td>Willst du in der Mensa essen?</td><td>Mein Zug fährt gleich ab.</td></tr>
<tr><td>Willst du allein wohnen?</td><td>Wollen wir bei mir etwas kochen?</td></tr>
<tr><td>Ich habe Sabine gefragt.</td><td>Geht es dir gut?</td></tr>
</table>

(handwritten: und, with arrow connecting "Meine Eltern kommen morgen." to "Ich zeige ihnen meine Wohnung.")

aber versus *sondern*

Aber and **sondern** are both translated with English "but." Both express a contrast, but they are *not* interchangeable. **Sondern** *must* be used when "but" means "but . . . instead," "but rather."

> Er bleibt zu Hause, **aber** sie geht einkaufen.
> *He's staying home, but she's going shopping.*
> Er bleibt nicht zu Hause, **sondern** geht einkaufen.
> *He's not staying home, **but** is going shopping **instead.***

Sondern *always* follows a *negative* statement and expresses *mutually exclusive alternatives.* Note that the clause following **sondern** often leaves out elements it has in common with the first clause. Such deletion is called *ellipsis.*

> Er bleibt nicht zu Hause, sondern [er] geht einkaufen.
> Das ist kein Wein, sondern [das ist] Wasser.
> Käthe hat es nicht getan, sondern die Kinder [haben es getan].

2 **Übung:** *Aber* oder *sondern?*

Combine each pair of simple sentences into a compound sentence, using **aber** or **sondern** as appropriate. Use ellipsis where possible.

1. Sie fliegt nach Italien. Ihr Mann fährt mit dem Zug.

2. Sie haßt mich nicht. Sie liebt mich.

3. Es ist noch nicht sieben Uhr. Er ist schon zu Hause.

4. Ich fahre nicht mit dem Auto. Ich komme zu Fuß.

5. Ich trage keinen Mantel. Ich trage meine Jacke.

6. Bernd mag dieses Bier nicht. Lutz trinkt es gern.

Position of *nicht* before *sondern*

You have learned that in negations, **nicht** *follows* the direct object and expressions of definite time (p. 79). However, if these elements are followed by an alternative introduced by **sondern, nicht** will *precede* them. When **nicht** negates only a single element, it immediately precedes that element.

Ich kaufe den Mantel nicht.	*but*	Ich kaufe **nicht den Mantel,** sondern die Jacke.
Johanna arbeitet heute nicht.	*but*	Johanna arbeitet **nicht heute,** sondern morgen.[3]

3 **Übung:** Nein, nicht x, sondern y.

Answer your instructor's questions negatively, using **sondern.**

BEISPIEL: Wollen Sie *um sieben* frühstücken?
Nein, ich will nicht um sieben frühstücken, sondern um zehn.

1. Suchen Sie *die Thermosflasche?*

2. Gehen Sie *am Mittwoch* ins Kino?

3. Gehen Sie *mit Ursula* in die Stadt?

4. Gehen Sie mit Ursula *in die Stadt?*

5. Wollen Sie mir *die Fotos* zeigen?

6. Waren Sie *gestern* in der Bibliothek?

Verbs with Dative Objects

A few German verbs require an object in the dative case rather than the accusative. Two of these are **helfen** and **antworten.**

Ich sehe den Mann.	*I see the man.*
but	
Ich helfe **dem** Mann.	*I'm helping the man.*
Du fragst die Frau.	*You ask the woman.*
but	
Du antwortest **der** Frau.	*You answer the woman.*

This chapter introduces the following verbs with dative objects:

antworten	*to answer* (someone)
danken	*to thank*
gefallen	*to please*
gehören	*to belong to*
glauben	*to believe* (someone)[4]
helfen	*to help*

---

3. When the contrast expressed by **sondern** is especially strong, the sentence can even begin with **nicht:** Nicht den Mantel kaufe ich, sondern die Jacke. *It's not the coat I'm buying, but the jacket.*

4. **Glauben** takes an accusative inanimate object, but a dative personal object: **Ich glaube das.** but **Ich glaube dir.** One can thus say: **Ich glaube dir das.** = *I believe you when you say that.*

The dative object is usually a person.

Marie dankt **dem Lehrer.**	*Marie thanks the teacher.*
Wem gehört dieser Wagen?	*Who owns this car? (Literally: To whom does this car belong?)*
Diese Stadt gefällt **mir.**	*I like this city. (Literally: This city pleases me.)*

Note the translation of the last example above. **Gefallen** is another way of saying "to like something" (see pp. 107–108), but subject and object are the reverse of English. Remember that the verb must agree in number with the subject.

Diese Städte **gefallen** mir.

I like these cities.

4 **Übung** Wem helfen die Kinder?

Die Kinder wollen heute helfen. Sagen Sie, wem sie helfen.

5 **Übung:** Wem gehört das Buch?

Tell your instructor what belongs to whom.

> BEISPIEL: Wem gehört dieses Buch?
> Es gehört mir.

6 **Übung:** Was gefällt Ihnen?

Your instructor asks if you like various things. Say whether you do or not.

> BEISPIEL: Gefällt Ihnen das Wetter heute?
> Ja, es gefällt mir. *oder* Nein, es gefällt mir nicht.

1. Gefällt Ihnen ihre Arbeit?
2. Gefällt Ihnen dieses Buch?
3. Gefällt Ihnen mein Hemd?
4. Gefällt Ihnen das Wetter heute?
5. Gefallen Ihnen die Vorlesungen an der Uni?
6. Gefallen Ihnen diese Bilder?
7. Gefallen Ihnen meine Schuhe?
8. Gefällt Ihnen dieses Zimmer?

7 **Partnerarbeit:** Wer kann mir helfen?

Your instructor asks a general question. Turn to your partner and direct the question specifically to him or her. Your partner answers with anything that makes sense. Reverse roles for the next question.

> BEISPIEL: Wer kann mir helfen?
> A: Kannst *du* ihr helfen?
> B: Nein, ich kann ihr nicht helfen. Ich habe keine Zeit.

1. Wer glaubt mir?
2. Wer kann mir antworten?
3. Wem gehört denn dieser Regenschirm?

4. Wem gefällt das Wetter heute?
5. Wer kann mir heute helfen?

Personal Dative

The dative case is also used to indicate a person's involvement in or reaction to a situation. This *personal dative* is often translated by English "to" or "for."

Ist es **Ihnen** zu kalt?	*Is it too cold **for you**?*
Es wird **mir** zu dunkel.	*It's getting too dark **for me**.*
Wie geht es **dir**?	*How are you? (Literally, How goes it **for you**?)*
Wie geht es **deiner Mutter**?	*How is **your mother**?*
Das ist **mir** egal.	*It's all the same **to me**.*

The personal dative may often be omitted without changing the basic meaning of the sentence.

> Ist es zu kalt?   Es wird zu dunkel.   Wie geht es?

It may *not* be omitted in the following idiom:

> **Das tut mir leid.**   *I'm sorry about that.*

8 **Übung:** Ist es Ihnen zu kalt?

Your instructor asks how you feel about something. Give your opinion, then ask your neighbor for an opinion.

> BEISPIEL: Ist es Ihnen hier zu kalt?
> A: Mir ist es nicht zu kalt. Und dir?
> B: Mir ist es zu kalt.

1. Ist es Ihnen zu dunkel hier?
2. Ist Ihnen dieses Zimmer zu heiß?
3. Ist Ihnen dieses Buch zu teuer?
4. Ist Ihnen dieser Stuhl hoch genug?
5. Macht Ihnen Deutsch Spaß?
6. Ist Ihnen der Winter hier zu kalt?

9 Partnerarbeit: Das tut mir leid / Das ist mir egal

Say something (invented or real) about how things are going for you, what you're doing at the moment, etc. Your partner must decide whether to respond with indifference or sympathy. Then switch roles.

BEISPIEL: Ich habe morgen eine Klausur.
Oh, das tut mir leid. *oder* Das ist mir egal.

Using *würden* + infinitive

To express intentions, opinions, preferences, and polite requests the verb **würden** is used with an infinitive.

Würden Sie mir den Koffer **tragen?**	*Would you carry my suitcase?*
Was **würdest** du gerne **tun?**	*What would you like to do?*
Ich **würde** das nicht **machen.**	*I wouldn't do that.*

The German equivalent of English "would" is **würden.**[5] It functions like a modal verb, with a dependent infinitive in final position. **Würden** is conjugated like **möchten** (see p. 76):

Ich **würde** sagen . . .	Wir **würden** sagen . . .
Du **würdest** sagen . . .	Ihr **würdet** sagen . . .
Er/sie **würde** sagen . . .	Sie/sie **würden** sagen . . .

10 Gruppenarbeit: Würden Sie bitte . . . ?

Ask your instructor to do a favor for you. Some possibilities are listed below.

BEISPIEL: Würden Sie bitte das Fenster schließen?

mir den Koffer tragen	für uns ein Foto machen
mir eine Brezel kaufen	Lebensmittel einkaufen
das Mittagessen kochen	Ihre Arbeit beschreiben
mir den Bahnhof zeigen	mir den Staßenatlas geben

---

5. **Würden** is the present subjunctive form of **werden.** See pp. 417–22 for an explanation of the general subjunctive.

11 **Kettenreaktion:** Ich würde gern . . .

Was würden Sie gerne heute abend machen? Sagen Sie es, und dann fragen Sie weiter.

> BEISPIEL: Heute abend würde ich gern _____. Und du?
> Ich würde gern·_____.

More on Two-way Prepositions

There is an important group of verb pairs used with the two-way prepositions. One verb shows destination and always takes the accusative case. The other shows location and always takes the dative case.

Destination (accusative)	Location (dative)
Weak Transitive Verbs	*Strong Intransitive verbs*
legen, hat gelegt *to lay (down), put*	**liegen, hat gelegen** *to lie, be lying*
Ich lege das Buch **auf den Schreibtisch** *I'm putting the book on the desk.*	Das Buch liegt **auf dem Schreibtisch** *The book is (lying) on the desk.*
setzen, hat gesetzt *to set (down), put*	**sitzen, hat gesessen** *to sit, be sitting*
Sie setzt das Kind **auf den Stuhl.** *She's putting the child on the chair.*	Das Kind sitzt **auf dem Stuhl.** *The child is (sitting) on the chair.*
stellen, hat gestellt *to place (down), put*	**stehen, hat gestanden** *to stand, be standing*
Ich stelle die Flasche **auf den Tisch.** *I'll put the bottle on the table.*	Die Flasche steht **auf dem Tisch.** *The bottle is (standing) on the table.*
hängen, hat gehängt *to hang up*	**hängen, hat gehangen** *to be hanging*
Er hat die Karte **an die Wand** gehängt. *He hung the map on the wall.*	Die Karte hat **an der Wand** gehangen. *The map hung on the wall.*

Note that **hängen** has one infinitive form but a weak participle (**gehängt**) and a strong participle (**gehangen**).

Legen and **liegen** are used when objects are *laid down* or are *lying* in a horizontal position. **Stellen** and **stehen** are used when objects are *stood up* or are *standing* in a vertical position.

> Ich **lege** das Buch auf den Tisch.　　*I'm putting the book (down flat) on the table.*
>
> *but*
> Ich **stelle** das Buch ins Bücherregal.　　*I'm putting the book (upright) in the bookcase.*

Frau Schneider is working around the house. Describe what she is doing in the left-hand pictures, then the results of her efforts in the right-hand pictures.

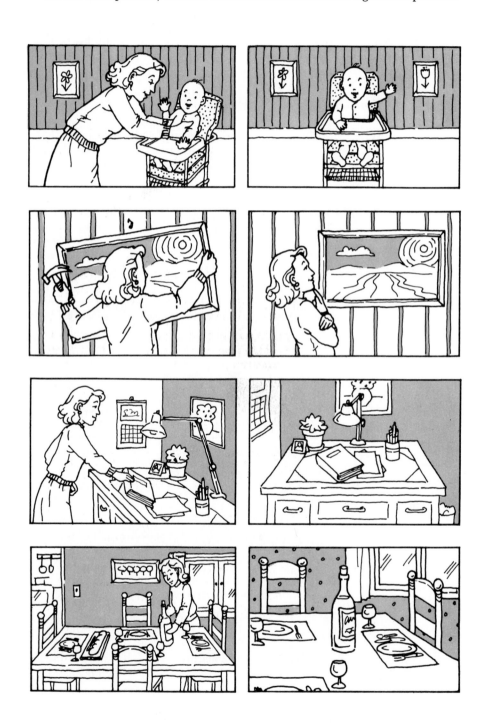

Der-words versus ein-words

The **der**-words and the **ein**-words modify nouns. All the **der**-words have the same endings that show case, gender, and number. The **ein**-words have the same set of endings with three exceptions. Here is a list of the most common **der**-words in the nominative case. You already know the first three. The last two are new.

masc.	neut.	fem.	plur.	
der	das	die	die	the; that (when stressed)
dieser	dieses	diese	diese	this, these
jeder	jedes	jede	alle	each, every; (plur.) all
solcher	solches	solche	solche	such
welcher	welches	welche	welche	which?

Since the endings of the definite article (**der, das, die**) are slightly irregular, **dieser** is used here to review the **der**-word endings in the three cases you know so far.

	der-word endings			
	masc.	*neut.*	*fem.*	*plural*
nom.	dieser Stuhl ⎫			
acc.	diesen Stuhl ⎬	dieses Buch	diese Uhr	diese Bücher
dat.	diesem Stuhl	diesem Buch	dieser Uhr	diesen Büchern

The **ein**-words are **ein, kein,** and all the possessive adjectives (**mein, dein, sein, ihr/Ihr, unser, euer**). They have the same endings as **der**-words *except in three cases* where they have *no* endings, as highlighted in the following table.

	ein-word endings			
	masc.	*neut.*	*fem.*	*plural*
nom.	**mein** Stuhl	**mein Buch** ⎫		
acc.	meinen Stuhl	**mein Buch** ⎬	meine Uhr	meine Bücher
dat.	meinem Stuhl	meinem Buch	meiner Uhr	meinen Büchern

▓ Übung

Your instructor makes a statement. Student A asks for clarification. Student B specifies what's being talked about.

> BEISPIEL: PROFESSOR: Das Zimmer ist klein.
> STUDENT A: Welches Zimmer ist klein?
> STUDENT B: Dieses Zimmer ist klein.

1. Das Hemd ist teuer.
2. Die Turnschuhe sind neu.
3. Der Lehrling heißt Martin.
4. Die Gruppe fährt nach Europa.
5. Der Pulli ist häßlich.
6. Die Brötchen sind frisch.

 ## ▓ Übung

Respond to what your instructor says, as in the example.

> BEISPIEL: Dieser Berg ist steil.
> Ja, aber nicht jeder Berg ist steil.

1. Diese Stadt ist langweilig.
2. Dieses Studentenwohnheim ist neu.
3. Dieser Tourist kann Deutsch.
4. Diese Arbeit macht mich müde.
5. Dieser Laden macht früh auf.
6. Dieser Zug fährt schnell.
7. Dieser Artikel ist kurz.

▓ Übung: Wem gehört das?

Someone's been stealing things in your dorm. The police come around asking suspicious questions about things in your room. Say that everything is yours.

> BEISPIEL: Wem gehört dieses Radio?
> Dieses Radio ist mein Radio. Es gehört mir.

1. Wem gehört dieser Koffer?
2. Wem gehört dieses Bett?
3. Wem gehört dieses Referat?
4. Wem gehört dieser Ausweis?
5. Wem gehört diese Lampe?
6. Wem gehört dieser Stadtplan?
7. Wem gehört diese Uhr?
8. Wem gehören diese Bücher?
9. Wem gehört dieses Geld?
10. Wem gehören diese Briefe?

Perfect Tense of Modal Verbs

You know that modal verbs are used with a dependent infinitive.

Ich muß viel **lesen.**	*I have to read a lot.*
Wir wollen nach Hause **gehen.**	*We want to go home.*

Here are the same sentences in the perfect tense:

Ich habe viel **lesen müssen.**	*I had to read a lot.*
Wir haben nach Hause **gehen wollen.**	*We wanted to go home.*

A modal verb with a dependent infinitive uses its own *infinitive* form instead of a past participle to form the perfect tense.[6] The infinitive of the modal verb *follows* the dependent infinitive. This construction is called a "double infinitive."

Note that the modal verbs always use **haben** as their auxiliary in the perfect tense, regardless of the dependent infinitive.

Wir **sind** nach Hause gegangen.	*We went home.*
but	
Wir **haben** nach Hause gehen wollen.	*We wanted to go home.*

16 Übung

Change these sentences from present to perfect tense, using the double infinitive construction.

BEISPIEL: Wir dürfen nicht laut singen.
Wir haben nicht laut singen dürfen.

1. Ich will in der Stadt bleiben.

2. Ich muß manchmal lachen.

3. Ich muß meiner Freundin Geld geben.

4. Ich kann den Bahnhof nicht finden.

5. Kann dir die Frau helfen?

6. Leider kann ich es nicht verstehen.

7. Ich darf leider nicht bleiben.

6. All the modal verbs are mixed verbs and have past participles on the pattern ge- + stem + -t (**dürfen–gedurft, können–gekonnt, mögen–gemocht, müssen–gemußt, sollen–gesollt, wollen–gewollt**). These past participles, however, are used *only* when there is *no* dependent infinitive.

Das hat er nicht **gekonnt.**	*He wasn't able to do that.*
Sie hat mich nicht **gemocht.**	*She didn't like me.*
Das habe ich nicht **gewollt.**	*I didn't want that (to happen).*

Tips zum Lesen und Lernen

Tips zum Vokabelnlernen und Wortschatzerweiterung

Translating English "to spend"   The reading passage in this chapter talks of spending time and money. Note the different verbs that German uses to distinguish between these two kinds of "spending."

> *verbringen*
>
> | | |
> |---|---|
> | Wir **verbringen** unsere Ferien in den Alpen. | *We're spending our vacation in the Alps.* |
> | Sie hat den Nachmittag zu Hause **verbracht.** | *She spent the afternoon at home.* |
>
> *ausgeben*
>
> | | |
> |---|---|
> | Wieviel muß man für ein Zimmer **ausgeben?** | *How much do you have to spend for a room?* |
> | Wir haben sehr viel Geld **ausgegeben.** | *We spent a lot of money.* |

Verbal Nouns   In principle, any German infinitive may act as a noun. It is then capitalized and is always neuter.

> reisen → **das Reisen**   *(traveling)*
> Das Reisen ist heutzutage leicht.   *Traveling is easy nowadays.*

These verbal nouns correspond to English gerunds (the form ending in **-ing**); some have additional, more specific meanings. For instance, **das Essen** means "eating" but also "food" and "meal." Here are some other examples:

das **Lernen**	*learning, studying*	das **Wissen**	*knowing;*
das **Leben**	*living; life*		*knowledge*
das **Sein**	*being; existence*	das **Fliegen**	*flying*

Leicht zu merken

hektisch
der **Horizont, -e**   Horizont
das **Instrument, -e**   Instrument
die **Kamera, -s**
packen
reservieren   reservieren
spontan
das **Ticket, -s**
die **Wanderlust**

„Unterwegs per Autostop oder mit der Bahn" describes how German young people travel in Europe. For a first impression of this text, do not read it, but simply skim it. Look for familiar vocabulary that is related to travel. In addition, watch for context clues that point to new travel-related vocabulary. As you skim, also keep an eye out for obvious cognates such as **Instrument.**

After skimming the text, go back and read it once through. Use the following questions as a guide to highlight some main ideas. See whether you can answer them after a first reading.

Wie kann man durch Europa reisen?
Warum reisen diese Menschen gern?
Wie kann man beim Reisen Geld sparen?
Wo kann man unterwegs Menschen kennenlernen?
Wo kann man auf der Reise übernachten?

Wortschatz 2

Verben

aus·steigen, ist ausgestiegen to get out (*of a vehicle*)
benutzen to use
hoffen to hope
mit·nehmen (nimmt mit), hat mitgenommen to take along
quatschen (*colloq.*) 1. to talk nonsense, 2. to chat
sparen to save (*money or time*)
trampen (*pronounced „trämpen"*), **ist getrampt** to hitchhike
übernachten to spend the night
verbringen, hat verbracht to spend (*time*)

Substantive

der **Abend, -e** evening
  am Abend in the evening
der **Platz, ⸚e** seat
der **Rucksack, ⸚e** rucksack, backpack

das **Abteil, -e** railway compartment
das **Ausland** (*sing.*) foreign countries
  im Ausland abroad
das **Ding, -e** thing
(das) **Florenz** Florence
das **Flugzeug, -e** airplane
das **Foto, -s** photograph
  ein Foto machen to take a picture
das **Ziel, -e** goal
  Reiseziel destination

die **Bahn** railroad; railway system
die **Fahrkarte, -n** ticket (*for means of transportation*)
die **Freiheit, -en** freedom
die **Jugendherberge, -n** youth hostel
die **Tasche, -n** pocket; hand/shoulder bag

Adjektive und Adverbien

bequem comfortable
pünktlich punctual, on time

so so
sympathisch friendly, congenial, likeable
verrückt crazy, insane

Nützliche Ausdrücke

Das macht (mir) Spaß. That is fun (for me).
in der Nähe von near, nearby
egal wohin (wer, warum, usw.) no matter where (who, why, etc.)

Gegensätze

aussteigen ≠ einsteigen to get out ≠ to get in

Mit anderen Worten

per Autostop reisen = trampen

Unterwegs per Autostop
oder mit der Bahn

Mit dem Sommer kommt wieder die Waunderlust. Dann
packt man den Koffer oder den Rucksack und macht eine
Reise. Viele Menschen fahren mit dem eigenen° Wagen oder   own
mit dem Flugzeug. Aber junge Leute mit wenig Geld in der
5   Tasche wollen nicht so viel ausgeben. Sie fahren lieber mit
der Bahn oder reisen per Autostop. Ein paar erzählen uns
hier von ihren Reiseerfahrungen.°   travel experiences

Adrienne, 18, Azubi° aus Kaisersaschern   = Lehrling
„Trampen erweitert° den Horizont. Ich bin in den Som-   broadens
10 merferien mit meinem Freund Markus nicht nur in
Deutschland, sondern auch im Ausland getrampt. Wir haben
Glück gehabt: Überall waren die Menschen sympathisch
und wir haben auch eine Menge Geld gespart. In Italien war
es einfach super. Ein Autofahrer hat uns von Venedig nach
15 Florenz mitgenommen. Er hat ein bißchen Deutsch verstanden, und wir haben dann drei Tage bei seiner Familie
gewohnt. Mit meiner Kamera habe ich ein paar schöne Fotos
von seinen Kindern gemacht. Das hat uns Spaß gemacht,
und ich hoffe, wir können sie nächstes Jahr wieder besuchen.
20 Ja, im Zug lernt man die Menschen einfach nicht so gut
kennen."

Thomas, 21, Student aus Tübingen
„Ich trampe schon in der Nähe von Tübingen, aber für eine
25 lange Reise würde ich immer ein Interrail-Ticket kaufen.
Das kostet unter DM 500 für vier Wochen, und man kann

(*links*) Trämper in der Nähe von
Heidelberg. (*rechts*) Im Speisewagen
[*dining car*]. (Schweiz)

durch 24 Länder in Europa reisen. Mit diesem Ticket habe ich viel Freiheit: Da kann man spontan weg, egal wohin.

Freunde von mir benutzen den Zug als „rollendes° Hotel." Am Tag besuchen sie eine neue Stadt. Am Abend steigen sie wieder ein und schlafen dann im Zug unterwegs zum nächsten° Reiseziel. Dieses Tempo ist mir aber zu hektisch. Ich übernachte lieber in der Jugendherberge und verbringe ein paar Tage in jeder Stadt."

rolling

next

Herbert, 29, Assistenzarzt° aus Ulm

resident (physician)

„Früher bin ich viel per Autostop gereist, aber heutzutage würde ich das nicht mehr machen. Die Unsicherheit° ist mir zu stressig, und ich habe nicht mehr so viel Freizeit. Das Reisen mit der Bahn gefällt mir, denn es ist sehr praktisch und bequem. Man geht einfach zum Bahnhof, kauft eine Fahrkarte, und steigt in den Zug ein. Und man weiß, man kommt pünktlich an.

uncertainty

Im Abteil quatsche ich gern ein bißchen mit den Mitreisenden° über viele Dinge. Letztes Wochenende bin ich zum Beispiel nach Berlin gefahren. Im Abteil hat ein Musikstudent aus Leipzig gesessen. Er ist in Wittenberg⁷ ausgestiegen, und ich habe ihm mit seinem Gepäck geholfen. Er hatte° nicht nur einen Rucksack und einen Koffer mit, sondern auch eine Baßgeige!° Für sein Instrument hat er einen zweiten° Platz reservieren müssen. Verrückt, nicht?"

fellow passengers

had
double bass
second

Fragen zum Lesestück

1. Warum reisen viele Leute so gern im Sommer?
2. Wie kann man im Urlaub Geld sparen?
3. Wohin ist Adrienne getrampt?
4. Hat es ihr Spaß gemacht? Warum?
5. Wo kann man Menschen unterwegs kennenlernen?
6. Wie kann man mit der Bahn billig reisen?
7. Wie kann man den Zug als „rollendes Hotel" benutzen?
8. Wo kann man billig übernachten?
9. Warum kann das Trampen stressig sein?
10. Warum würde Herbert heutzutage nicht mehr trampen?
11. Wem hat er im Zugabteil geholfen?

---

7. Leipzig (in the state of Saxony), Wittenberg (in the state of Saxony-Anhalt). Martin Luther is buried in Wittenberg. Johann Sebastian Bach spent the greater part of his life in Leipzig.

Situationen aus dem Alltag

Reisen und Verkehr   *(Travel and Traffic)*

Some of these words are already familiar.

Verben

abfahren ≠ ankommen
einsteigen ≠ aussteigen
um·steigen   to transfer, change *(buses, trains, etc.)*

Substantive

der **Bahnhof, ⸚e**
der **Bus, -se**   *bus*
der **Flughafen, ⸚**   *airport*
der **Verkehr**   *traffic*
der **Wagen, -**
der **Zug, ⸚e**
das **Auto, -s**
das **Flugzeug, -e**
die **Autobahn, -en**   *expressway, high-speed highway*
die **Fahrkarte, -n**

ERHOLUNG AUF DEM RHEIN.
DIE BAHN BRINGT SIE ZUM SCHIFF.

KD Köln-Düsseldorfer ▦ Deutsche Bundesbahn

Nützliche Ausdrücke

Ich fahre **mit dem Wagen.**   . . . *by car.*
            mit dem Bus.   . . . *by bus.*
            mit der Bahn.   . . . *by train.*

Partnerarbeit: Was habe ich zuerst gemacht?

Here are eight statements about a train trip. Number them in the order that
the events most likely happened. Then read them aloud in order.

_____ Ich habe mit meinem Nachbarn im Abteil geredet.

_____ Ich habe mir eine Fahrkarte gekauft.

_____ Ich habe im Abteil einen Roman gelesen.

_____ Ich habe eine Reise ins Ausland machen wollen.

_____ Ich bin in den Zug eingestiegen.

_____ Ich habe mir eine Landkarte gekauft.

_____ Ich bin zum Bahnhof gegangen.

_____ Ich bin pünktlich angekommen.

Gruppenarbeit: Planen wir unsere Reise.   *4 Personen*

Planen Sie zusammen eine Reise nach Europa. Besprechen Sie diese Fragen miteinander. Benutzen Sie die Landkarte.

Welche Länder wollen wir besuchen?

Wie lange wollen wir bleiben?

Wie wollen wir durch Europa reisen? Mit der Bahn? Per Autostop?

Wo wollen wir übernachten? In einer Jugendherberge? Im Hotel?

Was wollen wir mitnehmen? Machen wir eine Liste.

Haben wir etwas vergessen?

Partnerarbeit: Rollenspiel

Spielen Sie diese Situation mit Ihrem Partner. Ein Partner spielt den Autofahrer, der andere (*other*) spielt den Tramper. Der Tramper steht seit einer Stunde im Regen. Endlich hält ein Auto. Der Tramper steigt ein und spricht mit dem Fahrer über das Trampen und die Ferien.

Sie können Ihr Gespräch (*conversation*) dann vor der ganzen Klasse spielen.

Fahrplanauszug

Sommer

27. Mai bis 29. September

Hannover ➡ Nürnberg

465 Km

Verkehrszeiten	ab	Zug	an	Service	Umsteigen in	an	ab	Zug
werktags außer Sa, nicht 14.VI.	1.28	*D*2187	6.52		Würzb	5.11	5.22	N6237
	1.28	*D*2187	7.05	🚃				
Mo bis Sa, nicht 4.VI.	6.45	*IC*781	10.43		Würzb	9.41	9.48	*EC*29
	7.45	*IC*581	11.43		Würzb	10.41	10.48	*EC*13
	8.45	*IC*583	12.43		Würzb	11.41	11.48	*EC*21
	9.45	*IC*681	13.43					
	10.21	*FD*1983	15.08	🚃				
	10.45	*IC*783	14.43		Würzb	13.41	13.48	*IC*621
	11.45	*EC*91	15.42					
	12.45	*IC*785	16.43		Würzb	15.41	15.48	*IC*521
täglich außer Sa, nicht 3.VI.	13.45	*IC*683	17.43					
	14.45	*IC*787	18.43		Würzb	17.41	17.48	*EC*27
täglich außer Sa, nicht 3.VI.	15.45	*IC*685	19.43					
	16.45	*IC*687	20.43					
täglich außer Sa, nicht 3.VI.	17.45	*IC*585	21.46		Würzb	20.41	20.48	*IC*721
	18.40	*D*2787	22.46		Würzb	21.42	21.48	*IC*623
	20.58	*D*499	1.58					
	23.04	*D*2181	4.45					

Abweichungen siehe Abfahrtplan
Angaben ohne Gewähr. Änderungen vorbehalten.

EC Zuschlag 6,00 DM
IC Zuschlag 6,00 DM

Zum Schluß

Sprechen wir miteinander!

A Gruppenarbeit: Was gefällt euch hier?

Was gefällt Ihnen an Ihrer Uni? Was gefällt Ihnen nicht? Machen Sie miteinander zwei Listen (*lists*).

das Essen in der Mensa	die Hausaufgaben
das Leben im Studentenwohnheim	der Streß
die Vorlesungen	die Studentenzeitung
	usw.

B Gruppenarbeit: Was mache ich jetzt?

The class is divided into two groups. The instructor does various things, and each team in turn tries to describe the action. A correct answer scores a point. If your team answers incorrectly, the other team has a chance to describe the same action.

BEISPIEL: Was mache ich jetzt?
Sie stellen die Flasche auf den Stuhl.

C Partnerarbeit: Am Telefon

Situation: Barbara Hinrich phones her father to tell him when she's arriving this evening. He asks where she is and whether she's going to have dinner at home tonight. She says she's going to a restaurant with friends and won't be home until late. Her father says he'll see her later. They say good-bye (on the telephone: **Auf Wiederhören**).

Complete this conversation with your partner.

VATER: Hallo? Hinrich.
BARBARA: Hallo _____! Hier ist _____.
VATER: Ach _____! Wo _____?
BARBARA: _____.
VATER: Wirklich? _____?
BARBARA: _____.
VATER: Also, _____.
Auf Wiederhören!
BARBARA: _____!

D Partnerarbeit

Now choose one of the following situations and invent your own telephone conversation. Since long distance rates are expensive, be brief and convey as much information as efficiently as you can.

1. Phone a friend to report you have just returned from abroad.

2. Phone home to say you have arrived somewhere.

3. Phone your roommate to say you've forgotten something.

4. Find out whether a youth hostel or hotel has room for you.

E Gruppeninterview: Wer ist schon weit gereist?

Wie viele Studenten haben schon eine lange Reise gemacht? Die anderen (*other*) Studenten interviewen sie und fragen zum Beispiel:

Wann?   **Wohin?**   **Mit wem?**   **Warum?**

F Partnerarbeit: Was würdest du lieber machen?

Here are some choices you might make when traveling. Ask each other which you would rather do. State a preference and give a reason.

BEISPIEL: ┌─────── **sprechen** ───────┐
                                ↓   ↓
            Ihre Muttersprache?   eine Fremdsprache?

Ich würde lieber eine Fremdsprache sprechen, denn das macht mehr Spaß.

┌────── **übernachten** ──────┐
↓   ↓
im Hotel?   in einer Jugendherberge?

┌────── **reisen** ──────┐
↓   ↓
per Autostop?   mit der Bahn?

┌────── **tragen** ──────┐
↓   ↓
einen Rucksack?   einen Koffer?

┌────── **eine Woche verbringen** ──────┐
↓   ↓
in der Stadt?   auf dem Land?

┌────── **kennenlernen** ──────┐
↓   ↓
Touristen aus Ihrem Land?   Studenten aus dem Ausland?

┌────── **sitzen** ──────┐
↓   ↓
im Konzert?   im Café?

Schreiben Sie zu Hause

G **Wanderlust**   Complete the sentences below so that they constitute a short essay on traveling inexpensively.

1. Manchmal will ich einfach _____.

2. Natürlich braucht man Geld für _____.

3. Ohne viel Geld in der Tasche kann _____.

4. Man kann aber immer _____.

5. Das ist manchmal schön, denn _____.

6. Mit meinem Interrail-Ticket kann _____.

7. Das Tempo darf nicht _____.

8. Ich würde wahnsinnig gern _____.

9. Nächstes Jahr _____.

10. Hoffentlich ist _____.

H Die Reise war super. Ein Brief aus Florenz

Auf Seite 206 hat Adrienne von ihrer Reise mit ihrem Freund erzählt. Natürlich hat sie im Ausland eigentlich viel mehr gemacht. Was hat sie ihren Eltern aus Italien geschrieben? Wie war es bei dieser Familie, warum hat es soviel Spaß gemacht, usw.? Schreiben Sie Adriennes Brief nach Hause. (*Review letter-writing conventions in Kapitel 6, p. 176.*)

I Schreiben Sie das Gespräch (*conversation*) zwischen Herbert und dem Musikstudenten aus Leipzig in dem Zugabteil (siehe S. 207).

J Wie sagt man das auf deutsch?

1. Did you take a trip this year?

2. Yes, we went to Venice.

3. Did you take the children along?

4. Yes, and they liked Italy very much. (*use* **gefallen**)

5. Does this suitcase belong to you?

6. Not to me, but to my brother.

7. Where should I put it?

8. Would you please put it under the table?

9. How's your husband?

10. He's not very well.

11. Oh, I'm sorry.

Auf der Fähre [*ferry*] nach Helgoland. (Nordsee)

Almanach

Jugendherbergen   *Youth Hostels*

There are about 585 **Jugendherbergen** in Germany, 125 in Austria, and 125 in Switzerland. They are meeting places for young travelers from all over the world. In addition to providing inexpensive food and lodging, they offer a variety of courses and organized trips.

Below is a copy of a page from the Youth Hostel handbook for Germany as well as a key explaining the symbols used.

Membership in the **AYH** (*American Youth Hostels*) entitles the cardholder to privileges in hostels all over the world. Membership costs as of 1991: under 18 years of age, $10.00; 18–54, $25.00; over 54, $15.00. In Bavaria you must be under 26 years of age to stay in a youth hostel. To apply for membership, write to:

American Youth Hostels, Inc.
P.O. Box 37613
Washington, D.C. 20013–7613
(202) 783–6161

Kurzinformationen über alle Jugendherbergen

Postleitzahl	Jugendherberge / Adresse / Herbergseltern	Lvb	Telefon	Betten	Tagesräume	Hobby- und Sporträume	Warmwasser	Dusche	Familienzimmer	Kochgelegenheit	Vollverpflegung	B	Freibad	Hallenbad	Wintersport-Möglichkeiten	ev Kirche	kath. Kirche	Bahnhof	Bus	Straßenbahn	Besondere Bedingungen	Seite
2720	**Rotenburg/Wümme** Verdener Str. 104 Gästehaus	Unt.-Ems.	04261 4051	152	3	1	x	x	—		x	—	20	20	—	x	x	30	—	—	—	S. 332
8803	**Rothenburg o.d.T.** Roßmühle Doris u. Eduard Schmitz	Bayern	09861 4510	141	1	x	x	x	4	x	x	—	15	15	x	x	x	20	x	—	—	S. 178
8803	**Rothenburg o.d.T.** „Spitalhof" Pf. 1206 Klaus u. Beate Moll	Bayern	09861 889	90	3	—	x	x	—	—	x	—	15	15	—	x	x	20	x	—	—	S. 178
8774	**Rothenfels „Burg"** Verwaltung Burg Rothenfels	Bayern	09393 1015	200	4	1	x	x	—	—	x	○	—	—	—	—	x	—	15	—	—	S. 178
7210	**Rottweil a. Neckar** Lorenzgasse 8 Elisabeth u. Hans-Peter Schobel	Schwab.	0741 6274	78	2	—	x	x	—	—	x	—	15	15	—	x	x	20	—	—	—	S. 309
7820	**Rudenberg-Neustadt** Titisee Neustadt Rudenberg 6 Irene und Horst Brömel	Baden	07651 7360	138	5	2	x	x	2	—	x	○	30	x	x	x	x	30	—	—	○	S. 137
6220	**Rüdesheim** Am Kreuzberg Hella u. Manfred Alt	Hessen	06722 2711	222	4	1	x	x	2	—	x	—	—	20	—	x	x	20	20	—	•○	S. 226
6090	**Rüsselsheim** Hauptm.-Scheuermann-Weg 6 Gisela u. Konrad Merz	Hessen	06142 42346	116	6	1	x	x	—	—	x	—	10	15	—	x	x	15	5	—	•○	S. 226
4784	**Rüthen** Am Rabenknapp 5 Cläre und Herbert Gillert	Westf.-L.	02952 483	108	4	1	—	x	1	—	x	○	1	—	—	x	x	—	15	—	—	S. 363

KAPITEL 8

Das Leben in der Stadt

Communicative Goals
- Talking about food and shopping
- Discussing city life
- Finding your way around a new town and traveling by public transportation
- Asking directions
- Ordering in a restaurant

Cultural Goal
- Learning something about life in German cities

Lyrik zum Vorlesen   Heinrich Heine, „Die Loreley"

Grammatik   Subordinate Clauses and Subordinating Conjunctions   •   Infinitive Constructions with *zu*   •   Genitive Case   •   Official Time-telling   •   Nouns of Measure, Weight, and Number   •   Translating English "to"

Lesestück   Aspekte der Großstadt

Situationen aus dem Alltag   Unterwegs in der Stadt; In der Konditorei

Almanach   Kulturleben und Freizeit in der Großstadt

Dialoge

„Zahlen bitte!"

KELLNERIN: So, hat es Ihnen geschmeckt?

GAST: Ausgezeichnet!

KELLNERIN: Möchten Sie noch etwas bestellen?

GAST: Danke,[1] ich möchte zahlen, bitte.

KELLNERIN: Sie haben Schnitzel, Pommes frites, einen Salat und ein Bier gehabt, nicht wahr?

GAST: Ja, und auch eine Tasse Kaffee.

KELLNERIN: Das macht zusammen DM 25,80, bitte sehr.

„Was brauchen wir noch?"

DORA: Heute morgen habe ich Max zum Abendessen eingeladen. Weißt du, ob er kommt?

FRANZ: Ja, aber er hat mir gesagt, daß er erst um halb sieben kommen kann. Wieviel Uhr ist es jetzt?

DORA: Halb sechs. Also muß ich noch schnell zum Supermarkt, um ein paar Sachen einzukaufen. Was brauchen wir noch?

FRANZ: Wir brauchen noch ein Kilo Kartoffeln, 200 Gramm Leberwurst, Käse, eine Flasche Rotwein und etwas zum Nachtisch.

DORA: Ist das alles?

FRANZ: Ich glaube ja.

Ein Stadtbummel

Marianne besucht ihren Freund Helmut in Köln. Er hat ihr die Stadt noch nicht gezeigt, weil es geregnet hat.

HELMUT: Du, der Regen hat endlich aufgehört! Hast du jetzt Lust, einen Stadtbummel zu machen?

MARIANNE: Ja gerne. Aber ich hab' jetzt Hunger. Können wir zuerst essen?

HELMUT: Selbstverständlich! In der Nähe des Doms gibt es ein Restaurant, wo wir griechisch essen können.

MARIANNE: Hmmm, das klingt lecker!

HELMUT: Nachher können wir dann den Dom besuchen, und von da ist es nicht mehr weit zum Kunstmuseum.

---

1. **Danke** = „Nein, danke."

"Check please!"

WAITRESS: Did you enjoy your meal?[2]
PATRON: Excellent!
WAITRESS: Would you like to order anything else?
PATRON: No thanks. I'd like the check, please.
WAITRESS: You had a cutlet, French fries, a salad, and a beer, right?
PATRON: Yes, and also a cup of coffee.
WAITRESS: All together that comes to 25 Marks 80, please.

"What else do we need?"

DORA: This morning I invited Max to supper. Do you know if he's coming?
FRANZ: Yes, but he told me that he couldn't come until 6:30. What time is it now?
DORA: 5:30. So I need to make a quick trip to the supermarket to buy a few things. What else do we need?
FRANZ: We still need a kilo of potatoes, 200 grams of liverwurst, cheese, a bottle of red wine, and something for dessert.
DORA: Is that all?
FRANZ: I think so.

A Stroll Through Town

Marianne is visiting her friend Helmut in Cologne. He hasn't shown her around town yet, because it's been raining.

HELMUT: Hey look, the rain's finally stopped! Do you want to take a stroll through town now?
MARIANNE: Sure. But I'm hungry now. Can we eat first?
HELMUT: Of course. Near the cathedral there's a restaurant where we can eat Greek food.
MARIANNE: Hmmm, that sounds delicious!
HELMUT: Then we can visit the cathedral afterwards, and from there it's not far to the art museum.

Wortschatz 1

Verben

bestellen to order
ein·laden (lädt ein), hat eingeladen to invite
klingen, hat geklungen to sound
schmecken to taste; to taste good
   Wie schmeckt es dir? How does it taste? How do you like it?
zahlen to pay

Substantive

der Bummel, - stroll, walk
   einen Stadtbummel machen to take a stroll through town
der Dom, -e cathedral
der Durst thirst
der Gast, ⁼e guest; patron
der Hunger hunger
der Kaffee coffee
der Käse cheese
der Kellner, - waiter
der Liter liter
der Nachtisch dessert
   zum Nachtisch for dessert
der Salat, -e salad; lettuce
der Supermarkt, ⁼e supermarket
das Abendessen supper, evening meal
   zum Abendessen for dinner
das Gebäude, - building
das Glas, ⁼er glass
das Gramm gram
das Kilogramm kilogram
   das Kilo (*short for* **Kilogramm**)
(das) Köln Cologne

das Museum, Museen museum
das Restaurant, -s restaurant
das Schnitzel, - cutlet, chop
die Kartoffel, -n potato
die Kellnerin, -nen waitress
die Kunst, ⁼e art
die Sache, -n (personal) possession; matter, affair
die Tasse, -n cup
die Wurst, ⁼e sausage
   die Leberwurst liverwurst

Adjektive und Adverbien

ausgezeichnet excellent
griechisch Greek
lecker tasty, delicious
weit far, far away
zuerst first, at first

Andere Vokabeln

daß (*sub. conj.*) that
noch etwas something else, anything more
ob (*sub. conj.*) whether, if
um . . . zu in order to

Nützliche Ausdrücke

Ich glaube ja. I think so.
griechisch (italienisch, französisch, usw.) essen to eat Greek (Italian, French, etc.) food
Hunger haben to be hungry
Durst haben to be thirsty
Lust haben (etwas zu tun) to want to (do something)

---

2. Literally: "Well, did it taste good (to you)?"

in der Nähe (+ *gen.*)   near, nearby
Zahlen bitte!   (May I have the) check please!
Wieviel Uhr ist es? = Wie spät ist es?

weit ≠ nah(e)   far ≠ near
zuerst ≠ zuletzt   at first ≠ finally, last of all
Ich glaube ja. ≠ Ich glaube nein.   I think so. ≠ I don't think so.

der Kram (*colloq.*) = **die Sachen; alte Sachen**

Variationen

A **Persönliche Fragen**

1. Haben Sie heute gefrühstückt? Was haben Sie denn gegessen? Hat's Ihnen geschmeckt?
2. Kennen Sie ein Restaurant, wo man sehr gut essen kann? Wie heißt es?
3. Essen Sie gern griechisch? italienisch? französisch? deutsch?
4. Trinken sie viel Kaffee? Was trinken Sie sonst?
5. Was essen Sie gern zum Nachtisch?
6. Laden Sie oft Freunde zum Abendessen ein?
7. Kaufen Sie im Supermarkt ein? Wie oft?
8. Marianne hat Lust, einen Stadtbummel zu machen. Haben Sie Lust, heute etwas zu machen? Was denn?
9. Gehen Sie gern ins Kunstmuseum? Welche Künstler (*artists*) mögen Sie?

```
        15-08-90 #0000

GAST/TISCH # 161
  2 PAELLA VAL.    *40.00
  1 SCHNITZEL PA   *14.00
  1 KINDERTELLER    *9.00
  1 FL WASSER       *3.50
  1 FL LIMO         *3.50
  1 MÄRZEN 0.5      *2.80
  1 WEIZEN          *3.50
  1 MÄRZEN 0.3      *1.80
BROT               *2.00
BAR        *80.10
ENTH.MWST14%       *9.59

BESTEN DANK
COSTA DEL SOL
```

B **Übung:** Raten Sie mal!   *Take a Guess!*

Marianne und Helmut wollen einen Stadtbummel machen. Das heißt, sie haben ein bißchen freie Zeit und können langsam durch die Stadt gehen. Um einen Bummel zu machen, braucht man also Zeit. Raten Sie mal, was diese Wörter bedeuten:

1. Sie machen einen **Schaufensterbummel.**
2. Ich hab' ein bißchen Geld in der Tasche. Machen wir doch einen **Einkaufsbummel.**
3. Der Zug hat an jedem kleinen Bahnhof gehalten. Ich fahre nie wieder mit diesem **Bummelzug!**
4. Fritz studiert seit 13 Semestern an dieser Uni und ist immer noch nicht fertig. Er ist ein **Bummelstudent!**
5. Die Arbeiter arbeiten immer noch, aber sehr langsam. Sie machen einen **Bummelstreik.**

C Übung: Schmeckt es Ihnen, oder nicht?

Ihre Professorin nennt (*names*) etwas zu essen oder trinken. Sagen Sie, ob es Ihnen schmeckt oder nicht.

BEISPIEL: Essen Sie gern Tomatensuppe?
Nein, das schmeckt mir nicht.

Käse	Kaffee	Pommes frites
Bier	Brot	Leberwurst
Pizza	Salat	griechisches Essen
Kartoffeln	Wienerschnitzel	Wein

Lyrik zum Vorlesen

The cliff called the Loreley is on the Rhine River at its deepest spot. In his famous poem „Ich weiß nicht, was soll es bedeuten" (1823), Heinrich Heine invented a Romantic myth about this place. Set to music by the composer Silcher, it achieved the status of a folk song.

Ich weiß nicht, was soll es bedeuten („Die Loreley")

Ich weiß nicht, was soll es bedeuten,
daß ich so traurig° bin;
ein Märchen aus alten Zeiten,
das kommt mir nicht aus dem Sinn.°

sad

das . . . Sinn = das kann ich nicht vergessen

Die Luft ist kühl und es dunkelt,°
und ruhig° fließt° der Rhein;
der Gipfel° des Berges funkelt°
im Abendsonnenschein.

es dunkelt = es wird dunkel
peacefully / flows
mountain top / glistens

Die schönste Jungfrau° sitzet°
dort oben° wunderbar,
ihr goldenes Geschmeide° blitzet,°
sie kämmt° ihr goldenes Haar.

most beautiful maiden / **sitzet = sitzt** */ high above*
jewelry / glistens
combs

Sie kämmt es mit goldenem Kamme,°
und singt ein Lied dabei;°
das hat eine wundersame,°
gewaltige° Melodei.

comb
while doing so
= wunderbare
powerful

Den Schiffer° im kleinen Schiffe°
ergreift° es mit wildem Weh;°
er schaut° nicht die Felsenriffe,°
er schaut nur hinauf in die Höh.°

sailor / boat
is gripped / longing
= sieht */ submerged rock*
up to the heights

Ich glaube die Wellen° verschlingen°
am Ende Schiffer und Kahn;°
und das hat mit ihrem Singen
die Loreley getan.

waves / swallow
boat

Heinrich Heine (1797–1856)

Grammatik

Subordinate Clauses and Subordinating Conjunctions

Subordinating conjunctions, like coordinating conjunctions (see pages 193–95), join two clauses together. The clause beginning with a subordinating conjunction, however, becomes *subordinate to*, or *dependent on*, the other clause (called the *main clause*). A subordinate clause is *not* an independent sentence and cannot stand alone.

> *main clause   subordinate clause*
>   I know   that they still remember me.

The subordinate clause "that they still remember me" is not a complete sentence. In this chapter you will learn the following subordinating conjunctions:

da	*since* (causal, not temporal)
daß	*that*
ob	*whether, if* (when it means "whether")
weil	*because*
wenn	*if*

Verb-Last Word Order in the Subordinate Clause

Unlike coordinating conjunctions, which do not affect word order, subordinating conjunctions *move the inflected verb to the end of the subordinate clause.*

> Wir essen um halb sieben.

Ich glaube, **daß** wir   um halb sieben essen.
I think that we're eating at 6:30.

> Brauchen wir noch etwas?

Weißt du, **ob**   wir noch etwas brauchen?
Do you know whether we need anything else?

> Ich habe gerade gegessen.

Ich habe keinen Hunger, **weil** ich   gerade gegessen habe.
I'm not hungry because I've just eaten.

> Ich habe Zeit.

Ich helfe dir, **wenn** ich   Zeit habe.
I'll help you if I have time.

1 **Übung:** Ich weiß, daß . . .

Sie planen miteinander ein Abendessen. Ihre Professorin sagt Ihnen etwas. Sagen Sie, daß Sie das wissen.

> BEISPIEL: Die Wurst ist teuer.
> Ich weiß, daß sie teuer ist.

1. Wir essen um sieben.
2. Wir brauchen Rotwein.
3. Der Käse schmeckt gut.
4. Die Kinder wollen essen.

5. Tante Marie kommt zum Abendessen.
6. Wir haben keinen Salat.
7. Wir brauchen etwas zum Nachtisch.
8. Tante Marie trinkt keinen Kaffee.

 2 **Übung:** Ich weiß nicht, ob . . .

Ihr Professor ist neu in dieser Stadt. Er hat viele Fragen, aber Sie sind auch neu und können ihm keine Antworten geben.

> BEISPIEL: Ist dieses Restaurant teuer?
> Ich weiß nicht, ob es teuer ist.

1. Gibt es hier einen Automechaniker?
2. Ist dieses Hotel gut?
3. Ist die Uni weit von hier?
4. Gibt es eine Buchhandlung in der Nähe?
5. Kann man den Dom besuchen?
6. Kann man hier einen Stadtplan kaufen?

3 **Kettenreaktion:** Warum lernst du Deutsch?

In turn, ask each other why you do the things listed below. Give your reason, then ask the next student.

> BEISPIEL: Warum lernst du Deutsch?
> Ich lerne Deutsch, *weil* es interessant ist. Warum . . .?

Deutsch lernen
zur Buchhandlung gehen
trampen
jetzt essen

einen Rucksack tragen
bis 9.00 schlafen
draußen sitzen

Question Words as Subordinating Conjunctions

The question words (**wann, warum, was, wer,** etc.) act as subordinating conjunctions when they introduce an indirect question (i.e., a question restated as a subordinate clause).

> *question:*　　　　　　　　Was brauchen wir zum Abendessen?
>
> *indirect question:* Weißt du, **was** wir zum Abendessen brauchen?
>
> *Do you know what we need for supper?*

$$\text{Wer ist das?}$$

Ich kann Ihnen nicht sagen, wer ▭ das ist.
I can't tell you who that is.

 4 Übung: Die Tramper

Ein Freund von Ihnen will mit anderen Studenten eine Reise per Autostop machen. Ihre Professorin hat Fragen über ihre Reise, aber Sie wissen die Antworten nicht.

> BEISPIEL: Wer plant die Reise?
> Ich weiß nicht, wer die Reise plant.

1. Wohin fahren die Tramper?
2. Wo wollen sie übernachten?
3. Warum trampen Ihre Freunde?
4. Wen wollen sie besuchen?
5. Wann kommen die Tramper zurück?
6. Was packen sie in den Rucksack?
7. Welche Route fahren sie?

Verbs with Separable Prefixes in Subordinate Clauses

You know that when a verb with a separable prefix is used in a main clause, the prefix is separated from the verb and placed at the end of the clause.

> Dort **kaufe** ich immer **ein.**

In a subordinate clause, the verb moves to the end of the clause and the prefix is attached to it.

> Weißt du, warum ich ▭ immer dort einkaufe?

 5 Übung: Was hat sie gefragt?

Die Professorin spricht zu leise (*quietly*). Student A hört sie nicht richtig, und fragt Student B, was sie gesagt hat. Student B antwortet.

> BEISPIEL: PROFESSORIN: Wann stehen Sie auf?
> STUDENT A: Was hat sie gefragt?
> STUDENT B: Sie hat gefragt, wann du aufstehst.
>
> PROFESSORIN: Kommt Bernd vorbei?
> STUDENT A: Was hat sie gefragt?
> STUDENT B: Sie hat gefragt, ob Bernd vorbeikommt.

1. Wann fängt das Semester an?
2. Kommt Ingrid vorbei?
3. Warum geht Regine weg?
4. Bringt Maria die Kinder mit?
5. Hört die Musik bald auf?
6. Mit wem geht Hans spazieren?
7. Wo steigt man in die Straßenbahn ein?
8. Wo steigen wir aus?
9. Wer macht das Fenster zu?

Order of Clauses in the Sentence

Subordinate clauses may either follow or precede the main clause.

1   2

Ich spreche langsam, da ich nicht viel Deutsch gelernt habe.

1   2

Da ich nicht viel Deutsch gelernt habe, spreche ich langsam.

In the latter case, the *entire* subordinate clause is considered the first element in the sentence. The verb of the main clause therefore follows it immediately in second position. *The two inflected verbs are directly adjacent to each other, separated by a comma.*

    subordinate clause   main clause
Wenn ich Zeit **habe, gehe** ich ins Museum.
Ob er sympathisch **ist, weiß** ich nicht.

 6 Übung

Ihre Professorin hat Fragen, aber Sie wissen die Antworten nicht.

BEISPIEL: Wie ist das Wetter?
            Wie das Wetter ist, weiß ich nicht.

1. Wer ist das?
2. Wem gehört das?
3. Wohin fährt er?
4. Was kostet das?
5. Wie heißt sie?
6. Warum ist er müde?
7. Wessen Koffer ist das?
8. Wen kennt sie?

Infinitive Constructions with *zu*

The German infinitive is sometimes preceded by **zu.** For the most part, this construction parallels the use of the English infinitive with *to:*

Was gibt's hier **zu sehen?**   *What's there to see here?*
Hast du Zeit, diesen Brief **zu lesen?**   *Do you have time to read this letter?*

Note especially the second sentence above. In German, *the infinitive with* **zu** *comes at the end of its phrase.* In English, the infinitive with *to* comes at the beginning of its phrase.

When a separable-prefix verb is used, the **zu** is inserted between the prefix and the stem infinitive.

ab**zu**fahren   spazieren**zu**gehen

Ich hoffe, bald **abzufahren.**   *I hope to leave soon.*
Hast du Lust, mit mir **spazierenzugehen?**   *Would you like to go for a walk with me?*

Here are some cases in which the infinitive with **zu** is used:

- as a complement of verbs like **beginnen, anfangen, aufhören, helfen, hoffen, lernen, planen, scheinen,** and **vergessen.**

Fangen wir an **zu essen.**[3]	Let's start to eat.
Sie hofft, **Geschichte zu studieren.**	She's hoping to study history.
Ich habe vergessen, **dir von meiner Reise zu erzählen.**	I forgot to tell you about my trip.

■ as a complement of constructions like **Lust haben, Zeit haben,** and **Spaß machen.**

Hast du Lust, **einen Stadt-bummel zu machen?**	Do you want to take a walk through town?
Ich habe keine Zeit, **einkaufen zu gehen.**	I have no time to go shopping.

■ as a complement of many adjectives such as **dumm, einfach, schön,** and **wichtig.**

Es ist sehr wichtig, **das zu verstehen.**	It's very important to understand that.
Es ist schön, **dich wiederzusehen.**	It's nice to see you again.

 7 Übung: Es macht mir Spaß . . .

Ihr Professor fragt, ob Sie etwas gerne machen. Antworten Sie, daß es Ihnen Spaß macht.

BEISPIEL: Gehen Sie gern ins Museum?
Ja, es macht mir Spaß, ins Museum zu gehen.

1. Trampen Sie gern?
2. Reisen Sie gern mit der Bahn?
3. Essen Sie gern im Restaurant?
4. Quatschen Sie gern am Telefon?
5. Spielen Sie gern Tennis?
6. Leben Sie gern in der Stadt?

8 Gruppenarbeit: Was hast du vergessen?

Sie haben alle vergessen, etwas zu tun. Sagen Sie, was Sie vergessen haben, dann fragen Sie den nächsten Studenten.

BEISPIEL: Ich habe vergessen, meine Hausaufgaben zu schreiben. Was hast du vergessen?
Ich habe vergessen, . . .

Diese Liste gibt Ihnen einige Möglichkeiten (*possibilities*):

to invite my friends	to order dessert	to buy potatoes
to order tickets	to shop	to show you my photographs

3. Note on punctuation: The infinitive with **zu** is not set off by a comma if it has no complements of its own. If it has complements, it *must* be set off by a comma: (Ich fange an **zu essen.** Ich fange an, **Brot zu essen.**)

Infinitives with *um . . . zu* and *ohne . . . zu*

um . . . zu = *in order to*

> Ich muß in die Stadt, **um Lebens-mittel einzukaufen.**
>
> *I have to go to town (in order) to buy groceries.*
>
> Ich fahre nach Deutschland, **um Deutsch zu lernen.**
>
> *I'm going to Germany in order to learn German.*

ohne . . . zu = *without . . . -ing*

> Sie ist abgefahren, **ohne mich zu besuchen.**
>
> *She left without visiting me.*
>
> Ich habe das Buch gelesen, **ohne es zu verstehen.**
>
> *I read the book without understanding it.*

9 Übung

Restate each sentence, changing the **weil**-clause to an **um . . . zu** phrase and eliminating the modal verb and its subject.

> BEISPIEL: Ich gehe in die Stadt, weil ich einkaufen will.
> Ich gehe in die Stadt, *um einzukaufen.*

1. Ich gehe ins Restaurant, weil ich etwas essen will.
2. Sie sitzt am Fenster, weil sie die Straße sehen möchte.
3. Oft trampen Studenten, weil sie Geld sparen wollen.
4. Manchmal fährt man ins Ausland, weil man mehr lernen möchte.

10 Übung

Sagen Sie, warum Sie etwas machen.

> BEISPIEL: Warum gehen Sie zum Supermarkt?
> Um Brot zu kaufen.

1. Warum gehen Sie zur Uni?
2. Warum gehen Sie nach Hause?
3. Warum arbeiten Sie diesen Sommer?
4. Warum sparen Sie Geld?
5. Warum rufen Sie Ihre Eltern an?
6. Warum gehen Sie ins Museum?

11 Übung

Combine these sentences, changing the second one to an **ohne . . . zu** phrase.

> BEISPIEL: Er hat den Koffer genommen. Er hat mich nicht gefragt.
> Er hat den Koffer genommen, ohne mich zu fragen.

1. Sie sind abgefahren. Sie haben nicht „auf Wiedersehen" gesagt.
2. Ich arbeite in einem Geschäft. Ich kenne den Chef nicht.

3. Karin hat ein Zimmer gefunden. Sie hat nicht lange gesucht.

4. Geh nicht spazieren. Du trägst keinen Mantel.

5. Geh nicht weg. Du hast kein Frühstück gegessen.

6. Sie können nicht ins Konzert. Sie haben keine Karten gekauft.

Genitive Case

The genitive case is the fourth and last case to be learned. It expresses possession (*John's* books) or a relationship between two nouns marked in English by the preposition *of* (the color *of your eyes*). Here are some examples of genitive phrases:

der Wagen **meiner Mutter**	*my mother's* car
die Freunde **der Kinder**	*the children's* friends
das Haus **meines Bruders**	*my brother's* house
das Ende **des Tages**	the end *of the day*
Egons Freundin	*Egon's* girlfriend

Forms of the Genitive Case

The **der**-words and the **ein**-words (see p. 201) all share the same set of genitive endings. (Nominative, accusative, and dative—the cases you have already learned—are included in the following table for comparison and review.)

Genitive Case

	masc.	*neut.*	*fem.*	*plural*
nom.	der Mann	das Kind	die Frau	die Leute
acc.	den Mann	das Kind	die Frau	die Leute
dat.	dem Mann	dem Kind	der Frau	den Leuten
gen.	-es -(e)s	-es -(e)s	-er	-er
	des Mannes	des Kindes	der Frau	der Leute
	eines Mannes	eines Kindes	einer Frau	keiner Leute
	meines Mannes	eures Kindes	Ihrer Frau	unserer Leute
	dieses Mannes	jedes Kindes	welcher Frau	dieser Leute

In addition to the genitive ending of the **der**- or **ein**-word, in the masculine and neuter singular *the noun itself adds the ending* **-s** (d**es** Bahnhof**s**). Monosyllabic nouns such as **Mann** and **Kind** may take the ending **-es** (des Mann**es**).

The masculine N-nouns (see page 175), however, do *not* add an **-s** to the noun, but rather the same **-en** or **-n** ending as in the accusative and dative.

Kennen Sie die Frau **dieses Herrn?**	*Do you know this gentleman's wife?*
Kennen Sie die Freundin **meines Studenten?**	*Do you know my student's friend?*

Use of the Genitive Case

In German, the genitive generally *follows* the noun it modifies. In English, the possessive precedes the noun (**das Haus meines Bruders** *my brother's house*). Proper names and kinship titles used as names, however, usually *precede* the nouns they modify, as in English (**Egons Freundin** *Egon's girlfriend*, **Muttis Wagen** *Mom's car*). Proper names simply add **-s** *without an apostrophe* in the genitive.

German uses the genitive case for both persons and things, whereas English usually reserves the possessive ending *'s* for people and animals and uses *of* for things.

das Haus **meines Bruders**	*my brother's* house
die Häuser **der Stadt**	*the houses* **of the city**

 12 Übung

Change these noun phrases from nominative to genitive.

BEISPIEL: der Zug
           des Zuges

1. ein Arzt	5. das Kind	9. der Student
2. mein Freund	6. die Leute	10. dieser Herr
3. unser Vater	7. jede Uni	11. das Essen
4. die Lehrerin	8. eine Mutter	12. diese Zimmer

Note on Usage

a friend of my brother's	**ein Freund von meinem Bruder**
a cousin of mine	**eine Kusine von mir**
Is Max a friend of yours?	**Ist Max ein Freund von dir?**

---

 13 Übung: Wie sagt man das auf deutsch?

BEISPIEL: *your girlfriend's sister*
           die Schwester deiner Freundin

1. the walls of my room	10. the rooms of the house
2. the end of the week	11. Maria's students
3. Karl's major	12. the cities of Europe
4. the children's pictures	13. the windows of this room
5. the history of the war	14. your mother's car
6. his brother's house	15. the history of these countries
7. her sister's boyfriend	16. Grandpa's clock
8. the cities of Switzerland	17. a friend of yours
9. a student's letter	18. a student of mine

Prepositions with the Genitive

There is a small group of prepositions that take the genitive case.

statt or **anstatt**	*instead of*	Schreib eine Karte **statt eines Briefes.**
trotz[4]	*in spite of, despite*	**Trotz des Wetters** sind wir ans Meer gefahren.
während	*during*	**Während der Woche** fährt er oft in die Stadt.
wegen	*because of, on account of*	**Wegen seiner Arbeit** kann er nicht kommen.

Note: **Statt** and **anstatt** are interchangeable and equally correct.

14 Übung

Form prepositional phrases with the elements provided, then give English equivalents. Then invent your own completions for these sentences.

BEISPIEL: während / Sommer
während des Sommers (*during the summer*)
Während des Sommers habe ich gearbeitet.

1. trotz / Wetter
2. während / Ferien
3. statt / Straßenkarte
4. wegen / mein / Mutter

5. wegen / mein / Studium
6. trotz / Arbeit
7. während / Tag
8. anstatt / Hotel

15 Übung: Warum tun Sie das?

Ihr Professor möchte wissen, warum Sie etwas tun. Sagen Sie es ihm. Die Liste von Gründen (*reasons*) hilft Ihnen.

BEISPIEL: Warum arbeiten Sie so viel?
Wegen meines Studiums.

Studium	Eltern	Wetter
Klausur	Schnee	Klima
Arbeit	Regen	Streß

1. Warum bleiben Sie heute zu Hause?
2. Warum wollen Sie im Süden wohnen?
3. Warum dürfen Sie heute abend nicht mitkommen?
4. Warum brauchen Sie Ferien?
5. Warum brauchen Sie manchmal Aspirin?
6. Warum müssen die Kinder heute im Haus spielen?
7. Warum wollen Sie heute draußen sitzen?

---

4. In spoken German **trotz** and **wegen** are frequently used with the dative case, but the genitive is considered more correct, especially with **wegen**.

Official Time-telling

You already know how to tell time in German (see p. 16). For official time-telling, however, there is another system. One gives the full hour and the number of minutes past it. In addition, rather than A.M. or P.M., the twenty-four hour clock is used. This is the way the time is given in the media, in train schedules, on announcements of events, etc. Subtract 12 to get the P.M. time as expressed in English.

written	*spoken*	
1.40 Uhr	Es ist ein Uhr vierzig.	*It's 1.40 A.M.*
7.55 Uhr	Es ist 7 Uhr 55.	*It's 7:55 A.M.*
13.25 Uhr	Es ist 13 Uhr 25.	*It's 1:25 P.M.*
20.00 Uhr	Es ist zwanzig Uhr.	*It's 8:00 P.M.*

16 Übung: Wieviel Uhr ist es?

Sagen Sie die Uhrzeit auf deutsch!

BEISPIEL: 11:20 P.M.
Es ist 23.20 Uhr („dreiundzwanzig Uhr zwanzig").

1. 1:55 P.M.   3. 11:31 A.M.   5. 10:52 P.M.
2. 6:02 P.M.   4. 9:47 P.M.   6. 2:25 A.M.

Wann kann man Dr. Niederstadt donnerstags im Büro besuchen?

17 Übung: Wann kommt der Zug an?

Sie arbeiten am Hauptbahnhof in Mannheim und geben Auskunft über die Züge. Ihr Professor bittet um (*asks for*) Auskunft. Sie müssen die Antworten auf dem Fahrplan finden.

BEISPIEL: Entschuldigung, wann kommt der Zug aus Hamburg in Mannheim an?
Er kommt um 14.22 Uhr an.
Um wieviel Uhr fährt er in Hamburg ab?
Um 9.33 Uhr.

Mannheim Hbf (Hauptbahnhof)					
Ankunft (arrivals)			**Abfahrt** (departures)		
Zug-Nr.	ab[5]	an[5]	Zug-Nr.	ab	an
6342	Hamburg 9.33 Uhr	Mannheim 14.22 Uhr	1338	Mannheim 5.42 Uhr	Zürich 8.12 Uhr
7422	München 10.03 Uhr	Mannheim 13.10 Uhr	2472	Mannheim 6.06 Uhr	Nürnberg 9.33 Uhr
1387	Frankfurt 11.20 Uhr	Mannheim 12.01 Uhr	6606	Mannheim 7.55 Uhr	Straßburg 8.40 Uhr
7703	Wien 10.10 Uhr	Mannheim 17.56 Uhr	2203	Mannheim 10.12 Uhr	Innsbruck 15.46 Uhr
9311	Berlin 11.05 Uhr	Mannheim 19.16 Uhr	3679	Mannheim 13.23 Uhr	Prag 20.09 Uhr

[5]**ab:** time and place of departure; **an:** time and place of arrival.

	DEPART **ABFAHRT**		DEPARTURE		
[14 24]					(i)
Zeit		Über	Nach	Gleis	Später
1431	Nahverkehr	St Ingbert	Homburg	16	
1432	Nahverkehr	Völklingen-Saarlouis	Saarhölzbach	3	
1433	Nahverkehr	Brebach	Hanweiler	6	

Nouns of Measure, Weight, and Number

Nouns indicating measure and weight are *not* followed by a prepositional phrase, as they are in English.

ein Glas Bier	a glass **of** beer
eine Flasche Wein	a bottle **of** wine
eine Tasse Kaffee	a cup **of** coffee
ein Kilo Kartoffeln	a kilo **of** potatoes
ein Liter Milch	a liter **of** milk
ein Stück Brot	a piece **of** bread
eine Portion Pommes frites	an order/helping **of** French fries

Masculine and neuter nouns of measure *remain in the singular*, even following numerals greater than one.

drei **Glas** Bier	three glass**es** of beer
zwei **Kilo** Kartoffeln	two kilo**s** of potatoes
vier **Stück** Brot	four piece**s** of bread

Feminine nouns of measure, however, *do* use their plural forms.

zwei Tass**en** Kaffee	two cups of coffee
drei Flasch**en** Wein	three bottles of wine
drei Portion**en** Pommes frites	three portions of french fries

18 Übung

Sie sitzen mit Freunden in einem Restaurant in Deutschland. Ihre Freunde können kein Deutsch. Sagen Sie der Kellnerin, was sie bestellen wollen.

BEISPIEL: *I'd like a cup of coffee.*
Bringen Sie uns bitte eine Tasse Kaffee.

1. . . . a glass of wine and two cups of coffee.

2. . . . three glasses of water and two glasses of beer.

3. . . . a bottle of wine and two orders of French fries.

4. . . . three glasses of beer, two glasses of wine, and a cup of coffee.

Translating English "to"

The all-purpose English preposition indicating destination is *to*: We're going *to Germany, to the ocean, to the train station, to the movies, to Grandma's.* German has several equivalents for English *to*, depending on the destination:

- **nach** with cities, states, and most countries.

        Wir fahren **nach Wien.**
              nach Kalifornien.
              nach Deutschland.
              nach Europa.
and in the idiom: **nach Hause.**

- **zu** with people and some locations.

        Ich gehe **zu meinen Freunden.**
              zu meiner Großmutter.
              zum Bahnhof.
              zur Buchhandlung.
              zur Post (*post office*).

- **in** with countries whose names are feminine or plural, and with some locations.

        Ich fahre **in die Schweiz.**
              in die Bundesrepublik.
              in die USA.

        Wir gehen **ins Kino.**
              ins Bett.
              ins Konzert.
              ins Museum.
              ins Restaurant.
              ins Theater.
              in die Stadt (= *downtown*).
              in die Kirche (*church*).
              in die Mensa.

Here is a rough rule-of-thumb for deciding whether to use **zu** or **in** with a destination within a city: **in** is usually used with destinations where one will spend a relatively long time (**ins Kino, in die Kirche, ins Bett**); **zu** is usually used with destinations involving a briefer visit (**zum Bahnhof, zur Post**).

Lesestück

Aspekte der Großstadt

Tips zum Lesen und Lernen

Tips zum Vokabelnlernen

The topic of this chapter is **die Stadt.** Compound nouns with **Stadt** define various kinds of cities. You have already encountered, for example, **Altstadt,** the "old city" or medieval core of modern German cities. In the following reading, other kinds of cities are mentioned: **Großstadt, Kleinstadt,** and **Hafenstadt** (*port city*).

Übung

Try to describe in German the following kinds of cities:

Industriestadt

Touristenstadt

Universitätsstadt

Kulturstadt

Weltstadt

Ferienstadt

Leicht zu merken

der **Aspekt, -e**	As*pekt*
elegant	ele*gant*
(das) **England**	
die **Metropole**	Metro*pole*
(das) **Skandinavien**	
der/die **Sozialarbeiter/in**	Sozial*arbeiter*
die **Tour, -en**	

Einstieg in den Text

The following reading is called **Aspekte der Großstadt.** In it, an American exchange student and a German social worker talk about their lives in Hamburg and Munich, two of Germany's largest cities. Before reading it, think about your own experiences in or impressions of cities. Write a few sentences in German about what you find good or bad about big cities.

Das Stadtleben

Das gefällt mir   Das gefällt mir nicht

Wortschatz 2

Verben

ärgern   to annoy, offend
**rad·fahren (fährt Rad), ist
radgefahren**   to bicycle
**ski·fahren (fährt Ski), ist
skigefahren** (*pronounced
„Schifahren"*)   to ski
steigen, ist gestiegen   to
climb

Substantive

der **Alltag**   everyday life
der **Eindruck, ¨e**   impression
der **Einwohner, -**   inhabitant
der **Fußgänger, -**   pedestrian
der **Hafen, ¨**   port, harbor
der **Preis, -e**   price

das **Jahrhundert, -e**   century
(das) **München**   Munich
das **Rad, ¨er**   wheel; bicycle
das **Fahrrad, ¨er**   bicycle
(das) **Rußland**   Russia

die **Ecke, -n**   corner
   an der Ecke   at the corner
   um die Ecke   around the
   corner
die **Fußgängerzone, -n**
   pedestrian zone closed to
   vehicles
die **Großstadt, ¨e**   large city
   (*over 500,000 inhabitants*)
die **Kleinstadt, ¨e**   town
   (*5,000 to 20,000
   inhabitants*)

Adjektive und Adverbien

geradeaus   straight ahead
links   to/on the left
rechts   to/on the right
trotzdem   in spite of that,
nevertheless

Andere Vokabeln

gar kein . . .   no . . . at all,
   not a . . . at all
obwohl (*sub. conj.*)   although
viele (*pl. pronoun*)   many
people

Nützliche Ausdrücke

auf dem Land   in the
   country (i.e., rural area)
aufs Land   to the country
im Gegenteil   on the
   contrary

Mit anderen Worten

riesengroß = sehr sehr groß

SEIT 1390
HISTORISCHES

**Hotel·Restaurant
Goldener Adler**

GOETHE·STUBE · BATZENHÄUSL
Besitzer· Familie Cammerlander
Direktion Karl Pokorny

6020 INNSBRUCK
Herzog·Friedrich·Str. 6. Tel. 26 3 34

Aspekte der Großstadt

Die meisten° Deutschen leben in Städten mit über 80 000 Einwohnern. Welche Vorteile und Nachteile° gibt es, wenn man in einer Großstadt wohnt?

Eindrücke eines Amerikaners

5 *Mark Walker, Student:* Dieses Jahr verbringe ich zwei Semester als Austauschstudent an der Universität Hamburg.[6] Da ich aus einer Kleinstadt in Colorado komme, schien mir Hamburg zuerst riesengroß. Es war schwer zu verstehen, wie die Deutschen so dicht zusammengedrängt°
10 leben können.

   Aber das bedeutet nicht, daß Hamburg mir nicht gefällt. Im Gegenteil! Ich finde es phantastisch, daß es in der Stadt so viel zu tun gibt. Wenn ich Lust habe, kann ich jeden Tag ins Konzert, ins Kino, oder ins Museum gehen. Hamburg ist
15 die zweitgrößte° Stadt der Bundesrepublik und eine internationale Metropole. Weil es eine Hafenstadt ist, gibt es seit Jahrhunderten Verbindungen° mit England, Skandinavien, Rußland und vielen anderen° Ländern.

   Wenn das Stadtleben mir zu viel wird, dann ist es sehr
20 leicht, mein Fahrrad zu nehmen, in die Bahn zu steigen, und aufs Land zu fahren. In der Lüneburger Heide[7] südlich von° Hamburg kann man schöne Radtouren machen. Dieser Kontrast zwischen Stadt und Land scheint mir besonders typisch für Deutschland. Das Land ist den Einwohnern der Städte
25 sehr wichtig als Erholung° vom Streß des Alltags.

most
advantages and disadvantages

dicht zusammengedrängt = *crowded together*

second largest

ties
other

south of

relaxation

Rudern [*rowing*] auf dem Alster (Hamburg).

6. Large deep-water port on the Elbe river. Population 1.6 million.
7. The Lüneburg Heath, an extensive nature preserve on the North German plain, south of Hamburg and north of Hannover.

„Ich wohne gern hier"

Beate Kreuz, Sozialarbeiterin in München:[8] Ich arbeite mit Jugendlichen° aus Gastarbeiterfamilien.[9] Sie haben oft keinen Schulabschluß° und können keine Arbeit finden. Ich sehe also jeden Tag die Probleme einer Großstadt wie München. Trotz dieser Probleme wohne ich sehr gerne hier. Obwohl die Wohnungsnot° in München schlimm ist, haben ein paar Freunde und ich eine Wohnung in einem alten Gebäude finden können. Ich kann mit der S-Bahn° überall hinfahren° und brauche gar kein Auto. Im Sommer gehen wir in der Isar[10] schwimmen oder im Englischen Garten[11] radfahren, und im Winter fahren wir in den Alpen Ski. In der Kaufinger Straße[12] gibt es eine große Fußgängerzone, wo viele gern einen Schaufensterbummel machen. An jeder Ecke gibt es ein elegantes Geschäft, aber in meinem Beruf sehe ich so viel Arbeitslosigkeit,° daß mich der Konsumzwang° und die hohen° Preise ärgern. Trotzdem kann man auch ohne viel Geld in der Tasche gut leben.

mit Jugendlichen = mit jungen Leuten
diploma

housing shortage

Stadtbahn = *commuter rail service*
überall hin- = *everywhere*

unemployment
pressure to buy / high

Einkaufen am Markt (München)

8. **München** (English *Munich*), capital city of Bavaria (German **Bayern**), pop. 1.2 million.
9. Families of foreign or "guest" workers. These are workers from Turkey, Italy, Yugoslavia, and other southern European countries, principally employed in heavy industry and construction.
10. Munich is located on the Isar, a 160-mile-long tributary of the Danube, originating in the Austrian Alps.
11. A large park designed by the American Benjamin Thompson, Count Rumford (1753–1814).
12. Formerly a major traffic thoroughfare in central Munich.

1. Woher kommt Mark Walker?

2. Was macht er in Hamburg?

3. Welchen Eindruck hat Hamburg zuerst auf ihn gemacht? Warum?

4. Wie gefällt ihm die Stadt?

5. Was kann er jeden Tag tun, wenn er Lust hat?

6. Was können die Menschen in der Stadt machen, wenn ihnen der Streß des Alltags zu viel wird?

7. Was ist Beate Kreuz von Beruf?

8. Warum braucht sie gar kein Auto?

9. Was macht sie in ihrer Freizeit im Sommer? im Winter?

10. Welche Probleme des Stadtlebens sieht sie in ihrer Arbeit?

Situationen aus dem Alltag

Unterwegs in der Stadt

Gebäude und Orte (*Buildings and Places*)

die **Apotheke, -n**	*pharmacy*
die **Brücke, -n**	*bridge*
das **Café, -s**	*café*
die **Haltestelle, -n**	*streetcar or bus stop*
das **Kaufhaus, ⁻er**	*department store*
die **Kirche, -n**	*church*
die **Konditorei, -en**	*pastry café*
die **Post**	*post office*
das **Rathaus, ⁻er**	*city hall*

Verkehrsmittel (*Means of Transportation*)

der **Bus, -se**	*bus*
das **Taxi, -s**	*taxicab*
die **Straßenbahn**	*streetcar*
die **U-Bahn**	*subway*

Fragen wir nach dem Weg. (*Let's ask for directions.*)

Entschuldigung, wie komme ich **zur Post?**

                     . . . **zum Bahnhof?**

Das ist gleich in der Nähe.
Das ist nicht weit von hier.
Gehen Sie über die Straße, und dann geradeaus.

                     . . . nach links.

                     . . . nach rechts.

                     . . . um die Ecke.

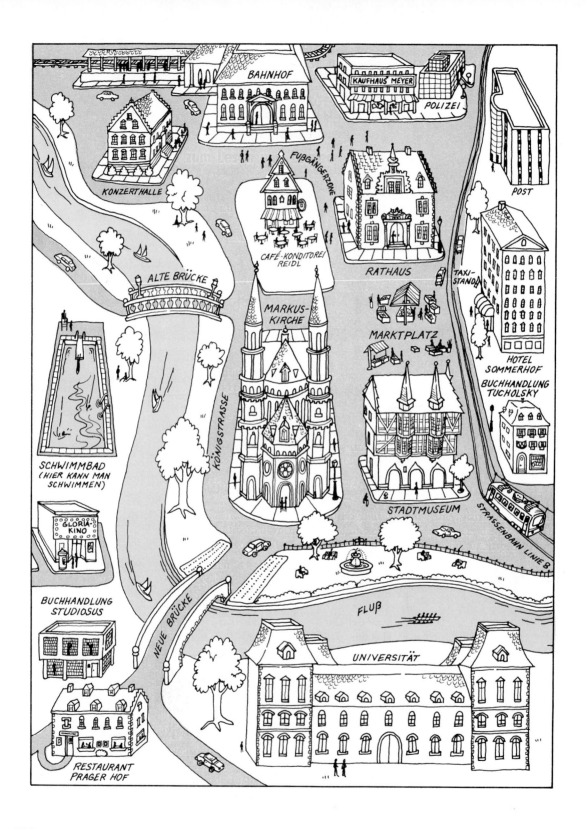

Partnerarbeit: Wie komme ich zu . . . ?

Partner A ist fremd in dieser Stadt. Er oder sie benutzt den Stadtplan, um nach dem Weg zu fragen. Partner B ist hier zu Hause und sagt Partner A den Weg durch die Stadt. Dann tauschen Sie die Rollen aus (**austauschen** = *switch*).

1. Sie stehen vor der Post und wollen zum Marktplatz.
2. Sie sind im Museum und müssen zum Hotel zurück, um zu Mittag zu essen.
3. Sie sind in der Fußgängerzone und haben Hunger. Sie brauchen Hilfe (*help*), um ein Restaurant zu finden.

Gruppendiskussion: Was machen wir denn morgen?

Mit einer Studentengruppe machen Sie eine Reise durch Deutschland. Heute abend sind Sie in einer Großstadt angekommen und übernachten im Hotel Sommerhof (siehe Stadtplan). Besprechen Sie, was Sie morgen machen wollen.

Wohin wollen wir gehen?

Was gibt es dort zu tun oder zu sehen?

Wo wollen wir essen?

Was machen wir dann am Abend?

Wie kommen wir hin (*get there*)? Zu Fuß, mit einem Taxi, oder mit der Straßenbahn?

In der Konditorei

Am Tisch

1. die Serviette, -n
2. die Gabel, -n
3. der Teller, -
4. das Messer, -
5. der Löffel, -
6. das Glas, ¨er
7. die Speisekarte, -n

Was gibt's zum Essen und zum Trinken?

Das wissen Sie schon:

das Bier	der Kaffee	der Salat
das Brot	der Käse	die Tasse
das Brötchen, -	die Kartoffel, -n	das Wasser
die Flasche, -n	der Nachtisch	der Wein
	die Pommes frites	die Wurst

Auf der Speisekarte der Konditorei finden Sie auch:

die **Butter**	*butter*
das **Ei, -er**	*egg*
das **Eis**	*ice cream*
das **Kännchen, -**	*small (coffee or tea) pot*
der **Kuchen, -**	*cake*
die **Milch**	*milk*
die **Portion, -en**	*serving of, order of*
der **Saft, ¨e**	*juice*
die **Sahne**	*cream*
der **Schinken**	*ham*
der **Tee**	*tea*

❖ *Café-Konditorei Reidel*

Warme Getränke

Tasse Kaffee	2,30
Kännchen Kaffee	4,60
Tasse Mocca	4,40
Kännchen Mocca	5,40
Tasse Kaffee Hag. . . .	2,40
Kännchen Kaffee Hag . .	4,80
Tasse Kakao mit Sahne . . .	2,40
Kännchen Kakao mit Sahne .	4,80
Glas Tee mit Milch oder Zitrone .	2,30
Glas Tee mit Rum	4,50
Glas Pfefferminztee . . .	2,30
Glas Grog von Rum 4 cl . .	5,00
Glas Glühwein 0,21	4,50
Glas heiße Zitrone	2,60

Eis und Eisgetränke

Portion gemischtes Eis . .	3,20
Portion gemischtes Eis mit Sahne	3,90
Früchte-Eisbecher „Florida" .	6,50
Eis-Schokolade	4,00

Kalte Getränke

Flasche Mineralwasser . . .	2,10
Flasche Coca Cola	2,10
Flasche Orangeade . . .	2,10
Pokal Apfelsaft	2,40
Glas Orangensaft	2,80
Glas Tomatensaft	2,80
Glas Zitrone natur	2,60

Frühstück

Kleines Gedeck	6,00

1 Kännchen Kaffee, Tee od. Schokolade, 2 Brötchen, Butter, Konfitüre

Großes Gedeck	7,90

1 Kännchen Kaffee, Tee od. Schokolade, 2 Brötchen, Butter, Konfitüre, 1 gek. Ei, 1 Scheibe Schinken od. Käse

Ergänzung zum Frühstück

1 gekochtes Ei	1,00
1 Portion Konfitüre	0,80
1 Portion Butter	0,80
1 Scheibe Käse	1,60
1 Scheibe Schinken	1,80
1 Brötchen oder 1 Scheibe Brot	0,60

Gruppenarbeit: In der Konditorei   *3 oder 4 Studenten*

Sie sitzen zusammen in der Café-Konditorei Reidl und bestellen etwas zu essen und trinken. Jemand in der Gruppe spielt den Kellner oder die Kellnerin. Die anderen bestellen von der Speisekarte.

Zum Schluß

Sprechen wir miteinander!

A **Übung:** Wann machen Sie das?

Ihr Professor fragt, wann Sie etwas machen. Sagen Sie es ihm. Die Liste der Zeitangaben (*time phrases*) hilft Ihnen.

> BEISPIEL: Wann haben Sie Zeit, eine Reise zu machen?
> Während der Ferien. / Im Sommer. / usw.

am	*im*	*während*
Morgen	Frühling	Woche
Abend	Herbst	Ferien
Wochenende	Winter	Vorlesung
Montag (usw.)	Januar (usw.)	Konzert

1. Wann gehen Sie zur Deutschstunde?

2. Wann haben Sie Zeit, einzukaufen?

3. Wann schreiben Sie Briefe?

4. Wann schlafen Sie gern?

5. Wann haben Sie Lust, ins Ausland zu fahren?

6. Wann haben Sie keine Zeit, ins Kino zu gehen?

B **Partnerarbeit:** Wie findest du das?

On the left are some adjectives you can use to describe your attitude toward the activities listed on the right. Take turns telling each other what you think.

> BEISPIEL: Ich finde es wunderschön, schwimmen zu gehen.

altmodisch	einen Stadtbummel zu machen
bequem	Deutsch zu lernen
barbarisch	schwimmen zu gehen
blöd	Hausaufgaben zu schreiben
einfach	meine Eltern anzurufen
furchtbar	um 6 Uhr aufzustehen
gut	Frühstück zu essen
interessant	Romane zu lesen
klug	ins Museum zu gehen
leicht	Geld zu sparen
nett	im Sommer zu arbeiten
phantastisch	Freunde einzuladen
schwierig	Kaffee zu trinken
stinklangweilig	ein Zimmer zu finden

C **Partnerarbeit:** Wessen . . . ist das?

Pictured below are Ute's family and some things that belong to them. Take turns asking what belongs to whom.

> BEISPIEL: Wessen Buch ist das?
> Das ist das Buch ihrer Schwester.

Schwester   Bruder   Eltern

D **Gruppenarbeit:** Warum tun Sie das?

Your instructor asks you why you do certain things. Answer with an **um . . . zu** phrase.

> BEISPIEL: Warum gehen Sie in die Altstadt?
> Um einen Schaufensterbummel zu machen.

1. Warum gehen Sie ins Wasser?
2. Warum lernen Sie Deutsch?
3. Warum fahren Studenten oft per Autostop?
4. Warum bringt man eine Kamera mit, wenn man reist?
5. Warum fährt man im Winter in die Alpen?
6. Warum rufen Sie Ihre Freunde an?

E Partnerarbeit: *Warum machst du das gern?*

Jetzt fragen Sie andere Studenten in der Klasse, was sie gern machen und warum. Sie antworten mit **um . . . zu** oder **weil.**

> BEISPIEL: So fängt es an: A: Was machst du denn gern?
> B: Ich gehe oft gern in die Stadt.
> A: Warum?
> B: *Um* ins Kino *zu* gehen. *oder*
> *Weil* ich gern ins Kino gehe.

Schreiben Sie zu Hause

F **Die ideale Stadt** Sie sind Städteplaner/in von Beruf und kennen viele Städte. Einige haben Ihnen sicher gefallen, einige nicht. Jetzt dürfen Sie die ideale Stadt planen. Beschreiben Sie diese Stadt. Was würde sie haben, was würde sie nicht haben? Warum?

G **Ein Brief nach Hause** Sie kennen schon die Stadt auf Seite 236. Sie haben den Tag dort verbracht. Jetzt sitzen Sie am Abend im Hotel und schreiben einen Brief nach Hause. Beschreiben Sie Ihrer Familie, wie der Tag war. Was sind Ihre Eindrücke von der Stadt und von den Menschen?

H Wie sagt man das auf deutsch?

1. Can you please tell me where the cathedral is?

2. It isn't far from here. If you go around the corner, you'll see it.

3. Thanks very much.

4. What do you do when city life gets too stressful for you?

5. Sometimes I go to the country and go for a walk.

6. Do I still have time to go shopping?

7. Yes, of course. If you go right away, I'll come along.

8. My brother's girlfriend has a birthday tomorrow and I want to give her something.

Almanach

Kulturleben und Freizeit in der Großstadt

These pages give you some idea of the rich cultural and recreational offerings of German cities. See how much you can understand.

ZOOLOGISCHER GARTEN KÖLN
Riehler Str. 173 · 5000 Köln 60 · Tel. 76 30 66

Öffnungszeiten:

ZOO
Sommer
9.00 – 18.00 Uhr
Winter
9.00 – 17.00 Uhr

AQUARIUM
9.30 – 18.00 Uhr
ganzjährig

Straßenbahnen: 11, 15, 16!
Linienbus: 134 und 148.
Mülheimer Boote · Rheinseilbahn direkt an der Brücke

Werden Sie Mitglied
des Fördervereins

„FREUNDE
DES KÖLNER ZOOS e.V."

„Casino Jivers"

Die Casio Jivers treffen mit ihrem straighten Pow-Swing direkt in die Beine ihres Publikums. Ingo Berg zaubert auf seinem Stand-Drum einen unermüdlichen treibenden Swing, während Stephan Baumgardt sein kraftvollen, melodieösen Linien auf dem Kontrabass beisteu... Rudi Blondscheck, der den Großteil der Songs kom... getextet hat, rundet mit seiner jazzgeprägten ganze ab. Zusammen bringen die d... temperamentvollen Show ein... der jedes Publikum s...

Ägyptisches Museum
Berlin

11 13 15

Ägyptisches Museum Berlin

**Staatliche Museen
Preußischer Kulturbesitz**

Öffnungszeiten:
Täglich 9-17 Uhr, freitags
geschlossen. Eintritt frei.

Verkehrsverbindungen:
Bus 54, 62, 74
U-Bahn Linie 1, Station
Sophie-Charlotte-Platz
Linie 7, Station
Richard-Wagner-Platz
(ca. 10 Min. Fußweg)

Führungen:
– für Berliner Schulklassen,
Montag bis Freitag, 8-15 Uhr,
Telefon 8301-465;
– für auswärtige Schul-
klassen, Gruppen oder
Einzelpersonen, Montag
bis Donnerstag, 8-12 Uhr,
Telefon 8301-466;
oder nach schriftlicher
Anmeldung.

Adresse:
Schloßstraße 70
1 Berlin 19, gegenüber dem
Schloß Charlottenburg

Telefon (030) 32091-261/267

VILLA – STUCK

Salonmusik
der
Jahrhundertwende
Christian Mattick – Flöte
Mathias Huth – Klavier

spielen

Werke von Raff, Grieg, Liszt u.a.

im Salon der Villa Stuck

Prinzregenten Str. 60

8000 München 80

Eintritt: 15.– / erm. 10.– nur Abendkasse

• Donnerstag, 22. Juni, 20⁰⁰ Uhr •

Zusammenfassung und Wiederholung

Kapitel 5–8

FORMS

1. Verbs

A. Separable prefix verbs (prefix is stressed)   p. 136

anfangen	**aus**steigen	**spazieren**gehen
aufstehen	**rad**fahren	**kennen**lernen
einkaufen	**ski**fahren	**mit**kommen

The prefix separates in the present tense:

	inflected stem		*prefix*
Wir	**fangen**	bald	**an.**
Sie	**steht**	um sieben	**auf.**
Wann	**gehen**	wir denn	**spazieren?**

p. 136

The prefix separates in the imperative:

inflected stem		*prefix*
Fangen	Sie bald	**an!**
Steht	um sieben	**auf!**
Komm	bitte	**mit!**
Fahren	wir doch	**Ski!**

p. 136

The perfect tense of separable prefix verbs:

Prefix + **ge** + Stem   p. 168

vorbeikommen → Bärbel ist vorbei**ge**kommen.
zumachen → Wer hat diese Tür zu**ge**macht?
mitbringen → Ich habe dir etwas mit**ge**bracht.

B. Inseparable prefix verbs (prefix is not stressed)   p. 138
The following prefixes are inseparable: **be-, ent-, er-, ge-, ver-, zer-.**

bedeuten, enttäuschen, erzählen, gefallen, vergessen
Er vergißt alles.
Vergeßt eure Hausaufgaben nicht!

Perfect tense of inseparable prefix verbs: *no* **ge-!**   p. 169

Hast du deinen Mantel **vergessen?**
Das habe ich nicht **verstanden.**

C. The simple past tense of **sein** *to be*   p. 163

ich **war**	wir **waren**
du **warst**	ihr **wart**
Sie **waren**	Sie **waren**
er/es/sie **war**	sie **waren**

Wo wart ihr letzte Woche?   Wir waren auf dem Land.

D. Perfect tense

pp. 163–70

1. Inflected Auxiliary (**haben** or **sein**) + Past Participle

auxiliary		*past participle*
Ich **habe**	den Bahnhof	**gesucht.**
Sie **ist**	nach Wien	**geflogen.**

2. **sein** as auxiliary in the perfect tense p. 166
The verb must both be *intransitive* and show *change of location or condition.*

Wir **sind** nach Hause gegangen.	*(change of location)*
Ich **bin** schnell gelaufen.	*(change of location)*
Hans **ist** groß geworden.	*(change of condition)*

Exceptions are **bleiben** and **sein.**

Sie **sind** zehn Tage **geblieben.**
Er **ist** oft im Ausland **gewesen.**

3. Participles of weak vs. strong verbs

Participles of Weak Verbs   **ge-** + stem + **-(e)t**   p. 164

---

sagen	Was hast du ihm **gesagt?**
ärgern	Das hat mich **geärgert.**
kosten	Es hat viel **gekostet.**
arbeiten	Ich habe heute viel **gearbeitet.**

Verbs ending in **-ieren** are always weak but never add the prefix **ge-** in the past participle:

studieren   Ich habe in Freiburg **studiert.**

Participles of Strong Verbs   **ge-** + stem + **-en**   p. 165

---

geben	Vater hat mir Geld **gegeben.**
helfen	Sie haben uns nicht **geholfen.**
fahren	Ich bin nach Deutschland **gefahren.**
trinken	Was habt ihr denn **getrunken?**

The perfect stem is not always predictable from the infinitive. Past participles must be memorized.

Participles of Mixed Verbs   **ge-** + changed stem + **-t**   p. 169

---

bringen	Er hat den Brief zur Post **gebracht.**
verbringen	Wo haben Sie die Ferien **verbracht?**
kennen	Ich habe sie gut **gekannt.**
wissen	Hast du das nicht **gewußt?**

---

4. Perfect tense of modal verbs p. 203

auxiliary	*double infinitive*
Sie **haben** das nicht	**verstehen können.**
Sie **hat**	**mitgehen dürfen.**

E. Verbs with dative objects pp. 195–97

The following verbs require a dative object.

antworten	Antworten Sie **mir**, bitte.
danken	Er hat **mir** für den Roman gedankt.
gefallen	Das gefällt **mir** sehr.
gehören	**Wem** gehört das?
glauben	Ich kann **Ihnen** nicht glauben.
helfen	Hilf **mir**, bitte!

2. Nouns and pronouns

A. Noun phrases

1. with **der**-words p. 139, pp. 201–2, p. 225

Definite Article + Noun			
		Singular	*Plural*
masculine	*nom.*	der Mann	die Männer
	acc.	den Mann	die Männer
	dat.	dem Mann	den Männer**n**
	gen.	des Mann**es**	der Männer
neuter	*nom.*	das Kind	die Kinder
	acc.	das Kind	die Kinder
	dat.	dem Kind	den Kinder**n**
	gen.	des Kind**es**	der Kinder
feminine	*nom.*	die Frau	die Frauen
	acc.	die Frau	die Frauen
	dat.	der Frau	den Frauen
	gen.	der Frau	der Frauen

Dative plural of all nouns ends in **-n** (except when the plural form is **-s:** den Hotels, den Kinos).

The genitive singular of masculine and neuter nouns takes **-es** when the noun is one syllable: des Kindes. Otherwise, add **-s:** des Vaters, des Problems.

2. with **ein**-words

ein-word + Noun				p. 201
		Singular	*Plural*
masculine	*nom.*	kein Mann	keine Männer
	acc.	keinen Mann	keine Männer
	dat.	keinem Mann	keinen Männer**n**
	gen.	keines Mann**es**	keiner Männer

		Singular	Plural
neuter	*nom.*	kein Kind	keine Kinder
	acc.	kein Kind	keine Kinder
	dat.	keinem Kind	keinen Kinder**n**
	gen.	keines Kind**es**	keiner Kinder
feminine	*nom.*	keine Frau	keine Frauen
	acc.	keine Frau	keine Frauen
	dat.	keiner Frau	keinen Frauen
	gen.	keiner Frau	keiner Frauen

B. Masculine N-Nouns

p. 175, p. 225

	Singular	*Plural*
nom.	der Student	die Studen**ten**
acc.	den Studen**ten**	die Studen**ten**
dat.	dem Studen**ten**	den Studen**ten**
gen.	des Studen**ten**	der Studen**ten**

Similarly:

der Bauer, -n, -n	*farmer*
der Herr, -n, -en	*gentleman; Mr.*
der Journalist, -en, -en	*journalist*
der Korrespondent, -en, -en	*correspondent*
der Kunde, -n, -n	*customer*
der Mensch, -en, -en	*person, human being*
der Tourist, -en, -en	*tourist*

C. Personal Pronouns

Singular			*Plural*		
nom.	*acc.*	*dat.*	*nom.*	*acc.*	*dat.*
ich	mich	mir	wir	uns	uns
du	dich	dir	ihr	euch	euch
Sie	Sie	Ihnen	Sie	Sie	Ihnen
er	ihn	ihm			
es	es	ihm	sie	sie	ihnen
sie	sie	ihr			

3. Prepositions

pp. 143–44

A. Prepositions with dative case

aus	*out of; from* (country or city)
außer	*except for; besides; in addition to*
bei	*near; at; in the home of*
mit	*with*

nach	*after; to* (with country and city names)
seit	*since* (temporal); *for* (when scanning the past)
von	*from; of; by*
zu	*to* (with people and some locations)

B. Two-way prepositions (with accusative or dative) pp. 170–73

	Destination ***Wohin?*** *with accusative*	**Location** ***Wo?*** *with dative*
an	*to, toward*	*at, alongside of*
auf	*onto*	*on, upon, on top of*
hinter	*behind*	*behind*
in	*into, to*	*in*
neben	*beside, next to*	*beside, next to*
über	*over, above; across*	*over, above*
unter	*under*	*under; beneath*
vor	*in front of*	*in front of*
zwischen	*between*	*between*

Verb pairs used with two-way prepositions: p. 199

Destination ***Wohin?*** *with accusative* *Weak verbs*	**Location** ***Wo?*** *with dative* *Strong verbs*
hängen (hat gehängt)	hängen (hat gehangen)
legen	liegen
setzen	sitzen
stellen	stehen

C. Standard contractions of *preposition + article*

an das → **ans**	in dem → **im**
an dem → **am**	von dem → **vom**
bei dem → **beim**	zu dem → **zum**
in das → **ins**	zu der → **zur**

D. Prepositions with the genitive p. 227

statt, anstatt	*instead of*
trotz	*in spite of*
während	*during*
wegen	*because of, on account of*

WORD ORDER

1. Word order of nouns and pronouns p. 142

A. Word order of direct and indirect objects. Note the parallel to English word order.

Ich zeige **meiner Mitbewohnerin den Artikel.**	*I'm showing my roommate the article.*
Ich zeige **ihn meiner Mitbewohnerin.**	*I'm showing it to my roommate.*

Ich zeige **ihr den Artikel.**

I'm showing her the article.

Ich zeige **ihn ihr.**

I'm showing it to her.

B. Pronoun word order
Personal pronouns are either in first position

Er ist gern allein.

or immediately after the inflected verb in the order nominative, accusative, dative.

Heute gebe **ich es ihm.**

2. Word order in compound sentences and infinitive phrases

A. Coordinating conjunctions: **aber, denn, oder, sondern, und**   pp. 193–95
Coordinating conjunctions do not affect word order.

Clause 1	*Coordinating*	*Clause 2*
(verb second)	*Conjunction*	*(verb second)*

Ich bleibe nicht.   Ich gehe nach Hause.
Ich bleibe nicht, **sondern** ich **gehe** nach Hause.

B. Subordinating conjunctions: **da, daß, ob, obwohl, weil, wenn** and   pp. 219–22
question words introducing subordinate clauses: **wann, warum, was, wem, wen, wer, wessen, wie, wo, woher, wohin.** Subordinating conjunctions require verb-last word order.

Main Clause	*Subordinating*	*Subordinate Clause*
(verb second)	*Conjunction*	*(verb last)*

Ich **weiß** nicht,   **ob**   sie in München **wohnt.**

or

Subordinate Clause	*Main Clause*
(verb last)	*(verb first, i.e., in second position)*

Ob sie in München **wohnt,** **weiß** ich nicht.

C. Infinitive phrases with **zu**
   1. The infinitive with **zu** comes at the end of its phrase: pp. 222–23

   Es war schön.   Ich habe Sie endlich kennengelernt.
   Es war schön, Sie endlich **kennenzulernen.**

   2. **um . . . zu** = *in order to*   p. 224

   Ich reise nach Deutschland.   Ich möchte dort studieren.
   Ich reise nach Deutschland, **um** dort **zu studieren.**

   3. **ohne . . . zu** = *without (doing something)*

   Ich habe ein Jahr dort gelebt.   Ich habe ihn nicht kennengelernt.
   Ich habe ein Jahr dort gelebt, **ohne** ihn **kennenzulernen.**

FUNCTIONS

1. Expressing intentions, preferences, opinions, and making polite requests: *würden* + *infinitive*.
p. 198

Würden Sie mir bitte den Koffer **tragen?**
Ich **würde sagen,** daß du zu kritisch bist.
Würdest du gern **schwimmen gehen,** oder lieber **Tennis spielen?**

2. Uses of dative case

A. To show recipient or beneficiary of action (indirect object)
pp. 138–39

Meine Freundin hat **mir** einen Rucksack geschenkt.
Zeigen Sie **dem Professor** Ihr Referat.

B. To show personal involvement and reactions (personal dative)
p. 197

Wie geht es **Ihnen?**
Wie schmeckt **dir** der Kaffee?
Das ist **mir** egal.

3. Use of genitive case

Genitive case shows a relation of one noun to another, expressed in English by the possessive (*John's* book—**Johanns** Buch) or by the preposition *of* (*the color of your jacket*—die Farbe **deiner** Jacke). In German, genitive case usually *follows* the noun it modifies.

genitive
pp. 225–26

der Wagen meines Freundes — *my friend's car*
die Kinder seiner Schwester — *his sister's children*
die Gebäude dieser Stadt — *the buildings of this city*

Exception: Proper names in the genitive precede the noun they modify.

Beethovens Symphonien
Utes Freundin

4. Translating English "to"
p. 230

A. **nach**—with cities and most countries

Fahren wir **nach** Berlin!

B. **zu**—with people and some locations

Ich gehe heute abend **zu** Inge.
Jetzt müssen wir schnell **zum** Bahnhof.

C. **in**—with countries whose names are preceded by an article

Wir wollen im Sommer **in die** Schweiz.
Damals haben wir eine Reise **in die** Sowjetunion gemacht.

And with some locations:

Kommst du mit **ins** Konzert?
Ich gehe gern mit ihr **ins** Kino.

SITUATIONS, IDIOMS, EXPRESSIONS

1. **In stores and restaurants**

   Ich esse gern italienisch.
   Was darf es sein?
   Eine Tasse Kaffee und zwei Glas Bier, bitte sehr.
   Zwei Kilo Kartoffeln, bitte.

   Wieviel kostet das bitte?
   Sonst noch etwas?
   Zahlen bitte!
   Das macht zusammen . . .

2. **Eating and drinking**

   Was ißt du gern?

		Was trinkst du gern?
Bauernbrot	Kuchen	Bier
Brezeln	Leberwurst	Kaffee mit/ohne Sahne
Brot mit/ohne Butter	Nachtisch	Milch
Brötchen	Obst	Saft
Eier	Pommes frites	Wasser
Eis	Salat	Wein
Fleisch	Schinken	Tee
Gemüse	Suppe	
Kartoffeln	Wurst	
Käse		

3. **Greetings, opinions, and feelings**

   Herzlich willkommen!
   Bitte sehr.
   Ich habe die Nase voll.
   Quatsch!
   Es tut mir leid.
   Es macht nichts.
   Es ist mir egal.
   Das macht mir Spaß.

   Egal wohin (wer, warum, usw.).
   Ich glaube ja.
   Im Gegenteil.
   Einverstanden?
   Ist gut.
   Ich habe Hunger. Ich habe Durst.
   Ich habe Lust, ins Kino zu gehen.

4. **Place and time**

   Gibt es ein Restaurant **in der Nähe**?
   Wir fahren **aufs Land.**
   Meine Großeltern wohnen **auf dem Land.**

   Wieviel Uhr ist es? / Wie spät ist es?
   Es ist 8.15 Uhr.
   Es ist 19.20 Uhr.

5. **Mit anderen Worten: Slang im Kontext**

   Dieter Hillebrandt, Student in Berlin, erzählt:

   Letztes Jahr habe ich **das Abi** geschafft, und jetzt studiere ich an **der Uni.** Weil ich keine **Bude** in der Stadt gefunden habe, wohne ich in einer **WG.** Ich habe nicht genug Platz für meinen **Kram**, aber **das ist mir Wurscht**, denn es gefällt mir hier.

   Diese Woche war eine **Katastrophe.** Im Moment habe ich wirklich **eine Menge** Arbeit, weil ich nächste Woche im Seminar ein Referat über Hegel halten muß. Ich sitze von morgens bis abends am Schreibtisch und arbeite **wie wahnsinnig.** Es ist **blöd**, wenn die Arbeit so **stressig** wird, aber ich muß es einfach tun.

TEST YOUR PROGRESS

A. Fill in the blank with the correct preposition or contraction (*preposition + article*).

1. Ich bin _____ vier Semestern _____ dieser Uni.
2. _____ Professor Brinkmann möchte ich eine Dissertation _____ Kafka schreiben.
3. Ich habe seinen Namen nicht _____ Vorlesungsverzeichnis gefunden.
4. Jeden Tag fahre ich _____ meiner Freundin _____ meinem Motorrad _____ Uni.
5. _____ dem Semesterende wollen wir _____ den Ferien zusammen _____ Österreich fahren.
6. _____ dem Schreibtisch _____ mir zu Hause liegen alle meine Bücher _____ (except for) dem Geschichtsbuch.

B. Form questions to which these are the answers.

1. Er fliegt nach Wien.
2. Sie kommt aus Berlin.
3. Doch, das stimmt.
4. Doch, natürlich habe ich Zeit für dich.
5. Das hat mein Großvater immer gesagt.
6. Die Landkarte gehört meinem Freund.
7. Am Dienstag sollen wir das machen.
8. Die Kinder sind heute bei ihrer Tante.

C. Fill in the blank with the correct prepositional phrase containing a German equivalent of "to."

1. Kommst du mit _____ Kino?
2. Nein, leider nicht. Ich fahre heute abend _____ meiner Kusine.
3. Mußt du also _____ die Schweiz?
4. Ja, ich muß zuerst _____ Basel und dann mit dem Zug _____ Zürich fahren.
5. Warte, ich komme mit dir _____ Bahnhof und gehe später _____ Hause.

D. Complete the sentence according to the English cue. In the second sentence of each pair, substitute pronouns for objects.

1. Die Großmutter erzählt _____ _____.
   (*the children*) (*a fairy-tale*)
   Sie erzählt _____ _____ am Abend.
   (*it*) (*to them*)
2. Ich habe _____ _____ gezeigt.
   (*my friend*) (*the article*)
   Dann hat er _____ * _____ erklärt.
   (*it*) (*to me*)

E. Restate the following sentences in the perfect tense.

1. Karin bleibt heute zu Hause.
2. Meine Freunde wohnen nicht in München.
3. Um wieviel Uhr stehst du denn auf?
4. Ich schreibe meiner Familie einen Brief.

5. Ich muß eine Stunde bleiben.
6. Die Schüler sind oft müde.
7. Ich habe leider keine Zeit.
8. Sie wird Lehrerin.

F. Combine the sentences with the conjunctions cued in English.

1. Kommst du mit? (*or*) Bleibst du hier?
2. (*because*) Ich habe keine Zeit. Ich kann Ihnen nicht helfen.
3. Hamburg liegt nicht im Süden Deutschlands. (*but rather*) Es liegt im Norden.
4. Ich weiß nicht. (*whether*) Ist er hier?
5. (*since*) Wir haben wenig Geld. Wir müssen trampen.
6. (*if*) Du kannst mir helfen. Ich bin bald fertig.
7. Jan hat nicht studiert. (*but*) Er weiß viel über Geschichte.
8. Hast du gehört? (*that*) Tante Karoline besucht uns morgen.
9. (*although*) Sie ist nie in Europa gewesen. Sie spricht gut Deutsch.

G. Complete these sentences, using the genitive phrases cued in English.

1. Wir nehmen (*my friend's car*).
2. Kennen Sie schon (*the end of this story*)?
3. Nein, aber (*Karl's brother*) sagt, es soll gut sein.
4. (*My teacher's house*) liegt gleich um die Ecke.
5. Mir gefällt (*the language of these people*) sehr.
6. Mir gefällt mein Studium (*in spite of the work*).
7. (*Because of my work*) kann ich leider nicht kommen.
8. Ist denn (*the life of a student*) so schwer?

H. Give the German equivalents for these sentences with time expressions.

1. What time is it, please?
2. It is almost seven-thirty.
3. When is the train supposed to arrive?
4. It arrives at eight fifty-nine P.M.
5. What are you doing at quarter to eight?

I. Look at the cues at the beginning of each sentence. Insert the correct German form in the blank and supply the preposition (or contraction) needed.

1. (*to lie*) Manchmal _____ ich bis neun _____ Bett.
2. (*to lay*) Du kannst deine Tasche _____ den Stuhl _____.
3. (*to put*) Sollen wir Ihren Schreibtisch _____ Büro _____.
4. (*to stand*) Ja bitte, aber er soll nicht direkt _____ Fenster _____.
5. (*to sit*) Darf ich ein paar Minuten hier _____ Tisch _____?

J. Combine these sentences by changing the one in italics into an infinitive phrase.

BEISPIEL: Es ist sehr schön. *Wir gehen im Sommer hier schwimmen.*
Es ist sehr schön, im Sommer hier schwimmen zu gehen.

1. Wir haben keine Lust. *Wir sollen Onkel Georg besuchen.*
2. *Sie wollen etwas über Kunst lernen.* (um . . . zu) Sie sind ins Museum gegangen.
3. Es war sehr nett von ihr. *Sie hat mir eine Karte aus Köln geschickt.*
4. Gehst du schon? *Du hast Julia nicht auf Wiedersehen gesagt.* (ohne . . . zu)

KAPITEL

9

Unsere
Umwelt

Communicative Goals
- Using adjectives to describe things
- Giving the date
- Discussing ecology and recycling
- Talking about sports

Cultural Goal
- Discussing German and global environmental issues

Lyrik Zum Vorlesen   Jürgen Werner,
„Die Lorelei 1973"

Grammatik   Attributive Adjectives and
Adjective Endings   •   Word Order of
Adverbs: Time / Manner / Place   •   Ordinal
Numbers and Dates

Lesestück   Unsere Umwelt in Gefahr

Situationen aus dem Alltag   Der Sport

Almanach   Seid ihr schlaue Umweltfüchse?

Dialoge

Recycling in unserem Wohnhaus

Frau Berger trifft Herrn Rehhagel auf der Treppe.

FRAU BERGER: Mensch, wohin mit dem riesengroßen Sack?

HERR REHHAGEL: In den Keller. Die neuen Container sind da. Jetzt können wir Altglas und Altpapier hier im Haus[1] sammeln.

FRAU BERGER: Na, endlich! Jetzt brauche ich meinen Müll nicht mehr zum Recycling zu schleppen.

HERR REHHAGEL: Ja, das ist jetzt nicht mehr nötig. Wenn alle Häuser der Stadt mitmachen, dann ist das ein großer Fortschritt.

Ein umweltfreundliches Geburtstagsgeschenk

DANIEL: Was hat dir Marianne zum Geburtstag geschenkt?

FRANK: Ein neues Fahrrad, weil wir unseren Zweitwagen verkauft haben.

DANIEL: Wieso denn?

FRANK: Er war ja sowieso kaputt, und da wir in die Stadt umgezogen sind, kann ich mit dem Rad zur Arbeit fahren.

DANIEL: Da sparst du aber viel Geld.

FRANK: Ja, und ich habe auch ein gutes Gefühl, weil ich etwas gegen die Luftverschmutzung mache.

Treibst du Sport?

JUNGE: Sag mal, treibst du gern Sport?

MÄDCHEN: Klar. Ich verbringe das ganze Wochenende auf dem Tennisplatz. Spielst du auch Tennis?

JUNGE: Ja, das ist mein Lieblingssport, aber ich bin kein guter Spieler.

MÄDCHEN: Da kann ich dir einen wunderbaren Tennislehrer empfehlen.

Notes on Usage

da   At the beginning of a clause, the adverb **da** often means "then," "in that case," "under those circumstances," "for that reason":

Da sparst du aber viel Geld.
Da kann ich dir einen wunderbaren Tennislehrer empfehlen.

The Flavoring Particle *aber*   As a flavoring particle, **aber** is often used to intensify a statement. It adds the sense of "really," "indeed."

Da sparst du **aber** viel Geld.   *Then you'll really save a lot of money.*

The particle **aber** can add a note of surprise or admiration:

Mensch, das ist **aber** teuer!   *Wow, that's really expensive.*

---

1. **Haus** can also be used to mean "building."

Recycling in Our Apartment Building

Ms. Berger meets Mr. Rehhagel on the stairs.

MS. BERGER: Wow, where to with that huge sack?

MR. REHHAGEL: To the cellar. The new trash containers are here. Now we can collect waste glass and waste paper here in the building.

MS. BERGER: At last! Now I don't have to haul my trash to the recycling center anymore.

MR. REHHAGEL: Yes, that's not necessary anymore. If all the buildings in town participate, then that's great progress.

An Ecological Birthday Present

DANIEL: What did Marianne give you for your birthday?

FRANK: A new bicycle, because we sold our second car.

DANIEL: How come?

FRANK: It was kaput anyway, and since we've moved to the city, I can ride my bike to work.

DANIEL: Then you're saving a lot of money.

FRANK: Yes, and it also feels good to be doing something against air pollution.

Do You Play Sports?

BOY: Hey, do you like to play sports?

GIRL: Sure. I spend all weekend on the tennis court. Do you play tennis too?

BOY: Yes, that's my favorite sport, but I'm not a good player.

GIRL: Then I can recommend a wonderful tennis teacher to you.

Wortschatz 1

Verben

empfehlen (empfiehlt), hat empfohlen to recommend
mit·machen to participate, cooperate
sammeln to collect
schleppen (*colloq.*) to drag, lug (along), haul
treffen (trifft), hat getroffen to meet
treiben, hat getrieben to drive, force, propel
Sport treiben to play sports
um·ziehen, ist umgezogen to move, change residence

Substantive

der **Container, -** large trash container
der **Fortschritt, -e** progress
der **Geburtstag, -e** birthday
zum Geburtstag for (your/her/my/etc.) birthday
der **Junge, -n, -n** boy
der **Keller, -** cellar, basement
der **Müll** trash, refuse
der **Sack, ¨e** sack
der **Sport** sport
der **Tennisplatz, ¨e** tennis court

der **Zweitwagen, -** second car

das **Gefühl, -e** feeling
das **Geschenk, -e** present
das **Mädchen, -** girl
das **Papier, -e** paper
das **Recycling** recycling; recycling center
das **Tennis** tennis
das **Wohnhaus, ¨er** apartment building

die **Luft** air
die **Luftverschmutzung** air pollution
die **Gefahr, -en** danger
die **Treppe** staircase, stairs
auf der Treppe on the stairs
die **Umwelt** environment
die **Verschmutzung** pollution

Adjektive und Adverbien

ganz whole, entire
das ganze Wochenende all weekend, the whole weekend
kaputt (*colloq.*) broken, kaput; exhausted
klar clear; (*colloq.*) sure, of course

nötig necessary
schmutzig dirty
sportlich athletic
umweltfreundlich environmentally beneficial, non-polluting
zweit-[2] second

Andere Vokabeln

Lieblings- (*noun prefix*) favorite
   Lieblingssport favorite sport
wieso? How come? How's that? What do you mean?

Nützliche Ausdrücke

na endlich! at last! high time!

Gegensätze

nötig ≠ unnötig necessary ≠ unnecessary
schmutzig ≠ sauber dirty ≠ clean

> **Mit anderen Worten**

dreckig (*colloq.*) = **schmutzig**

Variationen

A Persönliche Fragen

1. Ist man in Ihrem Studentenwohnheim umweltfreundlich? Was macht man da für die Umwelt?

2. Auch als Hobby kann man Dinge sammeln, z.B. Briefmarken (*stamps*), Münzen (*coins*) oder Schallplatten. Sammeln Sie etwas? Was?

3. Frau Berger hat früher ihren Müll zum Recycling geschleppt. Was müssen Sie jeden Tag (z.B. in Ihrem Rucksack) mitschleppen?

4. Zum Geburtstag hat Frank ein neues Fahrrad bekommen. Was würden Sie gern zum Geburtstag bekommen?

5. Besitzt Ihre Familie zwei Wagen? Braucht sie wirklich zwei?

6. Fährt jemand in Ihrer Familie mit dem Rad zur Arbeit? Wenn nicht, warum nicht?

7. Meinen Sie, daß die Luftverschmutzung hier ein Problem ist? Wie ist es bei Ihnen zu Hause?

8. Treiben Sie Sport? Wie oft in der Woche?

9. Was ist Ihr Lieblingssport? -film? -buch? Und Ihre Lieblingsstadt? -schallplatte?

B Warum ich Geld brauche.

Sagen Sie, warum Sie Geld brauchen.

    BEISPIEL: Warum brauchen Sie Geld?
             Ich brauche Geld, *um* ein Rad *zu* kaufen.

---

2. The hyphen indicates that this adjective cannot be used without an ending. For adjective endings, see pp. 259–62.

C Welche Farbe hat das?

Sagen Sie, welche Farbe diese Dinge haben.

> BEISPIEL: Welche Farbe hat Georgs Hemd?
> Es ist rot.

Welche Farbe hat/haben . . .

der Wald?   der Wein?

der Kaffee?   das Hemd dieses Jungen?

das Meer?   diese Landkarte?

die Wände dieses Zimmers?   diese Bäume im Sommer? im Herbst?

die Bluse dieser Studentin?   ihr Pulli?

Lyrik zum Vorlesen

Um diese Parodie zu verstehen, muß man „Die Loreley" von Heinrich Heine schon kennen. Lesen Sie noch einmal Heines Gedicht (*poem*) auf Seite 218 und dann diesen Text.

Die Lorelei 1973

Ich weiß nicht, was soll es bedeuten,
daß ich so traurig bin;
ein Alptraum° aus unseren Zeiten,   *nightmare*
er geht mir nicht aus dem Sinn.

Die Luft ist schwül° und verdunkelt,   *close, heavy*
und dreckig fließt der Rhein;
kein Gipfel des Berges funkelt,
wo sollt' auch die Sonne sein?

Am Ufer° des Rheines sitzt sie,   *bank*
die deutsche Chemie-Industrie;
dort braut° sie gefährliche Gifte,°   *brews / poisons*
die Luft macht erstickend° sie.   *suffocating*

Sie kümmert sich° nicht um den Abfall,°   **kümmert sich** = *cares about /*
der° aus den Rohren° fließt;   *garbage / that / pipes*
er kommt aus dem chemischen Saustall,°   *pig-sty*
wo er in den Rhein sich ergießt.°   **sich ergießt** = *pours*

Dem Schiffer im Tankerschiffe,
ihm macht das Atmen Müh';°   **ihm . . . Müh** = *has trouble*
er schaut nicht die Felsenriffe,   *breathing*
er schaut nur die dreckige Brüh'.°   *brew*

Ich weiß, die Wellen verschlingen
einst° nicht nur Schiffer und Kahn;   *some day*
und das hat mit ihren Giften
die Industrie getan.

Jürgen Werner (geboren 1939)

Grammatik

Attributive Adjectives and Adjective Endings

Predicate Adjectives versus Attributive Adjectives

Adjectives in both English and German are used in one of two ways in a sentence:

- They may follow "linking" verbs such as *to be, to become, to remain,* and *to seem* (**sein, werden, bleiben, scheinen**), in which case they are called *predicate adjectives* because they constitute the second part of the predicate. Most of the adjectives you have encountered so far have been predicate adjectives.

Das Rad ist **neu.**	*The bicycle is **new.***
Meine Großeltern werden **alt.**	*My grandparents are getting **old.***
Der Kaffee ist **heiß.**	*The coffee is **hot.***

Predicate adjectives in German have *no endings*.

- Adjectives may also occur *before* a noun. In this position they are called *attributive adjectives.*

das **neue** Rad	*the **new** bicycle*
meine **alten** Großeltern	*my **old** grandparents*
heißer Kaffee	***hot** coffee*

German attributive adjectives *always* have endings.

The Noun Phrase

Attributive adjectives occur in noun phrases. A noun phrase consists of a noun and the words directly associated with it. English and German noun phrases have similar structures. They consist typically of three types of words: *limiting words, attributive adjectives,* and *nouns.*

Limiting words are the **der**-words and the **ein**-words you already know:

der-*words*	**ein-*words***	
der	ein	
dieser	kein	
jeder	mein ⎫	
solcher	dein ⎪	
welcher	sein ⎪	
alle[3]	ihr ⎬ possessive adjectives	
	unser ⎪	
	euer ⎪	
	ihr ⎭	

---

3. **Alle** is plural and takes the primary plural endings, i.e., **alle** (*nom.* and *acc.*), **allen** (*dat.*), **aller** (*genitive*). **Alle** is often followed by a second limiting word. They will both have the same primary ending: **alle meine Freunde, alle diese Leute.**

They are called "limiting words" because they *limit* the noun in some way rather than describing it: **dieses Fahrrad** (**this** bicycle, not that one), **meine Großeltern** (**my** grandparents, not yours).

Here are some examples of noun phrases. Note that the noun phrase does not necessarily contain both a limiting word and an attributive adjective.

limiting word	*attributive adjective*	*noun*	
das	neue	Fahrrad	*the new bicycle*
jede		Woche	*every week*
alle	deutschen	Studenten	*all German students*
	heißer	Kaffee	*hot coffee*
meine	kleine	Schwester	*my little sister*

German adjective endings have acquired the reputation of being a formidable obstacle for the learner. However, the system is conceptually quite simple and mainly requires practice in using it automatically in spoken German. To be able to use attributive adjectives, you only need to know two sets of endings—called the *primary endings* and the *secondary endings*—and three rules for their use. Half of the system is already familiar to you: the primary endings are simply the endings of the **der**-words that show gender, number, and case.

Primary Endings			
	masc.	*neut.*	*fem.*	*plur.*
---	---	---	---	---
nom.	dieser	dieses	diese	diese
acc.	diesen	dieses	diese	diese
dat.	diesem	diesem	dieser	diesen
gen.	dieses	dieses	dieser	dieser

There are only two secondary endings, **-e** and **-en**. They occur in the following pattern:

Secondary Endings			
	masc.	*neut.*	*fem.*	*plur.*
---	---	---	---	---
nom.	-e	-e	-e	-en
acc.	-en	-e	-e	-en
dat.	-en	-en	-en	-en
gen.	-en	-en	-en	-en

Note that the **-en** occurs *throughout the plural* as well as *throughout the dative and genitive cases.*

Rules for the Use of Adjective Endings

- Within every noun phrase, a primary ending *must* be present. (In most noun phrases, the primary ending will be on the limiting word.)

limiting word with primary ending	attributive adjective with secondary ending	noun
dies**es**	schöne	Bild
mit mein**er**	gut**en**	Freundin

- Some noun phrases have no limiting word. Others have an **ein**-word without an ending. In such phrases, the *attributive* adjective takes the primary ending.[4]

no limiting word or ein-word without ending	attributive adjective with primary ending	noun
	alte	Häuser
	heiß**er**	Kaffee
ein	alt**es**	Haus

- Attributive adjectives in succession have the same ending.

  ein groß**es** alt**es** Haus
  groß**e** alt**e** Häuser
  gut**er** heiß**er** Kaffee

Pay special attention to the three instances in which **ein**-words have no endings. They are the *only* instances in which **ein**-words differ from **der**-words.

masculine nominative	*neuter nominative and accusative*
ein alt**er** Mann	ein klein**es** Kind
	but
der alte Mann	dieses kleine Kind

Neue Mode: Alte Häuser

---

4. There is one exception to rule 2: In the masculine and neuter genitive singular, the attributive adjective not preceded by a limiting word takes the *secondary ending* **-en** rather than the primary ending.

   trotz tief**en** Schnees   *in spite of deep snow*
   wegen schlecht**en** Wetters   *because of bad weather*

Such phrases are quite rare. Moreover, note that the primary ending *is* present on the noun itself.

Let's summarize. The tables below show the complete declension of an adjective in noun phrases using a **der**-word, noun phrases using an **ein**-word, and noun phrases without limiting words.

Adjective Endings Following a **der**-word

	masc.	neut.	fem.	plur.
nom.	dieser junge Mann	dieses junge Kind	diese junge Frau	diese jungen Leute
acc.	diesen jungen Mann	dieses junge Kind	diese junge Frau	diese jungen Leute
dat.	diesem jungen Mann	diesem jungen Kind	dieser jungen Frau	diesen jungen Leuten
gen.	dieses jungen Mannes	dieses jungen Kindes	dieser jungen Frau	dieser jungen Leute

Adjective Endings Following an **ein**-word

	masc.	neut.	fem.	plur.
nom.	ein junger Mann	ein junges Kind	eine junge Frau	meine jungen Leute
acc.	einen jungen Mann	ein junges Kind	eine junge Frau	meine jungen Leute
dat.	einem jungen Mann	einem jungen Kind	einer jungen Frau	meinen jungen Leuten
gen.	eines jungen Mannes	eines jungen Kindes	einer jungen Frau	meiner jungen Leute

Adjective Endings without a Limiting Word

	masc.	neut.	fem.	plur.
nom.	kalter Wein	kaltes Wasser	kalte Milch	kalte Suppen
acc.	kalten Wein	kaltes Wasser	kalte Milch	kalte Suppen
dat.	kaltem Wein	kaltem Wasser	kalter Milch	kalten Suppen
gen.	kalten Weines	kalten Wassers	kalter Milch	kalter Suppen

1 **Übung:** Welcher Tisch ist das?

Below is a list of some classroom objects and people, arranged by gender, as well as a list of adjectives that you can use to describe them. Your instructor will point to objects and people and ask you which they are. Describe them with adjectives.

> BEISPIEL: Welches Bild ist das?
> Das ist *das neue Bild.*

masc.	neut.	fem.	plur.	adjectives
Bleistift	Bild	Gruppe	Jeans	billig
Junge	Buch	Hose	Schuhe	bunt
Kugelschreiber	Fenster	Jacke	Studenten	doof
Mantel	Foto	Kamera	Bücher	freundlich
Pulli	Glas	Landkarte		groß
Radiergummi	Heft	Studentin		herrlich
Stadtplan	Hemd	Tafel		höflich
Student	Kleid	Tasche		kaputt
Stuhl	Mädchen	Tür		kurz
	Papier	Uhr		langweilig
	Poster	Zeitschrift		neu
	Wörterbuch	Zeitung		wunderbar
				typisch
				alt
				blau, rot, grün, usw.
				fleißig
				toll
				schrecklich

2 **Übung:** Sehen Sie den Tisch?

Now your instructor asks whether you see certain objects or people. You're not sure which ones are meant, so you ask for more information.

> BEISPIEL: Sehen Sie den Tisch?
> Meinen Sie den *grünen* Tisch?

Fragewort

Was für . . . ? *What kind of . . . ?*

Was für ein Artikel ist das?	*What kind of article is that?*
Was für einen Wagen hast du?	*What kind of car do you have?*
Mit **was für** Menschen arbeitest du zusammen?	*What kind of people do you work with?*

---

3 **Übung:** Was für ein Buch ist das?

Jetzt fragt Ihr Professor zum Beispiel, was für ein Buch das ist. Sie beschreiben das Buch.

> BEISPIEL: Was für ein Buch ist das?
> Das ist ein interessantes Buch.

4 **Partnerarbeit:** Nicht wahr?

Take turns confirming each other's impressions. One partner asks the question and the other responds. Then switch roles.

> BEISPIEL: Das Haus ist schön, nicht wahr?
> Ja, das ist ein schönes Haus.

1. Die Kneipe ist alt, nicht?
2. Der Junge ist klug, nicht wahr?
3. Das Hotel ist teuer, nicht wahr?
4. Der Automechaniker ist gut, nicht?
5. Das Kind ist müde, nicht wahr?
6. Die Buchhandlung ist phantastisch, nicht?
7. Das Bett ist bequem, nicht?
8. Der Tag ist warm, nicht?

Now invent your own sentences on the same pattern.

5 **Übung:** Was für ein Buch brauchen Sie?

Jetzt möchte Ihre Professorin wissen, was für Sachen Sie brauchen, tragen, usw. Sagen Sie es ihr.

> BEISPIEL: PROF.: Was für ein Buch brauchen Sie?
> STUD.: Ich brauche ein neues Buch.
>
> PROF.: Was für Schuhe tragen Sie heute?
> STUD.: Heute trage ich alte Turnschuhe.

6 **Übung:** Wir haben keinen neuen Wagen.

Ihr Professor fragt Sie nach (*about*) etwas. Sie antworten, daß Sie es nicht haben.

> BEISPIEL: Ist Ihr Wagen neu?
> Nein, ich habe keinen neuen Wagen.

1. Ist Ihr Fahrrad neu?
2. Sind diese Bücher langweilig?
3. Ist der Tennislehrer wunderbar?
4. Ist der Sportplatz groß?
5. Ist die Wurst frisch?
6. Sind Ihre Freunde sportlich?
7. Sind diese Kleider schmutzig?
8. Ist Ihr Schlafzimmer groß?

7 **Übung:** Was machen Sie lieber?

Der Professor fragt Sie, was Sie lieber machen.

> BEISPIEL: Dieser Zug fährt langsam, aber dieser fährt schnell. Mit welchem Zug fahren Sie lieber?
> Ich fahre lieber mit dem langsamen Zug.

1. Dieser Kaffee ist heiß, aber dieser ist kalt. Welchen trinken Sie lieber?
2. Dieses Hemd ist rot, und dieses ist gelb. Welches gefällt Ihnen besser?
3. Diese Kartoffeln sind groß, aber diese sind klein. Welche nehmen Sie?
4. Dieser See ist warm, aber dieser ist kühl. In welchem würden Sie lieber schwimmen?
5. Diese Stadt ist schön, aber diese ist häßlich. In welcher würden Sie lieber wohnen?
6. Dieses Zimmer ist hell, aber dieses ist dunkel. Welches gefällt Ihnen?
7. Dieses Hotel ist alt, aber dieses ist neu. In welchem würden Sie lieber übernachten?
8. Diese Brezeln sind frisch, aber diese sind alt. Welche würden Sie lieber essen?

Word Order of Adverbs: Time / Manner / Place

You learned in *Kapitel 1* that adverb sequence in German is time before place.

> Ich fahre **morgen nach Kopenhagen.**
> Wir bleiben **heute zu Hause.**

If an adverb or adverbial phrase of manner (answering the question **wie?** or **mit wem?**) is also present, the sequence is *time—manner—place.*

> Ich fahre morgen **mit der Bahn** nach Kopenhagen.

A good mnemonic device is that the adverbs answer the following questions in alphabetical order:

wann: (morgen)   **wie?** (mit der Bahn)   **wo(hin)?** (nach Kopenhagen)

8 **Übung**

1. Wie können wir morgen nach Berlin fahren?

   Wie viele Möglichkeiten gibt es für eine Reise nach Berlin?

   BEISPIEL: Wir können morgen <u>mit der Bahn</u> nach Berlin fahren.

2. Mit wem gehen Sie abends ins Kino?

   BEISPIEL: Ich gehe abends <u>mit meinem Freund</u> ins Kino.

Ordinal Numbers and Dates

The ordinal numbers (i.e., **first, second, third,** etc.) are adjectives and in German take the usual adjective endings.

From one to nineteen, add **-t-** to the cardinal number and then the appropriate adjective ending. Note the three irregular forms in boldface.

der, das, die	**erste**	1st	elfte	11th
	zweite	2nd	zwölfte	12th
	dritte	3rd	dreizehnte	13th
	vierte	4th	vierzehnte	14th
	fünfte	5th	fünfzehnte	15th
	sechste	6th	sechzehnte	16th
	siebte	7th	siebzehnte	17th
	achte	8th	achtzehnte	18th
	neunte	9th	neunzehnte	19th
	zehnte	10th		

From twenty on up, add **-st-** and the adjective ending to the cardinal number.

der, das, die	zwanzigste	20th
	einundzwanzigste	21st
	zweiundzwanzigste	22nd
	dreiundzwanzigste	23rd
	usw.	
	dreißigste	30th
	vierzigste	40th
	hundertste	100th
	tausendste	1000th

In German, an ordinal number is seldom written out in letters. It is usually indicated by a period after the numeral.

der **10.** November = der zehnte November

Dates in German

Here is how to ask for and give the date:

Den wievielten haben wir heute? ⎫
　　　　　　　or ⎬ *What's the date today?*
Der wievielte ist heute? ⎭ (literally: *"The how manyeth do we have today / is today?"*)

Heute haben wir **den dreizehnten.** ⎫
　　　　　　　or ⎬ *Today is the thirteenth.*
Heute ist **der dreizehnte.** ⎭

Here is how to say on what date something occurs or occurred:

Das war **am zehnten** August.   *That was on the tenth of August.*
Wir fliegen **am achtzehnten.**   *We're flying on the eighteenth.*

In German, the full date is given in the order: day, month, year.

den 1.2.1992   *February 1, 1992*

VHS
Das neue Semester beginnt.

Am 11. Febr.

9 Übungen

A. Der wievielte ist heute?
   Heute ist der . . .

   1. 3. August
   2. 9. Februar
   3. 1. Mai
   4. 17. Juli
   5. 2. Januar
   6. 8. April

B. Den wievielten haben wir heute?
   Heute haben wir den . . .

   7. 5. März
   8. 13. Juni
   9. 11. November
   10. 19. September
   11. 7. Dezember
   12. 28. Oktober

10 Übung

Wann kommt Frank? Er kommt am . . .

1. 4. Januar

2. 30. September

3. 6. April

4. 25. Juli

5. 31. Oktober

6. 20. Februar

11 **Partnerarbeit:** Wann reist Susanne nach München?

Hier sehen Sie eine Seite (*page*) aus Susannes Terminkalender für Februar. Fragen Sie einander, wann sie alles macht.

BEISPIEL: A: Wann besucht sie Heinz?
          B: Sie besucht ihn am ersten.

FEBRUAR	
1 Heinz besuchen	9 im Computerzentrum arbeiten
2	10
3 ins Theater gehen („Mutter Courage")	11 ins Kino („Männer")
4	12
5	13
6 mit Jörg und Katja essen gehen	. . .
7 schwimmen gehen (19 Uhr)	20 Reise nach München
8	21 in die Berge fahren

Lesestück   Unsere Umwelt in Gefahr

Tips zum Lesen und Lernen

Tips zum Vokabelnlernen

Identifying Noun Gender   Now that you have acquired a vocabulary of several hundred words in German, you can begin to recognize some patterns in the gender and formation of nouns. You have already learned that agent nouns ending in **-er** are always masculine (**der Lehrer**) and that the ending **-in** always designates a female (**die Lehrerin**).

The gender of many nouns is determined by a suffix. Here are some of the most common suffixes that form nouns.

■ Nouns with the following suffixes are *always feminine* and *always* have the plural ending **-en**:

> **-ung, -heit, -keit, -schaft, -ion, -tät**

-ung forms nouns from verb stems:

lösen (*to solve*) →	**die Lösung, -en** (*solution*)
zerstören (*to destroy*) →	**die Zerstörung** (*destruction*)
verschmutzen (*to pollute*) →	**die Verschmutzung** (*pollution*)

-heit and **-keit** form nouns on adjective stems and from other nouns:

frei →	**die Freiheit, -en** (*freedom*)
freundlich →	**die Freundlichkeit** (*friendliness*)
gesund →	**die Gesundheit** (*health*)

-schaft forms collective and more abstract nouns from concrete nouns:

Studenten →	**die Studentenschaft** (*student body*)
Land →	**die Landschaft, -en**
Freund →	**die Freundschaft, -en** (*friendship*)

-ion and **-tät**: Words borrowed from French or Latin. Most have English cognates:

die Diskussion, -en	**die Generation, -en**
die Universität, -en	**die Elektrizität**

■ The suffixes **-chen** and **-lein** form diminutives. The stem vowel of the noun is umlauted wherever possible, and the noun automatically becomes *neuter*. Plural is always identical to singular.

die Karte →	**das Kärtchen, -** (*little card*)
das Stück →	**das Stückchen, -** (*little piece*)
das Brot →	**das Brötchen, -**
die Magd (archaic: *maid*) →	**das Mädchen, -**
die Frau →	**das Fräulein, -** (*Miss; young woman*)
das Buch →	**das Büchlein, -** (*little book*)

Übung: Raten Sie mal! *Take a guess!*

Was bedeuten diese Wörter?

1. die Möglichkeit
2. die Wanderung
3. die Ähnlichkeit
4. die Mehrheit
5. die Meinung
6. die Lehrerschaft
7. die Wohnung
8. die Schönheit
9. die Dummheit
10. die Studentenschaft
11. die Radikalität
12. die Gesundheit
13. die Schwierigkeit
14. das Brüderlein
15. das Liedchen
16. das Städtchen
17. das Würstchen
18. das Häuschen
19. die Kindheit

Leicht zu merken

aktiv	*aktiv*
akut	
das **Atom, -e**	*Atom*
die **Basis**	
demonstrieren	*demonstrieren*
die **Elektrizität**	*Elektrizität*
die **Energie**	*Energie*
enorm	
die **Generation, -en**	*Generation*
die **Konsequenz, -en**	*Konsequenz*
der **Lebensstandard**	
die **Natur**	*Natur*
das **Ökosystem**	
das **Plastik**	
politisch	
produzieren	*produzieren*
radikal	*radikal*
sowjetisch	*sowjetisch*
der **Supertanker, -**	

Umweltschutz

Heute schon an morgen denken!

Der Bundesminister des Innern

Einstieg in den Text

The following text discusses environmental problems. These issues concern not just Americans, but people all over the globe. They are particularly crucial in densely populated Europe.

Look over *Wortschatz 2*, then read the following hypotheses about the environment. Do you agree or disagree with them? Compare your responses to the opinions expressed in the reading.

1. Wir sind heute immer noch sehr abhängig von der Natur.

2. Die Großindustrie ist für die Umweltverschmutzung verantwortlich.

3. Die Atomenergie ist eine gute Alternative zum Öl.

4. Der Durchschnittsbürger (*average citizen*) kann im Alltag viel gegen die Umweltverschmutzung tun.

5. Die Politiker müssen viel mehr für die Umwelt tun.

Wortschatz 2

Verben

führen to lead
lösen to solve
retten to rescue, save
verbrauchen to consume, use up
verschmutzen to pollute; dirty
verschwenden to waste
werfen (wirft), hat geworfen to throw
  weg·werfen to throw away, discard
zerstören to destroy

Substantive

der **Abfall, ⁓e** waste product, refuse; trash
der **Fisch, -e** fish
der **Politiker, -** politician
der **Unfall, ⁓e** accident
der **Vogel, ⁓** bird

das **Beispiel, -e** example
das **Kraftwerk, -e** power plant
  das **Atomkraftwerk** atomic power plant
das **Öl** oil
das **Tier, -e** animal

die **Chance, -n** chance
die **Dose, -n** (tin) can
die **Gesellschaft, -en** society
die **Gesundheit** health
die **Jugend** (*sing.*) youth; young people
die **Kraft, ⁓e** power; strength
die **Lösung, -en** solution
die **Menschheit** mankind, human race
die **Partei, -en** political party
die **Pflanze, -n** plant
die **Politik** politics; policy
die **Technik** technology
die **Ware, -n** product

Adjektive und Adverbien

abhängig von dependent on
bereit prepared, ready
eigen- own
erstaunlich astounding
gefährlich dangerous
gesund healthy
hoch (*predicate adj.*), **hoh-** (*attributive adj.*) high
Das Gebäude ist **hoch.**
aber
Das ist ein **hohes** Gebäude.

jährlich annually
stark strong

Andere Vokabeln

mancher, -es, -e many a (*in plural* = some)

Nützliche Ausdrücke

im Jahr(e) 1989 in 1989
nicht nur . . . sondern auch not only . . . but also

Gegensätze

abhängig ≠ unabhängig dependent ≠ independent
führen ≠ folgen (+ *dat.*) to lead ≠ to follow
gesund ≠ krank healthy ≠ sick
die **Gesundheit ≠** die **Krankheit** health ≠ sickness
hoch ≠ niedrig high ≠ low
stark ≠ schwach strong ≠ weak

Unsere Umwelt in Gefahr

Das Problem: Der Mensch gegen die Natur?

Wir leben heute in Europa und Nordamerika in einer hoch-
industrialisierten° Welt. Wir lieben unseren Luxus° und
brauchen unsere Technik, denn sie sind die Basis unseres
hohen Lebensstandards. Aber unseren erstaunlichen Fort-
5   schritt haben wir teuer bezahlt.° Manchmal vergessen wir,
daß wir immer noch von der Natur abhängig sind.

   Um unsere Lebensweise° möglich zu machen, brauchen
wir enorm viel Energie. Obwohl die Nordamerikaner und
10   Westeuropäer nur zirka 15% der Weltbevölkerung° aus-
machen,° verbrauchen sie zirka 65% aller produzierten
Energie. Spätestens° seit der Katastrophe im sowjetischen
Atomkraftwerk in Tschernobyl am 26. April 1986 weiß man
aber, wie gefährlich diese Energiequelle° für unser Ökosys-
15   tem sein kann. Ein zweites Beispiel ist die Exxon-Valdez-
Katastrophe vom Jahre 1989; das Öl aus diesem verunglück-
ten° Supertanker hat das Meer verschmutzt und Fische und
Vögel weit und breit° in Gefahr gebracht. Die schlimmen
Folgen° von solchen Unfällen können jahrelang fortdauern.°
20   Leider aber sind alle unsere Hauptenergiequellen (Öl,
Kohle,° Atomkraft) schädlich° für die Natur und für unsere
Gesundheit.

highly industrialized / luxury

teuer bezahlt = *paid a high price for*

way of life

world population
comprise
at the latest

energy source

grounded
far and wide
*consequences / **jahrelang fortdauern** =*
   persist for years
coal / harmful

(*links*) Im Schwarzwald. (*rechts*) Waldsterben.

Aber nicht nur die Großindustrie muß für die Umwelt verantwortlich sein, sondern auch jeder einzelne° Mensch.
Wir fahren zu viel Auto, wir essen zu viel in Fast-Food-Restaurants, wir benutzen zu viele Spraydosen° und produzieren zu viel Abfall. Die Konsequenzen sind: der saure Regen von den Abgasen,° Müllhalden° voll von unnötigen Plastikverpackungen° und die Zerstörung der Ozonschicht.° Das Problem ist im dicht besiedelten° Deutschland besonders akut. Dort wirft jeder Bürger jährlich zirka 300 bis 400 kg Müll weg! Man möchte wirklich fragen: Sind wir Menschen denn die Feinde° der Natur?

individual

aerosol cans

exhaust gases / trash dumps
plastic packaging / ozone layer
dicht besiedelt = *densely populated*

enemies

Die Lösung: aktiv umweltfreundlich sein!

Besonders die junge Generation in Deutschland zeigt für diese Probleme starkes Engagement.° Manche finden bei den Grünen[5] eine radikale Alternative zu der Umweltpolitik der großen Parteien. Viele demonstrieren gegen neue Atomkraftwerke und suchen auch in ihrem eigenen Leben Alternativen zu der Wegwerfgesellschaft. Aber nicht nur die umweltbewußte° Jugend, sondern Deutsche aus allen Altersgruppen° sind heute bereit, ihr Leben zu ändern,° um Meere, Wälder, Tiere und Pflanzen zu retten.[6]

Wie kann man denn ein umweltfreundliches Leben führen? Man kann z.B. mehr radfahren und zu Fuß gehen und weniger° Auto fahren. Man sollte° nur Waren ohne unnötige Verpackung kaufen und den Hausmüll sammeln

commitment

environmentally conscious
age groups / change

less / should

BITTE VERLASSEN SIE DIESEN PLANETEN SO, WIE SIE IHN VORZUFINDEN WÜNSCHEN!

Es geht auch OHNE PVC

5. The "Greens," the environmental and anti-nuclear party, first won seats in the Bundestag in 1983. Although they lost these seats in the 1990 federal elections, they are still represented at the state level in some **Länder.** The Greens draw much of their support from younger voters.

6. An indication of environmental consciousness in Germany is the fact that in 1990, the Federal Republic became the first nation to ban the production and use of ozone-depleting chlorofluorocarbons.

und zum Recycling bringen. Man kann auch so wenig Wasser und Elektrizität wie° möglich verschwenden. Diese
Vorschläge° für den Alltag sind zwar° ein Anfang, aber längst
nicht° genug. Man muß natürlich auch von den Politikern
mehr Umweltbewußtsein° fordern.° Die Menschheit hat
nicht mehr viel Zeit. Nur wenn alle Länder politisch zusam-
menarbeiten, haben wir noch eine Chance, unsere Umwelt
zu retten.

50

55

so . . . wie = *as . . . as*
suggestions / indeed
längst nicht = *not nearly*
environmental awareness / demand

Fragen zum Lesestück

1. Von welchen Umweltkatastrophen haben Sie schon gehört?

2. Wann war die Katastrophe in Tschernobyl?

3. Wie können Umweltkatastrophen für die Natur gefährlich sein?

4. Wer soll denn für die Umwelt verantwortlich sein?

5. Nennen Sie unsere Hauptenergiequellen.

6. Kennen Sie alternative Energiequellen?

7. Wie kann unser modernes Alltagsleben für die Umwelt gefährlich sein?

8. Wie können wir ein umweltfreundliches Leben führen?

Situationen aus dem Alltag

Der Sport

„Wer Sport treibt, bleibt fit!" sagt man. Was meinen Sie? Treiben Sie Sport,
um fit und gesund zu bleiben, oder nur, weil es Ihnen Spaß macht? Hier sind
einige nützliche Wörter für eine Diskussion über Sport.

Substantive	*Verben*
das **Spiel, -e** *game*	**gewinnen, hat gewonnen** *to win*
die **Mannschaft, -en** *team*	**schlagen, hat geschlagen** *to beat*
die **Konkurrenz** *competition*	**trainieren** *to train*

Gruppenarbeit: Was spielst du gern?

Hier sind einige Piktogramme aus den Olympischen Spielen. Welchen Sport treiben Sie gern?

> BEISPIEL: Ich schwimme gern. Und du?
> Ich _____.

laufen
der **Läufer,** -
die **Läuferin, -nen**

schwimmen
der **Schwimmer,** -
die **Schwimmerin,
-nen**

skifahren
der **Skifahrer,** -
die **Skifahrerin, -nen**

boxen
der **Boxer,** -

Fußball spielen
der **Fußballspieler,** -
die **Fußballspielerin,
-nen**

Volleyball spielen
der **Volleyballspieler,** -
die **Volleyballspielerin,
-nen**

radfahren
der **Radfahrer,** -
die **Radfahrerin, -nen**

(Eis)hockey spielen
der **Hockeyspieler,** -

Gruppenarbeit: Sprechen wir über Sport   *2 oder 3 Personen*

1. Welchen Sport treibst du?
2. Warum gefällt dir dieser Sport?
3. Bist du in einer Universitätsmannschaft? Warst du in einer Schulmannschaft?

Klassendiskussion: Was meinen Sie?

1. Kann man fit bleiben, ohne Sport zu treiben?
2. In Deutschland gibt es nur selten Universitätsmannschaften. Sind solche Mannschaften an amerikanischen Unis gut oder nicht gut? Warum?

Zum Schluß

Sprechen wir miteinander

A **Gruppenarbeit:** Beschreiben wir das Klassenzimmer.

> BEISPIEL: Dort hängt ein großes Bild an der Wand.
> Dort steht ein kleiner Tisch.

Was sehen Sie sonst? Benutzen Sie Adjektive!

B **Gruppenarbeit:** Wer trägt was?

Benutzen Sie Adjektive, um die Kleider eines Studenten oder einer Studentin im Zimmer zu beschreiben. Die anderen müssen raten (*guess*), wen Sie meinen. Sie können auch Ihre eigenen Kleider beschreiben.

> BEISPIEL: A: Wer trägt heute eine alte Hose und ein häßliches Hemd?
> B: Meinst du Rick?

C **Übung:** Ich habe ein interessantes Bild gefunden.

Suchen Sie in einem Bilderbuch oder einer Zeitschrift ein interessantes Bild oder Foto. Beschreiben Sie es vor der Klasse. Benutzen Sie viele Adjektive!

> BEISPIEL: Ich habe dieses schöne Bild in einem alten Buch gefunden. Hier sieht man viele Häuser in einem kleinen Dorf. In der Mitte des Bildes steht eine alte Kirche und vor dieser schönen Kirche geht ein alter Mann mit einem jungen Kind spazieren. Hinter dem Dorf sieht man auch einen dunklen Wald, usw.

D **Gruppenarbeit:** Es gibt eine Alternative!

Hier sind einige Beispiele der Umweltverschmutzung. Können Sie Alternativen geben?

> BEISPIEL: Einen Plastiklöffel muß man wegwerfen.
> *Alternative*: Aber ich brauche nicht mit Plastiklöffeln zu essen.

1. Meine Familie wirft jede Woche viele Flaschen weg.
2. Sonntags fahre ich gern im eigenen Auto aufs Land.
3. Im Supermarkt sind die Lebensmittel alle in Plastik verpackt.
4. Manchmal werfen Menschen Papier auf die Straße.
5. Mein Kugelschreiber hat fast keine Tinte (*ink*) mehr.
6. In unserem Studentenwohnheim gibt es keine Recyclingcontainer.

Jeden Tag verbrauchen wir viele Sachen. Aber wir verschwenden auch eine Menge, besonders Dinge aus Plastik. Machen Sie eine Liste von solchen Dingen aus Ihrem Alltag. Was haben Sie in den letzten Tagen wegwerfen müssen? Warum?

Liste: „Das haben wir in letzter Zeit weggeworfen."

F **Gruppenarbeit:** Wann? Wie? Wo? Wohin?

Ask each other when or how you do the activities listed in the right-hand column. Answer with complete sentences, using the cues in the other two columns or inventing your own answers.

BEISPIEL: *Wann* reist du ins Ausland?
Ich reise *bald* ins Ausland.

Wann?	*Wie?*	*Tätigkeiten* (activities)
am 10. Oktober	mit meinen Freunden	ins Ausland reisen
nächsten Dienstag	allein	im Bett liegen
morgen	mit dem Zug	zum Recycling gehen
gestern	mit dem Auto	ins Kino gehen
bald	ziemlich schnell	in der Bibliothek lesen
1990	fleißig	in der Jugendherberge übernachten

Schreiben Sie zu Hause

G Rewrite this narrative, filling in each blank with an appropriate adjective. Don't forget to add the endings where they are needed.

Heute ist der _____ Mai und es ist ein _____ Tag. Ich bin mit meiner _____ Freundin Laura im _____ Wald spazierengegangen. Die Sonne war _____, und im Wald war es sehr _____. Wir haben unser Mittagessen mitgebracht und um ein Uhr waren wir schon hungrig. Aber wir haben vergessen, eine Flasche Wein mitzubringen. Wir haben gewußt, daß es im Wald ein _____ Restaurant gibt, und nach _____ Stunden haben wir es gefunden. Dort haben wir also eine _____ Flasche Wein gekauft. Die Kellnerin war eine sehr _____ Frau. Mit ihr haben wir über das Wetter gesprochen. Sie hat auch ein _____ Kind gehabt, und wir haben ein bißchen mit diesem _____ Mädchen gespielt. Später haben wir meinen _____ Freund Hannes getroffen. Er hat uns seinen _____ Wagen gezeigt. Am Ende dieses _____ Tages sind wir dann mit der Straßenbahn in die _____ Stadt zurückgefahren.

H Construct sentences from the elements provided. Be prepared to translate your sentences into English. / / = *comma*

1. mein / umweltfreundlich / Mitbewohner / tragen / Müll / in / Keller

2. alle / neu / Einwohner / unser- (*gen.*) / Studentenwohnheim- / mitmachen

3. nach / unser / lang / Wanderung / können / wir / in / ein / billig / Restaurant / ein / kalt / Bier / trinken

4. das / riesengroß / Zimmer / ist / sonnig / / und / ich / haben / mein / eigen / Schreibtisch

5. die / klein / Schüler / aus / d- / dritt- / Klasse / sammeln / leer / Flaschen / für / d- / Umweltaktion

6. ich / war / in / ein / phantastisch / Jugendherberge / in / d- / Schweiz / / wo / ich / in / ein / altmodisch / Bett / schlafen (*perfect tense*)

7. um / ein / lang / gesund / Leben / haben / / sollen / jed- / Mensch / aktiv / bleiben

8. bei / dies- / schön / Wetter / wir / wollen / zusammen / zum / neu / Tennisplatz / gehen

9. ich / haben / ein / gut / Gefühl / / wenn / ich / mein- / schmutzig / alt / Dosen / zum / Recycling / schleppen

I Wie sagt man das auf deutsch?

1. What's the date today?

2. It's April 5th. Why do you ask?

3. My old friend Markus has a birthday today, and I haven't called him up yet.

4. Can you recommend a good restaurant to me?

5. Do you like to eat French food?

6. Of course. Do you know a good French restaurant?

7. Yes. My favorite restaurant is in the old part of town (Altstadt).

8. Are you throwing these old bottles away, Frau Schuhmacher?

9. Yes, I don't have time to carry them to the cellar.

10. Would you give them to me? I'm collecting bottles to earn money.

Die Wälder sterben- nach den Wäldern sterben die Menschen.

Seid ihr schlaue Umweltfüchse?

Der „Bund für Umwelt und Naturschutz Deutschland" ist eine Lobby von umweltfreundlichen Menschen. In einer Broschüre geben sie Tips zum Schutz (*protection*) der Umwelt.

Umweltfüchse wissen, . . .

- daß Wasser ein Lebensmittel ist.
- daß jeder Deutsche pro Tag zirka 150 Liter Trinkwasser verbraucht.

Schlaue Umweltfüchse . . .

- werfen keine Medikamente in die Toilette, sondern bringen sie zur Sammelstelle für Giftmüll.
- duschen lieber, als ein Vollbad zu nehmen, weil sie beim Duschen nur 50 bis 100 Liter Wasser verbrauchen, statt 200 Liter beim Baden.

Umweltfüchse wissen, . . .

- daß die Bundesrepublik jedes Jahr einen Müllberg produziert, der so groß wie die Zugspitze ist.
- daß nur 11 Prozent dieses Mülls echter Müll sind. 98 Prozent wäre recyclebar.

Schlaue Umweltfüchse . . .

- kaufen Recyclingprodukte, z.B. Umweltschutzpapier.
- sortieren ihren Müll und bringen Glasflaschen, Metall, und Papier zu Containern oder direkt zum Recycling.

Recyclingcontainer. (Garmisch-Partenkirchen, Bayern)

UMWELTTIPS
für jeden Tag
Haus · Garten · Verkehr

Bund für
Umwelt und
Naturschutz
Deutschland
e. V.

BUND

Deutschland im 20. Jahrhundert

Communicative Goals
- Narrating events in the past
- Describing lost objects
- Telling how long ago something happened and how long an action lasted

Cultural Goal
- Learning about the Weimar Republic

Lyrik zum Vorlesen   Bertolt Brecht, „Mein junger Sohn fragt mich"

Grammatik   Simple Past Tense • Equivalents for "when": *als, wenn, wann* • Past Perfect Tense • More Time Expressions

Lesestück   Besuch einer Ausstellung historischer Plakate

Situationen aus dem Alltag   Die Politik

Almanach   The Bundestag and Political Parties in Germany Today

Dialoge

Damals

Am Nachmittag sitzen zwei Senioren auf einer Bank.

HERR ZIEGLER: Wie lange wohnen Sie schon hier?

FRAU PLANCK: Seit letztem Jahr. Vorher habe ich in Mainz gewohnt.

HERR ZIEGLER: Ach, das wußte ich ja gar nicht. Als ich ein Kind war, habe ich immer den ganzen Sommer dort bei meinen Großeltern verbracht.

FRAU PLANCK: Damals vor dem Krieg war die Stadt natürlich ganz anders.

„Was ist denn los?"

JÜRGEN: Heinz, was ist denn los? Du siehst so besorgt aus.

HEINZ: Ach, Barbara hat mir vor zwei Wochen ihren neuen Kassettenrecorder geliehen . . .

JÜRGEN: Na und? Du hast ihn doch nicht verloren, oder?

HEINZ: Keine Ahnung. Ich hatte ihn in meiner Tasche, aber vor zehn Minuten konnte ich ihn dann plötzlich nicht mehr finden.

JÜRGEN: So ein Mist! Meinst du, jemand hat ihn dir geklaut?

HEINZ: Nee, denn mein Geldbeutel fehlt nicht.

Schlimme Zeiten

STEFFI: Oma, für die Schule sollen wir unsere Großeltern über die Kriegszeit interviewen.

OMA: Nun, was willst du denn wissen, Steffi?

STEFFI: Also . . . wann bist du eigentlich geboren?

OMA: 1935. Als der Krieg anfing, war ich noch ein kleines Mädchen.

STEFFI: Erzähl mir bitte, wie es euch damals ging.

OMA: Gott sei Dank lebten wir auf dem Land, und zuerst ging es uns relativ gut, obwohl wir nicht reich waren.

STEFFI: Was ist dann passiert?

OMA: Das dauerte nur bis 1943. Dann ist mein Bruder in Rußland gefallen, und ein Jahr später starb meine Mutter.

Note on Usage

In *Kapitel 4,* you learned that **doch** can soften a command to a suggestion. In a statement, **doch** adds emphasis in the sense of "surely," "really." In the second dialogue, Jürgen fears the worst and says to Heinz:

Du hast ihn **doch** nicht verloren, oder?

(Surely) you haven't lost it, have you?

Back Then

Two senior citizens are sitting on a bench in the afternoon.

MR. ZIEGLER: How long have you lived here?

MRS. PLANCK: Since last year. Before that, I lived in Mainz.

MR. ZIEGLER: Oh, I didn't know that. When I was a child, I always spent the whole summer there with my grandparents.

MRS. PLANCK: Of course back then before the war the city was very different.

"What's wrong?"

JÜRGEN: Heinz, what's wrong? You look so worried.

HEINZ: Oh, Barbara loaned me her new cassette player two weeks ago . . .

JÜRGEN: So? You haven't lost it, have you?

HEINZ: No idea. I had it in my bag, but then ten minutes ago I suddenly couldn't find it.

JÜRGEN: What a drag! You think somebody ripped it off?

HEINZ: Nope, because my wallet's not missing.

Tough Times

STEFFI: Grandma, for school we're supposed to interview our grandparents about the war years.

GRANDMA: Well, what do you want to know, Steffi?

STEFFI: Let's see . . . when were you born, anyway?

GRANDMA: In 1935. When the war began I was still a little girl.

STEFFI: Please tell me what it was like for you back then.

GRANDMA: Thank goodness we lived in the country, and at first things were relatively good.

STEFFI: What happened then?

GRANDMA: That lasted only until 1943. Then my brother was killed in action in Russia and my mother died a year later.

Wortschatz 1

Verben

dauern to last; take (time)
fallen (fällt), fiel, ist gefallen to fall; die in battle
fehlen to be missing; to be absent
interviewen, hat interviewt to interview
leihen, lieh, hat geliehen to lend, loan; borrow
passieren, passierte, ist passiert to happen
stehlen (stiehlt), stahl, hat gestohlen to steal
verlieren, verlor, hat verloren to lose

Substantive

der **Geldbeutel, -** wallet, change purse
der **Kassettenrecorder, -** cassette player
der **Monat, -e** month
der **Nachmittag, -e** afternoon
am Nachmittag in the afternoon
der **Senior, -en, -en** senior citizen

die **Bank, ⸚e** bench

Adjektive und Adverbien

besorgt worried, concerned
damals at that time, back then
letzt- last
plötzlich sudden
reich rich
vorher before that, previously

Andere Vokabeln

als (*sub. conj.*) when, as
doch (*flavoring particle, see p. 281*)
nun now; well; well now

Nützliche Ausdrücke

(Ich habe) keine Ahnung. (I have) no idea.
den ganzen Sommer (Tag, Nachmittag, usw.) all summer (day, afternoon, etc.)
Na und? And so? So what?
So ein Mist! (*crude, colloq.*) 1. What a drag! 2. What a lot of bull!
Wann sind Sie geboren? When were you born?

Gegensätze

besorgt ≠ unbesorgt concerned ≠ carefree
reich ≠ arm rich ≠ poor
vorher ≠ nachher before that ≠ after that

Mit anderen Worten

klauen (*colloq.*) = **stehlen**

Variationen

A Persönliche Fragen

1. Jürgen sieht besorgt aus, weil er etwas verloren hat. Haben Sie je etwas verloren? Was?

2. Was machen Sie, wenn Sie etwas nicht finden können?

3. Würden Sie jemand Ihren Kassettenrecorder leihen? Warum oder warum nicht?

4. Wissen Sie, wann und wo Ihre Eltern geboren sind? Ihre Großeltern?

5. Wie lange wohnen Sie schon in dieser Stadt?

6. Herr Ziegler hat seine Sommerferien bei seinen Großeltern verbracht. Was haben Sie als Kind im Sommer gemacht?

7. Steffi muß für Geschichte jemand interviewen. Haben Sie schon einen Senioren interviewt? Was haben Sie gelernt?

B Übung: Fundbüro *Lost and Found*

Sie gehen zum Fundbüro, weil Sie etwas verloren haben. Unten ist eine Liste von verlorenen Dingen im Fundbüro. Sagen Sie, was Sie verloren haben. Dann beschreiben Sie es.

> BEISPIEL: PROF.: Was haben Sie verloren?
> STUDENT: Ich habe meine Kamera verloren.
> PROF.: Können Sie sie beschreiben?
> STUDENT: Es war eine _____ Kamera.

Fahrrad

Kassettenrecorder

Jacke

Koffer

Tasche

Wörterbuch

Pulli

Turnschuhe

Bundesbahnfundbüro
(Bundesbahnbezirksdirektion Köln)
Döppersberg 37, 5600 Wuppertal-Elberfeld
Tel. 0202/35 55 42

C Übung: Was ist gestern passiert?

Gestern war sehr viel los. Ihre Professorin möchte hören, was passiert ist.

> BEISPIEL: Können Sie uns sagen, was gestern passiert ist?
> Ja, gestern _____.

Your instructor will ask how long you did things. Answer that you did them all morning, all day, all week, all semester, and so on.

BEISPIEL: Wie lange sind Sie in Europa gewesen?
Ich war *den ganzen Sommer* da.

1. Wie lange haben Sie gestern Tennis gespielt?

2. Wie lange waren Sie in der Bibliothek?

3. Wie lange waren Sie mit Ihren Freunden zusammen?

4. Wie lange sind Sie im Bett geblieben?

5. Wie lange haben Sie an Ihrem Referat gearbeitet?

Lyrik zum Vorlesen

Bertolt Brecht (1898–1956) fled Germany in 1933 to settle first in France, then in Scandinavia. This poem, written in Finland during World War II, is the sixth of the short cycle "1940." It reflects events of that year.

Mein junger Sohn fragt mich

Mein junger Sohn fragt mich: Soll ich
   Mathematik lernen?
Wozu,° möchte ich sagen. Daß zwei   *what for!*
   Stück Brot mehr ist als eines
Das wirst du auch so merken.°   *you'll notice anyway*
Mein junger Sohn fragt mich: soll
   ich Französisch lernen?
Wozu, möchte ich sagen. Dieses Reich
   geht unter.° Und   *empire will collapse*
Reibe° du nur mit der Hand den Bauch°   *rub / belly*
   und stöhne°   *groan*
Und man wird dich schon verstehen.
Mein junger Sohn fragt mich: Soll
   ich Geschichte lernen?
Wozu, möchte ich sagen. Lerne du nur
   deinen Kopf in die Erde stecken°   *to stick your head in the sand*
Da wirst du vielleicht übrig bleiben.°   *will . . . survive*

Ja, lerne Mathematik, sage ich
Lerne Französisch, lerne Geschichte!

Bertolt Brecht (1898–1956)

›Der Klassiker der Vernunft‹

Bertolt Brecht
Große kommentierte Berliner und
Frankfurter Ausgabe in 30 Bänden
Suhrkamp

Grammatik

Simple Past Tense

Simple past tense is used in written German to narrate a series of interconnected events in the past. Most novels are written in the simple past. Although the perfect tense is the usual past tense in spoken German, the frequently occurring verbs **sein, haben,** and the modal verbs are used with the simple past in conversation. (You learned the simple past tense of **sein** in *Kapitel 6.*) The simple past tense of weak and strong verbs is formed in different ways.

Simple Past of Weak Verbs

The marker for the simple past is **-te**. Weak verbs form the simple past by adding the following endings to the verb stem:

ich wohn**te**	*I lived*	wir wohn**ten**	*we lived*
du wohn**test**	*you lived*	ihr wohn**tet**	*you lived*
Sie wohn**ten**		Sie wohn**ten**	
er wohn**te**	*he lived*	sie wohn**ten**	*they lived*

Verbs whose stems end in **-d** or **-t** add **-e-** between the stem and these endings:

ich arbeit**ete**	*I worked*	wir arbeit**eten**	*we worked*
du arbeit**etest**	*you worked*	ihr arbeit**etet**	*you worked*
Sie arbeit**eten**		Sie arbeit**eten**	
sie arbeit**ete**	*she worked*	sie arbeit**eten**	*they worked*

For weak verbs, the only form you need to know to generate all other possible forms is the infinitive: **wohnen, wohnte, hat gewohnt** or **arbeiten, arbeitete, hat gearbeitet.**

1 **Übung:** Doras Einkaufstag

Here is a present-tense narrative of Dora's day in town. Retell it in the simple past tense.

Dora **braucht** Lebensmittel. Sie **wartet** bis zehn Uhr, dann **kauft** sie in einer kleinen Bäckerei ein. Sie **bezahlt** ihre Brötchen und **dankt** der Verkäuferin. Draußen **schneit** es, und sie **hört** Musik auf der Straße. Sie **sucht** ein Restaurant. Also **fragt** sie zwei Studenten. Die Studenten **zeigen** ihr ein gutes Restaurant gleich in der Nähe. Dort **bestellt** sie etwas zu essen und eine Tasse Kaffee. Es **schmeckt** ihr sehr gut, aber die Menschen am nächsten Tisch **quatschen** zu laut, und das **ärgert** sie ein bißchen.

Simple Past of Strong Verbs

The strong verbs do *not* have the marker **-te.** Instead, the verb stem is changed. The changed stem is called the *simple past stem,* e.g., nehmen, **nahm,** hat genommen. This new stem takes the following personal endings in the simple past tense:

ich nahm	*I took*	wir nahmen	*we took*
du nahmst	} *you took*	ihr nahmt	} *you took*
Sie nahmen		Sie nahmen	
er nahm	*he took*	sie nahmen	*they took*

Note that the **ich-** and the **er-**form of strong verbs have *no* endings in the simple past: **ich nahm, er/es/sie nahm.**

Principal Parts of Strong Verbs

The simple past stem is one of the *principal parts* of a strong German verb. The principal parts are the three (or sometimes four) forms you must know in order to generate all other forms of a strong verb. You have now learned all of them.

infinitive	*(3rd person sing. present)*[1]	*simple past stem*	*auxiliary + past participle*
nehmen	**(nimmt)**	**nahm**	**hat genommen**

The following table contains the principal parts of all the strong verbs you have learned so far. As an aid to memorization, they have been arranged into groups according to the way their stem-vowels change in the past tenses. Memorize their simple past stems and review your knowledge of the other principal parts.

---

1. All verbs that change their stem vowel in the present tense **du-** and **er-**forms are strong. The principal parts of all strong verbs used in the book will be found in Appendix 1. Neither the Appendix nor the following list includes verbs formed by adding prefixes to stems you know, e.g., **abfahren, beschreiben,** etc.

Principal Parts of Strong Verbs

Infinitive	3rd sing. pres.	Simple past	Perfect	English
anfangen	fängt an	fing an	hat angefangen	to begin
fallen	fällt	fiel	ist gefallen	to fall
halten	hält	hielt	hat gehalten	to hold, stop
schlafen	schläft	schlief	hat geschlafen	to sleep
verlassen	verläßt	verließ	hat verlassen	to leave
einladen	lädt ein	lud ein	hat eingeladen	to invite
fahren	fährt	fuhr	ist gefahren	to drive
tragen	trägt	trug	hat getragen	to carry, wear
essen	ißt	aß	hat gegessen	to eat
geben	gibt	gab	hat gegeben	to give
lesen	liest	las	hat gelesen	to read
sehen	sieht	sah	hat gesehen	to see
vergessen	vergißt	vergaß	hat vergessen	to forget
empfehlen	empfiehlt	empfahl	hat empfohlen	to recommend
helfen	hilft	half	hat geholfen	to help
nehmen	nimmt	nahm	hat genommen	to take
sprechen	spricht	sprach	hat gesprochen	to speak
stehlen	stiehlt	stahl	hat gestohlen	to steal
sterben	stirbt	starb	ist gestorben	to die
treffen	trifft	traf	hat getroffen	to meet
werfen	wirft	warf	hat geworfen	to throw
bleiben		blieb	ist geblieben	to stay
entscheiden		entschied	hat entschieden	to decide
leihen		lieh	hat geliehen	to lend
scheinen		schien	hat geschienen	to shine, seem
schreiben		schrieb	hat geschrieben	to write
steigen		stieg	ist gestiegen	to climb
treiben		trieb	hat getrieben	to drive, propel
beginnen		begann	hat begonnen	to begin
schwimmen		schwamm	ist geschwommen	to swim
finden		fand	hat gefunden	to find
klingen		klang	hat geklungen	to sound
trinken		trank	hat getrunken	to drink
singen		sang	hat gesungen	to sing
liegen		lag	hat gelegen	to lie
sitzen		saß	hat gesessen	to sit
fliegen		flog	ist geflogen	to fly
fließen		floß	ist geflossen	to flow
schließen		schloß	hat geschlossen	to close
verlieren		verlor	hat verloren	to lose
ziehen		zog	hat/ist gezogen	to pull; move
anrufen		rief an	hat angerufen	to call up
gehen		ging	ist gegangen	to go
hängen		hing	hat gehangen	to be hanging
heißen		hieß	hat geheißen	to be called
kommen		kam	ist gekommen	to come
laufen	läuft	lief	ist gelaufen	to run
sein	ist	war	ist gewesen	to be
stehen		stand	hat gestanden	to stand
tun		tat	hat getan	to do

2 Übung

Change the following sentences to the simple past tense.

1. Mir gefällt sein neues Fahrrad.
2. Barbara ruft um halb fünf an.
3. Sie schwimmt das ganze Jahr, um fit zu bleiben.
4. Ich finde das Buch interessant.
5. Jede Woche schreibt sie uns eine Postkarte.
6. Der Film beginnt um 20.30 Uhr.
7. Er hilft mir gern mit meinen Hausaufgaben.
8. Sie heißt Dora Schilling.
9. Um acht gehen die Senioren miteinander essen.
10. Er liegt immer gern im Bett und liest die Zeitung.
11. Ich finde es komisch, daß er nichts trinkt.
12. Am Montag kommt Bert züruck.
13. Sie kommt um 10 Uhr an und bleibt den ganzen Tag da.
14. Sie sieht ihren Freund und läuft schnell zu ihm.

3 Übung: Ein Brief

Complete this letter by filling in the verbs in the simple past tense. Some of the verbs are strong and some are weak.

Liebe Martine,

Weißt du, was dem armen Ulrich vorgestern passiert ist? Er hat mich gestern angerufen und _____ (erzählen) es mir. Er _____ (kennenlernen) im Park eine sympatische junge Studentin _____. Sie _____ (aussehen) ganz elegant und reich _____. Zusammen _____ (sitzen) sie auf einer Bank und _____ (sprechen) über das Studium. Ulrich _____ (tragen) eine Jacke, aber weil es sehr warm war, _____ (legen) er sie auf die Bank. Alles _____ (scheinen) gut zu gehen, und Ulrich _____ (einladen) sie in ein Konzert _____. Sie _____ (sagen) ja und _____ (geben) ihm ihre Adresse und Telefonnummer. Nach einer Stunde _____ (stehen) die Studentin auf und _____ (gehen) in die Bibliothek zurück. Am Abend_____ (kommen) er zu Hause an und _____ (suchen) seinen Hausschlüssel in der Tasche seiner Jacke. Aber dort _____ (finden) er keinen Schlüssel, und auch sein Geld _____ (sein) weg. Er _____ (rufen) die Nummer der Studentin an, aber sie _____ (wohnen) gar nicht da. So ein Mist, nicht?

Jetzt muß ich gehen. Viele Grüße,

Deine Annelies

Simple Past of Modal Verbs

The modal verbs form their simple past with the **-te** marker, like the weak verbs. But those modals that have an umlaut in the infinitive *drop* it in the past tense.

müssen, **mußte**		
ich muß**te** *I had to*	wir muß**ten** *we had to*	
du muß**test** ⎱ *you had to*	ihr muß**tet** ⎱ *you had to*	
Sie muß**ten** ⎰	Sie muß**ten** ⎰	
er muß**te** *he had to*	sie muß**ten** *they had to*	

Similarly:

dürfen	ich **durfte**	*I was allowed to*
können	ich **konnte**	*I was able to*
mögen	ich **mochte**[2]	*I liked*
sollen	ich **sollte**	*I was supposed to*
wollen	ich **wollte**	*I wanted*

4 Übung

1. Sagen Sie, was Sie gestern machen mußten.
   BEISPIEL: Ich mußte gestern zwei Bücher lesen.

2. Jetzt sagen Sie, was Sie und Ihre Freunde gestern machen wollten.
   BEISPIEL: Wir wollten gestern skifahren gehen.

3. Was durften Sie als Kind nicht machen?
   BEISPIEL: Ich durfte nie allein schwimmen gehen.

Simple Past of Mixed Verbs

The mixed verbs (see p. 169) use the **-te** marker for the simple past but attach it to the *changed* stem, which you already have learned for the past participles:

wissen, **wußte,** hat gewußt		
ich wuß**te** *I knew*	wir wuß**ten** *we knew*	
du wuß**test** ⎱ *you knew*	ihr wuß**tet** ⎱ *you knew*	
Sie wuß**ten** ⎰	Sie wuß**ten** ⎰	
sie wuß**te** *she knew*	sie wuß**ten** *they knew*	

Similarly:

bringen, **brachte,** hat gebracht
kennen, **kannte,** hat gekannt

---

2. Note that **mögen,** in addition to dropping the umlaut, has a consonant change in the simple past.

Simple Past of *haben* and *werden*

Only **haben** and **werden** are irregular in the simple past tense.

haben, **hatte**, hat gehabt			
ich hatte	*I had*	wir hatten	*we had*
du hattest ⎤ Sie hatten ⎦	*you had*	ihr hattet ⎤ Sie hatten ⎦	*you had*
er hatte	*he had*	sie hatten	*they had*

werden, **wurde**, ist geworden			
ich wurde	*I became*	wir wurden	*we became*
du wurdest ⎤ Sie wurden ⎦	*you became*	ihr wurdet ⎤ Sie wurden ⎦	*you became*
sie wurde	*she became*	sie wurden	*they became*

5 Übung

Retell the following short narrative in the simple past.

Andreas **kennt** Mainz sehr gut, weil seine Großeltern dort **wohnen.** Als er 11 Jahre **wird, darf** er allein mit dem Zug nach Mainz fahren. Er **verbringt** jeden Sommer dort. Die Großeltern **wissen** alles über die Stadt, denn sie **leben** seit Jahren in Mainz. Er **bringt** ihnen immer ein Geschenk mit, und das **haben** sie immer gern.

Use of the Simple Past Tense

In English, there is a difference in *meaning* between past tense and perfect tense. Compare these sentences:

> *I saw Marion in the restaurant.*
> *I have seen Marion in the restaurant.*

"I saw Marion" refers to a unique event in the past, while "I have seen Marion" implies that Marion has been in the restaurant and may be there again.

In German, there is *no* difference in meaning between simple past and perfect tense. They both simply convey that the action is in the past:

> Ich **sah** Marion im Restaurant. ⎤
> Ich **habe** Marion im ⎬ *I saw Marion in the restaurant.*
>   Restaurant **gesehen.** ⎦

The difference between German simple past and perfect tense is mainly one of *usage:* they are used under different circumstances. As you have already learned, perfect tense is the *conversational past,* used in conversation to refer to events in the past. Simple past tense is used in conversation *only* with frequently occurring verbs such as **sein, haben,** and the modal verbs.

—Wo **warst** du denn gestern? Ich
  habe auf dich gewartet.
—Ich **hatte** kein Geld mehr und
  mußte nach Hause.

—*Where were you yesterday? I
  waited for you.*
—*I didn't have any more money
  and had to go home.*

The primary use of simple past tense is in *written* German. It is used in letters, newspaper reports, short stories, novels, etc., to narrate a series of connected events in the past. Here, for example, is the beginning of the fairy tale „Hänsel und Gretel":

Vor einem Wald **wohnte** ein
Holzhacker mit seinen zwei
Kindern. Sie **hießen** Hänsel
und Gretel. Sie **hatten** wenig
zu essen, und ihre Stief-
mutter **wollte** sie los
werden.

*At the edge of a forest lived a
woodcutter with his two children. Their names were Hansel
and Gretel. They had little to eat
and their stepmother wanted to
get rid of them.*

Simple Past after the Conjunction *als*

After the subordinating conjunction **als** ("when" or "as" referring to a point or stretch of time in the past), *simple past tense is required.*

Hans hat uns oft besucht, **als** er
in New York **wohnte.**

*Hans often visited us when he
lived in New York.*

Als wir aus dem Haus **kamen,** hat
der Regen angefangen.

*As we came out of the house the
rain began.*

 6 **Übung:** Es war schon spät

Sagen Sie, daß es schon spät war, als etwas passierte.

BEISPIEL: Das Konzert fing an.
          Es war schon spät, als das Konzert anfing.

1. Ich fand den Laden.
2. Er ging endlich.
3. Wir kamen in München an.

4. Sie fuhr ab.
5. Das Telefon klingelte.
6. Meine Freunde kamen vorbei.

7 **Partnerarbeit:** Wie geht's weiter?

Take turns completing the following sentences with an **als**-clause.

1. Jürgen konnte seinen Schlüssel nicht finden, als . . .
2. Herr Ziegler hat jeden Sommer seine Großeltern besucht, als . . .
3. Es ging der Großmutter nicht gut, als . . .
4. Ute lief schnell ins Haus, als . . .
5. Alle Schüler lachten, als . . .

Now restate the sentences, beginning with your **als**-clause.

BEISPIEL: *Als* Jürgen nach Hause kam, konnte er seinen Schlüssel nicht finden.

Equivalents for "when": als, wenn, wann

It is important to distinguish among three German subordinating conjunctions, each of which may be translated by English "when."

- **als** = *when* (in the past), *as*   **Als** refers to an event or state *in the past* and requires the simple past tense.

Als wir in Wien waren, haben wir Andreas besucht.	*When we were in Vienna, we visited Andreas.*

- **wenn** = *when/if; whenever*   **Wenn** means "when" in reference to an event *in the present or future*. Since it can also mean "if," clauses with **wenn** can be ambiguous.

Wenn wir in Wien sind, besuchen wir Andreas.	*When (If) we're in Vienna, we'll visit Andreas.*

  Wenn also means "whenever" in reference to habitual or repeated action *in the past or present*. It is often used together with an adverb such as **immer** to avoid ambiguity between "whenever" and "if."

Wenn Hans nach Wien kommt, geht er **immer** ins Kaffeehaus.	*Whenever Hans comes to Vienna, he always goes to a coffee house.*

  Note carefully the difference in meaning between **als** and **wenn** used with simple past tense.

Als sie das sagte, wurde er rot.	*When she said that, he turned red.*
Wenn sie das sagte, wurde er immer rot.	*Whenever she said that, he always turned red.*

- **Wann** = *when?*   **Wann** is always a question word, used both in direct questions

Wann kommt der Zug an?	*When does the train arrive?*

  and in indirect questions:

Ich weiß nicht, **wann** er ankommt.	*I don't know when it's arriving.*

8 **Übung:** Als, wenn oder wann?   *Mit offenen Büchern*

1. Mutti, _____ darf ich spielen?
   _____ du deine Hausaufgaben gemacht hast.

2. _____ fängt das Konzert an?
   Ich weiß nicht, _____ es anfängt.
   Karl kann es uns sagen, _____ er zurückkommt.
   Wir haben viele Konzerte gehört, _____ wir in Berlin waren.
   Das möchte ich auch tun, _____ ich nach Berlin fahre.

3. _____ ich gestern an der Uni war, habe ich Angelika getroffen. Sie hat gesagt, sie kommt heute abend mit.
   Gut! _____ Angelika mitkommt, macht es mehr Spaß.

9 **Partnerarbeit:** Wie sagt man das auf deutsch?

Sagen Sie diese Dialoge auf deutsch mit Ihrem Partner.

1. A: When did you meet Claudia?
   B: I met her when I studied in Vienna. Whenever I'm there, I always write her a postcard.
   A: I don't know when I'll go to Vienna again.

2. A: When I was young I hitchhiked a lot.
   B: When I go to Europe, I'll do that too.
   A: When are you going to Europe?
   B: When I have enough money.

Past Perfect Tense

The past perfect tense is used for an event in the past which *preceded* another event in the past.

Als Hans aufstand, **hatte** Ulla schon **gefrühstückt.**

*When Hans got up, Ulla **had** already **eaten breakfast.***

The form of the past perfect tense is parallel to that of the perfect tense, but the auxiliary verb (**haben** or **sein**) is in the *past tense* instead of the present (**haben → hatte, sein → war**).

ich	**hatte gegessen**	*I had eaten*
du	**hattest gegessen** ⎫	
Sie	**hatten gegessen** ⎬	*you had eaten*
er	**hatte gegessen**	*he had eaten*
wir	**hatten gegessen**	*we had eaten*
ihr	**hattet gegessen** ⎫	
Sie	**hatten gegessen** ⎬	*you had eaten*
sie	**hatten gegessen**	*they had eaten*

ich	**war aufgestanden**	*I had gotten up*
du	**warst aufgestanden** ⎫	
Sie	**waren aufgestanden** ⎬	*you had gotten up*
sie	**war aufgestanden**	*she had gotten up*
wir	**waren aufgestanden**	*we had gotten up*
ihr	**wart aufgestanden** ⎫	
Sie	**waren aufgestanden** ⎬	*you had gotten up*
sie	**waren aufgestanden**	*they had gotten up*

Look at the following timetable of morning events at Hans and Ulla's house, then at how they are combined in the sentences that follow.

> 8.00 Uhr: Ulla hat gefrühstückt.
> 9.00 Uhr: Hans ist aufgestanden.
> 10.00 Uhr: Ulla ist zur Uni gegangen.
> 11.00 Uhr: Hans hat gefrühstückt.

event 1	event 2

Ulla **hatte** schon **gefrühstückt,**   als Hans aufstand.
Ulla had already eaten,   *when Hans got up.*

The order of the clauses may of course be reversed:

event 2	event 1

Als Hans aufstand,   **hatte** Ulla schon **gefrühstückt.**
When Hans got up,   *Ulla had already eaten.*

The subordinating conjunction **nachdem** (*after*) is often used with the past perfect tense.

> **Nachdem** Ulla gefrühstückt hatte,   *After Ulla had eaten breakfast,*
> ging sie zur Uni.   *she went to the university.*

 10 **Übung:** Als Ulla nach Hause kam

Sie spielen die Rolle von Hans. Sagen Sie, was Sie schon gemacht hatten, als Ulla nach Hause kam. Die Liste hilft Ihnen.

> BEISPIEL: Als Ulla nach Hause kam, hatte ich schon Lebensmittel eingekauft.

Kartoffeln gekocht   abgefahren

zur Uni gegangen   alles sauber gemacht

ins Restaurant gegangen   eine Zeitschrift gelesen

die Kinder ins Bett gebracht   ein paar Briefe geschrieben

alles gefunden

More Time Expressions

vor + dative = "ago"

vor fünf Minuten	*five minutes ago*
vor einer Stunde	*an hour ago*
vor drei Tagen	*three days ago*
vor einem Monat	*a month ago*
vor hundert Jahren	*a hundred years ago*

11 **Übung:** Wann war das?

Sagen Sie auf deutsch, wann Karl abgefahren ist.

> BEISPIEL: Wann ist Karl abgefahren?
> (*two days ago*): Vor zwei Tagen.

1. a minute ago
2. an hour ago
3. three years ago
4. five hours ago
5. ten days ago

12 **Übung**

Sagen Sie auf deutsch, wann Sie Ihre Großeltern besucht haben.

1. a week ago
2. two weeks ago
3. a year ago
4. six months ago
5. a month ago

13 **Partnerarbeit:** Wann hast du zuletzt . . . gemacht?

Benutzen Sie diese Vokabeln, um einander Fragen zu stellen.

> BEISPIEL: Wann hast du zuletzt deine Oma besucht?
> Ich habe sie vor drei Monaten besucht.

deine Oma besuchen

Geld ausgeben

einen Stadtbummel machen

einen langen Roman lesen

in ein neues Haus umziehen

Sport treiben

etwas für die Umwelt tun

einen Brief bekommen

Duration Ending in the Past

There is a difference between German and English in the way they show whether an action or state ended in the past or whether it is continuing at the moment of speaking. English makes this distinction by using different verb tenses.

> We **lived** in Berlin for three years. *Past tense* for a state ending in the past (i.e., we don't live there any more).
>
> We **have lived** in Berlin for three years. *Perfect tense* for a state continuing at the moment of speaking (i.e., we're *still* living there).

In German, however, *both simple past and perfect tense* are used for a state ending in the past.

> Wir **wohnten** drei Jahre in Berlin.
> Wir **haben** drei Jahre in Berlin **gewohnt.**
> We **lived** in Berlin for three years.

Duration Beginning in the Past but Continuing in the Present

For a state beginning in the past but continuing at the moment of speaking, German uses *present tense* and one of these adverbial phrases:

schon (+ accusative)   →   **schon drei Jahre**
seit (+ dative)   →   **seit drei Jahren**

Wir **wohnen schon drei Jahre** in Berlin.
Wir **wohnen seit drei Jahren** in Berlin.[3]

*We **have lived** in Berlin for three years.*

Note carefully the difference between verb tenses in the two languages!

Note on Usage

Notice the different ways to express "for a long time."

Ich hoffe, du kannst **lange** bleiben.	*I hope you can stay for a long time.* (continuing into the future)
Ich wohne **schon lange** hier. Ich wohne **seit langem** hier.	*I've lived here for a long time.* (continuing from the past)

---

14 Übung: Wie lange schon?

Ihre Professorin möchte wissen, wie lange Sie etwas schon machen. Sagen Sie, Sie machen es schon zwei Jahre.

BEISPIEL: Wie lange arbeiten Sie schon hier?
Ich arbeite schon zwei Jahre hier.

Antworten Sie mit schon.

1. Wie lange studieren Sie schon hier?
2. Wie lange lernen Sie schon Deutsch?
3. Wie lange treiben Sie schon Sport?
4. Wie lange wohnen Sie schon im Studentenwohnheim?
5. Wie lange fahren Sie schon Rad?

Antworten Sie mit seit.

6. Seit wann kennen Sie mich?
7. Seit wann haben Sie kurze Haare?
8. Seit wann studieren Sie hier?
9. Seit wann sammeln Sie Altglas?
10. Seit wann spielen Sie ein Musikinstrument?

---

3. Also possible is the combination **Wir wohnen schon seit drei Jahren in Berlin.**

15 Übung: Seit wann?

Jetzt können Sie sagen, wie es wirklich ist (freie Antworten).

1. Wie lange studieren Sie schon hier?
2. Seit wann lernen Sie Deutsch?
3. Wie lange lernen Sie schon Fremdsprachen?
4. Seit wann tragen Sie diese Hose?
5. Wie lange kennen Sie mich schon?
6. Seit wann gibt es diese Uni?
7. Wie lange können Sie schon Auto fahren?
8. Seit wann können Sie einen Computer benutzen?

16 Partnerarbeit: Wie sagt man das auf deutsch?

Übersetzen Sie diese Sätze mit Ihrem Partner.

1. We've known him for a year.
2. She's lived here for two weeks.
3. We've been shopping here for a long time.
4. Barbara has already been here five days.
5. She has studied in Halle for two semesters.
6. For ten years there's been an excellent restaurant here.
7. Michael has been reading this book for a long time.
8. I've been hungry for two days.

**Die ersten freien Wahlen
in der ehemaligen DDR.**

Besuch einer Ausstellung
historischer Plakate

Tips zum Lesen und Lernen

Wortschatzerweiterung

The following reading mentions several concepts such as National Socialism, Communism, and anti-Semitism. English words ending in *-ism* denote a system of belief, a doctrine, or a characteristic. Their German equivalents end in the suffix **-ismus.** These words are all *masculine* in German.

der Antisemitismus   der Kommunismus
der Extremismus   der Optimismus
der Idealismus   der Pessimismus

See if you can guess more such words.

City Names as Adjectives   The reading also mentions the *Weimar* Republic, the *Versailles* Treaty, and the *New York* Stock Exchange. When the names of cities are used as adjectives in German, they are capitalized and simply add the ending **-er** in all cases.

Ich bin oft mit der **New Yorker** U-Bahn gefahren.	*I often rode on the New York subway.*
Der **Prager** Frühling 1968 wollte den „Sozialismus mit einem menschlichen Gesicht."	*The Prague Spring of 1968 wanted "socialism with a human face."*

Leicht zu merken

die **Demokratie, -n**	Demokra*tie*
demokratisch	
der **Direktor, -en**	
die **Epoche, -n**	*E*poche
extrem	
die **Form, -en**	
historisch	
ideologisch	
illegal	*il*legal
die **Inflation**	Infla*tion*
katastrophal	katastro*phal*
manipulieren	manipu*lieren*
die **Methode, -n**	Me*th*ode
die **Monarchie, -n**	Monar*chie*
die **Opposition, -en**	Opposi*tion*
die **Republik, -en**	Repub*lik*
die **Situation, -en**	Situa*tion*
symbolisch	
terroristisch	terror*is*tisch

Einstieg in den Text

In the following reading, you will encounter quite a bit of factual historical information about an important period in modern German history: the Weimar Republic. Much of the information will probably be new to you, but you already know enough German to be able to understand complex issues.

When reading the text through for the first time, keep the following basic information questions in mind as a guide:

Was war die Weimarer Republik?
Wann war diese historische Epoche?
Wer hat damals eine Rolle gespielt?
Warum war diese Zeit so wichtig?

Before reading, also examine the illustrations that accompany and are referred to in the reading. These convey an impression of the content of the reading and will help you to understand the issues discussed.

Was für Plakate sind das?
Aus welcher Zeit kommen sie?
Was zeigen die Bilder?
Welche Wörter oder Namen können Sie schon verstehen?

Wortschatz 2

Verben

erklären to explain
nennen, nannte, hat genannt
  to name, call
stören to disturb
unterbrechen (unterbricht),
  unterbrach, hat
  unterbrochen to interrupt
versuchen to try, attempt
wachsen (wächst), wuchs, ist
  gewachsen to grow
wählen to choose; to vote
zählen to count
zusammen·kommen,
  kam zusammen, ist
  zusammengekommen to
  come together, congregate

Substantive

der **Arm, -e** arm
der **Besuch, -e** visit
der **Schriftsteller, -** writer
  (*m.*)

der **Staat, -en** state
der **Wähler, -** voter

das **Plakat, -e** poster
das **Reich, -e** empire, realm
das **Volk, ̈-er** people, nation,
  folk

die **Arbeitslosigkeit**
  unemployment
die **Ausstellung, -en**
  exhibition
die **Bedeutung, -en** meaning,
  significance
die **Dame, -n** lady
die **Idee, -n** idea
die **Schriftstellerin, -nen**
  writer (*f.*)
die **Wahl, -en** choice;
  election

Adjektive und Adverbien

arbeitslos unemployed
ausländisch foreign
bekannt known; well
  known

hart hard; tough; harsh
unruhig restless, uneasy,
  troubled

Andere Vokabeln

bevor (*sub. conj.*) before
nachdem (*sub. conj.*) after

Nützliche Ausdrücke

zu Ende sein to end, be
  finished, be over
  1918 war der Krieg zu
  Ende. The war ended in
  1918.
eine Frage stellen to ask a
  question
meine Damen und Herren
  ladies and gentlemen

Gegensätze

bekannt ≠ unbekannt
  known ≠ unknown
unruhig ≠ ruhig
  restless ≠ calm, peaceful

Besuch einer Ausstellung historischer Plakate

Im Hessischen Landesmuseum° gibt es eine Ausstellung politischer Plakate aus der Weimarer Republik (1919–1933). Der Museumsdirektor führt eine Gruppe ausländischer Studenten durch die Ausstellung.

    „Meine Damen und Herren, herzlich willkommen im Landesmuseum! Bevor wir in die Ausstellung gehen, möchte ich Ihnen ein paar Worte über die Geschichte der Weimarer Republik sagen. Vielleicht ist Ihnen diese Epoche schon bekannt, aber wenn Ihnen etwas nicht klar ist, können Sie jederzeit° Fragen stellen—das stört mich gar nicht.

    Was war das eigentlich, die Weimarer Republik? So nennen wir den deutschen Staat in der Zeit zwischen dem Ende des Ersten Weltkrieges 1918 und dem Anfang des Dritten Reiches[4] im Januar 1933. Es war Deutschlands erster Versuch,° eine demokratische Staatsform zu entwickeln.° Unsere Plakate zeigen die extremen ideologischen Gegensätze° dieser Epoche. Aber sie zeigen auch, wie man gegensätzliche° Ideen oft mit ähnlichen Bildern darstellen° kann."

    Hier unterbrach ein Student mit einer Frage: „Entschuldigung, aber können Sie uns erklären, warum es die ‚Weimarer' Republik hieß? War Berlin nicht damals die Hauptstadt Deutschlands?"

    „Sicher. Berlin blieb auch die Hauptstadt, aber die Politiker kamen 1919 in der Stadt Weimar zusammen, um die neue demokratische Verfassung zu beschließen.° In Berlin

Hessian State Museum

at any time

attempt / develop

polarities
contradictory / represent

Verfassung . . . beschließen *ratify the constitution*

4. **The Third Reich:** the Nazis' own name for their regime (1933–1945).

war die politische Situation damals sehr unruhig, und außerdem° hatte Weimar wichtige symbolische Bedeutung als die Stadt, wo die großen Schriftsteller Goethe und Schiller[5] früher gelebt und gearbeitet hatten.

30   Die ersten Jahre der Republik waren eine Zeit der Arbeitslosigkeit und hohen Inflation. Deutschland hatte den Ersten Weltkrieg verloren, und die Monarchie war zu Ende.[6] Unter dem harten Versailler Friedensvertrag[7] mußte der neue demokratische Staat 20 Milliarden° Goldmark an die

35 Siegermächte° (besonders an Frankreich) zahlen. Unser erstes Plakat, aus der Zeit vor 1925, zeigt den deutschen Reichsadler° durch den Versailler Vertrag gefesselt.°

moreover

billion
victors

imperial eagle / fettered

5. Johann Wolfgang von Goethe (1749–1832); Friedrich von Schiller (1759–1805). 6. Kaiser Wilhelm II abdicated in November 1918 and went into exile in the Netherlands. 7. The Peace Treaty of Versailles. This treaty officially ended the First World War in 1919.

Als die New Yorker Börse° 1929 stürzte,° wurde die Wirt-
schaftskrise° in den Industrieländern Europas katastrophal.
40 Man zählte im Februar 1930 schon mehr als° 3,5 Millionen
arbeitslose Menschen in Deutschland.

Diese Wirtschaftskrise brachte die junge deutsche
Demokratie in Gefahr, denn schon 1932 waren sieben Millionen Menschen arbeitslos. Es gab damals mehr als dreißig
45 politische Parteien, und besonders die antidemokratischen
konnten schnell wachsen. Auf diesem zweiten Plakat sieht
man, wie die 'starke Hand' der katholischen Zentrums-
partei[8] die extremen Parteien erwürgt.° In den Wahlen
nach 1930 stieg aber die Macht der Nationalsozialisti-
50 schen Deutschen Arbeiterpartei (NSDAP)—der Nazis—bis
sie die stärkste° im Reichstag[9] wurde. Ihr Führer Adolf Hitler
benutzte den Antisemitismus und Antikommunismus, um
die Ängste des Volkes zu manipulieren. Ein Plakat der Nazis
zeigt den symbolischen 'starken Mann,' der° Deutschland
55 retten soll. Die Opposition sehen Sie noch auf diesem Plakat
von 1931, wo starke Arme versuchen, das Hakenkreuz° der
Nazis zu zerreißen."°

Eine Studentin stellte eine Frage: „Ist denn Hitler nicht
illegal an die Macht gekommen?"°
60 „Eigentlich nicht", antwortete der Museumsdirektor.
„Nachdem die Wähler den Nazis die meisten Stimmen°
gegeben hatten, mußte man Hitler zum Reichskanzler
ernennen.° Erst als er Kanzler geworden war, konnte er mit
terroristischen Methoden die Republik in eine Diktatur ver-
65 wandeln.° Deutschland ist also ein gutes Beispiel für die
Zerstörung einer schwachen Demokratie durch wirtschaftliche Not° und politischen Extremismus."

stock market / crashed
economic crisis
mehr als = *more than*

strangles

strongest

who

swastika
rip apart

an . . . gekommen = *came to power*

(here) votes

zum . . . ernennen = *appoint*
  chancellor
in . . . verwandeln = *transform into a*
  dictatorship
wirtschaftliche Not = *economic*
  hardship

8. The conservative Center Party, consisting mainly of Catholic voters.
9. The name of the German Parliament until 1945.

Fragen zum Lesestück

1. Warum haben die Studenten das Museum besucht?

2. Aus welcher Zeit waren die Plakate dieser Ausstellung?

3. Wer führte die Gruppe durch die Ausstellung?

4. Was für Plakate haben die Studenten im Museum gesehen?

5. Was zeigen die Bilder auf den Plakaten?

6. Warum hieß der deutsche Staat damals die „Weimarer" Republik?

7. Wie war die Situation in Deutschland nach dem Ersten Weltkrieg? Beschreiben Sie die Probleme.

8. Warum war die junge Demokratie in Gefahr?

9. Wann wurde Hitler Reichskanzler?

10. Wie ist er an die Macht gekommen?

Situationen aus dem Alltag

Die Politik

In dem Lesestück haben Sie nicht nur etwas über Geschichte, sondern auch etwas über Politik gelernt. Was hat denn diese politische Diskussion mit unserem Leben zu tun? Wir sind alle politische Menschen, und die Politik spielt eine Rolle in unserem Alltag, ob wir wollen oder nicht.

Spielen wir jetzt ein bißchen mit der Sprache und den Bildern der Politik. Zuerst einige Wörter (viele sind Ihnen schon bekannt):

die Freiheit
der Frieden
der Krieg, -e
die Politik
der Politiker / die Politikerin
die Regierung, -en   *government in power, administration*

der Staat
die Umwelt
das Volk
die Wahl
 wählen
 Wähler

Gründen Sie (*found*) eine neue politische Partei.

Der Name unserer Partei: _____
Unsere Plattform:
Wir sind für _____, _____, usw.
Wir sind gegen _____, _____, usw.
Wir sehen viele Probleme in der modernen Welt:

_____

Unsere Lösungen sind:

_____

Unsere Parole (*slogan*) für die Wahl:

_____

Gruppenarbeit

Ihre politische Partei braucht auch ein Symbol für das Wahlplakat. Wie Sie gerade gelesen haben, waren Tiere wichtige Symbole auf den Plakaten in der Weimarer Republik. Sie können ein Tier als Symbol Ihrer Partei wählen, denn Tiere können Ideen symbolisieren.

der Adler, -	*eagle*
der Bär, -en, -en	*bear*
der Elefant, -en, -en	*elephant*
der Esel, -	*donkey*
der Löwe, -n, -n	*lion*
die Schlange, -n	*snake*
die Taube, -n	*dove*

Gruppenarbeit: Wahlkampagne *Election Campaign*

Jetzt zeigen Sie den anderen Studenten Ihr Wahlplakat. Erklären Sie, warum man Ihre Partei wählen soll. Die „Wähler" können natürlich Fragen stellen oder kritisieren.

Unser Plakat zeigt . . .
Wählt unsere Partei, weil . . .

Gruppenarbeit: Zur Diskussion

Ist es wichtig für Politiker, die Geschichte ihres Landes zu kennen? Was meinen Sie?

Zum Schluß

Sprechen wir miteinander

A **Kettenreaktion:** Ich suche . . . *Mit offenen Büchern*

Student/in A wählt ein Adjektiv und ein Substantiv und sagt, was er/sie sucht. B sagt, er/sie hat das nicht. Dann geht's weiter.

BEISPIEL: A: Ich suche deutsche Zeitungen.
B: Leider haben wir keine deutschen Zeitungen. Ich suche . . .

Adjektive		*Substantive*	
amerikanisch	bunt	Romane	Fahrräder
kurz	frisch	Menschen	Alternativen
bekannt	freundlich	Pullis	Politiker
gesund	kostenlos	Geschenke	Restaurants
toll	leer	Brötchen	Arbeiter
deutsch	nagelneu	Rucksäcke	Gebäude
lang	riesengroß	Flaschen	Kleider
ehrlich	sportlich	Bücher	Wälder
besser	umweltfreundlich	Professoren	Plakate
interessant		Ideen	

B **Gruppenspiel:** Wer war ich?

Wählen Sie eine bekannte historische Person. Spielen Sie diese Person vor der Klasse. Sie müssen den anderen Studenten genug Information geben, so daß sie Ihre Identität erraten (*guess*) können.

BEISPIEL: Ich bin im 18. Jahrhundert in Österreich geboren und ging später nach Frankreich. Der französische König war mein Mann. Ich sagte einmal: „Wenn das Volk kein Brot hat, dann soll es Kuchen essen." In der Revolution verlor ich dann meinen Kopf. Wer war ich?

C **Partnerarbeit:** Als meine Großeltern jung waren.

Interviewen Sie einander über die Jugend ihrer Großeltern. Füllen Sie den Fragebogen aus (*fill out the questionnaire*).

1. Wo sind deine Großeltern geboren? _____

2. Wo lebten sie als Kinder? _____

3. Kamen sie aus großen Familien? _____

4. Wo und wie lernten sie einander kennen? _____

5. Wie war ihre Kindheit und Jugend anders als heute? _____

D **Gruppenarbeit:** Schreiben wir eine Geschichte zusammen   *4–5 Studenten*

Unten haben Sie eine Liste von Verben zur Auswahl (*to choose from*). Benutzen Sie diese Verben, um zusammen eine kurze Geschichte zu schreiben. Sie brauchen einen Sekretär oder eine Sekretärin. Er oder sie soll die Geschichte aufschreiben (*write down*). Der erste Satz der Geschichte ist: „Vor vielen Jahren lebte ein armer Student in einem alten Gebäude in der Altstadt." Student A wählt ein Verb von der Liste und sagt den zweiten Satz. Student B sagt einen dritten Satz, usw. (Sie dürfen natürlich auch andere Verben benutzen.)

aufstehen	aufmachen	aussehen	beginnen
benutzen	besitzen	bleiben	einkaufen
essen	dauern	frühstücken	heißen
hoffen	kochen	bekommen	liegen
machen	nehmen	schlafen	trinken
sitzen	spazierengehen	klauen	lernen
verdienen	verlieren	sagen	zahlen
versuchen	helfen	sterben	übernachten

Lesen Sie einander Ihre Geschichten vor. (**vorlesen** *to read aloud*)

Schreiben Sie zu Hause

E   Create sentences with a verb from column 1, an indirect object from column 2, and a direct object from column 3. Don't forget to add adjective endings where necessary.

BEISPIEL: Ich habe meinem lieben Onkel einen langen Brief geschrieben.

1	2	3
geben	mein lieber Onkel	ein langer Brief
schenken	die nette Austauschstudentin	das neue Restaurant
kaufen	die kleinen Kinder	unsere schöne Altstadt
zeigen	unsere neuen Freunde	unser großer Straßenatlas
erzählen	meine Großeltern	ein Geburtstagsgeschenk
schreiben	das sympathische Mädchen	neue Turnschuhe
beschreiben	mein sportlicher Freund	ein neuer Kassettenrecorder
empfehlen	die ausländischen Touristen	das alte Märchen
leihen	meine gute Freundin	dieser neue Roman

F   Write a friend a note about your visit to the poster exhibition. Use the simple past and the past perfect tenses.

1. nachdem / ich / essen (*past perfect tense*) // ich / treffen / mein / Freunde / vor / Museum

2. dort / es / geben / interessant / Ausstellung / von / politisch / Plakate

3. wir / wollen / sehen / Ausstellung // um . . . zu / lernen / über / modern / Geschichte

4. wir / unterbrechen / der Museumsdirektor // um . . . zu / Fragen / stellen

5. Plakate / zeigen / die / viel / Partei / während / dies- / Zeit

6. Nachdem / wir / bleiben / ganz / Nachmittag / da *(past perfect tense)* // gehen / miteinander / in / Café

G Freies Schreiben

1. Take the story you composed orally with your classmates in exercise D and polish it as a written assignment.

2. Können wir aus der Geschichte der Weimarer Republik etwas lernen? Finden Sie Parallelen zu unserer Zeit?

H Wie sagt man das auf deutsch?

1. How long have you lived in this house?

2. We've been here for two years and we like it a lot.

3. When we worked in Rostock, we only had a small apartment.

4. You look worried. Did something happen to you?

5. I think that somebody stole my new backpack.

6. I had it beside me in the restaurant and suddenly it was gone.

7. I hope you had your I.D. and your money in your pocket.

8. When were you in Heidelberg?

9. Two years ago, when I was an exchange student in Germany.

10. I tried all year to find an old friend of my parents, but he had died.

Wahlplakat der CDU.

Almanach

The Bundestag and Political Parties in Germany Today

On December 2, 1990, with the addition of the five new **Länder** (*states*) from the former German Democratic Republic, a united Germany held its first free elections in fifty-eight years. The last had been in November 1932, just before Hitler's seizure of dictatorial powers. In order to prevent the profusion of small parties that had weakened the Reichstag during the Weimar Republic, the framers of the post-war **Grundgesetz** ("Basic Law" or constitution of the Federal Republic of Germany) in 1949 added a requirement that a

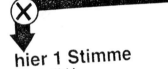

Stimmzettel
für die Wahl zum Deutschen Bundestag im Wahlkreis 66 Oberbergischer Kreis

Sie haben 2 Stimmen

hier 1 Stimme
für die Wahl
eines/einer Wahlkreis-
abgeordneten

hier 1 Stimme
für die Wahl
einer Landesliste (Partei)
— maßgebende Stimme für die Verteilung der
Sitze insgesamt auf die einzelnen Parteien —

Erststimme

Zweitstimme

#	Erststimme		Zweitstimme	
1	**Beucher,** Friedhelm Julius Lehrer **SPD** Sozialdemokratische Bergneustadt Partei Hauptstr. 56 a Deutschlands	◯	◯ SPD	Sozialdemokratische Partei Deutschlands Willy Brandt, Anke Fuchs, Dr. Christoph Zöpel, Franz Müntefering, Ingrid Matthäus-Maier
2	**Dr. Waffenschmidt,** Horst Parl. Staatssekretär, **CDU** Christlich Stadtdirektor a.D. Demokratische Waldbröl Union Deutschlands Weidenfeld 2	◯	◯ CDU	Christlich Demokratische Union Deutschlands Dr. Norbert Blüm, Dr. Dorothee Wilms, Dr. Norbert Lammert, Dr. Horst Waffenschmidt, Irmgard Karwatzki
3	**Albowitz,** Ina Werbekauffrau, **F.D.P.** Freie Hausfrau Demokratische Gummersbach Partei Hagener Str. 108	◯	◯ F.D.P.	Freie Demokratische Partei Hans-Dietrich Genscher, Dr. Otto Graf Lambsdorff, Dr. Irmgard Adam-Schwaetzer, Jürgen W. Möllemann, Dr. Burkhard Hirsch
4	**Meyer,** Friedrich Versicherungs- **GRÜNE** DIE GRÜNEN angestellter Gummersbach Grotenbachstr. 36	◯	◯ GRÜNE	DIE GRÜNEN Marie-Theresia Knapper, Gerd Braun, Tatjana Behm, Wolfgang Templin, Kottwitz
			◯ CM	CHRISTLICHE MITTE Maria-Adelgunde Mertensacker, Kraus, Dr. Franz Erd, Christine Saggau, Heinrich Kerstnig
6	**Freis,** Gertrud Angestellte **DIE GRAUEN** Initiiert vom Senioren- Engelskirchen Schutz-Bund "Graue Hermann-Löns-Weg 15 Panther" e.V. ("SSB-GP")	◯	◯ DIE GRAUEN	DIE GRAUEN Initiiert vom Senioren-Schutz-Bund "Graue Panther" e.V. ("SSB-GP") Gertrud Unruh, Lisbeth Mroß, Dr. Volkmar Schön, Günter Niemeck, Schemmy
7	**Dr. Grumbrecht,** Volker Selbst. Unternehmer **REP** DIE REPUBLIKANER Berlin	◯	◯ REP	DIE REPUBLIKANER Heuß, Weiner, Dr. Ziegler, Schönhuber, Boschan, Weber FRAUENPARTEI

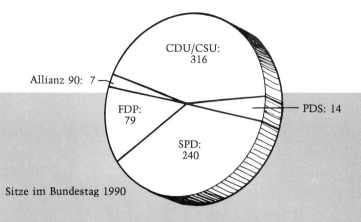

CDU/CSU:
316

Allianz 90: 7

FDP:
79

PDS: 14

SPD:
240

Sitze im Bundestag 1990

party must receive at least 5% of the popular vote to be represented in the Bundestag (*Federal Parliament*). This provision has effectively excluded small extremist parties of both the Right and the Left.

The victors in the election of 1990 were the conservative and liberal coalition partners already in power, who had backed speedy unification of the two Germanies. Helmut Kohl's CDU (**Christlich-Demokratische Union**) with its Bavarian sister party the CSU (**Christlich-Soziale Union**) form the conservative end of the German political spectrum and have consistently received 45–50% of the popular vote. Their coalition partner is the liberal FDP (**Freie Demokratische Partei**) under the leadership of the Foreign Minister Hans-Dietrich Genscher, a principal architect of unification. The FDP has in the past received 5–10% of the popular vote, but has an influence out of proportion to its size because the larger parties need it as a coalition partner to achieve a majority in the Bundestag.

The losers in the all-German elections were those parties that feared economic and social dislocations and therefore advocated a more gradual process of unification. The SPD (**Sozialdemokratische Partei Deutschlands**) is the oldest party in the Bundestag, with a history stretching back to the beginnings of socialism in the 19th century. Today's SPD is dedicated to the welfare state, with only a minority supporting a program of more radical socialism. It traditionally receives 35–45% of the popular vote from industrial workers, students, and young professionals. The environmental and anti-nuclear party known as the Greens (**Die Grünen**) first won parliamentary representation in 1983. These newcomers to the German political scene forced the traditional parties to adopt more environmentally conscious platforms. Factional disputes and their opposition to quick unification, however, lost the Greens so many votes that they failed to clear the 5% hurdle in the 1990 election.

A special ruling applying only to the 1990 elections made it possible for two parties from the former GDR to be represented in the present Bundestag without meeting the 5% requirement: the PDS (**Partei des Demokratischen Sozialismus**), the former East German Communist Party; and the **Allianz 90,** a local eastern German Green party. These parties are unlikely to be able to retain their seats in subsequent elections.

Wahlplakat der Grünen.

Deutschland nach der Mauer

Communicative Goals
- Talking about parts of the body and clothing
- Describing morning routines
- Specifying amounts
- Talking about where people are from

Cultural Goal
- Understanding contemporary Germany's role in Europe

Lyrik zum Vorlesen Hoffmann von Fallersleben, „Das Lied der Deutschen"

Grammatik Reflexive verbs • Dative Pronouns with Clothing and Parts of the Body • Adjectival Nouns • Adjectives and Pronouns of Indefinite Number: *einige, mehrere,* etc. • More on *bei*: Setting a Scene • Designating Decades: The 90s, etc.

Lesestück Deutschland im europäischen Haus

Situationen aus dem Alltag Morgens nach dem Aufstehen

Almanach Zeittafel zur deutschen Nachkriegsgeschichte

Dialoge

Am Brandenburger Tor

Helen aus USA besucht ihre Verwandten in Berlin. Sie steht mit ihrer Kusine Anke am Brandenburger Tor.[1]

ANKE: Du kannst dir gar nicht vorstellen, wie es am 9. November 1989 hier aussah. So was hab' ich noch nie erlebt.

HELEN: Du meinst, als die DDR die Mauer öffnete?

ANKE: Genau. Als wir das im Fernsehen sahen, sind wir sofort zur Mauer gelaufen. Es stimmte: Die Grenze war offen . . . *und* die Beamten waren freundlich. Alle haben sich wahnsinnig gefreut.

HELEN: Was hast du zuerst im Westen gemacht?

ANKE: Lach nicht, aber ich hab' mir einige Bananen gekauft. Die waren für mich etwas Herrliches.

Ein Unfall: Stefan bricht sich das Bein

Stefans Mutter macht das Licht im Schlafzimmer an.

MUTTER: Markus, zieh dich schnell an und komm mit!

VATER: Was ist denn los?

MUTTER: Stefan hat sich beim Radfahren verletzt! Ich fürchte, er hat sich das Bein gebrochen.

VATER: Um Gottes Willen! Beeilen wir uns!

Anna besucht Stefan im Krankenhaus

ANNA: Wie geht's dir denn, du Armer?

STEFAN: Hallo Anna! Schön, daß du gekommen bist.

ANNA: Fühlst du dich heute besser, oder tut dir das Bein noch weh?

STEFAN: Ach, es geht. Ich kann mich schon selber waschen, aber ich darf noch nicht aufstehen.

ANNA: Schade! Schau mal, ich habe dir Schokolade und Blumen mitgebracht.

STEFAN: Oh, die sind hübsch! Danke, das ist aber lieb von dir!

ANNA: Nichts zu danken! Gute Besserung!

Note on Usage

In colloquial spoken German, the definite article can replace the personal pronoun. This is somewhat more emphatic than the personal pronoun and usually comes at the beginning of the sentence.

Die (= sie) waren für mich etwas Herrliches.

*For me **they** were something marvelous.*

Die (= sie) sind hübsch!

***Those** are pretty.*

---

1. The Brandenburg Gate, a triumphal arch built in the late 18th century, located just east of where the Berlin wall once stood.

At the Brandenburg Gate

Helen, from the USA, is visiting her relatives in Berlin. She's standing at the Brandenburg Gate with her cousin Anke.

ANKE: You just can't imagine how it looked here on November 9, 1989. I've never experienced anything like that.

HELEN: You mean when the GDR opened the Wall?

ANKE: Exactly. When we saw it on TV, we immediately ran to the Wall. It was true: the border was open . . . *and* the officials were friendly. Everybody was incredibly happy.

HELEN: What was the first thing you did in the West?

ANKE: Don't laugh, but I bought myself some bananas. For me they were something marvelous.

An Accident: Stefan Breaks His Leg

Stefan's mother turns on the light in the bedroom.

MOTHER: Markus, get dressed quickly and come along!

FATHER: What's wrong?

MOTHER: Stefan hurt himself riding his bike! I'm afraid he's broken his leg.

FATHER: For heaven's sake! Let's hurry!

Anna Visits Stefan in the Hospital

ANNA: How are you, you poor guy?

STEFAN: Hi, Anna! Nice of you to come.

ANNA: Do you feel better today or does your leg still hurt?

STEFAN: Oh, it's all right. I can already wash myself, but they won't let me get up yet.

ANNA: Too bad. Look, I've brought you chocolate and flowers.

STEFAN: Oh, those are pretty. Thanks, that's really nice of you!

ANNA: Don't mention it. Get well soon!

Wortschatz 1

Verben

an·machen to turn on, switch on

sich² etwas an·sehen (sieht an), sah an, hat angesehen to take a look at something

sich an·ziehen, zog an, hat angezogen to get dressed

sich beeilen to hurry

brechen (bricht), brach, hat gebrochen to break

sich erkälten to catch a cold

erleben to experience

sich freuen to be happy

sich fühlen to feel (*intrans.*)

fürchten to fear

sich etwas leisten können to be able to afford something

Das kann ich mir nicht leisten. I can't afford that.

öffnen to open

schauen to look

schneiden, schnitt, hat geschnitten to cut

sich setzen to sit down

sich verletzen to injure oneself, get hurt

sich verspäten to be late

sich etwas vor·stellen to imagine something

waschen (wäscht), wusch, hat gewaschen to wash

weh tun, tat weh, hat weh getan (+ *dat. of person*) to hurt

Das tut (mir) weh. That hurts (me).

Substantive

der Arzt, ¨e doctor (*m.*)

der Beamte, -n (*adj. noun*) official, civil servant (*m.*)

der/die³ Bekannte, -n (*adj. noun*) acquaintance, friend

der Finger, - finger

der Kopf, ¨e head

der Mund, ¨er mouth

der/die Verwandte, -n (*adj. noun*) relative

der Zahn, ¨e tooth

das Auge, -n eye

das Bein, -e leg

das Fernsehen television

  im Fernsehen on TV

das Gesicht, -er face

das Krankenhaus, ¨er hospital

das Licht, -er light

das Ohr, -en ear

das Schlafzimmer, - bedroom

das Tor, -e gate

die Ärztin, -nen doctor (*f.*)

die Banane, -n banana

die Beamtin, -nen official, civil servant (*f.*)

die Blume, -n flower

die Deutsche Demokratische Republik (DDR) the German Democratic Republic (GDR)

die Grenze, -n border

die Mauer, -n (*free standing or outside*) wall

die Schokolade chocolate

---

2. **Sich** is a reflexive pronoun. This will be explained on p. 316.

3. Inclusion of both masculine and feminine articles indicates that this is an adjectival noun. See pp. 323–25.

ander- other, different
genau exact, precise
hübsch pretty, handsome
mehrere several, a few
wenige few

Andere Vokabeln

sich (*third person reflexive pronoun, see p. 316*)

Nützliche Ausdrücke

Gute Besserung! Get well soon!
schade too bad
Das ist schade! That's a shame! Too bad! What a pity!
Schau mal. Look. Look here.
so etwas something like that, anything like that

Gegensätze

sich anziehen ≠ **sich ausziehen** to get dressed ≠ to get undressed

schnell machen (*colloq.*) = **sich beeilen**
so was (*colloq.*) = **so etwas**

Variationen

A Persönliche Fragen

1. Helen besucht ihre Kusine in Berlin. Haben Sie Verwandte im Ausland? Wo leben sie? Haben Sie sie schon einmal besucht?

2. Anke sagt, die Bananen waren für sie etwas Herrliches. Was ist für Sie etwas Herrliches?

3. Am 9. November 1989 war die Berliner Mauer endlich offen. Wissen Sie noch, wo Sie an diesem Tag waren? Was war Ihre Reaktion damals?

4. Stefan hatte einen Unfall beim Radfahren. Haben Sie je einen Unfall gehabt? Mit dem Rad oder dem Auto?

5. Er hat sich verletzt. Ist Ihnen so was als Kind passiert? Wenn ja, wie?

6. Sind Sie je im Krankenhaus gewesen? Warum? Haben Ihnen Ihre Freunde etwas mitgebracht? Was denn?

7. Anna bringt Stefan Schokolade und Blumen mit. Was bringen Sie mir, wenn ich im Krankenhaus bin?

B Übung: Ich habe etwas Interessantes gemacht!

Choose from the list of adjectives below to characterize something you have done. Then say what it was you did.

BEISPIEL: A: Ich habe einmal etwas _____-es gemacht.
B: Wieso? Was hast du denn gemacht?
A: Ich habe/bin _____.

blöd	gefährlich	langweilig
interessant	schwierig	umweltfreundlich
wunderbar	wahnsinnig	intelligent
toll	neu	furchtbar

C Partnerarbeit: Wie geht's denn weiter?

Take these two lines from the second dialogue and compose your own continuation. Then perform your dialogue for the class.

A: Zieh dich schnell an und komm mit!

B: Was ist denn los?

A: _____

B: _____

A: _____

B: _____

Lyrik zum Vorlesen

The famous „Lied der Deutschen," also known as the „Deutschlandlied," is one of the most fervently nationalistic—and controversial—political songs ever composed. Although the first stanza is commonly associated with German military expansionism, the author was, ironically, an opponent of repressive government. His anti-authoritarian sentiments cost him his post as professor at the University of Breslau. The text proclaims abstract concepts ("unity, law, freedom") and calls for a unification of all German-speaking territories into one state. The idealistic dreams of unity were appropriate for Hoffmann's generation, which had survived the ravages of the Napoleonic Wars and were frustrated by the division of their nation into many small states.

Hoffmann wrote the text in 1841 to a favorite popular tune by Joseph Haydn in praise of the Austrian Emperor, „Gott erhalte Franz den Kaiser" (*God Preserve Kaiser Franz*, [1797]). Haydn also used this melody in his magnificent *Kaiserquartett* (Opus 76, no.3, second movement). The song did not become the German national anthem until 1922, when it was chosen by the young Weimar Republic. In 1945 it was banned by the allied military government. In 1952, when no satisfactory substitute could be found, the third stanza alone became the national anthem of the Federal Republic of Germany.

Das Lied der Deutschen

Deutschland, Deutschland über alles,
Über alles in der Welt,
Wenn es stets° zu Schutz und Trutze°   = **immer / Schutz . . . Trutze** =
Brüderlich zusammenhält;   *protection and defiance*
Von der Maas bis an die Memel,
Von der Etsch bis an den Belt:[4]
Deutschland, Deutschland über alles,
Über alles in der Welt!

4. The Maas River = the Meuse in Belgium. The Memel River = the Nemunas River in Lithuania. The Etsch River = the Adige River in South Tirol (now part of Italy). The Belt = seaway in the Baltic between two Danish islands.

Deutsche Frauen, deutsche Treue,°   *loyalty*
Deutscher Wein und deutscher Sang°   *song*
Sollen in der Welt erhalten°   *preserve*
Ihren alten, schönen Klang,°   *sound*
Uns zu edler Tat begeistern°   *inspire us to noble deeds*
Unser ganzes Leben lang:
Deutsche Frauen, deutsche Treue,
Deutscher Wein und deutscher Sang!

Einigkeit° und Recht° und Freiheit   *unity / law*
Für das deutsche Vaterland!
Danach laßt uns alle streben°   *strive*
Brüderlich mit Herz und Hand!
Einigkeit und Recht und Freiheit
Sind des Glückes Unterpfand:°   **des . . . Unterpfand** *guarantees*
Blüh° im Glanze° dieses Glückes,   *of happiness / flourish / glow*
Blühe, deutsches Vaterland!

August Heinrich Hoffman von Fallersleben
(1798–1874)

Deutschland nach der Mauer   **315**

Grammatik

Reflexive Verbs

Reflexive Verbs and Pronouns

In most sentences with objects, the subject and the object are two different people or things.

    subj.   *obj.*

Ich habe **ihn** verletzt.	*I injured **him**.*
Ich habe **ihm** geholfen	*I helped **him**.*

Sometimes, however, a verb's subject and object are the *same* person or thing. The verb is then called *reflexive*. The object of a *reflexive verb* is always a pronoun called a *reflexive pronoun*.

    subj.   *obj.*

Ich habe **mich** verletzt.	*I hurt **myself**.*
Ich habe **mir selbst**[5] geholfen.	*I helped **myself***

Reflexive pronouns in English end in -*self* or -*selves*, e.g., *myself, himself, herself, themselves*. German has both accusative and dative reflexive pronouns. Reflexive pronouns are identical to personal pronouns except in the third person and the formal second person, where the reflexive pronoun is **sich.**[6]

Reflexive Pronouns

	singular		*plural*
	acc.	*dat.*	*acc. & dat.*
1st person	mich	mir	uns
2nd person (fam.)	dich	dir	euch
2nd person (form.)	sich	sich	sich
3rd person	sich	sich	sich

In the plural, the reflexive pronouns often denote reciprocity and are the equivalent of English *each other*.

Wir treffen **uns** morgen.	*We'll meet **each other** tomorrow.*
Kennt ihr **euch**?	*Do you know **each other**?*
Sie kennen **sich** seit langem.	*They've known **each other** for a long time.*

---

5. The words **selbst** and **selber** are adverbs meaning *(by) myself, yourself, himself, ourselves,* etc.
    Ich kann das **selber** machen.   *I can do it (by) myself.*
Used after reflexive pronouns, they emphasize the reflexive.
    Wir müssen das Kind noch waschen.   *We still have to was the child.*
    Nein, er hat **sich** schon **selbst** gewaschen.   *No, he has already washed **himself**.*
6. Note on spelling: **sich** is not capitalized *even* when it refers to the polite second-person pronoun **Sie.**

Note on Usage

einander **each other**   Plural reflexive pronouns used reciprocally may be replaced by the reciprocal pronoun **einander** (*each other*).

Kennt ihr **euch?** = Kennt ihr **einander?**

Remember that **einander** can also combine with prepositions.

miteinander *with each other*
zueinander *to each other*

Verbs with Accusative Reflexive Pronouns

Any transitive verb may be used reflexively.[7] Here is a sample conjugation using **sich verletzen.**

Ich habe **mich** verletzt.   *I hurt **myself.***
Du hast **dich** verletzt.   *You hurt **yourself.***
Sie hat **sich** verletzt.   *She hurt **herself.***

Wir haben **uns** verletzt.   *We hurt **ourselves.***
Ihr habt **euch** verletzt.   *You hurt **yourselves.***
Sie haben **sich** verletzt.   *They hurt **themselves.*** (*You hurt **yourself/yourselves.***)

 1 **Übung:** Wer hat sich verletzt?

Die ganze Klasse war im Bus, als der Busfahrer einen kleinen Unfall hatte. Sagen Sie, wer sich verletzt hat.

BEISPIEL: Ich habe mich verletzt.

2 **Übung:** Er kennt nur sich selbst.

Answer your instructor's questions by saying that the person knows, sees, etc. only him or herself.

BEISPIEL: Wen kennt er denn?
Er kennt nur sich selbst.

1. Wen sieht sie denn?   5. Wen haben Sie denn verletzt?
2. Wen versteht er denn?   6. Wen hat er geärgert?
3. Wen lieben Sie denn?   7. Wen haben sie gerettet?
4. Wen brauche ich denn?

---

7. A transitive verb is a verb that takes a direct object (e.g., **sehen, tragen, verletzen**). An intransitive verb cannot take a direct object (e.g., **sein, werden, schlafen**).

3 **Partnerarbeit:** Wir verstehen uns.

Use each of the verbs below in the following routine:

> BEISPIEL: A: *Verstehst* du mich?
> B: Ja, ich verstehe dich. Verstehst du mich?
> A: Ja, ich verstehe dich auch.
> A & B: Wir verstehen uns! (Wir verstehen einander!)

verstehen	brauchen	morgen treffen
sehen	kennen	am Wochenende besuchen

German Reflexive Verbs That Are Not Reflexive in English

Some German reflexive verbs are not reflexive in English. Their English equivalents often use "get." Here are some examples.[8]

sich anziehen	*to get dressed*
sich waschen	*to get washed*
sich setzen	*to sit down*

Sie wäscht **sich.**	*She's getting washed.*
Er zog **sich** an.	*He got dressed.*
Bitte, setzen Sie **sich.**	*Please sit down.* (literally: *Please set yourselves down.*)

4 **Übung:** Bitte, setzen Sie sich!

Your instructor will tell you to stand up or sit down. Then say what you have done.

> BEISPIEL: Bitte stehen Sie auf!
> (*Student/in steht auf.*) Ich bin aufgestanden.
> Bitte setzen Sie sich.
> (*Student/in setzt sich.*) Ich habe mich gesetzt.

Verbs Requiring the Accusative Reflexive

Verbs like **anziehen** and **waschen** may be used either reflexively (**Ich wasche mich.**) or nonreflexively (**Ich wasche den Wagen.**) Some German verbs, however, must *always* be used with an accusative reflexive pronoun. Their English equivalents are *not* reflexive.

sich beeilen	*to hurry*
sich erkälten	*to catch cold*
sich freuen	*to be happy*
sich fühlen	*to feel*
sich verspäten	*to be late*

---

8. German transitive verbs *require* an accusative object even when that object is identical with the subject. Many English transitive verbs become intransitive when their subject performs an action on itself.

5 **Gruppenarbeit:** Wann freust du dich besonders?   *3 oder 4 Studenten*

Alle müssen sagen, wann sie sich besonders freuen. Die Bilder geben Ihnen einige Ideen, aber Sie dürfen auch frei antworten.

BEISPIEL: Ich freue mich, wenn die Sonne scheint. Wann freust du dich?

1.    2.   3.

6 **Gruppenarbeit:** Warum mußt du dich beeilen?

Jetzt sind Sie alle in Eile. Sagen Sie einander warum.

BEISPIEL: Ich muß mich beeilen, weil mein Zug bald abfährt. Warum mußt du dich beeilen?

1.    2.    3.

7 **Gruppenarbeit:** Wann hast du dich dieses Jahr verspätet?

Jeder verspätet sich manchmal. Erzählen Sie der Klasse, warum Sie sich einmal verspätet haben. Unten sind einige Möglichkeiten. Dann antworten Sie frei.

BEISPIEL: Ich habe mich einmal verspätet, weil . . .

krank sein	Fahrrad kaputt
spät aufstehen	die Deutschstunde vergessen
sich verletzten	Uhr verlieren
einen Unfall haben	einen Freund im Krankenhaus besuchen

Verbs with Dative Reflexive Pronouns

Verbs with Dative Objects   You have already seen that a verb like **helfen**, which requires a dative object, must be used with a reflexive pronoun when the subject and object are identical.

Ich kann **mir selber** helfen.	*I can help **myself.***

Reflexive Indirect Object   The subject and *indirect* object of a verb can also be identical. In this case the indirect object is a *dative* reflexive pronoun.

Ich kaufe **mir** Blumen.	*I'm buying **myself** flowers.*
Du kaufst **dir** Blumen. }	*You're buying **yourself** flowers.*
Sie kaufen **sich** Blumen. }	
Er kauft **sich** Blumen.	*He's buying **himself** flowers.*
Wir kaufen **uns** Blumen.	*We're buying **ourselves** flowers.*
Ihr kauft **euch** Blumen. }	*You're buying **yourselves** flowers.*
Sie kaufen **sich** Blumen. }	
Sie kaufen **sich** Blumen.	*They're buying **themselves** flowers.*

Note: Except for **mir** and **dir,** the dative reflexive pronouns are identical in form to the accusative reflexive pronouns.

The dative reflexive makes explicit the fact that the subject is the beneficiary of its own action. It may be omitted without changing the basic meaning of the sentence.

Ich kaufe mir eine Jacke.	*I'm buying myself a jacket.*
Ich kaufe eine Jacke.	*I'm buying a jacket.*

8 Übung: Einkaufsbummel

Jetzt gehen wir zusammen einkaufen. Jeder hat DM 200 und darf sich etwas kaufen. Erzählen Sie den anderen, was Sie sich kaufen. Die Bilder geben Ihnen einige Ideen, aber Sie dürfen sich natürlich auch andere Sachen kaufen.

BEISPIEL: Was kaufen Sie sich, Robert?
Ich kaufe mir ein neues Hemd und eine Zeitung.

Verbs Requiring the Dative Reflexive

There are some German verbs that must *always* be used with the dative reflexive pronoun. They all require a *direct object* as well. Their English equivalents are *not* reflexive.

German: dative reflexive	*English: not reflexive*
sich etwas ansehen	*to take a look at, look over*
Ich wollte **mir** den Wagen ansehen.	*I wanted to take a look at the car.*
sich etwas leisten können	*to be able to afford*
Kannst du **dir** ein neues Fahrrad leisten?	*Can you afford a new bicycle?*
sich etwas vorstellen	*to imagine*
Das kann ich **mir** nicht vorstellen.	*I can't imagine that.*

Note how to tell if a reflexive verb is used with an accusative or a dative reflexive pronoun. German reflexive verbs are conventionally indicated by the inclusion of the reflexive pronoun **sich. Sich,** however, can be either accusative or dative. Therefore, **etwas** is included with the verb if **sich** is a *dative* reflexive.

sich (*dative*) **etwas** (*accusative*) **ansehen**

Ich möchte mir das Auto ansehen.

9 Kettenreaktion: Die armen Studenten

Wie alle Studenten haben Sie nie genug Geld. Sagen Sie, was Sie sich nicht leisten können, und dann fragen Sie weiter.

BEISPIEL: PROFESSOR/IN: Was können Sie sich nicht leisten?
STUDENT/IN 1: Ich kann mir keine Europareise leisten. Was kannst du dir nicht leisten?
STUDENT/IN 2: Ich kann mir . . .

10 Partnerarbeit: Was wollen wir uns heute nachmittag ansehen?

Öffnen Sie Ihr Buch auf den Stadtplan, Seite 256. Sie verbringen den Nachmittag zusammen in dieser Stadt. Sagen Sie einander, was Sie sich ansehen möchten.

BEISPIEL: A: Ich möchte mir den Dom und _____ ansehen. Und du?
B: Ich möchte mir lieber _____ ansehen.

Dative Pronouns with Clothing and Parts of the Body

Unlike English, German does not usually use the genitive or possessive adjective (**mein, dein, sein,** etc.) with parts of the body or with articles of clothing when they are being put on or taken off. Instead, it uses the personal dative.

Die Mutter wäscht **dem Kind** die Hände.	*The mother washes **the child's** hands.*
Sie zog **ihm** den Mantel an.	*She put **his** coat on for him.*
Meine Freundin schneidet **mir** die Haare.	*My girlfriend cuts **my** hair.*

If the subject is performing the action on itself, the dative pronoun is of course *reflexive.*

Ich habe **mir** die Hände gewaschen.	*I washed **my** hands.*
Er zog **sich** den Mantel an.	*He put on **his** coat.*
Ich schneide **mir** selber die Haare.	*I cut **my** hair myself.*
Stefan hat **sich** das Bein gebrochen.	*Stefan broke **his** leg.*

11 **Übung:** Körperteile

Review your knowledge of parts of the body by identifying them in the picture below.

Rätsel (*Riddle*)
Was ist das? Hat Arme aber keine Hände, läuft und hat doch keine Füße.

die **Katze, -n** *cat*   der **Hund, -e** *dog*

12 Übung: Wo tut es Ihnen weh?

Stefan tut das Bein noch ein bißchen weh. Ihr Professor möchte wissen, wo es Ihnen weh tut.

> BEISPIEL: Wo tut es Ihnen weh?
> Mir tut der Kopf weh.

13 Übung

Sagen Sie Ihrem Professor, **wann** Sie sich heute angezogen haben, und dann, **was** Sie sich angezogen haben.

> BEISPIEL: Um wieviel Uhr haben Sie sich heute angezogen?
> Ich habe mich um halb acht angezogen.
> Was haben Sie sich angezogen?
> Ich habe mir _____, _____ und _____ angezogen.

Adjectival Nouns

Adjectival Nouns Referring to People

In English, adjectives such as *sick, rich,* and *famous* occasionally function as nouns referring *collectively* to a group of people.

> *Florence Nightingale cared for* **the sick.**
> *Life styles of* **the rich and famous.**

Adjectival nouns are more frequent in German than in English. Moreover, they can refer to individuals, not just to collective groups as in English. Masculine adjectival nouns denote men, feminine ones denote women, while plural adjectival nouns simply denote "people."

Like other nouns in German, adjectival nouns are capitalized, but they *receive adjective endings* as though they were followed by the nouns **Mann, Frau,** or **Menschen.** Here are some examples that include these nouns in brackets to make the structure clear. *Note the adjective endings!* As in any noun phrase, these endings will change depending on whether or not the adjectival noun is preceded by a limiting word.

Die Alte [Frau] lag im Bett.	*The old woman was lying in bed.*
Kennst du **den Großen** [Mann] da?	*Do you know that tall man there?*
Hier wohnt **ein Reicher** [Mann].	*A rich man lives here.*
Er wollte **den Armen** [Menschen] helfen.	*He wanted to help the poor.*

In principle, any adjective can be used as an adjectival noun. Here are some common ones you should learn:

der/die[9] **Alte, -n**	*old man/woman*
der/die **Arme, -n**	*poor man/woman*
der **Beamte, -n**	*official, civil servant*[10]
der/die **Bekannte, -n**	*acquaintance, friend*
der/die **Deutsche, -n**[11]	*German (man/woman)*
der/die **Grüne, -n**	*member of the Greens (the environmental political party)*
der/die **Kleine, -n**	*little boy/girl* or *short man/woman*
der/die **Kranke, -n**	*sick man/woman*
der/die **Verwandte,-n** (*from* **verwandt** =*related*)	*relative*

14 **Übung**

Complete each sentence with the appropriate form of **mein Bekannter** (*my friend, masculine*)

BEISPIEL: Das ist ____.
Das ist *mein Bekannter.*

1. Heute zum Mittagessen treffe ich ____.
2. Ich gehe oft mit ____ Volleyball spielen.
3. Das ist die Frau ____.
4. ____ heißt Robert.

Now use a form of **meine Bekannten** (*my friends*).

5. Das sind ____.
6. Kennen Sie ____?
7. Helfen Sie bitte ____!
8. Das sind die Kinder ____.

Now use a form of **die Deutsche** (*the German woman*).

9. Wie heißt denn ____?
10. Meinst du ____?
11. Ich trampe mit ____ nach Italien.
12. Ist das der Rucksack ____?

Now use a form of **die Alten** (*the old people*).

13. Das haben wir von ____ gelernt.
14. Morgen kommen ____.
15. Wer trägt denn die Koffer ____?
16. Machen wir etwas Schönes für ____.

Now use a form of **unser Verwandter** (*our relative, masculine*)

17. Helmut ist ____.
18. Kennst du ____?
19. Du sollst mit ____ sprechen.
20. Die Tochter ____ besucht uns morgen.

9. From now on, adjectival nouns will be listed in the *Wortschatz* in this way.

10. Note that *only the masculine form of this noun* is an adjectival noun. The feminine form ends in **-in: die Beamtin.**

11. This is the *only* noun of nationality that is adjectival.

Neuter Adjectival Nouns Referring to Qualities

Neuter adjectival nouns are abstract nouns designating qualities (e.g., the good, the bad, the ugly). They occur only in the singular, most frequently after the indefinite pronouns **etwas, nichts, viel,** and **wenig.** Note that since these pronouns are *not* limiting words, the following adjectival noun has the *primary* neuter ending **-es.**[12]

etwas Herrliches	*something marvelous*
nichts Neues	*nothing new*
viel Gutes	*much that is good*
wenig Interessantes	*little of interest*

15 **Übung:** Was haben Sie mir mitgebracht?

Ihre Professorin hatte einen Unfall und liegt im Krankenhaus. Sie besuchen sie und bringen ihr Geschenke mit. (*First choose an adjective from the left-hand column to describe your present, then tell her what it is.*)

BEISPIEL: STUDENT: Ich habe Ihnen etwas _____-es mitgebracht.
PROFESSORIN: Was denn?
STUDENT: Ein-_____.

neu	Pflanze
schön	Kassettenrecorder
teuer	frische Brötchen
interessant	Schokolade
herrlich	Fotos von unserer Reise
klein	Stück von der Mauer
lecker	Flasche Wein
umweltfreundlich	Zeitschriften
wunderbar	Blumen

Neuter adjectival nouns also can occur after the definite article. In this case, they are abstract nouns signaling the *quality* designated by the adjective. There are several English equivalents for this.[13]

Das Moderne gefällt mir.	*I like modern things.*
	I like what is modern.
Sie sucht immer **das Gute.**	*She's always seeking the good.*
	She's always seeking what's good.

---

12. Following **etwas, nichts,** etc., the only other ending that the adjectival noun can have is the primary neuter *dative* ending **-em.**
Beginnen wir mit **etwas Neuem.**   *Let's begin with something new.*

13. Do not confuse adjectival nouns with noun phrases which have omitted a redundant noun.
Das alte Haus gefällt dir, aber ***das neue*** gefällt mir.   *You like the old house, but I like **the new one.***
The noun ***Haus*** may be omitted because it has already been used in the immediately preceding noun phrase. In English, such a deleted noun must be replaced by *one.*

Adjectives and Pronouns of Indefinite Number

You have already learned as individual vocabulary words a group of adjectives used with plural nouns to indicate indefinite amounts.

wenige	*few*
einige	*some*
mehrere	*several*
andere	*other(s)*
viele	*many*

These adjectives are *not* limiting words. They are thus just like descriptive adjectives, i.e., when not preceded by a limiting word, they take *primary* endings.

Andere Leute waren da. *Other people were there.*
Ich habe **viele** Freunde in Bonn. *I have a lot of friends in Bonn.*

When a limiting word precedes them, they take *secondary* endings.

Die anderen Leute waren da. *The other people were there.*
Meine vielen Freunde schreiben *My many friends often write to me.*
  mir oft.

Remember that any descriptive adjectives following the adjective of indefinite number will *always* have the *same* ending it does.

Andere junge Leute waren da. *Other young people were there.*
Die anderen jungen Leute waren *The other young people were there.*
  da.

 16 Übung

Supply the correct adjective endings.

1. Darf ich einig ＿＿ schön ＿＿ Postkarten haben?

2. Sie hat schon mehrer ＿＿ deutsch ＿＿ Bücher gelesen.

3. Viel ＿＿ jung ＿＿ amerikanisch ＿＿ Schüler verstehen das nicht.

4. Haben Sie auch die ander ＿＿ neu ＿＿ Arbeiter kennengelernt?

5. Ich habe mit viel ＿＿ interessant ＿＿ Menschen gesprochen.

6. Deine viel ＿＿ neu ＿＿ Ideen gefallen mir sehr.

7. Das sind die Probleme der ander ＿＿ jung ＿＿ Journalisten.

8. Ich kenne einig ＿＿ gut ＿＿ Restaurants in Hamburg.

Indefinite Pronouns

Without a following noun, the indefinite plural adjectives become indefinite pronouns referring to human beings:

Viele sagen das. *Many (people) say that.*
Einige gehen ins Kino, **andere** ins *Some (people) are going to the*
  Theater. *movies, others to the theater.*

17 Übung: Einige und andere

Not everyone in your class likes doing the same things. Answer your instructor's questions by saying that *some* of you (**einige**) like doing one thing, *others* (**andere**) prefer something else.

> BEISPIEL: PROFESSOR: Gehen Sie gern ins Kino?
> STUDENT A: *Einige* gehen gern ins Kino.
> STUDENT B: *Andere* gehen lieber _____.

1. Spielen Sie gern Tennis?
2. Sprechen Sie gern über Politik?
3. Essen Sie gern Wurst?
4. Fahren Sie gern Ski?
5. Lesen Sie gern Zeitung?

6. Arbeiten Sie gern in der Bibliothek?
7. Trinken Sie gern Kaffee zum Frühstück?
8. Sitzen Sie gern vor dem Fernseher?

More on *bei*

In *Kapitel 5* you learned that the dative preposition **bei** has the spatial meanings "in the home of," "near," or "at." More frequently, however, **bei** is used to set a scene. It then has the meanings "during," "while . . . ing," or "at" (an activity or someone's home or business).

Er hat sich **beim Radfahren** verletzt.	*He injured himself while riding his bicycle.*
Marion is jetzt **bei der Arbeit.**	*Marion's at work now.*
Ich lese oft **beim Essen.**	*I often read during meals.*
Ich war gestern **beim Arzt.**	*I was at the doctor's yesterday.*

18 Übung; Wann passiert das?

Sagen Sie, wann etwas passiert oder nicht passiert. Benutzen Sie **bei** in Ihrer Antwort.

> BEISPIEL: Ich falle nie, wenn ich skifahre.
> Ich falle nie beim Skifahren.

1. Mein Mitbewohner stört mich, wenn ich lese.
2. Wir treffen uns oft, wenn wir radfahren.
3. Höfliche Kinder singen nicht, wenn sie essen.
4. Wenn wir spazierengehen, können wir miteinander sprechen.
5. Ich höre gern Musik, wenn ich Auto fahre.
6. Wenn ich arbeite, ziehe ich mir die Schuhe aus.

19 Übung

Antworten Sie mit **bei.**

> BEISPIEL: Wie hat er sich denn verletzt? (*while skiing*)
> Beim Skifahren.

1. Wie haben Sie sich erkältet? (*while swimming*)
2. Wo sind Sie morgens um zehn? (*at work*)
3. Wie lernt man viele Menschen kennen? (*while hitchhiking*)
4. Wann sprechen Sie nicht viel? (*when driving a car*)
5. Wo ist denn Ihre Frau? (*at the doctor's*)
6. Wie hast du so viel Geld verloren? (*playing cards*)
7. Wo hast du die Hilde kennengelernt? (*at the first lecture*)

Designating Decades: The 90s, etc.

These examples show how German designates decades (**das Jahrzehnt, -e**).

die 20er (Zwanziger) Jahre	*the 20s (Twenties)*
aus den 60er Jahren	*from the 60s*
in den 90er Jahren	*in the 90s*

Note that the cardinal number adds the ending **-er.** No other adjective ending is used, regardless of case.

20 Übung: Aus welchem Jahrzehnt?

Aus welcher Zeit kommen diese Bilder?

1.

2.

3.

Tips zum Lesen und Lernen

Wortschatzerweiterung

Country Names, Nouns, and Adjectives of Nationality   The only designation of nationality that is an adjectival noun is **der/die Deutsche.** Some other nouns of nationality have a masculine form ending in **-er** and a feminine in **-erin.** You already know some of these:

Country	Male Native	Female Native	Adjective
Amerika	der Amerikaner	die Amerikanerin	amerikanisch
England	der Engländer	die Engländerin	englisch
Italien	der Italiener	die Italienerin	italienisch
Österreich	der Österreicher	die Österreicherin	österreichisch
die Schweiz	der Schweizer	die Schweizerin	schweizerisch

Other nouns of nationality are N-nouns in the masculine that add **-in** (and sometimes an umlaut) in the feminine.

Frankreich	der Franzose, -n, -n	die Französin	französisch
Jugoslawien	der Jugoslawe, -n, -n	die Jugoslawin	jugoslawisch
Rußland (die Sowjetunion)	der Russe, -n, -n	die Russin	russisch

Remember that when stating a person's nationality, Germans do *not* use the indefinite article.

Sind Sie Deutsche?	*Are you a German?*
Nein, ich bin Jugoslawin.	*No, I'm a Yugoslav.*

Gruppenarbeit: Woher kommst du?

Sie sind auf einer internationalen Studentenkonferenz. Jeder bekommt vom Professor ein Stück Papier mit seinem Land. Jetzt stehen alle Studenten auf und sprechen miteinander. Am Ende sollen Sie wissen, woher alle anderen kommen.

> BEISPIEL: Woher kommst du denn?
> Ich komme aus England.
> Ach, du bist Engländerin!

Leicht zu merken

die **Demonstration, -en**	Demonstra*tion*
existieren	exis*tieren*
der **Kapitalismus**	Kapita*lismus*
der **Kommunismus**	Kommu*nismus*
die **Million, -en**	Milli*on*
Osteuropa	
der **Protest**	Prot*est*
reformieren	refor*mieren*
das **Regime**	
der **Respekt**	
die **Revolution, -en**	Revolu*tion*
separat	sepa*rat*
die **Sowjetunion**	Sow*jet*union
stoppen	
das **Symbol, -e**	Sym*bol*
die **UdSSR**	
zentral	zen*tral*
die **Zone, -n**	

Einstieg in den Text: Recognizing New Words in Context

Noun-building Suffixes   Look again at page 268 *Kapitel 9* to recall the feminine suffix **-schaft** that is used to make abstract nouns from concrete ones (e.g., **Freundschaft** from **Freund**). The following reading contains the nouns **Feindschaft** (line 29) and **Staatsbürgerschaft** (line 37). You can guess their meanings from the context in which they occur.

Past Participles as Adjectives   Past participles of verbs are often used as attributive adjectives. They take regular adjective endings.

bauen → **gebaut-**	*to build → built*
Das ist das neu **gebaute** Studentenwohnheim.	*That's the newly built dormitory*

The reading contains the following participles used as adjectives:

besiegen *to defeat* → **besiegt-** (line 10)
entnazifizieren *to denazify* → **entnazifiziert-** (line 11)
vereinen *to unite* → **vereint-** (line 15)
hassen *to hate* → **gehaßt-** (line 54)

Übung

Wie heißt das Adjektiv (mit Endung!)? Und wie heißt der Satz auf englisch?

BEISPIEL: Das sind _____ Waren. (stehlen)
Das sind gestohlene Waren. *Those are stolen goods.*

1. Ich schleppe das _____ Altpapier zum Recycling. (sammeln)

2. Man darf in diesem _____ Wasser nicht schwimmen. (verschmutzen)

3. Deutschland hat seine _____ Städte wiederaufgebaut. (zerstören)

4. Leider konnten wir uns die _____ Reise nicht leisten. (planen)

5. Das _____ Zimmer war uns zu teuer. (reservieren)

Wortschatz 2

Verben

ändern to change (*trans.*)
> **Sie hat ihr Leben geändert.**
> She changed her life.

sich ändern to change
(*intrans.*)
> **Ihr Leben hat sich geändert.** Her life changed.

auf·geben (gibt auf), gab auf, hat aufgegeben to give up

aus·wandern to emigrate

bauen to build

sich bewegen to move
(*intrans.*)

kritisieren to criticize

rufen, rief, hat gerufen to call, shout

tanzen to dance

vereinen to unite

verschwinden, verschwand, ist verschwunden to disappear

Substantive

der **Nachbar, -n, -n** neighbor
der **Schlüssel, -** key

der **Tod** death
der **Unterschied, -e** difference

das **Mitglied, -er** member
(das) **Ungarn** Hungary

die **Bewegung, -en** movement
die **Brücke, -n** bridge
die **Bundesrepublik Deutschland (BRD)** the Federal Republic of Germany (FRG)
die **Heimat** homeland; native country
die **Regierung, -en** government in power, administration
die **Seite, -n** side; page
die **Vereinigung** unification
die **Wirtschaft** economy
die **Zukunft** future

Adjective und Adverbien

beid- both
berühmt famous

europäisch European
offen open
tief deep
tot dead
verschieden various, different

Nützliche Ausdrücke

auf der einen Seite . . . auf der anderen Seite on the one hand . . . on the other hand

Gegensätze

auswandern ≠ einwandern to emigrate ≠ to immigrate
offen ≠ geschlossen open ≠ closed
der Tod ≠ das Leben death ≠ life
die Zukunft ≠ die Vergangenheit future ≠ past

Deutschland im europäischen Haus

Im Jahre 1989 ging eine Epoche der europäischen Geschichte zu Ende. Die Nachkriegszeit war endlich vorbei.° Besonders für die Länder Osteuropas sind die 90er Jahre eine Zeit des Neubeginns.° Mit seiner zentralen Lage° zwischen Ost und West und seiner starken Wirtschaft ist Deutschland in vielen Hinsichten° der Schlüssel zum neuen „europäischen Haus.“[14]

°over

°new beginning / °location

°in many respects

Historischer Hintergrund:° 1945 bis 1989

Im Jahre 1945 teilten die vier Alliierten° Amerika, England, Frankreich und die Sowjetunion das besiegte° Hitlerreich in vier Zonen auf,° mit dem Ziel, später einen neuen entnazifizierten° Staat zu bilden.° Aber bald änderte sich das politische Klima. Es begann der sogenannte° Kalte Krieg zwischen dem Kommunismus im Osten und dem Kapitalismus im Westen. Anstatt eines vereinten Landes gründete° man 1949 die Bundesrepublik Deutschland (BRD) und die Deutsche Demokratische Republik (DDR), zwei separate und sehr verschiedene Staaten.

°background
°allies
°defeated
teilten . . . auf = *divided*
°denazified / °form
°so-called

°founded

Bis 1961 konnten zirka 2,7 Millionen Menschen, darunter° viele junge Facharbeiter,° über° Berlin in den Westen auswandern. Die DDR verblutete.° Um diesen langsamen Tod aufzuhalten,° baute die Regierung 1961 eine Mauer mitten durch° Berlin. Auf der einen Seite war diese harte Maßnahme° erfolgreich,° denn es wurde praktisch° nicht mehr möglich, das Land zu verlassen. Auf der anderen Seite aber wurde die Berliner Mauer zu dem berühmten Symbol eines bankrotten° Regimes. Aber sie mußte 45 Jahre lang exis-

°among them / °skilled workers / °via
°was bleeding to death
°to prevent
°through the middle of
°measure / °successful / °for all practical
  purposes

°bankrupt

DDR-Wagen kurz vor der Wiedervereinigung. Was bedeutet „BRDDR“?

14. The common "European House" envisioned by the Soviet President Mikhail Gorbachov.

tieren, bis die zwei großen Siegermächte° USA und UdSSR
endlich ihre Feindschaft aufgaben.

November 1989: Die Grenze öffnet sich

30   Mit der „Glasnost–Politik" Michail Gorbatschows[15] wurde
es in den 80er Jahren endlich möglich, sich in der UdSSR
frei zu äußern° und die Regierung zu kritisieren. Dieses Tau-
wetter° weitete sich schnell auf die anderen Länder Osteu-
35 ropas aus.° Im Sommer 1989 begannen viele DDR–Bürger
über Ungarn und Österreich in die Bundesrepublik zu flie-
hen,° wo jeder automatisch die westdeutsche Staatsbürgerschaft und hundert Mark Begrüßungsgeld° bekam. Nun war
der Damm° gebrochen und die Regierung konnte den
40 Auswandererstrom° nicht mehr stoppen. Im November 1989
mußte sie die Grenze ganz öffnen.

  Viele° DDR-Bürger wollten aber ihre Heimat nicht verlassen, sondern reformieren. In Leipzig, Dresden und vielen
anderen Städten gab es riesengroße friedliche° Demonstra-
45 tionen gegen das Einparteiensystem.° „Wir sind das Volk",
riefen die Demonstranten, und später: „Wir sind *ein* Volk."
Diese Protestbewegung war die erste erfolgreiche gewalt-
lose° Revolution in der deutschen Geschichte. Sie führte zu
freien Wahlen und endlich zur Vereinigung der BRD und der
50 DDR.

  Die Bilder aus dem Herbst 1989 sind unvergeßlich:°
Deutsche aus beiden Staaten strömten° über die offene
Grenze und umarmten° sich. Manche tanzten auf der Mauer
und hackten Stücke aus ihr heraus.° Das gehaßte Symbol
55 des Kalten Krieges war endlich gefallen.

Deutschland im neuen Europa

Wie sieht denn die Zukunft des europäischen Hauses aus?
Die Deutschen fühlen sich immer weniger° abhängig von
der Sowjetunion und den USA und sehen sich heutzutage
60 eher° als starken Partner in der Europäischen Gemein-
schaft.[16] Als Mitglied der EG kann Deutschland die Rolle
einer Brücke zwischen Ost und West spielen. Aber die historischen Ängste der osteuropäischen Völker vor den
Deutschen sterben nicht so leicht aus.

65   Es dauert wahrscheinlich noch lange, bis solche Ängste
und die tiefen wirtschaftlichen Unterschiede zwischen Ost
und West ganz verschwinden. Aber in den fünfzig Jahren
seit dem Ende des Zweiten Weltkrieges ist der Prozeß der
Vergangenheitsbewältigung° so weit vorangeschritten,° daß
70 die Deutschen den Respekt ihrer Nachbarn im europäischen
Haus verdient haben.

15. The internal reforms in the Soviet Union referred to by the words
perestroika (restructuring) and *glasnost* (openness) were initiated under the
leadership of Mikhail Gorbachov. These sweeping changes spelled the end
of centralized control and the hegemony of the Communist Party.
16. The European Community (EC), the alliance among 12 western European
nations.

---

victorious powers

sich . . . äußern = *to express oneself*
thaw
weitete . . . aus = *spread*

flee
welcome money
dam
stream of emigrants

many

peaceful
one–party system

non–violent

unforgettable
streamed
embraced
hackten . . . heraus = *hacked out*

immer weniger = *less and less*

rather

*coming to terms with the past /
progressed*

1. Wer hat zuerst von einem „europäischen Haus" gesprochen? Was bedeutet das?

2. Warum ist Deutschlands Rolle so wichtig im neuen Europa?

3. Wie kam es zu zwei deutschen Staaten?

4. Warum waren die beiden deutschen Staaten so verschieden?

5. Warum hat die Regierung der DDR die Mauer mitten durch Berlin gebaut?

6. Was wurde mit der Glasnost-Politik möglich?

7. Wann hat die DDR-Regierung die Grenze ganz geöffnet?

8. Viele DDR-Bürger wanderten nicht in die BRD aus, sondern blieben in ihrer Heimat. Was taten sie dort?

9. Wie hat sich Deutschlands Rolle in Europa in den letzten Jahren geändert?

Situationen aus dem Alltag

Morgens nach dem Aufstehen

Das Wochenende war schon herrlich, aber alles Schöne geht zu Ende. Jetzt ist es wieder Montag. Sie müssen sich für den Tag fertig machen und gehen zum Badezimmer. Weil Sie alles selber machen müssen, müssen Sie eine Menge Reflexivverben benutzen.

Übung: Welcher Satz gehört zu welchem Bild?

Er kämmt sich die Haare.　　Er rasiert sich.　　　　　Sie schminkt sich.

Sie badet sich.　　　　　　Sie putzt sich die Zähne.　　Er duscht sich.

Übung: Was ist Ihre Routine am frühen Morgen?

In welcher Reihenfolge (*order*) machen Sie morgens diese Sachen? Antworten Sie mit ganzen Sätzen.

frühstücken	1. Zuerst stehe ich auf.
Kram in die Tasche packen	2. Dann _____
aufstehen	3. _____
sich zur Uni beeilen	4. _____
sich rasieren	5. _____
sich die Zähne putzen	6. _____
eine zweite Tasse Kaffee trinken	7. _____
sich anziehen	8. _____
sich duschen oder baden	9. _____

Zum Schluß

Sprechen wir miteinander!

A **Rollenspiel:** Schade, daß du im Krankenhaus bist! *3 Personen*

Lesen Sie zusammen diese Situation, und dann spielen Sie sie miteinander:

Ein Student spielt einen Verletzten. Er ist in einem Unfall gewesen und liegt jetzt im Krankenhaus. Die anderen zwei sind Freunde und besuchen ihn dort. Sie haben noch nichts Genaues über den Unfall gehört (Sie wissen z.B. nicht, wie er sich verletzt hat). Sie stellen ihm ein paar Fragen. Sie haben ihm natürlich auch Geschenke mitgebracht.

B **Gruppenarbeit:** Sprechen wir über die Fotos in diesem Kapitel.

Man sagt, ein Bild ist tausend Worte wert. Die Fotos in diesem Kapitel zeigen die menschliche Seite der Geschichte unserer Zeit. Sehen Sie sich diese Fotos noch einmal an, und versuchen Sie, so viel wie möglich auf dem Foto zu beschreiben. Dann stellen Sie sich vor, wie die Menschen auf diesen Fotos sich fühlen, was sie denken oder sagen.

C **Gruppendiskussion:**

Was hat sich geändert? Was muß sich noch ändern?

1. In Kapitel 10 and 11 haben Sie eine ganze Menge über deutsche Geschichte im 20. Jahrhundert gelesen. Versuchen wir mal, eine kurze Liste von einigen Tatsachen (*facts*) aus dieser Epoche an die Tafel zu schreiben. Was scheint Ihnen besonders wichtig zu sein? Warum?

2. Sie haben in diesem Kapitel über viele große Änderungen gelesen. Das Jahr 1989 bedeutete das Ende des Kalten Krieges. Müssen die USA und die UdSSR heute immer noch so viel Geld wie früher für Waffen (*weapons*) ausgeben? Stellen Sie sich mal vor, Sie sind Berater (*advisors*) des amerikanischen Präsidenten. Was würden Sie ihm sagen? Soll man dieses Geld jetzt für etwas anderes ausgeben? Was soll sich in unserem Land oder in der Welt ändern?

Schreiben Sie zu Hause

D **Gute Besserung!** Schreiben Sie diese Geschichte als Dialog zwischen Dr. Büchner und seinem Patienten Herrn Lenz. Der arme Herr Lenz liegt im Krankenhaus.

Dr. Büchner läuft morgens um 10.00 Uhr ins Krankenzimmer und sagt Herrn Lenz, es tut ihm leid, daß er sich verspätet hat. Er würde gern wissen, wie es Herrn Lenz geht und ob er sich besser fühlt. Er fragt, wo es ihm noch weh tut, und was er sonst noch braucht. Der Arzt sagt, daß er sich schon vorstellen kann, wie langweilig es ist, so lange im Bett liegen zu müssen.

Herr Lenz antwortet, daß es ihm nicht so gut geht, daß er noch sehr krank ist, daß es ihm überall weh tut, daß ihm das Essen im Krankenhaus nicht schmeckt und daß er das Fernsehen langweilig findet und einige neue Romane haben möchte.

Dr. Büchner sagt, es freut ihn zu sehen, daß Herr Lenz so viel besser aussieht. Er soll sich anziehen, denn er darf heute nach Hause.

E Fill in the blanks with appropriate nouns formed from adjectives. Choose from the following list:

gut	schön	verwandt	bekannt
deutsch	einfach	altmodisch	interessant
neu	kalt	toll	modern
besonder-	schlimm	herrlich	

1. Hast du etwas _____ zu berichten?

2. Ja, in der Stadt habe ich heute etwas ganz _____ gesehen!

3. Wirklich? In unserer langweiligen Stadt? Das ist schon etwas _____!

4. Kennst du Steffi Hartmann? Sie ist _____ und ist gerade aus Stuttgart angekommen.

5. Wie nett, dich kennenzulernen, Steffi! Eine alte _____ von mir aus der Schulzeit heißt Hartmann und wohnt auch in Stuttgart.

6. Ja, dann ist sie vielleicht sogar eine _____ von mir. Unsere Familie ist ziemlich groß.

7. Das _____ bei uns im Sommer ist nicht nur das Wetter, sondern auch die hohen Berge und die schöne Natur.

8. Super. Für mich ist das etwas _____. Ich bin in der Großstadt zu Hause.

9. Aber in unserem kleinen Dorf auf dem Lande ist das Leben manchmal noch wie im 19. Jahrhundert. Da gibt es wenig _____ zu sehen.

10. Das ist mir ja egal! So was gibt's in der Großstadt! Ich bin zu euch gekommen, um das _____ zu erleben.

F Machen Sie ganze Sätze. Vergessen Sie die Endungen nicht! (// = Komma)

1. wegen / dies- / Situation / viel- / Menschen / auswandern (*perfect tense*)

2. als / man / Mauer / bauen // können / wenig- / Menschen / nach / Westen / reisen (*simple past*)

3. Mauer / müssen / 45 Jahre / existieren (*simple past*) // bis / politisch / Situation / sich ändern (*past perfect*)

4. nach / Vereinigung / beid- / deutsch- / Staaten / Zukunft / anders / aussehen

5. all- / Menschen / sich freuen // wenn / Völker / Europa (*genitive*) / können / leben / in Frieden / miteinander

G Wie sagt man das auf deutsch?

1. When did your relatives immigrate to America?

2. Some emigrated from Germany sixty years ago.

3. Others arrived at the beginning of the nineteenth century.

4. Ute told me that you got hurt.

5. Yes, I broke my arm last week.

6. How did that happen?

7. I had an accident with my new bicycle.

8. Hurry up or we'll be late!

9. I still have to wash and get dressed.

10. Thank goodness we can afford a taxi.

11. Have the children already eaten?

12. Yes, and they've also brushed their teeth.

Almanach

Zeittafel, 1945–heute

1948 Währungsreform im Westen. Berlin-Blockade durch die Sowjets, Berliner Luftbrücke.

1949 Gründung der BRD und der DDR, Deutschland in zwei Staaten geteilt.

1945 9. Mai: Kapitulation Deutschlands. Der Zweite Weltkrieg ist zu Ende.

1955 BRD wird Mitglied der NATO, DDR wird Mitglied des Warschauer Paktes.

1950

1960

1953 Protestdemonstrationen in Ostberlin gegen zu hohe Arbeitsnormen.

1947 Marshall-Plan bringt den Westzonen ökonomische Hilfe. Der Wiederaufbau beginnt.

1946 Erste demokratische Kommunalwahlen seit 1933.

1989 Spätsommer: tägliche Flucht vieler DDR-Bürger über Ungarn. Erich Honecker tritt zurück. Millionen demonstrieren in Ost-Berlin, Leipzig und anderen Städten.
9. November: Die Regierung öffnet die Grenzen.

1961 Bau der Mauer zwischen Ost- und West-Berlin.

70er Jahre: Willi Brandts Ostpolitik. Normalisierung der Beziehungen zwischen BRD und DDR.

1990 März: erste demokratische Wahlen in der DDR.
Juli: Währungsunion der beiden deutschen Staaten.
Oktober: deutsche Vereinigung.
Dezember: erste gesamtdeutsche demokratische Wahlen seit 1932.

1970

1980

1990

1963 Besuch des US-Präsidenten John F. Kennedy an der Mauer.

1982 Beginn der Kanzlerschaft Helmut Kohls.

1987 750-Jahre-Feier in beiden Teilen der Stadt Berlin.

1991 Berlin wird wieder die Hauptstadt Deutschlands.

Erinnerungen

Schreibmaschine oder Computer?

HANS-PETER: Du, Karin, hast du das Buch mit, das ich dir geliehen habe?

KARIN: Ach, tut mir leid. Ich hab's wieder zu Hause gelassen. Ich arbeite noch an meinem Referat.

HANS-PETER: Ist ja egal. Du darfst es ruhig noch behalten. Willst du auch meine Schreibmaschine benutzen?

KARIN: Danke, aber ich schreibe die Arbeit[1] zum ersten Mal auf dem Computer. Ich hab' gehört, die Software ist idiotensicher.

Klatsch

PETRA: Wer war denn der Typ, mit dem Rita gestern weggegangen ist?

JÖRG: Der Mann, der so komisch angezogen war?

PETRA: Genau, den meine ich.

JÖRG: Das war der Rudi. Stell dir vor, sie hat sich mit ihm verlobt!

PETRA: Wenigstens sah er intelligenter aus als ihr letzter Freund.

Vor der Haustür

Frau Schwarzer, die neulich ins Haus eingezogen ist, redet nach der Arbeit mit ihrem Nachbarn Herrn Beck.

FRAU SCHWARZER: Ach Herr Beck, ich wollte Sie etwas fragen. Wo kann ich am billigsten meinen VW reparieren lassen?

HERR BECK: In der nächsten Querstraße gibt's den besten Mechaniker in der Gegend, aber der ist leider nicht der billigste.

FRAU SCHWARZER: Hmm . . . Im Augenblick bin ich etwas knapp bei Kasse. Ich glaub', ich mache es diesmal lieber selber.

HERR BECK: Na, viel Spaß. Also, dann wünsche ich Ihnen einen schönen Abend.

FRAU SCHWARZER: Danke, gleichfalls!

Notes on Usage

Contraction of *es*   In spoken German, the pronoun **es** is often contracted to **'s.**

Ich **hab's** wieder zu Hause gelassen.
In der nächsten Querstraße **gibt's** den besten Mechaniker.

etwas	Ich habe **etwas** vergessen.	*something*
	Ich bin **etwas** müde.	*somewhat, a little*
	Hast du **etwas** Geld?	*some*

---

1. Here **Arbeit** = schriftliche Arbeit, Referat.

Typewriter or Computer?

HANS-PETER: Karin, do you have the book with you that I lent you?

KARIN: Oh, sorry. I left it at home again. I'm still working on my paper.

HANS-PETER: Doesn't matter. Go ahead and keep it. Do you want to use my typewriter too?

KARIN: Thanks anyway, but I'm writing the paper on the computer for the first time. I've heard that the software is idiot proof.

Gossip

PETRA: Who was the guy Rita left with yesterday?

JÖRG: The man who was dressed so funny?

PETRA: Exactly. He's the one I mean.

JÖRG: That was Rudi. Just imagine, she's gotten engaged to him!

PETRA: At least he looked more intelligent than her last boyfriend.

At the Front Door

Ms. Schwarzer, who has recently moved into the building, is talking after work to her neighbor Mr. Beck.

MS. SCHWARZER: Oh Mr. Beck, I wanted to ask you something. Where can I get my VW repaired most cheaply?

MR. BECK: In the next cross street there's the best mechanic in the area, but he's unfortunately not the cheapest.

MS. SCHWARZER: Hmm . . . At the moment I'm somewhat short of cash. I think I'll do it myself this time.

MR. BECK: Well, have fun. Then I'll wish you a good evening.

MS. SCHWARZER: Thanks, you too.

Wortschatz 1

Verben

behalten (behält), behielt, hat behalten to keep, retain

erinnern an (+ *acc.*) to remind of

sich erinnern an (+ *acc.*) to remember

lassen (läßt), ließ, hat gelassen to leave (something or someone), leave behind; let; allow; cause to be done

reden to talk, speak

reparieren to repair

sich verloben mit to become engaged to

weg·gehen, ging weg, ist weggegangen to go away, leave

wünschen to wish

Substantive

der **Augenblick, -e** moment
   im Augenblick at the moment

der **Computer, -** computer

der **Idiot, -en, -en** idiot

der **Klatsch** gossip

der **Typ, -en** (*slang*) guy

das **Mal, -e** time (*in the sense of "occurrence"*)
   zum ersten Mal for the first time

die **Erinnerung, -en** memory

die **Gegend, -en** area, region

die **Maschine, -n** machine

die **Nacht, ̈e** night
   in der Nacht at night
   Gute Nacht. Good night.

die **Querstraße, -n** cross street

die **Schreibmaschine, -n** typewriter

die **Software** software

Adjektive und Adverbien

diesmal this time

etwas somewhat, a little

idiotensicher idiot proof, foolproof

intelligent intelligent

knapp scarce, in short supply
   knapp bei Kasse short of money

komisch peculiar, odd; funny

mit along

nächst- nearest; next

neulich recently

ruhig (*as sentence adverb*) feel free to, go ahead and
   Du kannst ruhig hier bleiben. Feel free to stay here.

übermorgen the day after tomorrow

vorgestern the day before yesterday

Andere Vokabeln

als (*with adj. or adv. in comparative degree*) than
   intelligenter / besser / netter als more intelligent / better / nicer than

na well . . .

(Einen) Augenblick, bitte!
Just a moment, please!
Danke, gleichfalls. Thanks,
you too. Same to you.
Viel Spaß! Have fun!

Gegensätze

sich erinnern ≠ vergessen
to remember ≠ to forget
**reden ≠ schweigen, schwieg,
hat geschwiegen**
to speak ≠ to be silent
reparieren ≠ kaputt machen
to repair ≠ to break
weggehen ≠ zurückkommen
to go away ≠ to come back
die Nacht ≠ der Tag
night ≠ day

Variationen

A Persönliche Fragen

1. Wie schreiben Sie Ihre Referate, auf einer Schreibmaschine oder einem Computer?

2. Leihen Sie Ihren Freunden Bücher, oder nicht? Wie ist es mit Schallplatten, Ihrem Fahrrad, oder mit Kleidern?

3. Was haben Sie heute zu Hause gelassen?

4. Jörg sagt, daß Rudi komisch angezogen war. Ziehen Sie sich manchmal komisch an? Was tragen Sie dann?

5. Wie alt soll man sein, bevor man sich verlobt? Was meinen Sie?

6. Besitzen Sie einen Wagen? Was für einen?

7. Sind Sie ein guter Mechaniker? Können Sie Ihr Auto selber reparieren?

B Übung: Was braucht man?

Um ihr Referat zu schreiben, braucht Karin Bücher, eine Schreibmaschine oder einen Computer, und vielleicht auch ein Wörterbuch. Was braucht man, um . . .

einen Brief zu schreiben?

das Frühstück zu machen?

eine Urlaubsreise zu machen?

eine Fremdsprache zu lernen?

einkaufen zu gehen?

eine Radtour zu machen?

eine Wanderung in den Bergen zu machen?

C **Übung:** Das Beste in der Gegend

Herr Beck weiß, wer der beste Mechaniker in der Gegend ist. Wissen Sie, wo man das Beste in der Gegend findet? Wo ist hier in unserer Gegend . . .

das beste griechische Restaurant? französische Restaurant?

das beste Kleidergeschäft?

das beste Hotel?

die beste Kneipe?

die beste Pizza?

das beste Sportgeschäft?

der beste Supermarkt?

D **Übung:** Sie dürfen das ruhig machen.

Ihr Professor sagt, er würde gern etwas machen. Antworten Sie ihm, er darf (oder soll) es **ruhig** machen.

BEISPIEL: Ich würde gern Ihren Kuli benutzen.
Klar, Sie dürfen ihn *ruhig* benutzen. *oder*
Benutzen Sie ihn *ruhig.*

1. Ich würde gerne Ihren Wagen länger behalten.
2. Heute abend würde ich gerne tanzen gehen.
3. Ich würde gern etwas Wichtiges sagen.
4. Ich würde meine Freunde gerne einladen.
5. Ich würde gern etwas essen.
6. Meinen Wagen würde ich gerne hier lassen.
7. Diese Flaschen würde ich jetzt gern zum Recycling bringen.
8. Ich würde gern meine Freundin Gertrud mitbringen.

Joseph von Eichendorff (1788–1857) was one of the foremost poets of the Romantic movement in Germany. Reverence for nature, longing for one's beloved, and nostalgia for one's homeland are all typical themes for the Romantics. The poem „Heimweh" (*Homesickness*) is from Eichendorff's story **Aus dem Leben eines Taugenichts** (*From the Life of a Good-for-Nothing*), in which the hero, in Italy, yearns for Germany and his beloved.

Heimweh

Wer in die Fremde° will wandern	= ins Ausland
Der muß mit der Liebsten° gehn,	*beloved*
Es jubeln° und lassen die andern	*rejoice*
Den Fremden alleine stehn.	
Was wisset ihr, dunkele Wipfel°	*treetops*
Von der alten, schönen Zeit?	
Ach, die Heimat hinter den Gipfeln,°	*peaks*
Wie liegt sie von hier so weit!	
Am liebsten° betracht° ich die Sterne,°	*most of all / contemplate /*
Die schienen, wie° ich ging zu ihr,	*stars / = als*
Die Nachtigall° hör ich so gerne,	*nightingale*
Sie sang vor der Liebsten Tür.	
Der Morgen, das ist meine Freude!°	*joy*
Da steig ich in stiller° Stund'	*quiet*
Auf den höchsten° Berg in die Weite,°	*highest / distance*
Grüß dich, Deutschland, aus Herzens	
Grund!°	*from the bottom of my heart*

Joseph von Eichendorff (1788–1857)

Zeichnung (*drawing*) von Ludwig Richter (19. Jhdt.)

Grammatik

Comparison of Adjectives and Adverbs

When adjectives or adverbs are used in comparisons, they can occur in three degrees.

- Positive degree (*basic form*)

  so interessant wie = *as interesting as*

Jörg ist **so interessant wie** Dieter.	*Jörg is **as interesting as** Dieter.*
Jutta läuft **schnell.**	*Jutta runs **fast.***

- Comparative Degree (*marker:* **-er**)

  interessanter als = *more interesting than*

Jörg ist **interessanter als** Helmut.	*Jörg is **more interesting than** Helmut.*
Jutta läuft **schneller als** ich.	*Jutta runs **faster than** I do.*

- Superlative Degree (*marker:* **-st**)

  am interessantesten = *most interesting*

In unserer Klasse ist Jörg **am interessantesten.**	*In our class, Jörg is **most interesting.***
Jutta läuft **am schnellsten.**	*Jutta runs **fastest.***

Formation of Comparative Degree

- To form the comparative degree of any adjective or adverb, add the marker **-er** to the basic form:

  basic form[2] **+ -er =** *comparative degree*

schnell	-er	**schneller**
schön	-er	**schöner**
interessant	-er	**interessanter**

English adjectives longer than two syllables form their comparative with *more: interesting—more interesting.* German does not follow this pattern. It simply adds **-er** to make the comparative, no matter how long the adjective is: **interessant—interessanter.**

---

2. Note on spelling: adjectives ending in **-el** and **-er** drop the **-e-** in the comparative: **dunkel—dunkler; teuer—teurer.**

- Attributive adjectives add the regular adjective endings *after* the comparative **-er-** ending.

> ***basic form* + -er- +** *adjective ending*
>
> schnell   -er-   -en
> interessant   -er-   -e
>
> Wir fuhren mit dem **schnelleren** Zug.   *We went by the faster train.*
>
> Jörg war der **interessantere** Student.   *Jörg was the more interesting student.*

- **als** = *than* when used with the comparative.

> Jörg ist interessanter **als** Helmut.   *Jörg is more interesting than Helmut.*

1 **Übung**

Your instructor is praising Jörg, but you respond that you are *more* everything than he is.

> BEISPIEL: Jörg ist interessant.
>   Aber ich bin interessanter als er.

1. Jörg ist hübsch.
2. Er ist ruhig.
3. Er läuft schnell.
4. Er ist ehrlich.
5. Jörg ist fleißig.
6. Er ist freundlich.
7. Er steht früh auf.
8. Er ist sportlich.

2 **Übung: Vergleichen wir!**   *Let's compare!*

Antworten Sie mit einem ganzen Satz.

> BEISPIEL: Was fährt schneller als ein Fahrrad?
>   Ein Auto fährt schneller als ein Fahrrad.

1. Was fährt langsamer als ein Zug?
2. Was schmeckt Ihnen besser als Salat?
3. Was ist moderner als eine Schreibmaschine?
4. Wer ist reicher als Sie?
5. Welches Auto ist teurer als ein Volkswagen?
6. Welche Energie ist umweltfreundlicher als Öl?
7. Welche Stadt ist sauberer als New York?
8. Welche Länder sind kleiner als Deutschland?

3 Übung: Im Kaufhaus

Sie sind Verkäufer im Kaufhaus. Ihr Professor spielt einen Kunden. Nichts scheint ihm zu gefallen. Sie versuchen, ihm etwas Schöneres, Billigeres, usw. zu zeigen.

BEISPIEL: Diese Blusen sind mir nicht dunkel genug.
Hier haben wir dunklere Blusen.

1. Diese Blumen sind mir nicht schön genug.

2. Diese Brötchen sind mir nicht frisch genug.

3. Diese Taschen sind mir nicht leicht genug.

4. Diese Bücher sind mir nicht billig genug.

5. Diese Fahrräder sind mir nicht leicht genug.

6. Diese Computer sind mir nicht schnell genug.

Formation of the Superlative

The superlative is formed in the following ways:

Adverbs   All adverbs form their superlative using the following pattern:

am _____-(e)sten[3]
am schnellsten *most quickly*

Jutta läuft **am schnellsten.**   *Jutta runs **fastest.***
Hans hat **am schönsten** gesungen.   *Hans sang **most beautifully.***

German has no superlative marker like English *most*. No matter how long an adverb is, simply add **-sten: am interessantesten** = *most interestingly.*

Attributive Adjectives   With attributive adjectives, add the regular adjective endings after the superlative **-(e)st-**, for example:

basic form + **-(e)st-** + *adjective ending*

interessant   -est-   -e
schnell-   -st-   -en

Meine **interessanteste** Studentin   *My **most interesting** student is*
  heißt Marianne.   *named Marianne.*
Wir fuhren mit dem **schnellsten**   *We took the **fastest** train.*
  Zug.

Predicate Adjectives   Predicate adjectives in the superlative may occur either in the **am _____-sten** pattern or with the definite article and regular adjective endings.

Albert ist **am interessantesten.**   *Albert is **most interesting.***
Albert ist **der interessanteste.**   *Albert is **the most interesting.***
Diese Bücher sind **die**   *These books are **the most interest-***
  interessantesten.   ***ing** (ones).*

3. Note on spelling: an extra **-e-** is added when the basic form ends in **-d, -t,** or a sibilant: **am mildesten, am heißesten.**

4 Übung: Christa ist nicht die beste.

Your instructor is praising Christa. You respond by praising yourself in the superlative.

> BEISPIEL: Christa läuft schnell.
> Aber ich laufe am schnellsten.

1. Christa ist freundlich.
2. Sie ist sehr fleißig.
3. Sie singt sehr schön.
4. Christa ist immer ruhig.
5. Sie sieht immer hübsch aus.
6. Sie ist sehr sportlich.

5 Gruppenarbeit: Ich bin der/die _____-ste!

Here are some adjectives you can use to describe yourself. Choose the one that you think you exemplify the best of anyone in the class. (Don't take this too seriously!) Then say, **Ich bin der/die _____-ste.**

> BEISPIEL: Ich bin der/die schönste hier!

aktiv	elegant	hungrig
altmodisch	faul	modern
clever	fleißig	radikal
doof	höflich	wahnsinnig

6 Übung: Im Laden

Sie sind wieder ein/e Verkäufer/in, und Ihre Professorin spielt eine Kundin. Sie sucht etwas, und Sie sagen, Sie haben das Neueste, Billigste, usw.

> BEISPIEL: Ich suche billige Weine.
> Hier sind die *billigsten* Weine.

1. Ich suche neue Schuhe.
2. Ich suche schöne Bilder.
3. Ich suche interessante Bücher.
4. Ich suche moderne Stühle.
5. Ich suche leichte Fahrräder.
6. Ich suche elegante Kleider.

Umlaut in Comparative and Superlative

Many one-syllable adjectives and adverbs whose stem vowels are **a, o,** or **u** (but *not* **au**) are umlauted in the comparative and superlative degrees. Here is a list of those you are already familiar with. Some occur in easy-to-remember pairs of opposites.

old	alt	älter	am ältesten
young	jung	jünger	am jüngsten
dumb	dumm	dümmer	am dümmsten
smart	klug	klüger	am klügsten
cold	kalt	kälter	am kältesten
warm	warm	wärmer	am wärmsten

short	kurz	kürzer	am kürzesten
long	lang	länger	am längsten
strong	stark	stärker	am stärksten
weak	schwach	schwächer	am schwächsten
sick	krank	kränker	am kränksten
healthy	gesund⁴	gesünder	am gesündesten
poor	arm	ärmer	am ärmsten
hard, harsh	hart	härter	am härtesten
often	oft	öfter	am öftesten
red	rot	röter	am rötesten
black	schwarz	schwärzer	am schwärzesten

healthy: gesund⁴ / *hard, harsh*: hart / *often*: oft (corrections already in table above)

7 **Gruppenarbeit:** kalt / kälter / am kältesten

The first student reads a sentence, and the next two respond with the comparative and superlative.

BEISPIEL: A: Meine Wohnung ist kalt.
           B: Meine Wohnung ist noch kälter.
           C: Aber meine Wohnung ist am kältesten.

1. Mein Bruder ist stark.
2. Mein Auto ist alt.
3. Mein Referat ist lang.
4. Mein Freund ist krank.

5. Meine Schwester ist jung.
6. Mein Zimmer ist warm.
7. Mein Besuch war kurz.
8. Mein Beruf ist hart.

Irregular Comparatives and Superlatives

Only a few adjectives and adverbs in German have irregular forms in the comparative and superlative. Here are the most frequent:

groß / größer / am größten	*big / bigger / biggest*⁵
gut / besser / am besten	*good, well / better / best*
hoch, hoh- / höher / am höchsten	*high / higher / highest*
nahe / näher / am nächsten	*near / nearer / nearest; next*
viel / mehr / am meisten	*much, many / more / most*
gern / lieber / am liebsten	*gladly, like to / preferably, rather / most like to, like best of all to*

■ The three degrees of **gern** are used to say how much you like to do things.

Ich gehe **gern** ins Kino.	*I like to go to the movies.*
Ich gehe **lieber** ins Theater.	*I'd rather go to the theater.*
Ich gehe **am liebsten** ins Konzert.	*Most of all, I'd like to go to a concert.*

4. **Gesund** is an exception to the rule that only one-syllable adjectives add an umlaut in the comparative and superlative.

5. The irregularity in the comparison of **groß** is that the superlative adds **-t** (**größt-**) rather than **-est** to the stem.

- **Viel** means *much* or *a lot of* and it has *no adjective endings*. **Viele** means *many* and *does* have regular plural endings.

> Ich esse **viel** Brot.   *I eat a lot of bread.*
> Ich habe **viele** Freunde.   *I have many friends.*

The comparative degree **mehr** *never* has adjective endings.

> Du hast **mehr** Freunde als ich.   *You have more friends than I.*[6]

The superlative degree **meist-** *does* take endings; in addition, it is used with the definite article, in contrast to English *most*.

> **Die meisten** Studenten essen   ***Most*** *students eat in the cafeteria.*
> in der Mensa.

8 **Übung:** gut, besser, am besten

Rank the items on the right according to the criteria on the left.

> BEISPIEL: schnell fahren   Bus, Fahrrad, Zug
> Ein Fahrrad fährt schnell, ein Bus fährt schneller, und ein Zug fährt am schnellsten.

1. gut schmecken   Schokolade, Wurst, Kartoffelsalat
2. hoch sein   die Alpen, Haus, Dom
3. nahe sein   Studentenwohnheim, Mensa, Bibliothek
4. viel wissen   Schüler, Professoren, Studenten

9 **Gruppenarbeit:** Was sind Ihre Präferenzen?

Rank your preferences, as in the example.

> BEISPIEL: trinken   Tee, Kaffee, Milch
> Ich trinke gern Milch. Ich trinke lieber Kaffee. Aber am liebsten trinke ich Tee.

1. lesen   Zeitungen, Gedichte, Romane
2. hören   Rockmusik, Jazz, klassische Musik
3. wohnen   in der Stadt, auf dem Land, am Meer
4. spielen   Fußball, Tennis, Volleyball
5. bekommen   Briefe, Geschenke, gute Noten
6. essen   Pommes frites, Sauerkraut, Bauernbrot

---

6. **Wenig,** the antonym of **viel,** functions in the same way.
> Ich esse *wenig* Brot.
> Ich habe *wenige* Freunde.
> Ich habe *weniger* Freunde als du.

Comparisons

genauso . . . wie = *just as . . . as*
nicht so . . . wie = *not as . . . as*

Heute ist es **genauso kalt wie** gestern.	*Today is **just as cold as** yesterday.*
Stuttgart ist **nicht so groß wie** Berlin.	*Stuttgart is **not as large as** Berlin.*

immer _____-er   shows progressive change

Das Kind wird **immer größer**.	*The child's getting **bigger and bigger**.*
Sie liest **immer mehr** Bücher.	*She's reading **more and more** books.*

je _____-er, desto _____-er = *the _____-er, the _____-er*

Je schneller, desto besser.	*The faster the better.*
Je länger ich lebe, **desto weniger** weiß ich.[7]	*The longer I live, the less I know.*

 10 Gruppenarbeit: Damals und jetzt

Vergleichen wir (*Let's compare*) damals und jetzt. Jeder sagt, wie es früher war, und wie sich alles immer mehr verändert.

> BEISPIEL: Früher hatte man mehr Zeit, heute ist man immer mehr in Eile.
> Früher war das Lebenstempo langsamer, jetzt wird es immer schneller.

11 Übung: Vergleiche   *Comparisons*

Bring in pictures or photos that you have drawn, taken, or found in books or magazines. Find similarities and differences in these pictures and compare them in German for the class.

> BEISPIELE: Diese Bäume sind höher als diese hier, aber dieser Berg ist genauso hoch wie der andere.
>
> Diese Mutter sieht nicht so jung aus wie diese hier, aber dieses Kind ist genauso alt wie das Kind da. Das dritte Kind ist das älteste.

---

7. Note the word order in this structure: when **je . . . desto** joins two full clauses, **je** is a subordinating conjunction and **desto** is a coordinating conjunction.

Relative Clauses

A relative clause is a subordinate clause which modifies or further clarifies a noun.

Das ist das **neue** Buch. *That's the **new** book.*

    main clause   *relative clause*

Das ist das Buch, **das du mir geliehen hast.** *That's the book **that you lent me.***

The relative clause **das du mir geliehen hast,** like the descriptive adjective **neue,** modifies **Buch** by telling *which* book is being talked about.

    Relative clauses begin with a relative pronoun (English: *who, whom, whose, that, which*). The German relative pronoun is almost identical to the definite article, which you already know. Study the following table and note especially the forms in bold, which are *different* from the definite article.

Relative Pronouns

	masc.	neut.	fem.	plur.
nom.	der	das	die	die
acc.	den	das	die	die
dat.	dem	dem	der	**denen**
gen.	**dessen**	**dessen**	**deren**	**deren**

Sentences having a relative clause can be thought of as a combination of two separate sentences sharing an identical element (a noun or the pronoun representing it). This element in the main clause is called the *antecedent* because it *antecedes* (i.e., precedes) the relative pronoun. In the relative clause, the *relative pronoun relates* (i.e., refers) back to the antecedent. Here are some examples. Note how the antecedent and the relative pronoun always denote the same person or thing.

                masc.
                sing.

    antecedent   *nom.*

1. Das ist **der Typ.**   **Er** war im Kino.

Das ist der Typ, **der** im Kino war.
        rel. pron.
That's the guy who was at the movies.

                fem.
                sing.

    antecedent   *dat.*

2. Kennst du **die Frau?**   Ich arbeite mit **ihr.**

Kennst du die Frau, mit **der** ich arbeite?
        rel. pron.
Do you know the woman [whom] I work with?

3. Das ist **der Schriftsteller.**

antecedent

masc.
sing.
gen.

Die Romane **des Schriftstellers** sind berühmt.

Das ist der Schriftsteller, **dessen** Romane berühmt sind.
rel. pron.
That's the writer whose novels are famous.

4. Hast du **die Bücher?**

antecedent

acc.
plur.

Ich habe **sie** dir geliehen.

Hast du die Bücher, **die** ich dir geliehen habe?
rel. pron.
Do you have the books [that] I lent you?

Rules for Relative Clauses

- The relative pronoun is *never* omitted in German, as it often is in English (examples 2 and 4 above).

- The relative pronoun *always* has the same gender and number as its antecedent, but its *case* is determined by its function in the relative clause.

  fem. *fem.*
  sing. *sing.*
  nom. *dat.*

  Das ist **die Frau,** mit **der** ich arbeite.

- If the relative pronoun is the object of a preposition, the preposition *always* precedes it in the relative clause (example 2 above). Although in English the preposition often comes at the end of the relative clause (e.g., *the woman I work with*), this is *never* the case in German (die Frau, **mit der ich arbeite**).

- The relative clause is *always a subordinate clause* with verb-last word order. The relative clause is *always* set off from the rest of the sentence by commas.

- The relative clause is usually placed immediately after its antecedent.

  Das Buch, das du mir geliehen hast, hat mir geholfen.

  The book that you lent me helped me.

 12 **Kettenreaktion**

Student A liest den ersten Satz auf deutsch vor. Studentin B gibt eine englische Übersetzung und liest dann den nächsten Satz vor, usw.

1. Das ist der Mann, der hier wohnt.

2. Das ist der Mann, den ich kenne.

3. Das ist der Mann, dem wir helfen.

4. Das ist der Mann, dessen Frau ich kenne.

5. Das ist das Fahrrad, das sehr leicht ist.

6. Das ist das Fahrrad, das sie gekauft hat.

7. Das ist das Fahrrad, mit dem ich zur Arbeit fahre.

8. Das ist das Fahrrad, dessen Farbe mir gefällt.

9. Das ist die Frau, die Deutsch kann.

10. Das ist die Frau, die wir brauchen.

11. Das ist die Frau, der wir Geld geben.

12. Das ist die Frau, deren Romane ich kenne.

13. Das sind die Leute, die mich kennen.

14. Das sind die Leute, die ich kenne.

15. Das sind die Leute, denen wir helfen.

16. Das sind die Leute, deren Kinder wir kennen.

13 **Übung**

Lesen Sie jeden Satz mit dem richtigen Relativpronomen vor.

1. Das ist ein Fluß, _____ durch Österreich fließt. (*that*)

2. Der Berg, _____ wir durch das Fenster sehen, ist die Zugspitze. (*that*)

3. Kennst du den Herrn, _____ dieser Wagen gehört? (*to whom*)

4. Der Professor, _____ Bücher dort liegen, kommt gleich zurück. (*whose*)

5. Das ist ein Schaufenster, _____ immer bunt aussieht. (*that*)

6. Mir schmeckt jedes Abendessen, _____ du kochst. (*that*)

7. Das Kind, _____ ich geholfen habe, ist wieder gesund. (*whom*)

8. Sie kommt aus einem Land, _____ Regierung undemokratisch ist. (*whose*)

9. Die Studentin, _____ neben mir sitzt, ist im zweiten Semester. (*who*)

10. Beschreiben Sie mir die Rolle, _____ ich spielen soll. (*that*)

11. Christa, _____ die Schreibmaschine gehört, leiht sie dir gerne. (*to whom*)

12. Die Touristengruppe, _____ Gepäck dort steht, ist aus England. (*whose*)

13. Wer sind die Leute, _____ dort vor der Mensa stehen? (*who*)

14. Da sind ein paar Studenten, _____ du kennenlernen sollst. (*whom*)

15. Es gibt viele Menschen, _____ dieser Arzt geholfen hat. (*whom*)

16. Sind das die Kinder, _____ Hund gestorben ist? (*whose*)

Antworten Sie wie im Beispielsatz.

> BEISPIEL: Arbeiten Sie für *diesen* Chef?
> Ja, das ist der Chef, für den ich arbeite.

1. Sind Sie durch *diese* Stadt gefahren?

2. Haben Sie in *diesem* Hotel übernachtet?

3. Haben Sie mit *diesen* Amerikanern geredet?

4. Haben Sie an *dieser* Uni studiert?

5. Erinnern Sie sich an *diesen* Roman?

6. Kommen Sie aus *dieser* Stadt?

7. Wohnen Sie bei *dieser* Familie?

8. Spricht er zu *diesen* Menschen?

9. Steht unser Wagen hinter *diesem* Gebäude?

10. Bekommst du Briefe von *diesen* Freunden?

11. Spielt er für *diese* Mannschaft?

15 Übung

Machen Sie aus den zwei Sätzen *einen* Satz. Den zweiten Satz müssen Sie in einen Relativsatz umändern (*change*).

> BEISPIEL: Ich kenne die Frau. (Du meinst sie.)
> Ich kenne die Frau, die du meinst.

1. Suchst du die Schreibmaschine? (Sie war hier.)

2. Nein, ich habe eine andere Schreibmaschine. (Ich habe sie selber mitgebracht.)

3. Ist das die Geschichte? (Horst hat sie erzählt.)

4. Ja, er erzählt Geschichten. (Man muß über seine Geschichten lachen.)

5. Das ist ein Buch. (Ingrid hat es schon letztes Jahr gelesen.)

6. Meinst du das Buch? (Es ist jetzt sehr bekannt.)

7. Ist das der Mann? (Sie haben ihm geholfen.)

8. Nein, ich habe einem anderen Mann geholfen. (Er war nicht so jung.)

9. Kennst du die Studenten? (Sie wohnen in der Altstadt.)

10. Ja, das sind die Studenten. (Ich esse in der Mensa zusammen mit ihnen.)

11. Wie heißt der Junge? (Sein Vater ist Professor.)

12. Er hat einen komischen Namen. (Ich habe ihn vergessen.)

13. Ist die Frau berufstätig? (Du wohnst bei ihr.)

14. Ja, sie ist eine Frau. (Ihre Kinder wohnen nicht mehr zu Hause.)

16 **Partnerarbeit:** Ist das ein neuer Mantel?

Fragen Sie einander, ob Ihre Kleider und andere Sachen neu sind. Antworten Sie, daß sie alles letztes Jahr gekauft haben. Benutzen Sie einen Relativsatz in Ihrer Antwort.

> BEISPIEL: Ist das ein neuer Mantel?
> Nein, das ist ein Mantel, *den* ich letztes Jahr gekauft habe.

The Relative Pronoun *was*

A relative clause following the pronoun antecedents **das, etwas, nichts, viel, wenig,** and **alles** begins with the relative pronoun **was.**

Das stimmt, **was** er uns erzählte.	*What he told us is right.* (literally: *That which he told us is right.*)
Gibt es noch **etwas, was** Sie brauchen?	*Is there something else [that] you need?*
Nein, Sie haben **nichts, was** ich brauche.	*No, you have nothing [that] I need.*
Alles, was er sagt, ist falsch.	*Everything [that] he says is wrong.*

Was must also begin a relative clause whose antecedent is a neuter adjectival noun (see p. 325):

Was war **das Interessante, was** du mir zeigen wolltest?	*What was the interesting thing [that] you wanted to show me?*
Ist das **das Beste, was** Sie haben?	*Is that the best [that] you have?*

Was also begins a relative clause whose antecedent is an entire clause (English uses *which*).

Rita hat sich verlobt, was ich nicht verstehen kann.	*Rita got engaged, which I can't understand.*

 17 **Übung:** Etwas, was mir gefällt. / Etwas, was mich ärgert.

Ihre Professorin sagt etwas und möchte Ihre Reaktion hören. Sagen Sie: Ist das etwas, was Sie ärgert, oder etwas, was Ihnen gefällt?

> BEISPIEL: Die Umwelt ist sehr verschmutzt.
> Das ist etwas, was mich ärgert!

1. Das Studium wird immer teurer.

2. Der Kalte Krieg ist zu Ende.

3. Ihr Mitbewohner spielt abends laute Rockmusik.

4. Heute abend in der Mensa gibt es Pizza zum Abendessen.

5. Die Ferien beginnen bald.

6. Morgen kommen viele Verwandte zu Besuch.

18 **Partnerarbeit:** Was war das Tollste, was du je gemacht hast?

Below are cues for asking each other questions such as, "What's the greatest thing you've ever done?" Take turns asking each other the questions.

> BEISPIEL: toll / machen
> A: Was war das Tollste, was du je gemacht hast?
> B: Ich habe 1989 auf der Berliner Mauer gesessen.

1. schwierig / machen
2. schön / sehen
3. gefährlich / machen
4. dumm / sagen

5. erstaunlich / hören
6. gut / essen
7. interessant / lesen
8. toll / bekommen

The Verb *lassen*

The verb **lassen** has several meanings in German:

- *to leave (something or someone), leave behind*

Lassen Sie uns bitte allein.	*Please leave us alone.*
Hast du deinen Mantel im Restaurant **gelassen?**	*Did you leave your coat in the restaurant?*

- *to allow, let:* **lassen** + infinitive

Man **läßt** uns **gehen.**	*They're letting us leave.*
Laß doch die Kinder **spielen!**	*Let the children play!*

- *to have or order something done:* **lassen** + infinitive
  Here **lassen** is used to show that the subject is not performing an action, but rather having it done by someone else.

Sie **läßt** ihren Wagen **reparieren.**	*She's having her car fixed.*

The accusative case is used to show the performer of the action:

Sie läßt **den Mechaniker** ihr Auto reparieren.	*She's having the mechanic fix her car.*

A dative reflexive pronoun shows explicitly that the subject is having something done for its own benefit.

Ich lasse **mir** ein Haus bauen.	*I'm having a house built (for myself).*

In the perfect tense **lassen** is used with the double infinitive construction. The structure is parallel to that of the modal verbs (see page 203).

	double infinitive	
Man hat uns	**gehen lassen.**	*They let us depart.*
Ich habe den Wagen **reparieren lassen.**		*I had my car repaired.*

19 Übung: Warum ist das nicht hier?

Sagen Sie, wo Sie diese Menschen oder Dinge gelassen haben. Rechts gibt es einige Möglichkeiten, aber Sie können auch frei antworten.

> BEISPIEL: Warum haben Sie heute keine Jacke?
> Ich habe sie zu Hause gelassen.

1. Warum sind Ihre Kinder nicht hier?   in der Schweiz
2. Warum tragen Sie heute keinen Hut?   im Rucksack
3. Warum haben Sie Ihr Referat nicht mit?   bei ihrer Großmutter
4. Warum haben sie Ihren Ausweis nicht mit?   auf dem Bett
5. Warum haben Sie Ihren Wagen nicht mit?   zu Hause
6. Warum ist Ihre Tochter nicht hier?   in der Manteltasche

20 Partnerarbeit: Wo hast du das gelassen?

Hat Ihre Partnerin heute etwas nicht mitgebracht? Fragen Sie sie, wo sie es gelassen hat.

> BEISPIEL: Wo hast du heute deine grüne Jacke gelassen?
> Ich habe sie im Zimmer gelassen.

21 Übung: Ich habe es machen lassen.

Manchmal will man nicht alles selber machen. Dann läßt man es machen. Sagen Sie, daß diese Leute etwas machen ließen.

> BEISPIEL: Hast du das selber gemacht?
> Nein, das habe ich machen lassen.

1. Hast du dieses Kleid selber gemacht?
2. Hat Herr Beck seinen Wagen selber repariert?
3. Haben Sie Ihren Koffer selbst getragen?
4. Hast du dir die Haare selber geschnitten?
5. Hat Frau Schwarzer den Brief selbst abgeschickt (*sent off*)?
6. Haben Sie dieses Referat selbst geschrieben?
7. Hat Robert seine Schuhe selber geputzt?

> ### Note on German Equivalents for English "leave"
>
> There are several German equivalents for English "leave," depending on whether it means "go away" (*intransitive*) or "leave something" (*transitive*), and also on how, what, or whom you are leaving.
>
> - Intransitive: **gehen, weggehen, abfahren** (= *leave by vehicle*)
>
> | | |
> |---|---|
> | Ich muß jetzt **gehen.** | *I have to leave now.* |
> | Er **ging weg,** ohne etwas zu sagen. | *He left without saying anything.* |
> | Um elf **fuhr** sie mit dem Zug **ab.** | *She left by train at eleven.* |
>
> - Transitive: **lassen** (= *leave something somewhere*), **verlassen** (= *leave a person or place*)
>
> | | |
> |---|---|
> | Ich habe meine Tasche zu Hause **gelassen.** | *I left my bag at home.* |
> | Viele wollten ihre Heimat nicht **verlassen.** | *Many did not want to leave their homeland.* |

22 **Übung:** Wie sagt man das auf deutsch?

1. Jörg left the house at seven.
2. Jörg left at seven.
3. Jörg's train left at seven.
4. Jörg left his book in the Mensa.

Time Phrases with *Mal*

The English word *time* has two German equivalents, **die Zeit** and **das Mal.**

Zeit denotes time in general.

Ich brauche mehr **Zeit.**	*I need more time.*

Mal denotes an occurrence.

Das erste **Mal** habe ich das Buch nicht verstanden.	*I didn't understand the book the first time.*
Wie viele **Male** hast du es gelesen?	*How many times did you read it?*

Learn the following idioms with **Mal.**

zum ersten Mal	*for the first time*
zum zweiten Mal	*for the second time*
zum letzten Mal	*for the last time*
diesmal	*this time*
jedesmal	*every time*
das nächste Mal	*(the) next time*

Note that **-mal** added as a suffix to cardinal numbers forms adverbs indicating repetition.

einmal	*once*
zweimal	*twice*
zwanzigmal	*twenty times*
hundertmal	*a hundred times*
zigmal	*umpteen times*

23 **Übung:** Wie oft haben Sie das schon gemacht?

Ihre Professorin möchte wissen, wie oft Sie etwas schon gemacht haben.

BEISPIEL: John, wie oft haben Sie schon Ihr Lieblingsbuch gelesen?
Ich habe es schon viermal gelesen.

1. Wie oft haben Sie schon Ihren Wagen reparieren lassen?

2. Wie oft sind Sie dieses Jahr schon nach Hause gefahren?

3. Wie oft sind Sie dieses Semester schon ins Kino gegangen?

4. Wie oft haben Sie dieses Semester schon Referate schreiben müssen?

5. Wie oft haben Sie dieses Semester schon Ihren besten Freund angerufen?

6. Wie oft sind Sie schon am Wochenende weggefahren?

24 **Gruppenarbeit:** Was haben Sie zum ersten Mal hier erlebt?

Wenn man Student wird, erlebt und lernt man viel Neues. Sagen Sie, was Sie hier an der Uni oder am College zum ersten Mal getan, erlebt, gelernt, gesehen, angefangen oder versucht haben.

BEISPIEL: Ich habe *zum ersten Mal* angefangen, Astronomie zu studieren.
Ich habe *zum ersten Mal* über Politik diskutiert.

25 **Übung:** Wie sagt man das auf deutsch?

1. We don't have enough time for you.

2. This time we understand better.

3. Please give me more time.

4. He said that every time.

5. Today is my first time here.

6. I need time and money.

Parts of the Day

German divides up the day in the following way:

gestern
$\begin{cases} \text{früh } oder \text{ morgen} \\ \text{nachmittag} \\ \text{abend} \end{cases}$
yesterday
$\begin{cases} morning \\ afternoon \\ evening \end{cases}$

heute
$\begin{cases} \text{früh } oder \text{ morgen} \\ \text{nachmittag} \\ \text{abend} \end{cases}$
this
$\begin{cases} morning \\ afternoon \\ evening \end{cases}$

morgen
$\begin{cases} \text{früh} \\ \text{nachmittag} \\ \text{abend} \end{cases}$
tomorrow
$\begin{cases} morning \\ afternoon \\ evening \end{cases}$

In addition, remember:

26 **Übung:** gestern, heute und morgen

Ihr Professor möchte wissen, wann Sie verschiedene Dinge zum letzten Mal gemacht haben.

BEISPIEL: Wann haben Sie zum letzten Mal Kaffee getrunken?
Gestern abend. *oder* Heute früh.

1. Wann haben Sie zum letzten Mal Ihren besten Freund gesehen?
2. Wann sind Sie zum letzten Mal einkaufen gegangen?
3. Wann haben Sie zum letzten Mal Hausaufgaben gemacht?
4. Wann sind Sie zum letzten Mal ins Kino gegangen?
5. Wann haben Sie zum letzten Mal telefoniert?
6. Wann haben Sie zum letzten Mal etwas gegessen?

27 Übung

Jetzt möchte Ihr Professor wissen, wann Sie verschiedene Dinge das nächste Mal machen.

> BEISPIEL: Wann fahren Sie das nächste Mal weg?
> Morgen früh.

1. Wann besuchen Sie das nächste Mal Ihre Eltern?
2. Wann gehen Sie das nächste Mal ins Konzert?
3. Wann gehen Sie das nächste Mal ins Museum?
4. Wann fahren Sie das nächste Mal Rad?
5. Wann treffen Sie das nächste Mal Ihre Freunde?
6. Wann schreiben Sie das nächste Mal Ihre Hausaufgaben für die Deutschstunde?

Gestern haben wir das Baby bei Oma gelassen.

Zwei Denkmäler

Tips zum Lesen und Lernen

Tips zum Vokabelnlernen

The Prefix *irgend-* When prefixed to question words like **wo, wie** and **wann,** the prefix **irgend-** creates indefinite adverbs like English *somewhere, somehow, sometime,* etc.

irgendwo	*somewhere (or other), anywhere*
irgendwie	*somehow (or other)*
irgendwann	*sometime (or other), any time*

Hast du meine Zeitung **irgendwo** gesehen?
Have you seen my newspaper anywhere?

Kommen Sie **irgendwann** vorbei?
Will you come by sometime?

Das können wir uns schon **irgendwie** leisten.
We can afford that somehow or other.

Im Lesetext für dieses Kapitel schreibt Anna Seghers:

Der Dom hat die Luftangriffe . . . **irgendwie** überstanden.
The cathedral survived the air raids somehow or other.

Einstieg in den Text

Like the poems in **Lyrik zum Vorlesen,** the following reading, „Zwei Denkmäler" by Anna Seghers, was written not for students learning German but rather for an audience of German speakers. Nonetheless, you have now learned enough German to read such a text with a little help from the marginal glosses.

„Zwei Denkmäler" is not a story, but rather a brief reflective essay *about* a story that Seghers never finished but could not "get out of her head" (**Das geht mir heute nicht aus dem Kopf**). She focuses on two symbolic "monuments" (**Denkmäler**)—one of grand cultural significance, the other of individual suffering on a human scale.

Now that you have learned how relative clauses work in German, you will notice how frequent they are in expository prose like „Zwei Denkmäler." During your first reading of the text, be on the lookout for the eight relative clauses it contains. List each antecedent and relative clause. Here is the first one:

1. . . . eine Erzählung, die der Krieg unterbrochen hat.
   . . . *a story that the war interrupted.*

Wortschatz 2

Verben

holen to fetch, get
vergleichen, verglich, hat vergleichen to compare
wieder·sehen (sieht wieder), sah wieder, hat wiedergesehen to see again, meet again
Auf Wiedersehen! Goodbye.

Substantive

der **Stein, -e** stone

das **Denkmal, ̈er** monument
das **Schiff, -e** ship

die **Ebene, -n** plain
die **Erde** earth
die **Erzählung, -en** story, narrative
die **Freude, -n** joy
die **Größe, -n** size; greatness
die **Macht, ̈e** power, might
die **Milch** milk

Adjektive und Adverbien

einzig- single, only
fern distant, far away
grausam terrible, gruesome; cruel
jüdisch Jewish

Nützliche Ausdrücke

Das geht mir nicht aus dem Kopf. = Das kann ich nicht vergessen.
werden aus to become of
Was ist aus ihm geworden?
What has become of him?

Zwei Denkmäler

Anna Seghers is the pseudonym of Netty Reiling, who was born in Mainz in 1900. She studied art history and sinology. Because of her membership in the Communist Party, she was forced to flee Germany in 1933. She sought asylum in France and Mexico. Much of her writing in exile reflects the turbulent existence of a refugee and committed antifascist. In 1947 she moved to the GDR, where she died in 1983.

In der Emigration° begann ich eine Erzählung, die der Krieg unterbrochen hat. Ihr Anfang ist mir noch in Erinnerung geblieben. Nicht Wort für Wort, aber dem Sinn nach.° Was mich damals erregt° hat, geht mir auch heute nicht aus dem
5 Kopf. Ich erinnere mich an eine Erinnerung.
   In meiner Heimat, in Mainz am Rhein, gab es zwei Denkmäler, die ich niemals° vergessen konnte, in Freude und Angst, auf Schiffen, in fernen Städten. Eins° ist der Dom. Wie ich als Schulkind zu meinem Erstaunen° sah, ist er auf
10 Pfeilern° gebaut, die tief in die Erde hineingehen°—damals kam es mir vor,° beinahe° so hoch wie der Dom hochragt.° Ihre Risse sind auszementiert worden° sagte man, in

here: in exile

dem . . . nach = *the sense of it*
excited

niemals = **nie**
one of them
astonishment
pillars / go into
kam . . . vor = *it seemed to me /*
  beinahe = *fast / looms up /* **Risse . . .**
  worden = *cracks have been patched*

<table>
<tr><td>

15

20

25

30

35

40

</td><td>

vergangener° Zeit, da, wo das Grundwasser Unheil stiftete.°
Ich weiß nicht, ob das stimmt, was uns ein Lehrer erzählte:
Die romanischen° und gotischen° Pfeiler seien haltbarer° als
die jüngeren.

Dieser Dom über der Rheinebene wäre mir in all seiner
Macht und Größe geblieben,° wenn ich ihn auch nie wieder
gesehen hätte.° Aber ebensowenig° kann ich ein anderes
Denkmal in meiner Heimatstadt vergessen. Es bestand nur
aus° einem einzigen flachen Stein, den man in das Pflaster°
einer Straße gesetzt hat. Hieß die Straße Bonifaziusstraße?
Hieß sie Frauenlobstraße? Das weiß ich nicht mehr. Ich
weiß nur, daß der Stein zum Gedächtnis° einer Frau ein-
gefügt wurde,° die im ersten Weltkrieg durch Bombensplitter
umkam,° als sie Milch für ihr Kind holen wollte. Wenn ich
mich recht erinnere, war sie die Frau des jüdischen Wein-
händlers° Eppstein. Menschenfresserisch,° grausam war der
erste Weltkrieg, man begann aber erst an seinem Ende mit
Luftangriffen° auf Städte und Menschen. Darum hat man
zum Gedächtnis der Frau den Stein eingesetzt, flach wie das
Pflaster, und ihren Namen eingraviert.°

Der Dom hat die Luftangriffe des zweiten Weltkriegs
irgendwie überstanden,° wie auch° die Stadt zerstört worden
ist.° Er ragt° über Fluß und Ebene. Ob der kleine flache Ge-
denkstein° noch da ist, das weiß ich nicht. Bei meinen
Besuchen habe ich ihn nicht mehr gefunden.

In der Erzählung, die ich vor dem zweiten Weltkrieg zu
schreiben begann und im Krieg verlor, ist die Rede von° dem
Kind, dem die Mutter Milch holen wollte, aber nicht heim-
bringen° konnte. Ich hatte die Absicht,° in dem Buch zu
erzählen, was aus diesem Mädchen geworden ist.

</td><td>

past / **Grundwasser . . . stiftete** =
groundwater caused damage /
romanesque / *gothic* / **seien haltbarer**
= *were more durable*
wäre . . . geblieben = *would have
remained* / **wenn . . . hätte** = *even if I
had never seen it again* / *no less*
bestand . . . aus = *consisted of* /
pavement

in memory of
eingefügt wurde = *had been set in*
durch . . . umkam = *was killed by
shrapnel*
wine merchant / *cannibalistic*

air raids

engraved

survived / **wie auch** = **obwohl**
zerstört . . . ist = *was destroyed* /
looms / *commemorative stone*

ist . . . von = *the story is about*

heimbringen = **nach Hause bringen** /
intention

</td></tr>
</table>

Anna Seghers

Fragen zum Lesestück

1. Was hat Anna Seghers' Erzählung unterbrochen?

2. Was war Anna Seghers' Heimatstadt?

3. Was konnte sie nie vergessen?

4. Über welche Denkmäler schreibt sie?

5. Vergleichen Sie diese zwei Denkmäler.

6. An wen sollte der Stein erinnern?

7. Hat Anna Seghers den Stein wieder gefunden?

8. Wann begann sie, die Erzählung zu schreiben?

9. Was wollte sie in dem Buch erzählen?

Situationen aus dem Alltag

„Das geht mir nicht aus dem Kopf"

In der kurzen Erzählung „Zwei Denkmäler" erinnert sich die Schriftstellerin an etwas, was vor vielen Jahren passiert ist. Sie sagt, sie erinnert sich „an eine Erinnerung." Am Anfang dieses Kapitels haben Sie das Gedicht „Heimweh" von Eichendorff gelesen, in dem er auch über seine Erinnerungen an die Heimat und die Geliebte spricht.

Jeder Mensch hat Erinnerungen, nicht nur Dichter und Schriftsteller. Jetzt sprechen wir ein bißchen über unsere eigenen Erinnerungen.

Neue Vokabeln

die **Erfahrung, -en**	*experience*
die **Gegenwart**	*present (time)*
das **Heimweh**	*homesickness*
der **Ort, -e**	*place; small town*

Diese Wörter und Ausdrücke kennen Sie schon.

Ich bin in _____ geboren.
sich erinnern an
alte Freunde
umziehen
die Vergangenheit
verlassen
wiedersehen

Gruppendiskussion: Wo haben Sie als Kind gewohnt?

Leben Sie noch in der Stadt, wo Sie geboren sind, oder sind Sie umgezogen? Gefällt es Ihnen besser, wo Sie jetzt wohnen? Besuchen Sie manchmal Ihren Geburtsort? Was wollen Sie dort sehen? Was hat sich dort geändert?

Partnerarbeit: Ich erinnere mich an etwas Besonderes.

Erzählen Sie einander eine wichtige Erinnerung aus Ihrer Kindheit.

Gibt es z.B. einen besonderen Menschen, an den Sie sich erinnern? Oder einen Lieblingsort oder ein Gebäude, wo Sie gewohnt haben oder Zeit verbracht haben? Warum geht es Ihnen nicht aus dem Kopf?

Zum Schluß

Sprechen wir miteinander

A **Gruppenarbeit:** Vergleichen wir.

Der Professor wählt 6 oder 7 Studenten, die dann nach vorne kommen. Zuerst sagen alle, wann sie geboren sind. Jetzt antworten die anderen auf diese Fragen:

1. Wer ist der/die älteste?
2. Wer ist der/die jüngste?
3. Wer ist der/die größte?

4. Wer ist der/die kleinste?
5. Wer hat die längsten/kürzesten Haare?
6. Wer ist heute am schönsten angezogen?

B **Partnerarbeit:** Ich bin älter als du.

Jetzt vergleichen Sie sich mit Ihrem Partner. Seien Sie nicht zu ernst (*serious*)!

> BEISPIEL: Ich bin intelligenter als du!
> Vielleicht, aber ich habe schönere Augen als du!

Wer ist gesünder? müder? optimistischer? pünktlicher? sportlicher? usw.

C **Weltrekorde**

Jeder von Ihnen stellt den anderen eine Frage über einen Weltrekord. Die anderen müssen die Antwort erraten (*guess*).

> BEISPIEL: Wie heißt der höchste Berg der Welt?
> Wer ist die beste Tennisspielerin der Welt?

D **Gruppenarbeit:** Was machen Sie selber? Was lassen Sie machen?

Sagen Sie, ob Sie etwas selber machen, oder ob Sie es lieber machen lassen.

> BEISPIEL: den Wagen reparieren
> Ich repariere den Wagen selber. *oder*
> Ich lasse den Wagen reparieren.

den Wagen reparieren

die Haare schneiden

das Mittagessen kochen

den Kaffee machen

Lebensmittel einkaufen

Referate schreiben

E Spiel: Ratet mal, wen ich meine!

Choose another student in the room to describe, but don't tell anyone who it is. When your turn comes, say **Ich denke an eine Studentin, die . . .** or **Ich denke an einen Studenten, der . . .** and then add some description. The others must guess whom you mean.

BEISPIEL: Ich denke an eine Studentin, die heute eine gelbe Bluse trägt.

Schreiben Sie zu Hause

F Antworten Sie mit Ihren eigenen Worten auf jede Frage. Benutzen Sie in Ihrer Antwort einen Relativsatz.

BEISPIEL: Mit was für Menschen verbringen Sie gern Ihre Freizeit?

Mögliche Antwort: Ich verbringe gern meine Freizeit mit Menschen, mit denen ich Sport treiben kann.

1. Was für Erzählungen würden sie gern lesen?

2. Mit was für Menschen leben Sie gern zusammen?

3. Aus was für einer Familie kommen Sie?

4. Was für Städte gefallen Ihnen besonders gut?

5. In was für einem Gebäude wohnen Sie?

6. Mit was für Menschen verbringen sie gern Ihre Freizeit?

G Aufsatzthemen Anna Seghers wollte eine Geschichte über das Mädchen schreiben, dessen Mutter im Ersten Weltkrieg Milch holen wollte.

1. Schreiben Sie den Anfang dieser Geschichte. *oder*

2. Schreiben Sie das Ende dieser Geschichte. Was ist aus dem Mädchen geworden? Was für Erinnerungen hat sie heute?

H Wie sagt man das auf deutsch?

1. Can you repair your car yourself?

2. No, I never learned that. I always have it repaired.

3. A German I know is the best mechanic in town.

4. Are German trains really more punctual than American trains?

5. Yes, but the trains in France are the fastest.

6. Have you heard the newest gossip?

7. Not yet. What's going on?

8. Rita went away with the richest guy in the office.

9. She left poor Rudi, who was always short of cash.

Almanach

Four Modern Women Writers

Ingeborg Drewitz (1923–1986)
Ingeborg Drewitz was born in Berlin and lived there her entire life. She published dramas, short stories, radio plays, and novels and also worked extensively as a journalist. Her partly autobiographical novel *Gestern war heute* (1978) tells the story of three generations of women whose personal lives reflect political and social developments in twentieth-century Berlin.

Ingeborg Bachmann (1926–1973)
Ingeborg Bachmann was born in Klagenfurt, Austria, and attended the University of Vienna. Although she first became famous for her lyric poetry, Bachmann also wrote radio plays and short stories, as well as an opera libretto and the novel *Malina* (1972), the first part of the unfinished *Todesarten* ("Kinds of Death") trilogy.

Christa Wolf (b. 1929)

Christa Wolf was born in Landsberg an der Warthe, in what is now Poland. Her novel *Kindheitsmuster* ("Childhood Pattern," 1976) reflects her childhood during the Third Reich. She worked as an editor before publishing her first fiction in 1961 and has traveled and lectured widely in the West. The novel *Kassandra* (1983) retells the story of the Trojan War from a feminist point of view.

Sarah Kirsch (b. 1935)

Sarah Kirsch was born in Limlingerode in the Harz Mountains. She is primarily a lyric poet whose verse is characterized by intensity of language and precise, pictorial images. Her love poetry is striking for its combination of melancholy and single moments of recollected joy. She also published an influential collection of interviews with women in the German Democratic Republic entitled *Die Pantherfrau* ("The Panther Woman," 1973).

Zusammenfassung und Wiederholung

(Kapitel 9–12)

FORMS

1. Verbs

A. Simple past tense

1. Weak verbs

p. 285

stem + **-te** + endings	
ich sagte	wir sagten
du sagtest	ihr sagtet
Sie sagten	Sie sagten
er, es, sie sagte	sie sagten

stem ending in **-t** + **-ete** + endings	
ich arbeitete	wir arbeiteten
du arbeitetest	ihr arbeitetet
Sie arbeiteten	Sie arbeiteten
er, es, sie arbeitete	sie arbeiteten

2. Mixed verbs

p. 289

changed stem + **-te** + ending	
wissen, **wußte**, hat gewußt	
ich wußte	wir wußten
du wußtest	ihr wußtet
Sie wußten	Sie wußten
er, es, sie wußte	sie wußten

Similarly:

bringen → **brachte**   nennen → **nannte**
mitbringen → **brachte mit**   kennen → **kannte**
verbringen → **verbrachte**

and the modal verbs *(no umlaut in past stem)*:

p. 289

dürfen → **durfte**   müssen → **mußte**
können → **konnte**   sollen → **sollte**
mögen → **mochte**   wollen → **wollte**

3. **haben** and **werden** (*irregular in the simple past*)   p. 290

haben, **hatte,** hat gehabt	
ich hatte	wir hatten
du hattest	ihr hattet
Sie hatten	Sie hatten
er, es, sie hatte	sie hatten

werden, **wurde,** ist geworden	
ich wurde	wir wurden
du wurdest	ihr wurdet
Sie wurden	Sie wurden
er, es, sie wurde	sie wurden

4. Strong verbs   p. 286

changed stem + endings

nehmen, **nahm,** hat genommen	
ich nahm	wir nahmen
du nahmst	ihr nahmt
Sie nahmen	Sie nahmen
er, es, sie nahm	sie nahmen

The simple past tense of strong verbs will be found in the table on page 287. In *Kapitel 10–12,* you learned these additional strong verbs. Review their principal parts.   p. 287

infinitive	*3rd sing. pres.*	*simple past*	*perfect*
brechen	bricht	**brach**	hat gebrochen
lassen	läßt	**ließ**	hat gelassen
rufen		**rief**	hat gerufen
schneiden		**schnitt**	hat geschnitten
vergleichen		**verglich**	hat verglichen
verschwinden		**verschwand**	ist verschwunden
wachsen	wächst	**wuchs**	ist gewachsen
waschen	wäscht	**wusch**	hat gewaschen

B. Past perfect tense   pp. 293–94

Simple past of the auxiliary + past participle

Ich **hatte** das schon **gesagt.**	*I had said it already.*
Sie **war** fünf Jahre da **gewesen.**	*She had been there for five years.*
Nachdem sie **gegessen hatten,** gingen sie ins Theater.	*After they had eaten, they went to the theater.*

C. The Verb **lassen**   pp. 358–60

1. *to leave* (something or someone), *leave behind* (perfect tense: **hat gelassen**):

   Lassen Sie mich allein.
   Hast du deine Kamera im Hotel **gelassen?**

2. *to allow, let* (perfect tense: double infinitive):   p. 358

   Sie **lassen** uns heute nacht hier schlafen.
   Sie haben uns bis neun Uhr **schlafen lassen.**

3. *to have or order something done* (perfect tense: double infinitive):

   Sie **läßt** den Arzt kommen.
   Sie **hat** den Arzt **kommen lassen.**

   A noun or pronoun in the dative indicates for whom the action is performed:

   Ich lasse **mir** das Essen bringen.

2. Reflexive verbs and pronouns   pp. 316–21

A. Accusative and dative reflexive pronouns

	sing.	*plur.*
1st person	mich / mir	uns
2nd person	dich / dir	euch (*familiar*)
	sich	sich (*formal*)
3rd person	sich	sich

p. 316

B. Accusative reflexives   pp. 317–18

Reflexive pronoun is *accusative* when the subject and direct object are the same person or thing.

subject		*acc. reflex. / dir. obj.*	
Ich	habe	**mich**	verletzt.
Wir	haben	**uns**	kennengelernt.
Stefan	muß	**sich**	beeilen.

p. 316

C. Dative reflexives

pp. 320–21

Reflexive pronoun is *dative* when the subject and indirect object are the same person or thing (something else is the direct object).

subject		dat. reflex. / indir. obj.	dir. obj.
Ich	kaufte	**mir**	einen Hut.
Du	bestellst	**dir**	ein Bier.
Wir	sehen	**uns**	die Altstadt an.

D. Reflexive verbs

The following reflexive verbs have been introduced through *Kapitel 12,* either in the **Wortschatz** or **Situationen aus dem Alltag.** Review your knowledge of them.

sich ändern	*to change*
sich etwas ansehen	*to have a look at something*
sich anziehen	*to get dressed*
sich ausziehen	*to get undressed*
sich baden	*to take a bath, bathe*
sich beeilen	*to hurry*
sich bewegen	*to move*
sich duschen	*to take a shower*
sich erinnern an	*to remember*
sich erkälten	*to catch a cold*
sich freuen	*to be happy*
sich fühlen	*to feel*
sich die Haare kämmen	*to comb one's hair*
sich etwas leisten können	*to be able to afford something*
sich rasieren	*to shave*
sich schminken	*to put on makeup*
sich setzen	*to sit down*
sich verletzen	*to hurt oneself*
sich verloben mit	*to get engaged to*
sich verspäten	*to be late*
sich etwas vorstellen	*to imagine something*
sich die Zähne putzen	*to brush one's teeth*

3. Relative clauses and relative pronouns

A. Relative pronouns

pp. 353–57

	masculine	*neuter*	*feminine*	*plural*
nominative	der	das	die	die
accusative	den	das	die	die
dative	dem	dem	der	**denen**
genitive	**dessen**	**dessen**	**deren**	**deren**

B. Rules for use   p. 354

 1. The relative pronoun refers to an antecedent that precedes it.

 2. The relative pronoun agrees with its antecedent in number and gender.

 3. The case of the relative pronoun is determined by its use in the relative
    clause.

 4. Only a preposition may precede the relative pronoun in the relative
    clause.

 5. The relative clause has verb-last word order.

	antecedent	*rel. pron.*	
	Das ist **der Film,**	**der**	jetzt läuft.
		an den	ich mich nicht erinnern konnte.
		von dem	sie sprachen.
		dessen	Anfang mir so gut gefällt.

C. **Was** as a relative pronoun   p. 357

   Was is the relative pronoun when the antecedent is:

   a. **etwas, nichts, viel, wenig, alles**

      Das war **alles, was** sie sagte.

   b. neuter adjectival noun

      Das war **das Schönste, was** ich je gesehen hatte.

   c. an entire clause

      Sie wollen jetzt schlafen, was ich gut verstehen kann.

4. Adjectives and Adverbs

A. Adjective endings

   1. Adjective endings following a **der**-word: pp. 259–62

      Der-word has primary ending, adjective has secondary ending.

	masc.	*neut.*	*fem.*	*plur.*
nom.	dieser junge Mann	dieses junge Kind	diese junge Frau	diese jungen Leute
acc.	diesen jungen Mann	dieses junge Kind	diese junge Frau	diese jungen Leute
dat.	diesem jungen Mann	diesem jungen Kind	dieser jungen Frau	diesen jungen Leuten
gen.	dieses jungen Mannes	dieses jungen Kindes	dieser jungen Frau	dieser jungen Leute

   2. Adjective endings following an **ein**-word:

      When the **ein**-word has no ending, the adjective has the primary ending
      (highlighted forms).

	masc.	*neut.*	*fem.*	*plur.*
nom.	ein junger Mann	ein junges Kind	eine junge Frau	meine jungen Leute
acc.	einen jungen Mann	ein junges Kind	eine junge Frau	meine jungen Leute
dat.	einem jungen Mann	einem jungen Kind	einer jungen Frau	meinen jungen Leuten
gen.	eines jungen Mannes	eines jungen Kindes	einer jungen Frau	meiner jungen Leute

3. Adjective endings without a limiting word:

Adjective has primary ending except in masculine and neuter genitive (highlighted forms).

	masc.	*neut.*	*fem.*	*plur.*
nom.	kalter Wein	kaltes Wasser	kalte Milch	kalte Suppen
acc.	kalten Wein	kaltes Wasser	kalte Milch	kalte Suppen
dat.	kaltem Wein	kaltem Wasser	kalter Milch	kalten Suppen
gen.	kalten Weines	kalten Wassers	kalter Milch	kalter Suppen

B. Adjectives and pronouns of indefinite number   p. 326

wenige	*few*	**andere**	*other(s)*
einige	*some*	**viele**	*many*
mehrere	*several*		

C. Adjectival nouns

Adjective nouns are capitalized and receive adjective endings.

1. Referring to people   pp. 323–24

   masculine and feminine singular and plural:

attributive adjective	*vs.*	*adjectival noun*
unsere kleine Tochter		**Unsere Kleine** ist heute krank.
		Our little girl is sick today.
ein deutscher Student	*vs.*	Dieser Student ist **Deutscher.**
		This student is a German.
mit den alten Leuten	*vs.*	Ich will mit **den Alten** arbeiten.
		I want to work with (the) old people.

   The following words are *always* adjectival nouns:

der/die **Bekannte**	*acquaintance, friend*
der/die **Deutsche**	*German*
der/die **Verwandte**	*relative*
der **Beamte**	*official (m.)*

   (but: **die Beamtin** is not an adjectival noun)

2. Referring to qualities   p. 325
   Neuter, singular only:

   Das ist **das Schönste,** was ich je gesehen habe.
   That's the most beautiful thing I've ever seen.
   Haben Sie **etwas Billigeres?**
   Do you have anything cheaper?
   Ich habe **nichts Interessantes** gehört.
   I have not heard anything interesting.

D. Comparison of adjectives and adverbs pp. 346–52

1. Basic forms

positive degree	comparative degree (+ er)	superlative degree (am -(e)sten)
glücklich	glücklicher	am glücklichsten
interessant	interessanter	am interessantesten

2. With adjective endings

eine	glückliche	Kindheit	*a happy childhood*
eine	glücklichere	Kindheit	*a happier childhood*
die	glücklichste	Kindheit	*the happiest childhood*

interessante	Ideen	*interesting ideas*
interessantere	Ideen	*more interesting ideas*
die interessantesten	Ideen	*the most interesting ideas*

Note the two possibilities in the superlative of predicate adjectives:

Diese Ideen sind **am interessantesten.**
Diese Ideen sind **die interessantesten.**

3. Adjectives and adverbs with umlaut in the comparative and superlative

pp. 349–50

old	alt	älter	am ältesten
young	jung	jünger	am jüngsten
dumb	dumm	dümmer	am dümmsten
smart	klug	klüger	am klügsten
cold	kalt	kälter	am kältesten
warm	warm	wärmer	am wärmsten
short	kurz	kürzer	am kürzesten
long	lang	länger	am längsten
strong	stark	stärker	am stärksten
weak	schwach	schwächer	am schwächsten
sick	krank	kränker	am kränksten
healthy	gesund	gesünder	am gesündesten
poor	arm	ärmer	am ärmsten
hard, harsh	hart	härter	am härtesten
often	oft	öfter	am öftesten
red	rot	röter	am rötesten
black	schwarz	schwärzer	am schwärzesten

4. Irregular comparatives and superlatives pp. 350–51

big	**groß**	**größer**	**am größten**
good, well	**gut**	**besser**	**am besten**
high	**hoch, hoh-**	**höher**	**am höchsten**
near	**nahe**	**näher**	**am nächsten**
much, many	**viel**	**mehr**	**am meisten**
gladly	**gern**	**lieber**	**am liebsten**
		(preferably, rather)	*(to like most of all to)*

FUNCTIONS

1. Comparisons

p. 352

A. **genauso ... wie** = *just as ... as* (with positive degree)

nicht so ... wie = *not as ... as*

Die zweite Geschichte war **nicht so interessant wie** die erste.

B. **als** = *than* (with comparative degree)
Jetzt sind die Preise **höher als** letztes Jahr.

C. **immer** + comparative degree indicates progressive change

Im Frühling werden die Tage **immer länger**.

D. **je ... desto** = *the ... the ...* (with comparative degree)

Je früher, desto besser.

Je mehr man lernt, **desto** mehr versteht man.
Note that **je** requires verb-last word order, while **desto** requires verb-second word order.

2. Enumerating: Ordinal numbers

From first to nineteenth: *cardinal number* + *-t-* + *adjective ending* (note irregular forms in boldface)

p. 266

der, das, die **erste**	1st	elfte	11th
zweite	2nd	zwölfte	12th
dritte	3rd	dreizehnte	13th
vierte	4th	vierzehnte	14th
fünfte	5th	fünfzehnte	15th
sechste	6th	sechzehnte	16th
siebte	7th	siebzehnte	17th
achte	8th	achtzehnte	18th
neunte	9th	neunzehnte	19th
zehnte	10th		

twentieth and above: *cardinal number* + *-st-* + *adjective ending*

der, das, die zwanzigste	20th
einundzwanzigste	21st
siebenundfünfzigste	57th

3. Specifying time

A. Dates, days, months, decades, and years p. 266

1. Asking for the date

nom. **Der wievielte** ist heute?
Heute ist **der erste Februar.**

acc. **Den wievielten** haben wir heute?
Heute haben wir **den ersten Februar.**

What's today's date?
Today is February first.

2. In what part of the day? p. 362

gestern abend	*yesterday evening*
heute abend	*this evening*
in der Nacht	*at night*
morgen früh	*tomorrow morning*
morgen nachmittag	*tomorrow afternoon*

3. On what day of the week? **am . . .** p. 266

Wann fährst du ab?
Am Donnerstag. Aber **am Montag** komme ich zurück.

4. On what day of the month? **am . . .** p. 266

Wann ist er angekommen?
Am 5. April. (am fünften April)

Wann kommen Sie zurück?
Ich komme **am 11. Oktober** zurück. (am elften Oktober)

5. In what month? **im . . .**

Wann waren Sie in Rom?
Im September. Aber **im Dezember** war ich wieder zu Hause.

6. In what year?

In welchem Jahr ist er gestorben?
Er ist **im Jahre 1955** gestorben. *or* Er ist **1955** gestorben.

7. In what decade? **die 30er (Dreißiger) Jahre** = the Thirties p. 328

die goldenen 20er (Zwanziger) Jahre	*the golden 20s (Twenties)*
während der 60er Jahre	*during the 60s*
in den frühen 90er Jahren	*in the early 90s*

The number does not inflect as an adjective, regardless of case.

B. Other time expressions

1. "When?"

Wann warst du dort?
Letzten Montag. / Letztes Jahr. / Letzte Woche.

Wann machst du das?
Nächsten Dienstag. / Nächstes Semester. / Nächste Woche.

2. "How often?"

Wie oft machst du das?
Jeden Tag. / Jedes Wochenende. / Jede Woche.

3. *ago* = **vor** + dative p. 294

Wann warst du in Rom?
Das war **vor drei Jahren.**

Wann ist der Unfall passiert?
Vor einer Stunde.

4. Expressing duration: "How long?"

a. time phrase in accusative case

Ich habe **einen Tag** gewartet.

Wie lange warst du dort?
Den ganzen Tag. / Das ganze Jahr. / Die ganze Woche.

b. If an action ends in the past, use simple past or perfect tense:

p. 295

Ich **studierte** vier Semester in Berlin.⎤ *I studied in Berlin (for)*
Ich **habe** vier Semester in Berlin ⎬ *four semesters.*
  studiert.⎦

c. If an action is continuing in the present, use present tense plus **schon**
or **seit.** p. 296

Ich **wohne schon ein Jahr** hier.⎤ *I've been living here for a year.*
Ich **wohne seit einem Jahr** hier.⎦

5. Time phrases with **Mal** pp. 360–61

a. **das Mal** = *time* (in the sense of "an occurrence")

das erste (zweite, dritte) Mal   *the first (second, third) time*
zum ersten (zweiten) Mal   *for the first (second) time*

b. cardinal number + **-mal** = *how many times*

Ich bin **einmal** dort gewesen.   *I've been there once.*
Den Film habe ich **dreimal** gesehen.   *I've seen the film three times.*
Das habe ich schon **zigmal** gesagt.   *I've said that umpteen times.*

6. Equivalents of English "when"

a. **wann** p. 292

Question word = *at what time?*

Wann ist das passiert?

Conjunction = *at what time*

Ich weiß nicht, **wann** das passiert ist.

b. **wenn**

Conjunction = *when* (in the present or future)

Wenn Sie uns besuchen, zeigen wir Ihnen die Stadt.

Conjunction = *whenever* (in past or present)

Wenn ich nach Berlin kam, haben wir uns immer gesehen.

Conjunction = *if*

Wenn ich kann, helfe ich dir gerne.

c. **als** = *when* (for a single event or period in the past—almost always used with simple past tense)

Als ich jung war, durfte ich nicht allein in die Stadt.

4. Talking about clothing and parts of the body
p. 322

German usually uses dative pronouns, not posssessive adjectives, when talking about clothing and parts of the body.

Meine Freundin schneidet **mir** die Haare.	*My girlfriend cuts **my** hair.*
Ziehen Sie **sich** den Mantel an.	*Put on **your** coat.*
Stefanie hat **sich** das Bein gebrochen.	*Stefanie broke **her** leg.*
Ich muß **mir** die Zähne putzen.	*I have to clean **my** teeth.*

5. Specifying Time, Manner, and Place: Word Order of Adverbs
p. 265

Think of the adverbs as answering the following questions in alphabetical order:

	wann?	*wie?*	*wo(hin)?*
Ich werde	*morgen*	*mit meinen Freunden*	*vor der Bibliothek* warten.
Gehen wir	*jetzt*	*schnell*	*zum Supermarkt!*

6. Setting a Scene with *bei*
p. 327

bei = *while . . . ing,* or *at* (an activity or someone's home or business)

Die laute Musik stört mich **beim Lesen.**
Marion ist heute **bei ihren Verwandten.**

USEFUL IDIOMS AND EXPRESSIONS

1. **Requesting information**

   Was ist los?
   Darf ich eine Frage stellen?
   Was hast du zum Geburtstag bekommen?
   Wieso?
   Was ist aus ihm geworden?

2. **Reactions and opinions**

   Das ist schade.
   Das tut mir weh.
   Na endlich!
   Augenblick bitte!
   Danke, gleichfalls!
   So ein Mist!
   Na und?
   Ich habe keine Ahnung.
   Viel Spaß!

3. **Colloquialisms**

   Ich bin leider **knapp bei Kasse.**
   Das war eine **dreckige** Arbeit!
   Jemand hat mir den Geldbeutel **geklaut!**

TEST YOUR PROGRESS

A. Complete these sentences, using the appropriate reflexive phrase cued in English.

1. Ich höre, dein Vater hat _____ (got hurt)   *sich verletzt*

2. Ja, aber Gott sei Dank _____ (he already feels) viel besser.   *fühlt er sich*   *sich verloben*

3. Stimmt es, daß Rita und Rudi _____ (have gotten engaged)?

4. Richtig, darum _____ (they're so happy) so sehr.

5. Komm doch, wir müssen _____ (hurry up).

6. Ich komme schon, aber ich muß _____ (comb my hair).

7. Hast du _____ (already gotten dressed)?

8. Noch nicht, die Zeitung möchte ich _____ (have a look at).

B. Complete this paragraph, using the appropriate word or phrase cued in English. Don't forget the adjective endings!

Wenn man (*this*) Monat ins (*old*) Landesmuseum geht, sieht man (*a new*) Ausstellung über (*German*) Geschichte in (*our*) Jahrhundert. Dort kann man sich (*various interesting*) Plakate ansehen und (*the political*) Kunst in der Zeit der (*first German*) Republik studieren. Man sieht auf (*these old*) Plakaten, wie die (*many*) Parteien versucht haben, die Ängste (*of the German people*) zu manipulieren. Das (*first*) Bild ist ein (*good*) Beispiel für (*such political*) Plakate während (*this important*) Epoche. Es zeigt (*a „strong*) Mann." Natürlich sollten die (*unemployed Germans*) an einen „Führer" denken.

C. Fill in the blanks with **wenn, wann,** or **als** as appropriate.

_____ ich jung war, wollte ich Fußballspieler werden. _____ mein Vater mich jeden Samstag zum Spiel mitnahm, habe ich mich immer gefreut. „_____ darf ich einen Fußball haben?" fragte ich immer. Vater sagte: „_____ du sechs bist." _____ ich aber sechs wurde, wollte ich Cowboy werden. Ich kann mich nicht erinnern, _____ ich Arzt werden wollte. _____ ich Ihnen jetzt sage, was ich bin, glauben Sie es mir nicht: ich bin doch Fußballspieler geworden!

D. Use the verb **lassen** in the German equivalents of these sentences.

1. Please let me stay!
2. Did you leave your luggage in the car?
3. I'm having the food brought to me.
4. Did you have the doctor come? (*use perfect tense*)
5. Leave your coat on the chair.
6. Can we let the children play for another hour?

E. Restate each sentence, putting the adjective or adverb into the comparative and then into the superlative.

  BEISPIEL: Unsere Kusine ist *eine gute* Schülerin.
      Unsere Kusine ist *eine bessere* Schülerin.
      Unsere Kusine ist *die beste* Schülerin.

1. Ich würde *gern* deutschen Wein trinken.
2. Die Menschen aus dieser Gegend sind *arm*.
3. Zum Frühstück esse ich *oft* Brot.
4. Das ist ja ein *starker* Kaffee.
5. Schmidts haben *viele* Kinder.
6. Mein Mantel ist *warm*.
7. Man hat hier *große* Gebäude gebaut.
8. *Viele* Menschen verstehen mich nicht.
9. Wer fand diese Geschichte *interessant*?
10. Du scheinst ein *kluges* Kind zu sein.

F. Fill in the blanks with the appropriate relative pronoun.

1. Wie heißt der Chef, für _____ Sie arbeiten?
2. Er heißt Kurt Martens, und sein Sohn, mit _____ ich zur Schule ging, heißt Knut.
3. Ist das nicht der Junge, _____ (whose) Foto in der Zeitung stand?
4. Ja, die Fußballmannschaft, für _____ er spielt, hat letzte Woche gewonnen.
5. 1990 war das letzte Jahr, _____ ich in Deutschland verbracht habe.
6. Was war das Schönste, _____ du dort gemacht hast?
7. Ich habe gute Freunde kennengelernt, mit _____ ich über alles reden konnte.
8. Die Professorin, bei _____ ich ein Seminar über deutsche Literatur belegte, hat mir wirklich geholfen.
9. Die deutschen Studenten, _____ im Studentenwohnheim wohnten, waren auch sehr sympathisch.
10. Ja, das war etwas, _____ ich nie vergessen kann.

G. Insert a phrase with **Mal** or **-mal** into these sentences.

1. Das war (the last time), daß ich sie gesehen habe.
2. Ich werde ihn (one more time) fragen.
3. Seid ihr mehr als (three times) in der Schweiz gewesen?
4. Ja, das (second time) war ich erst elf Jahre alt.
5. Aber (back then) konnte ich noch nicht so gut Deutsch wie jetzt.
6. Nächsten Sommer fahre ich (for the fourth time) nach Zürich.

H. Wie sagt man das auf deutsch?

1. What kind of a car do you have?
2. I broke my arm a month ago.
3. He drove to Berlin this morning.
4. When you came home you disturbed me.
5. How long have you been learning German?
6. Those are the students whose names I've forgotten.
7. I went to the station with them the day before yesterday.
8. The blue shirt was the most expensive.
9. After we had eaten, we went to the movies.
10. Back then we lived in a small apartment.
11. He is a friend of mine.
12. My sister is younger than I am.

Die Schweiz

Dialoge

Skifahren in der Schweiz

BRIGITTE: Ich freue mich sehr auf die Semesterferien!

JOHANNA: Hast du vor, wieder Ski zu fahren?

BRIGITTE: Ja, ich werde zwei Wochen in der Schweiz verbringen. Morgen früh flieg' ich nach Zürich.

JOHANNA: Da bin ich ja ganz baff! Früher hast du doch immer Angst vorm Fliegen gehabt!

BRIGITTE: Stimmt, aber ich habe mich einfach daran gewöhnt.

In der WG: Bei Nina ist es unordentlich.

UTE: Nina, hör mal zu, wann wirst du deinen Kram endlich aufräumen?

NINA: Ich mach' das gleich. Seid mir nicht böse—ich mußte mich heute morgen wahnsinnig beeilen.

LUTZ: Ja, das sagst du immer. Jetzt haben wir aber die Nase voll. Alle müssen doch mitmachen.

NINA: Ihr habt recht. Von jetzt an werde ich mich mehr um die Wohnung kümmern.

Am Informationsschalter in Basel

TOURIST: Entschuldigung. Darf ich Sie um Auskunft bitten?

BEAMTIN: Gerne. Wie kann ich Ihnen helfen?

TOURIST: Ich bin nur einen Tag in Basel und kenne mich hier nicht aus. Was können Sie mir empfehlen?

BEAMTIN: Es kommt darauf an, was Sie sehen wollen. Das Kunstmuseum lohnt sich besonders. Wenn Sie sich für das Mittelalter interessieren, dürfen Sie das nicht verpassen.

TOURIST: Ja, das interessiert mich schon. Wie komme ich bitte dahin?

BEAMTIN: Direkt vor dem Bahnhof ist die Haltestelle. Dort müssen Sie in die Straßenbahnlinie 2 einsteigen. Am Museum steigen Sie dann aus.

TOURIST: Das werde ich schon finden. Vielen Dank für die Hilfe.

BEAMTIN: Bitte sehr.

Note on Usage

The equivalent for English "must not" is **nicht dürfen.**

Das Kunstmuseum dürfen Sie nicht verpassen.	*You mustn't (really shouldn't) miss the art museum.*

Skiing in Switzerland

BRIGITTE: I'm really looking forward to the semester break!

JOHANNA: Do you plan to go skiing again?

BRIGITTE: Yes, I'll spend two weeks in Switzerland. Tomorrow morning I fly to Zürich.

JOHANNA: I'm flabbergasted! Before, you were always afraid of flying!

BRIGITTE: True, but I've simply gotten used to it.

In the Group Apartment: Nina's Place Is Messy

UTE: Listen, Nina, when are you finally going to straighten up your stuff?

NINA: I'll do it right away. Don't be mad at me—I was in a big rush this morning.

LUTZ: Yeah, you always say that. Now we're really fed up. Everybody has to pitch in.

NINA: You're right. From now on I'll take more care of the apartment.

At the Information Window in Basel

TOURIST: Excuse me. May I ask you for information?

OFFICIAL: Sure. How can I help you?

TOURIST: I'm only in Basel for a day, and I don't know my way around here. What can you recommend to me?

OFFICIAL: It depends on what you want to see. The art museum is especially worthwhile. If you're interested in the Middle Ages, you mustn't miss it.

TOURIST: Yes, that sounds interesting. How do I get there?

OFFICIAL: Right in front of the station is the streetcar stop. You have to get the number 2 streetcar. Then get out at the museum.

TOURIST: I'll find it all right. Thank you for the help.

OFFICIAL: You're welcome.

Wortschatz 1

Verben

Angst haben vor (+ *dat.*) to be afraid of

auf·räumen to tidy up, straighten up

sich aus·kennen to know one's way around
Ich kenne mich hier nicht aus. I don't know my way around here.

bitten, bat, hat gebeten um to ask for, request

sich freuen auf (+ *acc.*) to look forward to

sich gewöhnen an (+ *acc.*) to get used to

interessieren to interest

sich interessieren für to be interested in

sich kümmern um to look after, take care of; deal with

sich lohnen to be worthwhile, worth the trouble

verpassen to miss (*an event, opportunity, train, etc.*)

sich vor·bereiten auf (+ *acc.*) to prepare for

vor·haben to plan, have in mind

warten auf (+ *acc.*) to wait for

zu·hören (+ *dat.*) to listen (to)
Hören Sie gut zu! Listen carefully.
Hör mir zu. Listen to me.

Substantive

der **Schalter, -** counter, window

das **Mittelalter** the Middle Ages

die **Auskunft** information
die **Haltestelle, -n** (streetcar or bus) stop
die **Hilfe** help
die **Linie, -n** (streetcar or bus) line
die **Straßenbahn, -en** streetcar

Adjektive und Adverbien

böse (+ *dat.*) angry, mad (at)
Sei mir nicht böse. Don't be mad at me.
direkt direct(ly)
unordentlich disorderly, messy

Nützliche Ausdrücke

von jetzt an from now on
Es kommt darauf an, . . . It depends on . . .
Es kommt darauf an, was Sie sehen wollen. It depends on what you want to see.
Wie komme ich dahin? How do I get there?

Gegensätze

sich interessieren ≠ sich langweilen   to be interested ≠ to be bored
unordentlich ≠ ordentlich   disorderly, messy ≠ orderly, neat

baff sein (*colloq.*) = **sehr staunen, sprachlos sein**
schlampig (*colloq.*) = **unordentlich**

Variationen

A Persönliche Fragen

1. Brigitte freut sich auf die Semesterferien. Freuen Sie sich auf etwas?

2. Sie hat vor, Ski zu fahren. Was haben Sie am Wochenende vor?

3. Fahren Sie in den Semesterferien irgendwohin?

4. Bei Nina sieht's schlampig aus. Wie sieht es bei Ihnen im Zimmer aus?

5. Die anderen in der WG sind Nina böse, weil sie nicht aufräumt. Wann werden Sie böse?

6. Der Tourist kennt sich in Basel nicht aus, aber zu Hause kennt er sich natürlich sehr gut aus. In welcher Stadt kennen Sie sich besonders gut aus?

7. Der Tourist interessiert sich für das Mittelalter. Wissen Sie, wann das Mittelalter war?

8. Der Tourist will das Museum nicht verpassen. Haben Sie je etwas Gutes verpaßt? Was denn?

9. Was machen Sie, wenn Sie sich in einer fremden Stadt nicht auskennen?

B Übung: Wie sagt man das mit anderen Worten?

1. Wenn man sehr wenig Geld hat, ist man _____.

2. Wenn man zu viel von etwas gehabt hat, sagt man: „Ich habe _____ voll.“

3. Jemand, der besonders müde ist, nennt man _____.

4. Wenn Sie sich bei einer Vorlesung sehr gelangweilt haben, dann haben Sie sie _____ gefunden.

5. Etwas, was sehr groß ist, kann man auch _____ nennen.

6. Ein anderes Wort für *dumm* ist _____.

Übung: Es kommt darauf an   *It depends*

Ihr Professor spielt die Rolle eines Freundes, dem Sie verschiedene Dinge empfehlen sollen. Sie sagen ihm jedesmal, es kommt darauf an.

> BEISPIEL: Können Sie mir *etwas in der Stadt* empfehlen?
> Es kommt darauf an, *was Sie sehen wollen.*

1. etwas auf der Speisekarte

2. ein gutes Buch

3. eine neue Schallplatte

4. ein Reiseziel

5. ein ruhiges Hotel

6. einen guten Wein

7. einen guten Kassettenrecorder

8. einen neuen Beruf

D **Rollenspiel:** Am Informationsschalter   *Gruppen von 3 Studenten*

Zwei von Ihnen sind Touristen und kennen sich in dieser Stadt nicht aus. Der/
die dritte arbeitet am Infoschalter und gibt Auskunft. Vergessen Sie nicht, „Sie"
zueinander zu sagen. Fangen Sie so an:

> TOURISTEN: Entschuldigung. Dürfen wir Sie um Auskunft bitten?

> BEAMTER/BEAMTIN: Gerne. Wie kann ich Ihnen helfen?

**Ziegenherde (*goat herd*) in
den Straßen von Zermatt.**

Eugen Gomringer was born in Bolivia, to Swiss parents, in 1925. His typically polyglot Swiss background is reflected in the fact that he has written poems in German, Swiss-German dialect, French, English, and Spanish. Gomringer is a leading exponent of concrete poetry **(konkrete Poesie)**, which rejects metaphor, radically simplifies syntax, and considers the printed page a visual as much as a linguistic experience. The following poem consists entirely of nouns followed by relative clauses in strict parallelism. Readers must work out the interrelationships for themselves. Pay particular attention to the verb tenses as you read this poem aloud.

nachwort°   *afterword*

das dorf,° das ich nachts hörte   *village*
der wald, in dem ich schlief

das land, das ich überflog°   *flew across*
die stadt, in der ich wohnte

das haus, das den freunden gehörte
die frau, die ich kannte

das bild, das mich wach hielt°   *kept awake*
der klang,° der mir gefiel   *sound*

das buch, in dem ich las
der stein, den ich fand

der mann, den ich verstand
das kind, das ich lehrte°   *taught*

der baum, den ich blühen° sah   *blooming*
das tier, das ich fürchtete

die sprache, die ich spreche
die schrift,° die ich schreibe   *writing*

Eugen Gomringer (b. 1925)

Grammatik

Verbs with Prepositional Complements

Many verbs use a prepositional phrase to complete, expand, or change their meaning. Such phrases are called *prepositional complements.*

Ich spreche.	*I'm speaking.*
Ich spreche **mit ihm.**	*I'm speaking **with him.***
Ich spreche **gegen ihn.**	*I'm speaking **against him.***

In the examples above, English and German happen to use parallel prepositions. In many cases, however, they do not. For example:

Er wartet **auf** seinen Bruder.	*He's waiting **for** his brother.*
Sie bittet **um** Geld.	*She's asking **for** money.*

For this reason, you must learn the verb and the preposition used with it *together.* Be sure to learn **bitten (bat, hat gebeten) um,** to ask **for.**

Note: Sometimes the complete verbal idea also involves a noun, as in **Angst haben vor.** Sometimes the equivalent English verb is transitive and does *not* have a prepositional complement: **sich erinnern an** = *to remember.*

Here is a list of the verbs with prepositional complements that you already have learned in this and previous chapters.

Angst haben vor (+ *dat.*) *to be afraid of*

Hast du Angst vorm Fliegen?	*Are you afraid of flying?*

bitten um *to ask for, request*

Sie bat mich um Geld.	*She asked me for money.*

erinnern an (+ *acc.*) *to remind of*

Das erinnert mich an etwas Wichtiges.	*That reminds me of something important.*

sich erinnern an (+ *acc.*) *to remember*

Sie hat sich an meinen Geburtstag erinnert.	*She remembered my birthday.*

sich freuen auf (+ *acc.*) *to look forward to*

Ich freue mich auf die Ferien!	*I'm looking forward to the vacation!*

sich gewöhnen an (+ *acc.*) *to get used to*

Sie konnte sich nicht an das kalte Wetter gewöhnen.	*She couldn't get used to the cold weather.*

sich interessieren für *to be interested in*

Interessieren Sich sich für moderne Kunst?

Are you interested in modern art?

sich kümmern um *to look after, take care of, deal with*

Ich werde mich mehr um die
Wohnung kümmern.

*I'll take more care of the
apartment.*

sich verloben mit *to get engaged to*

Rita hat sich mit Rudi verlobt.

Rita got engaged to Rudi.

sich vor·bereiten auf (+ *acc.*) *to prepare for*

Wir bereiten uns auf seinen
Besuch vor.

We're preparing for his visit.

warten auf (+ *acc.*) *to wait for*

Auf wen warten Sie denn?

Whom are you waiting for?

**sprechen (schreiben, lesen, lachen,
usw.) über** (+ *acc.*)

*to talk (write, read, laugh, etc.)
about*

Er hat über seine Heimat
gesprochen.

He talked about his home.

The prepositional phrase is a verbal complement (see pp. 74–75) and constitutes
the second part of the predicate. This means that it will come at the end of
the sentence or phrase:

Sie **kümmert sich** seit Wochen
nicht mehr **um ihre Arbeit.**

*For weeks she hasn't been taking
care of her work.*

Note that when the preposition used with a verb is a two-way preposition,
you must also memorize the case it takes (dative or accusative). Don't just
learn **warten auf**, *to wait for*, but rather **warten auf** + *accusative, to wait for.*
It is useful to know that the two-way prepositions **auf** and **über** almost always
take accusative case when used as verbal complements in a non-spatial sense.

Spatial

Er wartet auf **der** Straße.
He's waiting on the street.

Das Bild hängt über **meiner** Tür.
The picture hangs above my door.

Non-spatial

Er wartet auf **die** Lehrerin.
He's waiting for the teacher.

Sie sprach über **meine** Heimat.
She talked about my homeland.

Note that some verbs have both a direct object *and* a prepositional
complement.

     d.o.   *prep. compl.*
Er bittet **die Beamtin um Auskunft.**

He asks the official for information.

     d.o.   *prep. compl.*
Das erinnert **mich an meine Heimat.**

That reminds me of my home.

Be careful not to confuse prepositional complements (**erinnern *an***) and separable prefixes (***an*kommen**). Although separable prefixes sometimes look like prepositions, they are not, because they have no object.

Prepositional Complement   *Separable Prefix*

object

Er erinnert mich **an meinen Bruder.**   Der Zug kommt um 9 Uhr **an.**

Fragewörter

To ask a question using a verb with a prepositional complement, German forms a question word by attaching the prefix **wo-** to the preposition: **wo- + vor = wovor.** (If the preposition begins with a vowel, the prefix is **wor-: wor- + auf = worauf.**)

Wovor hast du Angst?   ***What*** are you afraid of?
Worauf wartest du denn?   ***What*** are you waiting for?
Wofür interessieren Sie sich?   ***What*** are you interested in?

---

1 Kettenreaktion: Wovor hast *du* denn Angst?

Jeder hat manchmal Angst. Es gibt viele Sachen, vor denen man Angst haben kann. Sagen Sie, wovor Sie Angst haben, und fragen Sie dann weiter. Die Liste gibt Ihnen einige Beispiele, aber Sie können auch frei antworten.

BEISPIEL: Ich habe Angst vor großen Hunden. Wovor hast *du* denn Angst?
Ich habe Angst vor . . .

große Hunde	komplizierte Technik
tiefes Wasser	Klausuren
ein Besuch beim Zahnarzt	das Leben in der Großstadt
das Fliegen	ein neuer Krieg

2 Übung: Darf ich Sie um etwas bitten?

Jeder braucht etwas und bittet die Professorin darum. Was brauchen Sie?

BEISPIEL: STUDENT/IN: Darf ich Sie um Hilfe bitten?
PROFESSOR/IN: Natürlich. Ich helfe Ihnen gerne.

3 Kettenreaktion: Worauf wartest *du* denn?

Die ganze Klasse steht an einer Straßenecke und wartet auf etwas. Sagen Sie, worauf Sie warten, und dann fragen Sie weiter.

BEISPIEL: A: Ich warte auf die Staßenbahn, Linie 2. Worauf wartest *du* denn?
B: Ich warte auf _____.

4 **Kettenreaktion:** Worauf freust *du* dich?

Sagen Sie, worauf Sie sich besonders freuen, und dann fragen Sie weiter.

> BEISPIEL: A: Ich freue mich auf die Semesterferien. Worauf freust *du* dich?
> B: Ich freue mich auf _____.

5 **Kettenreaktion:** Wofür interessierst *du* dich?

Nicht alle interessieren sich für die gleichen Dinge. Sagen Sie, wofür Sie sich besonders interessieren, und dann fragen Sie weiter.

> BEISPIEL: A: Ich interessiere mich für das Mittelalter. Wofür interessierst *du* dich?
> B: Ich interessiere mich für _____.

6 **Übung:** Woran konnten Sie sich nicht gewöhnen?

Wenn man anfängt zu studieren, ist es manchmal schwer, sich an das Neue zu gewöhnen. Sagen Sie Ihrer Professorin, woran Sie sich am Anfang nicht so leicht gewöhnen konnten.

> BEISPIEL: Woran konnten Sie sich hier am Anfang nicht gewöhnen?
> Ich konnte mich nicht an das Klima gewöhnen.

Pronouns as Objects of Prepositions: *da*-compounds and *wo*-compounds

da-compounds

When noun objects of prepositions are replaced by pronouns (e.g., **für meinen Freund—für ihn**), a distinction is made in German between nouns referring to people and nouns referring to inanimate objects.

- Nouns referring to people are replaced by personal pronouns following the preposition, as in English.

Steht Christof hinter Gabriele?	*Is Christof standing behind Gabriele?*
Ja, er steht **hinter ihr.**	*Yes, he's standing **behind her.***
Sprichst du oft mit den Kindern?	*Do you often talk with the children?*
Ja, ich spreche oft **mit ihnen.**	*Yes, I often speak **with them.***
Wartet ihr auf Manfred?	*Are you waiting for Manfred?*
Ja, wir warten **auf ihn.**	*Yes, we're waiting **for him.***

- Nouns referring to inanimate objects, however, are *not* replaced by personal pronouns, but rather by the prefix **da-** attached to the preposition (**da-** + **mit** = **damit**). If the preposition begins with a vowel, the prefix is **dar-** (**dar-** + **auf** = **darauf**).

Steht dein Auto vor oder hinter dem Haus?	*Is your car in front of the house or behind it?*
Es steht **dahinter.**	*It's **behind it.***
Was machen wir mit diesem Schreibtisch?	*What shall we do with this desk?*
Ich weiß nicht, was wir **damit** machen.	*I don't know what we'll do **with it.***
Wie lange warten Sie schon auf den Zug?	*How long have you been waiting for the train?*
Ich warte schon 10 Minuten **darauf.**	*I've been waiting **for it** for 10 minutes.*

Darauf haben wir schon
lange gewartet.

 7 Übung

Antworten Sie wie im Beispielsatz.

    BEISPIEL: Stand er neben dem Fenster?
            Ja, er stand daneben.

1. Interessieren Sie sich für Fremdsprachen?

2. Hast du nach dem Konzert gegessen?

3. Fangt ihr mit der Arbeit an?

4. Hat er lange auf die Straßenbahn gewartet?

5. Hat sie sich an das Wetter gewöhnt?

6. Hat sie wieder um Geld gebeten?

7. Bereitest du dich auf die Deutschstunde vor?

8. Liegt meine Zeitung unter deinem Rucksack?

9. Erinnerst du dich an deinen Urlaub?

10. Haben Sie vor der Bibliothek gewartet?

8 Übung

Diesmal kommt es darauf an, ob das Objekt ein Mensch ist. Wenn nicht, dann müssen Sie mit **da-** antworten.

BEISPIEL: Steht Ingrid neben Hans–Peter?
Ja, sie steht *neben ihm.*

Steht Ingrid neben dem Wagen?
Ja, sie steht *daneben.*

1. Hast du dich an das Wetter gewöhnt?

2. Bist du mit Ursula gegangen?

3. Erinnern Sie sich an die guten alten Zeiten?

4. Können wir über dieses Problem sprechen?

5. Wohnst du bei Frau Lindner?

6. Demonstrieren Sie gegen diesen Politiker?

7. Demonstrieren Sie gegen seine Ideen?

8. Interessieren Sie sich für Sport?

9. Fährst du mit Karin in die Schweiz?

10. Hat er dir für das Geschenk gedankt?

wo-compounds

The same animate/inanimate distinction is made with information questions that begin with a prepositional phrase. To ask a question about a person, German uses the preposition + **wen** or **wem**.

Auf wen warten Sie denn?	*Whom* are you waiting for?
Mit wem spielen die Kinder?	*Whom* are the children playing with?

When asking about a thing, use the **wo**-compounds you have already learned.

Worauf warten Sie denn?	*What* are you waiting for?
Womit spielt das Kind?	*What* is the child playing with?

9 **Übung:** Die laute Party

Sie sind auf einer Party, wo alle sehr laut reden. Ihr Professor, der zu leise spricht, sagt etwas, was Sie nicht genau hören. Fragen Sie den nächsten Studenten, was er gesagt hat.

> BEISPIEL: PROFESSOR: Ich habe auf einen Brief gewartet.
> STUDENT A: Worauf hat er gewartet?
> STUDENT B: Auf einen Brief.
>
> PROFESSOR: Ich habe auf meine Kusine gewartet.
> STUDENT A: Auf wen hat er gewartet?
> STUDENT B: Auf seine Kusine.

1. Ich freue mich auf die Semesterferien.
2. Ich habe mit Professor Hauser gearbeitet.
3. Ich habe mich mit Rita verlobt.
4. Ich muß mich um die Wohnung kümmern.
5. Ich interessiere mich für deutschen Wein.
6. Ich habe Angst vor der Atomenergie.
7. Ich erinnere mich an meinen komischen Onkel.
8. Ich kann mich nicht an diese harte Arbeit gewöhnen.

10 **Partnerarbeit:** Persönliche Fragen

Stellen Sie einander diese Fragen. Freie Antworten.

> BEISPIEL: Wofür interessierst du dich besonders?
> Für das Mittelalter. Und du?
> Für _____.

1. Wofür interessierst du dich besonders?
2. Wovor hast du manchmal Angst?
3. Worauf freust du dich besonders?
4. Worauf mußt du dich im Moment vorbereiten?
5. Woran kannst du dich nicht gewöhnen?

Worüber freuen sich Schüler und Azubis?

Future Tense

Formation: *werden* + infinitive

The future is a compound tense, consisting of an inflected form of the verb **werden** plus a dependent infinitive in final position:

ich **werde schlafen**	*I shall sleep*	wir **werden schlafen**	*we shall sleep*
du **wirst schlafen** Sie **werden schlafen** }	*you will sleep*	ihr **werdet schlafen** Sie **werden schlafen** }	*you will sleep*
er **wird schlafen**	*he will sleep*	sie **werden schlafen**	*they will sleep*

Note: **Werden** as the auxiliary (helping) verb for future tense corresponds to *shall* or *will* in English. Do not confuse it with the modal verb **wollen.**

Er **wird** schlafen.	He **will** *sleep.*
Er **will** schlafen.	He **wants to** *sleep.*

Here is how the future tense of a modal verb is formed. Note that the order of the modal and its dependent infinitive is the *reverse* of English.

Wir werden es **tun müssen.**

We will **have to do** it.

Use of Future Tense

As you already know, German usually uses *present tense* to express future meaning, especially when a time expression makes the future meaning clear.

Er **kommt** morgen zurück.	*He's coming back tomorrow.*

Future tense makes the future meaning explicit, especially in the absence of a time expression such as **morgen.**

Er **wird** selbstverständlich **zurückkommen.**	*Of course he will come back.*

 11 **Übung:** Noch nicht, aber bald.

Sagen Sie, daß etwas noch nicht passiert ist, aber bald passieren wird.

BEISPIEL: Hast du schon gegessen?
Noch nicht, aber ich werde bald essen.

1. Hat es schon geregnet?
2. Hast du schon aufgeräumt?
3. Seid ihr schon skigefahren?
4. Ist er schon aufgestanden?
5. Haben sie schon Deutsch gesprochen?
6. Haben Sie das schon machen müssen?
7. Hat Susi schon angerufen?
8. Seid ihr schon essen gegangen?

Wanting X to Do Y

To express the idea that a person wants something to happen or be done, English uses a direct object and an infinitive phrase.

d.o.   infin.phrase

She would like **the music to stop.**
I don't want **him** **to think that.**

German uses **wollen** or **möchten** followed by a **daß**-clause to express the same idea.

Sie möchte, **daß die Musik aufhört.**
Ich will nicht, **daß er das glaubt.**

12 **Übung:** Der Chef will das so.

Sie arbeiten für einen Chef, der sehr streng (*strict*) ist. Heute zeigen Sie einem neuen Lehrling das Büro. Er fragt immer, ob man alles so machen *muß*. Sagen Sie ihm, der Chef *will*, daß man es so macht.

BEISPIEL: *Müssen* wir um acht im Büro sein?
            Ja, der Chef will, daß wir um acht im Büro sind.

1. *Müssen* wir den ganzen Tag hier bleiben?

2. *Muß* ich immer pünktlich sein?

3. *Dürfen* wir erst um *zehn* Kaffee trinken?

4. *Müssen* wir diese alten Computer benutzen?

5. *Müssen* wir auch samstags arbeiten?

6. *Muß* man immer eine Krawatte tragen?

13 **Übung:** Ich möchte etwas ändern.

Diese Situationen gefallen Ihnen nicht. Sagen Sie, wie Sie sie ändern möchten. Mehrere Antworten sind möglich.

BEISPIEL: Die Musik ist Ihnen zu laut.
            Ich möchte, daß sie leiser wird.
            . . . , daß sie aufhört.

1. Draußen regnet es.

2. Das Wetter ist Ihnen zu kalt.

3. Ihre Mitbewohner quatschen zu viel.

4. Ihr kleiner Bruder stört Sie bei der Arbeit.

5. Das Essen in der Mensa schmeckt Ihnen nicht.

6. Man verschwendet zu viel Glas und Papier.

7. Die Industrie verschmutzt unser Trinkwasser.

8. Ihre Mitbewohner sind Ihnen zu schlampig.

Lesestück Zwei Schweizer stellen ihre Heimat vor

Tips zum Lesen und Lernen

Tips zum Vokabelnlernen

German Equivalents for "only" When "only" is an adjective, use **einzig-**. Otherwise use **nur**.

Ich habe **nur** fünf Mark in der Tasche.	*I have **only** five marks in my pocket.*
Er ist der **einzige** Mechaniker in der Gegend.	*He's the **only** mechanic in the area.*

Übung: Wie sagt man das auf deutsch?

1. I have only one pencil.

2. My only pencil is yellow.

3. A cup of coffee costs only DM 1,00.

4. That was the only restaurant that was open.

Leicht zu merken

die **Barriere, -n** Barriere
(das) **Chinesisch**
der **Dialekt, -e** Dialekt
konservativ konservativ
neutral neutral
die **Neutralität** Neutralität
offiziell offiziell
das **Prozent**
romantisch
stabil stabil
die **Stabilität** Stabilität

Einstieg in den Text

In dem Lesestück auf Seite 403–5 sagt der Schweizer Dr. Anton Vischer, daß er sich manchmal über die Klischees ärgert, die er im Ausland über seine Heimat hört. Wenn man an die Schweiz denkt, denkt man z.B. automatisch an Schokolade, Schweizerkäse und gute Uhren. Diese Klischees sind Ihnen sicher auch bekannt. Aber interessanter ist sicher das Neue, was er über seine Heimat erzählt.

Nachdem Sie den Text gelesen haben, machen Sie sich eine Liste von wenigstens fünf neuen Dingen, die Sie über die Schweiz gelernt haben.

Wortschatz 2

Verben

antworten auf (+ *acc.*) to answer (something); respond to

sich ärgern (über + *acc.*) to get annoyed (at), be annoyed (about)

auf·wachsen (wächst auf), wuchs auf, ist aufgewachsen to grow up

denken, dachte, hat gedacht to think
denken an (+ *acc.*) to think of

sich erholen (von) to recover (from); get well; have a rest

gebrauchen to use

gehören zu to be a part of, be one of

reagieren auf (+ *acc.*) to react to

sich etwas überlegen to consider, ponder, think something over
Das muß ich mir überlegen. I have to think it over.

vor·stellen to introduce; to present
Darf ich meine Tante vorstellen? May I introduce my aunt?

sich wundern (über + *acc.*) to be surprised, amazed (at)

Substantive

der **Ort, -e** place; town
der **Rechtsanwalt, ⸚e** lawyer (*m.*)
der **Schweizer, -** Swiss (*m.*)

das **Gespräch, -e** conversation
das **Werk, -e** work (of art), musical composition

die **Firma,** die **Firmen** firm, company
die **Rechtsanwältin, -nen** lawyer (*f.*)

die **Schweizerin, -nen** Swiss (*f.*)
die **Schwierigkeit, -en** difficulty

Adjektive und Adverbien

froh happy
stolz auf (+ *acc.*) proud of

Andere Vokabel

beides (*sing.*) both things

Nützliche Ausdrücke

eines Tages some day (*in the future*); one day (*in the past or future*)
in Zukunft in the future

Gegensätze

froh ≠ **traurig** happy ≠ sad

Zwei Schweizer stellen ihre Heimat vor

Dr. Anton Vischer,
Rechtsanwalt aus Basel,[1] 45 Jahre alt

In meinem Beruf bin ich für die Investitionen° ausländischer
Firmen verantwortlich und reise darum viel ins Ausland.

5 Dort höre ich oft die alten Klischees über meine Heimat.
Wenn man sagt, daß man aus der Schweiz kommt, denken
viele Menschen automatisch an saubere Straßen, Schokolade, Uhren, Käse und an die Schweizergarde° im Vatikan.
Darüber ärgere ich mich immer ein bißchen. Ich möchte

10 lieber, daß andere wissen, was für eine politische Aus-
nahme° die Schweiz in Europa bildet.° Ich werde versuchen,
Ihnen etwas davon zu beschreiben.

Schon seit dem 13. Jahrhundert hat die Schweiz eine
demokratische Verfassung.° Sie gehört also zu den ältesten

15 und stabilsten Demokratien der Welt. In beiden Weltkriegen

investments

Swiss Guard

exception / constitutes

constitution

„In den Bergen kann man sich körperlich und seelisch erholen."

1. Basel (*French* Bâle), Swiss city on the Rhine.

Kinder mit Schlitten (*sleds*) in der Altstadt von Basel.

ist die Schweiz neutral geblieben, und sie hat sich ihre Neutralität und ihre politische Stabilität bis heute bewahrt.°

    Einige werden unsere Gesellschaft wohl zu konservativ finden. In einem Kanton² ist das Wahlrecht° der Frauen sogar noch beschränkt.° Aber man darf nicht vergessen, daß es in der Schweiz durchaus° auch einen Platz für soziale Kritik° gibt. Das zeigen die Werke unserer bekanntesten Schriftsteller wie Max Frisch und Friedrich Dürrenmatt.³

    Jemand fragte mich einmal, ob ich stolz bin, Schweizer zu sein. Darauf habe ich sofort mit „ja" reagiert, aber in Zukunft werde ich mir die Antwort genauer überlegen. Ich werde einfach sagen, ich bin *froh*, Schweizer zu sein, denn meine Heimat ist das schönste Land, das ich kenne. Da ich meine Freizeit immer auf Bergtouren verbringe, ist mein Leben mit der Alpenlandschaft eng verbunden.° Für mich sind die Alpen der einzige Ort, wo ich mich körperlich und seelisch° erholen kann. Das klingt vielleicht romantisch, aber eigentlich bin ich ein ganz praktischer Mensch."

hat . . . bewahrt = *preserved*

sufferage
restricted
definitely / criticism

eng verbunden = *closely connected*

körperlich . . . seelisch = *physically and emotionally*

---

2. Switzerland is composed of twenty–three cantons, each with considerable autonomy. Swiss women have full suffrage in all cantons except in local elections in Appenzell.

3. Max Frisch (1911–1991) and Friedrich Dürrenmatt (1921–1990). Each wrote novels, essays and plays.

Nicole Wehrli

Dolmetscherin° aus Biel, 24 Jahre alt — *interpreter*

„Ich bin in der zweisprachigen° Stadt Biel—auf französisch — *bilingual*
Bienne—aufgewachsen, direkt an der Sprachgrenze zwischen der französischen und der deutschen Schweiz. Bei
uns können Sie manchmal auf der Straße Gespräche hören,
in denen die Menschen beides—Französisch *und* Deutsch—
miteinander reden. In der Schule habe ich dann Latein,° — *Latin*
Englisch und Italienisch gelernt. Sie werden sich also nicht
wundern, daß ich mich für Fremdsprachen interessiere.
Eines Tages möchte ich sogar mit Chinesisch anfangen.

Die Eidgenossenschaft[4] ist wohl ein Unikum° in Europa, — *something unique*
denn sie ist viersprachig. Die Sprachbarrieren waren lange
Zeit ein großes Hindernis° für die politische Vereinigung der — *obstacle*
Kantone und machen uns heute noch manchmal Schwierigkeiten. Achtzehn Prozent der Bevölkerung° hat Franzö- — *population*
sisch als Muttersprache, zwölf Prozent sprechen Italienisch
und etwa° ein Prozent Rätoromanisch.[5] Unser „Schwyzer- — *approximately*
dütsch"[6] können die meisten Deutschen nicht verstehen.
Da unsere Kinder das Hochdeutsch° erst in der Schule lernen — *High German*
müssen, ist es für sie oft so schwer wie eine Fremdsprache.
Die geschriebene und offizielle Sprache in den Schulen
bleibt Hochdeutsch, aber nach dem Unterricht° gebrauchen — **nach . . . Unterrricht** = *after class*
Lehrer und Schüler den Dialekt, wenn sie miteinander
reden."

„Mi Wält!"

4. Confederation, i.e., *Confoederatio Helvetica:* official designation for the Swiss Republic.

5. Rhaetoromansch, or simply Romansh, is a Romance language—a remnant of the original Roman occupation in the Alpine territories—spoken by about 40,000 rural Swiss in the canton of Grisons (**Graubünden**). Long under threat of extinction, it was declared one of the four national languages in 1938.

6. In High German, Schweizerdeutsch (Swiss-German dialect).

1. Was ist Dr. Vischer von Beruf?

2. Wofür ist er verantwortlich?

3. Welche Klischees hört er über die Schweiz, wenn er im Ausland ist?

4. Wie reagiert er darauf?

5. Seit wann hat die Schweiz eine demokratische Verfassung?

6. Kennen Sie andere neutrale Länder?

7. Was macht Herr Vischer in seiner Freizeit?

8. Warum ist die Stadt Biel, wo Nicole Wehrli aufgewachsen ist, besonders interessant?

9. Was war die größte Schwierigkeit bei der Vereinigung der Schweiz?

10. Wie viele Schweizer sind deutschsprachig?

11. Warum haben manche Deutsche Schwierigkeiten, die Schweizer zu verstehen?

12. Was für Schwierigkeiten haben die Kinder in der Schweiz mit der deutschen Sprache?

Situationen aus dem Alltag

Wie stellt man sich vor?

Wie stellt man sich oder einen Bekannten auf deutsch vor? Es kommt auf die Situation an. Unten sind vier verschiedene Situationen, aber zuerst ein paar Bemerkungen (*comments*).

Unter jungen Menschen ist es nicht so formell: Man sagt einfach seinen Namen und „Hallo" oder „Tag," wie zum Beispiel in *Situation 1* (unten). Wie Sie schon wissen, sagen Studenten sofort „du" zueinander.

Wenn man ältere Menschen zum ersten Mal kennenlernt, ist es formeller (*Situationen 2* and *3*). Man sagt **angenehm** oder **freut mich** oder **sehr erfreut** (alle drei = *pleased to meet you*). Natürlich sagt man „Sie" statt „du."

In allen Situationen ist es höflich, einander die Hand zu geben (*shake hands*). Das machen die Europäer viel öfter als die Amerikaner.

1. Die Studentin Sonja stellt ihrem Freund Wolfgang ihre Freundin Margaret aus Amerika vor.

   SONJA: Hallo Wolfgang! Darf ich vorstellen? Das ist meine Freundin Margaret aus Chicago.

   WOLFGANG: (*gibt ihr die Hand*) Hallo Margaret!

   MARGARET: Hallo Wolfgang.

   WOLFGANG: Nett, dich kennenzulernen.

   MARGARET: Danke, gleichfalls.

2. Bernd, 20, stellt seiner Mutter einen Freund vor.

BERND: Mutter, ich möchte dir meinen Freund Theo vorstellen.
FRAU RINGSTEDT: Freut mich, Sie kennenzulernen, Theo.
THEO: Angenehm, Frau Ringstedt. (*Sie geben sich die Hände.*)

3. Der amerikanische Austauschstudent Michael Hayward stellt sich einem Professor in der Sprechstunde (*office hour*) vor.

MICHAEL HAYWARD: Guten Tag, Professor Mohr. Darf ich mich vorstellen? Mein Name ist Hayward. (*Gibt ihm die Hand.*)
PROF. MOHR: Guten Tag, Herr Hayward. Bitte nehmen Sie Platz.

4. Zwei Geschäftsleute treffen sich auf einer Konferenz.

FRAU MÜLLER: Guten Tag, mein Name ist Müller.
HERR BEHRENS: Freut mich, Frau Müller. Behrens.

Gruppenarbeit: Rollenspiele

1. Darf ich mich vorstellen?
Sie sind alle Studenten auf einer Party, wo sie einander noch nicht kennen. Stehen Sie alle auf und stellen Sie sich einander vor.

2. Ich möchte euch meine Freunde vorstellen.
Zwei Studenten spielen die Rollen der Eltern. Ein dritter Student bringt zwei Freunde nach Hause und stellt sie den Eltern vor.

3. Now pretend that you're all business people at a convention. Introduce yourselves to each other. (In this kind of situation, people usually give only their last names.)

Zum Schluß

Sprechen wir miteinander

A **Partnerarbeit:** Was wird sein?

Lesen Sie die Zukunft Ihres Partners aus seiner Hand. Wie sieht seine Zukunft aus?

BEISPIEL: Du wirst lange leben. Du wirst dich oft verloben und dreimal heiraten (*get married*). Du wirst . . .

B **Gruppenarbeit:** Seid ihr optimistisch oder pessimistisch?

Wie wird die Welt in fünfzig Jahren aussehen? Wird das Leben besser sein oder nicht? Werden die Menschen glücklicher sein? Sagen Sie Ihre eigene Meinung.

C **Partnerarbeit:** Woran denkst du denn?

Stellen Sie einander Fragen mit diesen Verben.

> BEISPIEL: A: Woran denkst du denn?
> B: Ich denke an unser Gespräch von gestern.

1. denken an
2. sich freuen auf
3. sich interessieren für
4. sich ärgern über
5. sich kümmern um

6. sich erinnern an
7. warten auf
8. Angst haben vor
9. sich wundern über
10. sich vorbereiten (müssen) auf

D **Gruppenarbeit:** Was ist Ihr Hobby?

Wie verbringen Sie Ihre Freizeit? Haben Sie ein Hobby? Sprechen wir ein bißchen darüber. Machen wir zuerst eine Liste von Möglichkeiten.

1. Was kann man sammeln? Zum Beispiel: Briefmarken (*stamps*)

2. Spielen Sie ein Musikinstrument? Welches? Zum Beispiel: Klavier (*piano*)

3. Machen Sie gern etwas Kreatives? Zum Beispiel: Fotografieren

4. Spielen Sie gern etwas oder treiben Sie Sport? Zum Beispiel: Schach (*chess*)

5. Jetzt sprechen wir über unsere Hobbies. Stellen Sie einander Fragen darüber. Hier sind einige Möglichkeiten:

    A: Wofür interessierst du dich?
    B: Ich interessiere mich für _____.
    A: Warum interessierst du dich dafür? usw.

    A: Wie lange sammelst du schon _____?
    B: Seit _____.
    A: Kostet das viel Geld? usw.

E **Gruppenarbeit:** Reaktionen: Das lohnt sich. / Das lohnt sich nicht.

Wer hat etwas Interessantes am Wochenende oder im nächsten Sommer vor? Sagen Sie, was Sie vorhaben. Die anderen müssen dann mit ihrer Meinung darauf reagieren.

> BEISPIEL: STUDENT A: Am Wochenende habe ich vor, den neuen Film „_____" zu sehen.
> STUDENT B: Ja, das lohnt sich! Ich habe ihn schon letzte Woche gesehen. *oder*
> Das lohnt sich nicht. Ich habe gehört, er ist blöd.

F **Partnerarbeit:** Ich will, daß du dich änderst.

Sagen Sie Ihrem Partner, wie er sein Leben ändern soll. Dann antwortet er darauf. (Das ist nur ein Spiel. Nehmen Sie es also nicht zu ernst!)

> BEISPIEL: A: Ich will, daß du früher aufstehst!
> B: Warum denn? Ich schlafe doch gern. *Ich möchte, daß du . . .*

Schreiben Sie zu Hause

G For each pair of sentences below, fill in the past participle cued in English in the first sentence. In the second sentence, it is used as an attributive adjective. Don't forget the adjective ending!

1. Wer hat im Zimmer _____? (*straightened up*)
   Es ist schön, in einem _____ Zimmer zu sitzen.

2. Letztes Jahr habe ich sehr viel Geld _____. (*saved*)
   Mit meinem _____ Geld will ich eine Reise ins Ausland machen.

3. Hat man dir den Rucksack _____? (*stolen*)
   Ja, und meine neue Kamera war leider im _____ Rucksack.

4. Ich habe meine Hemden _____. (*washed*)
   Die _____ Hemden hängen draußen hinter dem Haus.

5. Der Mann, mit dem sie sich verlobt hat, ist immer schön _____. (*dressed*)
   Nur schön _____ Männer gehen mit ihr aus.

6. Diese Schreibmaschine hat schon meine Mutter als Studentin _____ (*used*).
   Eine _____ Schreibmaschine kann man billig bekommen.

7. Frau Schwarzer hat ihren Wagen selber _____. (*repaired*)
   Ihr _____ Wagen läuft jetzt gut.

H **Aufsatzthemen** Wählen Sie eine Frage und schreiben Sie eine Seite darüber.

1. Gibt es Sprachbarrieren in Ihrer Heimat? Beschreiben Sie einige.

2. Kennen Sie Ausländer, die in Amerika leben und deren Muttersprache nicht Englisch ist? Was für Schwierigkeiten gibt es für solche Menschen? Vielleicht sind Sie selber Ausländer. Welche Schwierigkeiten haben Sie gehabt?

I Wie sagt man das auf deutsch?

1. Are you looking forward to the end of the semester?

2. Yes, I'm planning to go skiing in Switzerland.

3. That sounds good. Have a good trip.

4. What do you think of when you hear the word "Switzerland?"

5. I remember my father's aunt who came from Switzerland.

6. Excuse me, do you know your way around in the library?

7. A bit. How can I help you?

8. I'm interested in modern writers.

9. I'll have to think it over.

10. What are you so annoyed about?

11. My roommate asked me for money again this morning.

12. Will you give it to him?

Profile of Switzerland

Area: 41,288 square kilometers; 15,941 square miles
Population: 6,700,000, or 162 people per square kilometer (420 per square mile)
Currency: Swiss franc (*Schweizer Franken*); 1 sfr = 100 Rappen or Centimes
Major Cities: Berne (*Bern*, capital, pop. 136,292), Zürich (largest city, pop. 346,879), Basel, Geneva (*Genf*), Lausanne
Religions: 48% Roman Catholic, 44% Protestant

Switzerland has one of the highest per capita incomes in the world, as well as one of the highest standards of living. The literacy rate is 99.5%. The rivers of the Alps provide inexpensive hydroelectric power. The mountains also attract countless tourists, thus creating Switzerland's main service industry.

Switzerland has not sent its troops into foreign wars since 1515. It adheres to its neutrality even to the extent of staying out of the United Nations and the European Economic Community (Common Market). It is, however, a member of several special UN agencies. The second headquarters of the U.N. is in Geneva, which is also the seat of the International Red Cross and of the World Council of Churches.

Marktplatz und altes Rathaus. (Basel)

Man kauft schweizer Waren in der ganzen Welt.

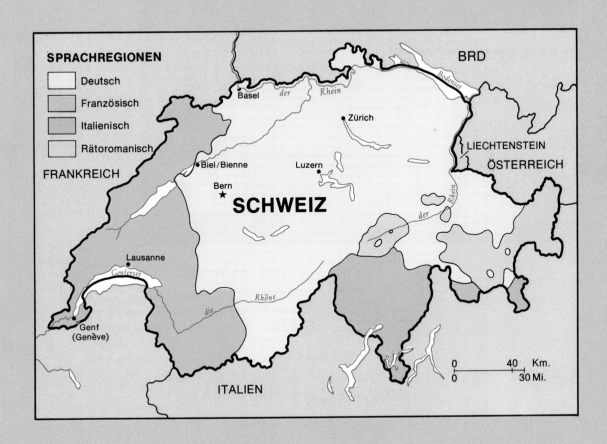

SPRACHREGIONEN

Deutsch
Französisch
Italienisch
Rätoromanisch

FRANKREICH

BRD

Basel

der Rhein

Zürich

LIECHTENSTEIN
ÖSTERREICH

Biel/Bienne

Luzern

Bern

★ SCHWEIZ

der Rhein

Lausanne

Genfersee

Rhône

die

Genf
(Genève)

0   40   Km.
0   30 Mi.

ITALIEN

Die Schweiz   411

Österreich

Communicative Goals
- Getting a room in a hotel
- Expressing wishes contrary-to-fact
- Talking about contrary-to-fact situations
- Making suggestions
- Making polite requests

Cultural Goal
- Learning about Austria

Lyrik zum Vorlesen   Ernst Jandl, „ottos mops"

Grammatik   General Subjunctive: Present Tense   •   Other Uses of the General Subjunctive   (Conditions Contrary to Fact   •   Wishes Contrary to Fact   •   Hypothetical Statements and Questions   •   Polite Requests)

Lesestück   Zwei Österreicher stellen sich vor

Situationen aus dem Alltag   Im Hotel

Almanach   Profile of Austria

Dialoge

Auf Urlaub in Österreich

RICHARD: Ursula, hast du noch österreichisches Geld?

URSULA: Nein, warum? Hast du keine Schillinge mehr?

RICHARD: Leider nicht. Wenn es nicht so spät wäre, könnte ich noch bei der Bank wechseln.

URSULA: Das macht ja nichts. An der Hotelkasse kannst du wechseln, oder wir zahlen im Restaurant entweder mit Kreditkarte oder mit Reiseschecks.

An der Rezeption

TOURIST: Grüß Gott! Hätten Sie noch ein Zimmer frei für heute nacht?

ANGESTELLTER: Wünschen Sie ein Einzelzimmer oder ein Doppelzimmer?

TOURIST: Am liebsten hätte ich ein Einzelzimmer mit Dusche.

ANGESTELLTER: Das könnte ich Ihnen erst morgen geben. Im Moment ist nur ein Doppelzimmer mit Bad frei.

TOURIST: Was würde das denn kosten?

ANGESTELLTER: 500 Schilling mit Frühstück.

TOURIST: Dürfte ich mir das Zimmer ansehen?

ANGESTELLTER: Selbstverständlich. (*Gibt ihm den Schlüssel*) Das wäre Zimmer Nummer 14 im ersten Stock.

Ausflug zum Heurigen

ANDREAS: Hast du heute abend etwas Besonderes vor?

ESTHER: Nein, warum?

ANDREAS: Dann könnten wir endlich nach Grinzing zum Heurigen[1] fahren.

ESTHER: Ja, höchste Zeit! Und es wäre auch schön, dort zu essen.

ANDREAS: Gute Idee! Ich hab' schon Riesenhunger.

ESTHER: Dann sollten wir gleich losfahren.

WEINGUT   HEURIGER
WELSER
1190 WIEN-HEILIGENSTADT
PROBUSGASSE 12

---

1. **Heurige** are taverns in the neighborhood of Vienna, each originally belonging to a vineyard and serving wine (called **Heuriger**) pressed from the previous October (**heuer** = *this year*). **Grinzing** is a suburb of Vienna.

On Vacation in Austria

RICHARD: Ursula, do you have any more Austrian money?

URSULA: No. Why? Haven't you got any more schillings?

RICHARD: Unfortunately not. If it weren't so late, I could still change money at the bank.

URSULA: That doesn't matter. You can change money at the hotel cashier, or we'll pay in the restaurant, either with credit card or with traveler's checks.

At the Reception Desk

TOURIST: Hello, would you still have a room free for tonight?

HOTEL CLERK: Do you want a single or a double room?

TOURIST: I'd prefer a single room with shower.

HOTEL CLERK: I couldn't give you that until tomorrow. At the moment there is only a double room with bath available.

TOURIST: What would that cost?

HOTEL CLERK: Five hundred schillings with breakfast.

TOURIST: May I please have a look at the room?

HOTEL CLERK: Of course. (Hands him the key) That would be room number 14 on the second floor.

Outing to a *Heuriger*

ANDREAS: Have you got anything special planned for tonight?

ESTHER: No, why?

ANDREAS: Then we could finally go to Grinzing to a *Heuriger*.

ESTHER: Yes, high time! And it would be nice to eat there too.

ANDREAS: Good idea! I'm already famished.

ESTHER: Then we ought to leave right away.

Wortschatz 1

Verben

los·fahren (fährt los), fuhr los, ist losgefahren   to depart, start, leave

wechseln   to change (money)

Substantive

der/die **Angestellte, -n**   employee

der **Ausflug, ¨e**   outing, excursion

der **Scheck, -s**   check
   der **Reisescheck, -s**   traveler's check

der **Schilling**   Austrian shilling

der **Stock**   floor (*of a building*)
   der **erste Stock**   the second floor
   im ersten Stock   on the second floor

das **Bad, ¨er**   bath
   ein Bad nehmen   to take a bath

das **Badezimmer, -**   bathroom

das **Doppelzimmer, -**   double room

das **Einzelzimmer, -**   single room

das **Erdgeschoß**   first floor, ground floor

die **Bank, -en**   bank

die **Dusche, -n**   shower

die **Kasse, -n**   cash register; cashier's office

die **Kreditkarte, -n**   credit card

die **Nummer, -n**   number

die **Rezeption**   (hotel) reception desk

Adjektive

österreichisch   Austrian

Andere Vokabeln

entweder . . . oder   either . . . or

Nützliche Ausdrücke

Grüß Gott!   Hello! (*in southern Germany and Austria*)

höchste Zeit   high time

Gegensätze

entweder . . . oder ≠ weder . . . noch   either . . . or ≠ neither . . . nor

Mit anderen Worten

der Riesenhunger = sehr großer Hunger

Variationen

A Persönliche Fragen

1. Haben Sie je Geld wechseln müssen? Warum?

2. Zahlen Sie im Restaurant mit Kreditkarte, Scheck oder Bargeld (*cash*)?

3. Haben Sie je in einem Hotel übernachtet? Wo war das?

4. Würden sie lieber in Jugendherbergen oder in Hotels übernachten, wenn Sie nach Österreich reisen? Warum?

5. Haben Sie ein Doppel- oder ein Einzelzimmer im Studentenwohnheim?

6. Andreas hat Riesenhunger. Man kann auch Riesendurst haben. Wann haben Sie Riesenhunger oder Riesendurst?

7. Grinzing ist ein Ausflugsort in der Nähe von Wien. Kennen Sie in dieser Gegend einen schönen Ausflugsort?

B Übung: Was ist ein Riese?

Ein berühmter Riese in der Bibel hieß Goliath. Sie kennen schon das Wort „riesengroß." So nennt man etwas sehr Großes. Jetzt wissen Sie auch, wenn man sehr hungrig ist, sagt man: „Ich habe Riesenhunger!" Also:

1. Einen riesengroßen Hunger nennt man auch *einen Riesenhunger*.

2. Einen sehr sehr großen Koffer nennt man auch _____.

3. Eine ganz große Freude ist _____.

4. Wenn viele Menschen zusammen demonstrieren, dann hat man _____.

5. Wenn ein Supertanker einen Unfall hat und sein Öl ins Meer fließt, dann ist das _____.

6. Ein sehr großes Hotel kann man auch _____ nennen.

C Übung: Wie wäre das?   *How would that be?*

Ihr Professor schlägt Ihnen etwas vor. Reagieren Sie darauf mit Ihren eigenen Worten: **Das wäre . . . !**

BEISPIEL: Sollen wir einen Ausflug machen?
Ja, das wäre toll!

ins Kino gehen?	uns die Stadt ansehen?
Geld wechseln?	zu Hause hocken?
Freunde einladen?	das Zimmer aufräumen?
skifahren gehen?	im Restaurant essen?
Theaterkarten kaufen?	eine Radtour machen?

Übung: entweder . . . oder

Sagen Sie, Sie machen entweder **dies** oder **das.**

> BEISPIEL: Was trinken Sie heute abend?
> Ich trinke entweder Tee oder Kaffee.

1. Wohin fahren Sie im Sommer?

2. Was möchten Sie gern essen?

3. Mit wem wollen Sie Tennis spielen?

4. Welche Fremdsprache werden Sie nächstes Jahr lernen?

5. Wer war denn das?

6. Wissen Sie, wo Ihr Hotelzimmer ist?

7. Wie kann man im Hotel zahlen?

8. Wann wollen Sie das nächste Mal skifahren?

Lyrik zum Vorlesen

The Austrian poet Ernst Jandl was born in Vienna in 1925. He has been a *Gymnasium* teacher since 1949. In the following poem, he shows that it is possible to tell a whole story using only one vowel. Reading it aloud will be a good review of the German long and short **o!**

ottos mops°   mutt

ottos mops trotzt°   *won't obey*
otto: fort° mops fort   *go away*
ottos mops hopst° fort   *hops*
otto: soso

otto holt koks°   *coal briquettes*
otto holt obst°   *fruit*
otto horcht°   *listens*
otto: mops mops
otto hofft

ottos mops klopft°   *knocks*
otto: komm mops komm
ottos mops kommt
ottos mops kotzt°   *pukes*
otto: ogottogott

Ernst Jandl (b. 1925)

Grammatik

General Subjunctive: Present Tense[2]

You can have various attitudes toward what you are saying. On the one hand, you can present something as a fact. On the other hand, you can present it as hypothetical, conjectural, or contrary to fact. Both German and English have two different sets of verb forms for these two possibilities, called the *indicative* and the *subjunctive moods* (from Latin *modus*, "manner, mode, way").

Up to now, you have been using the *indicative mood* to talk about what is definite, certain, and real.

Barbara **ist** nicht hier.	*Barbara **isn't** here.*
Ich **glaube** das.	*I **believe** that.*

The *subjunctive mood* (German: **der Konjunktiv**) is used to talk about hypothetical, uncertain, or unreal situations, and also to make polite statements and requests.

Wenn Barbara nur hier **wäre!**	*If only Barbara **were** here!*
Wenn ich mehr Zeit **hätte** . . .	*If I **had** more time . . .*
Würden Sie mir bitte helfen?	***Would** you please help me?*

English *present* subjunctive is signalled by what look like *past-tense* forms or by ***would*** + a verb.[3]

*If they **lived** nearby, we **would** visit them.*	(condition contrary to fact)
*If only **I had** more time!*	(wish contrary to fact)
***I would like** to have a room.*	(polite request)

Note that the verbs *lived* and *had* in the examples above are identical to the past in *form*, but have present tense meaning.

*If they **lived** nearby . . .*	(right now)
*If only **I had** more time!*	(right now)

Present Subjunctive of Weak Verbs

The present tense of the general subjunctive in German is also based on past indicative forms. In the case of *weak* verbs (see pp. 164, 285), the present subjunctive is *identical* to the simple past indicative you have already learned.

wenn ich wohnte	*if I lived*	wenn wir wohnten	*if we lived*
wenn du wohntest⎱ wenn Sie wohnten⎰	*if you lived*	wenn ihr wohntet⎱ wenn Sie wohnten⎰	*if you lived*
wenn sie wohnte	*if she lived*	wenn sie wohnten	*if they lived*

2. There is also a special subjunctive in German that you will learn in *Kapitel 16*.

3. The only separate subjunctive form in English is *were* in *I were* and *he were*.

Wishes Contrary to Fact

A contrary-to-fact wish is expressed in German by a **wenn**-clause in the subjunctive (verb last) with an added **nur**.

Wenn er **nur** näher **wohnte!**   *If **only** he **lived** closer!*

---

 1 Übung: Wenn es nur anders wäre!

Ihre Professorin beschreibt Ihnen eine Situation im Indikativ. Sie wünschen im Konjunktiv, daß es anders wäre.

BEISPIEL: Hans-Peter wohnt nicht hier.   *Hans-Peter doesn't live here.*
    Wenn er nur hier wohnte!   *If only he lived here!*

1. Petra kauft das nicht.

2. Georg beeilt sich nicht.

3. Der Urlaub dauert nicht länger.

4. Ich erhole mich nicht.

5. Die Gäste setzen sich nicht.

6. Maria macht die Tür nicht zu.

7. Robert bestellt nicht genug Bier.

8. Meine Freunde besuchen mich nicht.

9. Meine Großeltern wohnen nicht bei uns.

10. Inge wechselt ihr Geld nicht.

Present Subjunctive of Strong Verbs

The present subjunctive of strong verbs is also based on their past indicative forms, but these forms are *modified* according to the following three-step procedure.

Step 1: Take the simple past stem of the verb

   fahren → **fuhr-**   gehen → **ging-**   laufen → **lief-**   sein → **war-**

Step 2: Add an umlaut to the stem vowel whenever possible

   führ-   ging-   lief-   wär-

Step 3: Add the following personal endings:

ich wäre	*I would be*	wir wären	*we would be*	
du wärest		ihr wäret		
Sie wären	*you would be*	Sie wären	*you would be*	
er wäre	*he would be*	sie wären	*they would be*	

Note the difference between the present subjunctive endings and the past indicative endings of strong verbs:

present subjunctive (would go)	*past indicative* (went)
ich ginge	ich ging
du gingest	du gingst
sie ginge	sie ging
wir gingen	wir gingen
ihr ginget	ihr gingt
sie gingen	sie gingen

Only the **wir** and the plural **sie** endings are the same.

2 Übung

Review your knowledge of the simple past stems of these strong verbs.

BEISPIEL: laufen **lief**

scheinen	finden
kommen	gehen
anfangen	fahren
gefallen	sein
tun	schlafen
aussteigen	bekommen

3 Übung: Wenn es nur anders wäre!

Jetzt beschreibt Ihr Professor eine Situation im Indikativ. Sie wünschen im Konjunktiv, daß es anders wäre.

BEISPIEL: Meine Gäste gehen nicht nach Hause.
Wenn sie nur nach Hause gingen!

1. Gabi läuft nicht schnell.
2. Die Sonne scheint nicht.
3. Robert kommt nicht um zwölf.
4. Karin geht nicht mit uns spazieren.
5. Wir sind nicht alt genug.
6. Das Kind schläft nicht länger.
7. Wir bekommen kein Doppelzimmer.
8. Laura findet ihre Kreditkarte nicht.
9. Die Uhr geht nicht richtig.
10. Unsere Freunde fahren nicht nach Amerika.
11. Er fängt nicht an.
12. Die Wohnung gefällt uns nicht.
13. Das tut Marie nicht gern.
14. Hier steigen wir nicht aus.

Present Subjunctive of Modal Verbs

To form the present subjunctive of modal verbs, take the past indicative, *including endings,* and add an umlaut to the stem vowel of *only* those verbs that have an umlaut in their infinitive.

infinitive		*past indicative*	
dürfen	*to be allowed*	**ich durfte**	*I was allowed*

Present Subjunctive			
ich **dürfte**	*I would be allowed*	wir **dürften**	*we would be allowed*
du **dürftest** Sie **dürften**	*you would be allowed*	ihr **dürftet** Sie **dürften**	*you would be allowed*
er **dürfte**	*he would be allowed*	sie **dürften**	*they would be allowed*

Similarly:

past indicative		*present subjunctive*	
ich konnte	*I was able to*	ich **könnte**	*I could, would be able to*
ich mochte	*I liked*	ich **möchte**	*I would like to*
ich mußte	*I had to*	ich **müßte**	*I would have to*

The present subjunctive of **sollen** and **wollen,** however, is *not* umlauted, and so looks just like the past indicative.

ich sollte	*I was supposed to*	ich **sollte**	*I ought to*
ich wollte	*I wanted to*	ich **wollte**	*I would want to*

 4 **Übung:** Wenn es nur anders wäre!

Ihre Professorin beschreibt wieder eine Situation im Indikativ. Sie wünschen im Konjunktiv, daß es anders wäre.

> BEISPIEL: Christine kann kein Englisch.
> Wenn sie nur Englisch *könnte!*

1. Wir können kein Französisch.

2. Die Gäste müssen nach Hause.

3. Wir dürfen nicht länger bleiben.

4. Esther will nicht nach Grinzing.

5. Die Kinder können nicht mitfahren.

6. Unsere Freunde müssen bald abfahren.

7. Sie dürfen nicht alles sagen.

8. Andreas will nicht helfen.

5 Übung: Hören Sie gut zu! *Mit geschlossenen Büchern*

Listen to your instructor say each pair of sentences, then say which one is past indicative and which present subjunctive. Then, with open books, repeat each sentence aloud and give the English equivalent.

1. Durfte sie das machen? / Dürfte sie das machen?

2. Wir könnten ihn abholen. / Wir konnten ihn abholen.

3. Sie müßte das wissen. / Sie mußte das wissen.

4. Mochte er das Frühstück? / Möchte er das Frühstück?

Using Subjunctive to Make Suggestions

Wir **könnten** zusammen ausgehen.	*We **could** go out together.*
Wir **sollten** eigentlich hier bleiben.	*We really **ought** to stay here.*

---

6 Partnerarbeit: Was könnten wir heute machen?

Partner A sagt etwas Schönes, was Sie machen **könnten.** Partner B sagt aber, sie **sollten** eigentlich etwas anderes machen.

BEISPIEL: Wir *könnten* zusammen spazierengehen.
Aber wir *sollten* eigentlich das Zimmer aufräumen.

Hier haben Sie einige Möglichkeiten:

etwas Schönes	*etwas Wichtiges*
spazierengehen	das Zimmer aufräumen
Karten spielen	Hausaufgaben machen
tanzen gehen	Lebensmittel einkaufen
Musik hören	uns auf die Klausur vorbereiten

haben, werden, wissen

To form the present subjunctive of the verbs **haben, werden,** and **wissen,** take the past indicative, *including endings,* and add an umlaut to the stem vowel:

past indicative		*present subjunctive*	
ich hatte	*I had*	ich **hätte**	*I would have*
ich wurde	*I became*	ich **würde**	*I would become; I would*
ich wußte	*I knew*	ich **wüßte**	*I would know*

Polite Requests: subjunctive + *gern*

Ich hätte gern ein Einzelzimmer mit Bad.

I would like to have a single
room with bath.

Ich wüßte gern, wo die Kasse
ist.

I would like to know where the
cashier is.

7 **Kettenreaktion:** Was hätten Sie gern?

Sagen Sie, was Sie gern hätten.

> BEISPIEL: Ich hätte gern ein frisches Brötchen. Und du?
> Ich hätte gern ein-_____.

 8 **Kettenreaktion:** Was wüßten Sie gern?

Sagen Sie, Sie gern wüßten.

> BEISPIEL: Ich wüßte gern, wo ich Geld verdienen könnte. Und du?
> Ich wüßte gern, _____.

Present Subjunctive with *würden* + infinitive

In *Kapitel 7* you learned how to use the subjunctive construction **würde** +
infinitive to express intentions, opinions, preferences, and polite requests. This
construction is an alternative to the one-word present subjunctive forms you
have been learning in this chapter.

There is no difference in meaning between the following clauses:

Er **käme** . . .
Er **würde kommen** . . . } *He would come* . . .

The present subjunctive with **würden** often replaces the one-word form of
weak verbs that is indistinguishable from the past indicative. To avoid this
ambiguity:

Ich **sagte** das nicht.

*I didn't say that. / I wouldn't say
that.*

is replaced by:

Ich **würde** das nicht **sagen.**

I wouldn't say that.

Spoken German also avoids using the one-word form of many strong verbs by
replacing it with the subjunctive with **würden** (but *not* in the case of the
frequently used verbs **sein, haben,** and the modals).

Ich **tränke** Wein . . .
Ich **würde** Wein **trinken** . . .

is not as frequently heard as:
I'd drink wine . . .

**Ohne
Zeitung
hätten
Sie
weniger
zu
sagen.**

**DIE ZEITUNGEN
IN DEUTSCHLAND.**

9 Übung: Was würden Sie machen?

Sagen Sie, was Sie in diesen Situationen machen würden.

> BEISPIEL: Was würden Sie machen, wenn Sie diese Woche frei hätten?
> Ich würde nach Hause fahren.

Was würden Sie machen . . .

1. wenn Sie 500 Schilling hätten?

2. wenn Sie Hunger hätten?

3. wenn Sie Durst hätten?

4. wenn Sie Musik hören wollten?

5. wenn Sie Wanderlust hätten?

6. wenn Sie knapp bei Kasse wären?

7. wenn Sie Spaß haben wollten?

8. wenn Sie sich das Studium nicht leisten könnten?

Other Uses of the General Subjunctive

Conditions Contrary to Fact

A **wenn**-clause states the condition contrary to fact: "If x were true, then y would be true."

Wenn wir jetzt in Deutschland wären . . .	*If we were in Germany now . . .*
Wenn ich mehr Geld hätte . . .	*If I had more money . . .*

The main clause (with an optional **dann** as the first word) draws the unreal conclusion.

. . . (dann) würden wir sehr schnell Deutsch lernen.	*. . .(then) we would learn German very quickly.*
. . . (dann) brauchte ich nicht so viel zu arbeiten.	*. . . (then) I wouldn't need to work so much.*

Putting them together:

> Wenn wir jetzt in Deutschland wären, würden wir sehr schnell Deutsch lernen.
> Wenn ich mehr Geld hätte, dann brauchte ich nicht so viel zu arbeiten.

Conditional sentences may begin either with the **wenn**-clause (as in the two previous examples) *or* with the conclusion clause.[4]

> Wir würden sehr schnell Deutsch lernen, wenn wir jetzt in Deutschland wären.
> Ich brauchte nicht so viel zu arbeiten, wenn ich mehr Geld hätte.

4. The **wenn** is sometimes omitted from the **wenn**-clause. Its verb is then placed at the *beginning* of the clause. Compare the similar structure in English that omits *if:*
Hätte er das Geld, (dann) würde er mehr kaufen.   ***Had** he the money, he would buy more.*

It is important to note that not all conditional sentences are contrary to fact. They may leave open the question of whether or not the condition is fulfilled. Such "open conditions" use the indicative rather than the subjunctive. Notice the different implications:

open condition: **indicative**

> Wenn der Junge schon dreizehn **ist, darf** er den Film sehen.
>
> *If the boy is already thirteen, he may see the movie.*

(*Implication:* I don't know whether he is thirteen or not. He may be, in which case he may see the movie.)

condition contrary to fact: **subjunctive**

> Wenn der Junge schon dreizehn **wäre, dürfte** er den Film sehen.
>
> *If the boy were already thirteen, he would be allowed to see the movie.*

(*Implication:* Since I *know* he's *not* yet thirteen, he may *not* see the movie!)

 10 **Übung:** Wenn es anders wäre . . . *Mit offenen Büchern*

Ihr Professor beschreibt eine Situation im Indikativ. Sie sagen im Konjunktiv, wie es wäre, wenn die Situation *anders* wäre. (Note that the logic of these sentences demands changing positive to negative and vice versa).

> BEISPIEL: Weil es so kalt ist, können wir nicht schwimmen.
> Wenn es *nicht* so kalt *wäre, könnten* wir schwimmen.

1. Weil es so weit ist, können wir nicht zu Fuß gehen.
2. Weil ich keine Lust habe, mache ich es nicht.
3. Weil dieses Buch langweilig ist, lesen wir es nicht.
4. Weil der Dom geschlossen ist, können Sie ihn nicht besuchen.
5. Weil ich keine Zeit habe, kann ich keine Dusche nehmen.
6. Weil sie nicht aus Österreich kommt, sagt sie nicht „Grüß Gott."
7. Weil ich keinen Hunger habe, bestelle ich nichts.
8. Weil sie sich nicht für diesen Film interessiert, geht sie nicht mit.

 11 **Übung** *Mit offenen Büchern*

Wiederholen Sie, was Sie schon in *Übung 10* gemacht haben, aber diesmal beginnen Sie *nicht* mit **wenn.**

> BEISPIEL: Wir kommen zu spät, weil du nicht schneller fährst.
> Wir würden nicht zu spät kommen, wenn du schneller fahren würdest.

1. Wir bleiben hier, weil er uns braucht.
2. Ich muß jetzt wechseln, weil ich kein österreichisches Geld habe.
3. Wir gehen spazieren, weil die Sonne scheint.

4. Wir trampen nach Italien, weil wir keinen Wagen haben.

5. Ich lese die Zeitung nicht, weil ich so müde bin.

6. Er kann mir nicht danken, weil er meinen Namen nicht weiß.

7. Wir sehen uns nicht, weil er nicht mehr vorbeikommt.

8. Wir können nicht mit euch essen, weil ihr nicht bei uns übernachtet.

Wishes Contrary to Fact

There are two ways to form contrary-to-fact wishes:

Wenn sie nur hier wäre!	*If only she were here!*
Ich wünschte, sie wäre hier.	*I wish she were here.*

When you use the second expression, notice that *both* verbs are in the subjunctive **(wünschte, wäre).** The second clause of this construction *never* begins with **daß** but *always* has verb-second word order.

12 **Gruppenarbeit:** Buttje, Buttje, in der See

Es gibt ein bekanntes norddeutsches Märchen („Der Fischer und seine Frau"), in dem ein großer Butt (*flounder*) einem Fischer seine Wünsche erfüllt (*grants*). Der Fischer holt ihn immer wieder aus der See mit den Worten: „Buttje, Buttje, in der See," und sagt ihm, was er sich wünscht. Jetzt soll jeder von Ihnen den anderen sagen, was er/sie sich wünscht. Der Nächste sagt, ob er den Wunsch erfüllen kann oder nicht.

> BEISPIEL: Ich wünschte, es gäbe heute etwas Gutes in der Mensa.
> Das kann ich dir leider nicht erfüllen!

Hypothetical Statements and Questions

German also uses subjunctive for hypothetical statements and questions, where English uses *would, could,* or *ought to.*

Du **solltest** daran denken.	*You **ought to** think of that.*
Wir **könnten** nach Grinzing fahren.	*We **could** drive to Grinzing.*
Das **wäre** schön!	*That **would be** nice!*
Was **würde** das kosten?	*What **would** that cost?*

13 **Partnerarbeit:** Wie wäre das?

Sie wollen heute irgendetwas zusammen machen. Partner A macht einen Vorschlag (*suggestion*). Partner B reagiert darauf.

> BEISPIEL: A: Wir *könnten* eine Wanderung machen.
> B: Ja, das *wäre* schön! *oder* Nein, das *wäre* zu schwierig.

Polite Requests

Note the difference in the tone of the following two requests:

> **Can** you do this for me? vs. **Could** you do this for me?

It is more polite to soften the request with the subjunctive, as in the second sentence.

German uses the subjunctive in the same way to make polite requests. These are sometimes in the statement form you have already used.

Ich **hätte** gern eine Tasse Kaffee.	*I'd like to have a cup of coffee.*
Ich **wüßte** gern, wo der Bahnhof ist.	*I'd like to know where the train station is.*

Sometimes polite requests are questions.

Könnten Sie mir bitte helfen?	*Could you please help me?*
Würden Sie mir bitte den Koffer tragen?	*Would you please carry my suitcase?*
Dürfte ich eine Frage stellen?	*Might I ask a question?*

  14 **Übung:** Könnten Sie das bitte machen?

Benutzen Sie den Konjunktiv statt Indikativ, um höflicher zu sein.

> BEISPIEL: Können Sie mir bitte ein Kleid zeigen?
> Könnten Sie mir bitte ein Kleid zeigen?

1. Können Sie mir bitte sagen, wann der Zug nach Berlin abfährt?
2. Haben Sie Zeit, eine Tasse Kaffee mit mir zu trinken?
3. Darf ich mich hier setzen?
4. Tragen Sie mir bitte die Koffer? (Benutzen Sie *würden!*)
5. Ist es möglich, eine Zeitung zu kaufen?
6. Können Sie mir meinen Platz zeigen?
7. Haben Sie ein Einzelzimmer mit Dusche?
8. Wissen Sie, wo man Karten kaufen kann?

Tips zum Lesen und Lernen

Wortschatzerweiterung: adverbs of time

The suffix -*lang* To form the German equivalents of the English adverbial phrases *for days, for hours,* etc., add the suffix **-lang** to the plural of the noun.

minuten**lang**	*for minutes*
stunden**lang**	*for hours*
tage**lang**	*for days*
wochen**lang**	*for weeks*
monate**lang**	*for months*
jahre**lang**	*for years*
jahrhunderte**lang**	*for centuries*

Also learn the phrase

eine Zeitlang	*for a time, for a while*

In diesem Kapitel lesen Sie über Österreich. Das Lesestück spricht von der historischen Rolle Österreichs als Weltreich:

„Die Habsburger Dynastie regierte **jahrhundertelang** über Deutsche, Ungarn, Tschechen, Polen, Italiener, Serben und **eine Zeitlang** sogar über Mexikaner.“

Übung: Wie lange hat's gedauert?

Ihre Professorin möchte wissen, ob etwas lange gedauert hat. Wählen Sie das wahrscheinlichste Zeitadverb mit **-lang** für Ihre Antwort.

BEISPIEL: Haben Sie lange im Zug zwischen Paris und Berlin gesessen?
Ja, *stundenlang.*

Hat das elegante Abendessen lange gedauert?

Haben Sie lange auf den Bus warten müssen?

War's letzten Sommer sehr heiß?

War der Chef lange am Telefon?

Sind Sie manchmal schlechter Laune?

Waren die alten Römer lange Zeit in Nordeuropa?

analysieren	analys*ieren*
die **Dynastie, -n**	Dynast*ie*
der **Humor**	Hu*mor*
die **Ironie**	Iro*nie*
der **Kontakt**	Kon*takt*
kreativ	krea*tiv*
literarisch	literarisch
die **Melancholie**	Melancho*lie*
der **Patient, -en, -en**	Pati*ent*
philosophieren	philoso*phieren*
produktiv	produk*tiv*
die **Psychoanalyse**	Psychoana*lyse*

Einstieg in den Text

The two Austrians in the following reading selection use subjunctive mood mainly for conjectural and hypothetical statements. Below is one example of each type. After reading through the text once, write down other examples of subjunctive mood used for these purposes; be sure you understand them and can give English equivalents.

Hypothetical statements

Ich . . . könnte . . . bei meinen Eltern wohnen und an der Musikhochschule in Wien studieren.

Conjecture

. . . ohne Johann Strauß würde die Welt wahrscheinlich keine Walzer tanzen.

Alt und Jung ruhen sich auf einer Bank aus. (Tirol, Österreich)

Wortschatz 2

Verben

erwarten to expect
sich konzentrieren auf (+ *acc.*) to concentrate on
statt·finden, fand statt, hat stattgefunden to take place
träumen to dream

Substantive

der **Künstler, -** artist (*m.*)
der **Spiegel, -** mirror
der **Witz, -e** joke; wit

das **Klavier, -e** piano

die **Gegenwart** present (time)
die **Gelegenheit, -en** opportunity, chance

die **Hochschule, -n** university; institution of higher learning
die **Künstlerin, -nen** artist (*f.*)

Adjektive und Adverbien

begeistert von enthusiastic about, ecstatic about
ernst serious
  etwas ernst nehmen to take something seriously
gemütlich cozy, comfortable; quiet, relaxed
witzig witty, amusing
zunächst first (of all), to begin with

Andere Vokabeln

außerdem besides, in addition
beide (*pl. pronoun*) both (people)
zwar ... aber it's true ... but

Nützlicher Ausdruck

eine Zeitlang for a time, for a while

Gegensätze

ernst ≠ heiter
  serious ≠ cheerful
gemütlich ≠ ungemütlich
  cozy ≠ unpleasant, not cozy

Zwei Österreicher stellen sich vor

Marie-Therese Werdenberg
Musikstudentin in Salzburg

„Ich heiße Marie–Therese Werdenberg und bin Musikstudentin. Ich komme zwar aus Wien und könnte freilich° dort bei meinen Eltern wohnen und an der Musikhochschule in Wien studieren. Aber ich studiere lieber in Salzburg, weil ich mich hier besser auf das Klavierspielen konzentrieren kann. In Wien gäbe es zwar mehr Konzerte, in die man gehen könnte, aber hier ist es ruhiger und gemütlicher. Außerdem finden hier im Sommer die berühmten Festpiele[5] statt, und da habe ich die Gelegenheit, mit vielen Musikern° in Kontakt zu kommen.

5. The **Salzburger Festspiele**, an annual summer festival of drama and classical music.

freilich = natürlich

= Menschen, die Musik spielen

Salzburg bei Nacht.

Ja, was wäre Österreich ohne seine Musiktradition? Und umgekehrt:° Was wäre die Musikgeschichte ohne Öster-
reich? Salzburg ist Mozarts Geburtsort.° Auch Haydn, Schubert, Bruckner, Mahler und Schönberg sind alle in Österreich geboren. Beethoven und Brahms—beide deutsche Komponisten°—haben in Wien ihre wichtigsten Werke geschrieben. Und ohne Johann Strauß würde die Welt wahrscheinlich keine Walzer° tanzen.

Aber ich sollte nicht nur über Musik reden, bloß° weil das meine Leidenschaft° ist. Die Kulturgeschichte Österreichs hat der Welt eine ganze Menge gegeben. In Wien um 1900 gab es z.B. ein besonders produktives und faszinie-
rendes° Kulturleben. Die literarischen Werke von Hugo von Hofmannsthal und Arthur Schnitzler sind ein Spiegel dieser sehr kreativen Zeit. In der Malerei° arbeiteten Künstler wie Gustav Klimt und Oskar Kokoschka. Um diese Zeit begrün-
dete° Sigmund Freud die Psychoanalyse. Ich könnte noch viele Namen nennen, aber dann müßten wir fast den ganzen Tag hier sitzen."

Dr. Ulrich Kraus
Psychologe° aus Wien

„Mein Name ist Kraus, und ich bin Psychologe. Mit meinen Patienten und ihren Problemen habe ich mehr als genug zu tun; erwarten Sie also nicht von mir, daß ich den Durch-
schnittsösterreicher° analysiere. Ich könnte aber mindes-
tens° versuchen, diesen Menschen—den *homo austriacus*—
ein bißchen zu beschreiben.

Zunächst etwas Geschichte: ich möchte Sie daran erinnern, daß wir Österreicher auf eine sehr alte und große Tra-

vice versa
= Ort, wo man geboren ist

= Menschen, die Musik komponieren

waltzes
bloß = nur
passion

= sehr sehr interessantes

painting

founded

psychologist

average Austrian / **mindestens = wenigstens**

dition stolz sind. Die Habsburger Dynastie regierte° *ruled*
jahrhundertelang über Deutsche, Ungarn, Tschechen, Polen,
Italiener, Serben und eine Zeitlang sogar über Mexikaner.[6]
Was man vom englischen Weltreich sagt, könnte man auch
von Österreich sagen: Die Sonne ging nicht unter° über die- **ging . . . unter** = *set*
sem Reich.

Heute spielt unser kleines Land eine viel bescheidenere° *more modest*
politische Rolle. Aber der Kontrast zwischen Vergangenheit
und Gegenwart hat zu unserem Humor und unserer Selbst-
ironie beigetragen.° Manchmal habe ich das Gefühl, wir *contributed*
Österreicher sind unglücklich über unsere verlorene Größe,
aber wir sind wenigstens glücklich, daß wir unglücklich
sind. Verstehen Sie diese witzige Melancholie, die sich selbst
nicht ganz ernst nimmt?

Viele Österreicher würden den Unterschied zwischen
sich und den Deutschen so ausdrücken: Die Deutschen sind
fleißig, aber die Österreicher gemütlich. Die Wiener Kaffee-
häuser könnten nicht existieren, wenn der Österreicher
nicht gern stundenlang vor seinem Mokka[7] säße und
träumte. Er philosophiert gern darüber, wie die Welt sein
könnte. Darum nennt man Österreich manchmal das Land
des Konjunktivs: ‚Alles würde hier besser gehen, wenn wir
nur. . .' oder ‚Das wäre möglich, wenn . . .'"

Schloß Belvedere (Wien), nach einem alten Stich, zirka 1850 (der Stich, -e = *engraving*)

6. The Habsburgs ruled the Austrian Empire from 1278 to 1918. The empire
included Germans, Hungarians, Czechs, Poles, Italians, and Serbs. In 1864
Archduke Maximilian, brother of the Austrian emperor, was made Emperor
of Mexico. He was executed in 1867 by republican troops.

7. A strong aromatic coffee served in demitasse cups, named after a city in
Yemen. The drink was introduced into Vienna during the Turkish siege of
the city in 1683. Viennese cafes serve dozens of different styles of coffee,
each with its own name.

1. Woher kommt die Frau im ersten Teil des Textes, und was macht sie in Salzburg?

2. Warum studiert sie lieber dort als in Wien?

3. Was könnte sie öfter in Wien machen, wenn sie dort wohnte?

4. Nennen Sie einen berühmten Menschen, der in Salzburg geboren ist.

5. Kennen Sie andere berühmte Namen aus der Musikgeschichte Österreichs?

6. Warum war Wien um 1900 besonders interessant? Wer hat damals dort gelebt und gearbeitet?

7. Was wissen Sie von der Geschichte Österreichs?

8. Beschreiben Sie den größten Unterschied für die Österreicher zwischen der Vergangenheit und der Gegenwart ihres Landes.

9. Welche Unterschiede findet Dr. Kraus zwischen den Deutschen und seinen Landsleuten in Österreich?

10. Warum nennt man Österreich manchmal das Land des Konjunktivs?

Situationen aus dem Alltag

Im Hotel

Auf Seite 433 sehen Sie die Rezeption in einem Hotel. Hier ist eine Liste von Vokabeln, die Ihnen zum größten Teil (*for the most part*) schon bekannt sind.

Die Hotelgäste

sich anmelden	*to register*
das **Gepäck**	
der **Koffer, -**	
der **Reisepaß, -pässe**	
ein Zimmer reservieren	
ein Taxi bestellen	

An der Rezeption

der/die **Angestellte**	
die **Kasse**	
der **Zimmerschlüssel, -**	
der **Stadtplan, ⸚e**	
der **Stadtführer, -**	*city guidebook*
der **Speisesaal**	*dining room*
der **Lift**	*elevator*

Im Hotelzimmer

das **Bad**
die **Dusche**
das **Telefon (telefonieren)**
sich um·ziehen   *to change clothes*

Gruppenarbeit

Beschreiben Sie dieses Bild. Wer steht wo? Wer tut was?

Rollenspiele   *Gruppen von 3 Studenten*

Spielen Sie diese Situationen zusammen. Improvisieren Sie frei.

1. ***An der Rezeption***
   Zwei Touristen kommen gerade vom Flughafen im Hotel an. Sie haben ein
   Zimmer schon reserviert. Sie melden sich an der Rezeption an und stellen
   Fragen über das Zimmer.

2. *Eine Stunde später*

Die Touristen haben sich jetzt geduscht und umgezogen. Jetzt wollen sie ausgehen und sich die Stadt ansehen. An der Rezeption bitten sie um Auskunft. Der Angestellte gibt Ihnen viel Information über die Stadt, z.B., über das kulturelle Leben, Verkehrsmittel, Restaurants, usw. Bei ihm bekommen sie auch Stadtführer, Stadtpläne und Broschüren (*brochures*). Sie müssen auch Geld wechseln.

Zum Schluß

Sprechen wir miteinander

A **Partnerarbeit:** Was würdest du tun?

Unten sind einige Situationen. Besprechen Sie miteinander, was Sie in diesen Situationen tun würden.

> BEISPIEL: krank sein
> Was würdest du tun, wenn du krank wärest?
> Ich würde zunächst ins Bett gehen. Dann . . .

reich sein

in Europa sein

kein Student sein

wenig Geld haben

viel Zeit haben

jetzt Ferien haben

Hunger haben

Politiker sein

B **Gruppenarbeit:** Studentenreise nach Österreich   *4–5 Studenten*

Sie reisen nächstes Jahr mit einer Studentengruppe nach Österreich. Sie müssen sich jetzt darauf vorbereiten.

1. Was sollte man mitbringen?

2. Was für Bücher könnte man über Österreich lesen?

3. Was sollte man dort sehen? (Die Fotos in diesem Kapitel geben Ihnen vielleicht einige Ideen!)

4. Was würden Sie am liebsten in Österreich machen?

Spielen Sie diese Situationen zusammen. Seien Sie höflich und benutzen Sie den Konjunktiv! Seien Sie bereit, eine Situation vor der Klasse zu spielen.

1. **Kellner/in und Gast im Restaurant**

   Der Kellner fragt den Gast, was er/sie bestellen möchte. Der Gast fragt, ob man verschiedene Gerichte (*dishes*) hat und bestellt dann ein großes Essen. (You can use some food vocabulary from *Kapitel 8*, p. 238).

   KELLNER/IN: Bitte sehr? Was hätten Sie gern?

   GAST: Hätten Sie vielleicht . . .? Könnten Sie mir sagen . . .? Ich hätte gern . . .

2. **Hotelangestellte/r und Tourist/in**

   Die Touristin kommt im Hotel an und fragt, ob sie ein Zimmer haben könnte. Der Angestellte fragt sie, was für ein Zimmer sie haben möchte. Sie reist nicht allein, sondern ihre Familie wartet draußen im Auto.

D Übung: Eine witzige Anekdote aus Österreich

Provide the missing time word or phrase (in parentheses) in the following anecdote.

(Many years ago), (when) noch relativ wenige Touristen nach Österreich kamen, erzählte man eine Anekdote über eine reiche Amerikanerin, die *(one month)* in den österreichischen Alpen verbrachte. Sie wohnte in einem gemütlichen Hotel in einem kleinen Dorf, wo die Menschen sie sehr interessant fanden. *(Each morning), (when)* sie Frühstück aß, bestellte sie nur wenig zu essen: ein weich gekochtes Ei [soft-boiled egg] und eine Tasse Kaffee. *(Whenever)* das Wetter gut war, verbrachte sie *(the whole day)* draußen, und aß Brot und Käse aus ihrem Rucksack, *(when)* sie Hunger hatte. *(When)* die Dame endlich wieder nach Hause mußte, sagte sie dem Wirt [innkeeper] *(on Sunday)*, sie würde *(day after tomorrow)* abfahren. *(On Tuesday)* bat sie nach dem Frühstück um die Rechnung [bill]. Zunächst las sie die Rechnung und sagte *(for a while)* nichts. Darauf stand „für 28 Eier: 300 Schilling." Es stimmte, sie hatte *(for weeks every morning)* ein weiches Ei gegessen, aber sie konnte sich nicht erinnern, *(when)* sie je in ihrem Leben so teure Eier gegessen hatte. Sie ließ sofort den Wirt kommen und bat ihn um eine Erklärung. „*(When)* ich *(each morning)* mein Ei bestellte," sagte sie, „wußte ich nicht, daß sie bei Ihnen so selten [rare] sind. Der Wirt antwortete: „Ja, wissen Sie, gnädige Frau [Madame], die Eier sind bei uns *nicht* so selten, aber *Amerikanerinnen* sehr." Sie lachte, bezahlte die Rechnung und sagte, sie würde *(next year)* wiederkommen. „Hoffentlich sind *(then)* Amerikanerinnen *(no longer)* so selten und die Eier weniger teuer!"

Schreiben Sie zu Hause

E Schreiben Sie diese Sätze zu Ende.

1. Wenn ich Künstler/in wäre, . . .

2. Ich würde dich ernst nehmen, wenn . . .

3. Wenn ich die Gelegenheit hätte, dann . . .

4. Die Party könnte heute abend stattfinden, wenn . . .

5. Wenn du nur mit mir tanzen wolltest, . . .

6. Wir würden in diesem Hotel übernachten, wenn . . .

7. Wenn wir knapp bei Kasse wären, . . .

8. Wenn ich morgen nichts Besonderes vorhätte, dann . . .

F Machen Sie ganze Sätze mit diesen Vokabeln. Vergessen Sie die Endungen nicht. (// = Komma)

1. wenn / ich / nur / können / Klavier / spielen! (*wish contrary to fact*)

2. wir / würd- / gemütlich / sitzen / zusammen // wenn / wir / haben / mehr Zeit (*condition contrary to fact*)

3. wenn / ich / haben / Zimmer / im / erst- / Stock // Straßenbahn / würd- / mich / stören (*condition contrary to fact*)

4. wenn / wir / können / nicht / wechseln / Geld // wir / können / immer / zahlen / mit / Reisescheck (*open condition: indicative*)

5. ich / wissen / gern // wie / kommen / man / zum Museum (*first clause: polite subjunctive*)

6. ich / wünschen // ich / sein / bei / mein- / Freund / auf / Land (*wish contrary to fact*)

G **Wenn ich ein Vöglein wär'** You have learned that the subjunctive is used to express wishes contrary to fact. Obviously, this use of subjunctive occurs frequently in poems about love and longing. A well-known German folk song begins like this:

Wenn ich ein Vöglein wär'
Und auch zwei Flüglein° hätt'   *little wings*
Flög ich zu dir.
Weil's aber nicht kann sein,
Bleib ich allhier.°   **= hier**

Try creating a short poem of your own (either rhymed or not) in which you express such an unfulfillable wish.

Wenn ich . . .

. . .

Dann . . .

H **Aufsatzthema: Wenn ich die Welt regieren könnte** Stellen Sie sich vor, Sie könnten eine Woche lang die Welt regieren. Was würden Sie für die Völker der Erde tun? Was würden Sie ändern? Schreiben Sie eine Seite darüber.

I Wie sagt man das auf deutsch?

1. Would you like to go dancing with us tomorrow night?
2. That would be great, but unfortunately I've broken my leg.
3. That's a shame! You could come along anyway.
4. Your old friend Rainer will be there.

5. Max has been in Leipzig for weeks.
6. It would be nice to write him a postcard.
7. If only I knew where he is living now.
8. He's either in the Hotel Europa or somewhere in a youth hostel.

9. Can't you concentrate on your paper?
10. No, Marie always disturbs me with her loud music.
11. If you didn't have a piano in your room, you wouldn't have a problem.
12. That's right, but then I would have to look for a new roommate.

Das Hundertwasserhaus, Wien.

Profile of Austria

Area: 85,855 square kilometers; 32,376 square miles
Population: 7,600,000 or 89 people per square kilometer (235 people per square mile)
Currency: Schilling; 1 ÖS = 100 Groschen
Major cities: Vienna (*Wien*, capital, pop. 1,550,000), Graz, Linz, Salzburg, Innsbruck.
Religion: 98% Roman Catholic

Austria consists of nine states (*Bundesländer*). It is officially neutral, although its economic ties are primarily with Western Europe. Aside from basic industries such as machinery, iron and steel, textiles, and chemicals, tourism provides an important source of income. The literacy rate is 98%.

Austria plays a vital role in the United Nations, and Vienna has become a center of communication between East and West. With the opening of the "U.N.-City" in 1979, Vienna became the third seat of the U.N. It is also the headquarters for OPEC (the Organization of Petroleum Exporting Countries).

Straßenkonzert vor dem Stefansdom. (Wien)

Endlich ist der Frühling da. (Innsbruck mit Blick auf die Nordkette)

KAPITEL
15

Gastarbeiter in Deutschland

Communicative Goals
- Mailing a letter
- Talking about what could or might have happened in the past
- Talking about houses and apartments

Cultural Goal
- Learning about foreign workers in Germany

Lyrik zum Vorlesen   Aysel Özakin, „Wie lernt man in Deutschland eine merkwürdige Türkin kennen?"

Grammatik   General Subjunctive: Past Tense • Passive Voice • The Present Participle • Directional Prefixes: *hin-* and *her-*

Lesestück   Max von der Grün, „Leben im gelobten Land"

Situationen aus dem Alltag   Wohnen und Wohnungen

Almanach   Foreign Workers and Refugees in Germany

Dialoge

Wo liegt die Heimat?

Carlotta, Schülerin aus einer Gastarbeiterfamilie, wird für die Schülerzeitung interviewt.

INTERVIEWER: Es überrascht mich, daß du als Ausländerin so perfekt Deutsch kannst.

CARLOTTA: Kein Wunder. Ich bin hier geboren, und viele halten mich sogar für eine Deutsche.

INTERVIEWER: Aber ihr kommt doch aus Spanien, nicht? Wo fühlst du dich eigentlich zu Hause?

CARLOTTA: Das frag' ich mich auch. Hier kenne ich mich besser aus, aber mir ist klar, daß ich nicht von allen Deutschen akzeptiert werde.

Die verpaßte Geburtstagsfeier

LILLI: Bist du nicht zu Sonjas Geburtstagsfeier eingeladen worden?

FELIX: Doch, und ich wünschte, ich wäre dabei gewesen. Aber leider mußte ich arbeiten.

LILLI: Du hättest doch anrufen können, um ihr zu gratulieren.

FELIX: Da hast du recht. Das hätte ich machen sollen.

Vor der Post

Herr und Frau Becker gehen an der Hauptpost vorbei und sehen einen Briefkasten.

FRAU BECKER: Da kannst du deinen Brief einwerfen.

HERR BECKER: Augenblick. Hab' ich genug Briefmarken darauf? Vielleicht sollte ich hineingehen und ihn wiegen lassen.

FRAU BECKER: Zeig mal her . . . Aber Hartmanns sind doch umgezogen. Das ist ihre alte Adresse.

HERR BECKER: Verflixt nochmal! Das hätte ich nicht vergessen sollen.

FRAU BECKER: Ach, reg dich nicht auf! Wir kaufen schnell einen neuen Umschlag.

Where Is Home?

Carlotta, a pupil from a family of foreign workers, is being interviewed for the school newspaper.

INTERVIEWER: I'm surprised that, as a foreigner, you speak such perfect German.

CARLOTTA: No wonder. I was born here and many people even think I'm a German.

INTERVIEWER: But you come from Spain, don't you? Where do you actually feel at home?

CARLOTTA: I ask myself that too. I know my way around here better, but it's clear to me that I'm not accepted by all Germans.

The Missed Birthday Party

LILLI: Weren't you invited to Sonja's birthday party?

FELIX: Yes I was, and I wish I had been there. But unfortunately I had to work.

LILLI: You could have phoned to congratulate her.

FELIX: You're right. I should have done that.

In Front of the Post Office

Mr. and Mrs. Becker are going past the main post office and see a mailbox.

MRS. BECKER: You can mail your letter there.

MR. BECKER: Just a second. Do I have enough stamps on it? Maybe I should go in and have it weighed.

MRS. BECKER: Let me see . . . But the Hartmanns have moved. That's their old address.

MR. BECKER: Darn it all! I shouldn't have forgotten that.

MRS. BECKER: Oh, don't get upset! We'll just buy a new envelope.

Wortschatz 1

Verben

akzeptieren to accept

sich auf·regen (**über** + *acc.*) to get upset (about), get excited (about)

dabei sein to be present, attend

ein·werfen to mail (a letter)

sich fragen to wonder, ask oneself
  Ich frage mich, ob . . . I wonder if . . .

gratulieren (+ *dat.*) to congratulate
  Ich gratuliere dir zum Geburtstag! Happy birthday!

halten für to take for, regard as, think X is
  Ich halte es für möglich. I think it's possible.

überraschen to surprise

wiegen, wog, gewogen to weigh (*trans. and intrans.*)

Substantive

der **Ausländer, -** foreigner (*m.*)

der **Briefkasten, ⸚** mailbox

der **Gastarbeiter, -** foreign worker, guest worker (*m.*)

der **Umschlag, ⸚e** envelope

(das) **Spanien** Spain

die **Adresse, -en** address

die **Ausländerin, -nen** foreigner (*f.*)

die **Briefmarke, -n** stamp

die **Feier, -n** celebration, party
  die **Geburtstagsfeier** birthday party

die **Gastarbeiterin, -nen** foreign worker, guest worker (*f.*)

die **Post** post office; postal service; mail

Adjektiv oder Adverb

perfekt perfect

Andere Vokabeln

an (+ *dat.*) **. . . vorbei** (+ *verb*) (to go) past (something)
  Sie gehen an der Post vorbei. They're going past the post office.
  Ich fuhr am Dom vorbei. I drove past the cathedral.

hinein- (*prefix*) in, into (see p. 455)

Nützliche Ausdrücke

Kein Wunder! No wonder!

Zeig mal her. Let's see. Show it to me.

Mit anderen Worten

Verflixt nochmal! (*colloq.*) = **So ein Mist!** (Das sagt man, wenn man sich über etwas sehr ärgert.)

Variationen

A Persönliche Fragen

1. Der Interviewer ist überrascht, daß Carlotta so perfekt Deutsch spricht. Sind Sie auch manchmal überrascht? Was hat Sie zum Beispiel an dieser Uni überrascht, als Sie hier neu waren?

2. Carlotta weiß nicht genau, wo sie sich eigentlich zu Hause fühlt. Wo fühlen Sie sich zu Hause: wo Sie jetzt wohnen, wo Ihre Eltern wohnen, oder wo Sie geboren sind?

3. Felix hat Sonjas Geburtstagsfeier verpaßt. Haben Sie je etwas Wichtiges verpaßt? Erzählen Sie davon.

4. Schreiben Sie oft Briefe? An wen? Oder telefonieren Sie lieber?

5. Wo gibt es hier den nächsten Briefkasten?

6. Gehen Sie oft zur Post? Wann gehen Sie zur Post? Was lassen Sie dort machen?

B Gruppenarbeit: Reg dich nicht auf! *Take it easy!*

Manchmal regt man sich unnötig auf. In welchen Situationen regen Sie sich besonders auf? Wenn Sie etwas vergessen haben? Wenn Sie etwas Wichtiges vorhaben? Machen Sie zusammen eine Liste von solchen Situationen.

BEISPIEL: Ich rege mich auf, wenn ich ein Referat halten muß.

C Klassendiskussion: Geburtstagstraditionen

Was macht man in Ihrer Familie, wenn jemand Geburtstag hat? Gibt es bestimmte Familientraditionen? Feiern Sie zu Hause oder im Restaurant? Lädt man viele Gäste ein, oder ist es nur eine kleine Feier? Darf sich das Geburtstagskind (das heißt, die Person, die Geburtstag hat) sein Lieblingsessen bestellen?

Aysel Özakin ist 1942 in der Türkei geboren. Sie studierte Romanistik und Pädagogik in Ankara und Paris. Seit dem türkischen Militärputsch 1980 lebt sie in Deutschland. In der Türkei hat sie Romane und Kurzgeschichten veröffentlicht (*published*). Sie hat auch Werke auf deutsch geschrieben.

„Wie lernt man in Deutschland eine merkwürdige° Türkin kennen?"

merkwürdig = *strange, odd*

Wo kommst du her?
Du siehst aber nicht so aus.
Du siehst aus wie wir.
Bist du in Deutschland aufgewachsen?
Aha . . .
Das ist ja eine ganz andere Kultur.
Gibt es auch andere Türkinnen wie dich?

Du bist ja auch nicht typisch türkisch.
Kommst du aus der oberen Schicht?°

oberen Schicht = *upper class*

Ich meine . . .
Hast du Kontakte mit anderen Türkinnen hier?
Du sitzt ja zwischen zwei Stühlen.
Zwischen zwei Welten.
Kannst du wieder in der Türkei leben?
Du bist bestimmt° freier hier.

bestimmt = sicher

Warum denn nicht?
Wovon lebst du?
Wie hast du die Sprache gelernt?
Ich bin ja wirklich erstaunt.
Lebst du allein?
Ich könnte es mir gar nicht vorstellen.
. . .
. . .
Was ist denn daran schlimm?

Aysel Özakin (b. 1942)
Aus *Du bist willkommen*

DEUTSCHE BUNDESPOST

Grammatik

General Subjunctive: Past Tense

Past subjunctive is used to talk about hypothetical, uncertain, or contrary-to-fact situations *in the past* (e.g., *"I would have waited* for you yesterday"). Now that you have learned how to use present-tense subjunctive, past subjunctive will prove quite easy. Its form is similar to the *perfect tense* of the indicative. The only difference is that the auxiliary verb is in the *present subjunctive* (a form of **hätten** or **wären** instead of **haben** or **sein**).

Past Subjunctive

ich **hätte** gewartet	*I would have waited*	wir **hätten** gewartet	*we would have waited*
du **hättest** gewartet	*you would have waited*	ihr **hättet** gewartet	*you would have waited*
Sie **hätten** gewartet		Sie **hätten** gewartet	
sie **hätte** gewartet	*she would have waited*	sie **hätten** gewartet	*they would have waited*
ich **wäre** gekommen	*I would have come*	wir **wären** gekommen	*we would have come*
du **wärest** gekommen	*you would have come*	ihr **wäret** gekommen	*you would have come*
Sie **wären** gekommen		Sie **wären** gekommen	
er **wäre** gekommen	*he would have come*	sie **wären** gekommen	*they would have come*

Caution! Note that English uses the word *would* in both the present and past subjunctive, while German uses **würden** *only* in the present subjunctive, *not* in the past.

present Er **würde** mitkommen. He **would** come along.
past Er **wäre** mitgekommen. He **would have** come along.

Note also that the subjunctive mood has *only this one past tense*, unlike the indicative which has three past tenses (simple past, perfect, past perfect).

1 Übung: Aber *ich* hätte das gemacht.

Ihre Professorin sagt Ihnen, daß sie etwas nicht gemacht hat. Sie sagen, daß *Sie* es gemacht hätten.

BEISPIEL: Ich habe keinen Ausflug gemacht.
　　　　　Aber *ich* hätte einen Ausflug gemacht.

1. Ich habe nicht um Auskunft gebeten.

2. Ich habe Anna nicht geholfen.

3. Ich habe die Adresse nicht gewußt.

4. Ich bin nicht Ski gefahren.

5. Ich habe mir die Haare nicht gekämmt.

6. Ich bin nicht lange geblieben.

7. Ich habe den Plan nicht verstanden.

8. Ich bin nicht tanzen gegangen.

9. Ich habe mich nicht verspätet.

10. Ich habe mir keinen Computer gekauft.

2 **Übung**

Wie sagt man das auf deutsch?

1. I would have hated it.

2. Bernd wouldn't have waited.

3. We would have bought stamps.

4. I would have gotten up earlier.

5. That would have lasted a long time.

6. That would have cost too much.

7. You wouldn't have been happy.

8. I would have gotten used to it.

9. They would have stayed longer.

10. They would have showed us a double room.

 3 **Gruppenarbeit (Phantasiediskussion):** Was hätten Sie gemacht?

Sagen Sie, was **Sie** gemacht hätten . . .

wenn Sie letzten Sommer 20 000 Dollar im Lotto (*lottery*) gewonnen hätten.

wenn Ihr Professor sich gestern das Bein gebrochen hätte.

wenn Sie vor 100 Jahren gelebt hätten.

Past Subjunctive of Modal Verbs

The past subjunctive of modal verbs is also similar to the perfect indicative tense (see p. 203). Because modal verbs always use **haben** as their auxiliary, their past subjunctive is formed with **hätten** plus the *double infinitive.*

Du **hättest** doch **anrufen können.**	*You could have called.*
Das **hätte** ich **machen sollen.**	*I should have done that.*

In English, the past subjunctive of modal verbs uses *would have, could have,* or *should have.* Notice how simple and consistent German modals are compared to English.

Ich **hätte** kommen **dürfen.**	*I **would have been allowed** to come.*
Ich **hätte** kommen **können.**	*I **could have** come.*
Ich **hätte** kommen **müssen**	*I **would have had to** come.*
Ich **hätte** kommen **sollen.**	*I **should have** come.*
Ich **hätte** kommen **wollen.**	*I **would have wanted to** come.*

Caution: When the double infinitive structure occurs in a *subordinate* clause, the inflected auxiliary (**hätte** in the sentences above) must come *before* the double infinitive.

Er sagte mir, daß ich mehr Geld **hätte** wechseln sollen.

Ich fragte, wie ich das **hätte** wissen sollen.

This is the *only* case in German where the inflected verb is not in final position in a subordinate clause.

4 **Übung:** Das hätten Sie machen sollen

Ihr Professor hat vergessen, viele wichtige Dinge zu machen. Sagen Sie ihm, er hätte sie machen sollen.

BEISPIEL: Ich habe vergessen, meinen Regenschirm mitzubringen.
Sie hätten ihn mitbringen sollen.

1. Ich habe vergessen, mein Bett zu machen.

2. Ich habe vergessen, meine Bücher mitzubringen.

3. Ich habe vergessen, meine Frau anzurufen.

4. Ich habe vergessen, eine Zeitung zu kaufen.

5. Ich habe vergessen, das Fenster zu schließen.

5 **Übung**

Wie sagt man das auf deutsch?

1. We could have flown.

2. We would have had to buy tickets.

3. Frank should have come along.

4. He wouldn't have wanted to come along.

5. He wouldn't have been allowed to come along.

6 **Gruppenarbeit (Phantasiediskussion):** Was hätten Sie machen müssen?

Was hätten Sie machen müssen . . .

wenn Sie heute zu spät aufgestanden wären?

wenn Sie Ihren Zug verpaßt hätten?

wenn Ihr Wagen kaputt gewesen wäre?

wenn Sie sich das Bein gebrochen hätten?

7 **Gruppenarbeit:** Ich wünschte, ich hätte das nicht gemacht.

Als Kinder haben wir alle viel gemacht, was wir lieber nicht gemacht hätten. Sagen Sie, was Sie lieber gemacht oder nicht gemacht hätten.

BEISPIELE: Ich wünschte, ich hätte meine ältere Schwester nicht so oft geärgert.
Ich wünschte, ich hätte mehr Klavier geübt.
Ich wünschte, ich hätte . . .

Passive Voice

Compare the following sentences:

Die meisten Studenten lesen diese Zeitung.	*Most students read this newspaper.*
Diese Zeitung wird von den meisten Studenten gelesen.	*This newspaper is read by most students.*

Both sentences say essentially the same thing, but the first is in the *active voice* while the second is in the *passive voice*. The passive voice is used to emphasize that something is being *acted upon* (the *newspaper* is being read) rather than to emphasize the agent performing that action (the *students* who are reading it).

In active sentences, the grammatical subject is also the agent or performer of the action.

Die Studenten lesen.   *The students read.*

In passive sentences, the grammatical subject is the *object* of the action.

Die Zeitung wird gelesen.   *The newspaper is read.*

Every passive sentence can be thought of as the transformation of an active sentence *with a transitive verb and a direct object*. The direct object of the active sentence becomes the *subject* of the passive sentence.

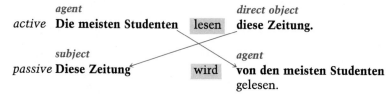

Formation of the German Passive Voice

The passive voice in English consists of the auxiliary verb *to be* plus a past participle.

active voice	*passive voice*		
		aux.	*part.*
He sees.	*He*	**is**	**seen.**
We never do that.	*That*	**is** *never*	**done.**

The passive voice in German consists of the auxiliary verb **werden** plus a past participle.

active voice	*passive voice*		
		aux.	*part.*
Er sieht.	Er	**wird**	**gesehen.**
Wir machen das nie.	Das	**wird** nie	**gemacht.**

Here is a table showing the formation of all tenses of **gesehen werden** (*to be seen*).

Passive Voice				
passive infinitive		**gesehen** werden	*to be*	*seen*
present	Er wird	**gesehen.**	*He is*	*seen.*
past	Er wurde	**gesehen.**	*He was*	*seen.*
future	Er wird	**gesehen** werden.	*He will be*	*seen.*
perfect	Er ist	**gesehen** worden.	*He has been*	*seen.*
			or	
			He was	*seen.*
past perfect	Er war	**gesehen** worden.	*He had been*	*seen.*

Note:

- In both German and English passive, the past participle (**gesehen**/*seen*) is invariable through all tenses. The auxiliary verb (**werden**/*to be*) is conjugated.

- The normal past participle of **werden** (**geworden**) is contracted to **worden** in the perfect tenses of the passive voice.

- The German passive infinitive is in the reverse order of English.

gesehen werden

to be seen

8 Übung: Das wird sofort gemacht!

Sie sind Hotelangestellte/r. Ihre Professorin ist Gast im Hotel und bittet Sie, verschiedene Sachen für sie zu machen. Sie sagen, alles wird sofort gemacht.

> BEISPIEL: Können Sie mir bitte diese Uhr reparieren?
> Ja, sie wird sofort repariert!

1. Können Sie mir bitte einen Brief einwerfen?

2. Können Sie mir bitte einen Tisch reservieren?

3. Können Sie mir bitte die Schuhe putzen?

4. Können Sie mir bitte das Zimmer aufräumen?

5. Können Sie mir bitte meine Kleider aufhängen?

6. Können Sie mir bitte das Bett machen?

7. Können Sie mir bitte das Frühstück bringen?

8. Können Sie mir bitte ein Taxi bestellen?

9 Übung

Change the sentences from the active to the passive. Be careful to keep the same tense as in the active sentence.

simple past tense

1. Im 18. Jahrhundert schrieb man viele Briefe.

2. In der ganzen Welt las man seinen ersten Roman.

3. Man zeigte den Film in jedem Kino.

4. Man kaufte viele Bananen.

future tense

5. Was wird man sagen?

6. Man wird dieses Wahlplakat nicht sehen.

7. Man wird neue Wohnungen für die Armen bauen.

8. Man wird dieses Thema besprechen.

Welches Haus wurde früher gebaut? Fachwerk-(*half-timbered*) und modernes Einfamilienhaus.

perfect tense

9. Man hat die alte Wohnung verkauft.

10. Man hat die Briefe eingeworfen.

11. Man hat den jungen Künstler eingeladen.

12. Man hat unsere Umwelt verschmutzt.

Passive Voice with a Modal Verb

Using passive voice with a modal verb is easy as long as you keep in mind that the dependent infinitive is the two-word *passive infinitive* (e.g. **getan werden**) rather than the one-word active infinitive **(tun).**

active	Er mußte es **tun.**	*He had to do it.*
passive	Es mußte **getan werden.**	*It had to be done.*

Here is a table showing the formation of all tenses with a modal verb:

<table>
<tr><td colspan="3" align="center">Passive with a Modal Verb</td></tr>
<tr><td>*present*</td><td>Das muß **getan werden.**</td><td>*That has **to be done.***</td></tr>
<tr><td>*past*</td><td>Das mußte **getan werden.**</td><td>*That had **to be done.***</td></tr>
<tr><td>*future*</td><td>Das wird **getan werden** müssen.</td><td>*That will have **to be done***</td></tr>
<tr><td>*perfect*</td><td>Das hat **getan werden** müssen.</td><td>*That had **to be done.***</td></tr>
<tr><td>*past perfect*</td><td>Das hatte **getan werden** müssen.</td><td>*That had had **to be done.***</td></tr>
</table>

10 Übung

Change the sentences from active to passive. Be sure to use the same tense as in the active sentence.

present

1. Wir müssen die Wohnung aufräumen.
2. Wir müssen noch den Wein kaufen.
3. Du darfst deine Freunde nicht einladen.
4. Man muß Oma nach Hause bringen.

past

5. Man mußte die Fenster schließen.
6. Man mußte die Kinder abholen.
7. Man konnte das Mädchen nicht interviewen.
8. Man durfte nichts kochen.

11 Gruppenarbeit: Was muß gemacht werden? *Mit offenen Büchern*

Sie diskutieren, was gemacht werden muß, um die Umwelt zu retten. Unten sind einige Möglichkeiten zum Kombinieren, aber Sie sollen auch Ihre eigenen Ideen benutzen.

BEISPIEL: Der Müll muß zum Recycling gebracht werden.

der Müll	schließen
das Altglas	finden
Alternativen	organisieren
Atomkraftwerke	zum Recycling bringen
Demonstrationen	ändern
unser Denken	bauen
umweltfreundliche Autos	sammeln

Passive Voice with an Agent

Most passive sentences make no mention of the agent performing the action.

Diese Häuser wurden sehr schnell gebaut.	*These houses were built very quickly.*
Das wird oft gesagt.	*That is often said.*

When an animate agent *is* expressed, **von** + dative is used.[1]

Diese Häuser wurden **von türkischen Gastarbeitern** gebaut.	*These houses were built by Turkish foreign workers.*
Das wird **von vielen Menschen** gesagt.	*That is said by many people.*

---

1. When the agent is some impersonal force, **durch** + *accusative* is used. See *Lesestück*, p. 460, lines 31–32.

12 Übung

Restate the following sentences in the passive. Use the same tense as in the active sentence.

BEISPIEL: Meine Freundin liest jetzt den Roman.
Der Roman wird jetzt von meiner Freundin gelesen.

1. Fast alle Physikstudenten belegen dieses Seminar.

2. Viele deutsche Schüler tragen gern Turnschuhe.

3. Unser Professor empfahl dieses Buch.

4. Alle Schüler in der Schweiz müssen Fremdsprachen lernen.

5. Michael hat mich eingeladen.

6. Die Gruppe hat das Thema besprochen.

7. Mein Freund hat die Gäste abgeholt.

8. Die Kinder singen immer dieses Lied.

9. Der Gepäckträger schleppte den Koffer zum Taxi.

10. Alle feiern Omas Geburtstag.

13 Übung: Von wem?

Sagen Sie, von wem diese verschiedenen Dinge gemacht werden (oder gemacht wurden).

BEISPIEL: Von wem werden Brötchen gebacken?
Sie werden vom Bäcker gebacken.

1. Von wem wird das Essen im Restaurant gebracht?

2. Von wem werden Autos repariert?

3. Von wem werden Romane geschrieben?

4. Von wem wird das Gepäck am Bahnhof getragen?

5. Von wem wurde „Hamlet" geschrieben?

6. Von wem wurde Beethovens Neunte Symphonie komponiert?

7. Von wem wird eine Vorlesung an der Uni gehalten?

8. Von wem werden Zeitungsartikel geschrieben?

The Present Participle

To form the present participle (English: *sleeping, reading,* etc.) of a German verb, simply add **-d** to the infinitive.

schlafend	*sleeping*
feiernd	*celebrating*
denkend	*thinking*
lesend	*reading*

The present participle is used

■ as an attributive adjective with the standard adjective endings.

> Wir wollen das **schlafende** Kind   *We don't want to disturb the*
>   nicht stören.   *sleeping child.*
> Lesen Sie die **folgenden** Seiten.   *Read the following pages.*

■ occasionally as an adverb:

> Sie sah mich **fragend** an.   *She looked at me questioningly.*

The German present participle is *not* used as a verbal noun. German uses the infinitive for this purpose: *No Parking* = **Parken verboten** (see p. 204). Nor is it used as a predicate adjective: *The child is sleeping* = **Das Kind schläft.** (There is no present progressive tense in German: see p. 28).

 14 Übung

Add the present participle of the cued verb as an adjective to each sentence.

> BEISPIEL: Wir können die Preise nicht mehr zahlen. (steigen)
>   Wir können die steigenden Preise nicht mehr zahlen.

1. Jeder Mensch weiß das. (denken)

2. Was meinen die Politiker? (führen)

3. Die Arbeitslosigkeit ist ein Problem. (wachsen)

4. Sie hörte die Kinder. (lachen)

5. Bitte stören Sie meinen Mitbewohner nicht. (schlafen)

Directional Prefixes: *hin-* and *her-*

German has two separable prefixes that combine with verbs of motion to show whether that motion is *toward the speaker* (**her-**) or *away from the speaker* (**hin-**). (You are already familiar with these directional indicators from the question words **woher?** *from where?* and **wohin?** *to where?*)

> Können wir nicht **hin**fahren?   *Can't we go **there?***
> Komm doch mal **her.**   *Come **here** a minute.*
> Wie komme ich (da)**hin?**   *How do I get **there?***

These directional indicators are often used in combination with other separable prefixes that indicate direction. Two sets of these are **auf und unter** (*up and down*) and **ein**[2] **und aus** (*in and out*). The two elements combine to make one separable prefix that can be attached to any verb of motion.

---

2. Notice that the preposition **in** is replaced by the prefix **ein**.

hinausgehen

herauskommen

hereinkommen

hineingehen

heraufsteigen

hinuntergehen

The prefixes **hin-** and **her-** must be used when the sentence does not contain a directional phrase such as **in die Post** or **ins Haus.** It is *incorrect* to say „Gehen wir ein." Correct is: **Gehen wir hinein.**[3]

Da ist die Hauptpost. Gehen wir **hinein.**	*There's the main post office. Let's go in.*
Draußen scheint die Sonne. Gehen wir **hinaus.**	*The sun is shining outside. Let's go out.*

Note: When someone knocks at the door, Germans simply say

Herein!   *Come in!*

3. Even when a prepositional phrase *is* used, the directional prefixes are sometimes added:
   Er ist aus dem Haus **heraus**gekommen.   *He came **out** of the house.*
   Sie ging in die Kirche **hinein.**   *She went **into** the church.*

15 **Gruppenarbeit:** Gehen wir hinein!

Complete these sentences by filling in the missing word.

*You're standing **outside** the house.*

1. Gehen wir _____. (in)

2. Karl, komm doch _____! (out)

3. Anna ist vor einer Minute _____. (gone in)

4. Bald kommen die Kinder aus dem Haus _____. (out)

*You're standing **inside** the house.*

5. Kommt Grete bald _____? (in)

6. Es ist so schön, ich möchte jetzt _____. (go out)

7. Wir sollten alle _____. (go out)

8. (*Es klingelt.*) _____! ("Come in!")

*You're standing **at the top** of the steps.*

9. Warum kommt ihr nicht _____? (up)

10. Jörg ist gerade _____. (gone down)

*You're standing **at the bottom** of the steps.*

11. Susi, ich brauche Hilfe! Komm mal schnell _____! (down here)

12. Ich bin jetzt müde. Ich gehe _____ und lege mich aufs Bett. (up)

16 **Partnerarbeit:** Wo kommt sie her? Wo geht er hin?

Beschreiben Sie, was diese Menschen machen:

Tips zum Lesen und Lernen

Tips zum Vokabelnlernen

German Equivalents for "think" The English verb "to think" has several meanings, for which German has various verbs (rather than just one). You have already learned most of these verbs as separate vocabulary items.

- When "think" = "to have an opinion," use **glauben, meinen,** or **finden.**

Ich **glaube/meine/finde** das auch.	*I think so too.*
Ich glaube ja.	*I think so.*
Ich glaube nein.	*I don't think so.*

- When "think" = "to think *of*," "keep in mind," use **denken an.**

Er **dachte an** seine Jugend.	*He was thinking of his youth.*
Denken Sie **an** die anderen.	*Think of the others.*

- When "think" = "to think x is . . . ," "to take x for . . . ," use **halten für.**

Ich **hielt** sie **für** eine Deutsche.	*I thought she was a German.*
Ich **halte** das **für** zu schwer.	*I think that's too difficult.*

- When "think" = "to think *about*," "ponder," use **sich etwas überlegen.**

Das muß ich mir **überlegen.**	*I have to think about that.*
Ich werde mir die Alternativen **überlegen.**	*I'll think about the alternatives.*

Übung: Wie sagt man das auf deutsch?

1. I often think of Karin.
2. I think she's a good doctor.
3. What do *you* think?
4. I have to think about the answer.
5. I think that's a great idea!
6. Do you think I'm crazy?
7. I don't think so.

Leicht zu merken

integrieren	integrieren
der **Kilometer,** -	Kilometer
die **Mentalität**	Mentalität
der **Ozean, -e**	
die **Religion, -en**	Religion
renovieren	renovieren

Recognizing the Passive Voice in Context   The following text contains seven passive constructions. You will recognize them by the fact that they all have some form of **werden** plus a past participle. Here is the first occurrence of passive:

> . . . weil sie nicht leicht integriert werden können. (line 2)

As you encounter the others, jot them down and make sure you understand them.

Leitfragen   In dem folgenden Text schreibt der Autor von den Problemen und Gefühlen eines türkischen Gastarbeiters in Dortmund. Er läßt auch den Arbeiter Osman Gürlük selbst über sein Leben reden. Die Sprache ist relativ einfach und direkt. Suchen Sie Antworten auf die folgenden Fragen, während Sie lesen:

1. Warum arbeitet dieser Mann in Deutschland und nicht in der Türkei?
2. Was sind seine Reaktionen auf Deutschland und die Deutschen?
3. Wie lebt er in Dortmund?
4. Warum ist es für die Türken in Deutschland besonders schwer?

Wortschatz 2

Verben

mieten   to rent (from somebody)

Substantive

der **Teil, -e**   part
der **Türke, -n, -n**   Turk (*m.*)

das **Heimweh**   homesickness

die **Kälte**   cold
die **Möglichkeit, -en**   possibility
die **Türkei**   Turkey
die **Türkin, -nen**   Turk (*f.*)

Adjektive und Adverbien

christlich   Christian
erstaunt   astonished
menschlich   human, like a human being; humane
türkisch   Turkish
verwandt (mit)   related (to)

Nützlicher Ausdruck

nach und nach   gradually, little by little

Gegensätze

die **Kälte** ≠ die **Hitze**
   cold ≠ heat

Leben im gelobten Land°

Im Jahre 1989 arbeiteten fast 1,6 Millionen Gastarbeiter in der Bundesrepublik. Weil sie nicht leicht integriert werden können, stellen diese Arbeiter ein ernstes soziales Problem dar.° Man braucht sie zwar für die deutsche Wirtschaft, aber
5 sie werden nicht wirklich akzeptiert. Max von der Grün, 1926 in Bayreuth geboren, von 1951 bis 1963 Bergmann,° jetzt freier° Schriftsteller in Dortmund, berichtete 1975 über das Leben eines türkischen Gastarbeiters in seinem Buch **Leben im gelobten Land,** aus dem hier einige Stellen° abge-
10 druckt° werden. Zunächst spricht der Arbeiter Osman Gürlük selbst:

„Diese Kälte hier in Deutschland macht mich krank; ich habe immer noch Heimweh, heute manchmal noch stärker als vor fünf Jahren; Heimweh ist eine Krankheit, und diese
15 Krankheit ist nur in der Türkei zu heilen;° aber in Anatolien[4] gibt es für mich keine Arbeit, keinen Verdienst,° keine Möglichkeit, irgendwann einmal nach oben zu kommen,° wie ein Mensch zu leben, mit Haus und geregeltem Einkommen:° ich muß vorerst° in Deutschland bleiben, muß mit
20 dieser Krankheit leben; in dieser Kälte; die Kälte hier in Deutschland, das sind die Menschen."

gelobten Land = *Promised Land*

stellen . . . dar = *to present*

miner
free–lance

passages
reprinted

ist nur . . . zu heilen = *can only be cured / wages*
nach . . . kommen = *to get ahead*

geregeltem Einkommen = *regular income / for the time being*

Autoaufkleber in Berlin

Max von der Grün

4. Anatolia, the eastern part of Turkey.

Osman Gürlük lebt heute mit seiner Frau und der drei-
jährigen° Tochter Ißek in einer Zweieinhalbzimmerwoh-
nung im Dortmunder Norden, in einem Viertel,° das aus-
schließlich° von Türken bewohnt° wird. Die Deutschen
25 sagen: Türkenviertel. Die deutschen Mieter sind nach und
nach, als immer mehr Türken in das Viertel kamen, in
andere Stadtteile gezogen,° in Neubauten.° Das „Türkenviertel" besteht ausschließlich aus° Altbauten, die von den
Eignern° heute nur noch notdürftig° renoviert werden, weil
30 die Häuser irgendwann einmal abgerissen° werden durch
die geplante Stadtsanierung° . . .
   Die Türken in der Bundesrepublik haben es von allen
Gastarbeitern am schwersten: sie sind weder Europäer, noch
35 gehören sie einer christlichen Religion an° und ihre Mentalität ist nicht mit der unseren° verwandt. Um einiger-
maßen° menschlich leben zu können, müssen sie dreitausend Kilometer entfernt° von ihrer Heimat arbeiten.
   Dazu sagt Osman Gürlük: „Ich will nicht klagen,° ich
40 bin nur immer wieder darüber erstaunt, daß dreitausend
Kilometer mehr sind als nur dreitausend Kilometer;
wahrscheinlich ist es leichter, den Ozean zu durchschwim-
men, als deutschen Arbeitern klar zu machen, daß wir Türken nichts anderes wollen als sie auch, nämlich° arbeiten,
45 um anständig° leben zu können; wir sind geduldet,° und das
auch nur, so lange wir gebraucht werden; das müssen meine
Landsleute begreifen° lernen.

= drei Jahre alte
= Stadtteil
= nur / *inhabited*

= umgezogen / = neue Gebäude
besteht . . . aus = *consists of*
= Besitzern / = minimal, sehr wenig
torn down
urban renewal

gehören . . . an = *are members of*
der unseren = unserer
= mehr oder weniger
= weit weg
complain

namely
decently / wir . . . geduldet = *we are
tolerated*
= verstehen

Fragen zum Lesestück

1. Wie viele Gastarbeiter arbeiteten 1985 in der Bundesrepublik?

2. Warum sind diese Arbeiter ein Problem für die deutsche Gesellschaft?

3. Wo kommt der Gastarbeiter Osman Gürlük her?

4. Wie beschreibt er sein Heimweh?

5. Wo hätte er dieses Gefühl nicht?

6. Warum mußte er seine Heimat verlassen?

7. Was meint er, wenn er von der Kälte in Deutschland spricht? Das Wetter?

8. Wo wohnt Osman Gürlük, und wie groß ist seine Familie?

9. Beschreiben Sie den Stadtteil, in dem er wohnt.

10. Was meint er, wenn er sagt: „3.000 Kilometer sind mehr als nur 3.000 Kilometer"?

Situationen aus dem Alltag

Wohnen und Wohnungen

Hier ist der Grundriß (*floorplan*) vom Erdgeschoß einer typischen deutschen Wohnung. Wahrscheinlich gibt es auch noch einen ersten Stock mit mehr Schlafzimmern. Wie ist diese deutsche Wohnung anders als eine amerikanische? In Deutschland gibt es zum Beispiel keine eingebauten Schränke (*built-in closets*) wie in Amerika, sondern man hat einen großen Kleiderschrank (*wardrobe*) im Schlafzimmer. Merken Sie andere Unterschiede?

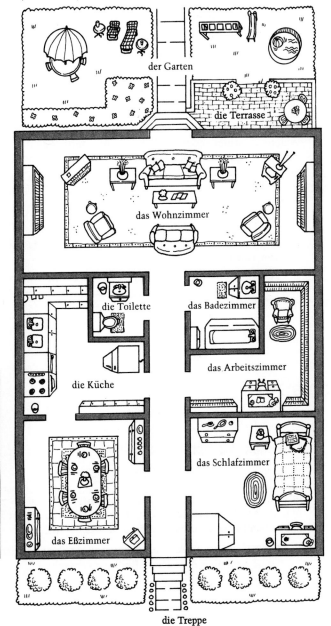

der Garten

die Terrasse

das Wohnzimmer

die Toilette

das Badezimmer

das Arbeitszimmer

die Küche

das Schlafzimmer

das Eßzimmer

die Treppe

die Garage

461

Um diese Übung zu machen, müssen Sie zuerst die Namen der Zimmer lernen.

1. Wo wird das Essen gekocht?
2. Wo wird das Auto geparkt?
3. Wo werden Referate, Briefe, usw. geschrieben?
4. Wo könnte man fernsehen und die Zeitung lesen?
5. Wo spielen die Kinder bei schönem Wetter?
6. Wo putzt man sich die Zähne?
7. Wo schläft man?
8. Wo nimmt man ein Bad?
9. Wo ißt die Familie zusammen?
10. Wo könnte man bei gutem Wetter sitzen und Kaffee trinken?

Partnerarbeit: Gehen wir hinein!

Sie stehen vor dem Haus auf Seite 461, dann gehen Sie zusammen hinein. Welche Zimmer möchten Sie sich ansehen? Was machen Sie dort? Wenn Sie fertig sind, sagen Sie den anderen Studenten, wohin Sie gegangen sind und was Sie dort gemacht haben.

Gruppenarbeit: Zur Diskussion

1. Wie wohnen Sie zu Hause? Beschreiben Sie das Haus oder die Wohnung Ihrer Familie.
2. Wie würde Ihr Traumhaus aussehen? Beschreiben Sie es.

Zum Schluß

Sprechen wir miteinander

A **Partnerarbeit:** Was hättest du lieber gemacht?

In den Sommerferien hat man nie genug Zeit, alles zu machen, was man machen möchte. Sagen Sie einander zuerst, was Sie letzten Sommer gemacht haben, und dann was Sie lieber gemacht hätten.

BEISPIEL: Ich mußte den ganzen Tag im Büro arbeiten, aber ich hätte lieber eine lange Radtour gemacht.

B Gruppenarbeit: Was hätten Sie gemacht, wenn . . .

So ist es *nicht* gewesen, aber es hätte anders sein können. Was hätten Sie gemacht, . . .

1. wenn Sie dieses Semester nicht studiert hätten?
2. wenn Sie letztes Jahr eine Million Dollar gewonnen hätten?
3. wenn Sie vor 10 000 Jahren gelebt hätten?
4. wenn Sie Beethoven gewesen wären?
5. wenn Sie gestern einen Autounfall gehabt hätten?

C Übung

Erzählen Sie die „Lebensgeschichten" der folgenden Dinge im Passiv. Das wird so gemacht:

> BEISPIEL: Zeitung: Journalisten / schreiben
> Die Zeitung wird zuerst von Journalisten geschrieben. (usw.)

1. die Zeitung: Journalisten / schreiben
   am Morgen auf der Straße / kaufen
   zwischen sieben und halb acht / lesen
   im Zug / vergessen
   alter Mann / finden und lesen

2. der Roman: Schriftsteller / schreiben
   in der Buchhandlung / kaufen
   zu Hause / lesen
   einem Freund / leihen
   vom Freund / verlieren

3. die Wurst: Metzger (*butcher*) / machen
   Hausfrau / kaufen
   im Wasser / kochen
   zum Mittagessen / essen

4. die Postkarte: in Italien / kaufen
   Barbara / schreiben
   zur Post / bringen
   in den Briefkasten / einwerfen
   Familie / lesen

Erzählen Sie weiter von den folgenden Objekten: der Tisch, das Auto, das Brötchen, das Frühstück, das Gepäck, die Weinflasche, das Foto.

D Gruppenarbeit: Trivial Pursuit   *2 Mannschaften*

Jetzt spielen Sie ein bißchen „Trivial Pursuit". Jede Mannschaft stellt der anderen Fragen über Geschichte, berühmte Personen, Kunst, Literatur, usw. Benutzen Sie den Passiv.

> BEISPIEL: Von wem wurde *Faust* geschrieben?
> Wo wurde Jazzmusik zuerst gespielt?

Schreiben Sie zu Hause

E Rewrite these sentences in passive voice. Keep the same tense.

1. Man akzeptiert mich fast überall.
2. Robert interviewt eine italienische Schülerin.
3. Man warf den Brief in den Briefkasten ein.
4. Die Studenten haben eine Europareise geplant.
5. Hat Klaus die Wohnung im ersten Stock gemietet?
6. Dort sprach man nur Türkisch.
7. Man muß dieses Problem verstehen.
8. Die Gäste haben meine Großmutter überrascht.

F Aufsatzthemen

1. Was für Schwierigkeiten hätten Sie in einem Land, wo kein Englisch gesprochen wird? Beschreiben Sie die Situation.
2. Gibt es Gastarbeiter in Nordamerika? Wie ist die Situation anders als in Europa?

G Phantasiefrage Wählen Sie eine historische Person und stellen Sie sich vor, Sie wären dieser Mensch gewesen. Wie hätten Sie gelebt? Hätten Sie etwas anderes gemacht?

BEISPIEL: Wenn ich Napoleon gewesen wäre . . .

H Wie sagt man das auf deutsch?

1. Would you have liked to live in the 19th century?
2. I have to think about that.
3. How would life have been different back then?
4. You would not have been able to work with a computer.
5. My paper has to be written soon.
6. When do you need my new typewriter?
7. Either today or the day after tomorrow.
8. What are you writing about?
9. About foreign workers in Austria and Switzerland.
10. A lot of books have been written about that.
11. There is the post office. Didn't you want to mail your letter?
12. Yes, let's go in. I could also buy some stamps.

Almanach

Foreign Workers and Refugees in Germany

During the past 45 years, Germany has attracted large numbers of foreigners. There are various reasons for this high immigration rate. In the economic growth that followed Europe's recovery from World War II, labor shortages existed in all the industrialized countries of northern Europe. From the 1960s to the early 1970s, workers from Turkey, Yugoslavia, Italy, Greece, Spain, and Portugal were brought into Germany. Germany still has the largest number of such "guest" workers in Europe (1.6 million in 1986) but actively discourages more from coming since the labor shortage is over.

Another large class of foreigners in Germany are those seeking asylum from political persecution in their native countries. The German Basic Law (*Grundgesetz* or constitution) states that "those being persecuted politically have a right to asylum." Now, however, the already densely-populated country is finding it increasingly difficult to support large numbers of political refugees. At the end of 1988, about 800,000 foreign refugees resided in Germany, 80,000 of them entitled to asylum.

The most acute immigration problem in the late 1980s and early 1990s resulted from the liberalization of Eastern Europe and the opening of what used to be called the "Iron Curtain." Ethnic Germans (*Volksdeutsche*) from Eastern European countries such as Poland, the Soviet Union, and Romania are granted automatic citizenship by the German constitution. In 1989, 377,000 of these Eastern European immigrants (the so-called *Aussiedler*) entered Germany. Many fear that the numbers could climb even higher in the coming years, straining German social services even further.

(*links*) Im BMW-Werk (München) (*rechts*) Junge Türkin in Berlin.

Die Frau: neue Wege und Rollen

Communicative Goal
- Reporting what others have said

Cultural Goal
- Discussing women in Germany and the changing social roles of both men and women

Lyrik zum Vorlesen   Bettina Wegner, „Ach, wenn ich doch als Mann auf diese Welt gekommen wär"

Grammatik   Impersonal Passive   •   Subjective Use of Modal Verbs   •   Indirect Quotation and Special Subjunctive   •   Subjunctive with *als ob*   •   Extended Modifiers

Lesestück   Gedanken über die Emanzipation der Frau

Situationen aus dem Alltag   Mit Gefühl! (Wie drückt man Gefühle aus?)

Almanach   Legal Protection for Pregnancy and Maternity

Dialoge

Kind oder Beruf?

MARTHA: Wie schafft ihr das, wenn euer Kind da ist? Wirst du deine Stelle aufgeben?

MARGARETE: Nee, eine so gut bezahlte Stelle ist schwer zu finden. Rolf kann vormittags auf das Baby aufpassen und nachmittags an seiner Diss arbeiten.

MARTHA: Wer paßt *dann* auf das Baby auf?

MARGARETE: Dann bin ich da. Ich habe meine Chefin schon gefragt, ob es möglich sei, halbtags zu arbeiten.

MARTHA: Was sagte sie dazu?

MARGARETE: Sie meinte, das ginge. Die ist ja selber verheiratet mit Kindern.

Goldene Hochzeit

HEINRICH: Liese, du siehst aus, als ob du kaum geschlafen hättest.

LIESE: Stimmt schon. Bei uns wurde bis halb vier gefeiert.

HEINRICH: Was wurde denn gefeiert?

LIESE: Die goldene Hochzeit meiner Großeltern.

HEINRICH: Sagenhaft! Und sie sehen noch so jung aus!

Mädchen in „Männerberufen":

Berufe für Männer und Frauen

Wortschatz 1

Child or Career?

MARTHA: How are you going to manage when your child is born? Will you quit your job?

MARGARETE: No, such a well-paying job is hard to find. Rolf can look after the baby in the mornings and work on his dissertation in the afternoons.

MARTHA: Who'll look after the baby then?

MARGARETE: Then I'll be here. I've already asked my boss whether it's possible to work part-time.

MARTHA: What did she say to that?

MARGARETE: She thought it would work. She's married and has kids herself.

Golden Wedding Anniversary

HEINRICH: Liese, you look as though you had hardly slept.

LIESE: That's right. Our party went on until 3:30.

HEINRICH: What were you celebrating?

LIESE: My grandparents' golden wedding anniversary.

HEINRICH: Incredible! And they still look so young!

Verben

auf·passen to pay attention; look out
aufpassen auf (+ *acc.*) to look after
heiraten to marry
verheiratet sein to be married

Substantive

das **Baby, -s** baby

die **Hochzeit, -en** wedding
die **goldene Hochzeit** golden wedding anniversary

Adjektive und Adverbien

golden golden
halbtags (*adv.*) half days
halbtags arbeiten to work part-time
kaum hardly, barely
vormittags (in the) mornings

Andere Vokabeln

als ob (+ *subjunctive*) as if, as though

Nützliche Ausdrücke

Was sagen/meinen Sie dazu? What do you say to that?
Sagenhaft! Incredible!

Gegensätze

verheiratet ≠ **unverheiratet/ ledig** married ≠ unmarried/single

Mit anderen Worten

die Diss = die Dissertation = die Doktorarbeit

Eine Aktion des Bundesministers für Jugend, Familie und Gesundheit

Mit machen macht Mut

FRAUEN KÖNNEN MEHR

Variationen

A Persönliche Fragen

1. Margarete sagt, sie wird ihre Stelle nicht aufgeben, um auf das Baby aufzupassen. Was würden Sie in dieser Situation machen, wenn Sie gerade ein Kind bekommen hätten?

2. Haben Sie je eine gute Stelle aufgegeben? Warum?

3. Wollen Sie eines Tages Kinder haben? Wie stellen Sie sich Ihr Leben mit Kindern vor?

4. Liese sagt, daß sie bis halb vier gefeiert hat. Haben Sie je so lange gefeiert? Wann war das?

5. Lieses Großeltern haben ihre goldene Hochzeit gefeiert. Nach wievielen Jahren feiert man goldene Hochzeit?

6. Waren Sie je bei einer goldenen Hochzeitsfeier dabei? Wie hat man gefeiert?

7. Leben Ihre Großeltern noch? Wenn ja, wissen sie, wie lange sie schon verheiratet sind?

B Gruppenarbeit: Was sagen Sie dazu?

Reagieren Sie auf die Sätze links mit einem passenden (*appropriate*) Ausdruck von der rechten Seite.

Heute habe ich Geburtstag.	Das wäre nett!
Du sprichst perfekt Deutsch.	Gott sei Dank!
Gehen wir zusammen Ski fahren?	Doch.
Möchten Sie etwas trinken?	Natürlich.
Darf ich meinen Freund Gerd vorstellen?	Kein Wunder!
Morgen früh wasche ich mir die Haare.	Lieber nicht.
Stefan hat sich das Bein gebrochen.	Sehr angenehm.
Wollt ihr viele Kinder haben?	Höchste Zeit!
Wir bekommen einen neuen Professor.	Gerne!
Ich war bis halb vier auf.	Wie schade!
Kannst du mich nicht verstehen?	Verflixt nochmal!
Ich hab meinen Geldbeutel verloren!	Ich gratuliere!
	Danke gleichfalls!
	Bist du verrückt?

C **Übung:** Das ist schwer zu finden

Margarete sagt, eine gute Stelle ist schwer zu finden. Antworten Sie auf die folgenden Fragen.

1. Was ist in dieser Gegend schwer zu finden?

2. Was ist manchmal schwer zu glauben?

3. Was ist für Sie schwer zu verstehen?

Lyrik zum Vorlesen

Bettina Wegner nannte man „die beste Liedermacherin der DDR." Sie ist 1947 in Berlin geboren. Sie singt von Liebe und Hoffnung, aber auch von Protest.

„Ach, wenn ich doch als Mann auf diese Welt gekommen wär" (1975)

Ach, wenn ich doch als Mann auf diese
    welt gekommen wär
da wär ich besser dran° und wüßte, wie   **da . . . dran = da ginge es mir**
    sie sind   **besser**
und alles, was ich machte, wäre sicher
    halb so schwer
und von der Liebe kriegte° dann der   **kriegte = bekäme**
    andere das Kind.

Ich hätte monatlich° nurmehr° noch   **= jeden Monat / = nur**
    finanzielle Sorgen°   *worries*
beim Tanzen könnte ich einfach fragen:
    Tanzen Sie?
Und würde ich mal wach° mit einem   **würde . . . wach** = *if I woke up*
    Schmerz im Kopf° am Morgen   **Schmerz im Kopf** = *headache*
Würd es nicht heißen: Deine Migräne,
    Liebling,° das ist Hysterie (. . .)   *Darling*

Ich hab genug von diesem kleinen
    Unterschied
ich will das gleiche° machen wie der   *the same*
    Mann
will, daß man einen Menschen in mir
    sieht
und daß ich wirklich gleichberechtigt°   *with equal rights*
    leben kann.

Ach Gott, da müßte ich ja schließlich
    auch zur Volksarmee.°   *former E. German army*
Na denn° lieber nee?   **na denn** = *well then*
Oder doch?
Und denn die kurzen Haare!
Na wärn ja bloß° anderthalb Jahre!°   **bloß = nur** / *1 1/2 years*
    (length of compulsory active
    Bettina Wegner (b. 1947)   *duty)*

Grammatik

Impersonal Passive

One German passive construction has no precise English equivalent. It is used to say that some human activity is going on, without mentioning who performs it. There is no expressed subject at all, and the verb is *always* in the third person singular.

Bis halb vier **wurde gefeiert.**	*The party went on until 3:30.*
Hier **wird** bis zwei Uhr morgens **getanzt und gesungen.**	*There's dancing and singing here until 2:00 A.M.*

If no other element occupies first position in the sentence, an impersonal **es** is used to fill it. This **es** is not a real subject and disappears if any other element occupies first position.[1]

Es wurde bis halb vier gefeiert.
Es wird hier bis zwei Uhr morgens getanzt.

 1 **Übung:** Anders gesagt

Diese Sätze mit **man** kann man auch als unpersönliche Passivsätze formulieren.

BEISPIEL: Heute ißt man um neun Uhr.
Heute wird um neun Uhr gegessen.

1. Hier singt man zu laut.

2. Beim Bäcker fängt man früh an.

3. In Leipzig demonstrierte man.

4. Damals arbeitete man schwer.

5. Morgen liest und schreibt man viel.

6. Jetzt kauft man ein.

7. Gestern tanzte man bis zwei Uhr.

8. In unserer Stadt baut man immer mehr.

---

1. Similarly, when verbs with dative objects (see p. 195) are used in the passive voice, their objects *remain* in the dative case and the passive is *always* in the third person singular. An impersonal **es** is in the first position if no other element occupies it.

active
Man hilft dem Alten.   *They're helping the old man.*

passive
Dem Alten wird geholfen. ⎫
Es wird dem Alten geholfen. ⎭   *The old man is being helped.*

2 **Übung:** Wo wird das in der Wohnung gemacht?

Antworten Sie auf die Fragen Ihres Professors.

> BEISPIEL: Wo wird in der Wohnung oder im Haus gekocht?
> In der Küche.
>
> Was wird im Abeitszimmer gemacht?
> Bücher werden dort gelesen.

1. Wo wird gegessen?

2. Was wird im Schlafzimmer gemacht?

3. Wo wird ferngesehen?

4. Was wird im Garten gemacht?

5. Wo wird der Wagen geparkt?

Moderne „Zusammen-
arbeit": so wird das
Essen gekocht.

Subjective Use of Modal Verbs

The modal verbs are sometimes used to show speakers' subjective attitudes toward what they are saying. By and large, this subjective use of the modal verbs parallels English.

- **mögen** expresses *possibility*

    Das **mag** sein.   *That may be.*

- **müssen** expresses *strong probability*

    Die Menschen drüben **müssen**   *The people over there must be*
    Touristen sein.   *tourists.*

- **sollen** expresses *hearsay*

    Sie **soll** eine gute Lehrerin sein.   *She's supposed to be a good teacher.*

    Sie **sollen** so glücklich sein.   *They are said to be so happy.*

- **können** expresses *fairly strong possibility* (sometimes = English *may*)

    Sie **kann** morgen schon hier sein.   *She may be here as early as tomorrow.*

    Kann das Richard sein?   *Can that be Richard?*

- **wollen** casts *doubt on someone else's claim* (no parallel in English)

    Er **will** viel über Musik wissen.   *He claims to know a lot about music.[2]*

3 Übung: Kann das sein?

Lesen Sie die folgenden Sätze laut vor. Dann geben Sie ein Äquivalent auf englisch, und sagen Sie, ob das Modalverb objektiv oder subjektiv gebraucht wird.

1. Kann das Utes Wagen sein?

2. Nein, das muß Richards Wagen sein.

3. Wieso, Ute wollte sich doch einen roten Wagen kaufen, nicht?

4. Mag sein. Wir müssen Ute fragen.

5. Ja, sie soll um drei wieder da sein.

6. Dann müssen wir zusammen in die Vorlesung.

4 Übung

Wie sagt man das auf deutsch?

1. She is supposed to be very famous.

2. That may be.

3. Roland must know a lot about politics.

4. He claims to know everything about politics.

5. It may be that they don't love each other any more.

6. But they are supposed to be so happy together!

---

2. The subjective modals also parallel English in the way they form their past tense. Note the difference between objective use (modal in the *simple past* with dependent *present* infinitive: **mußte . . . sein** = *had to be*) and subjective use (modal remains in *present tense* with dependent *past* infinitive: **muß . . . gewesen sein** = *must have been*).

objective Er **mußte** gestern in Wien **sein.**   *He had to be in Vienna yesterday.*
subjective Er **muß** gestern in Wien **gewesen sein.**   *He must have been in Vienna yesterday.*

Indirect Quotation and Special Subjunctive

Direct versus Indirect Quotation

There are two basic ways to report what someone has said: directly or indirectly. One can quote directly, repeating the original speaker's exact words.[3]

Bernd sagte: „Ich muß heute in die Bibliothek."	*Bernd said, "I have to go to the library."*

It is much more common, however, to report speech in *indirect* quotation, either without a conjunction:

Bernd sagte, er muß heute in die Bibliothek.	*Bernd said he has to go to the library today.*

or with the conjunction **daß** (*that*):

Bernd sagte, daß er heute in die Bibliothek muß.	*Bernd said that he has to go to the library today.*

Note that in indirect quotation, pronouns often have to be changed: „**Ich** muß in die Bibliothek."—Er sagte, **er** muß in die Bibliothek.

In the spoken language, many Germans simply use the indicative for indirect quotation, as in the previous examples and as we have done up to this point in this book. But it is also quite common to use *general subjunctive* for indirect quotation.

Bernd sagte, er **müßte** in die Bibliothek.	*Bernd said he had to go to the library.*
Meine Chefin meinte,[4] das **ginge.**	*My boss thought it would work.*

In formal written and spoken German, however (for example, in a term paper, newspaper article, television news report, or speech), indirect quotation *must* be expressed with forms called the *special subjunctive*.

Er sagte, er **müsse** in die Bibliothek.
Die Chefin meinte, das **gehe.**

Formation of the Special Subjunctive

To form the special subjunctive, add the endings from the general subjunctive of strong verbs (**-e, -est, -e; -en, -et, -en**) to the *unchanged infinitive stem* of the verb.

er/es/sie **gehe, laufe, könne, wisse, müsse, sehe,** usw.

---

3. Note on punctuation: German usually uses a colon before a direct quotation, while English uses a comma.

4. Notice that *thoughts* (Sie **meinte**) can also be reported in indirect quotation.

In practice, special subjunctive occurs *almost exclusively* in the third person singular.[5] This form is immediately recognizable for the following reasons:

- Unlike general subjunctive built on the *past* stem (e.g., **ging-**), it is built on the *infinitive* stem (**geh-**).

- Unlike the indicative ending in **-t** (**sie geht**), special subjunctive ends in **-e** (**sie gehe**).

The *only* German verb with a complete set of forms in special subjunctive is **sein**. Note that the **ich-** and **er-**forms lack endings.

ich **sei**	wir **seien**
du **seiest**	ihr **seiet**
er, es, sie **sei**	sie **seien**

Special subjunctive has only two additional tenses, future and past, each formed using the special subjunctive of the auxiliary verb.

future	sie **werde** das **sagen**	*she will say that*
past	er **habe** das **gewußt**	*he knew that*
	sie **sei** dort **gewesen**	*she was there*

Use of Special Subjunctive

You will encounter indirect quotation in special subjunctive introduced by a verb of saying or asking in the *indicative*. Once an environment of indirect quotation has been thus established, the economy of special subjunctive becomes evident: as long as special subjunctive continues to be used, it makes explicit that the person is still being quoted indirectly, and no further verbs of saying are required, as they sometimes are in English. Here are some examples of the kind you might hear on the evening news or read in the paper:

In Bonn sagte der Bundeskanzler, er **wisse** noch nicht, wie man dieses Problem lösen **werde**, aber er **glaube**, daß etwas bald entschieden werden **müsse**. Man **habe** nicht mehr viel Zeit.	*In Bonn the Federal Chancellor said he didn't know yet how they would solve this problem, but he believed that something had to be decided soon. (He continued that) there wasn't much time left.*

5. A note about forms. There are two reasons why special subjunctive occurs most often in the third person singular. First, any special subjunctive form that would be identical to an indicative form *does not exist*. Forms of the general subjunctive are used instead, as in the following paradigm:

ich **liefe** (la~~u~~fe)	wir **liefen** (la~~u~~fen)
du **laufest**	ihr **laufet**
er, es, sie **laufe**	sie **liefen** (la~~u~~fen)

Thus there is *no* **wir-** or **sie-**form in special subjunctive, because they would *always* be identical to indicative. An **ich-**form exists only for verbs with an irregular indicative singular, such as the modal verbs and **wissen: ich könne, ich wisse.**

The second reason for the high frequency of the third person singular is that special subjunctive is the *most formal* method for indirect quotation. As such, it is seldom used in the **ich-, du-,** or **ihr-**forms. It is usually used instead to quote formally some third person.

In einem exklusiven Interview
mit unserem Reporter sagte
Steffi Graf, sie **hoffe,** noch eine
lange Karriere vor sich zu haben.
Sie **sei** noch jung und **fühle** sich
sehr fit, besonders seit sie sich
von einer schlimmen Erkältung
erholt **habe.**

*In an exclusive interview with our
reporter, Steffi Graf said that she
hoped to have a long career still
ahead of her. (She said) she was
still young and felt very fit, especially since recovering from a
bad cold.*

Tenses in Indirect Quotation

As you can see from the examples above, there is a difference in the way
English and German handle tenses in indirect quotation. In English, the tense
of the introductory verb of saying influences the tense of the indirect quotation.

Direct Quotation
  Barbara said, "I have to go to the library."
Indirect Quotation   *Introductory Verb in the Present*
  *She **says** she **has** to go to the library.*
Indirect Quotation   *Introductory Verb in the Past*
  *She **said** she **had** to go to the library.*

In German, the tense of the introductory verb of saying has *no influence* on
the tense of the indirect quotation. The tense of the indirect quotation is *always
the same as the tense of the direct quotation* from which it derives. If the
tense of the direct quotation was *present,* use *present subjunctive* for the
indirect quotation.

  Bundeskanzler: „Ich **muß** mir das überlegen."

  Der Bundeskanzler sagt, } er **müsse** sich das überlegen.
  Der Bundeskanzler sagte,

If the tense of the direct quotation was *future,* use *future subjunctive.*

  Graf: „Ich **werde** mehr spielen."

  Graf sagt, } sie **werde** mehr spielen.
  Graf sagte,

If the tense of the direct quotation was *any past tense,* use *past subjunctive.*

  Graf: „Ich **habe** mich von der Erkältung **erholt.**"

  Graf sagt, } sie **habe** sich von der Erkältung **erholt.**
  Graf sagte,

If the original quotation is *already* in the subjunctive, the indirect quotation
simply *remains* in the subjunctive.

  Bundeskanzler: „Ich **möchte** nichts mehr darüber sagen."

  Der Bundeskanzler sagt, } er **möchte** nichts mehr darüber sagen.
  Der Bundeskanzler sagte,

5 Übung: Zeitungsartikel

Here are two examples of indirect quotation one might encounter in a news report. Reconstruct the original direct quotations, changing pronouns as necessary.

1. Der deutsche Außenminister berichtete, die Barrieren zur europäischen Vereinigung **seien** gefallen. Man **könne** jetzt beginnen, dem Europa-Parlament in Straßburg mehr Autorität zu geben. Es **werde** wahrscheinlich noch ein paar Jahre dauern, bis alle Probleme gelöst **seien.** Er persönlich **glaube** aber, daß man schon große Fortschritte gemacht **habe.**

2. Die Polizei meldete (*announced*) heute, ein schwerer Unfall auf der Autobahn zwischen Stuttgart und Heidelberg **habe** acht Verletzte und zwei Tote gekostet. Die Ursache (*cause*) des Unfalls **sei** das neblige Wetter im Neckartal gewesen. Alle Autofahrer **sollten** sich andere Routen nach Norden aussuchen.

6 Schriftliche Übung: Bericht über ein Interview

As a reporter for the student newspaper, you interview Frau Dr. Edenhof, a visiting lecturer on international affairs. Below is a transcript from your tape recorder. Now report what she said to you in indirect quotation. Begin your report with „Frau Dr. Edenhof sagte, . . .“ and be careful to change pronouns and possessive adjectives as necessary.

„Es freut mich sehr, hier an der Uni zu sein. Ich war vor zehn Jahren zum letzten Mal hier und habe damals viele nette Menschen kennengelernt. Ich finde diese Stadt wunderschön. Ich hoffe, ich werde diesmal mehr Zeit haben, um mir die Stadt anzusehen. Mein Thema für heute abend ist die Zukunft der Nato im neuen Europa. Ich weiß, daß es hier sehr viel Interesse für dieses aktuelle Problem gibt. Man kann natürlich in einer Stunde nicht alles sagen. Ich hoffe, am Ende meines Vortrags (*lecture*) eine gute Diskussion mit Ihnen zu haben.“

Questions and Commands in Indirect Quotation

- A yes/no question becomes an **ob**-clause in indirect quotation.

    Karin: „Hat Hans genug Geld?“

    Karin fragte, **ob** Hans genug Geld hat (habe, hätte).

- Information questions become subordinate clauses introduced by the question word.

    Tourist: „Wo ist der Bahnhof, bitte?“

    Der Tourist fragte, **wo** der Bahnhof ist (sei, wäre).

- Commands become statements with the verb **sollen**, with or without **daß.**

    Frau Henning: „Kauf das nicht, Heinz!“

    Frau Henning sagte ihrem Mann, er **soll** (solle, sollte) das nicht kaufen.
    Frau Henning sagte ihrem Mann, **daß** er das nicht kaufen **soll** (solle, sollte).

7 Übung: Was hat sie denn gesagt?

Ihre Professorin fragt Sie etwas oder sagt, Sie sollen etwas machen. Erzählen Sie dem nächsten Studenten, was die Professorin gesagt hat.

> BEISPIELE: PROFESSORIN: Bitte leihen Sie mir einen Bleistift.
> STUDENTIN: Sie sagte, ich soll ihr einen Bleistift leihen.
> PROFESSORIN: Wo ist Ihr Regenschirm?
> STUDENT: Sie fragte, wo mein Regenschirm wäre.

1. Wie fühlen Sie sich heute?

2. Arbeiten Sie oft mit dem Computer?

3. Was haben Sie zum Frühstück gegessen?

4. Empfehlen Sie mir bitte etwas Neues.

5. Helfen Sie mir bitte heute nachmittag.

6. Können Sie sich auf Ihre Arbeit konzentrieren?

7. Können Sie sich ein neues Fahrrad leisten?

8. Haben Sie Ihren Studentenausweis mit?

9. Passen Sie gut auf!

10. Seien Sie nicht frustriert!

Subjunctive with *als ob* ("as if," "as though")

The subordinating conjunction **als ob** (*as if, as though*) must be followed by a verb in the subjunctive.[6] Clauses with **als ob** are preceded by introductory phrases such as the following (note the special meaning of **tun** in the first example).

Du tust (so), als ob . . .	*You act as though . . .*
Du siehst aus, als ob . . .	*You look as if . . .*
Es war (so), als ob . . .	*It was as if . . .*
Er tut, als ob er nichts **wüßte.**	*He acts as if he didn't know anything.*
Du siehst aus, als ob du krank **wärest.**	*You look as though you're ill.*
Es war so, als ob wir uns immer **gekannt hätten.**	*It was as if we had always known each other.*

---

6. Either general *or* special subjunctive may be used, but general subjunctive is more frequent. Sometimes this conjunction is used in the abbreviated form of **als** alone (without **ob**). In that case, the verb immediately follows it rather than coming at the end of the clause: Du siehst aus, als **wärest** du krank.

8 Übung: Aber Sie tun doch, als ob Sie gesund wären!

Ihr Professor erzählt Ihnen etwas über sich selbst. Sagen Sie ihm, er tut, als ob das Gegenteil stimmte.

BEISPIEL: Ich fühle mich heute krank.
Aber Sie tun doch, als ob Sie gesund wären.

1. Ich bin traurig.

2. Ich bin knapp bei Kasse.

3. Ich bin von Natur faul.

4. Ich bin verheiratet.

5. Ich bin eigentlich ein schlampiger Mensch.

6. Ich bin fast immer ernst.

7. Eigentlich bin ich dumm.

9 Gruppenarbeit: Sie sehen aus, als ob . . .

Sehen Sie sich die Menschen in diesen Fotos an. Wie sehen sie aus? (Gefühle, Berufe, usw.)

BEISPIEL: Sie *sieht aus, als ob* sie viel zu tun *hätte*.

1.

2.

3.

Extended Modifiers

Look at the following phrases:

diese junge Schriftstellerin	*this young writer*
diese bekannte junge Schriftstellerin	*this well-known young writer*
diese sehr bekannte junge Schriftstellerin	*this very well-known young writer*

Both German and English can extend noun phrases by inserting a series of adjectives and adverbs between a limiting word (**diese** *this*) and its noun (**Schriftstellerin** *writer*). In German, however, such a series can be continued much further than in English.

diese unter Studenten sehr bekannte junge Schriftstellerin	*this young writer who is very well known among students*
diese unter Studenten in Deutschland sehr bekannte junge Schriftstellerin	*this young writer who is very well known among students in Germany*
diese heute unter Studenten in Deutschland sehr bekannte junge Schriftstellerin	*this young writer who is very well known among students in Germany today*

Such extended modifiers are encountered primarily in written German, and their use or avoidance is a matter of stylistic preference. You should *not* try to use this construction actively until you have had more experience with German, but you *should* be able to recognize and understand it.

The extended modifier is basically a substitute for a relative clause.

diese unter Studenten bekannte Schriftstellerin =
diese Schriftstellerin, die unter Studenten bekannt ist

Extended modifiers often contain a present or past participle functioning as an attributive adjective. This participle would be the conjugated verb in the corresponding relative clause.

Die Schüler freuten sich auf **die in zwei Tagen** *beginnenden* **Ferien.** =
Die Schüler freuten sich auf die Ferien, **die in zwei Tagen** *beginnen.*

Eine so gut *bezahlte* **Stelle** ist schwer zu finden. =
Eine Stelle, **die so gut** *bezahlt wird,* ist schwer zu finden.

10 **Übung:** Die Schriftstellerin

Read these sentences aloud, then make relative clauses from the extended modifiers.

> BEISPIEL: Die in Hamburg geborene Schriftstellerin wohnt heute in Berlin.
> Die Schriftstellerin, die in Hamburg geboren ist, wohnt heute in Berlin.

1. Ihr erstes, im Ausland kaum gelesenes Buch machte sie in Deutschland berühmt.
2. Ihre zwei Jahre jüngere Schwester ist Lehrerin in Düsseldorf.
3. In Berlin wohnt sie in einem alten, von Touristen kaum besuchten Stadtteil.
4. Aus allen Teilen Deutschlands bekommt sie Briefe von ihren oft sehr jungen Lesern.
5. Von ihr erwartet man Antworten auf viele für die Jugend immer ernster werdende Probleme.

(*links*) Heutzutage muß man sich im Büro mit dem Computer auskennen. (*rechts*) Lastwagenfahrerin (*truck driver*)

Tips zum Lesen und Lernen

Leicht zu merken

die **Emanzipation**	Emanzipat*i*on
ideal	ide*al*
industriell	industri*ell*
die **Karriere, -n**	Karri*er*e
parallel	para*ll*el
das **Phänomen, -e**	Phäno*men*
die **Position, -en**	Positi*on*
psychologisch	

Einstieg in den Text

Leitfragen   Das Lesestück in diesem Kapitel hat als Thema (*topic*) die Emanzipation der Frau. Dieses Thema ist nicht nur für Frauen, sondern auch für Männer wichtig. Als Vorbereitung auf das Lesen sollen Sie über Ihre eigenen Meinungen zu diesem Thema nachdenken. Hier sind einige Fragen, die Sie sich stellen könnten.

1. Ist Ihre Mutter Hausfrau?

2. Ist sie auch berufstätig?

3. Wie war es mit Ihrer Großmutter?

4. Wie ist das Leben Ihrer Mutter anders als das Leben Ihrer Großmutter?

5. Wollen Sie heiraten und Kinder haben? Wie stellen Sie sich Ihr Leben als Mann oder als Frau vor?

Identifying Special Subjunctive and Extended Modifiers in Context   The following reading contains several examples of both indirect quotation in special subjunctive and extended modifiers. After reading it through once, first see if you understand why special subjunctive is used in lines 8 and 35. Then look closely at the two examples of extended modifiers and see if you can translate them into English (the marginal glosses will help you).

(line 30) Heutige Frauen haben auch gelernt, **die trotz aller Schwierigkeiten errungenen Leistungen** dieser früheren Frauengeneration zu schätzen.

(line 48) **Die auch in Amerika bekannte Schriftstellerin** Christa Wolf schrieb über dieses Phänomen . . .

Wortschatz 2

Verben

bieten, bot, hat geboten to offer; provide

diskutieren to discuss; debate

erledigen to attend to, take care of, finish

frustrieren to frustrate

teil·nehmen (nimmt teil), nahm teil, hat teilgenommen an (+ *dat.*) to take part in

Substantive

der **Erfolg, -e** success

der **Gedanke, -ns,⁷ -n** thought

der **Lohn, ̈e** wage

der **Weg, -e** way, path

das **Geschlecht, -er** sex, gender

das **Gesetz, -e** law
   vor dem Gesetz under, in the eyes, of the law

das **Thema, Themen** topic, subject, theme

die **Aufgabe, -n** task, assignment

die **Gleichberechtigung** (*sing.*) equal rights

die **Küche, -n** kitchen

Adjektive und Adverbien

deutlich clear

gebildet educated

gesellschaftlich social

gleich equal

gleichberechtigt enjoying equal rights

kritisch critical

öffentlich public

Nützlicher Ausdruck

es geht um it's a question of . . . ; it's about . . . (*subject is always **es***)
   Worum geht es in dieser Diskussion? What's this discussion about?
   Es geht um die Gleichberechtigung. It's about equal rights.

Gegensätze

gebildet ≠ ungebildet educated ≠ uneducated

öffentlich ≠ privat public ≠ private

7. The nouns **Gedanke** and **Name** take an **-n** in every case except the nominative (Kennst du meinen Namen?) *and* add **-s** in the genitive. Proverb: **Der Wunsch ist Vater des Gedankens.**

Gedanken über die
Emanzipation der Frau

Die Rolle der Frau in der Gesellschaft ist in Deutschland
wie fast überall in der Welt in den letzten Jahren zum heißen
Diskussionsthema geworden. Es wird sowohl über soziale
als auch° über psychologische Fragen diskutiert. Es geht um
gleichen Lohn für gleiche Arbeit, aber auch um das Selbst-
bewußtsein° der Frau und um die Beziehungen° zwischen
den Geschlechtern.

　Ein altes Klischee sagt, die Frau solle sich nur um „Kinder, Küche und Kirche" kümmern. Für manche Frauen mag
das noch stimmen, aber für die meisten jungen Frauen nicht
mehr. Es ist das Ziel der Frauenbewegung, solche Klischees
zu bekämpfen° und allen Frauen neue Wege zu eröffnen.°
Heutzutage versuchen viele Frauen, aus dieser traditionellen
sozialen Rolle auszubrechen.

　In früheren Zeiten wurden fast alle jungen Mädchen auf
eine Zukunft als Mutter und Hausfrau vorbereitet. Sie mußten früh lernen, wie die „ideale" Frau sein sollte: beschei-
den,° ordentlich und kinderlieb.° Dieses traditionelle Bild
hatte sich nach und nach als selbstverständlich etabliert.°

　Im industriellen Zeitalter° wurde es aber immer deut-
licher, daß die Industrie die Arbeitskraft° der Frau brauchte.
Es waren die ungebildeten und armen Frauen aus der Arbei-
terklasse, die in gefährlichen, ungesunden Fabriken arbeiten

sowohl . . . als auch = both . . . and

self–esteem / relationships

= kämpfen gegen / = neue Chancen zu geben

modest / **= lieb zu Kindern**
established
= Epoche
labor

Friedensdemonstration (Berlin)

Politessen (*meter maids*) in Berlin

mußten, weil ihre Familien sonst verhungert° wären. Die
Damen der Oberschicht° aber konnten zu Hause Herrin°
sein, wo es ihre Aufgabe war, den Haushalt° zu führen und
gesellschaftliche Unterhaltung° zu bieten. Natürlich gab es
schon im 18. und 19. Jahrhundert gebildete und aktive
Frauen, wie z.B. Bettina von Arnim oder Rahel Varnhagen,
die Berliner Salons führten.[8] Heutige° Frauen haben auch
gelernt, die trotz aller Schwierigkeiten errungenen Leistung-
en° dieser früheren Frauengenerationen zu schätzen.°

Und wie ist es heute? Im Grundgesetz[9] der BRD (Artikel
3) steht zwar, daß alle Menschen vor dem Gesetz gleich
seien. Männer und Frauen seien gleichberechtigt. Aber ist
die offizielle Gleichberechtigung schon verwirklicht?°
Manche berufstätigen Frauen müssen noch die Hausarbeit
erledigen, obwohl sie den gleichen Arbeitstag haben wie ihre
Männer. Jede Frau, die so überfordert° ist, wird natürlich
frustriert.

Trotzdem hat sich viel im Leben der Frauen geändert.
Jungen Frauen stehen heute viel mehr Türen offen als vor
fünfzig Jahren. Immer mehr Frauen nehmen aktiv und kritisch am öffentlichen Leben ihres Landes teil. In der BRD
haben Frauen führende Positionen in politischen Parteien,
besonders bei den Grünen.

Viele Frauen wollen traditionelle Männerrollen nicht
einfach übernehmen, sondern auch ändern. Die auch in
Amerika bekannte Schriftstellerin Christa Wolf schrieb über
dieses Phänomen: „Die Möglichkeit, die unsere Gesellschaft [den Frauen] gab: zu tun, was die Männer tun, hat
sie . . . zu der Frage gebracht: Was *tun* die Männer über-
haupt?° Und will ich das eigentlich?"

Aber parallel zu den Verbesserungen° im Leben der Frau
ändert sich die Rolle des Mannes. Heutzutage wollen viele
Männer mehr Zeit mit ihren Familien verbringen und sich
weniger um Karriere und Erfolg kümmern. Die Frauenemanzipation bringt also viel mehr als nur bessere Berufs-
chancen für Frauen. Sie könnte auch eines Tages zu einem
besseren Leben für beide Geschlechter führen.

Zeile	Glosse
25	= an Hunger gestorben = der oberen Klasse / *mistress* *household* *entertainment*
30	= moderne **errungenen Leistungen** = *gained* *achievements* / *appreciate*
35	= wirklich geworden
40	*overtaxed*
50	*anyway, after all* *improvements*

8. The novelist and essayist Bettina von Arnim (1785–1859) and the prolific
letter writer Rahel Varnhagen von Ense (1771–1833) presided over influential
literary salons in Berlin.
9. The "Basic Law" or constitution of the Federal Republic of Germany.

1. Was sind die Ziele der Frauenbewegung?

2. Wie heißt das alte Klischee über das Leben der Frau?

3. Beschreiben Sie die traditionelle Rolle der Frau.

4. Wie wurde die soziale Rolle der Frau durch die Industrialisierung geändert?

5. Was für Frauen arbeiteten in den Fabriken?

6. Welche Möglichkeiten haben junge Frauen von heute, die die Frauen vor fünfzig Jahren nicht hatten?

7. Wie könnte die Frauenbewegung auch das Leben der Männer ändern?

Situationen aus dem Alltag

Mit Gefühl!

Sie haben schon viele Ausdrücke gelernt, mit denen Sie Gefühle und Reaktionen ausdrücken können. Die folgende Liste wiederholt solche Ausdrücke aus früheren Kapiteln.

sich freuen (die Freude, "joy")

Wunderbar!
Ich bin heute so glücklich!
Das ist ja wunderschön!
Ich gratuliere (dir)!
Ich bin begeistert!

Mitleid ausdrücken (das Mitleid, "sympathy")

Das tut mir leid.
Gute Besserung!
Schade!
Du siehst traurig aus.
 Was ist denn los?
Du Arme! Du Armer!

sich ärgern (der Ärger, "annoyance, anger")

Ich habe die Nase voll.
So ein Mist!
Verflixt nochmal!
Ich bin frustriert!

enttäuscht sein (die Enttäuschung, "disappointment")

Schade!
Ich habe Pech gehabt.
So ein Mist!

überrascht sein (die Überraschung, "surprise")

Um Gottes Willen!
Mensch!
So was!
Ich bin ganz baff!
Ich bin erstaunt!

„Total begeistert"

Gruppenarbeit: Mensch, bin ich . . . !

Diese Zeichnungen zeigen Menschen, die starke Gefühle haben. Welches Gefühl zeigt jedes Bild? Wie könnte man in jeder Situation die Emotion ausdrücken? (Es gibt natürlich verschiedene Möglichkeiten.)

Gruppendiskussion: Da war ich sehr aufgeregt.

Alle Menschen haben manchmal starke Gefühle. Beschreiben Sie eine Situation aus Ihrem Leben, in der Sie ein Gefühl von Ärger, Freude, Überraschung, Enttäuschung oder Mitleid gehabt haben.

BEISPIEL: Ich war einmal besonders überrascht, als . . .

Partnerarbeit: Mini-Dialoge

Unten werden verschiedene Situationen beschrieben. Erfinden Sie (*invent*) zu jeder Situation einen Mini-Dialog, in dem Sie Gefühle und Reaktionen ausdrücken. Spielen Sie dann einen von Ihren Dialogen vor der ganzen Klasse.

1. Sie wollen zusammen ausgehen. Ihre Freundin kann aber ihren Geldbeutel nicht finden.
2. Ein Partner ruft den anderen an und sagt, er müsse heute leider zu Hause bleiben, weil er plötzlich sehr krank geworden sei.
3. Ein Partner arbeitet für die Lotterie (*lottery*) und ruft den anderen an, um ihm zu gratulieren: er habe DM 100 000 gewonnen.
4. Sie freuen sich schon seit Monaten auf eine Reise nach Spanien. Jetzt hören Sie plötzlich, daß die Reise nicht mehr stattfinden kann, weil die Reisegesellschaft (*travel agency*) bankrott (*bankrupt*) ist.
5. Sie verbringen einen langweiligen Nachmittag vor dem Fernseher, und plötzlich klingelt es. Sie gehen an die Haustür, und da steht Ihr Lieblingsonkel Max, den Sie seit vier Jahren nicht mehr gesehen haben.

Zum Schluß

Sprechen wir miteinander

A Worum geht es?

Nennen Sie zuerst Filme oder Bücher, die Ihnen besonders gefallen. Dann sagen Sie bei jedem Werk, worum es geht.

> BEISPIEL: Mein Lieblingsfilm heißt „Casablanca". In dem Film geht es um Liebe, aber auch um Politik.

B Gruppenarbeit: Was wird hier gemacht?

Sagen Sie, was auf diesen Bildern gemacht wird.

> BEISPIEL: Hier werden Bücher gelesen. *oder*
> Hier wird gelesen.

C **Partnerarbeit:** Rollenspiel

Wählen Sie eine Situation aus, und seien Sie bereit, sie vor der ganzen Klasse
zu spielen.

1. **Abends um 18.00 Uhr**
   Margarete, die vor vier Monaten ein Baby bekommen hat, arbeitet wieder
   in ihrer alten Stelle. Ihr Mann Rolf schreibt an seiner Diss und bleibt bei
   dem Kleinen zu Hause. Margarete kommt nach einem harten Arbeitstag
   nach Hause.

2. **Umziehen oder hierbleiben?**
   Monika und Harald sind Studenten in ihrem letzten Semester an der Uni
   in München. Sie haben vor, bald zu heiraten. Harald hat gerade eine gut
   bezahlte Stelle an einem Gymnasium in Frankfurt bekommen. Monika hat
   noch keine Stelle gefunden und sie möchte München nicht verlassen.

3. **Mutter und Tochter**
   Anita (19 Jahre alt) fragt ihre Mutter (50), wie es damals war, als sie jung
   war. Frau Baumann erzählt ihrer Tochter, was sie als junge Frau gern
   gemacht hätte, oder was sie anders machen würde.

D **Klassendiskussion:** Unterschiede und Ähnlichkeiten

1. Besprechen Sie einige Unterschiede und Ähnlichkeiten . . .
   in der Erziehung (*upbringing*) von Mädchen und Jungen.
   im Leben von Studenten und Studentinnen an dieser Uni.

2. An einigen privaten Hochschulen in Amerika studieren *nur* Frauen (ohne
   Männer) oder *nur* Männer (ohne Frauen). Halten Sie das für gut? Warum
   oder warum nicht?

Schreiben Sie zu Hause

E Fernsehinterview Im Fernsehen gab es neulich ein Gespräch zwischen einem Interviewer und der bekannten Feministin Elisabeth Schmidt-Dengler. Lesen Sie diesen Bericht über das Interview und schreiben Sie das Gespräch, das die beiden geführt haben, als Dialog.

Der Interviewer fragte Frau Schmidt-Dengler, wie lange sie wohl noch für die Emanzipation der Frau kämpfen müsse. Das sei schwer zu sagen, meinte sie. Sie werde einfach nicht aufgeben, bis alle Frauen gleichberechtigt seien. Der Interviewer unterbrach und sagte, daß die Gleichberechtigung schon seit Jahren im Grundgesetz stehe. Frau Schmidt-Dengler lachte und sagte, ja, das stimme schon, und das sei auch wichtig. Auf der anderen Seite seien das Grundgesetz und die Wirklichkeit leider oft zwei verschiedene Sachen. Die Frauenemanzipation dürfe nicht nur im Gesetz stehen. Man müsse auch das traditionelle Denken über die Rollen von Mann und Frau ändern. Der Interviewer dankte Frau Schmidt-Dengler für das Gespräch.

F Aufsatzthema Was wäre in Ihrem Leben anders, wenn Sie eine Frau / ein Mann wären?

G Wie sagt man das auf deutsch?

1. Max told me that there was a new restaurant around the corner.
2. Yes, the food is supposed to be very good.
3. But the prices could be lower.
4. Max has eaten there three times already. He recommended it to me.

5. Did you ask Mimi whether she were coming to the wedding?
6. Yes, but she acted as if she had never heard of it.
7. Brigitte says she invited her last month.

8. Hello, Ruth! Why weren't you at Lina's birthday party on Friday night?
9. I'm sorry, but I was simply too tired.
10. You know, I've found a new job and I had a lot to take care of.
11. Too bad you missed it.
12. We celebrated until 1:30. (Use impersonal passive.)

Legal Protection for Pregnancy and Maternity

The laws known collectively as *Mutterschutz* (*Maternity Protection*) are a good example of the extensive social service safety net available to citizens of the Federal Republic.

Mutterschaftsgeld: A pregnant woman continues to receive the full amount of her previous pay (or disability pay, or a lump sum).

Mutterschaftsvorsorge: All expenses for prenatal care and delivery are covered.

Gefahrenschutz: A pregnant woman may not be forced to undertake tasks that endanger her or her child.

Kündigungsschutz: A woman cannot be fired during her pregnancy or in the four months following delivery (eight months if she chooses to take maternity leave).

Beschäftigungsverbot: A pregnant woman cannot be forced to work in the six weeks prior to her delivery date and may not work for eight weeks after delivery (twelve weeks for premature deliveries or multiple births).

Mutterschaftsurlaub: Maternity leave at reduced salary for up to four months may be taken after the 8–12 week protective period has expired. 93% of mothers take advantage of this leave to care for their newborn children.

Zusammenfassung und Wiederholung

(Kapitel 13–16)

FORMS

1. Future tense

Inflected form of **werden** + infinitive

p. 399

auxiliary   *infinitive*
Ich **werde** das am Montag **erledigen.**
Sie **wird** dich nicht   **verstehen.**

2. General subjunctive

pp. 417–26

A. Present tense of general subjunctive

1. Weak verbs

Present subjunctive has the same form as past indicative

p. 417

wenn ich wohnte	*if I lived*	wenn wir wohnten	*if we lived*
wenn du wohntest	*if you lived*	wenn ihr wohntet	*if you lived*
wenn sie wohnte	*if she lived*	wenn sie wohnten	*if they lived*

2. Strong verbs

Present subjunctive = simple past stem (**fuhr-**) + umlaut whenever possible (**führ-**) + subjunctive endings:

pp. 418–19

wenn ich **führe**	*if I drove*	wenn wir **führen**	*if we drove*
wenn du **führest**	*if you drove*	wenn ihr **führet**	*if you drove*
wenn er **führe**	*if he drove*	wenn sie **führen**	*if they drove*

3. Modal verbs

p. 420

Present subjunctive = past indicative (**ich sollte, ich durfte**) + umlaut when infinitive has umlaut (**ich sollte, ich dürfte**):

ich **dürfte**	*I would be allowed*	ich **müßte**	*I would have to*
ich **könnte**	*I could*	ich **sollte**	*I ought to*
ich **möchte**	*I would like to*	ich **wollte**	*I would want to*

p. 421

4. **haben, werden, wissen**

Present subjunctive = past indicative (**ich hatte, wurde, wußte**) + umlaut (**ich hätte, würde, wüßte**):

wenn ich **hätte**	*if I had*	wenn wir **hätten**	*if we had*
wenn du **hättest**	*if you had*	wenn ihr **hättet**	*if you had*
wenn sie **hätte**	*if she had*	wenn sie **hätten**	*if they had*

wenn ich **würde**	*if I became*	wenn wir **würden**	*if we became*
wenn du **würdest**	*if you became*	wenn ihr **würdet**	*if you became*
wenn er **würde**	*if he became*	wenn sie **würden**	*if they became*

wenn ich **wüßte**	*if I knew*	wenn wir **wüßten**	*if we knew*
wenn du **wüßtest**	*if you knew*	wenn ihr **wüßtet**	*if you knew*
wenn sie **wüßte**	*if she knew*	wenn sie **wüßten**	*if they knew*

5. Present subjunctive with **würde**

p. 422

ich **würde kommen**	*I would come*	wir **würden kommen**	*we would come*
du **würdest kommen**	*you would come*	ihr **würdet kommen**	*you would come*
er **würde kommen**	*he would come*	sie **würden kommen**	*they would come*

B. Past tense of general subjunctive

pp. 445–47

1. Without a modal verb

Use present subjunctive of **sein** or **haben** + past participle.

Ich **hätte** auf dich **gewartet**.	*I **would have waited** for you.*
Wir **wären** gestern abend **gekommen**.	*We **would have come** yesterday evening.*

2. With a modal verb

pp. 445–47

Use present subjunctive of **haben** + double infinitive.

Ihr **hättet** länger **warten sollen**.	*You **should have waited** longer.*
Sie **hätte** auch **mitkommen dürfen**.	*She **would have been allowed to come along** too.*

3. Special subjunctive (for indirect quotation)

pp. 474–76

A. Present tense of special subjunctive

pp. 474–75

Infinitive stem + subjunctive endings

Der Kanzler sagte, er **wisse** das schon.	*The Chancellor said he already **knew** that.*

| Frau Braun meint, daß sie das verstehen **könne.** | Mrs. Braun says that she **can** understand that. |

B. Future tense of special subjunctive   p. 475

Present special subjunctive of **werden** + infinitive

| Laura fragte, ob er bald **zurückkommen werde.** | Laura asked if he **would come back** soon. |

C. Past tense of special subjunctive   p. 475

Present special subjunctive of **haben** or **sein** + past participle

| Richard sagt, er **habe** das nicht **getan.** | Richard says he **didn't do** that. |
| Marie fragte, ob er schon **angekommen sei.** | Marie asked whether he **had** already **arrived.** |

4. Passive voice   pp. 448–52

A. Basic conjugation

Inflected Form of **werden** + past participle

passive infinitive		**gesehen werden**	*to be seen*
present	Er **wird**	**gesehen.**	*He is seen.*
past	Er **wurde**	**gesehen.**	*He was seen.*
future	Er **wird**	**gesehen werden.**	*He will be seen.*
perfect	Er **ist**	**gesehen worden.**	*He has been seen.* or *He was seen.*
past perfect	Er **war**	**gesehen worden.**	*He had been seen.*

B. Passive with a modal verb

Inflected modal + passive infinitive

present	Das	**muß**	**geändert werden.**	*That must be changed.*
past	Das	**mußte**	**geändert werden.**	*That had to be changed.*
future	Das	**wird**	**geändert werden müssen.**	*That will have to be changed.*
perfect	Das	**hat**	**geändert werden müssen.**	*That had to be changed.*
past perf.	Das	**hatte**	**geändert werden müssen.**	*That had had to be changed.*

C. Impersonal passive construction (for human activities)   p. 471

The verb is *always* third person singular. There is no expressed subject.

| Hier **wird** oft **getanzt.** | *There's often **dancing** here.* |

Impersonal **es** begins the sentence if no other element occupies first position.

Es wird hier oft getanzt.

5. Verbs with prepositional complements

pp. 392–94

A. Here is a list of all the verbs with prepositional complements that you have learned.

Angst haben vor (+ *dat.*)	*to be afraid of*
antworten auf (+ *acc.*)	*to answer something*
sich ärgern über (+ *acc.*)	*to get annoyed at, be annoyed about*
aufpassen auf (+ *acc.*)	*to look after; pay attention to*
sich aufregen über (+ *acc.*)	*to get upset, excited about*
bitten um	*to ask for, request*
denken an (+ *acc.*)	*to think of*
sich erholen von	*to recover from*
erinnern an (+ *acc.*)	*to remind of*
sich erinnern an (+ *acc.*)	*to remember*
sich freuen auf (+ *acc.*)	*to look forward to*
gehören zu	*to be part of, be one of*
sich gewöhnen an (+ *acc.*)	*to get used to*
halten für	*to take for, regard as, think X is*
sich interessieren für	*to be interested in*
sich konzentrieren auf (+ *acc.*)	*to concentrate on*
sich kümmern um	*to look after, take care of, deal with*
reagieren auf (+ *acc.*)	*to react to*
sprechen (schreiben, lesen, lachen, usw.) über (+ *acc.*)	*to talk (write, read, laugh, etc.) about*
teilnehmen an (+ *dat.*)	*to take part in*
sich verloben mit	*to become engaged to*
sich vorbereiten auf (+ *acc.*)	*to prepare for*
warten auf (+ *acc.*)	*to wait for*
sich wundern über (+ *acc.*)	*to be surprised, amazed at*

B. **da-** and **wo-**compounds

pp. 395–97

Use a **da-** or **wo-**compound instead of *preposition + pronoun* when the prepositional object is an inanimate noun.

animate noun object	*pronoun object*	
Er dachte **an seine Freundin.**	Er dachte **an sie.**	p. 395
Sie interessiert sich **für Goethe.**	**Für wen** interessiert sie sich?	

inanimate noun object	*da-* or *wo-compound*	
Er dachte an **die Deutschstunde.**	Er dachte **daran.**	p. 396
Sie interessiert sich **für Geschichte.**	**Wofür** interessiert sie sich?	

6. Participles

pp. 453–54

A. Present participles as adjectives and adverbs

infinitive + **-d**

schlafen + **-d** → **schlafend**	*sleeping*
spielen + **-d** → **spielend**	*playing*

As an adjective, the present participle takes the usual adjective endings.

Stört das **schlafende** Mädchen nicht.

*Don't disturb the **sleeping** girl.*

Spielende Kinder sind manchmal laut.

***Playing** children are sometimes loud.*

B. Past participles as adjectives   p. 330

Gut **vorbereitete** Studenten lernen am meisten.

*Well-**prepared** students learn the most.*

Ich muß meinen **reparierten** Wagen heute abholen.

*I have to pick up my **repaired** car today.*

FUNCTIONS

1. Making wishes and conditions contrary to fact: general subjunctive

pp. 423–24

A. Conditions contrary to fact

condition	*conclusion*
Wenn . . . (subjunctive verb),	(subjunctive verb) . . .
Wenn ich Zeit **hätte,**	**würde** ich Ihnen helfen.

conclusion	*condition*
. . . (subjunctive verb)	**wenn** . . . (subjunctive verb).
Ich **würde** Ihnen helfen,	**wenn** ich Zeit **hätte.**

B. Wishes contrary to fact   p. 425

1. **Wenn . . . nur . . .** (subjunctive verb)!

    Wenn du **nur** näher **wohntest!**   *If only you lived closer!*

2. **Ich wünschte, / Ich wollte, . . .** (subjunctive verb) . . .

    Ich **wünschte,** ich **könnte** mir etwas Besseres leisten.

    I wish I could afford something better.

2. Making polite requests: general subjunctive   p. 426

Use general subjunctive for polite requests. Note the difference in tone between indicative and subjunctive.

Können Sie nicht aufhören?
Könnten Sie bitte aufhören?

Can't you stop!
Could you please stop?

Haben Sie ein Zimmer frei?
Hätten Sie ein Zimmer frei?

Do you have a room free?
Would you have a room free?

3. Describing with *als ob*: general subjunctive

p. 478

Es war,
Er tut, } **als ob . . .** (subjunctive verb).
Sie sah aus,

Sie sehen aus, **als ob** Sie schlecht **geschlafen hätten.**

You look as if you had slept badly.

Sie spricht Deutsch, **als ob** es ihre Muttersprache **wäre.**

She speaks German as though it were her native language.

4. Quoting indirectly: special subjunctive

pp. 474–77

A. When special subjunctive is required

Formal German (such as journalistic reporting and research papers) requires special subjunctive for indirect quotation. In everyday conversation, most Germans use general subjunctive or indicative for indirect quotation.

B. Tenses in indirect quotation

p. 476

The tense of the indirect quote is the same as the tense of the direct quote from which it derives.

	Direct quotation	*Indirect quotation*	
present	„Ich **bin** müde.“	Luise sagte, sie **sei** müde.	*present*
past	„Ich **war** müde.“	Luise sagte, sie **sei** müde **gewesen.**	*past*
perfect	„Ich **bin** müde **gewesen.**“ }		
future	„Ich **werde** müde **sein.**“	Luise sagte, sie **werde** müde **sein.**	*future*

C. Yes/no questions in indirect quotation begin with **ob**

„Hast du Zeit?“ → Sie fragte, **ob** ich Zeit hätte.

D. Commands in indirect quotation use the verb **sollen**

„Denk daran!“ → Johann sagte, ich **sollte** daran denken.

5. Indicating direction

pp. 454–56

A. Away from the speaker: **hin**
B. Toward the speaker: **her**

6. Indicating possibility, probability, hearsay, and doubt with modal verbs

p. 472–73

A. Possibility: **mögen**

Die Arbeit **mag** hart sein, aber sie muß trotzdem gemacht werden.	*The work may be hard but it has to be done anyway.*

B. Strong probability: **müssen**

Sie **muß** schon in Europa sein.	*She must be in Europe already.*

C. Hearsay: **sollen**

Sie **sollen** doch so glücklich sein.	*They are supposed to be so happy.*

D. Fairly strong possibility: **können**

Er **kann** noch berühmt werden.	*He may yet become famous.*

E. Doubting a claim: **wollen**

Was? Dieser Politiker **will** ehrlich sein?	*What! This politician claims to be honest!*

7. Wanting *X* to do *Y*

p. 400

Use **möchten** or **wollen** followed by a **daß**-clause.

Wollen Sie, daß ich später vorbei-
komme?

Do you want me to come by later?

Nein, **ich möchte, daß** wir jetzt kurz
zusammen reden.

*No, I'd like us to talk briefly together
right now.*

USEFUL IDIOMS AND EXPRESSIONS

1. Specifying time

In Zukunft werde ich mehr Geld
brauchen.
Eines Tages müssen wir das erledigen.
Wir haben **jahrelang** darauf gewartet.

Ich habe **eine Zeitlang** in der Türkei
gearbeitet.
Höchste Zeit!

2. Requesting information

Kennen Sie sich hier aus?
Darf ich Sie um Auskunft bitten?

Wie komme ich dahin?
Worum geht es in dem Buch, das du
liest?

3. Expressing reactions and opinions

Das kann ich nicht ernst nehmen.
Kein Wunder!
Das mag sein.
Was sagen (meinen) Sie dazu?
Verflixt nochmal!

Sagenhaft!
Ich bin baff!
Das muß ich mir überlegen.
Es kommt darauf an.

4. Making requests and commands

Hören Sie gut zu!
Sei mir bitte nicht böse!

Passen Sie auf!
Zeig mal her.

5. Introducing people

Darf ich meinen Freund Jan vorstellen?
Darf ich mich vorstellen?
Angenehm. / Freut mich. / Sehr erfreut.

TEST YOUR PROGRESS

A. Provide the German prepositional phrase cued in English. Note that in some cases the English equivalent may not contain a preposition.

1. Wie lange warten Sie schon (*for something new*)?

2. Wie habt ihr (*to her idea*) reagiert?

3. Ich kann mich sehr gut (*my childhood*) erinnern.

4. Wir müssen uns (*for the test*) vorbereiten.

5. Kannst du dich bei diesem Wetter (*on your work*) konzentrieren?

6. Ich kümmere mich gar nicht (*with the test*).

7. Willst du (*in the discussion*) teilnehmen?

8. Nein, ich interessiere mich nicht (*in such problems*).

9. Ich kann mich nicht (*to your friends*) gewöhnen.

10. Denkt Rolf noch (*of me*)?

11. Natürlich. Er bat mich (*for your address*).

12. Meine Schwester hat sich (*to a German*) verlobt.

13. (*About this topic*) haben sich die Studenten sehr aufgeregt.

14. Er erinnert mich (*of his father*).

B. Answer the following questions affirmatively. Replace the prepositional phrase with a **da**-compound or the personal object with a pronoun.

> BEISPIEL: Bereiten Sie sich auf Ihre Reise vor?
> Ja, wir bereiten uns darauf vor.
> *oder*
> Erinnern Sie sich noch an meine ältere Schwester?
> Ja, ich erinnere mich noch an sie.

1. Haben Sie auf seinen Brief geantwortet?

2. Interessieren Sie sich für klassische Musik?

3. Kannst du dich an diesen Typ gewöhnen?

4. Hat Sabina sich um ihren Bruder gekümmert?

5. Hast du dich über seine Reaktion gewundert?

6. Habt ihr auch an die anderen Studenten gedacht?

C. Read the facts below and write conditional sentences contrary to these facts.

> BEISPIEL: Weil du viel Tennis spielst, bist du fit.
> Wenn du nicht viel Tennis spieltest, wärest du nicht fit.

1. Weil du nicht arbeitest, haben wir nicht genug Geld.

2. Wir haben nichts gekauft, weil der Laden noch nicht auf war.

3. Weil er nicht freundlich ist, kann man nicht leicht mit ihm reden.

4. Weil die Straßenbahn nicht weiter fährt, müssen wir jetzt laufen.

5. Ich habe ihr nicht gratuliert, weil ich nicht wußte, daß sie heute Geburtstag hat.

D. Read the facts below and use subjunctive to write wishes contrary to these facts. Use **Wenn . . . nur . . .** , **Ich wünschte . . .** , or **Ich wollte . . .** as indicated.

> BEISPIEL: Wir haben nicht genug Zeit. (wenn . . . nur)
> Wenn wir nur genug Zeit hätten!

1. Wir sind noch nicht angekommen. (wenn . . . nur)
2. Heute morgen haben wir die Wohnung nicht aufgeräumt. (ich wünschte)
3. In der Altstadt gibt es kein Café. (ich wollte)
4. Leider habe ich meine Reiseschecks vergessen. (wenn . . . nur)
5. Die Preise sind gestiegen. (ich wünschte)

E. Respond to each sentence by saying that the persons under discussion only *look* as though something were the case.

> BEISPIEL: Ist Rolf wirklich so optimistisch?
> Nein, er sieht nur aus, als ob er optimistisch wäre.

1. Sind deine Mitbewohner wirklich so ordentlich?
2. Haben deine Freunde wirklich so viel Geld?
3. Ist Jutta wirklich so konservativ geworden?
4. Ist Frank wirklich gerade aus den Ferien zurückgekommen?

F. Make these requests more polite by putting them into the subjunctive.

1. Können Sie mir helfen?
2. Darf ich eine Frage stellen?
3. Werden Sie mir das Gepäck tragen?
4. Haben Sie ein Zimmer mit Bad?
5. Wann soll ich das für Sie machen?

G. Restate the following sentences in the passive. Keep the same tense as the active sentence.

> BEISPIEL: Max baut dieses Haus.
> Dieses Haus wird von Max gebaut.

1. Karl hat diesen Brief geschrieben.
2. Hinter dem Dom baute die Stadt eine neue Schule.
3. Professor Müller hält die Vorlesung.
4. Viele Studenten haben diese Zeitung gelesen.
5. Mein Freund wird diese Arbeit erledigen.

H. Restate the sentences in the passive.

> BEISPIEL: Wer soll diese Arbeit machen?
> Von wem soll diese Arbeit gemacht werden?

1. Das kann der Chef eines Tages erledigen.
2. Das ganze Buch muß man bis Donnerstag lesen.
3. Unsren Zweitwagen müssen wir leider verkaufen.

4. Ein solches Klischee kann man nicht ernst nehmen.

5. Können alle die Frage verstehen?

I. Replace the verb in parentheses with an adjective formed from its present or past participle. Don't forget adjective endings.

>BEISPIEL: Wann werden die (bestellen) Bücher endlich ankommen?
>Wann werden die bestellten Bücher endlich ankommen?

1. Ich kann bei (schließen) Fenstern nicht schlafen.

2. Gott sei Dank habe ich das (verlieren) Geld wieder gefunden.

3. Der (übersetzen) Roman kann hoffentlich leichter gelesen werden.

4. Dieser Historiker hat viele (vergessen) Namen genannt.

5. Der gerade (abfahren) Zug fährt nach Madrid.

J. Wie sagt man das auf deutsch?

1. What are you thinking of?

2. I thought the book was very interesting.

3. I have to think about that for a while.

4. We could go to Grinzing. What do *you* think?

5. I think that's a good answer.

K. Restate the following sentences using the appropriate subjective modal.

>BEISPIEL: Es ist unglaublich, daß sie Ausländer sind.
>Sie können keine Ausländer sein.

1. Ich bin sicher, daß das unser alter Lehrer ist.

2. Man sagt, die Preise seien im Ausland niedriger.

3. Es ist möglich, daß das stimmt.

4. Vielleicht ist er schon dreißig.

5. Sie sagt, sie sei eine gute Künstlerin, aber ich glaube ihr nicht.

L. Report what Gabi said to you, using special subjunctive.

1. Ich war gestern in der Mensa. (Gabi sagte, sie . . .)

2. Das Essen hat mir gut geschmeckt.

3. Ich bereite mich jetzt auf eine Klausur vor.

4. Hat dich Heinz angerufen?

5. Ich bin jetzt ziemlich müde.

6. Zeig mir dein Referat über Kafka.

Answer Key to "Test Your Progress"

Test Your Progress 1 *(page 127)*

A.
1. scheint *to shine; to seem*
2. spielen *to play*
3. geht *to go*
4. bedeutet *to mean*
5. meine *to be of the opinion; to think; to mean*
6. läuft *to run; to go on foot; to walk*
7. stimmt *to be correct*
8. schläfst *to sleep*
9. fahren *to drive, go (by vehicle)*
10. besucht *to visit*
11. will *to want to*
12. darf *to be permitted to, may*
13. wirst *to become*
14. schneit *to snow*
15. bekommen *to get, receive*
16. liest *to read*
17. tragt *to carry; wear*
18. kann *to be able, can*
19. warte *to wait*
20. soll *to be supposed to, should*

B.
1. Barbara möchte schon nach Berlin.
2. Die Studenten wollen noch ein bißchen bleiben.
3. Was trägst du am Freitag?
4. Nimmt Karin ein Brötchen?
5. Liest du die Zeitung?
6. Schläft er bis neun?
7. Weiß Gisela, wie er heißt?
8. Wartet er bis zehn?
9. Ißt Oliver Pommes frites?
10. Horst läuft durch den Wald.

C.
1. die / Schulen
2. das / Hemden
3. die / Mütter
4. der / Schuhe
5. die / Sprachen
6. der / Freunde
7. die / Freundinnen
8. der / Brüder
9. die / Schwestern
10. das / Klischees
11. der / Söhne
12. die / Töchter
13. das / Häuser
14. die / Zeitungen
15. der / Berufe
16. das / Länder
17. der / Stühle
18. die / Frauen
19. der / Lehrer
20. die / Lehrerinnen

D.
1. Nein, ich bin noch nicht müde.
2. Nein, wir wohnen nicht mehr zu Hause.
3. Nein, sie ist keine Studentin mehr. *or:* . . . nicht mehr Studentin.
4. Nein, ich kenne deine Schwester noch nicht.
5. Nein, wir haben noch keine Kinder.
6. Nein, ich schreibe keine Briefe mehr.
7. Nein, Sie brauchen nicht mehr hier zu bleiben.
8. Nein, ich habe keine Angst mehr. *or:* . . . wir haben keine Angst mehr.

E.
1. Meine; keine
2. den *or* einen; kein
3. Ihren
4. meinen
5. unser
6. meine
7. Die
8. Ihre
9. Mein; meine
10. Das; keine

F.
1. ihr
2. sie
3. ihr
4. seine
5. ihr
6. Ihren
7. euch
8. Ihre
9. Ihr
10. sie

G.
1. Ich mag dich sehr. *or:* Ich habe dich sehr gern.
2. Mögen Sie (magst du) meine Freunde nicht? *or:* Haben Sie (hast du) meine Freunde nicht gern?
3. Ich möchte allein sein.
4. Ich bin gern allein.
5. Möchten Sie (möchtest du, möchtet ihr) schwimmen gehen?
6. Ich wandere gern.
7. Ich habe das Klima nicht gern. *or:* Ich mag das Klima nicht.

Test Your Progress 2 *(page 252)*

A.
1. seit; an
2. Bei; über
3. im
4. mit; auf; zur
5. Nach *or* Vor; in; nach
6. Auf *or* Unter *or* Neben *or* Hinter; bei; außer

B. 1. Wohin fliegt er? *or:* Wo fliegt er hin?
2. Woher kommt sie? *or:* Wo kommt sie her?
3. Stimmt das nicht?
4. Hast du keine Zeit für mich?
5. Wer hat das immer gesagt?
6. Wem gehört die Landkarte?
7. Wann sollen wir das machen?
8. Wo sind die Kinder heute?

C. 1. ins
2. zu
3. in
4. nach; nach
5. zum; nach

D. 1. den Kindern ein Märchen; es ihnen
2. meinem Freund den Artikel; ihn mir

E. 1. Karin ist heute zu Hause geblieben.
2. Meine Freunde haben nicht in München gewohnt.
3. Um wieviel Uhr bist du denn aufgestanden?
4. Ich habe meiner Familie einen Brief geschrieben.
5. Ich habe eine Stunde bleiben müssen.
6. Die Schüler sind oft müde gewesen.
7. Ich habe leider keine Zeit gehabt.
8. Sie ist Lehrerin geworden.

F. 1. Kommst du mit, oder bleibst du hier?
2. Weil ich keine Zeit habe, kann ich Ihnen nicht helfen.
3. Hamburg liegt nicht im Süden Deutschlands, sondern (es liegt) im Norden.
4. Ich weiß nicht, ob er hier ist.
5. Da wir wenig Geld haben, müssen wir trampen.
6. Wenn du mir helfen kannst, bin ich bald fertig.
7. Jan hat nicht studiert, aber er weiß viel über Geschichte.
8. Hast du gehört, daß Tante Karoline uns morgen besucht?
9. Obwohl sie nie in Europa gewesen ist, spricht sie gut Deutsch.

G. 1. den Wagen (das Auto) meines Freundes
2. das Ende dieser Geschichte
3. Karls Bruder
4. Das Haus meines Lehrers (meiner Lehrerin)
5. die Sprache dieser Menschen (dieser Leute)
6. trotz der Arbeit
7. Wegen meiner Arbeit
8. das Leben eines Studenten

H. 1. Wie spät ist es, bitte? (Wieviel Uhr ist es, bitte?)
2. Es ist fast halb acht.
3. Wann soll der Zug ankommen?
4. Er kommt um 20.59 Uhr an.
5. Was machst du (machen Sie) um Viertel vor acht?

I. 1. liege; im
2. auf *or* neben *or* unter (etc.); legen
3. ins; stellen
4. am; stehen
5. am; sitzen

J. 1. Wir haben keine Lust, Onkel Georg zu besuchen.
2. Sie sind ins Museum gegangen, um etwas über Kunst zu lernen.
3. Es war sehr nett von ihr, mir eine Karte aus Köln zu schicken.
4. Gehst du schon, ohne Julia auf Wiedersehen zu sagen?

Test Your Progress 3 *(page 383)*

A. 1. sich verletzt
2. fühlt er sich schon
3. sich verlobt haben
4. freuen sie sich
5. uns beeilen
6. mich kämmen (mir die Haare kämmen)
7. dich schon angezogen
8. mir ansehen

B. 1. diesen
2. alte
3. eine neue
4. deutsche
5. unserem
6. verschiedene interessante
7. die politische
8. ersten deutschen
9. diesen alten
10. vielen
11. des deutschen Volkes
12. erste
13. gutes
14. solche politischen
15. dieser wichtigen
16. einen starken
17. arbeitslosen Deutschen

C. 1. Als
2. Wenn
3. Wann
4. Wenn
5. Als
6. wann
7. Wenn

D. 1. Lassen Sie (Laß; Laßt) mich bitte bleiben!
2. Haben Sie Ihr (Hast du dein) Gepäck im Auto gelassen?
3. Ich lasse mir das Essen bringen.
4. Hast du (Haben Sie; Habt ihr) den Arzt kommen lassen?

5. Lassen Sie Ihren (Laß deinen) Mantel auf dem Stuhl.
6. Können wir die Kinder noch eine Stunde spielen lassen?

E.
1. lieber; am liebsten
2. ärmer; am ärmsten *or* die ärmsten
3. öfter; am öftesten
4. stärkerer; der stärkste
5. mehr; die meisten
6. wärmer; am wärmsten
7. größere; die größten
8. Mehr; Die meisten
9. interessanter; am interessantesten *or* die interessanteste
10. klügeres; das klügste

F.
1. den
2. dem
3. dessen
4. die
5. das
6. was
7. denen
8. der
9. die
10. was

G.
1. das letzte Mal
2. noch einmal
3. dreimal
4. das zweite Mal
5. damals
6. zum vierten Mal

H.
1. Was für einen Wagen (ein Auto) hast du?
2. Vor einem Monat habe ich mir den Arm gebrochen.
3. Heute morgen ist er nach Berlin gefahren.
4. Als du nach Hause kamst, hast du mich gestört.
5. Wie lange lernst du (schon) Deutsch?
6. Das sind die Studenten, deren Namen ich vergessen habe.
7. Ich bin vorgestern mit ihnen zum Bahnhof gegangen.
8. Das blaue Hemd war am teuersten (das teuerste).
9. Nachdem wir gegessen hatten, sind wir ins Kino gegangen.
10. Damals wohnten wir in einer kleinen Wohnung.
11. Er ist ein Freund von mir.
12. Meine Schwester ist jünger als ich.

Test Your Progress 4 *(page 500)*

A.
1. auf etwas Neues
2. auf ihre Idee
3. an meine Kindheit
4. auf die Prüfung
5. auf deine Arbeit
6. um die Prüfung
7. an der Diskussion
8. für solche Probleme
9. an deine Freunde
10. an mich
11. um deine Adresse
12. mit einem Deutschen
13. Über dieses Thema
14. an seinen Vater

B.
1. Ja, ich habe darauf geantwortet.
2. Ja, ich interessiere mich dafür.
3. Ja, ich kann mich an ihn gewöhnen.
4. Ja, sie hat sich um ihn gekümmert.
5. Ja, ich habe mich darüber gewundert.
6. Ja, wir haben auch an sie gedacht.

C.
1. Wenn du arbeitetest, hätten wir genug Geld.
2. Wir hätten etwas gekauft, wenn der Laden auf gewesen wäre.
3. Wenn er freundlich wäre, könnte man leicht mit ihm reden.
4. Wenn die Straßenbahn weiter führe, brauchten wir jetzt nicht zu laufen.
5. Ich hätte ihr gratuliert, wenn ich gewußt hätte, daß sie heute Geburtstag hat.

D.
1. Wenn wir nur schon angekommen wären!
2. Ich wünschte, wir hätten heute morgen die Wohnung aufgeräumt.
3. Ich wollte, es gäbe in der Alstadt ein Café.
4. Wenn ich meine Reiseschecks nur nicht vergessen hätte!
5. Ich wünschte, die Preise wären nicht gestiegen.

E.
1. Nein, sie sehen nur aus, als ob sie ordentlich wären.
2. Nein, sie sehen nur aus, als ob sie so viel Geld hätten.
3. Nein, sie sieht nur aus, als ob sie so konservativ geworden wäre.
4. Nein, er sieht nur aus, als ob er gerade aus den Ferien zurückgekommen wäre.

F.
1. Könnten Sie mir helfen?
2. Dürfte ich eine Frage stellen?
3. Würden Sie mir das Gepäck tragen?
4. Hätten Sie ein Zimmer mit Bad?
5. Wann sollte ich das für Sie machen?

G.
1. Dieser Brief ist von Karl geschrieben worden.
2. Hinter dem Dom wurde eine neue Schule von der Stadt gebaut.
3. Die Vorlesung wird von Professor Müller gehalten.
4. Diese Zeitung ist von vielen Studenten gelesen worden.
5. Diese Arbeit wird von meinem Freund erledigt werden.

H. 1. Das kann eines Tages vom Chef erledigt werden.
2. Das ganze Buch muß bis Donnerstag gelesen werden.
3. Unser Zweitwagen muß leider verkauft werden.
4. Ein solches Klischee kann nicht ernst genommen werden.
5. Kann die Frage von allen verstanden werden?

I. 1. geschlossenen   4. vergessene
2. verlorene   5. abfahrende
3. übersetzte   (abgefahrene)

J. 1. Woran denkst du?
2. Ich habe das Buch sehr interessant gefunden.
or: Ich hielt das Buch für sehr interessant.
3. Das muß ich mir eine Zeitlang überlegen.
4. Wir könnten nach Grinzing. Was meinst du?

5. Ich glaube (meine), das ist eine gute Antwort.
or: Das finde ich eine gute Antwort.

K. 1. Das muß unser alter Lehrer sein.
2. Die Preise sollen im Ausland niedriger sein.
3. Das mag (kann) stimmen.
4. Er kann (mag) schon dreißig sein.
5. Sie will eine gute Künstlerin sein, aber ich glaube ihr nicht.

L. 1. Sie sagte, sie sei gestern in der Mensa gewesen.
2. Sie sagte, das Essen habe ihr gut geschmeckt.
3. Sie sagte, sie bereite sich jetzt auf eine Klausur vor.
4. Sie fragte, ob Heinz mich angerufen habe.
5. Sie sagte, sie sei jetzt ziemlich müde.
6. Sie sagte, ich solle ihr mein Referat über Kafka zeigen.

Principal Parts of Strong and Irregular Verbs

The following table contains the principal parts of all the strong, mixed, and irregular verbs in *Neue Horizonte*. With a few exceptions, only the basic stem verbs are listed, e.g., **fahren, bringen,** and **kommen.** Verbs formed by adding a prefix—e.g., **radfahren, verbringen,** and **ankommen**—change their stems in the same way as the basic verb.

infinitive	3rd person sing. present	simple past	perfect	English
anfangen	fängt an	fing an	hat angefangen	*begin*
beginnen		begann	hat begonnen	*begin*
bieten		bot	hat geboten	*offer*
bitten		bat	hat gebeten	*ask for, request*
bleiben		blieb	ist geblieben	*stay*
brechen	bricht	brach	hat gebrochen	*break*
bringen		brachte	hat gebracht	*bring*
denken		dachte	hat gedacht	*think*
dürfen	darf	durfte	hat gedurft	*may, be allowed to*
einladen	lädt ein	lud ein	hat eingeladen	*invite*
empfehlen	empfiehlt	empfahl	hat empfohlen	*recommend*
entscheiden		entschied	hat entschieden	*decide*
essen	ißt	aß	hat gegessen	*eat*
fahren	fährt	fuhr	ist gefahren	*drive*
fallen	fällt	fiel	ist gefallen	*fall*
finden		fand	hat gefunden	*find*
fliegen		flog	ist geflogen	*fly*
fließen		floß	ist geflossen	*flow*
geben	gibt	gab	hat gegeben	*give*
gehen		ging	ist gegangen	*go*
gewinnen		gewann	hat gewonnen	*win*
haben	hat	hatte	hat gehabt	*have*
halten	hält	hielt	hat gehalten	*hold, stop*
hängen[1]		hing	hat gehangen	*be hanging*
heißen		hieß	hat geheißen	*be called*
helfen	hilft	half	hat geholfen	*help*
kennen		kannte	hat gekannt	*know, be acquainted with*
klingen		klang	hat geklungen	*sound*
kommen		kam	ist gekommen	*come*
können	kann	konnte	hat gekonnt	*can, be able to*
lassen	läßt	ließ	hat gelassen	*leave; let; allow to; cause to be done*
laufen	läuft	lief	ist gelaufen	*run*
leihen		lieh	hat geliehen	*lend*

1. When it is transitive, **hängen** is weak: **hängte, hat gehängt.**

infinitive	3rd person sing. present	simple past	perfect	English
lesen	liest	las	hat gelesen	read
liegen		lag	hat gelegen	lie
mögen	mag	mochte	hat gemocht	like
müssen	muß	mußte	hat gemußt	must, have to
nehmen	nimmt	nahm	hat genommen	take
nennen		nannte	hat genannt	name, call
rufen		rief	hat gerufen	call, shout
scheinen		schien	hat geschienen	shine, seem
schlafen	schläft	schlief	hat geschlafen	sleep
schlagen	schlägt	schlug	hat geschlagen	hit, beat
schließen		schloß	hat geschlossen	close
schneiden		schnitt	hat geschnitten	cut
schreiben		schrieb	hat geschrieben	write
schwimmen		schwamm	ist geschwommen	swim
sehen	sieht	sah	hat gesehen	see
sein	ist	war	ist gewesen	be
singen		sang	hat gesungen	sing
sitzen		saß	hat gesessen	sit
sollen	soll	sollte	hat gesollt	should
sprechen	spricht	sprach	hat gesprochen	speak
stehen		stand	hat gestanden	stand
stehlen	stiehlt	stahl	hat gestohlen	steal
steigen		stieg	ist gestiegen	climb
sterben	stirbt	starb	ist gestorben	die
tragen	trägt	trug	hat getragen	carry, wear
treffen	trifft	traf	hat getroffen	meet
treiben		trieb	hat getrieben	drive, propel
trinken		trank	hat getrunken	drink
tun		tat	hat getan	do
vergessen	vergißt	vergaß	hat vergessen	forget
vergleichen		verglich	hat verglichen	compare
verlassen	verläßt	verließ	hat verlassen	leave
verlieren		verlor	hat verloren	lose
verschwinden		verschwand	ist verschwunden	disappear
wachsen	wächst	wuchs	ist gewachsen	grow
waschen	wäscht	wusch	hat gewaschen	wash
werden	wird	wurde	ist geworden	become
werfen	wirft	warf	hat geworfen	throw
wiegen		wog	hat gewogen	weigh
wissen	weiß	wußte	hat gewußt	know (a fact)
wollen	will	wollte	hat gewollt	want to
ziehen		zog	hat/ist gezogen	pull; move

German-English Vocabulary

The following list contains all the words introduced in *Neue Horizonte* except for personal and relative pronouns, possessive adjectives, cardinal and ordinal numbers, and words glossed in the margins of the *Lesestücke*. The code at the end of each entry shows where the word or phrase is introduced in the text:

12–1	Kapitel 12, Wortschatz 1
9–2	Kapitel 9, Wortschatz 2
5–TLL	Kapitel 5, Tips zum Lesen und Lernen
	(in the section Leicht zu merken)
3–G	Kapitel 3, Grammatik
10–SA	Kapitel 10, Situationen aus dem Alltag

Strong and irregular verbs are listed with their principal parts: **nehmen (nimmt), nahm, hat genommen.** Weak verbs using **sein** as their auxiliary are shown by inclusion of the perfect: **reisen, ist gereist.**

Separable prefixes are indicated by a raised dot between prefix and verb stem: **ab·fahren.** This dot is *not* used in German spelling.

When a verb has a prepositional complement, the preposition follows all the principal parts: **teil·nehmen (nimmt teil), nahm teil, hat teilgenommen** *an* (+ *dat.*).

Adjectival nouns are indicated thus: der / die **Verwandte, -n**.

Masculine N-nouns like **der Student** and irregular nouns like **der Name** are followed by both the genitive singular and the plural endings: **der Student, -en, -en; der Name, -ns, -n.**

Adjectives followed by a hyphen may only be used attributively: **eigen-.**

If an adjective or adverb requires an umlaut in the comparative and superlative degrees, or if these forms are irregular, this is indicated in parentheses: **arm** (*ärmer*); **gern** (*lieber, am liebsten*).

The following abbreviations are used here and throughout *Neue Horizonte*.

acc.	accusative	*m.*	masculine
adj.	adjective	*neut.*	neuter
adj. noun	adjectival noun	*pers.*	person
adv.	adverb	*pl.*	plural
colloq.	colloquial	*prep.*	preposition
coor. conj.	coordinating conjunction	*sing.*	singular
dat.	dative	*sub. conj.*	subordinating
f.	feminine		conjunction
gen.	genitive	*trans.*	transitive
intrans.	intransitive	*usw.*	(= und so weiter) etc.

A

der **Abend, -e** evening, 7–2
  am Abend in the evening, 7–2
  Guten Abend! Good evening,
  Intro.
das **Abendessen, -** supper, evening
  meal, 8–1
  zum Abendessen for supper,
  8–1
abends (in the) evenings, 5–2
aber but (*coor. conj.*), 1–1;
  (*flavoring particle*), 9–1
ab·fahren (fährt ab), fuhr ab, ist
  abgefahren to depart, leave (by
  vehicle), 7–1
der **Abfall, ⁻e** waste product,
  refuse; trash, 9–2
abhängig von dependent on, 9–2
ab·holen to pick up, fetch, get,
  5–2
das **Abi** (*slang*) = Abitur, 5–1
das **Abitur** final secondary school
  examination, 5–1
das **Abteil, -e** railway
  compartment, 7–2
ach oh, ah, 2–1
das **Adjektiv, -e** adjective
die **Adresse, -n** address, 15–1
der **Adler, -** eagle, 10–SA
das **Adverb, -ien** adverb
ähnlich (+ *dat.*) similar (to), 3–2
  Sie ist ihrer Mutter ähnlich.
  She's like her mother.
die **Ähnlichkeit, -en** similarity,
  11–2
die **Ahnung** notion, inkling, hunch
  (Ich habe) keine Ahnung.
  (I have) no idea. 10–1
aktiv active, 9–TLL
aktuell topical, relevant, timely,
  5–2
akut acute, 9–TLL
akzeptieren to accept, 15–1
der **Almanach, -e** almanac
alle (*pl.*) all; everybody, 2–2
allein alone, 4–1
alles everything, 6–2
der **Alltag** everyday life, 8–2
die **Alpen** (*pl.*) the Alps, 4–TLL
als (*sub. conj.*) when, 10–1; as a,
  5–1; than (*with comparative*
  degree), 12–1
  als ob (+ *subjunctive*) as if, as
  though, 16–1
also well . . . 1–1; thus, 3–2

alt (älter) old, 2–2
die **Alternative, -n** alternative,
  2–TLL
altmodisch old-fashioned, 4–2
die **Altstadt, ⁻e** old city center,
  8–TLL
(das) **Amerika** America, 3–2
der **Amerikaner, -** American (*m.*),
  1–2
die **Amerikanerin, -nen** American
  (*f.*), 1–2
amerikanisch American, 3–2
an (+ *acc. or dat.*) to, toward; at,
  alongside of, 6–G
an (+ *dat.*) **vorbei** (+ *verb*) (to go)
  past (something), 15–1
  Sie gehen an der Post vorbei.
  They're going past the post
  office.
analysieren to analyze, 14–TLL
ander- other, different, 11–1
ändern to change (*trans.*), 11–2
sich ändern to change (*intrans.*),
  11–2
anders different, 2–2
der **Anfang, ⁻e** beginning, 6–1
  am Anfang at the beginning, 6–1
an·fangen (fängt an), fing an, hat
  angefangen to begin, start, 5–1
der **Anfänger, -** beginner, 5–TLL
angenehm pleasant; "pleasure to
  meet you," 13–SA
der / die **Angestellte, -n** employee,
  14–1
die **Anglistik** English studies,
  6–SA
die **Angst, ⁻e** fear, 3–2
  Angst haben to be afraid, 3–2
  Angst haben vor (+ *dat.*) to be
  afraid of, 13–1
an·kommen, kam an, ist
  angekommen to arrive, 5–1
an·kommen auf (+ *acc.*) to depend
  on, be contingent on
  Es kommt darauf an. It
  depends, 13–1
an·machen to turn on, switch on,
  11–1
sich an·melden to register (at a
  hotel, at the university, etc.),
  14–SA
an·rufen, rief an, hat angerufen to
  call up, 5–1
sich etwas an·sehen (sieht an), sah
  an, hat angesehen to take a
  look at something, 11–1

anstatt (+ *gen.*) instead of, 8–G
die **Antwort, -en** answer, 6–2
antworten (+ *dat.*) to answer (a
  person), 6–2
  antworten auf (+ *acc.*) to
  answer (something), respond
  to, 13–2
an·ziehen, zog an, hat angezogen
  to dress, 11–1
  sich anziehen to get dressed,
  11–1
der **Anzug, ⁻e** suit, 3–SA
die **Apotheke, -n** pharmacy, 8–SA
(der) **April** April, Intro.
die **Arbeit** work, 2–2
arbeiten to work, 1–1
der **Arbeiter, -** worker (*m.*), 5–2
die **Arbeiterin, -nen** worker (*f.*)
arbeitslos unemployed, 10–2
die **Arbeitslosigkeit**
  unemployment, 10–2
das **Arbeitszimmer, -** study, 15–SA
der **Ärger** annoyance, anger,
  16–SA
ärgern to annoy; offend, 8–2
  sich ärgern (über + *acc.*) to get
  annoyed (at), be annoyed
  (about), 13–2
der **Arm, -e** arm, 10–2
arm (ärmer, am ärmsten) poor,
  10–1
der **Artikel, -** article, 2–1
der **Arzt, ⁻e** doctor (*m.*), 5–SA,
  11–1
die **Ärztin, -nen** doctor (*f.*), 5–SA,
  11–1
der **Aspekt, -e** aspect, 8–TLL
das **Atom, -e** atom, 9–TLL
das **Atomkraftwerk** atomic power
  plant, 9–2
auch also, too, 1–1
auf (+ *acc. or dat.*) onto; on, upon,
  on top of, 6–G
die **Aufgabe, -n** task, assignment,
  16–2
auf·geben (gibt auf), gab auf, hat
  aufgegeben (*trans.* and *intrans.*)
  to give up, quit, 11–2
auf·hängen to hang up, 7–1
auf·hören (mit) to cease, stop
  (doing something), 5–1
auf·machen to open, 5–1
auf·passen to pay attention; look
  out, 16–1
auf·passen auf (+ *acc.*) to look
  after, 16–1

auf·räumen to tidy up, straighten up, 13–1

sich auf·regen (über + *acc.*) to get upset (about), get excited (about), 15–1

der Aufsatz, -̈e essay

das Aufsatzthema, -themen essay topic

auf·stehen, stand auf, ist aufgestanden to stand up; get out of bed, 5–1

auf·wachen, ist aufgewacht to wake up (*intrans.*), 7–1

auf·wachsen (wächst auf), wuchs auf, ist aufgewachsen to grow up, 13–2

das Auge, -n eye, 11–1

der Augenblick, -e, 12–1
  im Augenblick at the moment, 12–1
  (Einen) Augenblick, bitte. Just a moment, please. 12–1

(der) August August, Intro.

aus (+ *dat.*) out of; from, 5–G

aus·brechen (bricht aus), brach aus, ist ausgebrochen to break out

der Ausdruck, -̈e expression

der Ausflug, -̈e outing, excursion, 14–2

aus·geben (gibt aus), gab aus, hat ausgegeben to spend (money), 6–2

ausgezeichnet excellent, 8–1

sich aus·kennen, kannte aus, hat ausgekannt to know one's way around, 13–1

die Auskunft information, 13–1

das Ausland (*sing.*) foreign countries, 7–2
  im Ausland abroad, 7–2

der Ausländer, - foreigner (*m.*), 15–1

die Ausländerin, -nen foreigner (*f.*), 15–1

ausländisch foreign, 10–2

aus·packen to unpack, 11–SA

aus·sehen (sieht aus), sah aus, hat ausgesehen to appear, look (like), 5–2

außer (*prep.* + *dat.*) besides; in addition to, 5–G

außerdem (*adv.*) besides, in addition, 14–2

aus·steigen, steig aus, ist ausgestiegen to get out (of a vehicle), 7–2

die Ausstellung, -en exhibition, 10–2

der Austauschstudent, -en, -en exchange student, 6–1

aus·wandern, ist ausgewandert to emigrate, 11–2

der Ausweis, -e I.D. card, 6–2

aus·ziehen, zog aus, ist ausgezogen to move out, 6–1
  sich ausziehen to get undressed, 11–1

das Auto, -s car, 2–2

die Autobahn, -en expressway, high-speed highway, 7–SA

automatisch automatic, 6–TLL

der Automechaniker, - auto mechanic, 5–1

der Autostop hitchhiking
  per Autostop reisen to hitchhike, 7–2

B

das Baby, -s baby, 16–1

der Bäcker, - baker, 5–1

die Bäckerei, -en bakery, 5–1

das Bad bath, 14–1
  ein Bad nehmen to take a bath, 14–1

sich baden to take a bath, 11–SA

das Badezimmer, - bathroom, 14–1

baff sein to be flabbergasted, speechless, 13–1

die Bahn railroad, railway system, 7–2

der Bahnhof, -̈e train station, 7–1

bald soon, 3–1

die Banane, -n banana, 11–1

die Bank, -̈e bench, 10–1

die Bank, -en bank, 14–1

der Bär, -en, -en bear, 10–SA

barbarisch barbaric, 4–TLL

die Barriere, -n barrier, 13–TLL

die Basis basis, 9–TLL

bauen to build, 11–2

der Bauer, -n, -n farmer, 5–1

das Bauernbrot dark bread, 5–1

der Baum, -̈e tree, 4–2

der Beamte, -n (*adj. noun*) official, civil servant (*m.*), 11–1

die Beamtin, -nen official, civil servant (*f.*), 11–1

beantworten to answer (a *question, letter, etc.*), 6–2

bedienen to serve, 5–2

bedeuten to mean, signify, 1–2

die Bedeutung, -en meaning, significance, 10–2

sich beeilen to hurry, 11–1

begeistert von enthusiastic about, 14–2

beginnen, begann, hat begonnen to begin, 4–1

behalten (behält), behielt, hat behalten to keep, retain, 12–1

bei (+ *dat.*) in the home of; near; at, 5–1; during, while -ing, 11–G

beid- (*adj.*) both, 11–2

beide (*pl. pronoun*) both (people), 14–2

beides (*sing. pronoun*) both things, 13–2

das Bein, -e leg, 11–1

das Beispiel, -e example, 9–2
  zum Beispiel for example, 1–2

bekannt known, well known, 10–2

der / die Bekannte, -en acquaintance, friend, 11–1

bekommen, bekam, hat bekommen to receive, get, 4–1

belegen to register for, take (a university course), 6–2

benutzen to use, 7–2

bequem comfortable, 7–2

bereit prepared, ready, 9–2

der Berg, -e mountain, 3–1

bergig mountainous, 4–SA

berichten to report, 5–2

der Beruf, -e profession, vocation, 2–2 **Was sind Sie von Beruf?** What is your profession? 5–SA

berufstätig employed, 2–2

berühmt famous, 11–2

beschreiben, beschrieb, hat beschrieben to describe, 4–2

besitzen, besaß, hat besessen to own, 2–2

besonders especially, 5–2

besorgt worried, concerned, 10–1

besprechen (bespricht), besprach, hat besprochen to discuss, 3–2

die Besserung
  Gute Besserung!
  Get well soon! 11–1

best- *see* **gut**

bestellen to order, 8–1

der Besuch, -e visit, 10–2

besuchen to visit, 3–1

die **Betriebswirtschaft**
management, business, 6–SA

das **Bett, -en** bed, 6–1 **ins Bett
gehen** to go to bed, 7–1

bevor (*sub. conj.*) before, 10–2

sich **bewegen** to move (*intrans.*),
11–2

die **Bewegung, -en** movement,
11–2

bezahlen to pay, 6–2

die **Bibliothek, -en** library, 6–SA

das **Bier, -e** beer, 4–2

bieten, bot, hat geboten to offer;
provide, 16–2

das **Bild, -er** picture; image, 5–2

billig inexpensive, cheap, 6–2

die **Biologie** biology, 6–SA

bis (+ *acc.*) until, Intro.; by, 1–1
bis dann until then, 1–1

ein bißchen a little; a little bit; a
little while, 3–1

bitte (sehr) you're welcome, 2–1;
please, 3–2; here it is, there
you are, 5–1

bitten, bat, hat gebeten um (+
acc.) to ask for, request, 13–1
Er bittet mich um das Geld.
He's asking me for the money.

blau blue, 3–SA

bleiben, blieb, ist geblieben to
stay, remain, 2–2

der **Bleistift, -e** pencil, Intro.

blitzschnell quick as lightning,
3–2

blöd dumb, stupid, 5–1

die **Blume, -n** flower, 11–1

die **Bluse, -n** blouse, 3–2

der **Boden, ⸚** floor (of a room),
6–SA

böse (+ *dat.*) angry (at), 13–1

boxen to box, 9–SA

brauchen to need, 2–1

braun brown, 3–SA

die **BRD** (= **Bundesrepublik
Deutschland**) the FRG (= the
Federal Republic of Germany),
2–2

**brechen (bricht), brach, hat
gebrochen** to break, 11–1

die **Brezel, -n** soft pretzel, 5–1

der **Brief, -e** letter, 6–2

der **Briefkasten, ⸚** mailbox, 15–1

die **Briefmarke, -n** postage stamp,
15–1

der **Briefträger, -** mailman, 5–TLL

die **Brille** (*sing.*) (eye)glasses, 3–SA

bringen, brachte, hat gebracht to
bring, 6–1

das **Brot, -e** bread, 5–1

das **Brötchen, -** roll, 4–1

die **Brücke, -n** bridge, 8–SA; 11–2

der **Bruder, ⸚** brother, 2–1

das **Buch, ⸚er** book, Intro.

das **Bücherregal, -e** bookcase,
6–SA

die **Buchhandlung, -en** bookstore,
5–2

die **Bude, -n** (rented) student room,
6–2

der **Bummel, -** stroll, walk, 8–1
einen Bummel machen take a
stroll, 8–1

die **Bundesrepublik Deutschland**
the Federal Republic of
Germany, 11–2

bunt colorful, 3–SA, 5–2

der **Bürger, -** citizen, 6–2

das **Büro, -s** office, 1–1

der **Bus, -se** bus, 7–SA

die **Butter** butter, 8–SA

C

das **Café -s** café, 8–SA

campen to camp, 5–TLL

die **Chance, -n** chance, 9–2

der **Chef, -s** boss (*m.*), 5–1

die **Chefin, -nen** boss (*f.*), 5–1

die **Chemie** chemistry, 6–SA

(das) **Chinesisch** Chinese, 13–TLL

christlich Christian (*adj.*), 15–2

der **Computer, -** computer, 12–1

der **Container, -** container, 9–1

D

da there, 1–1; then, in that case,
9–1; since (*sub. conj., causal*),
8–G
da drüben over there, 2–1

dabei sein to be present, be there,
15–1

dahin Wie komme ich dahin?
How do I get there? 13–1

damals at that time, back then,
10–1

die **Dame, -n** lady, 10–2
meine Damen und Herren
ladies and gentlemen, 10–2

der **Dank** thanks
vielen Dank thanks a lot, 2–1

danke thanks, thank you, Intro.,
1–1
Danke, gleichfalls. You too.
Same to you. Intro., 12–1

danken (+ *dat.*) to thank, 7–1
Nichts zu danken! Don't
mention it! 2–1

dann then, 1–1

darum therefore, for that reason,
3–2

das sind (*pl. of* **das ist**) those are,
2–2

daß that (*sub. conj.*), 8–1

dauern to last; take (time), 10–1

die **DDR = Deutsche
Demokratische Republik**, 11–1

die **Decke, -n** ceiling, 6–SA

die **Demokratie, -n** democracy,
10–TLL

demokratisch democratic, 10–TLL

die **Demonstration, -en**
demonstration, 11–TLL

demonstrieren to demonstrate,
9–TLL

denken, dachte, hat gedacht to
think, 13–2
denken an (+ *acc.*) to think of,
13–2

das **Denkmal, ⸚er** monument,
12–2

denn (*flavoring particle in
questions*), 2–1; (*coor. conj.*)
for, because, 7–G

desto *see* **je . . . desto**

deutlich clear, 16–2

deutsch German, 2–2
auf deutsch in German, 1–2

(das) **Deutsch** German language,
3–2

der / die **Deutsche, -n** German,
1–2

die **Deutsche Demokratische
Republik** German Democratic
Republic (GDR), 11–1

die **Deutsche Mark (DM)** the
German mark, 5–1

(das) **Deutschland** Germany, 1–2

die **Deutschstunde, -n** German
class, 3–1

(der) **Dezember** December, Intro.

der **Dialekt, -e** dialect, 13–TLL

der **Dialog, -e** dialogue

der **Dichter, -** poet

(der) **Dienstag** Tuesday, Intro.

dieser, -es, -e; (*pl.*) **diese** this, these, 5–1

diesmal this time, 12–1

das **Ding, -e** thing, 7–2

direkt direct(ly), 12–1

der **Direktor, -en** director, 10–TLL

die **Diskussion, -en** discussion, 2–2

diskutieren to discuss; debate, 16–2

die **Diss** (*university slang*) dissertation, 16–1

die **Dissertation, -en** dissertation, 16–1

DM see **Mark**

doch (*stressed, contradictory*) yes I do, yes I am, yes he is, etc., 3–1; (*unstressed flavoring particle with commands*), 4–1; (*unstressed flavoring particle with statements*), 10–1

die **Doktorarbeit, -en** dissertation, 16–1

der **Dom, -e** cathedral, 8–1

(der) **Donnerstag** Thursday, Intro.

das **Doppelzimmer, -** double room, 14–1

das **Dorf, ̈er** village, 5–2

dort there, 2–1

die **Dose, -n** (tin) can, 9–2

draußen outside, 1–1

dreckig (*colloq.*) dirty, 9–1

dritt- third, 9–G

drüben over there, 2–1

dumm (dümmer) dumb, 5–1

dunkel dark, 3–SA

durch (+ *acc.*) through, 4–1

dürfen (darf), durfte, hat gedurft to be allowed to, 3–G
Was darf es sein? What'll it be? May I help you? 5–1

der **Durst** thirst
Durst haben to be thirsty, 8–1

die **Dusche, -n** shower, 14–1

sich duschen to take a shower, 11–SA

die **Dynastie, -n** dynasty, 14–TLL

E

die **Ebene, -n** plain, 12–2

die **Ecke, -n** corner, 8–2
an der Ecke at the corner, 8–2

um die Ecke around the corner, 8–2

egal + wo, wer, warum, usw. no matter where, who, why, etc., 7–2
Das ist (mir) egal. It doesn't matter (to me). I don't care. 7–1

ehrlich honest, 3–2

das **Ei, -er** egg, 8–SA

eigen- own, 9–2

eigentlich actually, in fact, 3–2

die **Eile** hurry **in Eile** in a hurry, 1–1

einander (*adv. and suffix*) each other, 5–G

der **Eindruck, ̈e** impression, 8–2

einfach simple, easy, 5–1

einige some, 6–2

ein·kaufen to shop for; go shopping, 5–2

ein·laden (lädt ein), lud ein, hat eingeladen to invite, 8–1

einmal once, 4–1
noch einmal once again, once more, 4–1

eins one, 1–2

ein·schlafen (schläft ein), schlief ein, ist eingeschlafen to fall asleep, 7–1

ein·steigen, stieg ein, ist eingestiegen to get in (a vehicle), 7–2

der **Einstieg, -e** entrance, way in

einverstanden Agreed. It's a deal. O.K. 5–1

ein·wandern, ist eingewandert to immigrate, 11–2

ein·werfen (wirft ein), warf ein, hat eingeworfen to mail (a letter), 15–1

der **Einwohner, -** inhabitant, 8–2

das **Einzelzimmer, -** single room, 14–1

ein·ziehen, zog ein, ist eingezogen to move in, 6–1

einzig, - single, only, 12–2

das **Eis** ice; ice cream, 8–SA

das **Eishockey** ice hockey, 9–SA

der **Elefant, -en, -en** elephant, 10–SA

elegant elegant, 8–TLL

die **Elektrizität** electricity, 9–TLL

die **Elektrotechnik** electrical engineering, 6–SA

die **Elektrotechniker, -** electrician; electrical engineer (*m.*), 5–SA

die **Elektrotechnikerin, -nen** electrician; eletrical engineer (*f.*) 5–SA

die **Eltern** (*pl.*) parents, 2–1

die **Emanzipation** emancipation, 16–TLL

empfehlen (empfiehlt), empfahl, hat empfohlen to recommend 9–1

das **Ende, -n** end, 6–2
Ende Februar at the end of February, 6–2
am Ende at the end, 6–1
zu Ende sein to end, be finished, be over, 10–2

endlich finally, 1–1

die **Energie, -n** energy, 9–TLL

(das) **England** England, 8–TLL

der **Engländer, -** Englishman, 11–TLL

die **Engländerin, -nen** Englishwoman, 11–TLL

englisch English, 11–TLL

(das) **Englisch** English language, 3–2

enorm enormous, 9–TLL

entscheiden, entschied, hat entschieden to decide, 3–2

Entschuldigung! Pardon me! Excuse me. 1–1

enttäuschen to disappoint, 6–2

die **Enttäuschung, -en** disappointment, 16–SA

entweder . . . oder either . . . or, 14–1

die **Epoche, -n** epoch, 10–SA

die **Erde** earth, 12–2

das **Erdgeschoß** ground floor, first floor, 14–2 (see **Stock**)

die **Erfahrung, -en** experience, 12–SA

erfinden, erfand, hat erfunden to invent

der **Erfolg, -e** success, 16–2

sich erholen (von) to recover (from), get well; have a rest, 13–2

erinnern an (+ *acc.*) to remind of, 12–1
sich erinnern an (+ *acc.*) to remember, 12–1

die **Erinnerung, -en** memory, 12–1

sich erkälten to catch a cold, 11–1

erklären to explain, 10–2
erleben to experience, 11–1
erledigen to attend to, take care of, finish, 16–2
erfreut pleased **Sehr erfreut.** Pleased to meet you. 13–SA
ernst serious, 14–2
    etwas ernst nehmen to take something seriously, 14–2
erst (*adv.*) not until; only, 5–1
erst- (*adj.*) first, 9–G
erstaunlich astounding, 9–2
erstaunt astonished, 15–2
erwarten to expect, 14–2
erzählen to tell, recount, 6–2
die Erzählung, -en story, narrative, 12–2
der Esel, - donkey, 10–SA
essen (ißt), aß, hat gegessen to eat, 2–1
das Essen food; meal, 2–2
das Eßzimmer, - dining room, 15–SA
etwas (*pronoun*) something, 3–1; (*adj. and adv.*) some, a little; somewhat, 12–1
    so etwas (*colloq.*: **so was**) something like that, anything like that, 11–1
(das) Europa Europe, 3–2
der Europäer, - European, 3–2
europäisch European, 11–2
existieren to exist, 11–TLL
extrem extreme, 10–TLL

F

die Fabrik, -en factory, 5–2
das Fach, ̈er area of study; subject, 6–SA
fahren (fährt), fuhr, ist gefahren to drive, go (by a vehicle), 3–1
die Fahrkarte, -n ticket (for bus, train, streetcar, etc.), 7–2
das Fahrrad, ̈er bicycle, 8–2
fallen (fällt), fiel, ist gefallen to fall; die in battle, 10–1
falsch false, incorrect, wrong, Intro.
die Familie, -n family, 2–1
die Farbe, -n color, 3–SA
fast almost, 2–2
faul lazy, 5–2
(der) Februar February, Intro.

fehlen to be missing; to be absent, 10–1
die Feier, -n celebration, party, 15–1
feiern to celebrate, 6–2
das Fenster, - window, Intro.
die Ferien (*pl.*) (university and school) vacation, 6–2
fern distant, far away, 12–2
fern·sehen (sieht fern), sah fern, hat ferngesehen to watch TV, 5–2
das Fernsehen television, 11–1
    im Fernsehen on TV, 11–1
der Fernseher, - TV set, 2–2
fertig (mit) done, finished (with); ready, 5–1
der Film, -e film, movie, 6–TLL
finanzieren to finance, 6–TLL
finden, fand, hat gefunden to find, 2–2
    Das finde ich auch. I think so too. 3–2
der Finger, - finger, 11–1
die Firma, die Firmen firm, company, 13–2
der Fisch, -e fish, 9–2
fit in shape, Intro., 3–1
flach flat, 4–2
die Flasche, -n bottle, 7–1
das Fleisch meat, 2–1
fleißig industrious, hard-working, 5–2
fliegen, flog, ist geflogen to fly, 1–1
(das) Florenz Florence (Italy), 7–2
der Flughafen, ̈ airport, 7–SA
das Flugzeug, -e airplane, 7–2
der Fluß, die Flüsse river, 4–2
folgen, ist gefolgt (+ *dat.*) to follow, 9–2
die Form, -en form, 10–TLL
formell formal, 1–TLL
formulieren to formulate
der Fortschritt, -e progress, 9–1
das Foto, -s photograph, 6–TLL; 7–2 **ein Foto machen** to take a picture, 7–2
die Frage, -n question, 2–1
    eine Frage stellen to ask a question, 10–2
der Fragebogen questionnaire
fragen to ask, 1–1
    sich fragen to wonder, ask oneself, 15–1
(das) Frankreich France, 5–2
der Franzose, -n, -n Frenchman, 11–TLL

die Französin, -nen Frenchwoman, 11–TLL
französisch French, 5–2
die Frau, -en woman, 1–1
    Frau Kuhn Mrs. / Ms. Kuhn, Intro.
das Fräulein, - young (unmarried) woman **Fräulein Schmidt** Miss Schmidt, Intro.
frei free, unoccupied, 2–1
die Freiheit, -en freedom, 7–2
(der) Freitag Friday, Intro.
die Freizeit free time, leisure time, 5–2
fremd strange; foreign, 3–2
die Fremdsprache, -n foreign language, 3–2
die Freude, -n joy, 12–2
freuen (Es) freut mich. "Pleased to meet you." Intro., 13–SA
sich freuen to be happy, 11–1
    sich freuen auf (+ *acc.*) to look forward to, 13–1
der Freund, -e friend, 2–1
die Freundin, -nen friend (*f.*), 3–1
freundlich friendly, 1–2
der Frieden peace, 6–2
frisch fresh, 5–1
froh happy, glad, 13–2
früh early, 3–1
der Frühling spring, 4–2
das Frühstück breakfast, 4–1
    zum Frühstück for breakfast, 4–1
frühstücken to eat breakfast, 4–1
frustrieren to frustrate, 16–2
sich fühlen to feel (*intrans.*), 11–1
führen to lead, 9–2
für (+ *acc.*) for, 1–1
furchtbar terrible, Intro.
fürchten to fear, 11–1
der Fuß, ̈e foot **zu Fuß** on foot, 3–2
der Fußball soccer; soccer ball, 5–2
der Fußgänger, - pedestrian, 8–2
die Fußgängerzone, -n pedestrian zone, 8–2

G

die Gabel, -n fork, 8–SA
ganz entire, whole, 9–1
    ganz gut pretty good, 1–1

den ganzen Sommer (Tag, Nachmittag, usw.) all summer (day, afternoon, etc.)

gar gar nicht not at all, 3–2

gar kein no . . . at all, not a . . . at all, 8–2

die **Garage, -n** garage, 15–SA

der **Garten, ¨** garden, 15–SA

der **Gast, ¨e** guest; patron, 8–1

der **Gastarbeiter, -** foreign worker (*m.*), 15–1

die **Gastarbeiterin, -nen** foreign worker (*f.*), 15–1

das **Gebäude, -** building, 8–1

geben (gibt), gab, hat gegeben to give, 2–2

es gibt (+ *acc.*) there is, there are, 2–2

gebildet educated, 16–2

geboren born

Wann sind Sie geboren? When were you born? 10–1

gebrauchen to use, 13–2

der **Geburtstag, -e** birthday, 9–1

Wann hast du Geburtstag? When is your birthday? Intro.

zum Geburtstag for (one's) birthday, 9–1

der **Gedanke, -ns, -n** thought, 16–2

das **Gedicht, -e** poem

die **Gefahr, -en** danger, 9–1

gefährlich dangerous, 9–2

gefallen (gefällt), gefiel, hat gefallen (+ *dat. of person*) to please, appeal to, 7–1

das **Gefühl, -e** feeling, 9–1

gegen (+ *acc.*) against, around, about (with time) 4–G

die **Gegend, -en** area, region, 12–1

der **Gegensatz, ¨e** opposite

der **Gegenteil im Gegenteil** on the contrary, 8–2

die **Gegenwart** present (time), 12–SA; 14–2

gehen, ging, ist gegangen to go; walk, 1–1

Wie geht es Ihnen / dir? How are you? Intro.

Wie geht's? How are you? Intro.

Es geht. It's all right. 4–1

es geht um . . . it's a question of . . .; it's about . . . (*subject is always es*), 16–2

gehören (+ *dat. of person*) to belong to (a person), 7–1

gehören zu (+ *dat.*) to be a part of, be one of, 13–2

gelb yellow, 3–SA

das **Geld** money, 2–2

der **Geldbeutel, -** wallet, change purse, 10–1

die **Gelegenheit, -en** opportunity, chance, 14–2

das **Gemüse** vegetables, 2–1

gemütlich cozy, comfortable; quiet, relaxed, 14–2

genau exact, precise, 11–1

genauso . . . wie just as . . . as, 12–G

die **Generation, -en** generation, 9–TLL

genug enough, 3–1

die **Geographie** geography, 4–TLL

geographisch geographical, 4–TLL

das **Gepäck** luggage, 7–1

der **Gepäckträger, -** porter, redcap, 7–1

gerade just, at this moment, 6–2

geradeaus straight ahead, 8–2

die **Germanistik** German studies, 6–SA

gern (lieber, am liebsten) gladly, with pleasure, 4–1

etwas gern haben to like something, 4–G

gern (+ *verb*) like to, 4–1

lieber (+ *verb*) prefer to, would rather, 4–1

Lieber nicht. I'd rather not. No thanks. Let's not. 4–1

das **Geschäft, -e** business; store, 5–2

die **Geschäftsfrau, -en** businesswoman, 5–SA

der **Geschäftsmann, die Geschäftsleute** businessman, businesspeople, 5–SA

das **Geschenk, -e** present, 9–1

die **Geschichte, -n** story; history, 6–2

das **Geschlecht, -er** sex, gender, 16–2

geschlossen closed (*see* **schließen**), 11–2

die **Geschwister** (*pl.*) siblings, 2–SA

die **Gesellschaft, -en** society, 9–2

gesellschaftlich social, 16–2

das **Gesetz, -e** law, 16–2

vor dem Gesetz under the law, in the eyes of the law, 16–2

das **Gesicht, -er** face, 11–1

das **Gespräch, -e** conversation, 13–2

gestern yesterday, 6–1 **gestern früh** yesterday morning, 12–G **gestern abend** yesterday evening, 12–G

gesund healthy, 9–2

die **Gesundheit** health, 9–2

gewinnen, gewann, hat gewonnen to win, 9–SA

sich gewöhnen an (+ *acc.*) to get used to, 13–1

das **Glas, ¨er** glass, 8–1

glauben (+ *dat. of person*) to believe; think, 4–1

Ich glaube ja. I think so. 8–1

Ich glaube nein. I don't think so. 8–1

gleich right away, immediately, 5–1; equal, 16–2

gleichberechtigt enjoying equal rights, 16–2

die **Gleichberechtigung** (*sing.*) equal rights, 16–2

das **Gleis, -e** track, 7–1

das **Glück** happiness; luck, 6–2

Glück haben to be lucky, 6–2

glücklich happy, Intro.

golden golden, 16–1

die **goldene Hochzeit** golden wedding anniversary, 16–1

der **Gott, ¨er** god

Gott sei Dank Thank goodness, 4–G

Grüß Gott Hello (in southern Germany and Austria), 14–1

Um Gottes Willen! For heaven's sake! 3–1

das **Gramm** gram, 8–1

die **Grammatik** grammar

gratulieren (+ *dat. of person*) to congratulate, 15–1

grau gray, 3–SA

grausam terrible, gruesome, cruel, 12–2

die **Grenze, -n** border, 11–1

griechisch Greek, 8–1

groß (größer, am größten) big, 2–1

die **Größe, -n** size, greatness, 12–1

die **Großeltern** (*pl.*) grandparents, 2–2

die **Großmutter, ⸚** grandmother, 2–2

die **Großstadt, ⸚e** large city (over 500,000 inhabitants), 8–2

der **Großvater, ⸚** grandfather, 2–2

grün green, 3–SA

der **Grund, ⸚e** reason

die **Gruppe, -n** group, 1–2

grüßen to greet, say hello to, 1–2

    Grüß Gott hello (in southern Germany and Austria), Intro., 14–1

gut (besser, am besten) good, well, Intro., 1–1

    Ist gut. (*colloq.*) OK. Fine by me. 5–1

    ganz gut pretty good, 1–1

    Guten Abend! Good evening! Intro.

    Guten Morgen! Good morning! Intro.

    Guten Tag! Hello! Intro.

    Gute Reise! Have a good trip! 1–1

das **Gymnasium, die Gymnasien** secondary school (prepares pupils for university), 3–2

H

das **Haar, -e** hair, 6–2

    sich die Haare kämmen to comb one's hair, 11–SA

haben (hat), hatte, hat gehabt to have, Intro., 2–1

der **Hafen, ⸚** port, harbor, 8–2

halb (*adv.*) half

    halb acht seven-thirty, Intro.

halbtags (*adv.*) half days, 16–1

    halbtags arbeiten to work part time, 16–1

Hallo! Hello! Intro.

halten (hält), hielt, hat gehalten to stop (*intrans.*); hold, 3–1

    halten für (+ *acc.*) to take for, regard as, think X is, 15–1

die **Haltestelle, -n** (streetcar or bus) stop, 8–SA; 13–1

die **Hand, ⸚e** hand, 5–1

der **Handschuh, -e** glove, 3–SA

hängen (*trans.*) to hang, 7–1

hängen, hing, hat gehangen (*intrans.*) to be hanging, 7–1

hart (härter) hard; tough; harsh, 10–2

hassen to hate, 3–2

häßlich ugly, 1–1

Haupt- (*noun prefix*) main, chief, primary, most important, 4–TLL

das **Hauptfach, ⸚er** major field (of study), 6–2

die **Hauptstadt, ⸚e** capital city, 4–TLL

das **Haus, ⸚er** house; building, 1–2

    nach Hause home (as in destination of motion), 3–1

    zu Hause at home, 2–2

die **Hausaufgabe, -n** homework assignment, 3–2

die **Hausfrau, -en** housewife, 2–2

das **Heft, -e** notebook, Intro.

die **Heimat** native place or country, homeland, 11–2

das **Heimweh** homesickness, 12–SA; 15–2

heiraten to marry, get married, 16–1

heiß hot, Intro.

heißen, hieß, hat geheißen to be called, 2–1

    das heißt that means, in other words, 6–2

    Ich heiße . . . My name is . . . , Intro.

    Wie heißen Sie? What's your name? Intro.

heiter cheerful, 14–2

hektisch hectic, 7–TLL

helfen (hilft), half, hat geholfen (+ *dat.*) to help, 7–1

hell bright, light, 3–SA

das **Hemd, -en** shirt, 3–2

her- (*prefix*) *indicates motion toward the speaker*, 15–G

der **Herbst** fall, autumn, 4–2

der **Herr, -n, -en** gentleman, 1–1

    Herr Lehmann Mr. Lehmann, Intro.

    meine Damen und Herren Ladies and Gentlemen, 10-2

herrlich great, terrific, marvelous, Intro.

herzlich willkommen heartily welcome, 6–2

heute today, Intro.

    heute abend this evening, tonight, 1–1

    heute morgen this morning, 5–1

    heute nachmittag this afternoon, 12–G

heutzutage nowadays, 3–2

hier here, 1–1

die **Hilfe** help, aid, 13–1

hin- (*prefix*) *indicates motion away from speaker*, 15–G

hinein- (*prefix*) in, into, 15–1

hinter (+ *acc. or dat.*) behind, 6–G

historisch historic, 10–SA

die **Hitze** heat, 15–2

hoch (*pred. adj.*), **hoh-** (*attributive adj.*) (**höher, am höchsten**) high, 4–2

    höchste Zeit high time, 14–1

die **Hochschule, -n** university, institute of higher learning, 14–2

die **Hochzeit, -en** wedding, 16–1

    die goldene Hochzeit golden wedding anniversary, 16–1

hoffen to hope, 7–2

hoffentlich (*adv.*) I hope, 4–1

höflich polite, 1–2

holen to fetch, get, 12–2

hören to hear, 3–2

der **Horizont, -e** horizon, 7–TLL

die **Hose, -n** trousers, pants, 3–2

das **Hotel, -s** hotel, 4–1

hübsch pretty, handsome, 11–1

der **Hügel, -** hill, 4–2

hügelig hilly, 4–SA

der **Humor** humor, 14–TLL

der **Hund, -e** dog, 11–G

der **Hunger** hunger, 8–1

    Hunger haben to be hungry, 8–1

hungrig hungry, 4–1

der **Hut, ⸚e** hat, 3–SA

I

ideal ideal, 16–TLL

die **Idee, -n** idea, 10–2

ideologisch ideological, 10–TLL

der **Idiot, -en, -en** idiot, 12–1

idiotensicher idiot proof, foolproof, 12–1

illegal illegal, 10–TLL

immer always, 1–2

    immer noch still, 4–2

    immer größer bigger and bigger, 12–G

in (+ *acc. or dat.*) in, 1–1; into, 6–G

der **Indikativ** indicative

die **Industrie, -n** industry, 5–TLL

industriell industrial, 16–TLL
die Inflation inflation, 10–TLL
der Ingenieur, -e engineer (m.), 5–SA
die Ingenieurin, -nen engineer (f.), 5–SA
die Informatik computer science, 6–SA
das Instrument, -e instrument, 7–TLL
integrieren to integrate, 15–TLL
intelligent intelligent, 12–1
interessant interesting, 3–1
interessieren to interest, 13–1
sich interessieren für (+ acc.) to be interested in, 13–1
international international, 3–TLL
interviewen to interview, 10–1
irgend- (prefix) **irgendwann** sometime or other, any time, 12–G
    irgendwie somehow or other, 12–G
    irgendwo somewhere or other, anywhere, 12–G
die Ironie irony, 14–TLL
(das) Italien Italy, 4–2
der Italiener, - Italian (m.), 11–TLL
die Italienerin, -nen Italian (f.), 11–TLL
italienisch Italian, 11–TLL

J

ja yes; (unstressed flavoring particle), 1–1
die Jacke, -n jacket, 3–2
das Jahr, -e year, 5–1 **im Jahr(e) 1992** in 1992, 9–2
jahrelang (adv.) for years, 14–TLL
das Jahrhundert, -e century, 8–2
jahrhundertelang (adv.) for centuries, 14–TLL
jährlich annually, 9–2
(der) Januar January, Intro.
je ever, 6–2 **je größer, desto besser** the bigger, the better, 12–G
die Jeans (pl.) jeans, 3–TLL
jeder, -es, -e each, every, 5–2
    jeder (pronoun) everyone
jedesmal every time, 12–G
jemand somebody, someone, 2–2
jetzt now, 3–1
    von jetzt an from now on, 13–1

der Joghurt yoghurt, 2–1
der Journalist, -en, -en journalist, 5–2
jüdisch Jewish, 12–2
die Jugend (sing.) youth; young people, 9–2
die Jugendherberge, -n Youth Hostel, 7–2
(das) Jugoslawien Yugoslavia, 5–2
der Jugoslawe, -n, -n Yugoslavian (m.), 11–TLL
die Jugoslawin, -nen Yugoslavian (f.), 11–TLL
jugoslawisch Yugoslavian, 11–TLL
(der) Juli July, Intro.
jung (jünger) young, 2–2
der Junge, -n, -n boy, 9–1
(der) Juni June, Intro.
Jura (study of) law, 6–SA

K

der Kaffee coffee, 8–1
kalt (kälter) cold, Intro.
die Kälte cold, 15–2
die Kamera, -s camera, 7–TLL
kämmen to comb
    sich die Haare kämmen to comb one's hair, 11–SA
(das) Kanada Canada, 5–TLL, 6–1
das Kännchen, - small (coffee or tea) pot, 8–SA
der Kapitalismus capitalism, 11–TLL
das Kapitel, - chapter
kaputt (colloq.) broken, kaput; exhausted, 9–1
    kaputt machen to break, 12–1
die Karriere, -en career, 16–TLL
die Karte, -n card; ticket; map, 4–1
die Kartoffel, -n potato, 8–1
der Käse cheese, 8–1
die Kasse, -n cashier; cashier's office, 14–1
der Kassettenrecorder, - cassette player, 10–1
katastrophal catastrophic, 10–TLL
die Katastrophe, -n catastrophe, 6–2
die Katze, -n cat, 11–G
kaufen to buy, 4–1
das Kaufhaus, ⁻er department store, 8–SA
kaum hardly, barely, 16–1

kein not a, not any, no, 3–1
    kein . . . mehr no more . . . , not a . . . any longer, 4–G
der Keller, - cellar, basement, 9–1
der Kellner, - waiter, 5–SA; 8–1
die Kellnerin, -nen waitress, 5–SA; 8–1
kennen, kannte, hat gekannt to know, be acquainted with, 2–1
kennen·lernen to get to know; meet, 5–1
die Kette, -n chain
die Kettenreaktion, -en chain reaction
das Kilo (= **das Kilogramm**), 8–1
das Kilogramm kilogram, 8–1
der Kilometer, - kilometer, 15–TLL
das Kind, -er child, 1–1
die Kindheit, -en childhood, 9–TLL
das Kino, -s movie theater, 6–2
die Kirche, -n church, 8–SA
klar clear; (colloq.) sure, of course, 9–1
die Klasse, -n class; grade, 1–2
der Klatsch gossip, 12–1
klauen (colloq.) to rip off, steal, 10–1
die Klausur, -en written test, 6–2
das Klavier, -e piano, 14–2
das Kleid, -er dress (pl. = dresses or clothes), 3–2
der Kleiderschrank, ⁻e clothes cupboard, wardrobe, 6–SA
die Kleidung clothing, 3–SA
klein little, small, 2–1
die Kleinstadt, ⁻e town (5,000 to 20,000 inhabitants), 8–2
das Klima climate, 4–2
klingen, klang, hat geklungen sound, 8–1
klingeln to ring, 7–1
das Klischee, -s cliché, 2–2
klischeehaft cliché, stereotyped, 13–SA
klug (klüger) smart, bright, 5–1
knapp scarce, in short supply, 12–1
    knapp bei Kasse short of cash, 12–1
die Kneipe, -n tavern, bar, 6–2
kochen to cook, 2–2
der Koffer, - suitcase, 7–1
(das) Köln Cologne, 8–1
die Kolonie, -n colony, 4–TLL
komisch peculiar, odd; funny, 12–1

kommen, kam, ist gekommen to come, Intro., 1–1

kommen aus to come from, Intro.

der **Kommunismus** Communism, 11–TLL

die **Konditorei, -en** pastry café, 8–SA

der **Konflikt, -e** conflict, 2–TLL

der **Konjunktiv** subjunctive

die **Konkurrenz** competition, 9–SA

können (kann), konnte, hat gekonnt can, be able to, 3–1

Ich kann Deutsch. I can speak German. 3–G

die **Konsequenz, -en** consequence, 9–TLL

konservativ conservative, 13–TLL

der **Kontakt, -e** contact, 14–TLL

der **Kontrast, -e** contrast, 4–TLL

sich konzentrieren auf (+ *acc.*) to concentrate on, 14–2

das **Konzert, -e** concert, 6–TLL

der **Kopf, ⸚e** head, 11–1

Das geht mir nicht aus dem Kopf. I can't forget that. 12–2

der **Korrespondent, -en, -en** correspondent, 5–TLL

kosten to cost, 5–1

Wieviel kostet das bitte? How much does that cost, please? 5–1

kostenlos free of charge, 6–2

die **Kraft, ⸚e** power; strength, 9–2

das **Kraftwerk, -e** power plant, 9–2

der **Kram** (*colloq.*) things, stuff; junk, 8–1

krank (kränker) sick, Intro.

das **Krankenhaus, ⸚er** hospital, 11–1

der **Krankenpfleger, -** nurse (*m.*), 5–SA

die **Krankenschwester, -n** nurse (*f.*), 5–SA

die **Krankheit, -en** sickness, 9–2

die **Krawatte, -n** tie, 3–SA

kreativ creative, 14–TLL

die **Kreide** chalk, Intro.

der **Krieg, -e** war, 6–2

kritisch critical, 5–TLL; 16–2

kritisieren to criticize, 11–2

die **Küche, -n** kitchen, 15–SA; 16–2

der **Kuchen, -** cake, 8–SA

der **Kugelschreiber, -** ball-point pen, Intro.

kühl cool, Intro.

die **Kultur, -en** culture, 4–TLL

sich kümmern um (+ *acc.*) to look after, take care of, deal with, 13–1

der **Kunde, -n, -n** customer (*m.*), 5–1

die **Kundin, -nen** customer (*f.*), 5–1

die **Kunst, ⸚e** art, 8–1

die **Kunstgeschichte** art history, 6–SA

der **Künstler, -** artist (*m.*), 5–SA; 14–2

die **Künstlerin, -nen** artist (*f.*), 5–SA; 14–2

kurz (kürzer) short, for a short time, 4–1

die **Kusine, -n** cousin (*f.*), 2–SA

L

das **Labor, -s** lab, 6–SA

lachen to laugh, 3–2

lachen über (+ *acc.*) to laugh about

der **Laden, ⸚** shop, store, 5–1

die **Lampe, -n** lamp, 6–SA

das **Land, ⸚er** country, 4–2

auf dem Land in the country, 8–2

aufs Land to the country, 8–2

die **Landkarte, -n** map, Intro.

die **Landschaft, -en** landscape, 4–2

die **Landsleute** compatriots

der **Landwirt, -e** farmer (*m.*), 5–SA

die **Landwirtin, -nen** farmer (*f.*), 5–SA

die **Landwirtschaft** agriculture, 6–SA

lang(e) (länger) long; for a long time, 4–1

langsam slow, Intro., 3–2

sich langweilen to be bored, 13–1

langweilig boring, 3–1

lassen (läßt), ließ, hat gelassen to leave (something or someone), leave behind; let, allow; cause to be done, 12–1

laufen (läuft), lief, ist gelaufen to run; (*colloq.*) to go on foot, walk, 3–1

die **Laune** mood

guter / schlechter Laune in a good / bad mood, Intro.

laut loud, Intro.

leben to live, be alive, 2–2

das **Leben** life, 4–2

die **Lebensmittel** (*pl.*) groceries, 5–2

der **Lebensstandard** standard of living, 9–TLL

die **Leberwurst, ⸚e** liverwurst, 8–1

lecker tasty, delicious, 8–1

ledig single (= unmarried), 16–1

leer empty, 5–1

legen to lay, put down, 6–1

der **Lehrer, -** teacher (*m.*), Intro.

die **Lehrerin, -nen** teacher (*f.*), Intro.

der **Lehrling, -e** apprentice, 5–1

leicht light (in weight); easy, 3–1

leid Das tut mir leid. I'm sorry about that, Intro., 7–1

leider unfortunately, Intro., 3–1

leihen, lieh, hat geliehen to lend, loan; borrow, 10–1

leise quiet, soft, Intro.

leisten sich etwas leisten können to be able to afford something, 11–1

die **Leitfrage, -n** guiding question

lernen to learn, 3–2

lesen (liest), las, hat gelesen to read, 2–1

lesen über (+ *acc.*) to read about, 2–1

das **Lesestück, -e** reading selection

letzt- last, 10–1

die **Leute** (*pl.*) people, 2–1

das **Licht, -er** light, 11–1

lieb dear; nice, sweet, 6–2

Lieber Fritz! Dear Fritz, (salutation in letter), 6–2

lieben to love, 3–2

lieber preferably, would rather (see **gern**)

Lieblings- (*noun prefix*) favorite, 9–1

am liebsten most like to, like best of all to (see **gern**)

das **Lied, -er** song, 4–2

liegen, lag, hat gelegen to lie; be situated, 4–2

der **Lift, -s** elevator, 14–SA

die **Limnologie** limnology

die **Linguistik** linguistics, 6–SA

die **Linie, -n** (streetcar or bus) line, 13–1

links to the left; on the left, 8–2

die **Liste, -n** list

der **Liter** liter, 8–1
literarisch literary, 14–TLL
der **Löffel, -** spoon, 8–SA
der **Lohn, ̈e** wage, 16–2
sich lohnen to be worthwhile, worth the trouble, 13–1
los Was ist los? What's the matter? What's going on? 3–1
lösen to solve, 9–2
los·fahren (fährt los), fuhr los, ist losgefahren to depart, start, leave, 14–1
die **Lösung, -en** solution, 9–2
der **Löwe, -n, -n** lion, 10–SA
die **Luft** air, 4–SA; 9–1
die **Luftverschmutzung** air pollution, 9–1
die **Lust** desire
Ich habe keine Lust. I don't want to. 3–1
Lust haben (etwas zu tun) to want to do (something), 8–1
die **Lyrik** poetry

M

machen to make; do, 1–1
Es macht (doch) nichts. It doesn't matter, 7–1
Das macht (mir) Spaß. That is fun (for me). 7–2
Das macht zusammen . . . . All together that comes to . . . , 5–1
die **Macht, ̈e** power, might, 12–2
das **Mädchen, -** girl, 9–1
mag (*see mögen*)
(der) **Mai** May, Intro.
das **Mal, -e** time (in the sense of occurrence), 12–1
zum ersten Mal for the first time, 12–G
das nächste Mal (the) next time, 12–G
mal (*flavoring particle with commands, see p. 99*), 4–1
man one (*indefinite pronoun*), 1–2
mancher, -es, -e many a, 9–2
manche (*pl.*) some
manchmal sometimes, 2–2
manipulieren to manipulate, 10–TLL
der **Mann, ̈er** man; husband, 2–1

die **Mannschaft, -en** team, 5–2
der **Mantel, ̈** coat, 3–2
das **Märchen, -** fairy tale, 4–2
die **Mark** (die **Deutsche Mark, DM**) mark (the German mark), 5–1
(der) **März** March, Intro.
die **Maschine, -n** machine, 12–1
die **Mathematik** mathematics, 6–SA
die **Mauer, -n** (free-standing or exterior) wall, 11–1
der **Mechaniker, -** mechanic, 5–1
die **Medizin** (field of) medicine, 6–SA
das **Meer, -e** sea, 4–2
mehr more, 2–2
nicht mehr no longer, not any more, 2–2
mehrere several, 11–1
meinen to be of the opinion, think, 1–2; to mean, 2–1
Was meinen Sie dazu? What do you say to that? What do you think of that? 16–1
die **Meinung, -en** opinion
meist- most (see **viel**)
meistens mostly, usually, 5–2
die **Melancholie** melancholy, 14–TLL
die **Menge, -n** quantity; crowd
eine Menge a lot, lots of, 6–2
die **Mensa** university cafeteria, 1–1
der **Mensch, -en, -en** person, human being, 6–1
Mensch! Man! Wow! 3–1
die **Menschheit** mankind, human race, 9–2
menschlich human, like a human being; humane, 15–2
die **Mentalität, -en** mentality, 15–TLL
merken to notice, remember
das **Messer, -** knife, 8–SA
die **Methode, -n** method, 10–TLL
die **Metropole, -n** metropolis, 8–TLL
mieten to rent (from somebody), 15–2
die **Milch** milk, 8–SA, 12–2
mild mild, 4–TLL
die **Million, -en** million, 11–TLL
die **Minute, -n** minute, 3–1
minutenlang (*adv.*) for minutes, 14–TLL

der **Mist** manure
So ein Mist! (*crude and colloq.*) What a drag. What a lot of bull. 10–1
mit (+ *dat.*) with, 2–1; (*adv.*) along, 12–1
der **Mitbewohner, -** fellow occupant, roommate, housemate (*m.*), 3–1
die **Mitbewohnerin, -nen** fellow occupant, roommate, housemate (*f.*), 3–1
mit·bringen, brachte mit, hat mitgebracht to bring along, take along, 6–1
miteinander with each other, together, 13–2
das **Mitglied, -er** member, 11–2
mit·kommen, kam mit, ist mitgekommen to come along, 5–1
das **Mitleid** sympathy, 16–SA
mit·machen to participate, cooperate, pitch in, 9–1
mit·nehmen (nimmt mit), nahm mit, hat mitgenommen to take along, 7–2
das **Mittagessen** midday meal, lunch, 5–2
das **Mittelalter** the Middle Ages, 13–1
(das) **Mitteleuropa** Central Europe, 3–2
(der) **Mittwoch** Wednesday, Intro.
die **Möbel** (*pl.*) furniture, 6–SA
möbliert furnished, 6–SA
modern modern, 4–2
mögen (mag), mochte, hat gemocht to like, 4–1
möchten would like to, 3–1
Das mag sein. That may be. 16–G
möglich possible, 6–1
die **Möglichkeit, -en** possibility, 15–2
der **Moment, -e** moment **im Moment** at the moment, 1–1
die **Monarchie, -n** monarchy, 10–TLL
der **Monat, -e** month, 10–1
monatelang (*adv.*) for months, 14–TLL
(der) **Montag** Monday, Intro.
der **Morgen, -** morning, 1–1
Guten Morgen! Good morning! 1–1

morgen tomorrow, Intro., 1–1
  morgen abend tomorrow evening, 12–G
  morgen früh tomorrow morning, 12–G
  morgen nachmittag tomorrow afternoon, 12–G
morgens (*adv.*) in the morning(s), 4–1
das **Motorrad, -̈er** motorcycle, 5–1
müde tired, weary, Intro.
der **Müll** trash, refuse, 9–1
(das) **München** Munich, 8–2
der **Mund, -̈er** mouth, 11–1
munter lively, cheerful, Intro.
das **Museum,** die **Museen** museum, 8–1
die **Musik** music, 3–2
die **Musikwissenschaft** musicology, 6–SA
müssen (muß), mußte, hat gemußt must, have to, 3–1
die **Mutter, -̈** mother, 2–2
die **Muttersprache, -n** native language, 5–2
die **Mutti, -s** mama, mom, 2–2
die **Mütze, -n** cap, 3–SA

N

na well . . . , 12–1
  na endlich! at last! high time! 9–1
  Na und? And so? So what? 10–1
nach (+ *dat.*) after, 5–G; to (with cities and countries), 1–1
  nach Hause home (as destination of motion), 3–1
  nach und nach gradually, little by little, 15–2
der **Nachbar, -n, -n** neighbor (*m.*), 11–2
die **Nachbarin, -nen** neighbor (*f.*), 11–2
nachdem (*sub. conj.*) after, 10–2
nachher later on, after that, 4–1
der **Nachmittag, -e** afternoon, 10–1
  am Nachmittag in the afternoon, 10–1
nachmittags (in the) afternoons, 5–TLL
nächst- next; nearest, 12–1
  nächstes Semester next semester, 2–1

die **Nacht, -̈e** night, 1–1
  Gute Nacht. Good night. 12–1
  in der Nacht in the night, at night, 12–1
der **Nachtisch, -e** dessert, 8–1
  zum Nachtisch for dessert, 8–1
nachts at night, 5–TLL
nah(e) (näher, am nächsten) near, 8–1
die **Nähe** nearness, vicinity **in der Nähe** (**von** or + *gen.*) near, nearby, 7–2
der **Name, -ns, -n** name, 5–1
die **Nase, -n** nose, 5–1
  Ich habe die Nase voll. I'm fed up. I've had it up to here. 5–1
naß wet, damp, 4–2
die **Natur** nature, 9–TLL
natürlich natural, naturally; of course, 1–1
der **Nebel** fog, mist, 4–SA
neben (+ *acc. or dat.*) beside, 6–G
das **Nebenfach, -̈er** minor field (of study), 6–2
neblig foggy, misty, Intro.
nee (*colloq.*) no, 6–1
nehmen (nimmt), nahm, hat genommen to take, 2–1
nein no, Intro.
nennen, nannte, hat genannt to name, call, 10–2
nett nice, 6–1
neu new, 3–2
neulich recently, 12–1
neutral neutral, 13–TLL
die **Neutralität** neutrality, 13–TLL
nicht not, Intro., 1–1
  gar nicht not at all, 3–2
  nicht mehr no longer, not any more, 2–2
  nicht nur . . . sondern auch not only . . . but also, 9–2
  nicht wahr? isn't it? can't you? doesn't she? etc., 3–1
nichts nothing, 3–1
  Nichts zu danken! Don't mention it! 2–1
  Es macht nichts. It doesn't matter. 7–1
nie never, 1–2
niedrig low, 6–2
niemand nobody, no one, 2–2
noch still, 2–2
  noch ein another, an additional, 2–2

  noch einmal once again, once more, 4–1
  noch etwas something else, anything more, 8–1
  noch immer still, 4–2
  noch kein- not a . . . yet, not any . . . yet, 4–G
  noch nicht not yet, 4–1
(das) **Nordamerika** North America, 2–TLL
der **Norden** the north, 4–2
normal normal, 2–2
die **Note, -n** grade, 5–1
nötig necessary, 9–1
(der) **November** November, Intro.
die **Nummer, -n** number, Intro., 14–1
nun now; well . . . , well now, 10–1
nur only, 2–1
nützlich useful

O

ob (*sub. conj.*) if, whether, 8–1
oben (*adv.*) above; on top
objektiv objective, 13–SA
das **Obst** fruit, 2–1
obwohl (*sub. conj.*) although, 8–2
oder or (*coor. conj.*), 1–2
offen open, 11–2
öffentlich public, 16–2
offiziell official, 13–TLL
öffnen to open, 11–1
oft (öfter) often, 1–2
ohne (+ *acc.*) without, 4–1
  ohne . . . zu without -ing, 8–G
das **Ohr, -en** ear, 11–1
das **Ökosystem, -e** ecosystem, 9–TLL
(der) **Oktober** October, Intro.
das **Öl** oil, 9–2
die **Oma, -s** grandma, 2–2
der **Onkel, -** uncle, 2–2
der **Opa, -s** grandpa, 2–2
die **Opposition, -en** opposition, 10–TLL
optimistisch optimistic, 3–TLL
ordentlich tidy, orderly, 13–1
der **Ort, -e** place; town, 12–SA; 13–2
der **Osten** the East, 4–2
(das) **Österreich** Austria, 4–1
der **Österreicher, -** Austrian (*m.*), 11–TLL

die **Österreicherin, -nen** Austrian (f.), 11–TLL
österreichisch Austrian, 14–1
(das) **Osteuropa** Eastern Europe, 11–TLL
der **Ozean, -e** ocean, 15–TLL

P

ein paar a couple (of), a few, 6–2
packen to pack, 7–TLL
die **Pädagogik** (field of) education, 6–SA
das **Papier, -e** paper, Intro., 9–1
parallel parallel, 16–TLL
die **Partei, -en** political party, 9–2
der **Partner, -** partner, 5–TLL
die **Party, -s** party, 6–TLL
der **Paß,** die **Pässe** passport, 7–SA
passieren, ist passiert to happen, 10–1
der **Patient, -en, -en** patient, 14–TLL
die **Pause, -n** break; intermission, 3–1
  eine Pause machen to take a break, 3–1
Pech haben to have bad luck, be unlucky, 6–2
per by
  per Autostop reisen to hitchhike, 7–2
perfekt perfect, 15–1
pessimistisch pessimistic, 3–TLL
die **Person, -en** person
persönlich personal
die **Pflanze, -n** plant, 9–2
das **Phänomen, -e** phenomenon, 16–TLL
phantastisch fantastic, 2–1
die **Philosophie** philosophy, 6–TLL
philosophieren to philosophize, 14–TLL
die **Physik** physics, 6–SA
das **Plakat, -e** (political) poster, 10–2
planen to plan, make plans, 7–1
das **Plastik** plastic, 9–TLL
der **Platz, ̈e** place; space; city square, 6–1; seat, 7–2
plötzlich suddenly, 10–1
(das) **Polen** Poland, 6–2
die **Politik** politics; policy, 9–2
der **Politiker, -** politician (m.), 5–SA; 9–2

die **Politikerin, -nen** politician (f.), 5–SA
die **Politikwissenschaft** political science, 6–SA
politisch political, 9–TLL
die **Pommes frites** (pl.) French fries, 3–2
die **Portion, -en** portion, order, helping, 8–SA
die **Position, -en** position, 16–TLL
die **Post** post office; postal service; mail, 8–SA
das **Poster, -** poster, Intro.
die **Postkarte, -n** postcard, 5–2
praktisch practical, 6–TLL
der **Präsident, -en, -en** president, 10–SA
der **Preis, -e** price, 8–2
prima terrific, great, Intro., 1–1
privat private, 6–TLL
das **Problem, -e** problem, 2–2
produktiv productive, 14–TLL
produzieren to produce, 9–TLL
der **Professor, -en** professor (m.), Intro.
die **Professorin, -nen** professor (f.), Intro.
das **Programm, -e** program, 6–TLL
der **Programmierer, -** programmer (m.), 5–SA
die **Programmiererin, -nen** programmer (f.), 5–SA
der **Protest, -e** protest, 11–TLL
das **Prozent** percent, 13–TLL
die **Prüfung, -en** examination
die **Psychoanalyse** psychoanalysis, 14–TLL
die **Psychologie** psychology, 6–SA
psychologisch psychological, 16–TLL
der **Pulli, -s** (short for **Pullover**), 3–2
der **Pullover, -** pullover, jersey, 3–2
pünktlich punctual, on time, 7–2
putzen to clean, 11–SA

Q

Quatsch! Rubbish! Baloney! Nonsense! 5–1
quatschen (colloq.) to talk nonsense, to chat, 7–2
die **Querstraße, -n** cross street, 12–1

R

das **Rad, ̈er** wheel; bicycle, 8–2
rad·fahren (fährt Rad), fuhr Rad, ist radgefahren to bicycle, 8–2
das **Radiergummi** eraser, Intro.
radikal radical, 9–TLL
das **Radio, -s** radio, 6–SA
sich rasieren to shave, 11–SA
raten (rät), riet, hat geraten to guess
  Raten Sie mal! Take a guess!
das **Rathaus, ̈er** town hall, 8–SA
reagieren auf (+ acc.) to react to, 13–2
die **Reaktion, -en** reaction
recht
  recht haben (hat recht), hatte recht, hat recht gehabt to be right, 4–1
rechts to the right; on the right, 8–2
der **Rechtsanwalt, ̈e** lawyer (m.), 5–SA; 13–2
die **Rechtsanwältin, -nen** lawyer (f.), 5–SA; 13–2
das **Recycling** recycling; recycling center, 9–1
reden to talk, speak, 12–1
das **Referat, -e** oral report; written term paper, 6–2
  ein Referat halten to give a report, 6–SA
  ein Referat schreiben to write a paper, 6–SA
reformieren to reform, 11–TLL
der **Regen** rain, 4–SA
der **Regenschirm, -e** umbrella, 3–SA
das **Regime** regime, 11–TLL
die **Regierung** government in power, administration (U.S.), 10–SA; 11–2
die **Region, -en** region, 4–TLL
regnen to rain, Intro., 1–1
regnerisch rainy, 4–SA
reich rich, 10–1
das **Reich, -e** empire; realm, 10–2
die **Reise, -n** trip, journey, 3–2
  eine Reise machen to take a trip, 3–2
  Gute Reise! Have a good trip! 1–1
der **Reiseführer, -** guide book, 5–1
reisen, ist gereist to travel, 5–2
  per Autostop reisen to hitchhike, 7–2

der **Reisescheck, -s** traveler's check, 14–1

das **Reiseziel, -e** destination, 7–2

relativ (*adj. and adv.*) relative, 2–TLL

die **Religion, -en** religion, 15–TLL

renovieren to renovate, 15–TLL

reparieren to repair, 12–1

die **Republik, -en** republic, 10–TLL

reservieren to reserve, 7–TLL

der **Respekt** respect, 11–TLL

das **Restaurant, -s** restaurant, 8–1

retten to save, rescue, 9–2

die **Revolution, -en** revolution, 11–TLL

die **Rezeption** hotel reception desk, 14–1

der **Rhein** the Rhine River, 4–TLL

richtig right, correct, Intro.

der **Riese, -n, -n** giant

riesengroß gigantic, 8–2

riesen- (*noun and adj. prefix*) gigantic

    riesengroß huge, gigantic

    Ich habe Riesenhunger. I'm famished / hungry as a bear. 14–2

der **Rock, ̈e** skirt, 3–SA

die **Rolle, -n** role, 2–2

    eine Rolle spielen to play a part; be of importance, 2–2

der **Roman, -e** novel, 5–2

romantisch romantic, 13–TLL

rot (röter) red, 3–SA

der **Rucksack, ̈e** rucksack, backpack, 7–2

rufen, rief, hat gerufen to call, shout, 11–2

ruhig calm, peaceful, 10–2; (*as sentence adv.*) "feel free to," "go ahead and," 12–1

(das) **Rumänien** Romania, 6–2

der **Russe, -n, -n** Russian (*m.*), 11–TLL

die **Russin, -nen** Russian (*f.*), 11–TLL

russisch Russian, 11–TLL

(das) **Rußland** Russia, 8–2

S

die **Sache, -n** thing, object; matter, affair, 8–1

der **Sack, ̈e** sack, 9–1

der **Saft, ̈e** juice, 8–SA

der **Satz, ̈e** sentence

sagen to say; tell, 1–2

    Was sagen Sie dazu? What do you say to that? What do you think of that? 16–1

sagenhaft! incredible! 16–1

die **Sahne** cream, 8–SA

der **Salat, -e** salad; lettuce, 8–1

sammeln to collect, 9–1

(der) **Samstag** Saturday, Intro.

sauber clean, 9–1

sauer sour, acidic, 5–2; (*colloq.*) ticked off, sore, Intro.

schade too bad, 11–1

    Das ist schade! That's a shame! What a pity! 11–1

schaffen handle, manage, get done, 3–1

die **Schallplatte, -n** (phonograph) record, 6–SA

der **Schalter, -** counter, window, 13–1

schauen to look, 11–1

    Schau mal. Look. Look here. 11–1

das **Schaufenster, -** store window, 5–2

der **Scheck, -s** check, 14–1

scheinen, schien, hat geschienen to shine; seem, 1–1

schenken to give (as a gift), 5–1

schicken to send, 6–2

das **Schiff, -e** ship, 12–2

der **Schilling, -e** Austrian shilling, 14–1

der **Schinken** ham, 8–SA

schlafen (schläft), schlief, hat geschlafen to sleep, 3–1

das **Schlafzimmer, -** bedroom, 11–1

schlagen (schlägt), schlug, hat geschlagen to hit; beat, 9–SA

schlampig (*colloq.*) messy, disorderly, 13–1

die **Schlange, -n** snake, 10–SA

schlecht bad, Intro., 1–1

schleppen (*colloq.*) to drag, lug (along), haul, 9–1

schließen, schloß, hat geschlossen to close, 5–2

schließlich after all, finally, 15–1

schlimm bad, 6–2

der **Schluß, die Schlüsse** end, conclusion

    zum Schluß in conclusion, finally

der **Schlüssel, -** key, 6–SA, 11–2

schmecken to taste (*trans. and intrans.*); taste good, 8–1

sich schminken to put on make-up, 11–SA

schmutzig dirty, 9–1

der **Schnee** snow, 4–2

schneiden, schnitt, hat geschnitten to cut, 11–1

schneien to snow, Intro.

schnell fast, Intro., 3–2

    schnell machen (*colloq.*) to hurry, 11–1

das **Schnitzel, -** cutlet, chop, 8–1

die **Schokolade** chocolate, 11–1

schon already; (*flavoring particle*), 3–1

    schon lange for a long time, 10–G

schön beautiful, 1–1

schrecklich terrible, 4–2

schreiben, schrieb, hat geschrieben to write, 3–2

    schreiben über (+ *acc.*) to write about, 3–2

    Wie schreibt man das? How do you write (spell) that? Intro.

die **Schreibmaschine, -n** typewriter, 6–SA, 12–1

der **Schreibtisch, -e** desk, 6–1

der **Schriftsteller, -** writer (*m.*), 10–2

die **Schriftstellerin, -nen** writer (*f.*), 10–2

der **Schuh, -e** shoe, 3–2

die **Schule, -n** school, 2–1

der **Schüler, -** secondary school pupil (*m.*), Intro.

die **Schülerin, -nen** secondary school pupil (*f.*), Intro.

das **Schulsystem, -e** school system, 3–TLL

schwach (schwächer) weak, 9–2

schwarz (schwärzer) black, 3–SA

schweigen, schwieg, hat geschwiegen to be silent, 12–1

die **Schweiz** Switzerland, 4–2

der **Schweizer, -** Swiss (*m.*), 13–2

die **Schweizerin, -nen** Swiss (*f.*), 13–2

schweizerisch Swiss, 11–TLL

schwer heavy; hard, difficult, 3–1

die **Schwester, -n** sister, 2–1

schwierig difficult, 5–1

die **Schwierigkeit, -en** difficulty, 13–2

schwimmen, schwamm, ist geschwommen to swim, 4–1

der **See, -n** lake, 4–1
   am See at the lake
sehen (sieht), sah, hat gesehen to
   see, 2–1
sehr very, 1–1
sein (ist), war, ist gewesen to be,
   Intro., 1–1
   dabei sein to be present,
   attend, 15–1
seit (+ *dat.*) since, 5–1
   seit 5 Jahren for (the past) 5
   years, 5–1
   seit langem for a long time,
   10–G
die **Seite, -n** side; page, 11–2
   **auf der einen Seite / auf der
   anderen Seite** on the one hand
   / on the other hand, 11–2
der **Sekretär, -e** secretary (*m.*),
   5–SA
die **Sekretärin, -nen** secretary (*f.*),
   5–SA
selber / selbst by oneself (myself,
   yourself, ourselves, etc.), 6–2
selbstverständlich "It goes
   without saying that . . . ", 4–G
selten seldom, 1–2
das **Semester, -** semester, 2–1
   nächstes Semester next
   semester, 2–1
die **Semesterferien** (*pl.*) semester
   break, 6–2
das **Seminar, -e** (university)
   seminar, 4–1
der **Senior, -en, -en** senior citizen,
   10–1
separat separate, 11–TLL
(der) **September** September, Intro.
die **Serviette, -n** napkin, 8–SA
setzen to set (down), put, 7–1
   sich setzen to sit down, 11–1
sich (*third pers. reflexive pronoun*)
   himself, herself, themselves,
   yourself, yourselves (*formal
   second person*), 11–1
sicher certain, sure, 2–1
siebt- seventh, 9–G
singen, sang, hat gesungen to sing,
   3–2
die **Situation, -en** situation,
   10–TLL
sitzen, saß, hat gesessen to sit,
   6–2
(das) **Skandinavien** Scandinavia,
   8–TLL
**ski·fahren (fährt Ski), fuhr Ski, ist
   skigefahren** to ski, 8–2

so like this, 1–2; so, 7–2
   so etwas (*colloq.*: **so was**)
   something / anything like that,
   11–1
sofort immediately, right away,
   6–2
die **Software** software, 12–1
sogar even, in fact, 2–2
der **Sohn, ̈e** son, 2–1
solcher, -es, -e such, 7–G
die **Solidarität** solidarity, 1–TLL
sollen (soll), sollte, hat gesollt
   should, be supposed to, 3–1
der **Sommer** summer, 4–2
das **Sommersemester** spring term
   (usually May–July), 6–SA
sondern but rather, instead (*coor.
   conj.*), 7–1
   nicht nur . . . sondern auch not
   only . . . but also, 9–2
(der) **Sonnabend** Saturday, Intro.
die **Sonne** sun, 1–1
sonnig sunny, Intro.
(der) **Sonntag** Sunday, Intro.
sonst (*adv.*) otherwise, apart from
   that, 6–2
   Sonst noch etwas? Will there
   be anything else? 5–1
sowieso anyway, 7–1
sowjetisch soviet, 9–TLL
die **Sowjetunion** the Soviet Union,
   6–TLL
sozial social, 2–TLL
der **Sozialarbeiter, -** social worker,
   8–TLL
die **Soziologie** sociology, 6–SA
(das) **Spanien** Spain, 15–1
sparen to save (money or time),
   7–2
der **Spaß** fun
   Das macht (mir) Spaß. That is
   fun (for me). 7–2
   Viel Spaß. Have fun. 12–1
spät late, 3–1
   Wie spät ist es? What time is
   it? Intro., 8–G
später later, 4–1
**spazieren·gehen, ging spazieren, ist
   spazierengegangen** to go for a
   walk, 5–2
die **Speisekarte, -n** menu, 8–SA
der **Speisesaal** (hotel) dining room,
   14–SA
der **Spiegel, -** mirror, 14–2
das **Spiel, -e** game, 9–SA
spielen to play, 1–1
spontan spontaneous, 7–TLL

der **Sport** sport, 5–TLL; 9–1
   Sport treiben to play sports,
   9–1
sportlich athletic, 9–1
die **Sprache, -n** language, 3–2
**sprechen (spricht), sprach, hat
   gesprochen** to speak, talk, 2–1
   sprechen über (+ *acc.*) to talk
   about, 2–1
der **Staat, -en** state, 10–2
stabil stabile, 13–TLL
die **Stabilität** stability, 13–TLL
die **Stadt, ̈e** city, 4–2
der **Stadtbummel, -** stroll through
   town, 8–1
der **Stadtführer, -** city guidebook,
   14–SA
der **Stadtplan, ̈e** city map, 6–2
stark (stärker) strong, 9–2
statt (+ *gen.*) instead of, 8–G
**statt·finden, fand statt, hat
   stattgefunden** to take place,
   14–2
staunen to be amazed, surprised,
   6–2
stehen, stand, hat gestanden to
   stand, 5–1
**stehlen (stiehlt), stahl, hat
   gestohlen** to steal, 10–1
steigen, stieg, ist gestiegen to
   climb, 8–2
steil steep, 3–1
der **Stein, -e** stone, 12–2
steinalt old as the hills, 3–2
die **Stelle, -n** job, position, 2–2
stellen to put, place, 7–1
   eine Frage stellen to ask a
   question, 10–2
sterben (stirbt), starb, ist gestorben
   to die, 5–2
die **Stereoanlage, -n** stereo, 6–SA
die **Stimme, -n** voice, 5–2
stimmen to be right (*impersonal
   only*), 1–2
   das stimmt that's right, that's
   true
   Stimmt schon. That's right.
   3–2
stinklangweilig extremely boring,
   3–1
das **Stipendium, die Stipendien**
   scholarship, stipend, 6–2
der **Stock** floor (of a building), 14–2
   der erste Stock the second
   floor (*see* **Erdgeschoß**)
   im ersten Stock on the second
   floor

stolz auf (+ *acc.*) proud of, 13–2
stoppen to stop, 11–TLL
stören to disturb, 10–2
die **Straße, -n** street; road, 1–1
die **Straßenbahn, -en** streetcar, 8–SA; 13–1
der **Straßenatlas** road atlas, 7–1
der **Streß, die Stresse** stress, 5–2
stressig stressful, 5–2
das **Stück, -e** piece, 5–1
   sechs Stück six (of the same item) 5–1
   ein Stück Kuchen a piece of cake, 8–G
der **Student, -en, -en** university student (*m.*), Intro.
die **Studentin, -nen** university student (*f.*), Intro.
der **Studentenausweis, -e** student I.D., 6–2
das **Studentenwohnheim, -e** student dormitory, 6–1
studieren to attend a university; study (a subject); major in, 1–2
   studieren an (+ *dat.*) to study at, 6–SA
das **Studium** university studies, 6–2
der **Stuhl, ⁻e** chair, Intro.
die **Stunde, -n** hour; class hour, 3–1
stundenlang (*adv.*) for hours, 14–TLL
subjektiv subjective, 13–SA
das **Substantiv, -e** noun
suchen to look for, seek, 2–1
der **Süden** the south, 4–2
super super, 4–1
der **Supermarkt, ⁻e** supermarket, 8–1
der **Supertanker, -** supertanker, 9–TLL
die **Suppe, -n** soup, 1–1
das **Symbol, -e** symbol, 11–TLL
symbolisch symbolic, 10–TLL
sympathisch friendly, congenial, likeable, 7–2
das **System, -e** system, 3–TLL

T

die **Tafel, -n** blackboard, Intro.
der **Tag, -e** day, 1–1
   eines Tages some day (in the future); one day (in the past or future), 13–2

   Guten Tag! Hello! Intro.
   jeden Tag every day, 5–2
   Tag! Hi! Hello! Intro.
tagelang (*adv.*) for days, 14–TLL
das **Tal, ⁻er** valley, 4–2
die **Tante, -n** aunt, 2–2
tanzen to dance, 11–2
die **Tasche, -n** pocket, shoulderbag, 3–SA, 7–2
die **Tasse, -n** cup, 8–1
die **Taube, -n** dove, pigeon, 10–SA
das **Taxi, -s** taxicab, 8–SA
die **Technik** technology, 9–2
der **Tee** tea, 8–SA
der **Teil, -e** part, 15–2
teilen to divide, 11–2
teil·nehmen (nimmt teil), nahm teil, hat teilgenommen an (+ *dat.*) to take part in, 16–2
das **Telefon, -e** telephone, 6–SA; 7–2
telefonieren to telephone, make a phone call, 14–SA
der **Teller, -** plate, 8–SA
das **Tempo** pace, speed, tempo, 6–2
das **Tennis** tennis, 9–1
der **Tennisplatz, ⁻e** tennis court, 9–1
der **Teppich, -e** rug, 6–SA
der **Termin, -e** appointment, 6–2
die **Terrasse, -n** terrace, 15–SA
terroristisch terrorist (*adj.*), 10–TLL
teuer expensive, 6–2
der **Text, -e** text
das **Theater, -** theater, 6–TLL
das **Thema, die Themen** topic, subject, theme, 16–2
die **Thermosflasche, -n** thermos bottle, 7–1
das **Ticket, -s** (airline) ticket, 7–TLL
tief deep, 11–2
das **Tier, -e** animal, 9–2
der **Tip, -s** tip, hint, suggestion
der **Tisch, -e** table, Intro.
die **Tochter, ⁻** daughter, 2–2
der **Tod** death, 11–2
todmüde (*colloq.*) dead tired, 4–1
die **Toilette, -n** lavatory, 15–SA
toll (*colloq.*) great, terrific, 3–2
das **Tor, -e** gate, 11–1
tot dead, 11–2
die **Tour, -en** tour, 8–TLL

der **Tourist, -en, -en** tourist (*m.*), 1–TLL
die **Touristin, -nen** tourist (*f.*), 1–2
die **Tradition, -en** tradition, 11–TLL
traditionell traditional, 2–TLL
tragen (trägt), trug, hat getragen to carry; wear, 3–1
trainieren to train, 9–SA
trampen, ist getrampt to hitchhike, 7–2
träumen to dream, 14–2
traurig sad, 13–2
treffen (trifft), traf, hat getroffen to meet, 9–1
treiben, trieb, hat getrieben to drive, force, propel, 9–1
   Sport treiben to play sports, 9–1
die **Treppe** staircase, stairs, 9–1
   auf der Treppe on the stairs, 9–1
trinken, trank, hat getrunken to drink, 4–2
trocken dry, 4–2
trotz (+ *gen.*) in spite of, despite, 8–G
trotzdem in spite of that, nevertheless, 8–2
Tschüs! So long! Intro.
das **T-Shirt, -s** T-shirt, 3–SA
tun, tat, hat getan to do, 3–1
   Es tut mir leid. I'm sorry (about that). 7–1
   Das tut mir weh. That hurts (me). 11–1
   Er tut, als ob . . . (+ *subj.*) He acts as if . . . , 16–G
die **Tür, -en** door, Intro.
der **Türke, -n, -n** Turk (*m.*), 15–2
die **Türkin, -nen** Turk (*f.*), 15–2
die **Türkei** Turkey, 15–2
türkisch Turkish, 15–2
der **Turnschuh, -e** sneaker, gym shoe, 3–2
der **Typ, -en** type; (*slang*) guy, 12–1
typisch typical, 1–1

U

die **U-Bahn** (= **Untergrundbahn**) subway train, 8–SA
üben to practice, Intro.
über (+ *acc.*) about, 2–1; (+ *acc.*

or dat.) over, across; above, 6–G

überall everywhere, 2–2

sich etwas überlegen to consider, ponder, think something over, 13–2

übermorgen the day after tomorrow, 12–1

übernachten to spend the night, 7–2

überraschen to surprise, 15–1

die **Überraschung, -en** surprise, 16–SA

übersetzen to translate, Intro.

übrigens by the way, 1–1

die **Übung, -en** exercise

die **UdSSR** the USSR, 11–TLL

die **Uhr, -en** clock, Intro.

    9 Uhr 9 o'clock, Intro., 5–1

    Wieviel Uhr ist es? What time is it? 8–G

um at (with times), 1–1; around (the outside of), 4–G

um . . . zu in order to, 8–1

der **Umschlag, ̈e** envelope, 15–1

um·steigen, stieg um, ist umgestiegen to transfer, change (trains, buses, etc.), 7–SA

die **Umwelt** environment, 3–2

umweltfreundlich ecologically beneficial, non-polluting, 9–1

um·ziehen, zog um, ist umgezogen to move, change residence, 9–1

    sich um·ziehen to change clothes, 14–SA

unabhängig independent, 9–2

unbekannt unknown, 10–2

unbesorgt unconcerned, carefree, 10–1

und and (*coor. conj.*), 1–1

der **Unfall, ̈e** accident, 9–2

(*das*) **Ungarn** Hungary, 11–2

ungebildet uneducated, 16–2

ungemütlich unpleasant, not cozy, 14–2

die **Uni, -s** (*colloq.*) university, 6–1

    an der Uni at the university, 6–1

die **Universität, -en** university, 5–TLL; 6–1

    an der Universität at the university, 6–1

unmöglich impossible, 6–1

unnötig unnecessary, 9–1

unordentlich messy, disorderly, 13–1

unruhig restless, troubled, 10–2

unten (*adv.*) below, on the bottom

unter (+ *acc. or dat.*) under, beneath; among, 6–1

unterbrechen (unterbricht), unterbrach, hat unterbrochen to interrupt, 10–2

der **Unterschied, -e** difference, 11–2

unterwegs on the way, en route; on the go, 4–1

unverheiratet unmarried, 16–1

unwichtig unimportant, 2–2

der **Urlaub, -e** vacation (from a job), 4–1

    Urlaub machen to take a vacation, 5–2

    in Urlaub gehen / fahren to go on vacation

die **USA** (*pl.*) the USA, 5–2

usw. (= **und so weiter**) etc. (= and so forth), 1–1

V

die **Variation, -en** variation

der **Vater, ̈** father, 2–1

der **Vati, -s** papa, dad, 2–2

(*das*) **Venedig** Venice (Italy), 7–1

verantwortlich für responsible for, 6–2

das **Verb, -en** verb

verboten forbidden, prohibited

verbrauchen to consume, use up, 9–2

verbringen, verbrachte, hat verbracht to spend (time), 7–2

verdienen to earn, 2–2

der **Verein, -e** club, organization, 5–2

vereinen to unite, 11–2

die **Vereinigung** unification, 11–2

Verflixt nochmal! Darn it all! 15–1

die **Vergangenheit** past (time), 11–2

vergessen (vergißt), vergaß, hat vergessen to forget, 5–2

vergleichen, verglich, hat verglichen to compare, 12–2

verheiratet sein to be married, 16–1

verkaufen to sell, 4–1

der **Verkäufer, -** salesman, 5–SA

die **Verkäuferin, -nen** saleswoman, 5–SA

der **Verkehr** traffic, 7–SA

verlassen (verläßt), verließ, hat verlassen to leave (a person or place), 5–1

sich verletzen to injure oneself, get hurt, 11–1

verlieren, verlor, hat verloren to lose, 10–1

sich verloben mit (+ *dat.*) to become engaged to, 12–1

verpassen to miss (an event, opportunity, train, etc.), 13–1

verrückt crazy, insane, 7–2

verschieden different, various, 11–2

verschmutzen to pollute; dirty, 9–2

die **Verschmutzung** pollution, 9–1

verschwenden to waste, 9–2

verschwinden, verschwand, ist verschwunden to disappear, 11–2

sich verspäten to be late, 11–1

verstehen, verstand, hat verstanden to understand, 3–1

versuchen to try, attempt, 10–2

verwandt (mit + *dat.*) related (to), 15–2

der / die **Verwandte, -n** relative, 11–1

der **Vetter, -n** cousin (*m.*), 2–SA

viel (mehr, am meisten) much, a lot, 1–1

viele many, 1–2; (*pronoun*) many people, 8–2

    vielen Dank many thanks, 2–1

vielleicht maybe, perhaps, 1–1

das **Viertel** quarter

    Viertel vor / nach sieben quarter to / past seven, Intro.

der **Vogel, ̈** bird, 9–2

die **Vokabel, -n** word (*in pl.* = vocabulary)

das **Volk, ̈er** people, nation, folk, 10–2

das **Volkslied, -er** folk song, 4–2

voll full, 5–1

der **Volleyball** volleyball, 9–SA

von (+ *dat.*) from, 4–2; of; by, 5–G

vor (+ *acc. or dat.*) in front of, 6–G

    vor einem Jahr a year ago, 10–G

vorbei (see **an . . . vorbei**)

vorbei·kommen, kam vorbei, ist vorbeigekommen to come by, drop by, 5–2 sich vor·bereiten auf (+ acc.) to prepare for, 13–1

vorgestern the day before yesterday, 12–1

vor·haben (hat vor), hatte vor, hat vorgehabt to plan, have in mind, 13–1

vorher before that, previously, 10–1

vor·lesen (liest vor), las vor, hat vorgelesen to read aloud

die Vorlesung, -en university lecture, 6–1

das Vorlesungverzeichnis, -se university catalogue, list of lectures and courses, 6–1

vormittags (in the) mornings, 16–1

der Vorschlag, ¨e suggestion

vor·stellen to introduce, present, 13–2

    sich vor·stellen to introduce oneself, 13–2

    sich etwas vor·stellen to imagine something, 11–1

das Vorurteil, -e prejudice, 13–SA

W

wachsen (wächst), wuchs, ist gewachsen to grow, 10–2

der Wagen, - car, 3–1

die Wahl, -en choice; election, 10–2

wählen to choose; to elect, 10–2

der Wähler, - voter, 10–2

wahnsinnig (adv. colloq.) extremely, incredibly, awfully; (adj.) crazy, insane, 3–1

wahr true, 3–1

    nicht wahr? isn't it? can't you? doesn't she? etc., 3–1

während (+ gen.) during, 8–G

die Wahrheit, -en truth, 13–SA

wahrscheinlich probably, 1–2

der Wald, ¨er forest, 4–2

die Wand, ¨e (interior) wall, Intro.

die Wanderlust wanderlust, 7–TLL

wandern, ist gewandert to hike, wander, 4–2

die Wanderung, -en hike, 5–2

wann? when? Intro.

die Ware, -n product, 9–2

warm (wärmer) warm, Intro.

warten to wait, 4–1

warten auf (+ acc.) to wait for, 13–1

Warte mal! Wait a second! Hang on! 4–1

warum? why? 1–1

was? what? Intro.

    was für? what kind of? 9–G

    Was ist los? What's the matter? What's going on? 3–1

waschen (wäscht), wusch, hat gewaschen to wash, 11–1

das Wasser water, 4–1

wechseln to change (money), 14–1

der Wecker, - alarm clock, 6–SA

weder . . . noch neither . . . nor, 14–1

der Weg, -e way, path, 16–2

weg (adv.) away, gone, 4–1

wegen (+ gen.) because of, on account of, 8–G

weg·gehen, ging weg, ist weggegangen to go away, leave, 12–1

weg·werfen (wirft weg), warf weg, hat weggeworfen to throw away, 9–2

weh tun, tat weh, hat weh getan (+ dat. of person) to hurt, 11–1

weil (sub. conj.) because, 8–G

der Wein, -e wine, 4–2

weinen to cry, 3–2

weiß white, 3–SA

weit far, far away, 8–1

welcher, -es, -e? which? 7–G

die Welt, -en world, 3–2

wem? (dat.) to whom? for whom? 5–G

wen? (acc.) whom? 2–G

wenig little bit, not much, 1–1

wenige few, 11–1

wenigstens at least, 2–2

wenn (sub. conj.) if, 8–G; when, whenever, 10–G

wer? (nom.) who? Intro.

werden (wird), wurde, ist geworden to become, get (in the sense of "become"), 4–1

werfen (wirft), warf, hat geworfen to throw, 9–2

das Werk, -e work (of art), musical composition, 13–2

wessen? whose? 2–G

der Westen the west, 4–2

das Wetter weather, Intro., 1–1

die WG (= Wohngemeinschaft) communal living group, shared apartment, 6–1

wichtig important, 2–2

wie how, Intro.; like, as, 1–1

    Wie bitte? I beg your pardon? What did you say? Intro.

    wie lange? how long? 3–G

wieder again, 1–1

wiederholen to repeat, Intro.

die Wiederholung, -en repetition; review

wieder·sehen (sieht wieder), sah wieder, hat wiedergesehen to see again, meet again, 12–2

    Auf Wiedersehen! Good-bye! Intro.

wiegen, wog, hat gewogen (trans. and intrans.) to weigh, 15–1

(das) Wien Vienna, 1–1

wieso? How come? How's that? What do you mean? 9–1

wieviel? how much? 5–1

    Wieviel kostet das, bitte? How much does that cost, please? 5–1

    Wieviel Uhr ist es? What time is it? 8–G

wie viele? how many? 2–1

wievielt-

    Den wievielten haben wir heute? What's the date today? 9–G

wild wild, 4–TLL

willkommen welcome, 6–2

    herzlich willkommen heartily welcome, 6–2

der Wind wind, 4–SA

windig windy, Intro.

der Winter, - winter, 4–1

    im Winter in the winter, 4–1

das Wintersemester fall term (usually October-February), 6–SA

wirklich real, 6–1

die Wirtschaft economy, 11–2

die Wirtschaftswissenschaft economics, 6–SA

der Wischer, - (blackboard) eraser, Intro.

wissen (weiß), wußte, hat gewußt to know (a fact), 2–1

die Wissenschaft, -en science; scholarship; field of knowledge, 6–SA

der Witz, -e joke; wit, 14–2

witzig witty, amusing, 14–2

wo? where? Intro.

die **Woche, -n** week, 5–2

das **Wochenende, -n** weekend, 5–2
    am Wochenende on the
    weekend, 5–2
    Schönes Wochenende! (Have a)
    nice weekend! Intro.

wochenlang (*adv.*) for weeks,
    14–TLL

woher? from where? Intro.

wohin? to where? 3–G

wohl probably, 6–2

wohnen to live, dwell, Intro.

die **Wohngemeinschaft, -en**
    communal living group, shared
    apartment, 6–1

das **Wohnhaus, ⁻er** apartment
    building, 9–1

die **Wohnung, -en** apartment, 6–2

das **Wohnzimmer, -** living room,
    15–SA

die **Wolke, -n** cloud, 4–SA

wolkig cloudy, Intro.

wollen (will), wollte, hat gewollt
    to want to, intend to, 3–1; to
    claim to, 16–G

worden (*special form of the past
    participle of* **werden** *used in
    the perfect tenses of the
    passive voice*)

das **Wort** word (*2 pl. forms:* die
    Worte = words in context, die
    Wörter = unconnected words,
    as in a dictionary), 5–2

das **Wörterbuch, ⁻er** dictionary,
    5–2

der **Wortschatz** vocabulary

die **Wortschatzerweiterung**
    vocabulary expansion

das **Wunder, -** miracle
    Kein Wunder! No wonder!
    15–1

wunderbar wonderful, 7–1

sich wundern (über + *acc.*) to be
    surprised, amazed (at)

wunderschön very beautiful, 1–1

wünschen to wish, 12–1

die **Wurst, ⁻e** sausage, 8–1
    Das ist mir Wurst (*or*
    Wurscht). I don't give a darn.
    7–1

Z

zahlen to pay, 8–1
    Zahlen bitte! Check please!
    8–1

zählen to count, 10–3

der **Zahn, ⁻e** tooth, 11–SA
    sich die Zähne putzen to
    brush one's teeth, 11–SA

zeigen to show, 5–1
    Zeig mal her. Let's see. Show
    it to me. 15–1

die **Zeile, -n** line (of text)

die **Zeit, -en** time, 3–2
    höchste Zeit high time, 14–1

Zeitlang
    eine Zeitlang for a time, for a
    while, 14–2

die **Zeitschrift, -en** magazine, 5–2

die **Zeitung, -en** newspaper, 2–1

zentral central, 11–TLL

zerstören to destroy, 9–2

die **Zerstörung** destruction

ziehen, zog, hat gezogen to pull,
    6–1

das **Ziel, -e** goal, 7–2

ziemlich fairly, quite, 1–2

zigmal umpteen times, 12–G

das **Zimmer, -** room, 2–1

zirka circa, 4–TLL

die **Zone, -n** zone, 11–TLL

zu to; too, 1–1
    zu Fuß on foot, 3–1
    zu Hause at home, 2–2

zuerst first, at first, 8–1

der **Zug, ⁻e** train, 7–1

zu·hören (+ *dat.*) to listen (to),
    13–1

die **Zukunft** future, 11–2
    in Zukunft in the future, 13–2

zuletzt last of all, finally, 8–1

zu·machen to close, 5–2

zunächst first (of all), to begin
    with, 14–2

zurück back, 1–1

**zurück·bringen, brachte zurück,
    hat zurückgebracht** to bring
    back

**zurück·kommen, kam zurück, ist
    zurückgekommen** to come
    back, 1–1

zusammen together, Intro., 4–1

die **Zusammenfassung** summary

**zusammen·kommen, kam
    zusammen, ist
    zusammengekommen** to come
    together, congregate, 10–2

zwar ... aber it is true, to be sure
    . . . but, 14–2

zweimal twice, 12–G

zweit- second, 9–1

der **Zweitwagen, -** second car, 9–1

zwischen (+ *acc. or dat.*) between,
    2–2

English-German Vocabulary

Strong and irregular verbs are marked by an asterisk: *brechen, *können, *bringen. Their principal parts can be found in Appendix 2.

A

able, be able to *können
about über (+ *acc.*)
    it's about X es geht um X
above oben (*adv.*); über (*prep.* + *dat. or acc.*)
abroad im Ausland
absent
    be absent fehlen
accept akzeptieren
accident der Unfall, ¨e
account
    on account of wegen (+ *gen.*)
acidic sauer
acquaintance der/die Bekannte, -n
acquainted
    be acquainted with *kennen
across über (+ *dat. or acc.*)
act
    He acts as if . . . Er tut, als ob . . . (+ *subj.*)
active aktiv
actually eigentlich
acute akut
address die Adresse, -n
adjective das Adjektiv, -e
administration, government in power die Regierung, -en
adverb das Adverb, -ien
affair, matter die Sache, -n
afford
    be able to afford something sich etwas leisten können
afraid of Angst haben (vor + *dat.*)
after nach (*prep.* + *dat.*); nachdem (*sub. conj.*)
after all schließlich
afternoon der Nachmittag, -e
    in the afternoon am Nachmittag
    (in the) afternoons nachmittags
    this afternoon heute nachmittag

afterward, after that nacher (*adv.*)
again wieder
against gegen (+ *acc.*)
ago vor (+ *dat.*)
    a year ago vor einem Jahr
agreed einverstanden
agriculture die Landwirtschaft
ah ach
aid die Hilfe
air die Luft
air pollution die Luftverschmutzung
airplane das Flugzeug, -e
airport der Flughafen, ¨
alarm clock der Wecker, -
alive
    be alive leben
all alle (*pl.*)
all summer (day, afternoon, etc.) den ganzen Sommer (Tag, Nachmittag, etc.)
allow *lassen
allowed
    be allowed to *dürfen
almanac der Almanach, -e
almost fast
alone allein
along mit (*adv.*)
alongside of an (+ *acc. or dat.*)
a lot viel (mehr, am meisten); eine Menge
Alps die Alpen (*pl.*)
already schon
also auch
alternative die Alternative, -n
although obwohl (*sub. conj.*)
always immer
amazed
    be amazed staunen
    be amazed (at) sich wundern (über + *acc.*)
America (das) Amerika
American der Amerikaner, -; die Amerikanerin, -nen; amerikanisch (*adj.*)
among unter (+ *acc. or dat.*)

amusing witzig
analyze analysieren
and und (*coor. conj.*)
anger der Ärger
angry (at) böse (+ *dat.*)
animal das Tier, -e
annoy ärgern
    get annoyed sich ärgern
annoyance der Ärger
annually jährlich
another, an additional noch ein
answer die Antwort, -en
    answer (a question, letter, etc.) beantworten
    answer (a person) antworten (+ *dat.*)
    answer (something) antworten auf (+ *acc.*)
anything
    anything like that so etwas; so was (*colloq.*)
    Anything more? (Sonst) noch etwas?
    Will there be anything else? Sonst noch etwas?
anyway sowieso
anywhere irgendwo
apart from that sonst
apartment die Wohnung, -en
apartment building das Wohnhaus, ¨er
appear *aus·sehen
appointment der Termin, -e
apprentice der Lehrling, -e
April (der) April
area die Gegend, -en
arm der Arm, -e
around, about (with time) gegen (+ *acc.*)
around (the outside of) um (+ *acc.*)
arrive *an·kommen
art history die Kunstgeschichte
art die Kunst, ¨e
article der Artikel, -
artist der Künstler, -; die Künstlerin, -nen

as a als
as wie
ask fragen
    ask a question eine Frage stellen
    ask for *bitten um
    ask oneself sich fragen
aspect der Aspekt, -e
assignment die Aufgabe, -n
astonished erstaunt
astounding erstaunlich
at bei (+ *dat.*)
at an (+ *acc. or dat.*)
at (with times) um (+ *acc.*)
at least wenigstens
At last! Na endlich!
athletic sportlich
atom das Atom, -e
atomic power plant das Atomkraftwerk, -e
attempt versuchen
attend to erledigen
August (der) August
aunt die Tante, -n
Austria (das) Österreich
Austrian der Österreicher, -; die Österreicherin, -nen; österreichisch (*adj.*)
auto mechanic der Automechaniker, -; die Automechanikerin, -nen
automatic automatisch
automobile das Auto, -s; der Wagen, -
autumn der Herbst
away weg (*adv.*)
awfully wahnsinnig (*colloq. adv.*)

B

baby das Baby, -s
back zurück
backpack der Rucksack, -̈e
bad schlecht; schlimm
baker der Bäcker, -; die Bäckerin, -nen
bakery die Bäckerei, -en
ball-point pen der Kugelschreiber, -
Baloney! Quatsch!
banana die Banane, -n
bank die Bank, -en
bar, tavern die Kneipe, -n
barbaric barbarisch
barely kaum
barrier die Barriere, -n

basement der Keller, -
basis die Basis
bath das Bad
    take a bath ein Bad *nehmen
bathroom das Badezimmer, -
be *sein
bear der Bär, -en, -en
beat *schlagen
beautiful schön
    very beautiful wunderschön
because weil (*sub. conj.*)
because, for denn (*coor. conj.*)
because of wegen (+ *gen.*)
become, get *werden
bed das Bett, -en
    get out of bed *auf·stehen
    go to bed ins Bett *gehen
bedroom das Schlafzimmer, -
beer das Bier, -e
before bevor (*sub. conj.*)
before that vorher (*adv.*)
begin *an·fangen; *beginnen
    to begin with zunächst (*adv.*)
beginner der Anfänger, -
beginning der Anfang, -̈e
    at / in the beginning am Anfang
behind hinter (+ *acc. or dat.*)
believe glauben (+ *dat. of person*)
belong to (a person) gehören (+ *dat.*)
below unten (*adv.*); unter (*prep.* + *acc. or dat.*)
bench die Bank, -̈e
beneath unter (+ *acc. or dat.*)
beside neben (+ *acc. or dat.*)
besides außer (+ *dat.*)
best best-
    like best of all to am liebsten (+ *verb*)
better besser
between zwischen (+ *acc. or dat.*)
bicycle *rad·fahren; das Fahrrad, -̈er; das Rad, -̈er
big groß (größer, größt-)
biology die Biologie
bird der Vogel, -̈
birthday der Geburtstag, -e
    for one's birthday zum Geburtstag
black schwarz (schwärzer)
blackboard die Tafel, -n
blouse die Bluse, -n
blue blau
book das Buch, -̈er
bookcase das Bücherregal, -e
bookstore die Buchhandlung, -en

border die Grenze, -n
bored
    be bored sich langweilen
boring langweilig
    extremely boring stinklangweilig
born geboren
borrow *leihen
boss der Chef, -s; die Chefin, -nen
both beid-
    both (people) beide (*pl. pronoun*)
    both (things) beides (*sing. pronoun*)
bottle die Flasche, -n
bottom
    at the bottom unten (*adv.*)
box boxen
boy der Junge, -n, -n
bread das Brot, -e
    dark bread das Bauernbrot
break *brechen; kaputt machen
    take a break eine Pause machen
break out *aus·brechen
break, intermission die Pause, -n
breakfast das Frühstück, -e
    eat breakfast frühstücken
    for breakfast zum Frühstück
bridge die Brücke, -n
bright, smart klug (klüger)
bright, light hell
bring *bringen
    bring along *mit·bringen
    bring back *zurück·bringen
broken kaputt (*colloq.*)
brother der Bruder, -̈
brown braun
brush one's teeth sich die Zähne putzen
build bauen
building das Gebäude, -
bus der Bus, -se
business das Geschäft, -e
businesspeople die Geschäftsleute
business (field of study) die Betriebswirtschaft
businessman der Geschäftsmann
businesswoman die Geschäftsfrau
but aber (*coor. conj.*)
    but rather sondern (*coor. conj.*)
butter die Butter
buy kaufen
by (a certain time) bis (+ *acc.*)
by von (+ *dat.*)
by the way übrigens

C

café das Café, -s
  pastry café die Konditorei, -en
cafeteria (at the university) die Mensa
cake der Kuchen, -
call *rufen
  call up *an·rufen
  be called *heißen
calm, peaceful ruhig
camera die Kamera, -s
camp campen
can, be able to *können
Canada (das) Kanada
cap die Mütze, -n
capitalism der Kapitalismus
car das Auto, -s; der Wagen, -
card die Karte, -n
care
  I don't care. Das ist mir egal.
  take care of sich kümmern um
  take care of, finish erledigen
career die Karriere, -n
carefree unbesorgt
carry *tragen
cashier, cashier's office die Kasse, -n
cassette player der Kassettenrecorder, -
cat die Katze, -n
catalogue (university) das Vorlesungsverzeichnis, -se
catastrophe die Katastrophe, -n
catastrophic katastrophal
cathedral der Dom, -e
cause to be done *lassen (+ infinitive)
cease auf·hören (mit)
ceiling die Decke, -n
celebrate feiern
celebration die Feier, -n
cellar der Keller, -
central zentral
century das Jahrhundert, -e
  for centuries jahrhundertelang
certain, sure sicher
chain die Kette, -n
chain reaction die Kettenreaktion, -en
chair der Stuhl, ⸚e
chalk die Kreide
chance die Gelegenheit, -en; die Chance, -n
change ändern (trans.); sich ändern (intrans.)
  change (clothes) sich *um·ziehen

change (money) wechseln
change (trains, buses, etc.), transfer *um·steigen
change purse der Geldbeutel, -
chapter das Kapitel, -
chat quatschen (colloq.)
cheap billig
check der Scheck, -s
  Check please! Zahlen bitte!
cheerful munter; heiter
cheese der Käse
chemistry die Chemie
chief Haupt- (noun prefix)
child das Kind, -er
childhood die Kindheit, -en
Chinese (das) Chinesisch
chocolate die Schokolade
choice die Wahl, -en
choose wählen
chop, cutlet das Schnitzel, -
Christian christlich
church die Kirche, -n
circa zirka
citizen der Bürger, -
city die Stadt, ⸚e
  capital city die Hauptstadt, ⸚e
  large city (over 500,000 inhabitants) die Großstadt, ⸚e
  old city center die Altstadt, ⸚e
  small city (5,000 to 20,000 inhabitants) die Kleinstadt, ⸚e
  city guidebook der Stadtführer, -
  city map der Stadtplan, ⸚e
civil servant der Beamte (adj. noun, m.); die Beamtin, -nen (f.)
claim to *wollen
class die Klasse, -n
class hour die Stunde, -n
clean putzen (verb); sauber (adj.)
clear klar; deutlich
cliché das Klischee, -s
cliché (adj.), stereotyped klischeehaft
climate das Klima
climb *steigen
clock die Uhr, -en
close *schließen, zu·machen
  closed geschlossen
clothes die Kleider (pl.)
clothes cupboard der Kleiderschrank, ⸚e
clothing die Kleidung
cloud die Wolke, -n
cloudy wolkig
club der Verein, -e
coat der Mantel, ⸚

coffee der Kaffee
cold kalt (kälter); die Kälte
  catch a cold sich erkälten
collect sammeln
Cologne (das) Köln
colony die Kolonie, -n
color die Farbe, -n
colorful bunt
comb kämmen
  comb one's hair sich die Haare kämmen
come *kommen
  All together that comes to . . . Das macht zusammen . . .
  come along *mit·kommen
  come back *zurück·kommen
  come by *vorbei·kommen
  come together *zusammen·kommen
  come from *kommen aus
comfortable bequem
communal living group die Wohngemeinschaft, -en; die WG, -s
Communism der Kommunismus
compare *vergleichen
compatriots die Landsleute (pl.)
competition die Konkurrenz
computer der Computer, -
computer science die Informatik
concentrate on sich konzentrieren auf (+ acc.)
concerned besorgt
concert das Konzert, -e
conclusion der Schluß, die Schlüsse
  in conclusion zum Schluß
conflict der Konflikt, -e
congenial sympathisch
congratulate gratulieren (+ dat. of person)
consequence die Konsequenz, -en
conservative konservativ
consider something sich etwas überlegen
consume verbrauchen
contact der Kontakt, -e
contingent
  be contingent on, depend on *an·kommen auf (+ acc.)
contrary
  on the contrary im Gegenteil
contrast der Kontrast, -e
conversation das Gespräch, -e
cook kochen
cool kühl
cooperate mit·machen

corner die Ecke, -n
>**around the corner** um die Ecke
>**at / on the corner** an der Ecke

correct richtig

correspondent der Korrespondent,
-en, -en

cost kosten

count zählen

counter, window der Schalter, -

country das Land, ⁻er
>**in the country** auf dem Land
>**to the country** aufs Land

couple
>**a couple (of)** ein paar

cousin der Vetter, -n; die Kusine,
-n

cozy, relaxed gemütlich

crazy verrückt; wahnsinnig

cream die Sahne

creative kreativ

critical kritisch

criticize kritisieren

cross street die Querstraße, -n

crowd die Menge, -n

cruel grausam

cry weinen

culture die Kultur, -en

cup die Tasse, -n

customer der Kunde, -n, -n; die
Kundin, -nen

cut *schneiden

cutlet das Schnitzel, -

D

dad der Vati, -s

damp naß

dance tanzen

danger die Gefahr, -en

dangerous gefährlich

dark dunkel

darn
>**Darn it all!** Verflixt nochmal!
>**I don't give a darn.** Das ist mir
>Wurst (or Wurscht).

date
>**What's the date today?** Der
>wievielte ist heute? Den
>wievielten haben wir heute?

daughter die Tochter, ⁻

day der Tag, -e
>**day after tomorrow**
>übermorgen
>**day before yesterday**
>vorgestern

for days tagelang

in those days damals

one day (in the past or future)
eines Tages

some day (in the future) eines
Tages

dead tot

deal with sich kümmern um

dear lieb

death der Tod, -e

December (der) Dezember

decide *entscheiden

deep tief

delicious lecker

democracy die Demokratie

democratic demokratisch

demonstrate demonstrieren

demonstration die Demonstration,
-en

depart *ab·fahren; *los·fahren

department store das Kaufhaus, ⁻er

depend on *an·kommen auf
(+ acc.)

dependent on abhängig von

describe *beschreiben

desire die Lust

desk der Schreibtisch, -e

despite trotz (+ gen.)

dessert der Nachtisch, -e
>**for dessert** zum Nachtisch

destination das Reiseziel, -e

destroy zerstören

destruction die Zerstörung

dialect der Dialekt, -e

dialogue der Dialog, -e

dictionary das Wörterbuch, ⁻er

die *sterben
>**die in battle** *fallen

difference der Unterschied, -e

different ander- (attributive adj.);
anders (predicate adj.)
>**different, various** verschieden

difficult schwer; schwierig

difficulty die Schwierigkeit, -en

dining room das Eßzimmer, -

dining room (hotel) der Speisesaal

direct(ly) direkt

director der Direktor, -en

dirty schmutzig; dreckig (colloq.)

disappear *verschwinden

disappoint enttäuschen

disappointment die Enttäuschung,
-en

discuss diskutieren; *besprechen

discussion die Diskussion, -en

disorderly schlampig (colloq.);
unordentlich

dissertation die Dissertation, -en;
die Diss (university slang); die
Doktorarbeit

distant fern

disturb stören

divide teilen

do machen; *tun

doctor der Arzt, ⁻e; die Ärztin,
-nen

dog der Hund, -e

done fertig

donkey der Esel, -

door die Tür, -en

dove die Taube, -n

drag schleppen (colloq.)

dream träumen

dress, get dressed sich *an·ziehen

dress das Kleid, -er

drink *trinken

drive *fahren

drive, propel *treiben

drop by *vorbei·kommen

dry trocken

dumb, stupid dumm (dümmer);
blöd

during während (+ gen.)
>**during, while -ing** bei

dwell wohnen

dynasty die Dynastie, -n

E

each jeder

each other einander

eagle der Adler, -

ear das Ohr, -en

early früh

earn verdienen

earth die Erde

east der Osten

easy, simple einfach; leicht

eat *essen

ecology
>**ecologically beneficial,**
>**non-polluting**
>umweltfreundlich

economics die
Wirtschaftswissenschaft

economy die Wirtschaft

ecosystem das Ökosystem, -e

educated gebildet

education (as field of study) die
Pädagogik

egg das Ei, -er

either . . . or entweder . . . oder

elect wählen
election die Wahl, -en
electrical engineer der
    Elektrotechniker, -; die
    Elektrotechnikerin, -nen
electrical engineering die
    Elektrotechnik
electrician der Elektrotechniker, -;
    die Elektrotechnikerin, -nen
electricity die Elektrizität
elegant elegant
elephant der Elefant, -en, -en
elevator der Lift, -s
emancipation die Emanzipation
emigrate aus·wandern
empire das Reich, -e
employed berufstätig
employee der / die Angestellte, -n
empty leer
en route unterwegs
end das Ende, -n; der Schluß, die
    Schlüsse
    at the end am Ende
    at the end of February Ende
    Februar
    end, be finished, be over zu
    Ende sein
energy die Energie
engaged
    become engaged to sich
    verloben mit
engineer der Ingenieur, -e; die
    Ingenieurin, -nen
England (das) England
English (language) (das) Englisch
English (adj.) englisch
English studies die Anglistik
Englishman der Engländer, -
Englishwoman die Engländerin,
    -nen
enormous enorm
enough genug
enthusiastic about begeistert von
entire ganz
entrance, way in der Einstieg, -e
envelope der Umschlag, ⁻e
environment die Umwelt
epoch die Epoche, -n
equal gleich
equal rights die
    Gleichberechtigung (sing.)
    enjoying equal rights
    gleichberechtigt
eraser das Radiergummi (pencil);
    der Wischer, - (blackboard)

especially besonders
essay der Aufsatz, ⁻e
    essay topic das Aufsatzthema,
    -themen
etc. usw. (= und so weiter)
Europe (das) Europa
    Central Europe (das)
    Mitteleuropa
    Eastern Europe (das) Osteuropa
European der Europäer, -; die
    Europäerin, -nen; europäisch
    (adj.)
even, in fact sogar
evening der Abend, -e
    good evening guten Abend
    in the evening am Abend
    (in the) evenings abends
    this evening, tonight heute
    abend
evening meal das Abendessen
ever je
every jeder
    every time jedesmal (adv.)
everybody alle (pl. pronoun)
everyday life der Alltag
everyone jeder (sing. pronoun)
everything alles
everywhere überall
exact genau
examination die Prüfung, -en; das
    Abitur (final secondary school
    exam); das Abi (slang)
example das Beispiel, -e
    for example zum Beispiel
excellent ausgezeichnet
exchange student der
    Austauschstudent, -en, -en
excursion der Ausflug, ⁻e
Excuse me. Entschuldigung.
exercise die Übung, -en
exhausted kaputt (colloq.)
exhibition die Ausstellung, -en
exist existieren
expect erwarten
expensive teuer
experience erleben; die Erfahrung,
    -en
explain erklären
expression der Ausdruck, ⁻e
expressway die Autobahn, -en
extreme extrem
extremely wahnsinnig (colloq.
    adv.)
eye das Auge, -n
eyeglasses die Brille (sing.)

F

face das Gesicht, -er
fact
    in fact eigentlich
    in fact, even sogar
factory die Fabrik, -en
fairly ziemlich
fairy tale das Märchen, -
fall *fallen
    fall asleep *ein·schlafen
fall, autumn der Herbst
    fall term das Wintersemester
false, incorrect falsch
family die Familie, -n
famous berühmt
fantastic phantastisch
far, far away weit; fern
farmer der Bauer, -n, -n; der
    Landwirt, -e; die Landwirtin,
    -nen
fast schnell
father der Vater, ⁻
favorite Lieblings- (noun prefix)
fear die Angst, ⁻e
February (der) Februar
Federal Republic of Germany
    (FRG) die Bundesrepublik
    Deutschland (BRD)
fed up
    I'm fed up. Ich habe die Nase
    voll.
feel sich fühlen (intrans.)
feeling das Gefühl, -e
fetch holen
    fetch, pick up ab·holen
few wenige
    a few ein paar
film der Film, -e
finally endlich; schließlich; zum
    Schluß; zuletzt
finance finanzieren
find *finden
Fine by me. Ist gut. (colloq.)
finger der Finger, -
finish, take care of erledigen
finished with fertig mit
firm, company die Firma,
    Firmen
first erst- (adj.); zuerst (adv.)
    at first zuerst
    first (of all) zunächst
fish der Fisch, -e
flabbergasted baff
flat flach

floor (of a building) der Stock
    ground floor, first floor das Erdgeschoß
    of a room der Boden, ⸚
    on the second floor im ersten Stock
    second floor der erste Stock
Florence (Italy) (das) Florenz
flower die Blume, -n
fly *fliegen
fog der Nebel
foggy neblig
folk das Volk, ⸚er
folk song das Volkslied, -er
follow folgen, ist gefolgt (+ *dat.*)
food das Essen
foolproof idiotensicher
foot der Fuß, ⸚e
    on foot zu Fuß
for für
    for years seit Jahren
    for a long time seit langem; schon lange
    for, because denn (*coor. conj.*)
forbidden verboten
foreign ausländisch
    foreign, strange fremd
    foreign countries das Ausland (*sing.*)
    foreign language die Fremdsprache, -n
    foreign worker der Gastarbeiter, -; die Gastarbeiterin, -nen
    foreigner der Ausländer, -; die Ausländerin, -nen
forest der Wald, ⸚er
forget *vergessen
    I can't forget that. Das geht mir nicht aus dem Kopf.
fork die Gabel, -n
form die Form, -en
formal formell
formulate formulieren
France (das) Frankreich
free time die Freizeit
free, unoccupied frei
free of charge kostenlos
freedom die Freiheit, -en
French fries die Pommes frites (*pl.*)
French (*adj.*) französisch
Frenchman der Franzose, -n, -n
Frenchwoman die Französin, -nen
fresh frisch
Friday (der) Freitag

friend der Freund, -e; die Freundin, -nen
friendly freundlich; sympathisch
from aus (+ *dat.*); von (+ *dat.*)
front
    in front of vor (+ *dat. or acc.*)
fruit das Obst
frustrate frustrieren
full voll
fun der Spaß
    Have fun. Viel Spaß.
    That is fun (for me). Das macht (mir) Spaß.
funny, peculiar komisch
furnished möbliert
furniture die Möbel (*pl.*)
future die Zukunft
    in the future in Zukunft

G

game das Spiel, -e
garage die Garage, -n
garden der Garten, ⸚
gate das Tor, -e
gender das Geschlecht, -er
generation die Generation, -en
gentleman der Herr, -n, -en
geographical geographisch
geography die Geographie
German der / die Deutsche, -n; deutsch (*adj.*)
    German (language) (das) Deutsch
    in German auf deutsch
    German class die Deutschstunde, -n
    German Democratic Republic (GDR) die Deutsche Demokratische Republik (DDR)
    German mark, Deutschmark die Deutsche Mark
    German studies die Germanistik
Germany (das) Deutschland
get, receive *bekommen
    get, become *werden
    get, fetch holen
    get, pick up ab·holen
    get in (a vehicle) *ein·steigen
    get out (of a vehicle) *aus·steigen

giant der Riese, -n, -n
gigantic riesengroß; riesen- (*noun and adj. prefix*)
girl das Mädchen, -
give *geben
    give (as a gift) schenken
    give up *auf·geben
glad froh
gladly, with pleasure gern(e) (*adv.*)
glass das Glas, ⸚er
glasses die Brille (*sing.*)
glove der Handschuh, -e
go *gehen
    go (by vehicle) *fahren
    go away *weg·gehen
    on the go unterwegs
goal das Ziel, -e
god der Gott, ⸚er
golden wedding anniversary die goldene Hochzeit
golden golden
gone weg
good gut (besser, best-)
    Good-bye! Auf Wiedersehen!
    Good evening! Guten Abend!
    Good morning! Guten Morgen!
    Have a good trip! Gute Reise!
    pretty good ganz gut
gossip der Klatsch
government in power die Regierung, -en
grade, class die Klasse, -n
grade (on a test, paper, etc.) die Note, -n
gradually nach und nach
gram das Gramm
grammar die Grammatik
grandfather der Großvater, ⸚
grandma die Oma, -s
grandmother die Großmutter, ⸚
grandpa der Opa, -s
grandparents die Großeltern (*pl.*)
gray grau
great herrlich
great prima
great, terrific toll (*colloq.*)
greatness die Größe
Greek griechisch (*adj.*)
green grün
greet grüßen
groceries die Lebensmittel (*pl.*)
group die Gruppe, -n
grow *wachsen
    grow up *auf·wachsen

gruesome grausam
guess *raten
    Take a guess! Raten Sie mal!
guest der Gast, ⸚e
guide book der Reiseführer, -
guy der Typ, -en (*slang*)
gym shoe der Turnschuh, -e

H

hair das Haar, -e
half halb (*adv.*)
    half days halbtags (*adv.*)
ham der Schinken
hand die Hand, ⸚e
    on the one / other hand auf
    der einen / anderen Seite
handle schaffen
handsome hübsch
hang hängen (*trans.*); *hängen
    (*intrans.*)
    hang up auf·hängen
happen passieren, ist passiert
happiness das Glück
happy glücklich, froh
    be happy sich freuen
harbor der Hafen, ⸚
hard hart (härter)
    hard, difficult schwer
hard-working fleißig
hardly kaum
harsh hart (härter)
hat der Hut, ⸚e
hate hassen
haul schleppen (*colloq.*)
have *haben
    have in mind *vor·haben
have to, must *müssen
head der Kopf, ⸚e
health die Gesundheit
healthy gesund (gesünder)
hear hören
heat die Hitze
heaven
    For heaven's sake! Um Gottes
    Willen!
heavy schwer
hectic hektisch
hello Grüß Gott! (in southern
    Germany and Austria); Guten
    Tag!; Hallo!
    say hello to grüßen
help *helfen (+ *dat.*); die Hilfe

helping, portion die Portion, -en
here hier (location); her
    (destination)
Here it is. Bitte.
Hi! Tag!
high hoch (*predicate adj.*), hoh-
    (*attributive adj.*) (höher,
    höchst-)
    High time! Höchste Zeit! Na
    endlich!
highway die Autobahn, -en
hike wandern, ist gewandert; die
    Wanderung, -en
hill der Hügel, -
hilly hügelig
hint der Tip, -s
historic historisch
history die Geschichte, -n
hit *schlagen
hitchhike per Autostop reisen;
    trampen, ist getrampt
hitchhiking der Autostop
hold *halten
home (as destination of motion)
    nach Hause
    at home zu Hause
    in the home of bei
homeland die Heimat
homesickness das Heimweh
homework assignment die
    Hausaufgabe, -n
honest ehrlich
hope hoffen
    I hope hoffentlich
horizon der Horizont, -e
hospital das Krankenhaus, ⸚er
hot heiß
hotel das Hotel, -s
hour die Stunde, -n
    for hours stundenlang
house das Haus, ⸚er
housemate der Mitbewohner, -;
    die Mitbewohnerin, -nen
housewife die Hausfrau, -en
how? wie?
    how come? Wieso?
    how long? wie lange?
    how many? wie viele?
    how much? wieviel?
however aber
human menschlich
    human being der Mensch, -en,
    -en
    human race die Menschheit
humane menschlich

humor der Humor
hunch die Ahnung, -en
Hungary (das) Ungarn
hunger der Hunger
hungry hungrig
    be hungry Hunger haben
hurry sich beeilen, schnell
    machen (*colloq.*); die Eile
    in a hurry in Eile
hurt weh *tun (+ *dat. of person*)
    That hurts (me). Das tut (mir)
    weh.
    get hurt sich verletzen
husband der Mann, ⸚er

I

I.D. card der Ausweis, -e
ice das Eis
    ice hockey das Eishockey
    ice cream das Eis
idea die Idee, -n
    (I have) no idea. Ich habe
    keine Ahnung.
ideal ideal
ideological ideologisch
idiot der Idiot, -en, -en
    idiot proof idiotensicher
if wenn (*sub. conj.*)
    if, whether ob (*sub. conj.*)
illegal illegal
image das Bild, -er
imagine something sich etwas
    vor·stellen
immediately gleich; sofort
immigrate ein·wandern
important wichtig
    most important Haupt- (*noun
    prefix*)
impossible unmöglich
impression der Eindruck, ⸚e
in in (+ *acc. or dat.*); hinein-
    (*prefix*)
incorrect, false falsch
Incredible! Sagenhaft!
incredibly wahnsinnig (*colloq.
    adv.*)
independent unabhängig
indicative der Indikativ
industrial industriell
industrious fleißig
industry die Industrie, -n
inexpensive billig

inflation die Inflation
information die Auskunft
inhabitant der Einwohner, -
injure oneself sich verletzen
inkling die Ahnung, -en
insane verrückt; wahnsinnig
instead of anstatt (+ *gen.*); statt
  (+ *gen.*)
instead sondern (*coor. conj.*)
instrument das Instrument, -e
integrate integrieren
intelligent intelligent
intend to *wollen
interest interessieren
  be interested in sich
  interessieren für
interesting interessant
intermission die Pause, -n
international international
interrupt *unterbrechen
interview interviewen
into in (+ *acc.*); hinein- (*prefix*)
introduce vor·stellen
  introduce oneself sich
  vor·stellen
invent *erfinden
invite *ein·laden
irony die Ironie
Italian der Italiener, -; die
  Italienerin, -nen; italienisch
  (*adj.*)
Italy (das) Italien

J

jacket die Jacke, -n.
January (der) Januar
jeans die Jeans (*pl.*)
jersey, pullover der Pullover, -; der
  Pulli, -s (*colloq.*)
Jewish jüdisch
job, position die Stelle, -n
joke der Witz, -e
journalist der Journalist, -en, -en
journey die Reise, -n
joy die Freude, -n
juice der Saft, ̈e
July (der) Juli
June (der) Juni
junk der Kram (*colloq.*)
just as . . . as genau so . . . wie
just, at the moment gerade

K

kaput kaputt (*colloq.*)
keep *behalten
key der Schlüssel, -
kilogram das Kilogramm; das Kilo
  (*colloq.*)
kilometer der Kilometer, -
kitchen die Küche, -n
knife das Messer, -
know (a fact) *wissen
  get to know kennen·lernen
  know, be acquainted with
  *kennen
  know one's way around sich
  *aus·kennen
known bekannt

L

lab(oratory) das Labor, -s
Ladies and Gentlemen meine
  Damen und Herren
lady die Dame, -n
lake der See, -n
  at the lake am See
lamp die Lampe, -n
landscape die Landschaft, -en
language die Sprache, -n
last letzt-
  last of all zuletzt
last, take time dauern
late spät
  be late sich verspäten
later on nachher (*adv.*)
laugh lachen
  laugh about lachen über
  (+ *acc.*)
lavatory die Toilette, -n
law das Gesetz, -e
  (study of) law Jura
  **under the law, in the eyes of
  the law** vor dem Gesetz
lawyer der Rechtsanwalt, ̈e; die
  Rechtsanwältin, -nen
lay, put down legen
lazy faul
lead *führen
learn lernen
**leave (something or someone),
  leave behind** *lassen
leave (a person or place)
  *verlassen

leave (by vehicle) *ab·fahren;
  *los·fahren
leave, go away *weg·gehen
lecture (university) die Vorlesung,
  -en
left
  to the left, on the left links
  (*adv.*)
leg das Bein, -e
leisure time die Freizeit
lend *leihen
let *lassen
letter der Brief, -e
lettuce der Salat, -e
library die Bibliothek, -en
lie, be situated *liegen
life das Leben
light das Licht, -er
  light (in color) hell
  light (in weight) leicht
like *mögen; wie (*conj.*)
  I like that. Das gefällt mir.
  to like something etwas gern
  haben
  like this so
  like to (do something) gern
  (+ *verb*)
  would like to möchten
likeable sympathisch
limnology die Limnologie
line (of text) die Zeile, -n
line (streetcar or bus) die
  Linie, -n
linguistics die Linguistik
lion der Löwe, -n, -n
list die Liste, -n
listen (to) zu·hören (+ *dat.*)
liter der Liter
literary literarisch
little klein
  a little etwas
  **a little; a little bit; a little
  while** ein bißchen
  little bit wenig
  little by little nach und nach
live leben
  live, dwell wohnen
lively munter
liverwurst die Leberwurst, ̈e
loan *leihen
long lang(e) (länger)
  for a long time schon lange,
  seit langem
  no longer nicht mehr

look schauen
    look after auf·passen auf
    (+ *acc.*); sich kümmern um
    look, appear *aus·sehen
    look for, seek suchen
    look forward to sich freuen auf
    (+ *acc.*)
    Look here. Schau mal.
    look out (for) auf·passen (auf +
    acc.)
    take a look at something sich
    etwas *an·sehen
lose *verlieren
lots of eine Menge
loud laut
love lieben
low niedrig
luck das Glück
    be lucky Glück haben
    be unlucky, have bad luck
    Pech haben
lug (along) schleppen (*colloq.*)
luggage das Gepäck
lunch, midday meal das
    Mittagessen

M

machine die Maschine, -n
magazine die Zeitschrift, -en
mail (a letter) *ein·werfen
mail die Post
mailbox der Briefkasten, ⸚
mailman der Briefträger, -
main Haupt- (*noun prefix*)
major field of study das
    Hauptfach, ⸚er
major in (a subject) studieren
make machen
make-up
    put on make-up sich
    schminken
mama, mom die Mutti, -s
man der Mann, ⸚er
Man! Mensch!
manage schaffen
management (field of study) die
    Betriebswirtschaft
manipulate manipulieren
mankind die Menschheit
many a mancher
many viele (*adj.*)
    many people viele (*pron.*)
map die Karte, -n; die Landkarte, -n
March (der) März

mark (the German mark) die Mark
marry, get married heiraten
    be married verheiratet sein
marvelous herrlich
mathematics die Mathematik
    (*sing.*)
matter
    It doesn't matter. Es macht
    (doch) nichts.
    It doesn't matter to me. Das
    ist mir egal.
    no matter where, who, why,
    etc. egal wo, wer, warum, usw.
    What's the matter? Was ist los?
matter, affair die Sache, -n
may, be allowed to *dürfen
    That may be. Das mag sein.
May (der) Mai
maybe vielleicht
meal das Essen
mean, think meinen
    What do you mean? Wieso?
mean, signify bedeuten
    that means, in other words das
    heißt
meaning die Bedeutung, -en
meat das Fleisch
mechanic der Mechaniker, -
medicine die Medizin
meet (for the first time)
    kennen·lernen
    meet again *wieder·sehen
    meet (by appointment) *treffen
melancholy die Melancholie
member das Mitglied, -er
mentality die Mentalität, -en
mention
    Don't mention it. Nichts zu
    danken.
menu die Speisekarte, -n
messy schlampig (*colloq.*);
    unordentlich
method die Methode, -n
metropolis die Metropole, -n
Middle Ages das Mittelalter (*sing.*)
might die Macht
mild mild
milk die Milch
million die Million, -en
minor field (of study) das
    Nebenfach, ⸚er
minute die Minute, -n
    for minutes minutenlang
miracle das Wunder, -
mirror der Spiegel, -
miss (an event, opportunity, train,
    etc.) verpassen

Miss Fräulein
missing
    be missing fehlen
mist der Nebel
misty neblig
modern modern
mom, mama die Mutti, -s
moment der Augenblick, -e; der
    Moment, -e
    at the moment im
    Augenblick; im Moment
    at the moment, just gerade
    Just a moment, please (Einen)
    Augenblick, bitte.
monarchy die Monarchie, -n
Monday (der) Montag
money das Geld
month der Monat, -e
    for months monatelang
monument das Denkmal, ⸚er
mood die Laune, -n
    in a good / bad mood guter /
    schlechter Laune
more mehr
    not any more nicht mehr
morning der Morgen, -
    Good morning! Guten
    Morgen!
    in the morning(s) morgens
    (*adv.*); vormittags (*adv.*)
    this morning heute morgen
most meist-
    most like to am liebsten
    (+ *verb*)
mostly meistens
mother die Mutter, ⸚
motorcycle das Motorrad, ⸚er
mountainous bergig
mouth der Mund, ⸚er
move (*intrans.*) sich bewegen
    move, change residence
    *um·ziehen
    move in *ein·ziehen
    move out *aus·ziehen
movement die Bewegung, -en
movie theater das Kino, -s
movie der Film, -e
Mr. Herr
Mrs. Frau
Ms. Frau
much viel (mehr, meist-)
    not much wenig
Munich (das) München
museum das Museum, die Museen
music die Musik
musicology die Musikwissenschaft
must *müssen

N

name *nennen; der Name, -ns, -n
    My name is . . . Ich heiße . . .
    What's your name? Wie
    heißen Sie?
napkin die Serviette, -n
nation, folk das Volk, ¨er
native language die
    Muttersprache, -n
native place or country die
    Heimat
natural natürlich
nature die Natur
near nah (näher, nächst-)
    near, nearby in der Nähe (von
    or + *gen.*)
nearness die Nähe
necessary nötig
need brauchen
neighbor der Nachbar, -n, -n; die
    Nachbarin, -nen
neither . . . nor weder . . . noch
neutral neutral
neutrality die Neutralität
never nie
nevertheless trotzdem
new neu
newspaper die Zeitung, -en
next nächst-
nice nett; lieb
night die Nacht, ¨e
    Good night. Gute Nacht.
    in the night, at night in der
    Nacht; nachts
no nein; nee (*colloq.*)
    no, not a kein (*negative
    article*)
    no more X kein X mehr
nobody, no one niemand
Nonsense! Quatsch!
normal normal
north der Norden
North America (das) Nordamerika
nose die Nase, -n
not nicht
    not a kein (*negative article*)
    not a . . . at all gar kein
    not any kein
    not any more, no longer nicht
    mehr
    not any X yet noch kein X
    not an X any longer kein X
    mehr
    not at all gar nicht
    not much wenig

    not only . . . but also nicht nur
    . . . sondern auch
    not yet noch nicht
notebook das Heft, -e
nothing nichts
notice merken
notion die Ahnung, -en
noun das Substantiv, -e
novel der Roman, -e
November (der) November
now jetzt; nun
    from now on von jetzt an
nowadays heutzutage
number die Nummer, -n
nurse der Krankenpfleger, -; die
    Krankenschwester, -n

O

o'clock Uhr (**3 o'clock** =
    3 Uhr)
object, thing die Sache, -n
objective objektiv
ocean der Ozean, -e
October (der) Oktober
odd komisch
of course natürlich
    of course, sure klar (*colloq.*)
of von (+ *dat.*)
offend ärgern
offer *bieten
office das Büro, -s
official der Beamte (*adj. noun, m.*);
    die Beamtin, -nen (*f.*); offiziell
    (*adj.*)
often oft (öfter)
oh ach
oil das Öl
OK Ist gut. (*colloq.*)
old alt (älter)
    old as the hills steinalt
old-fashioned altmodisch
on auf (+ *acc. or dat.*)
once einmal
    once again, once more noch
    einmal
one (*indefinite pronoun*) man
oneself
    **by oneself (myself, yourself,
    etc.)** selber, selbst
only nur (*adv.*)
    only, single einzig- (*adj.*)
onto auf (+ *acc. or dat.*)
open öffnen (*verb*); offen (*adj.*)

opinion die Meinung, -en
    be of the opinion, think
    meinen
opportunity die Gelegenheit, -en
opposite der Gegensatz, ¨e
opposition die Opposition, -en
optimistic optimistisch
or oder (*coor. conj.*)
order bestellen
    in order to um . . . zu
orderly ordentlich
organization, club der Verein, -e
other ander-
otherwise sonst
out of aus (+ *dat.*)
outing der Ausflug, ¨e
outside draußen (*adv.*)
over über (+ *dat. or acc.*)
    over there drüben; da drüben
own *besitzen; eigen- (*adj.*)

P

pace das Tempo
pack packen
page die Seite, -n
pants die Hose, -n
papa der Vati, -s
paper das Papier, -e
    written term paper das Referat
    write a paper ein Referat
    schreiben
parallel parallel
Pardon me. Entschuldigung.
    I beg your pardon? Wie bitte?
parents die Eltern (*pl.*)
part der Teil, -e
    take part in *teil·nehmen an
    (+ *dat.*)
participate mit·machen
partner der Partner, -
party (political) die Partei, -en
party die Party, -s
passport der Paß, die Pässe
past (time) die Vergangenheit
    to go past something an
    (+ *dat.*) . . . vorbei (+ *verb*)
path der Weg, -e
patient der Patient, -en, -en
patron der Gast, ¨e
pay bezahlen; zahlen
    pay attention auf·passen
peace der Frieden
peaceful, calm ruhig

peculiar komisch
pedestrian der Fußgänger, -
pedestrian zone die Fußgängerzone, -n
pen (ball-point) der Kugelschreiber, -
pencil der Bleistift, -e
people die Leute (*pl.*)
    people, nation, folk das Volk, ¨er
percent das Prozent
perfect perfekt
perhaps vielleicht
person der Mensch, -en,-en; die Person, -en
personal persönlich
pessimistic pessimistisch
pharmacy die Apotheke, -n
phenomenon das Phänomen, -e
philosophize philosophieren
philosophy die Philosophie
photograph das Foto, -s
physics die Physik (*sing.*)
piano das Klavier, -e
pick up ab·holen
picture das Bild, -er
    take a picture ein Foto machen
piece das Stück, -e
pigeon die Taube, -n
pity
    What a pity! Das ist schade!
place der Ort, -e; der Platz, ¨e
place, put stellen
plain die Ebene, -n
plan *vor·haben
    plan, make plans planen
plant das Pflanze, -n
plastic die Plastik
plate der Teller, -
play spielen
    play a part eine Rolle spielen
pleasant angenehm
please bitte
please, appeal to *gefallen (+ *dat.*)
Pleased to meet you. Sehr erfreut.
pleasure to meet you angenehm
pocket die Tasche, -n
poem das Gedicht, -e
poet der Dichter, -; die Dichterin, -nen
poetry die Lyrik
Poland (das) Polen
policy die Politik
polite höflich
political politisch
    political science die Politikwissenschaft

politician der Politiker, -; die Politikerin, -nen
politics die Politik
pollute verschmutzen
    non-polluting, ecologically beneficial umweltfreundlich
pollution die Verschmutzung
ponder something sich etwas überlegen
poor arm (ärmer)
port der Hafen, ¨
porter, redcap der Gepäckträger, -
portion die Portion, -en
position die Position, -en
    position, job die Stelle, -n
possibility die Möglichkeit, -en
possible möglich
post office die Post
postage stamp die Briefmarke, -n
postal service die Post
postcard die Postkarte, -n
poster das Poster, -
poster (political) das Plakat, -e
pot
    small (coffee or tea) pot das Kännchen, -
potato die Kartoffel, -n
power die Kraft, ¨e; die Macht, ¨e
power plant das Kraftwerk, -e
practical praktisch
practice üben
precise genau
prefer (to do something) lieber (+ *verb*)
preferably lieber
prejudice das Vorurteil, -e
prepare for sich vor·bereiten auf (+ *acc.*)
prepared, ready bereit
present das Geschenk, -e
    be present, be there *dabei·sein
    present (time) die Gegenwart
president der Präsident, -en, -en
pretty hübsch
pretzel die Brezel, -n
previously vorher
price der Preis, -e
primary Haupt- (*noun prefix*)
private privat
probably wahrscheinlich; wohl
problem das Problem, -e
produce produzieren
product, ware die Ware, -n
productive produktiv

profession der Beruf, -e
    What is your profession? Was sind Sie von Beruf?
professor der Professor, -en; die Professorin, -nen
program das Programm, -e
programmer der Programmierer, -; die Programmiererin, -nen
progress der Fortschritt, -e
prohibited verboten
propel *treiben
protest der Protest, -e
proud of stolz auf (+ *acc.*)
provide *bieten
psychoanalysis die Psychoanalyse
psychological psychologisch
psychology die Psychologie
public öffentlich
pull *ziehen
pullover, jersey der Pullover, -; der Pulli, -s (*colloq.*)
punctual pünktlich
pupil der Schüler, -; die Schülerin, -nen
put stellen
    put down, lay legen
    put down, set setzen

Q

quantity die Menge, -n
quarter das Viertel, -
    quarter to / past Viertel vor / nach
question die Frage, -n
    ask a question eine Frage stellen
    guiding question die Leitfrage, -n
    it's a question of es geht um
questionnaire der Fragebogen
quick as lightning blitzschnell
quiet leise
quit *auf·geben
quite ziemlich

R

radical radikal
radio das Radio, -s
railroad, railroad system die Bahn
railway compartment das Abteil, -e
rain regnen; der Regen

rainy regnerisch
rather
    I'd rather not. No thanks.
    Lieber nicht.
    would rather (do something)
    lieber (+ *verb*)
react to reagieren auf (+ *acc.*)
reaction die Reaktion, -en
read *lesen
    read about *lesen über (+ *acc.*)
    read aloud *vor·lesen
reading selection das Lesestück, -e
ready fertig
    ready, prepared bereit
real wirklich
realm das Reich, -e
reason der Grund, ¨e
receive *bekommen
recently neulich
reception desk die Rezeption
recommend *empfehlen
record (phonograph) die
    Schallplatte, -n
recover (from) sich erholen von
recycling das Recycling
red rot (röter)
reform reformieren
refuse, trash der Müll; der Abfall, ¨e
regard as *halten für
regime das Regime
region die Gegend, -en; die
    Region, -en
**register for, take (a university
    course)** belegen
    **register (at a hotel, the
    university, etc.)** sich
    an·melden
related (to) verwandt (mit)
relative der / die Verwandte, -n;
    relativ (*adj. and adv.*)
relevant aktuell
religion die Religion, -en
remain *bleiben
remember sich erinnern an (+ *acc.*)
remember sich merken
remind of erinnern an (+ *acc.*)
renovate renovieren
repair reparieren
repeat wiederholen
repetition die Wiederholung, -en
report berichten
    give a report ein Referat
    *halten
    oral report das Referat, -e
republic die Republik, -en
request *bitten um

rescue retten
reserve reservieren
respect der Respekt
respond to antworten auf (+ *acc.*)
responsible for verantwortlich für
rest
    have a rest sich erholen
restaurant das Restaurant, -s
restless unruhig
retain *behalten
review die Wiederholung
revolution die Revolution, -en
Rhine River der Rhein
rich reich
right, correct richtig
    be right recht *haben (*with
    person as subject*); stimmen
    (*impersonal only*)
    right away sofort; gleich
    That's right. Das stimmt.
    Stimmt schon.
    to the right, on the right
    rechts (*adv.*)
ring klingeln
rip off, steal klauen (*colloq.*)
river der Fluß, Flüsse
road die Straße, -n
    road atlas der Straßenatlas
role die Rolle, -n
roll das Brötchen, -
Romania (das) Rumänien
romantic romantisch
room das Zimmer, -
    dining room das Eßzimmer, -
    double room das
    Doppelzimmer, -
    living room das Wohnzimmer, -
    rented student room die Bude, -n
    single room das Einzelzimmer, -
roommate der Mitbewohner, -; die
    Mitbewohnerin, -nen
Rubbish! Quatsch!
rucksack der Rucksack, ¨e
rug der Teppich, -e
run *laufen
Russia (das) Rußland
Russian der Russe, -n, -n; die
    Russin, -nen; russisch (*adj.*)

S

sack der Sack, ¨e
sad traurig
salad der Salat, -e

salesman der Verkäufer, -
saleswoman die Verkäuferin, -nen
Saturday (der) Samstag, (der)
    Sonnabend
sausage die Wurst, ¨e
save, rescue retten
    save (money or time) sparen
say sagen
    What did you say? Wie bitte?
    What do you say to that? Was
    meinen / sagen Sie dazu?
Scandinavia (das) Skandinavien
scarce, in short supply knapp
schilling (Austrian currency) der
    Schilling, -e
scholarship die Wissenschaft
    scholarship, stipend das
    Stipendium, die Stipendien
school die Schule, -n; das
    Gymnasium, die Gymnasien
    (prepares pupils for university)
    school system das
    Schulsystem, -e
    secondary school pupil der
    Schüler, - (*m.*); die Schülerin, -
    nen (*f.*)
science die Wissenschaft, -en
sea das Meer, -e
seat der Platz, ¨e
second zweit-
    second car der Zweitwagen, -
secretary der Sekretär, -e; die
    Sekretärin, -nen
see *sehen
    Let's see. Zeig mal her.
    see again *wieder·sehen
seek, look for suchen
seem *scheinen
seldom selten
sell verkaufen
semester das Semester, -
    semester break die
    Semesterferien (*pl.*)
seminar das Seminar, -e
send schicken
senior citizen der Senior, -en, -en
sentence der Satz, ¨e
separate separat
September (der) September
serious ernst
    take something seriously
    etwas ernst *nehmen
serve bedienen
set (down) setzen
seventh siebt-
several mehrere

sex, gender das Geschlecht, -er
shame
    That's a shame! Das ist schade!
shape
    in shape fit
shared apartment die Wohngemeinschaft, -en; die WG, -s
shave sich rasieren
shine *scheinen
ship das Schiff, -e
shirt das Hemd, -en
shoe der Schuh, -e
shop, store der Laden, ¨
shop for, go shopping ein·kaufen
short kurz (kürzer)
    short of cash knapp bei Kasse
should *sollen
shoulderbag die Tasche, -n
shout *rufen
show zeigen
    Show it to me. Zeig mal her.
shower die Dusche, -n
    take a shower sich duschen
siblings die Geschwister (pl.)
sick krank (kränker)
sickness die Krankheit, -en
side die Seite, -n
significance die Bedeutung, -en
silent
    be silent *schweigen
similar (to) ähnlich (+ dat.)
similarity die Ähnlichkeit, -en
simple, easy einfach, leicht
since (temporal) seit (prep. + dat. and sub. conj.)
    since (causal) da (sub. conj.)
sing *singen
single, only einzig- (adj.)
    single, unmarried ledig
sister die Schwester, -n
sit *sitzen
    sit down sich setzen
situated
    be situated *liegen
situation die Situation, -en
size die Größe, -n
ski *ski·fahren
skirt der Rock, ¨e
sleep *schlafen
slow langsam
small klein
smart klug (klüger)
snake die Schlange, -n
sneaker der Turnschuh, -e

snow schneien; der Schnee
so so
    So what? Na und?
    So long! Tschüs!
soccer der Fußball
    soccer ball der Fußball, ¨e
social gesellschaftlich; sozial
social worker der Sozialarbeiter, -; die Sozialarbeiterin, -nen
society die Gesellschaft, -en
sociology die Soziologie
soft, quiet leise
software die Software
solidarity die Solidarität
solution die Lösung, -en
solve lösen
some etwas (sing.); einige (pl.); manche (pl.)
somebody jemand
somehow or other irgendwie
someone jemand
something else noch etwas
something etwas
    something like that so etwas, so was (colloq.)
sometime or other irgendwann
sometimes manchmal
somewhat etwas
somewhere or other irgendwo
son der Sohn, ¨e
song das Lied, -er
soon bald
sore, ticked off sauer (colloq.)
sorry
    I'm sorry about that. Das tut mir leid.
sound *klingen
soup die Suppe, -n
sour, acidic sauer
south der Süden
soviet sowjetisch
    Soviet Union die Sowjetunion
space der Platz, ¨e
Spain (das) Spanien
speak reden; *sprechen
    I can speak German. Ich kann Deutsch.
speechless baff
speed das Tempo
spell
    How do you spell that? Wie schreibt man das?
spend (money) *aus·geben
    spend (time) *verbringen
    spend the night übernachten

spite
    in spite of trotz (+ gen.)
    in spite of that, nevertheless trotzdem (adv.)
spontaneous spontan
spoon der Löffel, -
sport der Sport
    play sports Sport *treiben
spring der Frühling
    spring term das Sommersemester
square
    city square der Platz, ¨e
stabile stabil
stability die Stabilität
staircase die Treppe, -n
stairs die Treppe, -n
stamp die Briefmarke, -n
stand *stehen
    stand up *auf·stehen
standard of living der Lebensstandard
start *an·fangen
    start, depart (by vehicle) *los·fahren
state der Staat, -en
stay *bleiben
steal *stehlen
    steal, rip off klauen (colloq.)
steep steil
stereo die Stereoanlage, -n
stereotyped, cliché klischeehaft
still (adv.) noch; noch immer; immer noch
stipend das Stipendium, die Stipendien
stone der Stein, -e
stop *halten (intrans.); stoppen (trans.)
    stop (doing something) auf·hören (mit)
    stop (for streetcar or bus) die Haltestelle, -n
store das Geschäft, -e
    store, shop der Laden, ¨
story die Geschichte, -n
    story, narrative die Erzählung, -en
straighten up auf·räumen
strange, foreign fremd
street die Straße, -n
streetcar die Straßenbahn, -en
strength die Kraft, ¨e
stress der Streß, die Stresse
stressful stressig

stroll der Bummel, -
    take a stroll einen Bummel machen
    stroll through town der Stadtbummel, -
strong stark (stärker)
student (at university) der Student, -en, -en; die Studentin, -nen
    student dormitory das Studentenwohnheim, -e
    student ID der Studentenausweis, -e
studies (at university) das Studium
study das Arbeitszimmer, -
    study (a subject), major in studieren
    study at studieren an (+ *dat.*)
stupid blöd, dumm
subject, area of study das Fach, ̈er
    subject, topic das Thema, die Themen
subjective subjektiv
subjunctive der Konjunktiv
subway train die Untergrundbahn; die U-Bahn
success der Erfolg, -e
such solcher
suddenly plötzlich
suggestion der Vorschlag, ̈e; der Tip, -s
suit der Anzug, ̈e
suitcase der Koffer, -
summary die Zusammenfassung, -en
summer der Sommer
sun die Sonne
Sunday (der) Sonntag
sunny sonnig
super super
supertanker der Supertanker, -
supermarket der Supermarkt, ̈e
supper das Abendessen
    for supper zum Abendessen
supposed
    be supposed to *sollen
sure, of course klar (*colloq.*)
    to be sure . . . but zwar . . . aber
    sure, certain sicher
surprise überraschen; die Überraschung, -en
    be surprised staunen
    be surprised (about) sich wundern (über + *acc.*)
swim *schwimmen

Swiss der Schweizer, -; die Schweizerin, -nen; schweizerisch (*adj.*)
switch on an·machen
Switzerland die Schweiz
symbol das Symbol, -e
symbolic symbolisch
sympathy das Mitleid
system das System, -e

T

T-shirt das T-Shirt, -s
table der Tisch, -e
take *nehmen
    take along *mit·bringen; *mit·nehmen
    take (a university course) belegen
    take for *halten für
    take part in *teil·nehmen an (+ *dat.*)
    take place *statt·finden
talk reden; *sprechen
    talk about sprechen über (+ *acc.*)
    talk nonsense quatschen (*colloq.*)
tall groß
task die Aufgabe, -n
taste; taste good schmecken
tasty lecker
tavern die Kneipe, -n
taxicab das Taxi, -s
tea der Tee
teacher der Leher, -; die Lehrerin, -nen
team die Mannschaft, -en
technology die Technik
telephone telefonieren; das Telefon, -e
television das Fernsehen
    on TV im Fernsehen
    television set der Fernseher, -
    watch TV *fern·sehen
tell sagen
    tell, recount erzählen
tempo das Tempo
tennis das Tennis
    tennis court der Tennisplatz, ̈e
term paper das Referat, -e
terrace die Terrasse, -n
terrible furchtbar, grausam, schrecklich

terrific prima, herrlich, toll (*colloq.*)
terrorist terroristisch (*adj.*)
test die Prüfung, -en
    written test die Klausur, -en
text der Text, -e
than (+ *comparative degree*) als
thank danken (+ *dat.*)
    thank goodness Gott sei Dank
    thanks der Dank
    thanks, thank-you danke
    thanks a lot, many thanks vielen Dank
that daß (*sub. conj.*)
theater das Theater, -
theme das Thema, die Themen
then dann
    then, in that case da (*adv.*)
there da, dort
    How do I get there? Wie komme ich dahin?
    there is, there are es gibt (+ *acc.*)
therefore darum
thermos bottle die Thermosflasche, -n
thing das Ding, -e
    thing, object die Sache, -n
    things, stuff der Kram (*colloq.*)
think *denken; meinen, glauben
    I don't think so. Ich glaube nein.
    I think so. Ich glaube ja.
    I think so too. Das finde ich auch.
    think of *denken an (+ *acc.*)
    think something over sich etwas überlegen
    think X is *halten X für
    What do you think of that? Was meinen / sagen Sie dazu?
third dritt-
thirst der Durst
thirsty Durst haben
this, these dieser
thought der Gedanke, -ns, -n
through durch (+ *acc.*)
throw *werfen
    throw away *weg·werfen
Thursday (der) Donnerstag
thus also
ticked off, sore sauer (*colloq.*)
ticket die Karte, -n; die Fahrkarte, -n (bus, train, streetcar); das Ticket, -s (airline)

tidy ordentlich
    tidy up auf·räumen
tie die Krawatte, -n
time die Zeit, -en
    for a long time lang(e)
    for a short time, briefly kurz
    for a time eine Zeitlang
    high time höchste Zeit
    on time, punctual pünktlich
    take time, last dauern
    What time is it? Wie spät ist es? Wieviel Uhr ist es?
time (occurrence) das Mal, -e
    any time irgendwann
    at that time, back then damals
    for the first time zum ersten Mal
    (the) next time das nächste Mal
    this time diesmal (*adv.*)
    umpteen times zigmal
timely aktuell
tin can die Dose, -n
tip der Tip, -s
tired, weary müde
    dead tired todmüde
to rent (from somebody) mieten
to (*prep.*) an (+ *acc. or dat.*); nach (+ *dat., with cities and countries*); zu (+ *dat., with people and some places*)
today heute
together zusammen; miteinander
tomorrow morgen
    tomorrow afternoon morgen nachmittag
    tomorrow evening morgen abend
    tomorrow morning morgen früh
too auch; zu
    too bad schade
tooth der Zahn, ¨e
top
    on top oben (*adv.*)
topic das Thema, die Themen
topical aktuell
tough hart (härter)
tour die Tour, -en
tourist der Tourist, -en, -en; die Touristin, -nen
toward an (+ *acc. or dat.*)
town (5,000 to 20,000 inhabitants) die Kleinstadt, ¨e
    small town der Ort, -e

town hall das Rathaus, ¨er
track das Gleis, -e
tradition die Tradition, -en
traditional traditionell
traffic der Verkehr
train der Zug, ¨e
    train station der Bahnhof, ¨e
train (athletics) trainieren
transfer *um·steigen
translate übersetzen
trash der Abfall, ¨e; der Müll
trash container der Container, -
travel reisen
traveler's check der Reisescheck, -s
tree der Baum, ¨e
trip die Reise, -n
    Have a good trip! Gute Reise!
    take a trip eine Reise machen
trousers die Hose, -n
true wahr
    it is true . . . but zwar . . . aber
truth die Wahrheit, -en
try, attempt versuchen
Tuesday (der) Dienstag
Turk der Türke, -n, -n; die Türkin, -nen
Turkey die Türkei
Turkish türkisch
turn on an·machen
twice zweimal
type der Typ, -en
typewriter die Schreibmaschine, -n
typical typisch

U

ugly häßlich
umbrella der Regenschirm, -e
unconcerned unbesorgt
under unter (+ *acc. or dat.*)
understand *verstehen
undress, get undressed sich *aus·ziehen
uneducated ungebildet
unemployed arbeitslos
unemployment die Arbeitslosigkeit
unfortunately leider
unification die Vereinigung
unimportant unwichtig
unite vereinen
university die Universität, -en; die Uni, -s (*colloq.*); die

Hochschule, -n
    at the university an der Uni(versität)
    attend a university studieren
    university studies das Studium
unknown unbekannt
unmarried unverheiratet
unnecessary unnötig
unpack aus·packen
unpleasant ungemütlich
until bis
    not until erst
upon auf (+ *acc. or dat.*)
upset
    get upset (about) sich auf·regen (über + *acc.*)
USA die USA (*pl.*)
use benutzen; gebrauchen
    use up, consume verbrauchen
used to
    get used to sich gewöhnen an (+ *acc.*)
useful nützlich
USSR die UdSSR
usually meistens

V

vacation (university and school) die Ferien (*pl.*)
vacation (from a job) der Urlaub, -e
    go on vacation in Urlaub gehen / fahren
    take a vacation Urlaub machen
valley das Tal, ¨er
variation die Variation, -en
various verschieden
vegetables das Gemüse (*sing.*)
Venice (Italy) (das) Venedig
verb das Verb, -en
very sehr
vicinity die Nähe
Vienna (das) Wien
village das Dorf, ¨er
visit besuchen; der Besuch, -e
vocabulary expansion die Wortschatzerweiterung
vocabulary der Wortschatz
voice die Stimme, -n
volleyball der Volleyball
voter der Wähler, -

W

wage der Lohn, ⸚e
wait (for) warten (auf + *acc.*)
    Wait a second! Hang on! Warte mal!
waiter der Kellner, -
waitress die Kellnerin, -nen
wake up (*intrans.*) auf·wachen
walk *gehen; *laufen (*colloq.*); der Bummel, -
    go for a walk *spazieren·gehen
wall (free-standing or exterior) die Mauer, -n;
    (interior) die Wand, ⸚e
wallet der Geldbeutel, -
wander wandern
wanderlust die Wanderlust
want to *wollen
    I don't want to. Ich habe keine Lust.
    want to do something Lust haben, etwas zu tun
war der Krieg, -e
wardrobe der Kleiderschrank, ⸚e
warm warm (wärmer)
wash *waschen
waste product der Abfall, ⸚e
waste verschwenden
water das Wasser
way der Weg, -e
    on the way unterwegs
weak schwach (schwächer)
wear *tragen
weary, tired müde
weather das Wetter
wedding die Hochzeit, -en
Wednesday (der) Mittwoch
week die Woche, -n
    for weeks wochenlang (*adv.*)
weekend das Wochenende, -n
    on the weekend am Wochenende
weigh *wiegen
welcome willkommen
    heartily welcome herzlich willkommen
    You're welcome. Bitte (sehr).
well . . . also . . . ; na . . . ; nun . . .

well (*adv.*) gut
    get well sich erholen von
    Get well soon. Gute Besserung.
well known bekannt
west der Westen
wet naß
what kind of? was für?
what? was?
wheel das Rad, ⸚er
when als (*sub. conj.*), wann (*question word*), wenn (*sub. conj.*)
whenever wenn (*sub. conj.*)
where? wo?
    from where? woher?
    to where? wohin?
whether, if ob (*sub. conj.*)
which? welcher?
while während (*sub. conj.*)
    for a while eine Zeitlang
    while -ing bei
white weiß
who? wer?
whole ganz
whose? wessen?
why? warum?
wild wild
win *gewinnen
wind der Wind
window das Fenster, -
    store window das Schaufenster, -
    window, counter der Schalter, -
windy windig
wine der Wein, -e
winter (der) Winter
    in the winter im Winter
wish wünschen
wit der Witz, -e
with mit
    with each other miteinander
without ohne
    without -ing ohne . . . zu
witty witzig
woman die Frau, -en
    young unmarried woman das Fräulein, -
wonder, ask oneself sich fragen
    No wonder! Kein Wunder!

wonderful wunderbar
word das Wort, die Worte (*in context*), die Wörter (*unconnected*); die Vokabel, -n
work arbeiten; die Arbeit
    work part time halbtags arbeiten
    work (of art) das Werk, -e
worker der Arbeiter, -; die Arbeiterin, -nen
world die Welt, -en
worried besorgt
worthwhile
    be worthwhile, worth the trouble sich lohnen
Wow! Mensch!
write *schreiben
    write about schreiben über (+ *acc.*)
writer der Schriftsteller, -; die Schriftstellerin, -nen
wrong falsch

Y

year das Jahr, -e
    for years jahrelang
yellow gelb
yes ja
    yes I do, yes I am, etc. doch
yesterday gestern
    yesterday evening gestern abend
    yesterday morning gestern früh
yoghurt der Joghurt
young jung (jünger)
    young people die Jugend (*sing.*)
youth die Jugend
Youth Hostel die Jugendherberge, -n
Yugoslavia (das) Jugoslawien
Yugoslavian der Jugoslawe, -n, -n; die Jugoslawin, -nen; jugoslawisch (*adj.*)

Z

zone die Zone, -n

Credits

Text

Page 391, „nachwort" by Eugen Gomringer, reprinted by permission of the poet.

Page 416, „ottos mops" by Ernst Jandl, from *Der künstliche Baum*, 1970. Reprinted by permission of Hermann Luchterhand Verlag, Germany.

Page 459, „Turke" by Max von der Grün, from *Leben im gelobten Land*, 1975. Reprinted by permission of Hermann Luchterhand Verlag, Germany.

Page 470, „Ach, wenn ich doch als Mann auf diese Welt gekommen wär" by Bettina Wegner, from *Wenn meine Lieder nicht mehr stimmen*. Reprinted by permission of the poet.

Illustrations

Ruth J. Flanigan: 3–5, 7, 11, 12, 14, 16, 17, 24, 40, 50, 53, 63, 65, 83, 88, 106, 112, 134, 165, 173–175, 183, 185, 200, 236, 237, 240, 267, 319–322, 334, 362, 433, 455, 456, 461, 487–489, 497, 498
Matthew Hansen: 134 bottom
Richard Pusey: 411, 439, endpapers

Joseph Scharl: 425. From *Grimm's Fairy Tales*. Copyright 1944 by Pantheon Books, Inc. and renewed 1972 by Random House, Inc. Reprinted by permission of Pantheon Books, Inc., a division of Random House, Inc.

Photographs

Page 2 Judy Poe; **13** *(left)* Kevin Galvin/Stock Boston; **13** *(right)* Kevin Galvin; **15** Andrew Brilliant/Carole Palmer; **16** Andrew Brilliant/Carole Palmer; **19** Pierre Valette; **20** Ulrike Welsch; **21** Andrew Brilliant/Carole Palmer; **26** Ulrike Welsch; **36** *(left)* Owen Franken/Stock Boston; **36** *(right)* Beryl Goldberg; **39** Andrew Brilliant/Carole Palmer; **44** Bob Krist; **47** Kees ven den Berg/Photo Researchers; **57** Judy Poe; **60** Andrew Brilliant/Carole Palmer; **66** Eric Shambroom; **68** Owen Franken/Stock Boston; **86** Ulrike Welsch; **93** Helga Lada Fotoagentur; **94** Farrell Grehan/Photo Researchers; **95** Tony Freeman/PhotoEdit; **101** Mike Mazzachi/Stock Boston; **113** Jean-Yves Ruszniewski/Photo Researchers; **114** COMSTOCK/Sven Martson; **115** *(left)* Judy Poe; **115** *(middle)* Ulrike Welsch; **115** *(right)* Wolfgang Kaehler; **130** Transglobe/Jan Halaska/Photo Researchers; **146** Owen Franken; **150** Kevin Galvin/Stock Boston; **152** Kevin Galvin; **158** Margot Granitsas/The Image Works; **162** Robert S. Clagett; **177** Leo de Wys; **180** Kevin Galvin; **187** COMSTOCK/Hartman-Dewitt; **188** Kevin Galvin; **189** Eric Shambroom; **206** *(left)* Andrew Brilliant/Carole Palmer; **206** *(right)* Carl Purcell/Photo Researchers; **212** Paul Shambroom/Photo Researchers; **214** Wolfgang Kaehler; **228** Thomas S. Hansen; **233** Andrew Brilliant/Carole Palmer; **234** Kevin Galvin; **243** Kevin Galvin; **254** Helga Lade Fotoagentur; **270** *(left)* COMSTOCK/Russ Kinne; **270** *(right)* Interfoto-Preßebild-Fotoagentur; **273** *(left)* Kevin Galvin/Stock Boston; **273** *(right)* Interfoto-Preßebild-Fotoagentur; **278** Kevin Galvin; **280** Ulrike Welsch; **284** Kevin Galvin; **297** Pierre Valette; **309** Beryl Goldberg; **310** Owen Franken; **315** Owen Franken/Woodfin Camp; **328** *(left)* Photoreporters; **328** *(middle)* Photoreporters; **328** *(right)* The Bettmann Archive; **332** Margot Granitsas/The Image Works; **338** *(top left)* Keystone/The Image Works; **338** *(top right)* Keystone/The Image Works; **338** *(bottom)* The Bettmann Archive;

Index
of Grammatical, Lexical, and Orthographical Topics